Scotland and Beyond;

the Families of Donald Gunn (Tormsdale)

and

John Gunn (Dalnaha, Strathmore and Braehour)

Donald Gunn FIEAust, CPEng(Ret.)

and

Alastair J. Gunn B.A., Dip.Ed, B.Ed.

We particularly thank Sharon and Bill Gurney for their invaluable help.

Little is known of the ancestry or siblings of Donald Gunn (Tormsdale)[1]*. He may have had a brother John, for a John Gunn and Catherine McDonald witnessed the christening of Donald's sons Hugh and Alexander. John and Catherine were married in 1787, their first born son also being named John. Scottish naming customs of the time suggest that Donald's father may also have been named John.*

The Gunns of Dalnaha, Strathmore and Braehour are descended from John Gunn of Kilearnan and Navidale[2] *(573) the 5th Mackeamish of the Clan Gunn, by his second wife, Catherine Sinclair. John Gunn in Dalnaha, Strathmore and Braehour's father was Alexander Gunn of Dalnaglaton (242) b. c. 1688, m. c. 1720 to Janet / Jean MacLeod (241) of Dalnate b. c. 1700 and d. 29 June 1765, his father being John Gunn of Knockfinn (569) b. c. 1660; his father being George Gunn of Achintoul (568) and his father being John Gunn of Kilearnan and Navidale. For further detail see 'Burke's Peerage, Baronetage & Knightage' 107*th *edition.*

Version 1.2 May 2012

---

[1] From an email by Sharon Gurney October 2009. (It may be accurate but we are not yet convinced.) 'Re: Donald Gunn in Tormsdale—Parents John Gunn and Margaret, Siblings: John Gunn / Catherine MacDonald (Halkirk), Alexander Gunn / Janet Mackay (Bualchork), Margaret Gunn / George Gunn (Braehour).
1. John Gunn / Catherine MacDonald. Witnesses at Baptism of 2 children of Donald Gunn / Janet Mackenzie. Their son John was president of the Benevolent Society 1821.
2. Alexander Gunn / Ann Mackay lived in Edinburgh and Bualchork. Their daughter Margaret was born in Bualchork, 1796. Witness at baptism was Margaret Gunn of Bualchork and Donald Gunn Olgrinmore. Children were Janet, 1791, John, 1793, Margaret, 1796.
3. Margaret Gunn / George Gunn Their grandson Rev. James Gunn is buried beside families of John Gunn, 1764, and Nans? Mackay of Dorraairy? (Dorrery). (Halkirk Cemetery). James was a Minister in Uig parish and died in 1858, age 36. (Son of Alex Gunn and Ann Waters.)'

From an October 2010 email; 'William Gunn of Achlibster ... I have wondered if he was the father of John Gunn of Tormsdale and therefore the grandfather of Donald Gunn in Tormsdale. Achlibster and Tormsdale are 1½ miles apart and Donald's family are often recorded as being in Achlibster.'

And from a further email: 'Here is something very interesting for you—from the Thurso records—a marriage—John Gunn of Tormsdale, Helen Bain of Hoy, married 1742. It is interesting that John Gunn / Catherine MacDonald's second daughter was named Helen.'

And from a November 2009 email: '1742 John Gunn, Tormsdale, married Helen Bain, How, in Thurso Parish, 1774 / 75 Donald Gunn, Harpsdale, married Margaret Gunn, Tormsdale, in Halkirk Parish, Daughter Helen Gunn born 1778 in Mybster, Halkirk Parish, 1782 Donald Gunn, Tormsdale, married Janet MacKenzie, Children born in Tormsdale, 1804 Isabel Gunn, Tormsdale married Alexander Gunn, Bualmore, in Halkirk Parish, 1802 Isabel Gunn, Tormsdale witnessed bapt. of Christian Gunn, daughter of Donald Gunn and Janet Mackenzie, 1805 Catherine Gunn, Tormsdale witnessed bapt. of Marcus Gunn, son of Donald Gunn and Janet Mackenzie.'

And from a further email March 2010: 'There is never a mention in any early Church records of another Gunn family besides yours in Tormsdale. This family seems to have had close ties to the Achlibster area. Family trees have the Achlibster Gunns as descendents of the Crowner's son John. A tie to this family could explain a son of Donald Gunn / Janet Mackenzie having the name of Marcus.'

[2] Thomas Sinclair, *The Gunns,* pages 121-122.

Contents

Introduction

It is with a mixture of relief and trepidation that we present this book. It is something which we have worked on over many years and for one of us it is based on detailed material held within the family and worked on by generations. We are aware of shortcomings; this book is certainly not a simple read. It is a book to be explored—mined—to find material for other projects. It is best to view it, perhaps, as an old fashioned 'Papers relating to a Gunn family'.

Some points to note before proceeding—

- We wish to thank many people; most importantly, as already mentioned, Sharon and Bill Gurney. But many others have helped including Wendy Gunn, David Gunn, Edith Gunn Christoe, Susanne Christoe, Caroline Cottrell, Jan Wilkinson, Dorothy Jenkin, Iain Gunn, Roy and Carol Small, Judy Meyer, Bill Loader, the Learmonth and District Historical Society, Dundee City Archives, Catherine Sinclair, Judy Surman, Judy Meyer, Debbie Kuzub, Carol Small and all those responsible for the invention of the computer, family tree programs and the internet without whom this book would never have been possible.

- There are numbers against many names; for example Donald Gunn in Tormsdale (262). This is because genealogical programs assign unique identification numbers to people, and we have kept these numbers for clarity. Hence when people contact us we can be clear about the individual in question (one wonders how many distinct Donald Gunns there are in this book?). **Note the meaning of the words 'in' and 'of' when applied to people; 'in' means 'residing' and 'of' means ownership. We have tried to use these words in the correct way but we apologise if we have used them inaccurately.**

- We have not always entered Canada, Scotland or Australia; we have mainly done so when it is not clear from context. We have also used abbreviations for many places which we hope are self-evident (or rapidly become so); Vic for Victoria in Australia, Twp for Township in Canada being two examples.

- Some places, especially in Scotland, have defied being located; we note Inishmull and Loravack as examples. We assume transcription errors have been made, but some names may have changed over time and been lost.

- Spelling errors, in original documents, have been retained.

- In the family trees and charts we have generally excluded living people.

- We are aware of the difficulties presented by repetition, appendices and lack of an Index but we have decided it is much better to present that which we have, rather than toil indefinitely in the hope of perfection.

- Images of documents may have been resized as we have tried to ensure legibility. These images may also have been cropped (they are also often more ripped than they seem—many bills appear to have been written on scrap paper).

Finally we recognise that this book is not the last word on these matters; we are sure new information will come to light and look forward to supplementing this volume in the future.

Dirlot Cemetery 1996

Braehour Farm 1996

Brawlbin Farm 1996

Some Ramblings of a Very Amateur Australian Genealogist

Donald Gunn[3]

Uncle Norman (37) came to visit when I was a boy. I remember it well, for he drove a Singer motor car. Nobody in our family had a car except grandfather, but he was old and I cannot recall the car ever leaving the stables. They were still called the stables, even though there had been no horses for many years. It was summer. The car had no roof and red upholstery. It had a dicky seat. And Uncle Norman took me for a drive. The memory of that drive around the block, sitting in the dicky seat, has never left me.

I never saw Uncle Norman again. I know now that he died only a few years later, but it was many years before I wondered exactly who Uncle Norman was. There were lots of uncles and aunts, but I had no idea how they fitted. Maybe it was a budding engineer's understanding that everything needed to fit somewhere, but I started to create charts to visualise the links.

Various old relatives had scraps of paper tucked away in drawers on which someone, they thought their grandfather perhaps, had written down the names of his brothers and sisters, and maybe parents. They never seemed to correlate, and my charts languished. Then computers were invented, and imaginative people modified database programs to create genealogical software. Suddenly, everything could be recorded, kept together and visualised. And it was.

Once close relatives had been recorded, and assigned their proper place, it became a matter of contacting more distant relatives. I knew many second cousins when we were children, but with time contact had withered. Gradually though a record of the descendants of my great grandfather, who came to Australia in the mid 1850s, took shape. An early surprise was that descendants of great grandfather's daughters were not as keen to assist as the descendants of the sons. By now, for female descendants, the Gunn name was in the distant past, and irrelevant to the present. Nevertheless, eventually 428 of great-grandfather Donald Gunn's descendants were recorded down to the seventh generation.

We produced a chart which included a photo of great-grandfather. It was almost three and a half metres long, rolled into a cylinder. Not for display on the wall of a suburban house. It was popular, and many in the family ordered copies.

Uncle Norman was there. He was one of great grandfather's sons and had never married. He had volunteered, as was the case for all Australian servicemen, for the army in 1915 at the age of 42. He was evacuated from Gallipoli, wounded during the Somme battles, and returned to Australia a corporal in 1918. I have no other information about him except the date and place of his birth and death. There are no known photographs; he is not mentioned in any letters; he did not make a name for himself in any way; perhaps an

[3] Being a very slight modification of an article which was first published in "The Gunn Herald", No.70, October 2006—being the journal of the UK Clan Gunn Society.

address or two could be found from old telephone books or electoral rolls, but that is probably all. Nothing to conjure up an image of how he lived or what he did. Nothing except his military record at the National Archives of Australia and the memory of a Singer motor car.

Details of some of great grandfather's ancestors were also in the database. The eldest son of the eldest son of the eldest son of great grandfather's eldest son possessed papers and old letters from the early 1800s, which not only included details of ancestors, but letters to cousins and siblings that enabled more names to be added. In the mid 1990s, *The Gunn Herald* published descendant charts from the early MacKeamishs of the Clan Gunn, and it became possible to make connections, albeit with little detail.

Sources available to the amateur genealogist are many and varied, but records from before Britain started registering births and other details in 1837 are sparse. The pages of old parish registers had been photographed by the Church of Latter Day Saints and made available on searchable CDs. These were wonderful, but could create more problems than answers, for there would inevitably be records of several different families with the same parental names christening their children. I suspect many amateur genealogists have been guilty of recording as fact what was really wishful thinking.

The first British census was in 1841, and this is the real starting point for the amateur interested in moving back as far as possible. Like the parish records, the pages of each census had been photographed and, while readable page by page from reels of film, the data had not been entered into a searchable format. It now has, and it is wonderful. I now know that on 6 June 1841 there were 1,365 persons named Gunn and one named Gun recorded as residing in Caithness, and 465 persons named Gunn and 21 named Gun residing in Sutherland. Maybe this was well known to others, but to me it was a revelation. While history told that many Gunns had already emigrated, particularly after the clearances, many still intended to, and did. And these from the 1,852 left in the clan's home counties!

And in a moment of vanity, I found that 89 of the 633 males in Caithness went by the name of Donald Gunn.

Part 1—Donald Gunn in Tormsdale[4] (262); a genetic descendant chart

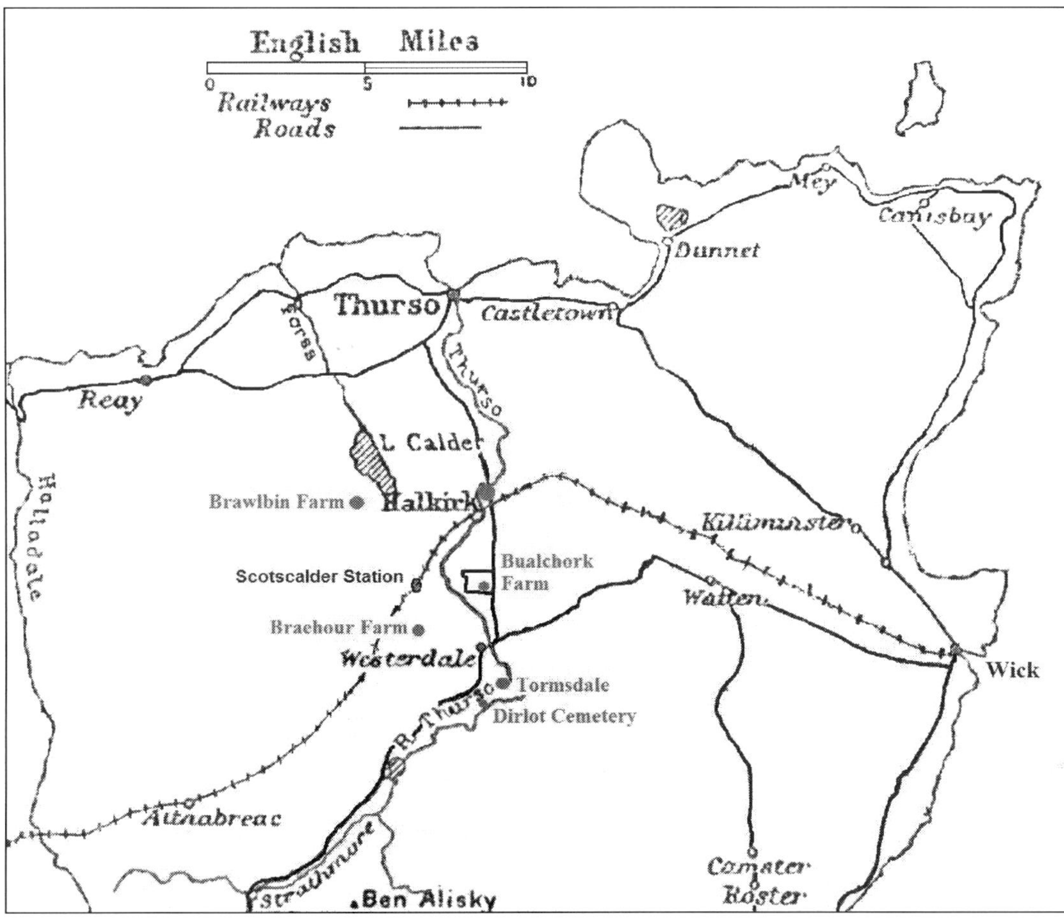

A map of north-east Scotland, showing some key places in our Gunn history.

---

[4]Tormsdale is "Tomnadale'; c. 5 buildings shown W Roy 1747-55. ... (later) a mortared farmhouse ruin of presumed 19th century date with associated footings and enclosures, some of which appear to pre-date the farmhouse.... Visited by OS 16 March 1982 ... A township comprising three roofed buildings, one of which is a long building, six unroofed buildings, three of which are long buildings, two enclosures, a sheepfold and some field walls are depicted on the 1st edition of the OS 6-inch map (Caithness 1876, sheet xxii). Eight unroofed buildings and four enclosures are shown on the current edition of the OS 1:10,560 map (1963). Information from RCAHMS (SAH) 27 November 1995'.
http://www.scotlandsplaces.gov.uk/search_item/index.php?service=RCAHMS&id=8250

Tormsdale, 2011, can be found from Westerdale village. There is a rough fishing track near the Church, which winds along the river from the centre of the village. Tormsdale consists, in 2011, of one run down house and many ruins.

Tormsdale 2011

Tormsdale 2011

Tormsdale 2011

The 1841 census records three households at Tormsdale, none of them Gunn.

Donald Gunn in Tormsdale (262), b. circa 1750 Tormsdale, Halkirk Parish, Caithness, d. circa 1840 Caithness
+**Janet MCKENZIE of Dunbeath** (703), b. circa 1765, m. 1782 Halkirk Parish, Caithness, d. after 1826

├── **John GUNN** (293), b. before 1783 Caithness, d. before 1784

├── **John GUNN of Tormsdale** (294), b. 1784 Tormsdale, Halkirk Parish, Caithness, d. 1857 Backlass, Watten Parish, Caithness

│ +**Anne / Ann GRANT** (3208), b. circa 1799, m. 1818 Halkirk Parish, Caithness, d. 1877 Banniskirk, Halkirk Parish, Caithness

│ ├── **Janet GUNN** (3211), b. 1820 Bualchork, Halkirk Parish, Caithness, d. before 1824

│ ├── **Margaret GUNN** (3212), b. 1821 Bualchork, Halkirk Parish, Caithness

│ ├── **Janet GUNN** (3213), b. Circa 1826 Caithness

│ ├── **Hector GUNN** (3214), b. 1826 Halkirk Parish, Caithness, d. 1904 Newlands, Watten Parish, Caithness

│ ├── **Donald GUNN of Olgrinbeg & Owen Sound** (3215), b. 1828 Olgrinbeg, Halkirk Parish, Caithness, d. 1895 Sydenham, Grey Co., Ontario

│ │ +**Janet MACKAY of Braehour** (3118), b. 1827 Caithness, m. 1852 Halkirk Parish, Caithness, d. 1914 Grey, Grey Co., Ontario

│ │ ├── **Angus Grant GUNN** (3218), b. 1850 Halkirk Parish, Caithness, d. 1864 Badnallie, Watten Parish, Caithness

│ │ ├── **Annie GUNN** (3134), b. 1852 Caithness, d. 1880 Owen Sound, Ontario

│ │ │ +**James ADAMS** (3219), m. 1877 Owen Sound, Ontario

│ │ ├── **Margaret GUNN** (3135), b. 1855 Caithness, d. 1942 Owen Sound, Ontario

│ │ ├── **Neil GUNN** (3136), b. 1857 Ontario, d. 1931 Sydenham, Ontario

│ │ │ +**Catherine CAMERON** (3143), b. 1873 Glengarry Co, m. 1892, d. 1928 Sydenham, Ontario

│ │ │ ├── **Allan Alexander GUNN** (3145), b. circa 1894, d. 1951

│ │ │ └── **Angus William GUNN** (3146), b. 1898, d. 1956 Sydenham, Ontario

│ │ ├── **John GUNN** (3137), b. 1859 Ontario, d. 1875

│ │ ├── **Donald McKay GUNN** (3138), b. 1861 Ontario, d. 1926

│ │ ├── **Angus Hector GUNN** (3142), b. 1864 Ontario, d. 1940 Prince George, British Colombia

│ │ ├── **Barbara Janet GUNN** (3139), b. 1866 Ontario, d. 1931 Ontario

│ │ │ +**William James CARNAHAN** (3147), b. 1869, d. 1948

│ │ │ └── **Margaret CARNAHAN** (3148)

│ │ ├── **Jemima GUNN** (3140), b. 1870 Ontario, d. 1870 Ontario

│ │ └── **William James GUNN** (3141), b. 1871 Ontario, d. 1890 Ontario

│ └── **Helen GUNN** (3216), b. 1835 Halkirk Parish, Caithness, d. 1931 Newton Moss, Watten Parish, Caithness.

│ +**Archibald SINCLAIR** (3217), m. 1858 Halkirk Parish, Caithness

│ ├── **John William SINCLAIR** (3220), b. 1858 Latheron Parish, Caithness

│ ├── **George SINCLAIR** (3221), b. 1860 Latheron Parish, Caithness, d. before 1869

│ ├── **Janet SINCLAIR** (3222), b. 1862 Watten Parish, Caithness

│ ├── **William G R SINCLAIR** (3223), b. 1863 Watten Parish, Caithness

│ ├── **Elizabeth SINCLAIR** (3224), b. 1865 Watten Parish, Caithness

│ ├── **Ann SINCLAIR** (3225), b. 1867 Watten Parish, Caithness

│ ├── **George SINCLAIR** (3226), b. 1869 Watten Parish, Caithness

│ ├── **Hector SINCLAIR** (3227), b. 1871 Watten Parish, Caithness

│ ├── **Archibald SINCLAIR** (3228), b. 1873 Watten Parish, Caithness

│ └── **Daniel G SINCLAIR** (3229), b. 1876 Watten Parish, Caithness

├── **Hugh Gunn in Tormsdale**[5] (295), b. 1787 Tormsdale, Halkirk Parish, Caithness, d. before 1851 Halkirk Parish, Caithness

│ +**Henrietta MCGREGOR of Dalnawillan** (752), b. 1795, m. 1814, d. 1890 Houstry, Dunbeath Parish, Caithness

│ ├── **William GUNN** (807), chr. 1815 Inishmull, Halkirk Parish, Caithness

│ ├── **Janet GUNN** (3230), chr. 1817 Inishmull, Halkirk Parish, Caithness, d. 1890 Houstry, Dunbeath Parish, Caithness

│ ├── **Catherine GUNN** (3231), chr. 1819 Inishmull, Halkirk Parish, Caithness d. 1913 Lybster, Latheron Parish, Caithness

│ ├── **Helen GUNN** (3232), b. 1822 Camster, Latheron Parish, Caithness

---

[5] For a more detailed chart of Hugh Gunn's descendants see page 471.

| ├── **Christina GUNN** (3233), b. 1825 Camster, Latheron Parish, Caithness, d. 1863 Houstry, Dunbeath Parish, Caithness

| ├── **Henrietta GUNN** (3234), b. 1827 Camster, Latheron Parish, Caithness

| ├── **Donald GUNN** (3235), b. 1829 Camster, Latheron Parish, Caithness, d. 1912 Latheron Parish, Caithness

| ├── **Mary GUNN** (3236), b. 1835 Camster, Latheron Parish, Caithness

| ├── **John GUNN** (3237), chr. 1837 Wick Parish, Caithness

| └── **Alexander GUNN** (3238), chr. 1839 Wick Parish, Caithness

| +**Christina GUNN** (3239), m. 1893 Latheron Parish, Caithness

| ├── **Henrietta GUNN** (808), b. 1894

| └── **Alexander M K GUNN** (3240), b. 1896

├── **Alexander GUNN of Bualchork and Brawlbin**[6] (1), b. 1789 Halkirk Parish, Caithness, d. 1847[7] Brawlbin, Reay Parish, Caithness

| +**Barbara GUNN**[8] **of Braehour** (6), b. 1810 Halkirk Parish, Caithness, m. 1829 Halkirk Parish, Caithness, d. 1844, Brawlbin, Reay Parish, Caithness

| ├── **Catherine GUNN** (119), b. 1830 Reay Parish, Caithness, d. 1912 Vic

| | +**James MILLER**[9] (117), b. 1826 Wick Parish, Caithness, m. 1857 Buninyong, Vic, d. 1918 Vic

| | ├── **Elizabeth MILLER** (278), b. 1858 Geelong, Vic, d. 1918 Vic

| | ├── **Alexander Gunn MILLER** (279), b. 1860 Geelong, Vic, d. 1938 Apollo Bay, Vic

| | ├── **John William Gunn MILLER** (280), b. 1862 Geelong, Vic, d. 1925 St Kilda, Vic

| | ├── **Jessie Barbara MILLER** (284), b. 1865 Emerald Hill, Vic d. 1936 Devon

| | | + **Charles James SWEARS** (282), m. circa 1885 Vic or London 1892, d. 1927 Devon

| | | ├── **Hugh Miller SWEARS** (286), b. 1894, d. 1917 France

| | | ├── **Marjorie Gertrude SWEARS**[10] (287), b. 1896 London, d. 1948 Worcestershire

| | | └── **Dorothy Catherine Swears** (4129), b. 1903

| | ├── **James Dunnet MILLER** (281), b. 1868 Emerald Hill, Vic, d. 1933 Heidelberg, Vic

| | └── **Katherine Margaret Mackay MILLER** (285), b. 1872 Emerald Hill, Vic, d. 1951 Sydney NSW

| | +**William Porter VINE** (283), b. 1857 Port Melbourne, Vic, m. 1895 Vic, d. 1923 Prahran, Vic

| | ├── **James Miller VINE**[11] (288), b. 1896 St Kilda, Vic

| | ├── **William Alan VINE** (290), b. 1898 St Kilda, Vic, d. 1917

| | ├── **Catherine Noel VINE** (291), b. 1900 St Kilda, Vic, d. 1903 Melbourne South, Vic

| | ├── **Francis Seymour VINE**[12] (292), b. 1904 St Kilda, Vic, d. 1961 Somers, Vic

| | ├── **Reginald Vernon VINE** (694), b. 1908 St Kilda, Vic, d. 1987 NSW

| | └── **Lesley Alison VINE**[13] (289), b. 1914 St Kilda, Vic, d. 1972

| ├── **Donald GUNN of Brawlbin & Ballarat** (3), b. 1832 Brawlbin, Reay Parish, Caithness, d. 1901 Ballarat, Vic[14]

| | +**Jane SURMAN** (41), b. 1836 Hampton Poyle, Oxfordshire, m. 1859 Buninyong, Vic, d. 1908 Ballarat, Vic

| | ├── **John Alexander GUNN (Hon.)**[15] (32), b. 1860 Buninyong, Vic, d. 1910 Sydney, NSW

---

6 It is also occasionally known as 'Braalbin' and can be found, as such, in various references; for example http://www.ambaile.org.uk/gd/newspapers/search_results.jsp?newspaper=5&PrimarySubject=0&startyear=1834&endyear=*&keywords=&StartRow=26400&MaxRows=.
The name seems to have derived from the ON compound appellative for 'broad field' also see http://books.google.co.uk/books?id=ISppAAAAMAAJ&q=brawlbin&dq=brawlbin&hl=en&ei=e6OkTJH3FsKSjAe7gemRDA&sa=X&oi=book_result&ct=result&resnum=9&ved=0CEgQ6AEwCDhG .

7 A receipt for the rent of Brawlbin (page 180) implies he died in 1844 and that Barbara was still alive in late 1845.

8 See Part 4 and later for Barbara's descent and further information relating to her side of the family; this marriage of two Gunn lines caused significant confusion to Alexander and Barbara's descendants for many years regarding the Chiefship. Also, an email from the Gurneys says '"The John O'Groat Journal'" published a birth on March 3, 1843-"Births-Gunn, Mrs Alex Brawlbin, a daughter."' We have no record for this child.

9 See Part 7.

10 She married the Rev. John Ernest Cocks Adams in Totnes, Devon in 1926.

11 Married Gwynneth Annie Archdall (3981) 1924, d. 25 Oct 1961, later he married Rosemary Caroline Stewart (1108) from whom at least one child was born, Patricia Louise Vine (1109) b. 1958, d. 1959 Fairfield Vic.

12 Married Elizabeth Smith Cuming (3982) 1929 Vic, d. 1931 Malvern Vic. They had two children, James Miller Vine (898) c. 1930 and Elizabeth Vine (3987) b. c. 1930, d. 1931 Malvern, Vic.

13 Married Charles Herbert Locke (3983) 1936 Vic.

14 Died at his residence 185 Lydiard Street Ballarat. http://newspapers.nla.gov.au/ndp/del/article/10535465?searchTerm=Gunn

| | | +**Jessie Marie TURNER**[16] (104), b. 1862 Beechworth, Vic, m. 1886 North Brighton, Vic, d. 1925 Randwick, NSW[17]
| | | |—— **Gladys Emily GUNN** (225), b. 1887 North Brighton, Vic, d. 1968 Melbourne, Vic
| | | |—— **Jessie Jean GUNN** (221), b. 1890 Ballarat, Vic, d. 1891 NSW
| | | |—— **Alexander Donald GUNN** (222), b. 1892 Ballarat, Vic, d. 1956 Melbourne, Vic
| | | └—— **Angus William GUNN** (223), b. 1895 Ballarat, Vic, d. 1926 Perth, WA
| | |—— **William Watkins GUNN** (33), b. 1861 Nr Ballarat, Vic, d. 1935 Crossover, Vic
| | | +**Margaret Jane BALHARRIE** (42), b. 1860 Perth, Tayside, m. 1891 Bloomfield, Vic, d. 1946 Frankston, Vic
| | | |—— **John William GUNN** (133), b. 1895 Ballarat, Vic, d. 1981 Frankston, Vic
| | | |—— **Jean Margaret GUNN** (139), b. 1896 Ballarat, Vic, d. 1975 Glenhuntly, Vic
| | | |—— **Violet Helen GUNN** (141), b. 1898 Warragul, Vic, d. 1968 Frankston, Vic
| | | |—— **Edith Mary GUNN** (134), b. 1899 Warragul, Vic, d. 1901 Sandringham, Vic
| | | |—— **Marjorie May GUNN** (135), b. 1904 Warragul, Vic, d. 1970 Launching Place, Vic
| | | └—— **Marcus Allan GUNN** (136), b. 1906 Crossover, Vic, d. 1981 Melbourne, Vic
| | |—— **Mary Jane GUNN** (34), b. 1864 Cardigan Nr Ballarat, Vic, d. 1934 Werribee, Vic
| | |—— **Donald GUNN** (35), b. 1865 Burrumbeet, Vic, d. 1933 Crossover, Vic
| | | +**Amy Agnes WAREHAM** (43), b. 1862 Cheshire, m. 1922 Middle Park, Vic, d. 1939 South Melbourne Vic
| | |—— **Marcus Daniel GUNN** (36), b. 1868 Buninyong, Vic, d. 1952 South Yarra, Vic
| | | +**Mary Jane CHENHALL**[18] (105), b. 1873 Chiltern, Vic, m. 1903 Corowa, NSW, d. 1941 Melbourne, Vic
| | | |—— **Keith Lindsay GUNN** (121), b. 1904 Corowa, NSW, d. 1967 Melbourne, Vic
| | | └—— **Norma Mary GUNN** (125), b. 1907 Corowa, NSW, d. 1971 Melbourne, Vic
| | |—— **Barbara GUNN** (106), b. 1870 Burrumbeet, Vic, d. 1941 Werribee, Vic
| | | +**Isaac PADGETT** (103), b. 1867 Mount Cole, Vic, m. 1899 Ballarat, Vic, d. 1937 Werribee, Vic
| | | |—— **Barbara Gunn PADGETT** (184), b. 1901 Ballarat, Vic, d. 1960
| | | |—— **Norman Gunn PADGETT** (180), b. 1903 Ballarat, Vic, d. 1952 Princhester, Qld
| | | └—— **Jean Gunn PADGETT** (186), b. 1913 Vic, d. 2002
| | |—— **Norman GUNN** (37), b. 1872 Burrumbeet, Vic, d. 1944 Williamstown, Vic
| | |—— **Hugh GUNN** (38), b. 1875 Burrumbeet, Vic, d. 1879 Burrumbeet, Vic
| | |—— **Arthur Gilbert GUNN** (9), b. 1878 Burrumbeet, Vic, d. 1933 Ivanhoe, Vic
| | | +**Louisa Maud Miriam RETALLICK** (10), b. 1875 Naseby, Otago, m. 1901 Ballarat, Vic, d. 1959 Elsternwick, Vic
| | | |—— **Malcolm Donald GUNN** (11), b. 1903 Ballarat, Vic, d. 1961 Heidelberg, Vic
| | | |—— **Kenneth Douglas GUNN** (23), b. 1905 Kalgoorlie, WA, d. 1951 Longreach, Qld
| | | |—— **Angus Norman GUNN** (24), b. 1912 Kalgoorlie, WA, d. 1994 Caringbah, NSW
| | | └—— **Colin GUNN** (29), b. 1915 Ballarat, Vic, d. 1916 Ballarat, Vic
| | └—— **Catherine Alexandrina GUNN** (39), b. 1880 Burrumbeet, Vic, d. 1960 Ormond, Vic
| |—— **Janet MacLeod GUNN**[19] (120), b. 1834 Brawlbin, Reay Parish, Caithness, d. 1913 Cardigan, Vic
| | +**John Watkins SURMAN** (118), b. 1831 Hampton Poyle, Oxfordshire, m. 1864 Cardigan, Vic, d. 1906 Ballarat, Vic
| | |—— **'Baby' SURMAN** (1550), b. 1865 Ballarat, Vic, d. 1865 Ballarat, Vic
| | |—— **John Daniel SURMAN** (272), b. 1866 Cardigan, Vic, d. 1935 Dunolly, Vic
| | | + (**Jessie**[20]) **Margaret COWLEY** (1553), b. 1866, m. 1895, d. 1951 Geelong, Vic
| | | |—— **Jessie Marguerite SURMAN** [21](1554), b. 1896 Armadale, Vic, d. 1955 Geelong, Vic

---

15 See Part 7.

16 Jessie Maria Turner's father, William Turner, was a noted banker. He was second—and sometimes third—in charge of the Commercial Bank of Australia for many years in the 1890s and was also a pamphleteer. An uncle was the noted early Geelong photographer Joseph Turner; he later worked at the Melbourne Observatory with the Great Melbourne Telescope.

17 http://newspapers.nla.gov.au/ndp/del/article/16209653?searchTerm=Gunn for the funeral notice.

18 Her brother was W.T. Chenhall M.D., M.B. B.S. F.R.C.S.. He was a notable Sydney surgeon until his death in 1923. http://newspapers.nla.gov.au/ndp/del/article/16112528?searchTerm=Gunn

19 We have kept the name Janet MacLeod. Although we have no primary source for the name MacLeod it has been commonly used by members of her family after her death.

20 In 'Digger Death Index Victoria 1921-1985' the death notice for her daughter gives Jessie as the first name for the mother.

└── **Thomas William SURMAN** (1555), b. 1899 Carlton, Vic, d. 1965 Melbourne, Vic

├── **Alexander Gunn SURMAN** (273), b. 1868 Ballarat, Vic, d. 1909 Ballarat, Vic

+**Esther KIRK** (676), b. 1864, m. 1891 Vic, d. 1938 Cardigan, Vic

├── **Jessie Beatrice SURMAN** (680), b. 1892 Ballarat, Vic, d. 1954 Caulfield, Vic[22]

├── **Linda Pearl SURMAN** (682), b. 1893 Ballarat, Vic[23]

├── **Eric SURMAN** (683), b. 1895 Haddon, nr Ballarat, Vic, d. 1959 Ballarat, Vic[24]

├── **Stella SURMAN** (681), b. 1897 Haddon, Vic, d. 1968 Ballarat, Vic[25]

├── **Tettie SURMAN** (679), b. 1898 Ballarat, Vic[26]

├── **Reginald Gunn SURMAN** (678), b. 1899 Haddon, Vic, d. 1943 Ballarat, Vic[27]

└── **Margery SURMAN** (687), b. 1904 Ballarat, Vic[28]

├── **Barbara Margaret McKay SURMAN** (274), b. 1870 Ballarat, Vic, d. 1928 Morwell, Vic

+**James BREWSTER** (1559), m. 1892

├── **Renee Grace Daphne BREWSTER**[29] (1577), b. 1893 Learmonth, Vic

├── **James William Ashley BREWSTER**[30] (1578), b. 1895 Ballarat, Vic, d. 1957 Sale, Vic

├── **John Watkins Surman BREWSTER**[31] (1579), b. 1897 Ballarat, Vic, d. 1975 Leongatha, Vic

├── **David Baxter BREWSTER** (1580), b. 1899 Yinnar, Vic

├── **Janet Barbara BREWSTER** (1581), b. 1902 Yinnar, Vic

├── **George Alan BREWSTER** [32](1582), b. 1904 Yinnar, Vic, d. 1985 Leongatha, Vic

├── **Hugh Gordon BREWSTER**[33] (1583), b. 1906 Leongatha, Vic, d. 1976 Leongatha, Vic

├── **Oswald Geoffrey BREWSTER** (1584), b. 1912 Morwell, Vic

└── **Robert Norman BREWSTER** (1585), b. 1913 Morwell, Vic

├── **Watkins SURMAN** (405), b. 1871 Sago Hill/Cardigan, Vic, d. 1875 Cardigan, Vic

├── **James William SURMAN** (275), b. 1873 Sago Hill, Vic, d. 1947 Horsham, Vic

+**Alice Maud Grace CURTIS** (677), b. 1874 Buninyong, Vic, m. 1894 Ballarat, Vic, d. 1956 Horsham, Vic

├── **Grace Jessie Frances SURMAN** (684), b. 1895 Wonwondah South, Vic, d. 1895 Mount Jeffcott, Vic

├── **Leslie Watkins SURMAN**[34] (685), b. 1896 Horsham, Vic, d. 1939 Scone NSW

├── **Hazel Marion SURMAN**[35] (686), b. 1901 Dunolly, Vic, d. 1984 Horsham, Vic

└── **Harry 'Jack' SURMAN**[36] (1561), b. 1917 Horsham, Vic, d. 2006 Drouin, Vic

├── **Irene Marian Catherine SURMAN** (693), b. 1874 Sago Hill, Vic, d. 1940 Melbourne, Vic

---

21 'Digger Death Index Victoria 1921-1985' Jessie Marguerite had a married name of Danier and she died in Geelong; her (second) husband was Gustav Danier (father Paul and mother Anna). He died in Geelong in 1958.

22 Jessie Surman married William George Nathanial Stephens (1556) in 1915 and they had children Joyce Wilma Stephens (3804) b. 1917 Elsternwick Vic and Edna Surman Stephens (3803) also b. 1917 Elsternwick Vic.

23 Linda Surman married George William Johnson (3801) 1923.

24 Eric Surman married Annie Walton (1557) b. 1897 d. 26 Jan 1965 Ballarat Vic. They had children: Alexander Geoffrey Surman (1558) b. 15 Jan 1923 Numurkah d. before 2008; Norma Surman (3004) b. after 1923 (who married 'unknown' Bell (3007); Joyce Surman (3005) b. after 1923 d. before 2008 and Elva Surman b. after 1923.

25 Stella Surman married David Davidson Draffin (2667) b. 1883 m. 1921 d. 1957 Ballarat. Their child was John Robert Draffin (3806) b. 1926 d. 1964.

26 Married Alfred Rupert Thompson (3802) b 1898, m. 1929 d. 1984 Surrey Hills, Vic.

27 Married Eva Draffin (2868) b. 1906, m. 1928, d. 24 Oct 1948 Ballarat Vic.

28 Margery Surman married James Clifford Sharp (995) b. 1903, m. 11 Mar. 1931 Ballarat Vic. d. 1968 Ballarat Vic.

29 Married Percy Osborne Scouller (2869) b. 1891, m. 1915, d. 1975 Heidelberg, Vic.

30 Married Elsie May Scouller (2870), 1926, with children Stanley Arthur Brewster (3989), b. 1918 Vic, d. 1975 Vic and Alan William Brewster (3988), b. 1924 Vic, d. 1978 Melbourne, Vic.

31 Married Marjory Letitia (unknown) (3773) before 1931.

32 Married Edith Mary (unknown) (3808) c. 1930 Vic.

33 Married Jessie Isabella Reilly (3807) b. 1908, m. circa 1930 d. 1982 Leongatha.

34 Married Eileen Avonia Fletcher (3776) b. 1902, m. 1931 Newcastle, d. 1947 Parkville, Vic. They had two daughters.

35 She married Robert Devlin 1884-1947 (1560) in 1925 and had three children; Jean, Jeffrey Watkins and Thomas Devlin.

36 A Surman Court exists at Jeeralang Junction and at Drouin, both of which were developed by Jack Surman and his son Gary Surman. He married Maude Elizabeth Hodges / Roadley and had children.

+**William O'CONNOR** (692), m. 1918 Vic

├── **Theodore Oswald SURMAN** (276), b. 1876 Cardigan, Vic, d. 1918 Melbourne South, Vic

└── **Geoffrey Eustace SURMAN** (277), b. 1878 Sago Hill, Vic, d. 1951 Heidelberg, Vic

+**Winifred May LITTLEHALES** (458), b. 1892 Vic, m. 1917 Ballarat, Vic, d. 1920 Ballarat, Vic

├── **Geoffrey Oswald SURMAN** (4), b. 1918 Ballarat, Vic, d. 1921 Sale, Vic

└── **John Watkins SURMAN**[37] (689), b. 1920 Ballarat, Vic, d. 1996 Brisbane, Qld

+**Ethel Stella TODD** (1552), b. 1901, m. 1926

├── **John GUNN** (12), b. 836 Reay Parish, Caithness, d. 1854 Port Melbourne, Vic

└── **William GUNN** (220), b. 1839 Reay Parish, Caithness, d. after 1864 Vic

├── **George GUNN of Tormsdale** (804), b. 1795 Tormsdale, Halkirk Parish, Caithness, d. 1868 Swiney Mains, Latheron Parish, Caithness

+**Ann MCDONALD** (942), b. circa 1801 Reay Parish, Sutherland, m. 1821 Halkirk Parish, Caithness, d. 1878 Swiney Mains, Latheron Parish, Caithness

├── **William GUNN of Bualchork** (3175), b. 1822 Bualchork, Halkirk Parish, Caithness, d. 1899 Rangag Forse, Latheron Parish, Caithness

├── **Margaret GUNN** (3176), b. 1824 Halkirk Parish, Caithness, d. 1895 Dunbeath, Caithness

├── **Hugh GUNN** (3177), b. 1825 Halkirk Parish, Caithness

├── **Janet GUNN** (3193), b. 1827 Halkirk Parish, Caithness, d. 1911 Knockglass, Dunbeath Parish, Caithness

+**John MACKAY** (3194), b. 1811 Latheron Parish, Caithness, m. 1853 Halkirk Parish, Caithness, d. 1899 Rangag Forse, Latheron Parish, Caithness

├── **Neil MACKAY** (3202), b. circa 1854

├── **Ann MACKAY** (3203), b. 1856 Halkirk Parish, Caithness, d. 1891 Halkirk Parish, Caithness

├── **Margaret MACKAY** (3204), b. 1857 Latheron Parish, Caithness

├── **Mary MACKAY** (3303), b. 1860 Rangag Forse, Latheron Parish, Caithness

├── **John MACKAY** (3207), b. 1862 Latheron Parish, Caithness

└── **Isabella Helen MACKAY** (3206), b. 1866 Latheron Parish, Caithness

├── **Donald GUNN** (3195), b. 1829 Bualchork, Halkirk Parish, Caithness, d. Halkirk Parish, Caithness

├── **Mary GUNN** (3196), b. 1831 Halkirk Parish, Caithness, d. 1904 Caithness

├── **Helen GUNN** (3197), b. 1834 Halkirk Parish, Caithness, d. 1909 Caithness

+**Charles M MUNRO** (3198), b. 1833 Wick Parish, Caithness, d. 1921 Latheron Parish, Caithness

├── **Isabella GUNN** (3199), b. 1836 Halkirk Parish, Caithness, d. 1866 Caithness

└── **Donald GUNN** (3200), b. 1840 Halkirk Parish, Caithness, d. 1895 Latheron Parish, Caithness

+**Mary Ann MUNRO** (3201)

├── **Donald GUNN of Bualchork** (296), b. 1796 Tormsdale, Halkirk Parish, Caithness

+**Ann MACKAY** (3244), b. circa 1809 Halkirk Parish, Caithness, m. 1827 Halkirk Parish, Caithness

├── **Hector GUNN** (3245), b. 1827 Halkirk Parish, Caithness

├── **Donald GUNN** (3246), b. 1829 Halkirk Parish, Caithness

├── **Janet GUNN** (3247), b. 1831 Halkirk Parish, Caithness

├── **Helen GUNN** (3248), b. 1833 Halkirk Parish, Caithness

├── **Margaret GUNN** (3249), b. 1835 Halkirk Parish, Caithness

├── **John GUNN (Sir) of Tormsdale**[38] (3250), b. 1837 Halkirk Parish, Caithness, d. 1918 Cardiff, Glamorgan

+**Sarah Jane HILL** (3311), m. 1871 Cardiff, Glamorgan, d. 1875

├── **John Donald GUNN** (3314), b. 1872 Cardiff, Glamorgan, d. 1872 Cardiff, Glamorgan

├── **Herbert Oswald GUNN** (3315), b. 1873 Cardiff, Glamorgan

└── **Arthur Hill GUNN** (3316), b. 1875 Cardiff, Glamorgan

+**Harriette BOYLE** (3312), b. circa 1846 Ballymacrea, Antrim, m. 1877 Belfast, d. 1914 Newport, Monmouthshire

├── **Annie Boyle GUNN** (3317), b. 1879 Cardiff, Glamorgan

+**Frederick George PENNY** (3318), m. 1905 Cardiff, Glamorgan

├── **Winifred Mackay GUNN** (3319), b. 1879 Cardiff, Glamorgan

+**Francis Brodie LODGE** (3320), b. 1880, m. 1909 Cardiff, Glamorgan, d. 1967

├── **Olive Mildred GUNN** (3323), b. 1881 Cardiff, Glamorgan

[37] Married Audrey Braker (1551) 28 Jun 1947.

[38] See Part 7.

Elsie Maud GUNN (3324), b. 1882 Cardiff, Glamorgan

Hester Boyle GUNN (3325), b. 1885 Cardiff, Glamorgan

John Boyle GUNN (3327), b. 1888 Cardiff, Glamorgan

Marjorie Lilian GUNN (3326), b. 1889 Cardiff, Glamorgan

+**Frederic STRATTON** (3328), m. 1913 Cardiff, Glamorgan

Christina GUNN (3251), b. 1839 Halkirk Parish, Caithness

Marcus GUNN[39] (3252), b. 1842 Bualchork, Halkirk Parish, Caithness, d. 1899 Cardiff, Glamorgan

+**Mary Elizabeth YEANDLE** (3313), b. 1855, m. 1877 Shurdington, Gloucestershire

Ernest GUNN (3329), b. 1878 Cardiff, Glamorgan, d. 1916 Cardiff, Glamorgan

Beatrice McKay GUNN (3330), b. 1880 Cardiff, Glamorgan

Marcus Sinclair GUNN (3331), b. 1890 Cardiff, Glamorgan

George GUNN (3253), b. 1842 Bualchork, Halkirk Parish, Caithness, d. before 1851 Halkirk Parish, Caithness

William GUNN[40] (297), b. 1799 Halkirk Parish, Caithness

Christian GUNN of Owen Sound (602), b. 1802 Halkirk Parish, Caithness

+**Alexander SUTHERLAND of Inshag** (3119), b. crca 1800 Caithness, m. 1825 Latheron Parish, Caithness

Christina SUTHERLAND (3130), b. 1826 Latheron Parish, Caithness, d. 1900

+**John MUNRO** (3166), m. circa 1850[41]

Donald SUTHERLAND (3127), b. 1828 Camster, Latheron Parish, Caithness, d. 1856

Janet SUTHERLAND (3256), b. 1830 Camster, Latheron Parish, Caithness, d. 1830 Caithness

Ann SUTHERLAND (3129), b. 1831 Camster, Latheron Parish, Caithness, d. 1914 Sydenham, Grey Co., Ontario

Janet SUTHERLAND (3131), b. 1833 Camster, Latheron Parish, Caithness, d.1908

+**James MACKAY** (3167), m. 1860[42]

Ellen SUTHERLAND (3120), b. 1835 Camster, Latheron Parish, Caithness, d. 1910

+**Hugh GORDON** (3121), b. 1830, m. 1855, d. 1915[43]

Alexander GORDON (3122), b. 1857, d. 1926

+**? FOSTER** (3125)

Ellen GORDON (3123)

Williamina SUTHERLAND (3132), b. 1838 Caithness, d. 1927 Grey, Grey Co., Ontario

Catherine SUTHERLAND (3133), b. 1839 Camster, Latheron Parish, Caithness, d. 1900

+**George MACDONALD** (3168), b. 1833, m. 1871, d. 1871 Grey, Grey Co., Ontario[44]

John SUTHERLAND (3128), b. 1842 Wentworth Co., Ontario, d. 1904

Marcus GUNN in Owen Sound (298), b. 1805 Halkirk Parish, Caithness, d. 1878 Owen Sound, Ontario

+**Barbara MACKAY** (3111), b. 1814 Halkirk Parish, Caithness, m. 1850 Sydenham, Grey Co., Ontario, d. 1881 Sydenham, Grey Co., Ontario

Janet GUNN (3113), b. 1851 Sydenham, Grey Co., Ontario, d. 1900 Owen Sound, Ontario

+**Herbert William JENKINS** (3117), b. 1850, m. 1876 Owen Sound, Ontario, d. 1941

Herbert Claude Marcus JENKINS (3160), b. 1877 Keppel, Grey Co., Ontario

+**Agnes Jane BROWN** (3290), b. 1877, m. 1902 Owen Sound, Ontario

Cecil Herbert JENKINS (2871), b. 1903 Owen Sound, Ontario

Nora Gertrude JENKINS (3310), b. 1903 Owen Sound, Ontario

Eva Elizabeth JENKINS (3159), b. 1880 Sydenham, Grey Co., Ontario, d. 1973 Owen Sound, Ontario

Norah Blanche JENKINS (3308), b. 1884 Sydenham, Grey Co., Ontario, d. 1885 Owen Sound, Ontario

---

[39] See Part 7.

[40] It is possible that William emigrated to Jamaica by 1819, see page 186 and the subsequent pages.

[41] With children John Munro b. c. 1852, Donald Munro, b. circa 1854, Margaret Munro, b. circa 1856, Christina Munro, b. circa 1858.

[42] With children Alexander MacKay, b. c. 1862, Catherine Innes MacKay, b. circa 1864, George MacKay, b.circa 1866, Wilhelmina MacKay, b. circa 1868.

[43] With other children: Mary Gordon, b. 2 Jan 1856, d. 2 Nov 1898, Charles Gordon, b. 20 Feb 1859, d. c. 1930, John Gordon, b. 11 Jan 1861, d. 13 Mar 1926, Christina Gordon, b. 19 Nov 1862, d. 12 Apr 1949, Donald Gordon, b. 14 Apr 1865, d. 16 Jan 1952, Thomas Gordon, b. 18 Jan 1867, d. 19 Aug 1934, Ann Sutherland Gordon, b. 31 Dec 1868. d. 1 Apr 1958, Elizabeth Gordon, b. 30 Dec 1872, d. 4 Feb 1935, Hugh Gordon, b. 5 Dec 1875, d. 10 Oct 1938.

[44] With child: Jessie MacDonald, b. circa 1871.

└── **Margaret GUNN** (3112), b. 1852 Sydenham, Grey Co., Ontario, d. 1920 Sarawak, Grey Co., Ontario
+**James Lindsay BOYD** (3116), b. 1848, m. 1871, d. 1918
├── **William John BOYD** (3153), b. 1872 Sydenham, Grey Co., Ontario, d. 1886 Sydenham, Grey Co., Ontario
├── **Barbara Jane BOYD** (3152), b. 1875 Sydenham, Ontario, d. 1973 Greenwood, Ontario
│ +**David REILLY** (3156), b. 1869 Ontario, m. 1897 Sydenham, Grey Co., Ontario, d. 1924 Owen Sound, Ontario
├── **Marcus Gunn BOYD** (3155), b. 1878 Sydenham, Grey Co., Ontario
│ +**Henrietta REILLY** (3158), b. 1878 Ontario, m. 1903 Sydenham, Grey Co., Ontario, d. 1929 Empress, Alberta
│ ├── **Opal Eileen BOYD** (3287), b. circa 1905
│ └── **Harold Elliott BOYD** (3288), b. circa 1907
├── **Robert John BOYD** (3150), b. 1880 Sydenham, Grey Co., Ontario, d. 1939 Owen Sound, Ontario
│ +**Sarah Alice COOK** (3157), b. 1887, d. 1968
│ ├── **James Henry Robert BOYD** (3268), b. 1910 Sydenham, Ontario, d. 1952
│ ├── **Norman BOYD** (3165), b. after 1911, d. after 1952
│ ├── **Earl BOYD** (3269), b. after 1911, d. after 1952
│ ├── **William James BOYD** (3270), b. after 1911, d. after 1952
│ └── **Edna BOYD** (3271), b. after 1911
└── **Catherine Margaret BOYD** (3154), b. 1882 Sydenham, Grey Co., Ontario, d. 1906 Sydenham, Grey Co., Ontario

Halkirk. 2011

Clan Gunn Centre, Latheron, 2011

Part 2—The descendants of Donald Gunn in Tormsdale (262); a journal with details

This Journal uses 'Generations'; and it is exactly that. Generation One is the 'founding' Donald (262), his wife and briefly their children, Generation Two is Donald's children, spouses and briefly their children and so on. The key purpose of the Journal is to flesh out the lives of the people, and provide evidence for these lives.

Generation One

1. Donald Gunn in Tormsdale (262) was born circa 1750 in Tormsdale, Halkirk Parish, Caithness. He married Janet McKenzie of Dunbeath (703), daughter of (--?--) McKenzie (805), on 19 Feb 1782 in Halkirk Parish, Caithness.[45] He died circa 1844[46] in Caithness. He was alive in 1826 when his son Hugh (295) wrote to him, but Donald is not recorded in either the 1841 or 1851 censuses. Another son, Marcus (298), wrote letters which from 1842 do not mention either parent. Marcus was living with a brother, and later also his sister Christian (602), by 1841, and death records from 1855 on do not include Donald.

Janet MCKENZIE of Dunbeath (703) was born circa 1765.[47] She died after 1826 as she was alive when their son Hugh wrote to his parents absolving them of all inheritance rights[48]. Hugh wrote in 1826 in Camster, Latheron Parish, Caithness—

Bolchork

'I Hugh Gunn tennant in Campster and lawfull son to Donald Gunn tennant Bolchork and to Janet McKenzie his lawfull married wife; do hereby and in presence of Donald Mcdonald and Benjaman Greay booth Shoemakers in Bolchork, Do Hereby acknowledge to have Received my full shair as their lawfull son of all that falls my shair of Hail(?) and whole their subject and in the presence of the Above specesifyed witnesses, Do Hereby Discharge them Their hears successors and asignies from any Cleam or Cleams relitive to the above specesifyed shair and for siverral good causes Do Hearby make void and Null all and Haill all my preferances Cleams or Considerations for my self my hears successors or assiginies forth from and for ever I am — your lawful son.

To Donald Gunn and
His Heirs tennant Bolchork'

On the back is written—'Discharge Hugh Gunn to his father + Heirs 1826'

This is an unusual document; why did he receive his inheritance rights early?

---

45 *The Church of Jesus Christ of Latter-day Saints*, CD-ROM, christenings at Halkirk, Caithness, of children born to Donald Gunn and Janet McKenzie: John 18 Jan 1783 and Hugh 7 Jan 1787, with Alexander 9 Jun 1789, Donald 19 Mar 1796, William 12 Mar 1799, Christian 30 Jan 1802, Marcus 9 Aug 1805 further described as born at Halkirk; Letter from Colin Gunn, Clan Gunn genealogist, to Donald Gunn, Jan 1998 banns read 19 Feb 1782.

46 See Brawlbin receipts page 159 on.

47 *LDS Church*, The parents of all Janet McKenzies born in Caithness or Sutherland between 1760 and 1770: Angus/---, Janet christened 17 Jun 1760, Dunnet, CAI, Angus/---, Janet christened 1 Apr 1770, Dunnet, CAI, David/Ann Waiter, Janet christened 12 Jul 1768, Watter, CAI, George/Isabel Smith, Janet christened 25 Sep 1768, Thurso, CAI, Hector/---, Janet christened 3 Aug 1769, Lairg, SUT. We have no evidence to prefer any as the parents of Janet.

48 For the original see page 21.

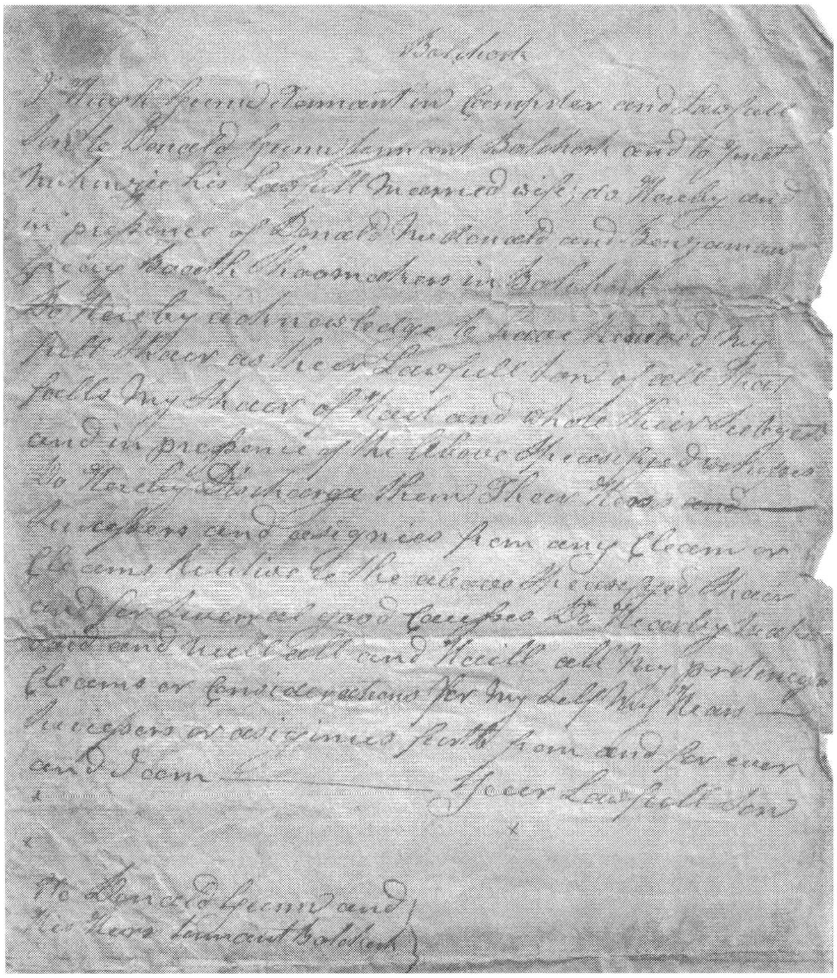
Balchork
I Hugh Gunn Tennant in Campster and Lawfull
Son to Donald Gunn Tennant Balchork and to Janet
McKenzie his Lawfull married wife; do Hereby and
in presence of Donald McDonald and Benjamin
Gray [illegible] Shoemakers in Balchork
Do Hereby acknowledge to have Received my
full Share as Their Lawfull Son of all Their
goods My Share of Meal and whole Their [illegible]
and in presence of the above Mentioned witnesses
Do Hereby Discharge them Their Heirs and
Successors and assignees from any Claim or
Claims Relative to the above Mentioned Share
and for Sundry good Causes Do Hereby [illegible]
[illegible] and [illegible] all and [illegible] all my pretences
Claims or Considerations for my Self My Heirs
Successors or assignees forth from and for ever
and I am ——— Their Lawfull Son
x
To Donald Gunn and
his Heirs tennant Balchork

Hugh Gunn's 1826 'discharge' document

Children of Donald Gunn in Tormsdale (262) and Janet McKenzie of Dunbeath (703) were:

- i. John GUNN (293) was christened on 18 Jan 1783 in Halkirk Parish, Caithness.[49] He was born before Jan 1783 in Caithness.[50] He died before 1784.
- 2 ii. John GUNN of Tormsdale (294).
- 3 iii. Hugh Gunn in Tormsdale (295).
- 4 iv. Alexander GUNN of Bualchork and Brawlbin (1).
- 5 v. George GUNN of Tormsdale (804).
- 6 vi. Donald GUNN of Bualchork (296).
- vii. William GUNN (297)[51] was born in 1799 in Halkirk Parish, Caithness.[52] He was christened on 12 Mar 1799 in Halkirk Parish, Caithness.[53]
- 7 viii. Christian GUNN of Owen Sound (602).
- 8 ix. Marcus GUNN in Owen Sound (298).

---

49 LDS Church
50 Ibidem
51 Ibidem
52 Ibidem
53 Ibidem

Generation Two

2. John GUNN of Tormsdale (294)[54] was born in 1784 in Tormsdale, Halkirk Parish, Caithness.[55] He was christened in Jun 1784 in Tormsdale, Halkirk Parish, Caithness. He married Anne / Ann Grant (3208), daughter of Hector Grant (3209) and Margaret Mackay (3210), on 02 Apr 1818/9 in Halkirk Parish, Caithness. He died on 29 Apr 1857 in Backlass, Watten Parish, Caithness. John and Anne (3208) appeared on the census of 06 Jun 1841 in Olgrinbeg, Halkirk Parish, Caithness.[56] They also appeared on the census of 30 May 1851 in Olgrinbeg, Halkirk Parish, Caithness.[57] He was a farmer.

Anne GRANT (3208) was born circa 1799. She died on 22 Apr 1877 in Banniskirk, Halkirk Parish, Caithness.

Children of John Gunn of Tormsdale (294) and Anne Grant (3208) were:

i. Janet GUNN (3211) was born in 1820 in Bualchork, Halkirk Parish, Caithness. She was christened on 20 Feb 1820 in Bualchork, Halkirk Parish, Caithness and died before 1824.

ii. Margaret GUNN (3212) was born in 1821 in Bualchork, Halkirk Parish, Caithness and was christened on 24 Aug 1821 in Bualchork, Halkirk Parish, Caithness. She appeared on the census of 06 Jun 1841 in the household of her parents John Gunn of Tormsdale (294) and Anne / Ann Grant (3208) in Olgrinbeg, Halkirk Parish, Caithness.[58]

iii. Janet GUNN (3213) was born in 1824 in Caithness. She appeared on the census of 06 Jun 1841 in the household of her parents John (294) and Anne (3208) in Olgrinbeg, Halkirk Parish, Caithness[59] and again on the census of 30 May 1851 in the household of her parents John (294) and Anne / Ann (3208) in Olgrinbeg, Halkirk Parish, Caithness.[60] She may have been a domestic servant.

iv. Hector GUNN (3214) was born in 1826 in Halkirk Parish, Caithness. He died on 13 Mar 1904 in Newlands, Watten Parish, Caithness. He appeared on the census of 06 Jun 1841 in the household of his parents John (294) and Anne / Ann (3208) in Olgrinbeg, Halkirk Parish, Caithness[61] and again on the census of 30 Mar 1851 in the household of his parents John (294) and

---

[54] *LDS Church*, christenings at Halkirk, Caithness, of children born to Donald Gunn and Janet McKenzie: John 18 Jan 1783 and Hugh 7 Jan 1787, with Alexander 9 Jun 1789, Donald 19 Mar 1796, William 12 Mar 1799, Christian 30 Jan 1802, Marcus 9 Aug 1805 further described as born at Halkirk.

[55] Bill & Sharon Gurney, e-mail message to Donald Gunn, 12 Sep 2008 and for much information on this page.

[56] UK Census 06 June 1841: John Gunn 50 farmer; Anne Gunn 40 wife; Margret Gunn 20 daughter; Janet Gunn 15 daughter; Hector Gunn 14 son; Helen Gunn 5 daughter; all resident at Olgrinbeg.

[57] Census 30 March 1851: John Gunn 70 head; Ann Gunn 50 wife; Jennet Gunn 25 daughter; Hector Gunn 22 son; Donald Gunn 22 son; Hellen Gunn 16 daughter; Angus Grant Gunn (3218) (or Aeneas Gunn, Grand-child aged 1) being the son of Donald of Ogrinbeg (3215) before marriage and left with his grandparents when parents emigrated from Scotland; all born Halkirk Parish, all resident Olgrinbeg. (These ages for John are from the census documents; he was christened in June 1784 so he was approximately 57 in 1841 and 67 in the 1851 census. Note: Census instructions for recording age were that if under 15, actual age; if over 15, record to the nearest 5 years below actual.)

[58] UK Census 06 June 1841.

[59] UK Census 06 June 1841.

[60] UK Census 30 March 1851.

[61] UK Census 06 June 1841.

Anne (3208) in Olgrinbeg, Halkirk Parish, Caithness.[62] He may have been a domestic servant. In the 1871 census he was at Banniskirk as Head of the family, aged 44, an unemployed labourer, living with with his mother and his grandson (?) Jasper Mackay aged 17. Their house had two rooms with one or more windows.[63]

9 v. Donald GUNN of Olginbreg & Owen Sound (3215). He appeared on the 1851 census, aged 22, as a domestic servant living in Olgrinbeg, Halkirk Parish, Caithness.

10 vi. Helen GUNN (3216).

3. Hugh Gunn in Tormsdale (295)[64] was born in 1787 in Tormsdale, Halkirk Parish, Caithness. He was christened on 07 Jun 1787 in Halkirk Parish, Caithness. He married Henrietta McGregor of Dalnawillan (752), daughter of William McGregor (753) and Catherine Gunn (754), on 28 Oct 1814.[65] He wrote an agreement with his parents discharging all inheritance rights in 1826 in Camster, Latheron Parish, Caithness (see page 21). Henrietta (752) and he appeared on the census of 06 Jun 1841 in Loravack, Latheron Parish, Caithness.[66] A letter from his brother Marcus indicates he was in Caithness and married with children in 1846.[67] He moved from Halkirk to Latheron between 1820 and 1821[68]. Hugh either died or left Caithness before 1851.

Henrietta MCGREGOR of Dalnawillan (752) was born in 1795; was aged 95 at death in 1890. She died on 15 Apr 1890 in Houstry, Dunbeath Parish, Caithness.[69] She appeared on the census of 30 Mar 1851 in Fly Glay[70], Halkirk Parish, Caithness[71] and again on the census of 30 Mar 1861 in Houstry, Latheron Parish, Caithness.[72]

Children of Hugh Gunn in Tormsdale (295) and Henrietta McGregor of Dalnawillan (752) were:

i. William GUNN (807) was christened on 24 Sep 1815 in Inishmull, Halkirk Parish, Caithness.

ii. Janet GUNN (3230) was christened on 04 Apr 1817 in Inishmull, Halkirk Parish, Caithness. She died on 15 Aug 1890 in Houstry, Dunbeath Parish, Caithness, at age 73. She appeared on the census of 30 Mar 1851 in the household of her mother Henrietta (752) in Fly Glay, Halkirk Parish,

---

62 Census 30 March 1851: John Gunn 70 head; Ann Gunn 50 wife; Jennet Gunn 25 daughter; Hector Gunn 22 son; Donald Gunn 22 son; Hellen Gunn 16 daughter; Aeneas Gunn grandson of John and Ann; all born Halkirk Parish, all resident Olgrinbeg.

63 Email from Catherine Sinclair to Alastair Gunn, Nov. 2011.

64 *LDS Church*, christenings at Halkirk, Caithness, of children born to Donald Gunn and Janet McKenzie: John 18 Jan 1783, John 8 June 1874 and Hugh 7 Jan 1787, with Alexander 9 Jun 1789, Donald 19 Mar 1796, William 12 Mar 1799, Christian 30 Jan 1802, Marcus 9 Aug 1805 further described as born at Halkirk.

65 Bill & Sharon Gurney, e-mail to Donald Gunn, 05 Sep 2008 for much information on this page.

66 UK Census 06 June 1841: Hugh Gunn 50 farmer; Harrietta Gunn 45 wife; Cathrine Gunn 20 daughter; Helen Gunn 18 daughter; Donald Gunn 12 son; Mary Gunn 6 daughter; John Gunn 4 son; Alexr Gunn 2 son; all resident Loravack.

67 See page 202.

68 From an email by Meg Stokes to Donald Gunn.

69 Ibidem

70 It is possible that this is a transcription error; 'Fleuchary' was perhaps the real place.

71 Census 30 March 1851: Henrietta Gunn 56 head; Janet Gunn 34; Catherine Gunn 31; Helen Gunn 29; Donald Gunn 22; Mary Gunn 16; John Gunn 14; Alexander Gunn 11.

72 Census 30 March 1861: Henrietta McGregor 65 head; Janet Gunn 44 daughter; Alexander Gunn son 21; Mary Campbell 7 granddaughter scholar.

Caithness[73] and again on the census of 30 Mar 1861 in the household of her mother Henrietta (752) in Houstry, Latheron Parish, Caithness. [74] She died unmarried. She was hampered by deafness, certainly by the time of her death and perhaps earlier[75].

iii. Catherine GUNN (3231) was christened on 10 Jan 1819 in Inishmull, Halkirk Parish, Caithness. She appeared on the census of 06 Jun 1841 in the household of her parents Hugh (295) and Henrietta (752) in Loravack, Latheron Parish, Caithness.[76] She appeared on the census of 30 Mar 1851 in the household of her mother Henrietta (752) in Fly Glay, Halkirk Parish, Caithness.[77]

iv. Helen GUNN (3232) was born on 29 Sep 1822 in Camster, Latheron Parish, Caithness. She was christened in Wick Parish, Caithness. She appeared on the census of 06 Jun 1841 in the household of her parents Hugh (295) and Henrietta (752) in Loravack, Latheron Parish, Caithness[78] and again on the census of 30 Mar 1851 in the household of her mother Henrietta (752) in Fly Glay, Halkirk Parish, Caithness.[79]

v. Christina GUNN (3233) was born in 1825 in Camster, Latheron Parish, Caithness. She was christened in Wick Parish, Caithness and died on 24 Apr 1863 in Houstry, Dunbeath Parish, Caithness.

vi. Henrietta GUNN (3234) was born in 1827 in Camster, Latheron Parish, Caithness.

vii. Donald GUNN (3235) was born in 1829 in Camster, Latheron Parish, Caithness. He appeared on the census of 06 Jun 1841 in the household of his parents Hugh (295) and Henrietta (752) in Loravack, Latheron Parish, Caithness.[80] He appeared on the census of 30 Mar 1851 in the household of his mother Henrietta (752) in Fly Glay, Halkirk Parish, Caithness.[81]

viii. Mary GUNN (3236) was born in 1835 in Camster, Latheron Parish, Caithness. She appeared on the census of 06 Jun 1841 in the household of her parents Hugh (295) and Henrietta (752) in Loravack, Latheron Parish, Caithness[82] and again on the census of 30 Mar 1851 in the household of her mother Henrietta (752) in Fly Glay, Halkirk Parish, Caithness.[83]

ix. John GUNN (3237) was christened on 10 Feb 1837 in Wick Parish, Caithness. He appeared on the census of 06 Jun 1841 in the household of his parents Hugh (295) and Henrietta (752) in Loravack, Latheron Parish,

---

73 Census 30 March 1851.

74 Census 30 March 1861.

75 Source; Bill & Sharon Gurney email 05 Sep 2008 and for further information on this page.

76 UK Census 06 June 1841: Hugh Gunn 50 farmer; Harrietta Gunn 45 wife; Cathrine Gunn 20 daughter; Helen Gunn 18 daughter; Donald Gunn 12 son; Mary Gunn 6 daughter; John Gunn 4 son; Alexr Gunn 2 son; all resident Loravack.

77 UK Census 30 March 1851: Henrietta Gunn 56 head; Janet Gunn 34; Catherine Gunn 31; Helen Gunn 29; Donald Gunn 22; Mary Gunn 16; John Gunn 14; Alexander Gunn 11.

78 UK Census 06 June 1841.

79 Census 30 March 1851.

80 UK Census 06 June 1841.

81 UK Census 30 March 1851.

82 UK Census 06 June 1841.

83 UK Census 30 March 1851.

Caithness.[84] He appeared on the census of 30 Mar 1851 in the household of his mother Henrietta (752) in Fly Glay, Halkirk Parish, Caithness.[85]

11 x. Alexander GUNN (3238).

4. Alexander GUNN of Bualchork and Brawlbin (1)[86] was born on 04 Jun 1789 in Halkirk Parish, Caithness. He was christened on 09 Jun 1789 in Halkirk Parish, Caithness. He married—and this was the cause of much family history confusion—Barbara Gunn of Braehour[87] (6), daughter of Donald Gunn (the Sennachie—the Historian of the Clan) of Braehour & Brawlbin (708) and Catherine Gunn of Osclay (3423), on 19 Mar 1829 in Halkirk Parish, Caithness.[88] He died on 29 Mar 1847[89] in Brawlbin, Reay Parish, Caithness, at age 57.[90] Bualchork is no longer recorded, even in Ordnance Survey maps, but a location, Bullechach is close to Tormsdale, Dirlot and Braehour, and is probably Alexander's birth location. See the map on page 9. Alexander (1) thought of emigrating to Jamaica in 1819.[91] He was a manager of the Loyal and United Benevolent Society of the Clan Gunn when it was formed on 18 Dec 1821 in Thurso Parish, Caithness and a shoemaker.[92] He was a farmer after 1828 in Brawlbin, Reay Parish, Caithness.[93] He entered into a 14 year lease of Brawlbin farm for £16/a on 30 Jun 1831.

He witnessed the marriage of Catherine Gunn (1120) and John Gunn in Durness (878) on 08 Jun 1836.[94] He and Barbara Gunn of Braehour (6) appeared on the census of 06 Jun 1841 in Brawlbin, Reay Parish, Caithness.

---

[84] UK Census 06 June 1841: Hugh Gunn 50 farmer; Harrietta Gunn 45 wife; Cathrine Gunn 20 daughter; Helen Gunn 18 daughter; Donald Gunn 12 son; Mary Gunn 6 daughter; John Gunn 4 son; Alexr Gunn 2 son; all resident Loravack.

[85] Census 30 March 1851: Henrietta Gunn 56 head; Janet Gunn 34; Catherine Gunn 31; Helen Gunn 29; Donald Gunn 22; Mary Gunn 16; John Gunn 14; Alexander Gunn 11.

[86] *LDS Church*, christenings at Halkirk, Caithness, of children born to Donald Gunn and Janet McKenzie: John 18 Jan 1783 and Hugh 7 Jan 1787, with Alexander 9 Jun 1789, Donald 19 Mar 1796, William 12 Mar 1799, Christian 30 Jan 1802, Marcus 9 Aug 1805 further described as born at Halkirk; Letter from Colin Gunn, Jan 1998—Alexander was the third recorded child of Donald Gunn, Tormesdale and Janet McKenzie. *Bible of Alexander Gunn*: Alexr Gunn was born 1789 and died on 29 Mar 1847; Chart from Colin Gunn, Clan Gunn Genealogist, as drawn for M. J. Gunn by Hugh Peskett.

[87] See Parts 4, 5, 6 and 7 of this book for detail of her side of the family.

[88] *LDS Church*, Marriage, Alexander Gunn, Barbara Gunn, 19 Mar 1829, Halkirk, Caithness; Clan Gunn Parish Records held at the Clan Gunn Heritage Centre, Latheron: Marriages 1829—Alexander of Bualchork married Barbara Gunn of Braehour.

[89] See page 27.

[90] See page 27.

[91] See page 126 and the following pages.

[92] Thomas Sinclair, *The Gunns*, pub. 1890, p.174; 'The Loyal and United Benevolent Society of the Clan Gunn, was instituted at Thurso, 18th December, 1821'. Alexander Gunn, shoemaker in Bualkork is named as one of the Society's managers. See Part 8.

[93] UK Census 06 June 1841: District of Brawlbin lying in the south part of the Parish of Reay. Each person who abode in each house on night of 6 June 1841: Alexander Gunn 50 farmer; Barbara Gunn 30; Kathrine Gunn 11; Donald Gunn 9; John Gunn 5; Janet Gunn 7; William Gunn 2; all born in Caithness. Note: Census instructions for recording age were that if under 15, actual age; if over 15, record to the nearest 5 years below actual ie Alexander Gunn was between 50 and 55 and Barbara between 30 and 35 on 6 June 1841. Birth years are thus Alexander 1786-1791 and Barbara 1806-1811. The summary notes that there were 40 occupied houses, 2 uninhabited houses, 78 males and 94 females comprising 40 families in the Brawlbin District.

[94] Parish Register, Wick Parish Register - 1835(6) - Marriage: John Gunn, farmer in Brawlbin, Parish of Reay; Catherine Gunn in Camster; witnesses Alexander Gunn, farmer, Brawlbin for the man; Donald Gunn, farmer, Brawlbin for the son; "Descent of the Gunns of Dalnaglaton & Braehour," Michael J Gunn, to Alastair Jack Gunn.

Brawlbin farm, 2011

Brawlbin farm, 2011

Barbara GUNN of Braehour (6)[95] was christened on 30 Mar 1810 in Halkirk Parish, Caithness, but her husband's family Bible records birth date as 17 Apr 1810.[96] It is unusual for the family Bible to be wrong; but still more so for the Halkirk Parish Register. She died on 28 Feb 1844 in Caithness aged 33.[97] See below—

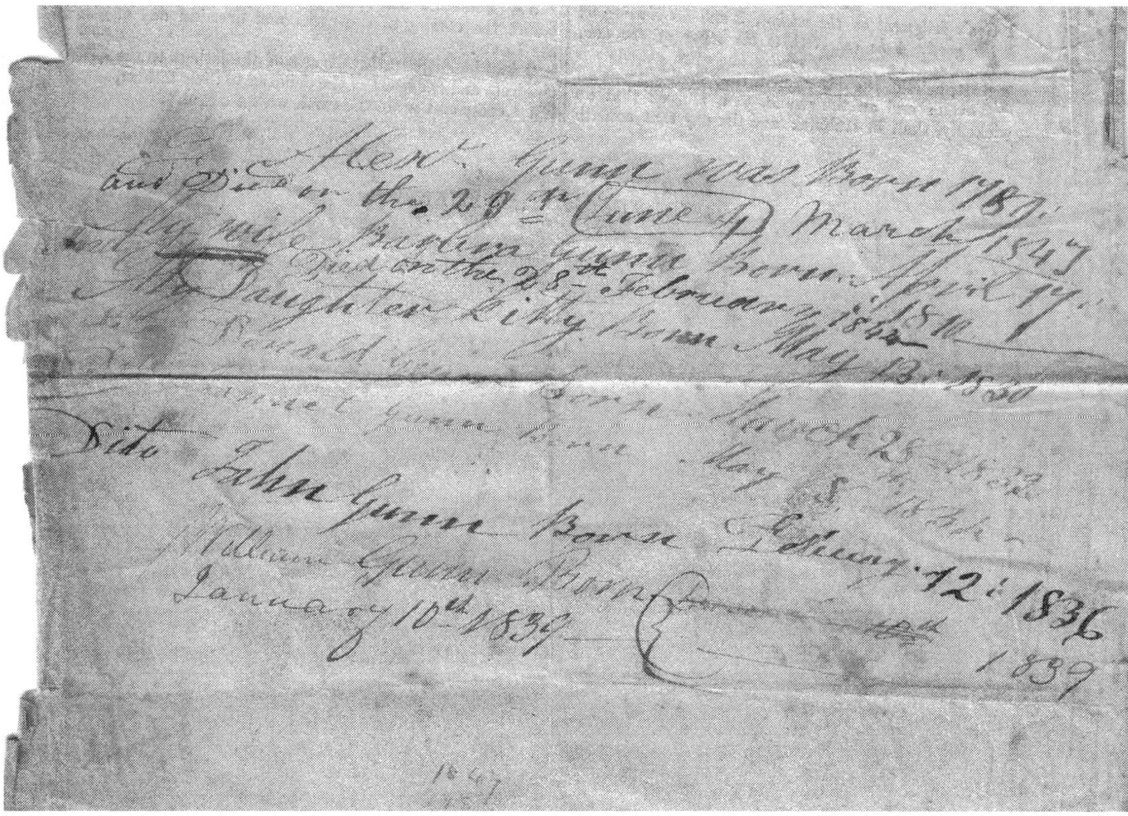
Alexr Gunn was Born 1787
and Died on the 20th June 4 March 1847
My wife Barbra Gunn Born April 17 1810
Died on the 28th February 1844
My Daughter Kity Born May 13 1830
Donald Gunn Born March 28 1832
Janet Gunn Born May 8 1834
John Gunn Born February 12 1836
William Gunn Born January 10th 1839

The family Bible page for Alexander and Barbara Gunn, written c. 1847

Children of Alexander Gunn of Bualchork and Brawlbin[98] (1) and Barbara Gunn of Braehour (6) were as follows:

12 i. Catherine GUNN (119) was born on 13 May 1830 Reay Parish, Caithness and died in Vic in 1912

13 ii. Donald GUNN of Brawlbin & Ballarat (3) was born on 28 Mar 1832 Reay Parish, Caithness and died on 14 Feb 1901 in Ballarat, Vic.

14 iii. Janet 'MacLeod' GUNN (120) was born 08 May 1834 in Brawlbin, Reay Parish Caithness and died on 30 May 1913 in Cardigan, Vic.

---

95 *LDS Church*, Christenings of children of Donald Gunn and Catherine Gunn: Barbara 1810, Mary 1812, Alexander 1814, Jean 1816, Lexy (Alexandrina?) 1825; Clan Gunn Parish Records.

96 Letter from Colin Gunn, Jan 1998: Barbara was the eldest daughter of Donald in Braehour, and later Brawlbin; *Bible of Alexander Gunn*: my wife, Barbra Gunn born April 17 1810.

97 *Bible of Alexander Gunn*: died on the 28th February 1844. See above.

98 See Part 3.

From a note by John Watkins Surman, who married Janet Gunn (consider the additional 'n' in her Janet and no 'Macleod'). It is assumed he wrote the note. See page 71 on—

Alexander Gunn –
Born June 4th 1789 –
Died Mar. 29th 1847.

Barbara Gunn
Born April 17th 1810.
Died Feby. 28th ~~1844.~~

Catherine Gunn.
Born May 13. 1830.

Donald Gunn –
Born March 28. 1832.

Jan[n]et Gunn
Born May 8th 1834

John Gunn
Born February 12. 1836
Died January 10. 1854.

William Gunn
Born January 10. 1839.

We are not convinced that John Gunn died in January 1854.

iv. John GUNN (12)[99] was born on 12 Feb 1836 in Reay Parish, Caithness.[100] He was christened on 20 Feb 1836 in Reay Parish, Caithness.[101] He appeared on the 1841 Census of Brawlbin, Reay Parish, Caithness, in the household of his parents Alexander Gunn of Bualchork and Brawlbin (1) and Barbara Gunn of Braehour (6).[102] He appeared on the 1851 Census of Brawlbin, Reay Parish, Caithness, in the household of Donald Gunn of Brawlbin & Ballarat (3).[103] He left Caithness by steamer for Glasgow, thence Liverpool on 11 Jul 1853. He emigrated on 23 Jul 1853 from Liverpool, Merseyside, per sailing ship 'Tasmania' for voyage to Australia. He arrived in Melbourne, Vic, listed in the ship's manifest as John Gum aged 24, on 25 Oct 1853. John was an impressive letter writer see 'Part 3'. It is probable that he died of sunstroke at Port Melbourne in December 1854 (or January 1855) whilst waiting for the ship carrying Donald and Catherine to arrive, but a death date of 10 Jan 1854 has been recorded, see the previous page.

v. William GUNN (220) was born on 10 Jan 1839 in Reay Parish, Caithness.[104] He died after June 1864 as a letter mentioning him—and written in Melbourne—exists.[105] William appeared on the 1841 Census of Brawlbin, Reay Parish, Caithness, in the household of his parents Alexander Gunn of Bualchork and Brawlbin (1) and Barbara Gunn of Braehour (6).[106] He appeared on the 1851 Census of Brawlbin, Reay Parish, Caithness, in the household of Donald Gunn of Brawlbin & Ballarat (3).[107] He probably emigrated on 01 Jul 1857 when the 'Donald McKay' left Liverpool as he

[99] *LDS Church*, Christenings of children of Barbara Gunn, father Alexander Gunn. Catherine, 18 May 1830, Halkirk; Donald, 9 Jun 1832, Reay; Janet, 19 Aug 1834, Reay; John, 29 Feb 1836, Reay.

[100] Clan Gunn Parish Records: Births 1836 John Gunn, parents Alexander, Brawlbin - Barbara; UK Census 06 June 1841: District of Brawlbin lying in the south part of the Parish of Reay. Each person who abode in each house on night of 6 June 1841: Alexander Gunn 50 farmer; Barbara Gunn 30; Kathrine Gunn 11; Donald Gunn 9; John Gunn 5; Janet Gunn 7; William Gunn 2; all born in Caithness. Note: Census instructions for recording age were that if under 15, actual age; if over 15, record to the nearest 5 years below actual ie Alexander Gunn was between 50 and 55 and Barbara between 30 and 35 on 6 June 1841. Birth years are thus Alexander 1786-1791 and Barbara 1806-1811. The summary notes that there were 40 occupied houses, 2 uninhabited houses, 78 males and 94 females comprising 40 families in the Brawlbin District; Census 30 March 1851: County of Caithness, Parish of Reay. Residents at Brawlbin. Donald Gunn head, unmarried 19, farmer, 16 acres, born Halkirk; Katherine Gunn sister, unmarried 20, general service, born Reay; Janet Gunn sister, unmarried 17, scholar, born Reay; John Gunn brother, unmarried 15, scholar born Reay; William Gunn brother, unmarried 12, scholar born Reay. Brawlbin comprised 39 occupied houses with 70 males and 93 females. The census district of Brawlbin and Oldenbruch (?) was 12 miles in length and 2 miles in breadth. The majority of homes, 39, was in Brawlbin, with 3 in Oldenbruch accommodating 24 people; see also the *Bible page of Alexander Gunn*: John Gunn born 12 February 1836.

[101] *LDS Church*, Christenings of children of Barbara Gunn, father Alexander Gunn; Catherine, 18 May 1830, Halkirk; Donald, 9 Jun 1832, Reay; Janet, 19 Aug 1834, Reay; John, 29 Feb 1836, Reay.

[102] UK Census 06 June 1841: District of Brawlbin lying in the south part of the Parish of Reay. Each person who abode in each house on night of 6 June 1841: Alexander Gunn 50 farmer; Barbara Gunn 30; Kathrine Gunn 11; Donald Gunn 9; John Gunn 5; Janet Gunn 7; William Gunn 2; all born in Caithness. Note: Census instructions for recording age were that if under 15, actual age; if over 15, record to the nearest 5 years below actual ie Alexander Gunn was between 50 and 55 and Barbara between 30 and 35 on 6 June 1841. Birth years are thus Alexander 1786-1791 and Barbara 1806-1811. The summary notes that there were 40 occupied houses, 2 uninhabited houses, 78 males and 94 females comprising 40 families in the Brawlbin District.

[103] Census 30 March 1851: County of Caithness, Parish of Reay. Residents at Brawlbin. Donald Gunn head, unmarried 19, farmer, 16 acres, born Halkirk; Katherine Gunn sister, unmarried 20, general service, born Reay; Janet Gunn sister, unmarried 17, scholar, born Reay; John Gunn brother, unmarried 15, scholar born Reay; William Gunn brother, unmarried 12, scholar born Reay. Brawlbin comprised 39 occupied houses with 70 males and 93 females. The census district of Brawlbin and Oldenbruch (?) was 12 miles in length and 2 miles in breadth. The majority of homes, 39, were in Brawlbin, with 3 in Oldenbruch accommodating 24 people.

[104] UK Census 06 June 1841, Census 30 March 1851; *Bible page of Alexander Gunn*: William Gunn born 10 Jan 1839.

[105] See Part 3.

[106] UK Census 06 June 1841.

[107] Census 30 March 1851.

arrived in Melbourne, Vic, aboard the 'Donald McKay'[108] of 2560 ton register carrying 595 passengers (which is the only shipping record of a William Gunn aged around 18 to travel to Melbourne between late 1854 and late 1858) in Sep 1857.[109] Letter from a William Gunn originally of Bualchork (3175)[110] to Donald Gunn (3), dated 11 Oct 1858, sends regards to William (220), showing William (220) was near to Donald (3). But no death details are recorded, which is unusual. Did he die in the bush? Did he emigrate?

5. George GUNN of Tormsdale (804) was born in 1795 in Tormsdale, Halkirk Parish, Caithness; unregistered. He married Ann McDonald (942), daughter of Hugh McDonald (3173) and Margaret McDonald (3174), on 09 Jan 1821 in Halkirk Parish, Caithness. The marriage is also recorded as 29 Dec 1820 in Reay, Sutherland.[111] He died on 19 Sep 1868 in Swiney Mains, Latheron Parish, Caithness, from disease of the liver and heart.[112] He was buried in Dirlot, Caithness.[113]

Ann MCDONALD (942) was born circa 1801 in Reay Parish, Sutherland. She died on 15 Apr 1878 in Swiney Mains, Latheron Parish, Caithness and was buried in Dirlot, Caithness.

Children of George Gunn of Tormsdale (804) and Ann McDonald (942) were as follows:

i. William GUNN of Bualchork (3175) was born in 1822 in Bualchork, Halkirk Parish, Caithness. He was christened on 14 Aug 1822 in Halkirk Parish, Caithness. He died on 13 Sep 1899 in Rangag Forse[114], Latheron Parish, Caithness.[115] He was buried in Dirlot, Caithness.[116] He was a Minister of the Scotland Free Church. He was a literary student in 1851 in Old Greyfriars, Edinburgh. He was an assistant manager, working with Rev. R R McKay in 1861 in E. Clyth, Latheron Parish, Caithness. He never married.

ii. Margaret GUNN (3176) was born in 1824 in Halkirk Parish, Caithness. She died on 15 Jun 1895 in the Hotel, Dunbeath, Caithness, while visiting her sister. She never married.

iii. Hugh GUNN (3177) was born on 07 Jul 1825 in Halkirk Parish, Caithness and christened on 08 Aug 1825 in Halkirk Parish, Caithness.

15 iv. Janet GUNN (3193).

---

108 http://www.eraoftheclipperships.com/page55.html for an excellent account of the clipper, along with an illustration.

109 Immigration to Victoria, British Ports 1852-1859, the only shipping record of a William Gunn aged around 18 to travel to Melbourne between late 1854 and late 1858 was per the Donald McKay of 2560 ton register carrying 595 passengers. He was recorded as a labourer and travelled alone. There is a further record of a William Gunn aged 21 arriving on the Delgany in Dec 1854. There are no other possible corrupted names on this passenger list.

110 See page 268.

111 Bill & Sharon Gurney, e-mail to Donald Gunn, 13 Sep 2008 and further information on this page.

112 Clan Gunn Parish Records: Latheron parish 1868 George Gunn, 72 years. Married to Ann McDonald, Died 19.9.1868 at Swiney Mains disease of liver and heart Informant Donald Gunn (son) Father Donald Gunn, farmer dec. Mother Janet Gunn ms McKenzie.

113 Bill & Sharon Gurney, e-mail to Donald Gunn, 13 Sep 2008; Dirlot cemetery tombstone: Tombstone No 10: George Gunn, Swiney Mains died Sept. 9, 1868; wife Ann Gunn died April 15, 1872; son Rev William Gunn died Sept 18, 1888 [1899] 76; Donald died infant; Isabella died Mar. 12, 1866 [?]; Donald Gunn 23 years, Inspector of Poor, Parish of Latheron Oct [26-28?] 1885 [1895] age 52; his wife Mary Ann Gunn Munro, Swiney House, Mar 12, 1917 age 63; Margaret Gunn June 15 1895 age 70.

114 Rangag 'is a farm /area half-way along the Causewaymire just north of Achavanich. There are a few old houses which all came under the name of Rangag' and 'Rangag is in the Forse Estate.' We presume that Rangag, Forse estate, is what is meant here. http://forum.caithness.org/showthread.php?t=45160

115 Ibidem

116 Bill & Sharon Gurney, e-mail to Donald Gunn, 13 Sep 2008.

v. Donald GUNN (3195) was born in 1829 in Bualchork, Halkirk Parish, Caithness. He was christened on 22 Dec 1829 in Halkirk Parish, Caithness, witnesses Mary Gunn and Ann McKay. He died in Halkirk Parish, Caithness, an infant and was buried in Dirlot, Caithness.

vi. Mary GUNN (3196)[117] was born in 1831 in Halkirk Parish, Caithness. She was christened on 27 Mar 1831 in Halkirk Parish, Caithness. She died on 10 Dec 1904 in Caithness. She appeared on the census of 1891 in the household of her sister and brother-in-law Charles M. Munro (3198) and Helen Gunn (3197). She appeared on the census of 1901 in the household of Charles M. Munro (3198) and Helen Gunn (3197).

vii. Helen GUNN (3197) was born in 1834 in Halkirk Parish, Caithness. She married Charles M. Munro (3198) and died on 01 Feb 1909 in Caithness. She and Charles appeared on the censuses of 1891 and 1901.

Charles M. MUNRO (3198) was born in 1833 in Wick Parish, Caithness. He died in 1921 in Latheron Parish, Caithness. He was a farmer in Knockglass, Dunbeath Parish, Caithness, a hotel keeper in 1891 in Knockglass, Dunbeath Parish, Caithness and was a farmer in 1901 at Norland Farm[118], Caithness.

viii. Isabella GUNN (3199) was born on 07 Nov 1836 in Halkirk Parish, Caithness. She was christened on 09 Dec 1836 in Halkirk Parish, Caithness and died on 12 Mar 1866 in Caithness at age 29. She was buried in Dirlot, Caithness.

ix. Donald GUNN (3200) was born on 10 Jul 1840 in Halkirk Parish, Caithness. He married Mary Ann Munro (3201). He died in 1895 in Latheron Parish, Caithness and was buried in Dirlot, Caithness. He was the informant of the death of George Gunn of Tormsdale (804) on 19 Sep 1868 in Swiney Mains, Latheron Parish, Caithness; disease of liver and heart.[119] He was the informant of the death of his mother Ann McDonald (942) on 15 Apr 1878 in Swiney Mains, Latheron Parish, Caithness. He and Mary Ann Munro (3201) had no children.

6. Donald GUNN of Bualchork (296)[120] was born in 1796 in Tormsdale, Halkirk Parish, Caithness.[121] He was christened on 19 Mar 1796 in Tormsdale, Halkirk Parish, Caithness.[122] He married Ann Mackay (3244) on 02 Feb 1827 in Halkirk Parish, Caithness. He witnessed the christening of Janet Gunn (3230) on 04 Apr 1817 in Inishmull, Halkirk Parish, Caithness.

---

117 Bill & Sharon Gurney, e-mail to Donald Gunn, 13 Sep 2008 and for further information on this page.

118 http://www.btinternet.com/~james.mckay/familyrecords/mackay5.htm for a previous owner.

119 Clan Gunn Parish Records: Latheron parish 1868 George Gunn, 72 years. Married to Ann McDonald Died 19.9.1868 at Swiney Mains disease of liver and heart Informant Donald Gunn (son) Father Donald Gunn, farmer dec. Mother Janet Gunn ms McKenzie.

120 *LDS Church*, christenings at Halkirk, Caithness, of children born to Donald Gunn and Janet McKenzie: John 18 Jan 1783 and Hugh 7 Jan 1787, with Alexander 9 Jun 1789, Donald 19 Mar 1796, William 12 Mar 1799, Christian 30 Jan 1802, Marcus 9 Aug 1805 further described as born at Halkirk.

121 *LDS Church*, christenings at Halkirk, Caithness; Bill & Sharon Gurney, e-mail to Donald Gunn, 17 Oct 2008; the family of Donald Gunn & Ann McKay of Halkirk Scotland.

122 Ibidem

He and Ann Mackay (3244) appeared on the census of 06 Jun 1841 in Achlibster[123], Halkirk Parish, Caithness[124] and on the census of 30 Mar 1851 in Bualchork, Halkirk Parish, Caithness.[125]

Ann MACKAY (3244) was born circa 1809 in Halkirk Parish, Caithness.[126]

Children of Donald Gunn of Bualchork (296) and Ann Mackay (3244) were as follows:

i. Hector GUNN (3245) was born in 1827 in Halkirk Parish, Caithness. He was christened on 05 Dec 1827 in Bualchork, Halkirk Parish, Caithness. He appeared on the census of 06 Jun 1841 in the household of his parents Donald (296) and Ann (3244) in Achlibster, Halkirk Parish, Caithness[127] and on the census of 30 Mar 1851 in the household of his parents Donald (296) and Ann (3244) in Bualchork, Halkirk Parish, Caithness.[128]

ii. Donald GUNN (3246) was born in 1829 in Halkirk Parish, Caithness. He was christened on 03 Jul 1829 in Halkirk Parish, Caithness. He appeared on the census of 06 Jun 1841 in the household of his parents Donald (296) and Ann (3244) in Achlibster, Halkirk Parish, Caithness.[129] He appeared on the census of 30 Mar 1851 in the household of his parents Donald (296) and Ann (3244) in Bualchork, Halkirk Parish, Caithness.[130]

iii. Janet GUNN (3247) was born in 1831 in Halkirk Parish, Caithness. She was christened on 08 Jul 1831 in Halkirk Parish, Caithness, witnesses were George McKay & Henrietta McKay of Achlibster. She appeared on the census of 06 Jun 1841 in the household of her parents Donald (296) and Ann (3244) in Achlibster, Halkirk Parish, Caithness.[131] She appeared on the census of 30 Mar 1851 in the household of her parents Donald (296) and Ann (3244) in Bualchork, Halkirk Parish, Caithness.[132]

iv. Helen GUNN (3248) was born in 1833 in Halkirk Parish, Caithness. She was christened on 28 Sep 1833 in Bualchork, Halkirk Parish, Caithness. She appeared on the census of 06 Jun 1841 in the household of her parents Donald (296) and Ann (3244) in Achlibster, Halkirk Parish, Caithness.[133] She appeared on the census of 30 Mar 1851 in the household of her parents Donald (296) and Ann (3244) in Bualchork, Halkirk Parish, Caithness.[134]

v. Margaret GUNN (3249) was born in 1835 in Halkirk Parish, Caithness. She was christened on 29 Jun 1835 in Bualchork, Halkirk Parish, Caithness,

---

123 http://her.highland.gov.uk/FullImage.aspx?imageID=45974&uid=MHG51358 for images of a typical Achlibster cottage.

124 UK Census 06 June 1841: Donald Gunn 40 farmer head; Ann Gunn 30 wife; Hector Gunn 13 son; Donald Gunn 11 son; Janet Gunn 9 daughter; Helen Gunn 7 daughter; Margaret Gunn 5 daughter; John Gunn 3 son; Christina Gunn 1 daughter; all resident at Achlipster.

125 Census 30 March 1851: Donald Gunn 52 head farmer of 14 acres; Ann Gunn 42; Hector Gunn 22; Donald Gunn 19; Janet Gunn 17; Helen Gunn 15; Margaret Gunn 13; John Gunn 11; Christina Gunn 9; Marcus Gunn 5; all resident at Bualchork.

126 Bill & Sharon Gurney, e-mail to Donald Gunn, 23 Sep 2008 and for further information on this page.

127 UK Census 06 June 1841.

128 UK Census 30 March 1851.

129 UK Census 06 June 1841.

130 UK Census 30 March 1851

131 UK Census 06 June 1841.

132 UK Census 30 March 1851.

133 UK Census 06 June 1841.

134 UK Census 30 March 1851.

witnesses were Marcus Gunn and Catherine Gunn. She appeared on the census of 06 Jun 1841 in the household of her parents Donald (296) and Ann (3244) in Achlibster, Halkirk Parish, Caithness.[135] She appeared on the census of 30 Mar 1851 in the household of her parents Donald (296) and Ann (3244) in Bualchork, Halkirk Parish, Caithness.[136]

16 vi. John GUNN (Sir)[137] of Tormsdale (3250).

vii. Christina GUNN (3251) was born in 1839 in Halkirk Parish, Caithness.[138] She was christened on 22 Dec 1839 in Bualchork, Halkirk Parish, Caithness, witnesses were George McKay and Henrietta McKay of Achlibster. She appeared on the census of 06 Jun 1841 in the household of her parents Donald (296) and Ann (3244) in Achlibster, Halkirk Parish, Caithness.[139] She appeared on the census of 30 Mar 1851 in the household of her parents Donald (296) and Ann (3244) in Bualchork, Halkirk Parish, Caithness.[140]

17 viii. Marcus GUNN[141] (3252).

ix. George GUNN (3253) was born on 05 May 1842 in Bualchork, Halkirk Parish, Caithness.[142] He was christened on 09 May 1842 in Bualchork, Halkirk Parish, Caithness.[143] He died before 1851 in Halkirk Parish, Caithness.[144] George and Marcus were twins.

7. Christian GUNN of Owen Sound (602)[145] was born in Jan 1802 in Halkirk Parish, Caithness.[146] She was christened on 30 Jan 1802 in Halkirk Parish, Caithness.[147] She married Alexander Sutherland of Inshag[148] (3119) on 23 Dec 1825 in Latheron Parish, Caithness.[149] She witnessed the christening of Janet Gunn (3230) on 04 Apr 1817 in Inishmull, Halkirk Parish, Caithness.[150] She and Alexander (3119) appeared on the census of

---

135UK Census 06 June 1841: Donald Gunn 40 farmer head; Ann Gunn 30 wife; Hector Gunn 13 son; Donald Gunn 11 son; Janet Gunn 9 daughter; Helen Gunn 7 daughter; Margaret Gunn 5 daughter; John Gunn 3 son; Christina Gunn 1 daughter; all resident at Achlipster.

136UK Census 30 March 1851: Donald Gunn 52 head farmer of 14 acres; Ann Gunn 42; Hector Gunn 22; Donald Gunn 19; Janet Gunn 17; Helen Gunn 15; Margaret Gunn 13; John Gunn 11; Christina Gunn 9; Marcus Gunn 5; all resident at Bualchork.

137See Part 7.

138Bill & Sharon Gurney, e-mail to Donald Gunn, 23 Sep 2008 and for further information on this page.

139UK Census 06 June 1841.

140Census 30 March 1851.

141See Part 7.

142Bill & Sharon Gurney, e-mail to Donald Gunn, 17 Oct 2008; The family of Donald Gunn & Ann McKay of Halkirk Scotland.

143Ibidem

144Ibidem

145Letter or email, Betty Warrilow to Donald Gunn, 14 Aug 2008; In the letters you will note Alexander Sutherland. He was married to Christian (Christina) Gunn born 1802. They had 8 children. I descend from their daughter Ellen who married Hugh Gordon, their son Alex named for his grandfather Alexander Sutherland, his daughter Ellen was my mother; *LDS Church*, christenings at Halkirk, Caithness, of children born to Donald Gunn and Janet McKenzie: John 18 Jan 1783 and Hugh 7 Jan 1787, with Alexander 9 Jun 1789, Donald 19 Mar 1796, William 12 Mar 1799, Christian 30 Jan 1802, Marcus 9 Aug 1805 further described as born at Halkirk.

146*LDS Church*, christenings at Halkirk, Caithness, of children born to Donald Gunn and Janet McKenzie: John 18 Jan 1783 and Hugh 7 Jan 1787, with Alexander 9 Jun 1789, Donald 19 Mar 1796, William 12 Mar 1799, Christian 30 Jan 1802, Marcus 9 Aug 1805 further described as born at Halkirk.

147Ibidem

148'Inshag' has nearly disappeared; it's at 58.419211N, 3.460216W and had four buildings in 1747-1755. http://www.scotlandsplaces.gov.uk/search_item/index.php?service=RCAHMS&id=8251

149*International Genealogical Index (IGI)*, Batch 7113908 Sheet 40.

150Bill & Sharon Gurney, e-mail to Donald Gunn, 05 Sep 2008.

06 Jun 1841 in Camster, Latheron Parish, Caithness.[151] She and Alexander (3119) emigrated in 1842 to Owen Sound, Canada. Christian (602) and Alexander (3119) appeared on the census of 1881 in Zorra East, Oxford North, Ontario. Census quotes Christian as aged 75, Presbyterian, in 1881.

Alexander SUTHERLAND of Inshag (3119) was born around 1800 in Caithness. He was a farmer whose concession was close to both Marcus (298) and Donald Gunn (3215) on 03 Nov 1845 in Lot 6, 11th Concession, Owen Sound, Ontario.[152] The census records Alexander (3119) as a farmer aged 88 (?), Presbyterian in 1881.

For letters from Marcus Gunn (298) concerning Alexander and Canada, refer to Part 3.

Children of Christian Gunn of Owen Sound (602) and Alexander Sutherland of Inshag (3119) were as follows:

i. Christina SUTHERLAND (3130)[153] was born in 1826 in Latheron Parish, Caithness.[154] She married John Munroe (3166) say 1850. She died in 1910.[155] She appeared on the census of 06 Jun 1841 in the household of her parents Alexander (3119) and Christian (602) in Camster, Latheron Parish, Caithness.[156] She and Ellen Sutherland (3120), Donald Sutherland (3127), Ann Sutherland (3129), Janet Sutherland (3131), and Catherine Sutherland (3133) emigrated with her parents in 1842 to Owen Sound, Canada. She was serving in the village for $4 a month on 14 Jul 1846. See the letter from Marcus Gunn in Part 3.

ii. Donald SUTHERLAND (3127)[157] was born in 1828 in Camster, Latheron Parish, Caithness. He died in 1856.[158] He appeared on the census of 06 Jun 1841 in the household of his parents Alexander (3119) and Christian (602) in Camster, Latheron Parish, Caithness.[159] He and Ellen Sutherland (3120), Ann Sutherland (3129), Christina Sutherland (3130), Janet Sutherland (3131), and Catherine Sutherland (3133) emigrated with their parents in 1842 to Owen Sound, Canada.

iii. Janet SUTHERLAND (3256) was born in 1830 in Camster, Latheron Parish, Caithness. She died in 1830 in Caithness.

---

151 UK Census 06 June 1841: Alexander Sutherland, cooper, 45; Christy Sutherland, 30; Christy Sutherland, 15; Donald Sutherland, 13; Ann Sutherland, 11; Jannet Sutherland. 9; Hellen Sutherland, 6; Williamina Sutherland, 4; Cathrine Sutherland, 2 and Marcus Gunn, 25. Note that census instructions for recording age were that if under 15, actual age; if over 15, record to the nearest 5 years below actual.

152 Letter or email, Betty Warrilow to Donald Gunn, 07 Aug 2008; Their farm was lot 6, 11th concession only a short distance from the farms of both Marcus and Donald Gunn.

153 Letter or email, Betty Warrilow to Donald Gunn, 07 Aug 2008; I descend from Alexander and Christian a.k.a. Christina Gunn Sutherland. Unfortunately their 2 sons died unmarried. The daughters ... are: Christina, Ann, Janet, plus the following: Ellen, Wilhemina, Catherine (Kate). All were born in Scotland except for the youngest son John who was born 1842 in Wentworth County, Ontario. Their son Donald was # 2 in the family born in 1829.

154 Ibidem

155 Letter or email, Betty Warrilow to Donald Gunn, 22 Aug 2008.

156 UK Census 06 June 1841: Alexander Sutherland, cooper, 45; Christy Sutherland, 30; Christy Sutherland, 15; Donald Sutherland, 13; Ann Sutherland, 11; Jannet Sutherland. 9; Hellen Sutherland, 6; Williamina Sutherland, 4; Cathrine Sutherland, 2 and Marcus Gunn, 25.

157 Letter or email, Betty Warrilow to Donald Gunn, 07 Aug 2008.

158 Letter or email, Betty Warrilow to Donald Gunn, 22 Aug 2008.

159 UK Census 06 June 1841.

iv. Ann SUTHERLAND (3129)[160] was born on 10 Sep 1831 in Camster, Latheron Parish, Caithness.[161] She died on 14 Aug 1914 in Sydenham, Ontario, at age 82.[162] She appeared on the census of 06 Jun 1841 in the household of her parents Alexander (3119) and Christian (602) in Camster, Latheron Parish, Caithness.[163] She and Ellen Sutherland (3120), Donald Sutherland (3127), Christina Sutherland (3130), Janet Sutherland (3131), and Catherine Sutherland (3133) emigrated with her parents in 1842 to Owen Sound, Canada. She was engaged in the village and earned 7/6d per month on 14 Jul 1846. See the letter from Marcus Gunn in Part 3.

v. Janet SUTHERLAND (3131)[164] was born on 06 Jul 1833 in Camster, Latheron Parish, Caithness.[165] She married James Mackay (3167) on 02 Feb 1860.[166] She died in 1908.[167] She appeared on the census of 06 Jun 1841 in the household of her parents Alexander (3119) and Christian (602) in Camster, Latheron Parish, Caithness.[168] She and Ellen Sutherland (3120), Donald Sutherland (3127), Ann Sutherland (3129), Christina Sutherland (3130), and Catherine Sutherland (3133) emigrated with their parents in 1842 to Owen Sound, Canada. She was keeping house for her uncle Marcus Gunn on 14 Jul 1846. See the letter by Marcus in Part 3.

18 vi. Ellen SUTHERLAND (3120).

vii. Williamina SUTHERLAND (3132)[169] was born on 12 May 1838 in Caithness.[170] She died on 02 Jul 1927 in Grey, Grey Co., Ontario, at age 89.[171] She appeared on the census of 06 Jun 1841 in the household of her parents Alexander (3119) and Christian (602) in Camster, Latheron Parish, Caithness.[172]

viii. Catherine SUTHERLAND (3133)[173] was born on 09 Jun 1839 in Camster, Latheron Parish, Caithness.[174] She married George Macdonald (3168), son of Hugh Macdonald (3169) and Barbara (--?--) (3170), in 1871.[175] She died

---

160Letter or email, Betty Warrilow to Donald Gunn, 07 Aug 2008.

161Ibidem

162Letter or email, Betty Warrilow to Donald Gunn, 22 Aug 2008.

163UK Census 06 June 1841: Alexander Sutherland, cooper, 45; Christy Sutherland, 30; Christy Sutherland, 15; Donald Sutherland, 13; Ann Sutherland, 11; Jannet Sutherland. 9; Hellen Sutherland, 6; Williamina Sutherland, 4; Cathrine Sutherland, 2 and Marcus Gunn, 25. Note that census instructions for recording age were that if under 15, actual age; if over 15, record to the nearest 5 years below actual.

164Letter or email, Betty Warrilow to Donald Gunn, 07 Aug 2008; I descend from Alexander and Christian a.k.a. Christina Gunn Sutherland. Unfortunately their 2 sons died unmarried. The daughters 3 of whom are mentioned in the letters are: Christina, Ann, Janet, plus the following: Ellen, Wilhemina, Catherine (Kate). All were born in Scotland except for the youngest son John who was born 1842 in Wentworth County, Ontario. Their son Donald was born in 1829.

165Ibidem

166Letter or email, Betty Warrilow to Donald Gunn, 22 Aug 2008.

167Ibidem

168UK Census 06 June 1841.

169Letter or email, Betty Warrilow to Donald Gunn, 07 Aug 2008.

170Ibidem

171Letter or email, Betty Warrilow to Donald Gunn, 22 Aug 2008.

172UK Census 06 June 1841.

173Letter or email, Betty Warrilow to Donald Gunn, 07 Aug 2008.

174Ibidem; Bill & Sharon Gurney, e-mail to Donald Gunn.

175Letter or email, Betty Warrilow to Donald Gunn, 22 Aug 2008.

in 1900.[176] She appeared on the census of 06 Jun 1841 in the household of her parents Alexander (3119) and Christian (602) in Camster, Latheron Parish, Caithness.[177] She and Ellen Sutherland (3120), Donald Sutherland (3127), Ann Sutherland (3129), Christina Sutherland (3130), and Janet Sutherland (3131) emigrated with their parents in 1842 to Owen Sound, Canada.

George MACDONALD (3168)[178] was born in 1833. He died on 31 Jan 1871 in Grey, Grey Co., Ontario.

ix. John SUTHERLAND (3128); born on passage[179] in Feb 1842 to Wentworth Co., Ontario.[180] He died on 17 Mar 1904 at age 62.[181] He witnessed the marriage of Herbert William Jenkins (3117) and Janet Gunn (3113) on 26 Dec 1876 in Owen Sound, Ontario.[182]

8. Marcus GUNN in Owen Sound (298)[183] was born in 1805 in Halkirk Parish, Caithness.[184] He was christened on 09 Aug 1805 in Halkirk Parish, Caithness.[185] He married Barbara Mackay (3111), daughter of Neil Mackay (3114) and Margaret Sutherland (3115), on 04 Jan 1850 in Sydenham, Ontario; performed by Rev. McKinnon.[186] He died 23 May 1878 in Owen Sound, Ontario. He was buried on 25 May 1878 in Greenwood, Ontario. In 1829 Marcus (298) was a cattle dealer.[187] He witnessed the christening of Sir John Gunn[188] (3250) on 04 Nov 1837 in Bualchork, Halkirk Parish, Caithness.[189] He appeared on the census of 06 Jun 1841 in the household of Alexander Sutherland (3119) and Christian Gunn (602) in Camster, Latheron Parish, Caithness.[190] He emigrated to Canada in 1842. On 27 Sep 1842 in Owen Sound, Ontario, Marcus (298) wrote to John Mackay in Caithness.[191] On 03 Nov 1845 in Owen Sound, Ontario, Marcus (298) wrote to brother Alexander.[192] On 04

---

176 Ibidem

177 UK Census 06 June 1841: Alexander Sutherland, cooper, 45; Christy Sutherland, 30; Christy Sutherland, 15; Donald Sutherland, 13; Ann Sutherland, 11; Jannet Sutherland. 9; Hellen Sutherland, 6; Williamina Sutherland, 4; Cathrine Sutherland, 2 and Marcus Gunn, 25. Note that census instructions for recording age were that if under 15, actual age; if over 15, record to the nearest 5 years below actual.

178 Letter or email, Betty Warrilow to Donald Gunn, 22 Aug 2008.

179 Letter or email, Betty Warrilow to Donald Gunn, 07 Aug 2008; I descend from Alexander and Christian a.k.a. Christina Gunn Sutherland. Unfortunately their 2 sons died unmarried. The daughters 3 of whom are mentioned in the letters (of 'Part 3') are: Christina, Ann, Janet, plus the following: Ellen, Wilhemina, Catherine (Kate). All were born in Scotland except for the youngest son John who was born 1842 in Wentworth County, Ontario. Their son Donald was \# 2 in the family born in 1829.

180 Ibidem

181 Letter or email, Betty Warrilow to Donald Gunn, 22 Aug 2008; Bill & Sharon Gurney, e-mail to Donald Gunn.

182 Carol Small, e-mail message to Donald Gunn, 01 Sep 2008: Herbert William Jenkins, 25, teacher, England, Keppel, son of George Jenkins & Elizabeth Hopkins, married Janet Gunn, 25, Owen Sound, same, daughter of Marcus Gunn & Barbara McKay, witness John Sutherland of Sydenham & Arthur H N Jenkins of Normanby, 26 Dec 1876 at Owen Sound.

183 *LDS Church*, christenings at Halkirk, Caithness, of children born to Donald Gunn and Janet McKenzie: John 18 Jan 1783 and Hugh 7 Jan 1787, with Alexander 9 Jun 1789, Donald 19 Mar 1796, William 12 Mar 1799, Christian 30 Jan 1802, Marcus 9 Aug 1805 further described as born at Halkirk.

184 Ibidem

185 Ibidem

186 Carol Small, e-mail to Donald Gunn, Aug 2008.

187 Implied in Part 3.

188 See Part 7.

189 Bill & Sharon Gurney, e-mail to Donald Gunn, 23 Sep 2008.

190 UK Census 06 June 1841.

191 See Part 3.

192 See Part 3.

Jul 1846 in Owen Sound, Ontario, Marcus (298) wrote to brother Alexander at Brawlbin, Caithness.[193] On 04 Jul 1846 in Owen Sound, Ontario, Marcus (298) wrote to his friend Robert Sinclair of Brawlbin in an addendum to a letter to his brother Alexander.[194] He was a farmer in Lot 14, Concession 11, Sydenham, Ontario.[195] He was a conscientious letter writer, see Part 3.

Barbara MACKAY (3111)[196] was born in 1814 in Halkirk Parish, Caithness,[197] and was christened on 08 Mar 1814 in Bualintagill, Halkirk Parish, Caithness.[198] She died on 23 Dec 1881 in Sydenham, Ontario, age 67.[199] She was buried on 25 Dec 1881 in Greenwood, Owen Sound, in the same plot as husband Marcus. She farmed with Marcus (298) in Lot 14, Concession 11, Sydenham (being the original name of Owen Sound), Ontario.[200]

Children of Marcus Gunn in Owen Sound (298) and Barbara Mackay (3111) both born in Sydenham, Ontario, were as follows:

19 i. Janet GUNN (3113).

20 ii. Margaret GUNN (3112).

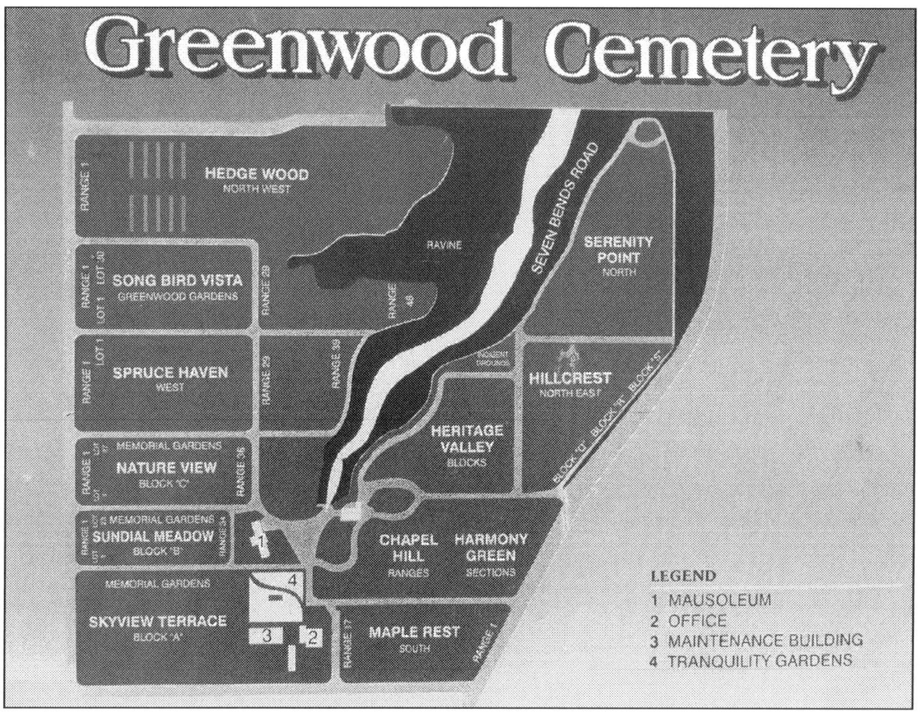

---

[193]See Part 3.

[194]See Part 3.

[195]Carol Small, e-mail to Donald Gunn, 04 Aug 2008.

[196]Carol Small, e-mail to Donald Gunn, Aug 2008.

[197]Bill & Sharon Gurney, e-mail to Donald Gunn, 03 Oct 2008: Family of Neil McKay & Margaret Sutherland of Caithness Scotland & Ontario Canada.

[198]Ibidem

[199]Ibidem

[200] Carol Small, e-mail to Donald Gunn, 04 Aug 2008. http://freepages.genealogy.rootsweb.ancestry.com/~wjmartin/grey8.htm

Generation Three

9. Donald GUNN of Olginbreg & Owen Sound (3215) was born in 1828 in Olgrinbeg, Halkirk Parish, Caithness.[201] He was christened on 20 Oct 1828 in Olgrinbeg, Halkirk Parish, Caithness. He married Janet Mackay of Braehour (3118), daughter of Neil Mackay (3114) and Margaret Sutherland (3115), on 04 Jun 1852 in Halkirk Parish, Caithness.[202] He died on 21 Apr 1895 in Sydenham, Ontario.[203] He was buried on 23 Apr 1895 in Greenwood, Ontario.[204] He was a teacher. He appeared on the census of 30 Mar 1851 in the household of his parents John (294) and Anne (3208) in Olgrinbeg, Halkirk Parish, Caithness.[205] He was a teacher in the log school SS\#1, Sydenham, Ontario.[206]

Janet MACKAY of Braehour (3118) was born in 1827 in Caithness. She was christened on 30 Sep 1827 in Halkirk Parish, Caithness.[207] She died on 15 Dec 1914 in Grey, Grey Co., Ontario, age 86. She was buried on 17 Dec 1914 in Greenwood, Ontario. She emigrated with Donald Gunn in 1857 from Caithness to Ontario, Canada after the death of his father; their son Neil was born en route.[208]

Children of Donald Gunn of Olginbreg & Owen Sound (3215) and Janet Mackay of Braehour (3118) were as follows:

i. Angus Grant GUNN (3218) was born in 1850 in Halkirk Parish, Caithness. He died on 27 Feb 1864 in Badnallie, Watten Parish, Caithness, of diphtheria. He was raised by his grandmother Ann Grant Gunn and uncle Hector Gunn.

ii. Annie GUNN (3134)[209] was born in 1852 in Caithness.[210] She married James Adams (3219) on 09 Oct 1877 in Owen Sound, Ontario.[211] She died in 1880 in Owen Sound, Ontario.[212] She emigrated with her parents in 1857

---

[201] Bill & Sharon Gurney, e-mail to Donald Gunn, 12 Sep 2008 and further information on this page.

[202] Carol Small, e-mail to Donald Gunn, 04 Aug 2008; Donald Gunn married Janet McKay in 1852. In his obituary, it says he was born in Reay, Caithness. But family story says that Marcus was Donald's uncle; Bill & Sharon Gurney, e-mail to Donald Gunn, 12 Sep 2008.

[203] Carol Small, e-mail to Donald Gunn, Aug 2008.

[204] Ibidem

[205] Census 30 March 1851: John Gunn 70 head; Ann Gunn 50 wife; Jennet Gunn 25 daughter; Hector Gunn 22 son; Donald Gunn 22 son; Hellen Gunn 16 daughter; Angus Grant Gunn 1; all born Halkirk Parish, all resident Olgrinbeg.

[206] Carol Small, e-mail to Donald Gunn, Aug 2008; Donald Gunn was a nephew of Marcus Gunn. He married Janet or Jenettie McKay in 1852, a sister of Barbara McKay wife of Marcus. They were daughters of Neil McKay (17..-) and Margaret Sutherland (1778-1878), natives of Caithnesshire (Thurso). They came to Canada about 1857 and are listed on lot 14 con.11, Sydenham Township. He was one of the teachers in the log school SS\#1 Sydenham (Gordon School) from 1852-1876 His son Neil liked to tease Annie Gordon b.1868 and called her his cousin.

[207] Bill & Sharon Gurney, e-mail to Donald Gunn, Family of Neil McKay & Margaret Sutherland of Caithness Scotland & Ontario Canada 03 Oct 2008.

[208] Carol Small, e-mail to Donald Gunn, Aug 2008.

[209] Carol Small, e-mail to Donald Gunn, 04 Aug 2008; Donald and Janet's children were Ann, Margaret, Neil, John, Donald MacKay Gunn, Barbara Janet, Jemima, William J and Angus Hector;

[210] Ibidem

[211] Bill & Sharon Gurney, e-mail to Donald Gunn, 12 Sep 2008; *The Owen Sound Advertiser*, Married - In Owen Sound, by Rev. J.I. Hindley, M.A., on the 9th inst., Mr James Adams, of Derby, to Miss Annie Gunn, of Sydenham; Certificate of Marriage, County of Grey, Division of Owen Sound: James Adams, 22 years of Owen Sound, b Canada bachelor, farmer, parents William Adams and Hannah Adams, to Annie Gunn b Scotland spinster, parents Donald Gunn and Janet Gunn, on 9 October 1877 at Owen Sound.

[212] Carol Small, e-mail to Donald Gunn, Aug 2008.

from Caithness to Ontario, Canada after death of her grandfather; her brother Neil was born en route.[213]

iii. Margaret GUNN (3135)[214] was born in 1855 in Caithness. She died on 04 May 1942 in Owen Sound, Ontario, age 88. She was buried on 06 May 1942 in Greenwood, Ontario. She emigrated with her parents in 1857 from Caithness to Ontario, Canada. She lived with brother Donald on land sold for a hospital. She was the informant of the death of Donald McKay Gunn (3138) in 1926.

21 iv. Neil GUNN (3136).

v. John GUNN (3137) was born in Oct 1859 in Ontario. He died on 28 Dec 1875 at age 16.[215]

vi. Donald McKay GUNN (3138) was born in 1861 in Ontario. He died in 1926. He lived with sister Margaret on land sold for hospital.

vii. Angus Hector GUNN (3142) was born in 1864 in Ontario. He died in 1940 in Prince George, British Colombia. He was a prospector in 1940.[216]

22 viii. Barbara Janet GUNN (3139).

ix. Jemima GUNN (3140)[217] was born in 1870 in Ontario. She died in 1870 in Ontario.

x. William James GUNN (3141) was born in 1871 in Ontario. He died on 10 Aug 1890 in Ontario. He was buried on 12 Aug 1890 in Greenwood, Ontario.

10. Helen / Ellen GUNN[218] (3216) was born in 1835 in Halkirk Parish, Caithness.[219] She married Archibald Sinclair (3217) on Tuesday 26 Jan 1858 in Halkirk. She appeared on the census of 06 Jun 1841 in the household of her parents John (294) and Anne (3208) in Olgrinbeg, Halkirk Parish, Caithness.[220] She appeared on the census of 30 Mar 1851 in the household of her parents John (294) and Anne (3208) in Olgrinbeg, Halkirk Parish, Caithness[221] where she is described as a domestic servant.

A direct relative of the family writes; 'On the marriage act, she appears to be living in Backlass, Watten before the marriage; she was a housemaid. Her brother Hector was a witness.

On the 1871 census Archibald 47 and Helen 34 appeared in Newlands, Watten, Caithness with their 6 surviving children: John William 13 (3220), see below, Janet 9 (3222), William R.G. 8 (3223), Elizabeth 6 (3224), Ann 4

213Carol Small, e-mail to Donald Gunn, Aug 2008.

214Carol Small, e-mail to Donald Gunn, 04 Aug 2008; Donald and Janet's children were Ann, Margaret, Neil, John, Donald MacKay Gunn, Barbara Janet, Jemima, William J and Angus Hector and for further information on this page.

215Carol Small, e-mail to Donald Gunn, Aug 2008; *Owen Sound Advertiser*, Died—In Sydenham, at his father's residence, 28th Dec, 1875, John, second eldest son of Mr Donald Gunn, age 16 years and 2 months.

216Bill & Sharon Gurney, e-mail to Donald Gunn, Family of Neil McKay & Margaret Sutherland of Caithness Scotland & Ontario Canada 03 Oct 2008 and for further inofmation on this page.

217Carol Small, e-mail to Donald Gunn, 04 Aug 2008.

218See http://catherine.sinclair.pagesperso-orange.fr/johngunn/pafg02.htm#33 for much more information about the children and their descendants than are given here.

219Bill & Sharon Gurney, e-mail to Donald Gunn, 12 Sep 2008.

220UK Census 06 June 1841: John Gunn 50 farmer; Anne Gunn 40 wife; Margret Gunn 20 daughter; Janet Gunn 15 daughter; Hector Gunn 14 son; Helen Gunn 5 daughter; all resident at Olgrinbeg.

221UK Census 30 March 1851: John Gunn 70 head; Ann Gunn 50 wife; Jennet Gunn 25 daughter; Hector Gunn 22 son; Donald Gunn 22 son; Hellen Gunn 16 daughter; Aeneas Gunn grandson of John and Ann 1; all born Halkirk Parish, all resident Olgrinbeg.

(3225) and George 2 (3226); except for the youngest, the children were all scholars. Archibald is described as an agricultural labourer; Helen does not work. They have 3 rooms with one or more windows.

Archibald had five attempts before managing to build his croft. In those days, the land belonged to the laird and the only way labourers could possess their own house was by building it within one night. At dawn, the laird would come and check that smoke was coming out of the chimney; if it was not, he was entitled to have the house demolished. Then the labourer had to try his luck again. No need to say that the whole community was giving a hand in such occasions! Archibald had a hard time before getting his own croft but he would certainly be happy and proud to know that it is still standing with its four walls, one of the only ones left in Watten ...

Helen Sinclair says that her grand-mother, Helen Gunn, was always very careful with her money and ruled the whole family, at least after her husband's death.[222]

Helen died of old age at 95, on Saturday, 17 Oct 1931 in Newton Moss, Watten.
Archibald SINCLAIR (3217), uncle, was the informant of the death of Angus Grant Gunn

Archibald SINCLAIR (3217), uncle, was the informant of the death of Angus Grant Gunn (3218) on 27 Feb 1864 in Badnallie, Watten Parish, Caithness; of diphtheria.[223]

Children of Helen Gunn (3216) and Archibald Sinclair (3217) were:

i. John William SINCLAIR (3220) was born in 1857/1858 in Latheron Parish, Caithness. He married Ann Henry in 1879 in Watten and had seven children between 1879-1890, in order Elizabeth 1879, Archibald 1880, David 1883, Janet 1886, James 1888, Helen 1890 and William 1890.

ii. George SINCLAIR (3221) was born in 1860 in Latheron Parish, Caithness.[224] He died before 1869.

iii. Janet SINCLAIR (3222) was born 16 May 1861 in Watten Parish, Caithness. She married George Sandison in 1881 in Watten and had Ellen Sandison in 1884.

iv. William G.R. SINCLAIR[225] (3223) was born in 1863 in Watten Parish, Caithness.

v. Elizabeth SINCLAIR (3224) was born on Saturday 24 Oct 1864 in Watten Parish, Caithness.

vi. Ann SINCLAIR (3225) was born on Thursday 21 Feb 1867 in Watten Parish, Caithness.

vii. George SINCLAIR (3226) was born on Friday, 02 Apr 1869 in Newlands, Watten Parish, Caithness and died 19 March 1943 in Lanergill. He married Georgina Sutherland 1876-1945 in 1907 and they had six children 1907-1921. From Catherine Sinclair;

Annie (1907-1964) Helen (or Ella) b. 1909, Jane (or Jean) 1911- c.1990s ... Janet (or Jenny) (1915-1981), Donald (1917-2009), Catherine Mackay (1921-deceased). He was a hard-working man, working both on his croft but also on other people's farms. He was very good

[222] From Catherine Sinclair, November 2011 email to Alastair Gunn.

[223] Bill & Sharon Gurney, e-mail to Donald Gunn, 12 Sep 2008.

[224] Bill & Sharon Gurney, e-mail to Donald Gunn, 12 Sep 2008 and further information on this page.

[225] Also known as William Aeneas Gunn Sinclair b. 04 Dec. 1862.

with his hands, especially very good at building. … He had been ill for a while but on the day he died, he got up from his bed, went to the fire-place where he was keeping his money and told his daughter Catherine who was there that this was the money for his funeral. He then went to his armchair, smoked his pipe and then went back to his bed and died a few minutes later.

George Sinclair, his wife Georgina Sutherland and their three eldest daughters—Jean, Helen and Annie

Being the other three children; Donald, Catherine and Jenny Sinclair

viii. Hector SINCLAIR (3227) was born on Wednesday 02 Aug 1871 in Watten Parish, Caithness. He married Hughina Sutherland.

ix. Archibald SINCLAIR[226] (3228) was born on Saturday 07 Jun 1873 in Watten Parish, Caithness.

x. Daniel Gunn SINCLAIR (3229) was born on Thursday 14 Dec 1876 in Watten Parish, Caithness. It was known that he emigrated to Australia (information from Catherine Sinclair in France). He emigrated to Queensland, Australia, probably in 1900 as a Daniel G. Sinclair was a passenger on the 'Duke of Norfolk' which arrived in Townsville, North Queensland, on 10 Aug 1900. He married Christina Ellen Anderson on 04 May 1904. Archibald Sinclair (4196) was born on 17 Jan 1905. Another child, Roderick James Sinclair (4197) was born on 01 Oct 1907[227] but died on 23 Aug 1910.[228] Ailsa Mavis Sinclair (4198) was born on 17 August 1908[229] but died 17 Aug 1910.[230] One newspaper reported they both died on the same day 26 Aug

[226]Probably another Archibald Sinclair was born in 1865.

[227]Australian Birth Index, Queensland, Reg. No. 001912.

[228]Australian Death Index, Queensland, Reg No. 000648.

[229]Australian Birth Index, Queensland, 1909 Reg No. 002031.

[230]Australian Death Index, Queensland, Reg. No. 000644.

1910 from 'ptomaine poisoning'[231]. 'Mrs Sinclair and two older children are in the hospital with symptoms similar to those of the children who died'.[232] In the 1905 Electoral Roll[233] Daniel Gunn Sinclair was at Stone River near Ingham, a labourer. Many Anderson families lived in the Stone River district, but whether they were related to Christina Ellen Anderson is not clear. The area is 'wet tropics'; its economy is rural and even then sugar cane was a major source of its income. The 1919 and 1925 Electoral Rolls record Daniel and Christina still at Stone River. In 1930 Helen Sinclair b. 07 Apr 1906 a daughter, (dressmaker) was with them at Victoria and Hardy Street, Ingham; an Archibald Sinclair was just above them in the Roll but does not have the same street address[234]. In 1936 and 1937 another daughter Alma Jean Sinclair was on the Electoral Roll with her parents at White Rock, along with Helen. It seems possible that Helen married an Unknown Weaver as a Helen Weaver is named as Next of Kin to her brothers in World War Two military records; Alma Jean Sinclair married Charles Henry Barclay of Townsville on 28 Dec 1939. There was a death notice for Daniel Gunn Sinclair for 06 Aug 1940 in Queensland, with father Archibald and mother Helen Gunn which shows he was 'our' Daniel Gunn Sinclair. He was buried in the Old Ingham cemetery, 'Uniting Church' section, plot 1355. The Daniel Gunn Sinclair who pleaded guilty to driving a utility without headlights on an Innisfail night, in late December 1946[235] was a son based on the name but no Queensland governmental birth/marriage/death paperwork can be found for him. He was born 21 Jun 1919 according to the Australian Army records, enlisted at Ingham and served in the Army in World War 2. In 1932 a Daniel G. Sinclair from north Queensland won a 'State Scholarship' to attend a Secondary School, but he was not in the top 1000 students. In 1954 a Daniel Gunn Sinclair was a carpenter in Leichardt.[236] He was probably still alive in 1977 in Cairns and married to Gladys, according to the Electoral Rolls. Another son, John William Sinclair (3220), was born 29 May 1914 and died on 22 Jul 1941.[237] It is possible that he died as a result of being shot when he went to assist two women who were struggling with a gunman in late September 1940. He was in a critical condition following that incident.[238] He may have killed a cow when driving in 1938.[239] He enrolled in World War 2 from Mount Isa in March 1940; he was a sergeant at his death.

[231] *The North Western Advocate and the Emu Bay Times*, Tas. 27 Aug 1910, page 5; the story appeared in many newspapers around the country.

[232] *The Brisbane Courier*, 26 Aug 1910, page 5,

[233] No other Daniel Gunn Sinclair is on the electoral roll for Queensland for any of these years.

[234] Later Electoral Rolls suggest he continued to live at Ingham until at least 1943, with wife Mona Margaret Tealby m.26 Mar 1930 at the Ingham Methodist Church. Alma Jean Sinclair was the bridesmaid; his sister.

[235] *Townsville Daily Bulletin,* 07 Dec 1946, page 5.

[236] *Townsville Daily Bulletin*, 22 Jan 1932, page 5.

[237] Australian Death Index, Queensland Reg. No 000296.

[238] *The Argus,* page 2, 01 Oct. 1940

[239] *Cairns Post*, page 6, 03 Jan 1938.

11. Alexander GUNN (3238) was born on 12 Jun 1839 in Camster, Latheron Parish, Caithness.[240] He was christened on 27 Jul 1839 in Wick Parish, Caithness. He married Christina Gunn (3239) in 1893 in Latheron Parish, Caithness. He appeared on the census of 06 Jun 1841 in the household of his parents Hugh (295) and Henrietta (752) in Loravack, Latheron Parish, Caithness.[241] He appeared on the census of 30 Mar 1851 in the household of his mother Henrietta (752) in Fly Glay, Halkirk Parish, Caithness.[242] He appeared on the census of 30 Mar 1861 in the household of his mother Henrietta (752) in Houstry, Latheron Parish, Caithness.[243] He was informant of the death of Henrietta McGregor of Dalnawillan (752) on 15 Apr 1890 in Houstry, Dunbeath Parish, Caithness.

Children of Alexander Gunn (3238) and Christina Gunn (3239) were as follows:

i. Henrietta GUNN (808) was born in 1894.
ii. Alexander M. K. GUNN (3240) was born in 1896.

12. Catherine GUNN (119)[244] was born on 13 May 1830 in Reay Parish, Caithness.[245] She was christened on 18 May 1830 in Halkirk Parish, Caithness.[246] She married James Miller [247](117), son of John Miller (934) and Elizabeth Dunnet (935), on 13 Mar 1857 in the residence of John W Surman, Buninyong, Vic.[248] She died in 1912 in Vic.[249] She appeared on the 1841 Census of Brawlbin, Reay Parish, Caithness, in the household of her parents Alexander Gunn of Bualchork and Brawlbin (1) and Barbara Gunn of Braehour (6).[250] She appeared on the 1851 Census of Brawlbin, Reay Parish, Caithness, in the household of

---

[240]Bill & Sharon Gurney, e-mail to Donald Gunn, 05 Sep 2008 and further information on this page.

[241]UK Census 06 June 1841: Hugh Gunn 50 farmer; Harrietta Gunn 45 wife; Cathrine Gunn 20 daughter; Helen Gunn 18 daughter; Donald Gunn 12 son; Mary Gunn 6 daughter; John Gunn 4 son; Alexr Gunn 2 son; all resident Loravack.

[242]UK Census 30 March 1851: Henrietta Gunn 56 head; Janet Gunn 34; Catherine Gunn 31; Helen Gunn 29; Donald Gunn 22; Mary Gunn 16; John Gunn 14; Alexander Gunn 11.

[243]UK Census 30 March 1861: Henrietta McGregor 65 head; Janet Gunn 44 daughter; Alexander Gunn son 21; Mary Campbell 7 granddaughter scholar.

[244]*LDS Church*, Christenings of children of Barbara Gunn, father Alexander Gunn. Catherine, 18 May 1830, Halkirk; Donald, 9 Jun 1832, Reay; Janet, 19 Aug 1834, Reay; John, 29 Feb 1836, Reay.

[245]UK Census 06 June 1841: District of Brawlbin lying in the south part of the Parish of Reay. Each person who abode in each house on night of 6 June 1841: Alexander Gunn 50 farmer; Barbara Gunn 30; Kathrine Gunn 11; Donald Gunn 9; John Gunn 5; Janet Gunn 7; William Gunn 2; all born in Caithness. Note: Census instructions for recording age were that if under 15, actual age; if over 15, record to the nearest 5 years below actual ie Alexander Gunn was between 50 and 55 and Barbara between 30 and 35 on 6 June 1841. Birth years are thus Alexander 1786-1791 and Barbara 1806-1811. The summary notes that there were 40 occupied houses, 2 uninhabited houses, 78 males and 94 females comprising 40 families in the Brawlbin District; Census 30 March 1851: County of Caithness, Parish of Reay. Residents at Brawlbinn. Donald Gunn head, unmarried 19, farmer, 16 acres, born Halkirk; Katherine Gunn sister, unmarried 20, general service, born Reay; Janet Gunn sister, unmarried 17, scholar, born Reay; John Gunn brother, unmarried 15, scholar born Reay; William Gunn brother, unmarried 12, scholar born Reay. Brawlbin comprised 39 occupied houses with 70 males and 93 females. The census district of Brawlbin and Oldenbruch (?) was 12 miles in length and 2 miles in breadth. The majority of homes, 39, was in Brawlbin, with 3 in Oldenbruch accommodating 24 people; see also *Bible of Alexander Gunn*: my daughter Kitty born May 13 1830 page 27.

[246]*LDS Church*, Christenings of children of Barbara Gunn, father Alexander Gunn
Catherine, 18 May 1830, Halkirk; Donald, 9 Jun 1832, Reay; Janet, 19 Aug 1834, Reay; John, 29 Feb 1836, Reay.

[247]See Part 7.

[248]Certificate of Marriage, 1857 130 Marriages solemnized in the District of Buninyong: James Miller, Ship Chandler, age 28, born Wick Scotland, Bachelor resident Geelong, father John Miller, Builder, mother Elizabeth Dunnet, married Catherine Gunn, Servant, age 26, born Reay Scotland, Spinster resident Geelong, father Alexander Gunn, Farmer, Mother Barbara Gunn, according to the Rites of the Presbyterian Church.

[249]See Part 7 for a more detailed version of this story.

[250]UK Census 06 June 1841: District of Brawlbin lying in the south part of the Parish of Reay. Each person who abode in each house on night of 6 June 1841: Alexander Gunn 50 farmer; Barbara Gunn 30; Kathrine Gunn 11; Donald Gunn 9; John Gunn 5; Janet Gunn 7; William Gunn 2; all born in Caithness. Note: Census instructions for recording age were that if under 15, actual age; if over 15, record to the nearest 5 years below actual so Alexander Gunn was between 50 and 55 and Barbara between 30 and 35 on 6 June 1841. Birth years are thus Alexander 1786-1791 and Barbara 1806-1811. The summary notes that there were 40 occupied houses, 2 uninhabited houses, 78 males and 94 females comprising 40 families in the Brawlbin District.

Donald Gunn of Brawlbin & Ballarat (3).[251] James Miller sent home for his childhood sweetheart Catherine Gunn (119) in 1854.[252] Catherine (119) and Donald (3) arrived in Melbourne, Vic, aboard the 'Herald of the Morning' in Dec 1854. Catherine appears to have travelled under her mother's name Barbara Gunn.[253]

James MILLER (117)[254] was born in 1826 in Wick Parish, Caithness; in the north of Scotland.[255] He died in 1918 in Vic at the age of 92, after 54 years with his company. He

---

251 UK Census 30 March 1851: County of Caithness, Parish of Reay. Residents at Brawlbin. Donald Gunn head, unmarried 19, farmer, 16 acres, born Halkirk; Katherine Gunn sister, unmarried 20, general service, born Reay; Janet Gunn sister, unmarried 17, scholar, born Reay; John Gunn brother, unmarried 15, scholar born Reay; William Gunn brother, unmarried 12, scholar born Reay. Brawlbin comprised 39 occupied houses with 70 males and 93 females. The census district of Brawlbin and Oldenbruch (?) was 12 miles in length and 2 miles in breadth. The majority of homes, 39, was in Brawlbin, with 3 in Oldenbruch accommodating 24 people.

252 *The James Miller Story.*

253 Unknown compiler, "Immigration to Victoria," *Ancestral File*, a Donald Gunn aged 27 arrived in Melbourne per the 'Herald of the Morning'. This is the only recorded Donald Gunn of the approximate age to arrive between late '54 & early '56. The ship's passenger list records John Raps(?), 22; Walter Williamson, 20; John Sutherland,19; Hugh Murray, 22; Donald Gunn, 27; Barbara Gunn, 29 and Hugh Matheson, 36 all travelling together. There are no other names listed on the passenger list that could possibly be corruptions of Catherine. WW Gunn states Donald & Catherine travelled together— could Catherine for some reason travel under her mother's name? It's odd but in one author's view—namely Don Gunn—"it is a case of accepting the only possible record found. The timing fits. There were only two Gunns on that ship, Donald, 27 & Barbara, 29, when they were really 22 & 24. Not right ages, but near enough for the time–note that John was recorded as John Gum (not Gunn), aged 24, when he was really 17. At least Barbara is not an unconnected name. There weren't any other Gunns that could possibly fit in any other ship, although in those years there were certainly many people unrecorded. There are several records suggesting that Donald and Catherine travelled together. The 'Herald of the Morning' arrived at a time of year when heat stroke was a distinct possibility in Melbourne. As to why she would do so, I can't imagine, but so many things were odd then. Might have been something to do with a single woman travelling with another man, and assuming a mantle of maturity. Maybe she didn't have papers in her own name, but her mother in some way had. I think John was recorded as being from Ireland.' Email to Alastair Gunn January 7, 2009.

254 Certificate of Marriage, 1857 879 marriages solemnized in the District of Buninyong.

255 *The James Miller Story*, James Miller, the son of a stonemason and builder, came to Australia in 1850 from Wick, a small seaport of Caithness in the north-east of Scotland. There he had learnt the age-old craft of sail making.
With only meagre savings behind him he worked for a while as a sailmaker in Van Diemen's Land, travelling on the ships trading between Van Diemen's Land and Norfolk Island. On one of these trips the cargo included a number of female convicts. The manner in which they were 'loaded' into the vessel, and the conditions under which they were carried, so disgusted the sailmaker that he left the ship in Sydney.
In the meantime the rush to the Victorian goldfields had set in. The discovery of the fabulously rich Ballarat and Bendigo fields, the first in Australia, resulted in fortunes for many diggers. James Miller decided to try his luck and, although he made no fortune, he was sufficiently successful to be able to establish his own small business as a ship chandler in Geelong.
In 1854 he sent home for his childhood sweetheart, Catherine Gunn, of Brawlbyn, Caithness, whom he married in 1857 in Geelong. They had six children, some of whom continued in the rope making business started by James.
James started his rope works at Emerald Hill, now South Melbourne, in 1862. A century later it was Australia's largest manufacturer of rope, cordage and associated products. Alexander Gray, another Scot, helped by providing capital for modern machinery. Then James brought to Australia his brothers-in-law: Peter Hogg, an experienced ropemaker, and George Murray, a carpenter.
In 1864, George Kinnear joined the staff to install and maintain machinery purchased from America. He was an engineer, but left the company in 1869 to establish his own successful enterprise.
With a nucleus of sound men, James was the first in Australia to introduce machinery for the preparing and spinning of vegetable fibres and the walk-laying of rope. The term 'ropewalk,' now a very old one, came from the spinner or ropemaker walking back and forth. The spinner wound a bunch of combed fibres around his waist, attached a few of the fibres to a hook and walked backwards while the driving wheel was turned by a fellow worker. As the hook revolved, the spinner fed out the fibre from the bundles around his waist. By the time he reached the end of the ropewalk a long piece of yarn had been spun. He repeated this operation until there were several yarns to twist together to form the 'strand.' Finally, three or more strands were twisted together thus 'laying' the rope. The James Miller enterprise was known originally not as a ropeworks but as a 'ropewalk.'
One day in 1888, James walked into the office and told the staff that he had sold the factory's South Melbourne site for 100,000 pounds. It was the height of the land boom. A deposit of 20,000 pounds was paid and the purchaser promptly resold at 125,000 pounds. And then the boom burst. Miller had only his deposit. Moreover he had contracted to build new works on a river frontage at Yarraville.
In the tragic years that followed, bank after bank closed its doors - including Miller's own bank. Left with the now unsaleable South Melbourne property on his hands, James was committed to substantial expenditure in the middle of the worst depression the colony had known. It must have been heartbreaking. Somehow the firm survived, the banks reconstructured and opened again, and by the time the depression was over, James' operations had all been transferred to Yarraville.
Not only were all debts paid, but James and his partner, Alexander Gray, managed to help friends who also faced ruin.
As a result of the land boom and the large number of bankruptcies that followed the crash of the 1890's, James and Gray, both now in their 70's, dissolved the partnership and formed a limited company on 7 Sep 1898, with James as Chairman and Gray one of the other two directors.

learned to be a ropemaker & sailmaker in Wick in 1845. He emigrated on 28 Jun 1850 from London in the sailing ship Australasia and he arrived in Hobart, Tas, in Oct 1850. He was employed as a sailmaker for three voyages in the 'Lady Franklin' between Hobart and Norfolk Island in 1851. He settled in Melbourne one week before gold was discovered at Clunes in Jun 1851. He walked all the way from Melbourne to Ballarat in 1851. He left the diggings in 1852 and started a coal yard and ship chandler business in Geelong, Vic. He sent for his childhood sweetheart, Catherine Gunn, of Brawlbin in 1854. He was a ship chandler on 13 Mar 1857.[256] He was the founder of Millers Ropes at Emerald Hill, now South Yarra, in partnership with Alexander Gray in 1862 in Vic. He sold the South Melbourne factory and bought river frontage at Yarraville in 1888. He dissolved the partnership and formed a limited company with son James as chairman and Gray as director on 07 Sep 1898. He wrote his reminscences in 1913. He retired as Chairman & Managing Director of Millers Ropes in 1916 in Melbourne, Vic. See *'The James Miller Story'* for full details and Part 7.

Children of Catherine Gunn (119) and James Miller (117) were as follows:

i. Elizabeth MILLER (278) was born in 1858 in Geelong, Vic.[257] She died in 1918 in Vic unmarried.

ii. Alexander Gunn MILLER (279) was born in 1860 in Geelong, Vic.[258] He died in 1938 in Apollo Bay, Vic.[259]

iii. John William Gunn MILLER (280) was born in 1862 in Geelong, Vic.[260] He died in 1925 in St Kilda, Vic.[261]

23 iv. Jessie Barbara MILLER (284).

v. James Dunnet MILLER (281) was born in 1868 in Emerald Hill, Vic.[262] He matriculated to the University of Melbourne from Wesley College in 1884. He was Secretary and a Director of Millers Ropes in 1918 and was known in Masonic and sporting circles.[263] He died in 1933 in Heidelberg, Vic.[264]

24 vi. Katherine Margaret Mckay MILLER (285).

13. Donald GUNN[265] of Brawlbin & Ballarat (3)[266] was born on 28 Mar 1832 in Brawlbin, Reay Parish, Caithness.[267] He was christened on 09 Jun 1832 in Reay Parish, Caithness.[268]

James Miller was a compassionate man. At the end of the first world war, and shortly before his death, the company built a canteen at the Yarraville factory. This was one of the very first to be provided by a company in Melbourne - at a time when concessions and benefits extended by employers to employees were a rarity. Full meals were not supplied, but light refreshments could be purchased. At James' direction, soup was supplied free to juveniles and female workers. It was his opinion that many arrived for work having had little or no breakfast and he considered they needed more than just the cold lunch they brought with them. This consideration toward employees and their personal problems is one reason that many grandchildren of original employees are on the payroll of the company today.
James died at 92 in 1918, six years after Catherine's death, after 54 years with the company he founded.
Source unknown. See Part 7.

256Certificate of Marriage, 1857 No. 879 marriages solemnized in the District of Buninyong.

257Register of BDMs - Victoria, 1858 2500.

258Register of BDMs - Victoria, 1860 3112.

259Register of BDMs - Victoria, 1938 17395.

260Register of BDMs - Victoria, 1862 14625.

261Register of BDMs - Victoria, 1925 15460.

262Register of BDMs - Victoria, 1869 2257.

263See Part 7.

264Register of BDMs - Victoria, 1933 460.

265See Part 7.

266*LDS Church*, Christenings of children of Barbara Gunn, father Alexander Gunn

He married Jane Surman (41), daughter of Daniel Surman (270) and Mary Ann Watkins (271), on 25 Mar 1859 in the Presbyterian school residence, Buninyong, Vic.[269] He died on 14 Feb 1901 in 185 Lydiard St, Ballarat, Vic, at age 68 of bronchial pneumonia and heart disease.[270] He was buried on 16 Feb 1901 in Old Cemetery Area DN Sec.14 Lot 5, Ballarat, Vic. He appeared on the 1841 Census of Brawlbin, Reay Parish, Caithness, in the household of his parents Alexander Gunn of Bualchork and Brawlbin (1) and Barbara Gunn of Braehour (6).[271] In Mar 1851 Donald Gunn of Brawlbin & Ballarat (3) was a farmer of 16 acres in Brawlbin, Reay Parish.[272] He appeared on the 1851 Census of Brawlbin, Reay Parish, Caithness, dated 30 Mar 1851. Donald (3) received a preliminary form for List of Candidates for a Passage on 24 May 1853 in Reay Parish.[273] He failed to gain passage to Australia on 30 Jun 1853 in Brawlbin, Reay Parish, Caithness. He was given a character reference by his Minister on 29 Jun 1854 in Brawlbin, Reay Parish, Caithness. He was given a second character reference on 03 Jul 1854 in Brawlbin, Reay Parish, Caithness. He emigrated on 21 Aug 1854 from Liverpool, Merseyside, per the 'Herald of the Morning' which is the only ship with a Donald Gunn as an unassisted passenger arriving between the range of known dates of Oct 1854 and Jun 1856. He was 47 years in Victoria.[274] Donald (3) and Catherine (119) arrived in Melbourne, Vic, aboard the 'Herald of the Morning' in Dec 1854. Catherine travelled

---

Catherine, 18 May 1830, Halkirk; Donald, 9 Jun 1832, Reay; Janet, 19 Aug 1834, Reay; John, 29 Feb 1836, Reay.

267Clan Gunn Parish Records: Births 1832 Donald Gunn, parents Alexander, Brawlbin - Barbara;

268*LDS Church*, Christenings of children of Barbara Gunn, father Alexander Gunn
Catherine, 18 May 1830, Halkirk; Donald, 9 Jun 1832, Reay; Janet, 19 Aug 1834, Reay; John, 29 Feb 1836, Reay.

269Register of BDMs - Victoria, 1859 No. 827; See Part 3—'Statement by Mr McKenzie taken down verbatim by William W. + Marcus D. Gunn sons of Donald Gunn late of Bralbin + Australia. June 20th 1928'. Married by Rev J Hastie, (ca. 1902); Certificate of Marriage, no.157 of marriages solemnized in the District of Buninyong, Donald Gunn, 26, bachelor, of Buninyong, farmer, married Jane Surman, 23, spinster, of Buninyong, teacher, on 25 March 1859; Letter or email, Dougal Gilmour to Donald Gunn, 8 Apr 1999.

270Register of BDMs - Victoria, 1901 253; *The Ballarat Courier*, Friday 15 Feb 1901, on the 14th February, at 185 Lydiard Street, Donald Gunn, aged 68 years. No flowers; John William Gunn—notes, held in 1996 by Dorothy Margaret Jenkin (nee Milner): Donald - whisky drinker and bought station near Ararat beyond Ercildoune. Lost his money. Died about 1902 Ballarat; Dorothy Margaret Milner; Letter or email, Dougal Gilmour to Donald Gunn, 8 Apr 1999; Certificate of Death, Vic 1901 24552 14 February 1901 at Lydiard Street, City of Ballarat, Donald Gunn, 68, insurance agent of broncho pneumonia, cardiac disease and asthma, duration about 3 months, father Alexander Gunn, farmer, mother Barbara Gunn, maiden name Gunn. Buried 16 February 1901 at Ballarat Old Cemetery. Born at Brawlbin, Reay, Caithness, Scotland, 47 years in Victoria, married at Buninyong at 27 years to Jane Surman, issue in order of birth, John Alexander, 41, William Watkins, 39, Mary Jane, 37, Donald, 35, Marcus Daniel, 32, Barbara, 30, Norman, 28, Hugh, died, Arthur Gilbert, 22, Catherine, 20. Signed by Donald Gunn, son, of Crossover, Gippsland.

271UK Census 06 June 1841: District of Brawlbin lying in the south part of the Parish of Reay. Each person who abode in each house on night of 6 June 1841: Alexander Gunn 50 farmer; Barbara Gunn 30; Kathrine Gunn 11; Donald Gunn 9; John Gunn 5; Janet Gunn 7; William Gunn 2; all born in Caithness. Note: Census instructions for recording age were that if under 15, actual age; if over 15, record to the nearest 5 years below actual ie Alexander Gunn was between 50 and 55 and Barbara between 30 and 35 on 6 June 1841. Birth years are thus Alexander 1786-1791 and Barbara 1806-1811. The summary notes that there were 40 occupied houses, 2 uninhabited houses, 78 males and 94 females comprising 40 families in the Brawlbin District.

272UK Census 30 March 1851: County of Caithness, Parish of Reay. Residents at Brawlbin. Donald Gunn head, unmarried 19, farmer, 16 acres, born Halkirk; Katherine Gunn sister, unmarried 20, general service, born Reay; Janet Gunn sister, unmarried 17, scholar, born Reay; John Gunn brother, unmarried 15, scholar born Reay; William Gunn brother, unmarried 12, scholar born Reay. Brawlbin comprised 39 occupied houses with 70 males and 93 females. The census district of Brawlbin and Oldenbruch (?) was 12 miles in length and 2 miles in breadth. The majority of homes, 39, were in Brawlbin, with 3 in Oldenbruch accommodating 24 people.

273See page 225 and the following pages.

274Letter or email, Dougal Gilmour to Donald Gunn, 8 Apr 1999; Certificate of Death: Vic 1901 24552 14 February 1901 at Lydiard Street, City of Ballarat, Donald Gunn, 68, insurance agent of broncho pneumonia, cardiac disease and asthma, duration about 3 months, father Alexander Gunn, farmer, mother Barbara Gunn, maiden name Gunn. Buried 16 February 1901 at Ballarat Old Cemetery. Born at Brawlbin, Reay, Caithness, Scotland, 47 years in Victoria, married at Buninyong at 27 years to Jane Surman, issue in order of birth, John Alexander, 41, William Watkins, 39, Mary Jane, 37, Donald, 35, Marcus Daniel, 32, Barbara, 30, Norman, 28, Hugh, died, Arthur Gilbert, 22, Catherine, 20. Signed by Donald Gunn, son, of Crossover, Gippsland.

under her mother's name Barbara Gunn.[275] He was a farmer in 1857 in Buninyong, Vic.[276] [277] He bought a farm for £250 in partnership with John Surman, his future brother-in-law in 1857 in Cardigan, Vic. He was the founding secretary, and still secretary of the Buninyong Highland Society on 01 Jan 1858 in Buninyong, Vic.[278] This society was the first Highland Society in Victoria, being founded in 1854—the Melbourne Society was founded in 1861 and the first Victorian Society not until 1864. He was the judge for the first sports meeting on 01 Jan 1858 of the Caledonian Society, Ballarat, Vic.[279] He was awarded a silver medal by the Buninyong Highland Society on 03 Jul 1859 in Ballarat, Vic.[280]

The medal was presented by the Highland Society of Ballarat for services in organising the first Highland Society in the (Australian) colonies and for acting as Secretary[281] for the first two years. The medallion originally had a large silver brooch attached but this has been lost.

---

[275]"Immigration to Victoria," a Donald Gunn aged 27 arrived in Melbourne per the Herald of the Morning. This is the only recorded Donald Gunn of the approximate age to arrive between late '54 & early '56. The ship's passenger list records John Raps(?), 22; Walter Williamson, 20; John Sutherland,19; Hugh Murray, 22; Donald Gunn, 27; Barbara Gunn, 29 and Hugh Matheson, 36 all travelling together.There are no other names listed on the passenger list that could possibly be corruptions of Catherine or William. W.W. Gunn states Donald & Catherine travelled together—could Catherine for some reason have travelled under her mother's name?

[276]Certificate of Marriage, no.157 of marriages solemnized in the District of Buninyong, Donald Gunn, 26, bachelor, of Buninyong, farmer, married Jane Surman, 23, spinster, of Buninyong, teacher, on 25 March 1859.

[277]*The Argus*, page 6, 13 July 1874 details his local work complaining about the Scab Act implementation in the Ballarat district.

[278]See Part 3; Anne Beggs Sunter, "The Buninyong Highland Society," *Buninyong & District Historical Society* (Feb 2006).

[279]Letter from Jack Alexander Gunn to Donald Gunn, 29 Jul 2001; William Bramwell Withers, *The History of Ballarat, from the First Pastoral Settlement to the Present Time* (40 Sturt Street: F W Niven & Co, 1887), The Caledonian Society was formed in November, 1858, and the first sports were held on New Year's Day, 1859, on what is now known as the Eastern Oval. Mr Hugh Gray was the first president, and with him as judges on that day were Charles Roy, Donald McDonald and Donald Gunn; "The Buninyong Highland Society."

[280]Letter, Jack Alexander Gunn to unknown recipient, 29 Jul 2001: awarded a silver medal from the Society for his work. The medal is 58 mm diameter (including the outer rim). The obverse has 'Highland Society / Instituted 1857' and in scroll 'Laimh na - ceartats.' There is a 40 mm high, raised Highland figure in the centre. The reverse has 'presented to / Donald Gunn Esq / late / Honorary Secretary / 3 July 1859.' The medal is held by a g.g.g.grandson of Donald in 2000 for his safekeeping for the family.; also information derived from a typed note by his daughter-in-law Jessie Maria Gunn (Turner) (104)

[281]*The Argus*, page 6, 5 January 1859 records the 'Second Gathering of the Highland Society of Buninyong' and notes 'The arrangements, under the energetic secretary, Mr. D. Gunn, were very good, as far as the clearing of the ground were concerned…' It is interesting to note that the above medal was presented at this show (it was made in Geelong); obviously the reverse side shows it was not presented to Donald at this time but later.
http://newspapers.nla.gov.au/ndp/del/article/7307469?searchTerm="Highland+society" and
http://newspapers.nla.gov.au/ndp/del/article/7144550?searchTerm="Highland+society" gives a further account of this second meeting. The third meeting in 1860 realised £340 17s, which left the Society £60 in credit

Donald Gunn (3)

---

http://newspapers.nla.gov.au/ndp/del/article/5695554?searchTerm="Highland+society" see
http://newspapers.nla.gov.au/ndp/del/article/5696136?searchTerm="Highland+society" for an account of the day.

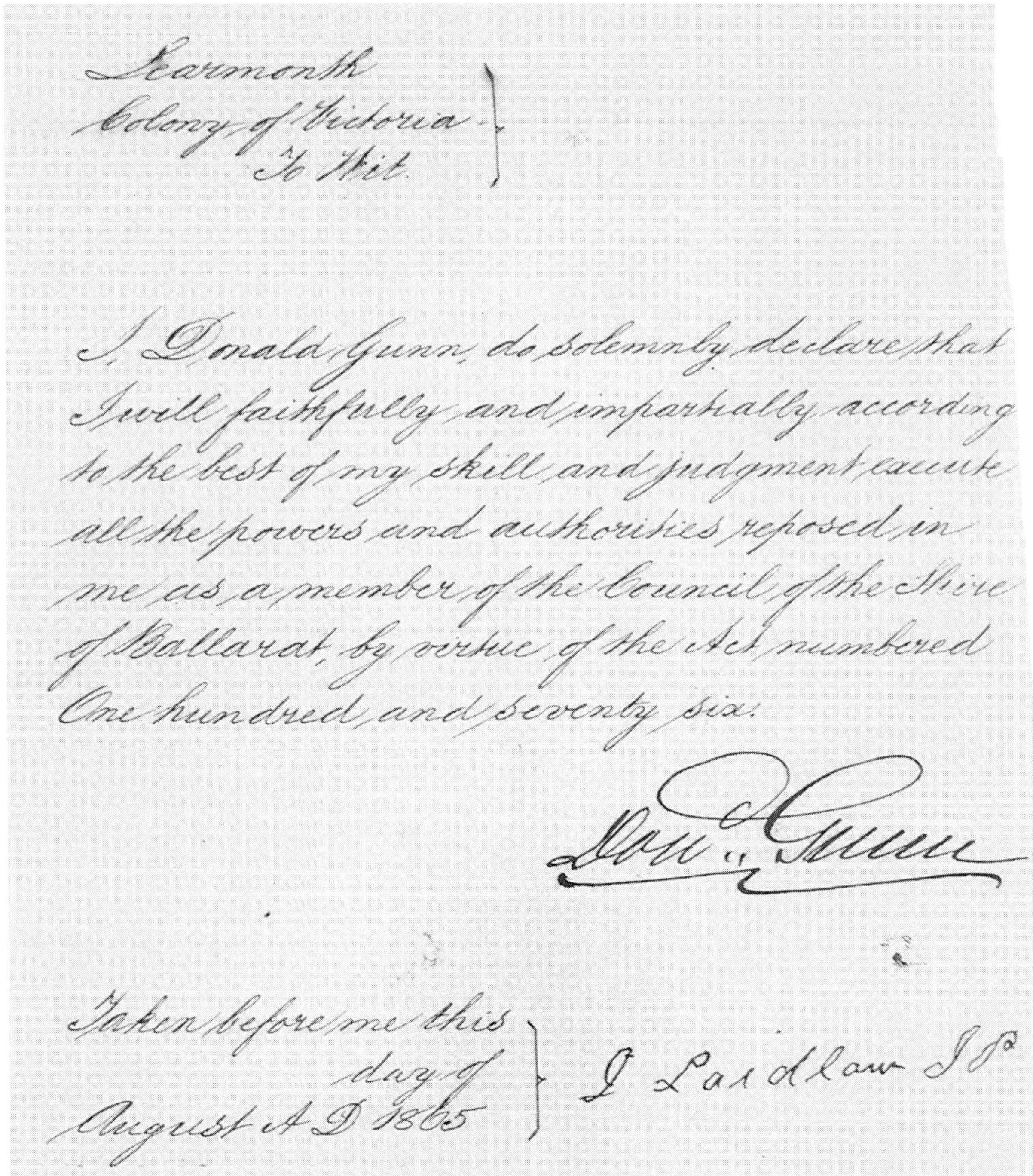
Learmonth
Colony of Victoria
To Wit.

I, Donald Gunn, do solemnly declare that I will faithfully and impartially according to the best of my skill and judgment execute all the powers and authorities reposed in me as a member of the Council of the Shire of Ballarat, by virtue of the Act numbered One hundred and seventy six.

Don. Gunn

Taken before me this
day of
August A D 1865 } J Laidlaw JP

Donald Gunn's declaration of office.

He was first elected as a Shire Councillor on 30 Aug 1865[282] in Ballarat, Vic.[283] He ended his first term as a Shire Councillor on 10 Jun 1867 in Ballarat, Vic.

[282] Interestingly *The Argus* records (page 6, 12 August 1865) that Donald Gunn was beaten for the Ballarat Shire South Riding a little more than two weeks earlier than when he joined the Council.
[283] See Part 7.

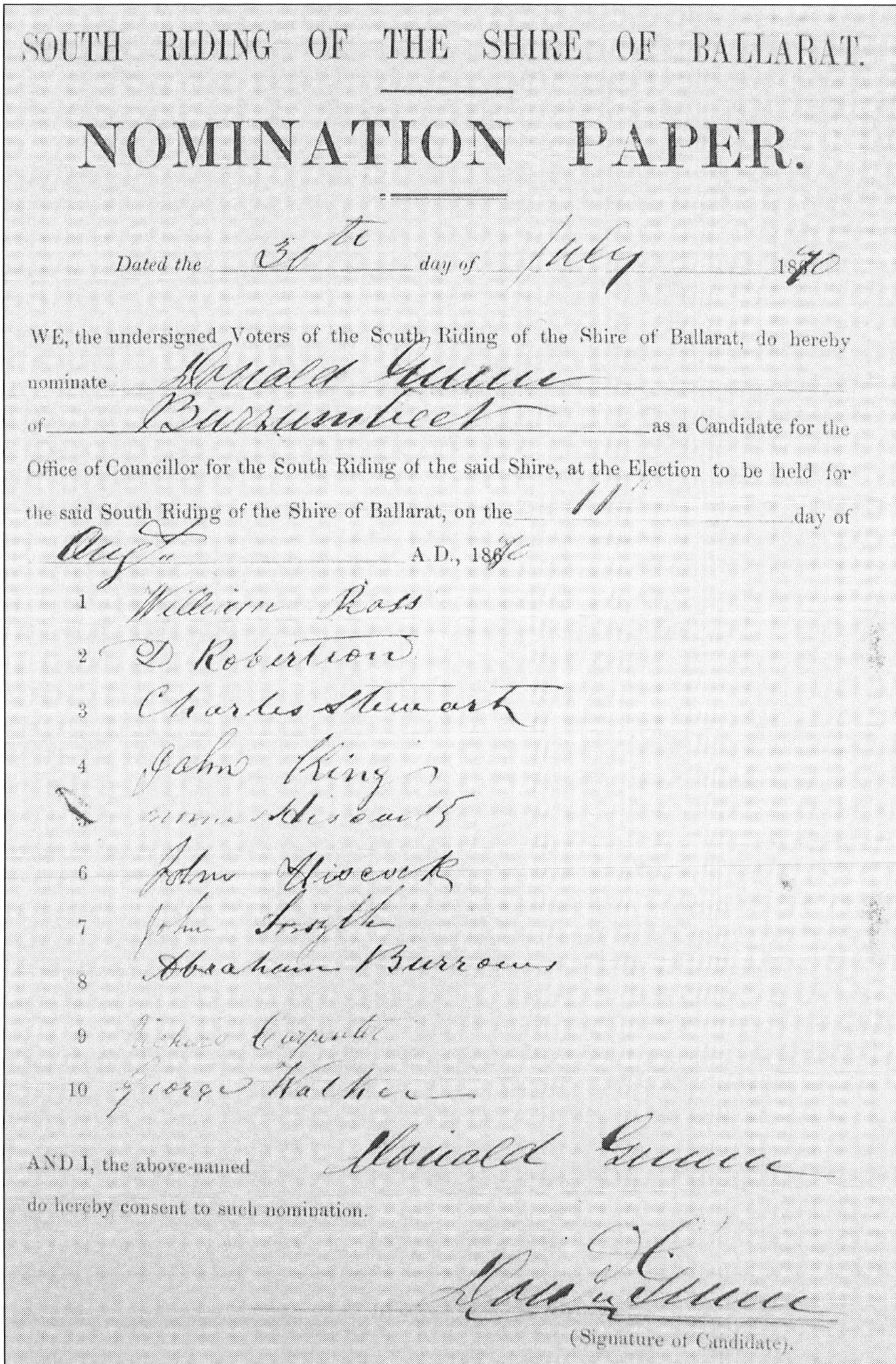

SOUTH RIDING OF THE SHIRE OF BALLARAT.

NOMINATION PAPER.

Dated the 30th *day of* July 1870

WE, the undersigned Voters of the South Riding of the Shire of Ballarat, do hereby nominate Donald Gunn of Burrumbeet as a Candidate for the Office of Councillor for the South Riding of the said Shire, at the Election to be held for the said South Riding of the Shire of Ballarat, on the 11th day of Aug A.D., 1870

1 William Ross
2 D Robertson
3 Charles Stewart
4 John King
5 [illegible]
6 John Hiscock
7 John Forsyth
8 Abraham Burrows
9 Richard Carpenter
10 George Walker

AND I, the above-named Donald Gunn do hereby consent to such nomination.

Donald Gunn
(Signature of Candidate).

Donald Gunn's 1870 nomination paper

He was elected for second term as a Shire Councillor on 15 Aug 1870 in Ballarat, Vic.[284] Donald (3) was elected Shire President[285][286] in Ballarat, Vic, on 11 Nov 1872. Donald (3) ended his service as Shire President on 12 Oct 1874 in Ballarat, Vic. Donald (3) ended service as a Shire Councillor[287] in 1876 in Ballarat, Vic. He was a member of the Ballarat Agricultural and Pastoral Society at least in 1871 (and presumably earlier) when he was elected Vice-President[288]. In 1872 he represented the society in Melbourne, helping appoint the Secretary to the Agricultural Department[289]. He is recorded as a J.P. in 1873[290] In the 'late summer of 1876-1877, while living at Burrumbeet, there was a heavy storm during the night and in the morning the tubs, buckets, plough furrows, and every depression that held water were full of a small fish similar to whitebait, and from 2 1/2 in. to 3 in. in length ...they must have numbered hundreds of thousands' recalled William Watkins Gunn in November 1920.[291] In 1883 the Ballarat Agricultural Society appointed Donald (of Burrumbeet) as an Inspector of sheep—he 'visits the stations and farms upon receipt of written notice, and after satisfying himself that the sheep have been evenly, equally and fairly shorn, will brand them and give the owner a certificate to that effect.'[292] His first report in April 1884 was interesting; 'with two exceptions, there was not a holding on which he did not find the sheep improperly shorn—in some instances as much as 50 per cent.'[293] The newspaper report also noted that 'There was a large attendance of members, in anticipation of an unfavourable report from the inspector'. He was an insurance agent in 1900.[294] Paperwork relating to him—especially the early years—can be found in 'Part 3'.

---

284 Ibidem

285 He represented the Shire on the Ballarat Forest Board in September 1873. 'The Argus' 9 September 1873

286 *The Argus* 10 September 1873 page 25 details some of his work as President when attending a conference on roads.

287 *The Argus*, 14 June 1876, page 3 describes one of his actions undertaken as Councillor; visiting a poor woman who was meant to be living in a hovel without the necessities of life.... As well *The Argus*, page 6, 8 December 1875 reports that he moved a motion saying the Shire Council would pay the medical fees of those contracting scarlet fever and not be able to pay for it themselves. He also was at the formal dinners (*The Argus* 19 April 1873, page 6).

288 *The Argus*, 11 May 1871, page 6.

289 *The Argus,* 09 Nov 1872, page 6.

290 *The Argus,* 21 May 1873, page 2S.

291 *The Argus*, 19 Nov 1920, page 4.

292 *The Argus,* 11 Oct 1883, page 5.

293 *The Argus*, 07 Apr 1884, page 7.

294 Letter or email, Dougal Gilmour to Donald Gunn, 8 Apr 1999; Certificate of Death: Vic 1901 24552 14 February 1901 at Lydiard Street, City of Ballarat, Donald Gunn, 68, insurance agent of broncho pneumonia, cardiac disease and asthma, duration about 3 months, father Alexander Gunn, farmer, mother Barbara Gunn, maiden name Gunn. Buried 16 February 1901 at Ballarat Old Cemetery. Born at Brawlbin, Reay, Caithness, Scotland, 47 years in Victoria, married at Buninyong at 27 years to Jane Surman, issue in order of birth, John Alexander, 41, William Watkins, 39, Mary Jane, 37, Donald, 35, Marcus Daniel, 32, Barbara, 30, Norman, 28, Hugh, died, Arthur Gilbert, 22, Catherine, 20. Signed by Donald Gunn, son, of Crossover, Gippsland.

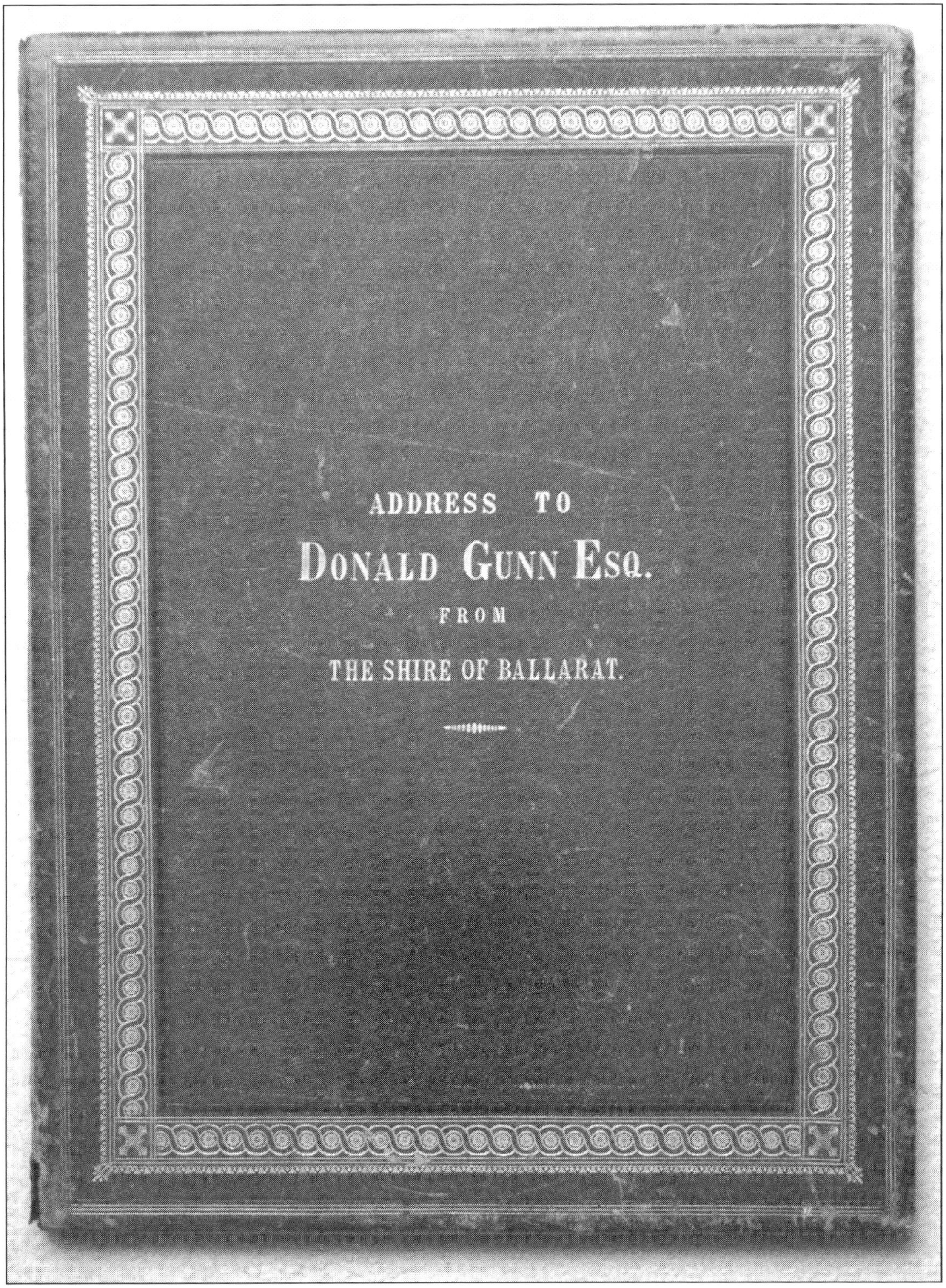
ADDRESS TO
DONALD GUNN ESQ.
FROM
THE SHIRE OF BALLARAT.

To

Donald Gunn Esq J.P.

BURRUMBEET.

Sir

We the President and Councillors of the Shire of Ballarat desire to convey to you our warm appreciation of the very energetic and valuable services rendered by you as a President of the Shire and Councillor for the South Riding.

We beg to acknowledge the impartial and gentlemanly manner in which you presided over all meetings of the Council during your term of Presidentship, and your steady and consistent advocacy of all measures affecting the welfare of the Shire, as a Councillor for a period extending over ten years.

In conclusion we sincerely wish you, Mrs Gunn and Family long life and prosperity.

As witness the Common Seal of the Corporation of the Shire of Ballarat affixed hereto this 11th Decr. [illegible] 1876, in the presence of:

James Mc Intosh President.

[illegible] Secretary.

Jane SURMAN (41) was born on 18 Jan 1836 in Hampton Poyle, Oxfordshire. She died on 14 Feb 1908 in 616 Lydiard St, Ballarat, Vic, at age 72.[295] She was buried on 15 Feb 1908 in Old Cemetery Area DN, Sec.14, Lot 5, Ballarat, Vic.[296] She appeared on the 1841 Census of Hampton Poyle, Oxfordshire, in the household of Daniel Surman (270).[297] She appeared on the 1851 Census of Hampton Poyle, Oxfordshire, in the household of Daniel Surman (270).[298] She emigrated with Daniel Surman (270) circa 1855 to Australia.[299] She was fifty-two years in Victoria.[300] She was a teacher[301] in Feb 1859 in Buninyong, Vic.[302]

(Left) Jane Surman (Gunn) with her mother Mary Ann Watkins (Surman) (271) and William Watkins Gunn (33)[303] c.1880 (Right) Jane Surman (Gunn)

---

[295]Register of BDMs - Victoria, 1908 219.

[296]Ballarat Old Cemetery records: Area DN, Sec.14, Lot 5.

[297]UK Census 06 June 1841: Daniel Surman 35 shoe maker, Mary Surman 30, John Surman 9, Jane Surman 5, Catherine Watkins 60.

[298]UK Census 30 March 1851: Hampton Poyle Daniel Surman head married 45 servant b Wokingham, Mary Surman wife married 40 schoolmistress b Oxford, Jane Surman daughter unmarried 15 scholar b Hampton Poyle, Catherine Watkins mother in law, widow 70 b Middlesex, London.

[299]*Unknown newspaper* 'in 1855 he arrived in Victoria with his parents and only sister, the latter being Mrs Gunn, of Doveton Street North'. Letter or email, Dougal Gilmour to Donald Gunn, 8 Apr 1999.

[300]*Unknown newspaper*' In 1855 he arrived in Victoria with his parents and only sister, the latter being Mrs Gunn, of Doveton Street North'; Letter or email, Dougal Gilmour to Donald Gunn, 8 Apr 1999.

[301]There was a Surman Common School at Windermere (Cardigan?) sometime in the 1860s-1870s which may be of relevance.

[302]Certificate of Marriage; Letter or email, Dougal Gilmour to Donald Gunn, 8 Apr 1999.

[303]Note the photographic studio of Willetts' is not recorded in *The Mechanical Eye in Australia Photography 1841-1900.*

Jane Surman (Gunn) (41) with two of her grandchildren, Alexander Donald Gunn (222) and Angus William Gunn (223) being sons of John Alexander Gunn.
Photographed in August 1904.

Back; *Donald 1865-1933, Barbara 1870-1941, John Alexander 1860-1910, Mary-Jane 1863-1934, Marcus Daniel 1868-1953*
Front; *William Watkins 1861-1935, Donald 1832-1901, Arthur Gilbert 1878-1933, Jane (Surman) 1836-1908, Norman 1872-1944*
Very front; *Catherine Alexandrina 1880-1960*

Children of Donald Gunn of Brawlbin & Ballarat (3) and Jane Surman (41) were as follows:

25 i. John Alexander GUNN (Hon.) (32).
See Part—7.

26 ii. William Watkins GUNN (33).

William Watkins Gunn

iii. Mary Jane GUNN (34) was born on 18 Jan 1864 in Cardigan Nr Ballarat, Vic.[304] She died on 05 May 1934 in Braemore, Werribee, Vic, at age 70.[305] She was buried on 07 May 1934 in Old Cemetery Area DN Sec.14 Lot 5, Ballarat, Vic.[306] She was on the electoral roll with John Alexander Gunn (Hon.) (32) in 1903 in Borambola Station, NSW.[307]

[304]Register of BDMs - Victoria, 1864 278.

[305]*Unknown newspaper*, 'on the 5th May, at Braemore, Werribee, Mary Jane, beloved eldest daughter of the late Donald and Jane Gunn, formerly of Burrumbeet. Deeply regretted'; Register of BDMs - Victoria, 1934 15340.

[306]Ballarat Old Cemetery records: Area DN Sec.14 Lot 5.

[307]Electoral Roll, 1903 Roll lists John Alexander Gunn, Station Manager, Marcus Daniel Gunn, Station Manager, Norman Gunn, Licensed Vaccinator, Mary Jane Gunn, Domestic Duties and Jessie Marie Gunn, Domestic Duties as residing at Borambola Station.

iv. Donald GUNN (35) was born on 20 Nov 1865 in Burrumbeet, Vic.[308] He was a partner in a mining lease with his brother William Watkins Gunn (and others) in South Warragul.[309] He married Amy Agnes Wareham (43), daughter of James Wareham (1697) and Mary Dalton (1114), on 16 Sep 1922 in St Anselms C of E, Middle Park, Vic.[310] He died on 29 Dec 1933 in 'The Shack', Crossover, Vic, at age 68 of cardiac failure.[311] He was buried on 30 Dec 1933 in Warragul, Vic.[312] He was with Ralph Milner gold mining circa 1900 in Buchan, Vic.[313] He was a sawmill employee in 1922.[314]

Donald Gunn.
The above photo was taken by 'Aaron Flegetaub School of Photography' which was in Ballarat 1888-1889; Donald was therefore about 24.

Amy Agnes WAREHAM (43)[315] was born in 1863 in Cheshire.[316] She married Francis Gumley (1115) in 1887.[317] She died in 1933 in Vic.

308Register of BDMs - Victoria, 1865 20736; "William Watkins Gunn;" Certificate of Birth, 1865 Births in the District of Burrumbeet in the Colony of Victoria, 20 Nov 1865, Donald Gunn, father Donald Gunn, farmer 33, mother Jane, 29.

309*The Argus,* 1 June 1892, page 7.

310Certificate of Marriage, No. 192 in Register of St Alsems C of E, Middle Park, 1922, BDM 7091 16 September 1922 between Donald Gunn, Bachelor, born Burrumbeet, sawmill employee age 56 of Crossover, and Amy Agnes Gumley, widow since 2 January 1901, 2 children, born Cheshire, England, house duties age 59 of Crossover, father James Walton (deceased), mother Mary (Dalton).

311*Unknown newspaper*, on the 29th December, at The Shack, Crossover, Donald, beloved husband of Amy, and son of late Donald and Jane Gunn, Burrumbeet; Certificate of Death: 1933 18730: On 29 December 1933 at The Shack, Crossover, Shire of Buln Buln, Donald Gunn, Timber Worker age 68, born Burrumbeet, married at Middle Park at age 56 to Amy Gumley, no issue, father Donald Gunn, Farmer, mother Jane Gunn formerly Surman.

312Certificate of Death: 1933 18730: On 29 December 1933 at The Shack, Crossover, Shire of Buln Buln, Donald Gunn, Timber Worker age 68, born Burrumbeet, married at Middle Park at age 56 to Amy Gumley, no issue, father Donald Gunn, Farmer, mother Jane Gunn formerly Surman.

313 William and brother Donald went to Buchan to mine quartz reef formations with Ralph Milner. Returns were good while Milner was in charge. William stayed under new managers, but Donald (and other family members?) retired. William carried on until the mine was abandoned about 1917. The mine was at Mt Tara, some 3-4 miles from Buchan in East Gippsland.

314Certificate of Marriage, No. 192 in Register of St Alsems C of E, Middle Park, 1922.

315Certificate of Marriage, Amy Agnes Gumley, widow since 2 January 1901.

27 v. Marcus Daniel GUNN (36).

Probably Marcus Daniel Gunn (from a portfolio holding all these near images); identified by elimination. Talma Studio operated in the years 1893-1900.

---

316 Certificate of Marriage, No. 192 in Register of St Alsems C of E, Middle Park, 1922, BDM 7091
16 September 1922 between Donald Gunn, Bachelor, born Burrumbeet, sawmill employee age 56 of Crossover, and Amy Agnes Gumley, widow since 2 January 1901, 2 children, born Cheshire, England, house duties age 59 of Crossover, father James Walton (deceased), mother Mary (Dalton).

317 Register of BDMs - Victoria, 1887 4462.

28 vi. Barbara GUNN (106).

Barbara Gunn and her husband Isaac Padgett (103);
Richards Art Studio operated from Sturt Street Ballarat in the years 1899-1900.
Barbara is wearing a wedding ring and she was married in 1899.

vii. Norman GUNN[318] (37) was born on 11 May 1872 in Burrumbeet, Vic.[319] He died in 1944 in Williamstown, Vic.[320] He was on the electoral roll with John Alexander Gunn (Hon.) (32) in 1903 at Borambola Station, NSW.[321] He was a stock and station agent, unmarried in 1915.[322] He began military service on 12 Apr 1915 in Melbourne, Vic, enlisted as Private, service number 1549, next of kin W.W. Gunn (brother).[323] He was discharged on 15 May 1918 from 22nd Battalion.

viii. Hugh GUNN (38) was born on 28 Oct 1875 in Burrumbeet, Vic.[324] He died on 24 Jun 1879 in Burrumbeet, Vic, at age 3.[325] He was buried on 25 Jun 1879 in Old Cemetery Area DN Sec.14 Lot 5, Ballarat, Vic.[326]

29 ix. Arthur Gilbert GUNN (9).

Richards Art Studio operated from Sturt Street Ballarat in the years 1899-1900. This makes Arthur Gilbert about twenty-one years old.

---

[318]See page 7. By repute he was apparently 'a bit of a lad' with the trace of a minor scandal.

[319]Register of BDMs - Victoria, 1872 7586.

[320]Register of BDMs - Victoria, 1944 11958.

[321]Electoral Roll: 1903 Roll lists John Alexander Gunn, Station Manager, Marcus Daniel Gunn, Station Manager, Norman Gunn, Licensed Vaccinator, Mary Jane Gunn, Domestic Duties and Jessie Marie Gunn, Domestic Duties as residing at Borambola Station.

[322]The AIF Project, online http://www.aif.adfa.edu.au:8080/index.html

[323]National Archives of Australia, Series B2455, control symbol Gunn N, barcode 4380098, born Ballarat; The AIF Project.

[324]Register of BDMs - Victoria, 1875 21520.

[325]Register of BDMs - Victoria, 1879 3921.

[326]Ballarat Old Cemetery records: Area DN Sec.14 Lot 5.

x. Catherine Alexandrina GUNN (39) was born on 13 Sep 1880 in Burrumbeet, Vic.[327] She died on 13 Aug 1960 in 13 Leila Road, Ormond, Vic, at age 79. She was living in Clarendon Street Ballarat with her mother in 1904[328]. She was an unmatriculated undergraduate at the University of Sydney in 1911 studying massage in a class of 16 unmatriculated women. She began military service on 06 Dec 1915 appointed as a member of Australian Army Masseuse Service[329] with grade of Masseuse.[330] She ended military service on 03 Apr 1925 in Prince of Wales Hospital, Randwick, NSW; resigned of own accord.[331] She travelled abroad; there is a record in her diary[332] of climbing Ben Nevis in Scotland on 14 Feb 1904 with a group of friends; she writes of it as a 'Kipling Campus trip'. 'Kit' (as she was known) in her diary included a piece of bark from a tree in Kashmir which a friend had sent her (amongst other foliage). The friend had written 'Dear Kit, Knowing how you appreciate anything out of the ordinary... Alice'. There was a leaf from Darjeeling in India, 1909. The diary also contained the normal 'Victorian' bits and pieces of sentimental poems. Her Electoral Roll addresses and occupations were—1903 District of Ballarat, Catherine Alexander Gunn, Clarendon St Ballarat; 1909 District of Ballarat, Catherine Alexandrina Gunn, 505 Mair St, Milliner (a time gap, presumably including Sydney); 1949 District of Melbourne, Catherine Alexandrina Gunn, 20 Ridgeway Place, Home Duties, at the same address were Joan White Gunn (the second wife of Alexander Donald Gunn (222)), Home Duties and Alexander Donald Gunn (222) and nephew of Catherine Alexandrina Gunn, Traveller; and 1954 District of Melbourne Ports, Catherine Alexandrina Gunn, 66 Evans St, Port Melbourne, Home Duties. She spent some time at Norfolk Island[333] as an envelope addressed to her at Burnt Pine Norfolk Island exists (sent from Melbourne 13 Apr 1942) as does a photo of her there.

An interesting woman, especially given her ten years of military service....

---

[327] Register of BDMs - Victoria, 1880 20818.

[328] Ballarat Directory 1904

[329] See http://www.awm.gov.au/cms_images/histories/15/chapters/14.pdf for a very detailed account of this nearly forgotten branch of the Australian Army and the early days of physiotherapy in Australia.

[330] Miscellaneous Army Form, Australian Army Massage Service, Appointment.
To Catherine A Gunn
By virtue of authority given by Regulations for the Australian Army Military Forces, you are hereby appointed to be a Member of the Australian Army Massage Service from the sixth day of December 1915. You are directed diligently to discharge your duty as such in the grade of Masseuse, or any higher grade to which you may be promoted or appointed.
Dated at Melbourne on the 16th day of November 1920. See the original on page 65.

[331] Miscellaneous Army Form, Department of Repatriation
Sydney, 16th April 1925
To Whom it may Concern
This is to certify that Miss Catherine A. Gunn, whose specimen signature appears at the foot hereof, was employed as Masseuse at the Prince of Wales Hospital, Randwick, from the 5th December 1915, to the 3rd April 1925 when she resigned of her own accord.
During this period Miss Gunn had considerable experience in Orthopaedic Massaging, and performed her duties in a conscientious and satisfactory manner. She is possessed of a thorough knowledge of her profession, and can be recommended to anyone desiring her services.
Issued without erasure or alteration,
Deputy Commissioner. See the original on page 66.

[332] Held by Alastair Gunn.

[333] From an email by Jan Tracy January 2010 (daughter of Jan Wilkinson and cousin to I.M. Gunn); her family was close to Kitty at one time. There is possibility of a romantic interest according to repute, see the photo on page 69.

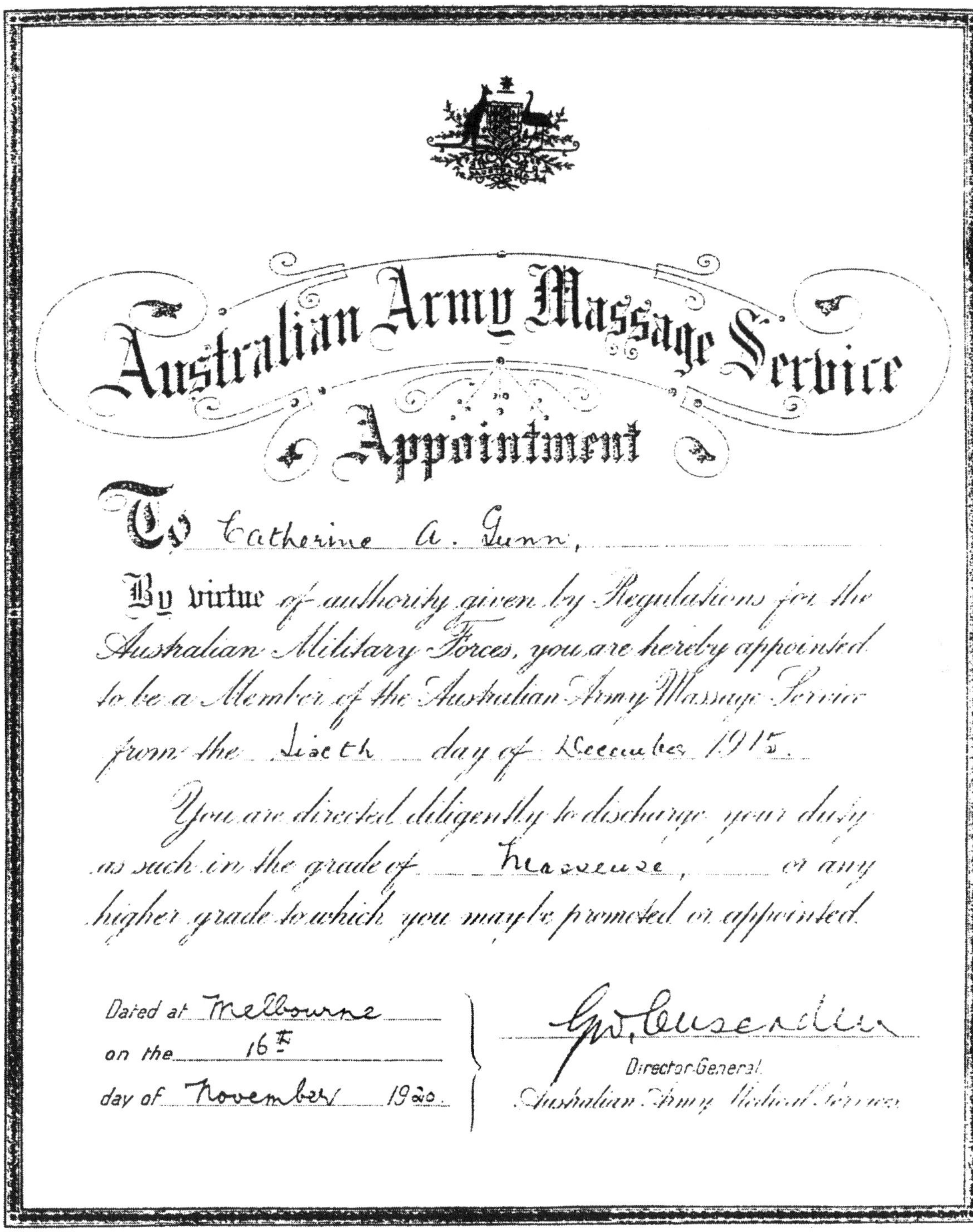

Australian Army Massage Service

Appointment

To Catherine A. Gunn,

By virtue of authority given by Regulations for the Australian Military Forces, you are hereby appointed to be a Member of the Australian Army Massage Service from the sixth day of December 1915.

You are directed diligently to discharge your duty as such in the grade of Masseuse, or any higher grade to which you may be promoted or appointed.

Dated at Melbourne
on the 16th
day of November 1920.

G.W. Cuscaden
Director-General
Australian Army Medical Services

PLEASE ADDRESS REPLY TO
THE DEPUTY COMMISSIONER,
AND QUOTE—
G .... / ....

TELEPHONES:
REDFERN 990 TO 997
(8 LINES)

COMMONWEALTH OF AUSTRALIA.

DEPARTMENT OF REPATRIATION.
NEW SOUTH WALES BRANCH.
CHALMERS ST.,

SYDNEY, 16th April, 1925.

TO WHOM IT MAY CONCERN.

This is to certify that Miss. Catherine A. Gunn, whose specimen signature appears at the foot hereof, was employed as Masseuse at the Prince of Wales' Hospital, Randwick, from the 5th December, 1915, to the 3rd April, 1925, when she resigned of her own accord.

During this period Miss. Gunn had considerable experience in Orthopaedic Massaging, and performed her duties in a conscientious and satisfactory manner. She is possessed of a thorough knowledge of her profession, and can be recommended to anyone desiring her services.

Issued without erasure or alteration.

Barrett
Deputy Commissioner.

C. A. Gunn

(Left) *Catherine on the left at No 4 Army General Hospital*[334] *1917. The badge on the bottom of the sleeve is that of Australian Army Massage Service 1914-1918. The person on the right is her relative Mary 'Molly' Robinson*[335].
(Right) *Catherine later in life.*

Garden Party at Admiralty House, Sydney, December 1917. Catherine is on the left and to the immediate right is, again, Mary 'Molly' Robinson. The person in the middle may be Sir Gerald Strickland, the then Governor of New South Wales.

---

[334]Opened at Randwick, July 1915.

[335]See footnote 450.

Catherine Gunn

Marcus Gunn, Catherine Gunn, Norman Gunn c.1940

The back of this 'real photograph' postcard states 'Mr Tolly (of Tolly's Winery S.A.) and … Aunty Kit – Norfolk Island at Aunt Em's boarding house (and in a different ink) Aunty Kits friend Norfolk Island' The writing was by Jan Wilkinson (130) who married a son of Marcus Daniel Gunn, a brother of Catherine. Wilkinsons remain on Norfolk Island in 2010.

It is possible that this is Leonard J. Tolley, son of one of the founders of the major brandy and wine firm of Tolley Scott and Tolley.

14. Janet 'MacLeod' GUNN (120)[336] was born on 08 May 1834 in Brawlbin, Reay Parish, Caithness.[337] She was christened on 19 Aug 1834 in Reay Parish, Caithness.[338] She married John Watkins Surman (118), son of Daniel Surman (270) and Mary Ann Watkins (271), on 12 May 1864 in house of bride's brother, Donald Gunn, Esquire, Cardigan, Vic.[339] She died on 30 May 1913 in Cardigan, Vic, at age 79.[340] She was buried on 02 Jun 1913 in Old Cemetery Area DN Sec.14 Lot 5A, Ballarat, Vic.[341] She appeared on the 1841 Census of Brawlbin, Reay Parish, Caithness, in the household of her parents Alexander Gunn of Bualchork and Brawlbin (1) and Barbara Gunn of Braehour (6).[342] She appeared on the 1851 Census of Brawlbin, Reay Parish, Caithness, in the household of Donald Gunn of Brawlbin & Ballarat (3).[343] She was living with, and looking after, aged grandparents in Nov 1859.[344] She planned to leave for Australia, but postponed in Mar 1863. She emigrated on 01 Oct 1863 from London per 'Chatsworth', 1129 tons register, 200 passengers. She arrived at Melbourne, Vic, aboard the 'Chatsworth' in company of Donald Campbell (3514) 20 and Eliz. K. Huxton (?) 25 on 16 Jan 1864. She arrived safely and was treated kindly by family in Jan 1864 in Ballarat, Vic. She was a teacher in 1864.[345]

---

336 *LDS Church*, Christenings of children of Barbara Gunn, father Alexander Gunn.
Catherine, 18 May 1830, Halkirk; Donald, 9 Jun 1832, Reay; Janet, 19 Aug 1834, Reay; John, 29 Feb 1836, Reay.

337 Clan Gunn Parish Records: Births 1834 Janet Gunn, parents Alexander, Brawlbin - Barbara; UK Census 06 June 1841: District of Brawlbin lying in the south part of the Parish of Reay. Each person who abode in each house on night of 6 June 1841: Alexander Gunn 50 farmer; Barbara Gunn 30; Kathrine Gunn 11; Donald Gunn 9; John Gunn 5; Janet Gunn 7; William Gunn 2; all born in Caithness.. Note: Census instructions for recording age were that if under 15, actual age; if over 15, record to the nearest 5 years below actual ie Alexander Gunn was between 50 and 55 and Barbara between 30 and 35 on 6 June 1841. Birth years are thus Alexander 1786-1791 and Barbara 1806-1811. The summary notes that there were 40 occupied houses, 2 uninhabited houses, 78 males and 94 females comprising 40 families in the Brawlbin District; Census 30 March 1851: County of Caithness, Parish of Reay. Residents at Brawlbin. Donald Gunn head, unmarried 19, farmer, 16 acres, born Halkirk; Katherine Gunn sister, unmarried 20, general service, born Reay; Janet Gunn sister, unmarried 17, scholar, born Reay; John Gunn brother, unmarried 15, scholar born Reay; William Gunn brother, unmarried 12, scholar born Reay. Brawlbin comprised 39 occupied houses with 70 males and 93 females. The census district of Brawlbin and Oldenbruch (?) was 12 miles in length and 2 miles in breadth. The majority of homes, 39, was in Brawlbin, with 3 in Oldenbruch accommodating 24 people; see the *Bible page of Alexander Gunn*: Janet Gunn born 8 May 1834 - see page 26.

338 *LDS Church*, Christenings of children of Barbara Gunn, father Alexander Gunn
Catherine, 18 May 1830, Halkirk; Donald, 9 Jun 1832, Reay; Janet, 19 Aug 1834, Reay; John, 29 Feb 1836, Reay.

339 Certificate of Marriage, 1864 1914 marriages solemnized in the District of Ballarat, John Watkins Surman, Teacher age 33, Bachelor born Hampton-Poyle, Oxon, England, residence Cardigan, father Daniel Surman, Farmer, mother Mary Ann Watkins, married Janet Gunn, age 30, Spinster born Reay, Caithness, Scotland, residence Cardigan, father Alexander Gunn, Farmer, mother Barbara Gunn, at the house of the Bride's Brother, Donald Gunn, Esq, Cardigan, according to the rites of the Presbyterian Church of Victoria. *The Star*, Ballarat, Page 2. 17 May 1864.

340 Register of BDMs - Victoria, 1913 4219; Letter or email, Dougal Gilmour to Donald Gunn, 8 Apr 1999.

341 Ballarat Old Cemetery records.

342 UK Census 06 June 1841.

343 UK Census 30 March 1851.

344 See Part 3 for further information.

345 Certificate of Marriage, 1864 1914 marriages solemnized in the District of Ballarat.

Janet Gunn

John Watkins Surman; Janet Gunn's husband

John Watkins SURMAN (118)[346] was born on 09 Oct 1831 in Hampton Poyle, Oxfordshire.[347] He was born in 1833 in Hampton Poyle, Oxfordshire.[348] He died on 11 Oct 1906 in Cardigan, Ballarat, Vic, at age 75.[349] He was buried on 13 Oct 1906 in Old Cemetery Area DN, Section 14, Lot 5A, Ballarat, Vic.[350] He appeared on the 1841 Census of Hampton Poyle, Oxfordshire, in the household of Daniel Surman (270).[351] He emigrated with Daniel Surman (270) to Australia in 1855.[352] He arrived in Melbourne, Vic. in 1855.[353] He was a schoolmaster[354], the first teacher at Windermere State School No.668, which he helped build and where he taught for thirty four years. He also helped build the Windemere church.

Cardigan State School (originally Windermere State School 668.)

He was the postmaster on a salary of £35/a in Cardigan, Vic, in 1868. On 26 Jun 1878 John Watkins Surman (118) reported that two more cases of scarlet fever had occurred in the vicinity of Windermere School in Ballarat, Vic.

---

346 *Unknown newspaper*, Undated. The death of another old resident, J.W. Surman, occurred on Thursday at his residence, Cardigan, aged 73 years. The deceased gentleman was born at Hampton Poyle, Oxfordshire, and was educated under Bishop Wilberforce at Oxford. In 1855 he arrived in Victoria with his parents and only sister, the latter being Mrs Gunn, of Doveton Street North. Two years later he settled in Buninyong, where he was engaged with the late Rev. J. Hastie in school work; and in August, 1860, he moved to Cardigan, opening a public school. Subsequently he entered the service of the Education Department, and retained his post until 1892, when he was retired. He was an earnest Sunday school and church worker, conducting the Sunday services for many years until the scattered congregations were able to build a church and obtain a settled minister. Deceased was married in 1864, and seven of his eight children survive. Of these five are sons and two daughters.

347 Certificate of Marriage, 1864 1914 states age as 33; email message from Judy Meyer to Donald Gunn, 02 Aug 2004.

348 *Unknown newspaper* '...was born at Hampton Poyle, Oxfordshire.'

349 Register of BDMs - Victoria, 1906 11573 - gives mother's name as Mary Ann Watkins; Judy Meyer, 02 Aug 2004.

350 Ballarat Old Cemetery records: Area DN, Section 14, Lot 5A.

351 UK Census 06 June 1841: Daniel Surman 35 shoe maker, Mary Surman 30, John Surman 9, Jane Surman 5, Catherine Watkins 60.

352 *Unknown newspaper* '...in 1855 he arrived in Victoria with his parents and only sister, the latter being Mrs Gunn, of Doveton Street North.'

353 Ibidem

354 Teacher reference number 2948.

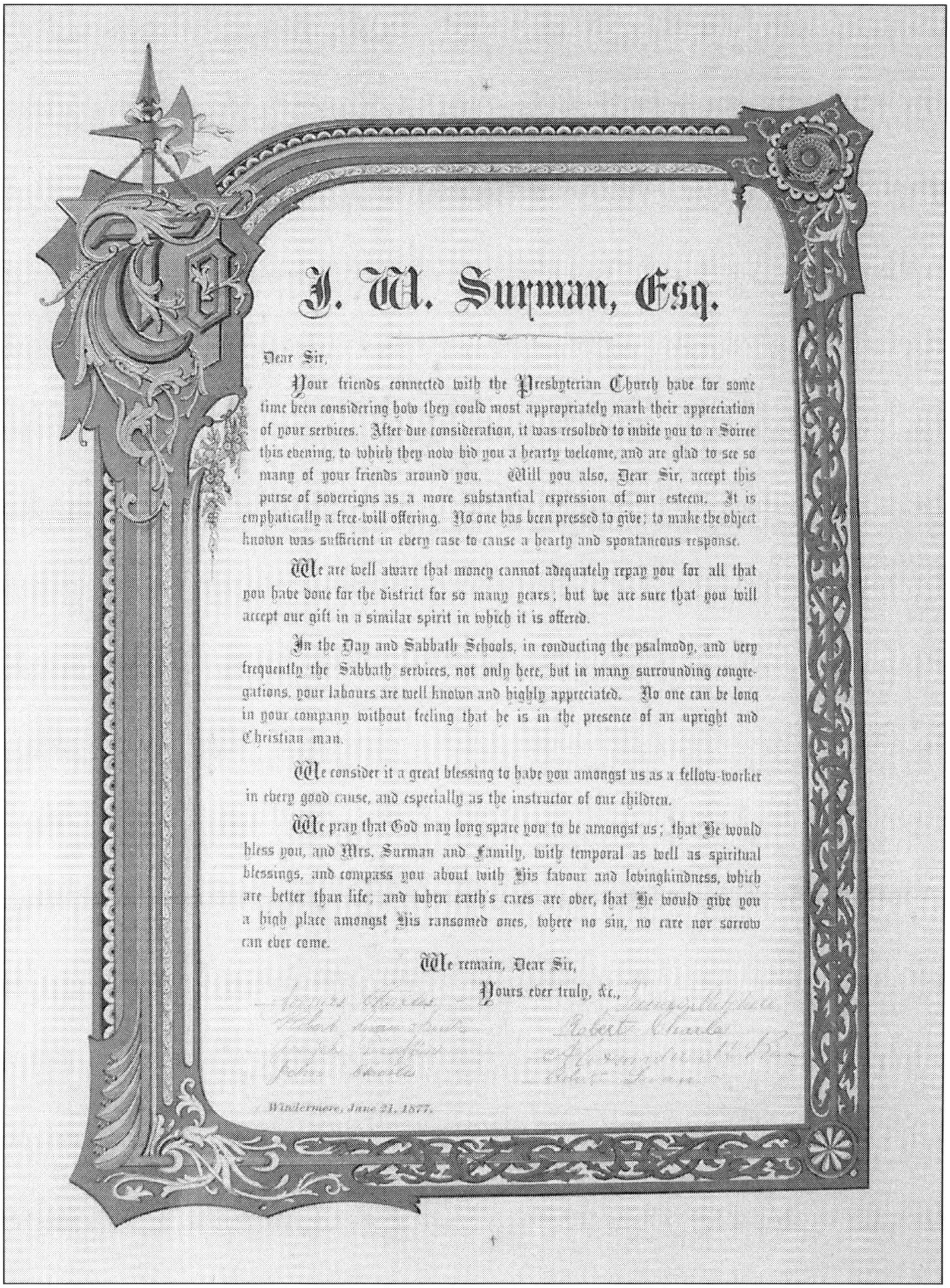
J. W. Surman, Esq.

Dear Sir,

Your friends connected with the Presbyterian Church have for some time been considering how they could most appropriately mark their appreciation of your services. After due consideration, it was resolved to invite you to a Soiree this evening, to which they now bid you a hearty welcome, and are glad to see so many of your friends around you. Will you also, Dear Sir, accept this purse of sovereigns as a more substantial expression of our esteem. It is emphatically a free-will offering. No one has been pressed to give; to make the object known was sufficient in every case to cause a hearty and spontaneous response.

We are well aware that money cannot adequately repay you for all that you have done for the district for so many years; but we are sure that you will accept our gift in a similar spirit in which it is offered.

In the Day and Sabbath Schools, in conducting the psalmody, and very frequently the Sabbath services, not only here, but in many surrounding congregations, your labours are well known and highly appreciated. No one can be long in your company without feeling that he is in the presence of an upright and Christian man.

We consider it a great blessing to have you amongst us as a fellow-worker in every good cause, and especially as the instructor of our children.

We pray that God may long spare you to be amongst us; that He would bless you, and Mrs. Surman and Family, with temporal as well as spiritual blessings, and compass you about with His favour and lovingkindness, which are better than life; and when earth's cares are over, that He would give you a high place amongst His ransomed ones, where no sin, no care nor sorrow can ever come.

We remain, Dear Sir,

Yours ever truly, &c.,

Robert Charles

Windermere, June 21, 1877.

He was presented with a citation from the Windermere community, signed by eight Windermere Presbyterian Church Elders (being James Charles, Robert Swan sen., Joseph Draffin, John Charles, James Mitchell, Robert Charles, Alexander McCrae and Robert Swan), for his services on 21 Jun 1887.[355] He was also presented with a purse of sovereigns.

355The J. W. Surman Citation, Learmonth District Historical Society.

Cardigan June 26th
1878 —

Windermere School
No. 668 —

The Secretary Ballarat Shire —

Sir,

I have the honor to report two more cases of Scarlet fever in the vicinity of this school — viz. the family of Mr James Charles and of Mr L Stewart

These make five families which have been attacked by the disease since the reopening of the school.

I have the honor to be
Sir
Your obedient servant
J. W. Surman —

An earlier March 1, 1878 letter concerning Scarlet fever had also been sent to the Shire Council. That earlier outbreak caused the School to be closed.

From the Family Registers of John Watkins Surman (held by a Surman descendant)—

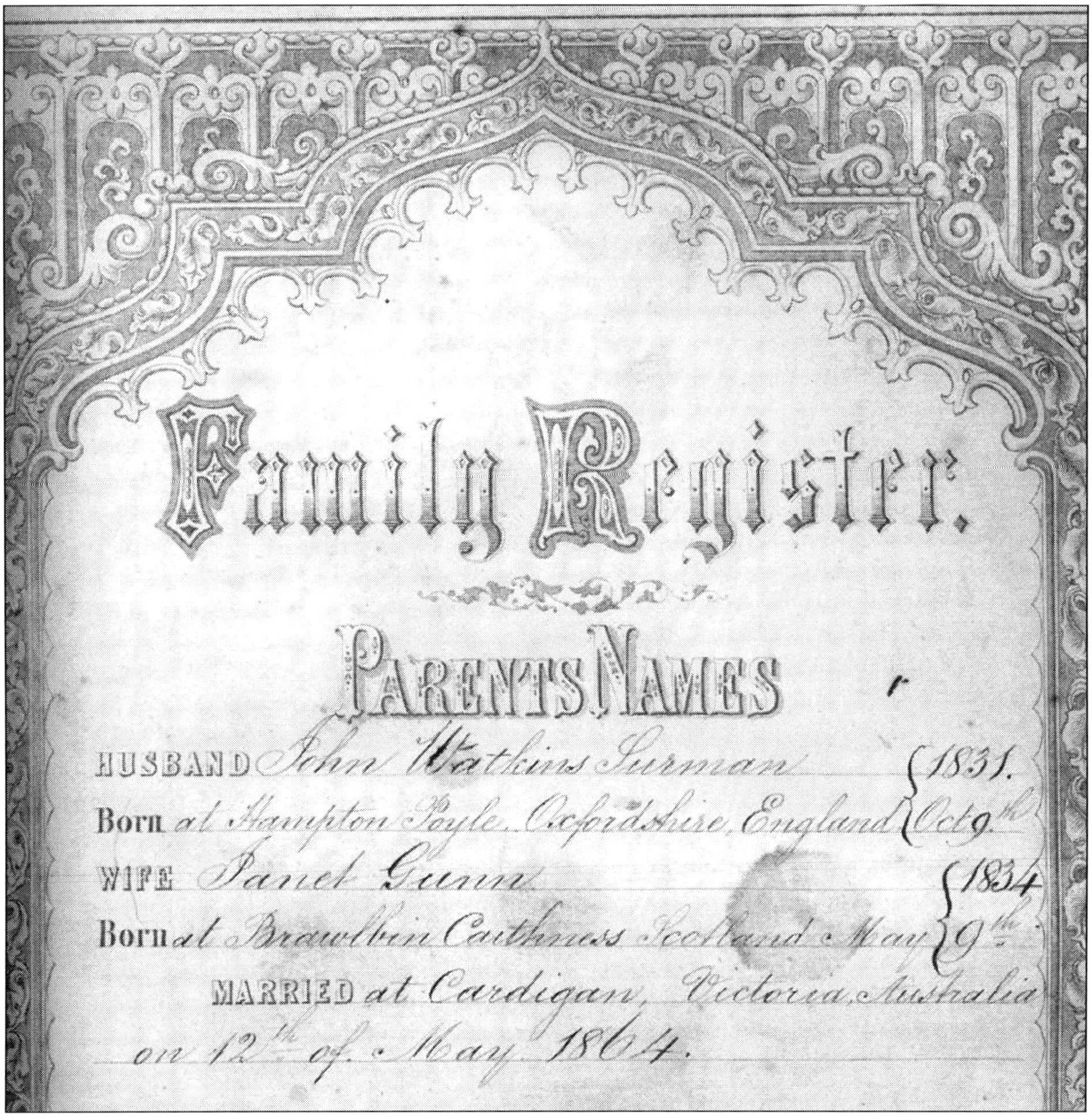

Family Register.

PARENTS NAMES

HUSBAND John Watkins Surman 1831.

Born at Hampton Poyle Oxfordshire, England Oct 9th

WIFE Janet Gunn 1834

Born at Brawlbin Caithness Scotland May 9th

MARRIED at Cardigan, Victoria Australia on 12th of May 1864.

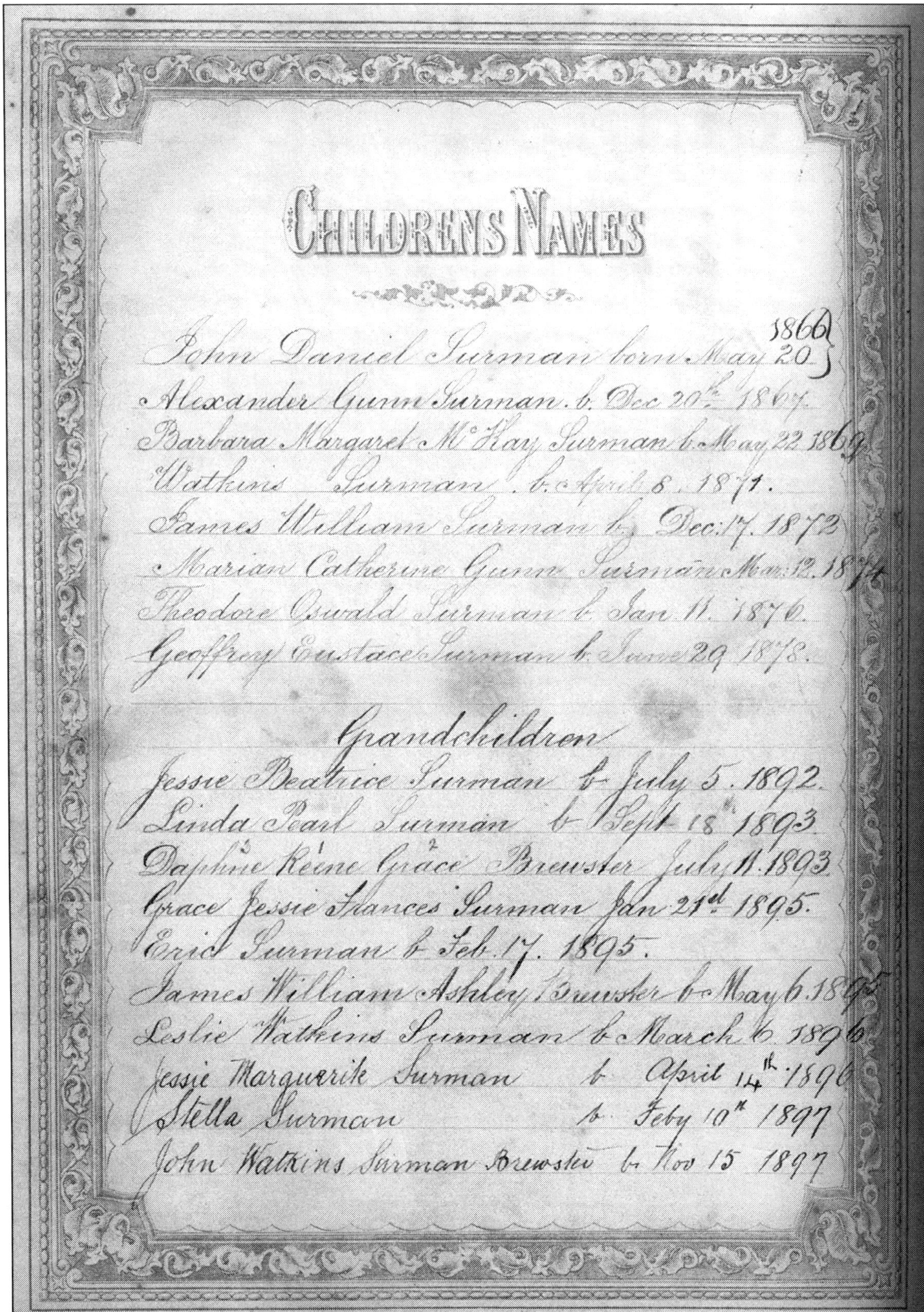

Childrens Names

John Daniel Surman born May 20 1866
Alexander Gunn Surman. b. Dec 20th 1867.
Barbara Margaret McKay Surman b. May 22 1869
Watkins Surman. b. April 8. 1871.
James William Surman b. Dec: 17. 1872
Marian Catherine Gunn Surman Mar: 12. 1874
Theodore Oswald Surman b. Jan. 11. 1876.
Geoffrey Eustace Surman b. June 29 1878.

Grandchildren

Jessie Beatrice Surman b. July 5. 1892.
Linda Pearl Surman b. Sept 18th 1893.
Daphne Reine Grace Brewster July 11. 1893
Grace Jessie Frances Surman Jan 21st 1895.
Eric Surman b. Feb. 17. 1895.
James William Ashley Brewster b. May 6. 1895
Leslie Watkins Surman b. March 6. 1896
Jessie Marguerite Surman b. April 14th 1896
Stella Surman b. Feby 10th 1897
John Watkins Surman Brewster b. Nov 15 1897

MARRIAGES

Alexander Gunn Surman married Sep 1891
to Esther Kirk
Barbara Margaret McKay Surman married
to James Brewster June 8th 1892.
James William Surman married to
Alice Curtis February 21st 1894
John Daniel Surman married to
Margaret Cowley Nov 6th 1895.

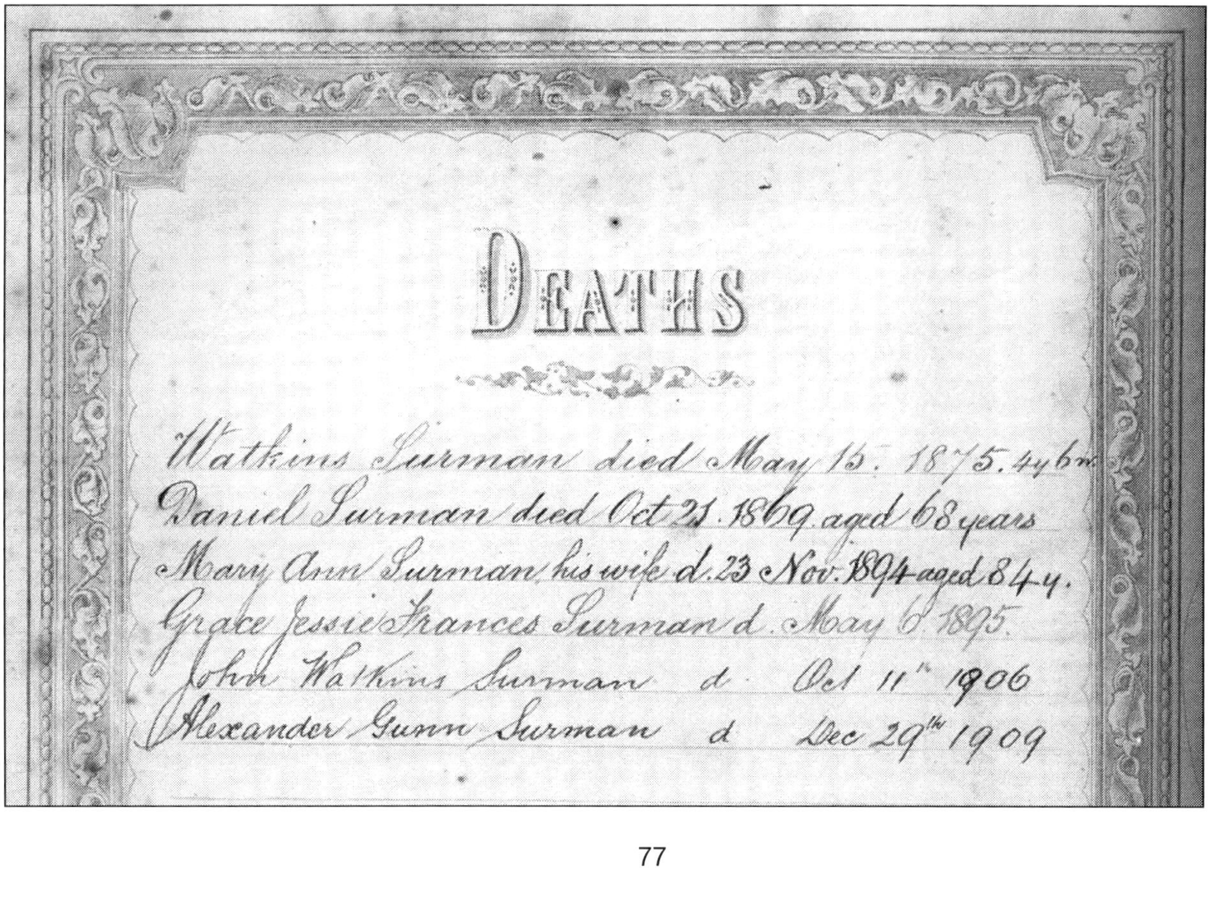

DEATHS

Watkins Surman died May 15. 1875. 4y6m
Daniel Surman died Oct 21. 1869 aged 68 years
Mary Ann Surman his wife d. 23 Nov. 1894 aged 84y.
Grace Jessie Frances Surman d. May 6 1895.
John Watkins Surman d. Oct 11th 1906
Alexander Gunn Surman d. Dec 29th 1909

Children of Janet MacLeod Gunn (120) and John Watkins Surman (118) were as follows:

- i. 'Baby' SURMAN (1550)[356] was born in Feb 1865 in Ballarat, Vic. and died on 24 Feb 1865 in Ballarat, Vic.
- 30 ii. John Daniel SURMAN (272).
- 31 iii. Alexander Gunn SURMAN (273).
- 32 iv. Barbara Margaret McKay SURMAN (274).
- v. Watkins SURMAN (405) was born in 1871 in Sago Hill / Cardigan, Vic.[357] He died on 15 May 1875 in Cardigan, Vic.[358]
- 33 vi. James William SURMAN (275). He was a school teacher.
- vii. Irene Marian Catherine SURMAN[359] (693) was born in 1874 in Sago Hill, Vic.[360] In 1903 and 1914, she was at home in Cardigan. She married William O'Connor (692) in 1918 in Vic.[361] She died in 1940 in Melbourne, Vic.

  William O'CONNOR (692) Marriage: 1918 [362].
- viii. Theodore Oswald SURMAN[363] (276) was born in 1876 in Cardigan.[364] He died on 17 May 1918 in Melbourne South, Vic.[365] He was buried in Morwell Cemetery, Plot D, Row R, Grave No. 282, Morwell, Vic.[366]

  He began military service on 04 Dec 1914 in Vic enlisted as Corporal, Regimental number 1614, Next of Kin, Mrs Barbara Brewster, Yinnar, Gippsland.[367]
- 34 ix. Geoffrey Eustace SURMAN (277).

15. Janet GUNN (3193)[368] was born in 1827 in Halkirk Parish, Caithness. She was christened on 10 Jul 1827 in Halkirk Parish, Caithness. She married John Mackay (3194), son of Neil Mackay (3114) and Margaret Sutherland (3115), on 18 Feb 1853 in Halkirk Parish, Caithness. She died on 23 Sep 1911 in Knockglass, Dunbeath Parish, Caithness and was buried in Dorrery, Caithness.[369]

John MACKAY (3194)[370] was born in 1811 in Latheron Parish, Caithness.[371] He was christened on 27 Dec 1811 in Halkirk Parish, Caithness. He died on 23 Dec 1899 in Rangag Forse, Latheron Parish, Caithness. He was buried in Dorrery, Caithness.

---

356 Judy Meyer, 02 Aug 2004 and further information on this page.

357 Register of BDMs - Victoria, 1871 19097.

358 Register of BDMs - Victoria, 1875 5572.

359 In Electoral Rolls (and perhaps elsewhere) the name is often Marion Catherine Surman.

360 Register of BDMs - Victoria, 1874 11626.

361 Register of BDMs - Victoria, 1918 5698.

362 Register of BDMs – Victoria.1918 5698.

363 See http://www.aif.adfa.edu.au:8080/showPerson?pid=292397 for the military file. He was in the Boer War as a civilian subordinate to 38 Co ASC and see http://naa12.naa.gov.au/scripts/imagine.asp?B=8097106&I=1&SE=1

364 Register of BDMs - Victoria, 1876 4937.

365 Register of BDMs - Victoria, 1918 5986; Judy Meyer, 02 Aug 2004.

366 The AIF Project.

367 Ibidem

368 Bill & Sharon Gurney, e-mail to Donald Gunn, 13 Sep 2008, and for further information on this page.

369 Bill & Sharon Gurney, e-mail to Donald Gunn, 13 Sep 2008; Dorrery cemetery tombstone: Janet Gunn, age 83, wife of John McKay, died 23/9/1911, died Knockglass, Dunbeath.

370 Bill & Sharon Gurney, e-mail to Donald Gunn, 13 Sep 2008 and for further information on this page.

Children of Janet Gunn (3193) and John Mackay (3194) were as follows:

i. Neil MACKAY (3202) was born say 1854. He died as an infant.

ii. Ann MACKAY (3203) was born in 1856 in Halkirk Parish, Caithness. She was christened on 24 Mar 1856 in Latheron Parish, Caithness and died in 1891 in Halkirk Parish, Caithness.

iii. Margaret MACKAY (3204) was born in 1857 in Latheron Parish, Caithness. She was christened on 09 Dec 1857 in Latheron Parish, Caithness.

iv. Mary MACKAY (3303) was born on 06 Jan 1860 in Rangag Forse and christened on 08 Jan 1860 in Rangag Forse, Latheron Parish, Caithness.

v. John MACKAY (3207) was born in 1862 in Latheron Parish, Caithness. He was christened on 09 Apr 1862 in Latheron Parish, Caithness. He witnessed the death of John Mackay (3194) on 23 Dec 1899 in Rangag Forse, Latheron Parish, Caithness.

vi. Isabella Helen MACKAY (3206) was born in 1866 in Latheron Parish, Caithness. She was christened on 13 Aug 1866 in Rangag Forse, Latheron Parish, Caithness.

16. John GUNN (Sir) of Tormsdale (3250)[372] was born on 28 Oct 1837 in Halkirk Parish, Caithness.[373] See Part 7. He was christened on 04 Nov 1837 in Bualchork, Halkirk Parish, Caithness.[374] He married Sarah Jane Hill (3311) in 1871 in Cardiff, Glamorgan. He married Harriette Boyle (3312) in 1877 in Belfast. He died on 20 Jan 1918 in Cardiff, Glamorgan, at age 80.[375] He appeared on the census of 06 Jun 1841 in the household of his parents Donald (296) and Ann (3244) in Achlibster, Halkirk Parish, Caithness.[376]

---

371 Bill & Sharon Gurney, e-mail to Donald Gunn, Family of Neil McKay & Margaret Sutherland of Caithness Scotland & Ontario Canada 03 Oct 2008.

372 Bill & Sharon Gurney, e-mail to Donald Gunn, 17 Oct 2008; The family of Donald Gunn & Ann McKay of Halkirk Scotland. Also see Part 7.

373 Bill & Sharon Gurney, e-mail to Donald Gunn, 23 Sep 2008; P R Myers, "Sir John Gunn, the Cardiff Business Entrepeneur from Caithness," *The Caithness Field Club Journal* (October 1983): See Part 7.

374 Bill & Sharon Gurney, e-mail to Donald Gunn, 23 Sep 2008.

375 Bill & Sharon Gurney, e-mail to Donald Gunn, 17 Oct 2008; and see Part 7.

376 UK Census 06 June 1841: Donald Gunn 40 farmer head; Ann Gunn 30 wife; Hector Gunn 13 son; Donald Gunn 11 son; Janet Gunn 9 daughter; Helen Gunn 7 daughter; Margaret Gunn 5 daughter; John Gunn 3 son; Christina Gunn 1 daughter; all resident at Achlipster.

Achlibster farm, 2011. 'Achlibster' is presumed to mean the farm, no village exists.

He appeared on the census of 30 Mar 1851 in the household of his parents Donald (296) and Ann (3244) in Bualchork, Halkirk Parish, Caithness.[377] He was educated in 1855 in Newport, Monmouthshire; began apprenticeship.[378] He was the principal promoter of a syndicate acquiring the Mount Stuart Dry Dock in 1872 in Cardiff, Glamorgan. He was present when Marcus Gunn (3252) was appointed manager of the Mount Stuart Dry Dock in 1874 in Cardiff, Glamorgan. He was elected president of the Chamber of Commerce in 1886 in Cardiff, Glamorgan and was re-elected president of the Chamber of Commerce in 1887. He was chairman of the Cardiff Shipowners' Association in 1891. He and Marcus Gunn (3252) were the owners of four ships, 'Dunedin', 'Cornelia', 'Dunbar' and 'Dunkeld' in 1892 (owned by John and Marcus Gunn & Co.). He was unsuccessful in contesting a Cardiff constituency on a Unionist ticket in 1892. He was re-elected president of the Chamber of Commerce in 1897 in Cardiff, Glamorgan. He was knighted in 1898. He had the 4395 gross ton 'Achlibster' built in honour of his birthplace in 1906 and he had the 'Bilbster', similar to the 'Achlibster', built in 1908. He passed managership of the 'Achlibster' and 'Bilbster' to Arthur Hill Gunn (3316)—his third son—and Ernest Gunn (3329)—his brother Marcus's oldest son—in 1911 in Cardiff, Glamorgan. He was a witness when Arthur Hill Gunn (3316) and Ernest Gunn (3329) took over managership of the ships 'Achlibster' and 'Bilbster' from John and Marcus Gunn in 1911 in Cardiff, Glamorgan. He also witnessed when Arthur Hill Gunn (3316) and Ernest Gunn (3329) added the steel screw steamer 'Chalister' to the family fleet in 1913.

Sarah Jane HILL (3311) died in 1875.

---

[377]UK Census 30 March 1851: Donald Gunn 52 head farmer of 14 acres; Ann Gunn 42; Hector Gunn 22; Donald Gunn 19; Janet Gunn 17; Helen Gunn 15; Margaret Gunn 13; John Gunn 11; Christina Gunn 9; Marcus Gunn 5; all resident at Bualchork.
[378]See Part 7.

Children of Sir John Gunn of Tormsdale (3250) and Sarah Jane Hill (3311) all born in Cardiff, Glamorgan, were as follows:

i. John Donald GUNN (3314) was born in 1872. He died in 1872 in Cardiff, Glamorgan.

ii. Herbert Oswald GUNN (3315) was born in 1873.

iii. Arthur Hill GUNN (3316) was born in 1875.[379] He and Ernest Gunn (3329) took over managership of the ships 'Achlibster' and 'Bilbster' from John and Marcus Gunn in 1911 in Cardiff, Glamorgan and added the steel screw steamer 'Chalister' to the family fleet in 1913. They sold the 'Achlibster' and 'Chalister' in 1919 and never resumed ship owning. He remained a director of the Mount Stuart Dry Locks Ltd in 1919 in Cardiff, Glamorgan.[380]

Harriette BOYLE (3312) was born circa 1846 in Ballymacrea, Antrim. She died in 1914 in Newport, Monmouthshire.

Children of Sir John Gunn of Tormsdale (3250) and Harriette Boyle (3312) all born in Cardiff, Glamorgan, were as follows:

i. Annie Boyle GUNN (3317) was born in 1879. She married Frederick George Penny (3318) in 1905 in Cardiff, Glamorgan.

ii. Winifred Mackay GUNN (3319) was born in 1879. She married Francis Brodie Lodge (3320), son of Sir Oliver Joseph Lodge (3321) and Mary Fanny Alexander Marshall (3322), in 1909 in Cardiff, Glamorgan.

Francis Brodie LODGE (3320) was born in 1880. He died in 1967. He and Alec Lodge (3432) took out a patent for an improved system of high tension ignition for motor vehicles in 1903[381]. He and Alec Lodge (3432) formed a partnership, Lodge Bros, in 1904 in 4 New Street, Birmingham, West Midlands. He and Alec (3432) opened their first workshop in 1907 in Wrentham Street, Birmingham, West Midlands. He was the founder, with his brother Alec, of the Lodge Plug Company, manufacturer of spark plugs for cars and aeroplanes. He assembled one of the world's largest collections of Chinese ceramics and bronzes.

iii. Olive Mildred GUNN (3323) was born in 1881.

iv. Elsie Maud GUNN (3324) was born in 1882.

v. Hester Boyle GUNN (3325) was born in 1885.

vi. John Boyle GUNN (3327) was born in 1888.

vii. Marjorie Lilian GUNN (3326) was born in 1889. She married Frederic Stratton (3328) in 1913 in Cardiff, Glamorgan.

17. Marcus GUNN (3252) was born on 05 May 1842 in Bualchork, Halkirk Parish, Caithness. He was christened on 09 May 1842 in Bualchork, Halkirk Parish, Caithness. He married Mary Elizabeth Yeandle (3313) in 1877 in Shurdington, Gloucestershire. He died in Sep 1899 in Cardiff, Glamorgan, at age 57. He appeared on the census of 30 Mar 1851 in

---

379Bill & Sharon Gurney, email to Donald Gunn, 17 Oct 2008; the family of Don Gunn & Ann McKay of Halkirk Scotland and for further information on this page.

380See Part 7.

381See http://www.macrugby.com/history-lodge.htm for further details about the fascinating Lodge family.

the household of his parents Donald (296) and Ann (3244) in Bualchork, Halkirk Parish, Caithness.[382] He, Marcus (3252), and George (3253), were twins. He was appointed manager of the Mount Stuart Dry Dock in 1874 in Cardiff, Glamorgan.[383] He and Sir John Gunn (3250) were the owners of four ships, 'Dunedin', 'Cornelia', 'Dunbar' and 'Dunkeld' in 1892 owned by 'John and Marcus Gunn & Co.'. He and Sir John Gunn (3250) had the 4395 gross ton 'Achlibster' built in honour of their birthplace in 1906. He and Sir John Gunn (3250) had the 'Bilbster', similar to the 'Achlibster', built in 1908. He was present when Arthur Hill Gunn (3316) and Ernest Gunn (3329) took over managership of the ships 'Achlibster' and 'Bilbster' from John and Marcus Gunn in 1911 in Cardiff, Glamorgan. He was present when Arthur Hill Gunn (3316) and Ernest Gunn (3329) added the steel screw steamer 'Chalister' to the family fleet in 1913.

Mary Elizabeth YEANDLE (3313) was born in 1855.

Children of Marcus Gunn (3252) and Mary Elizabeth Yeandle (3313) all born in Cardiff, Glamorgan, were as follows:

i. Ernest GUNN (3329) was born in 1878. He died in 1916 in Cardiff, Glamorgan.

He and Arthur Hill Gunn (3316) took over managership of ships Achlibster and Bilbster from John & Marcus Gunn in 1911 in Cardiff, Glamorgan. He and Arthur Hill Gunn (3316) added the steel screw steamer 'Chalister' to the family fleet in 1913. He and Arthur Hill Gunn (3316) sold the 'Achlibster' and 'Chalister' in 1919 and never resumed ship owning.

ii. Beatrice McKay GUNN (3330)[384] was born in 1880.

iii. Marcus Sinclair GUNN (3331) was born in 1890.

18. Ellen SUTHERLAND (3120)[385] was born on 21 Jul 1835 in Camster, Latheron Parish, Caithness.[386] She married Hugh Gordon (3121) in 1855.[387] She died on 27 Apr 1910 at age 74.[388] She appeared on the census of 06 Jun 1841 in the household of her parents Alexander (3119) and Christian (602) in Camster, Latheron Parish, Caithness.[389] She and Donald Sutherland (3127), Ann Sutherland (3129), Christina Sutherland (3130), Janet

---

[382]UK Census 30 March 1851: Donald Gunn 52 head farmer of 14 acres; Ann Gunn 42; Hector Gunn 22; Donald Gunn 19; Janet Gunn 17; Helen Gunn 15; Margaret Gunn 13; John Gunn 11; Christina Gunn 9; Marcus Gunn 5; all resident at Bualchork.

[383]See Part 7.

[384]Bill & Sharon Gurney, e-mail to Donald Gunn, 17 Oct 2008; The family of Donald Gunn & Ann McKay of Halkirk Scotland.

[385]Letter or email, Betty Warrilow to Donald Gunn, 14 Aug 2008; '... you will note Alexander Sutherland. He was married to Christian (Christina) Gunn born 1802. They had 8 children. I descend from their daughter Ellen who married Hugh Gordon, their son Alex named for his grandfather Alexander Sutherland, his daughter Ellen was my mother'.

[386]Letter or email, Betty Warrilow to Donald Gunn, 14 Aug 2008; Letter or email, Betty Warrilow to Donald Gunn, 07 Aug 2008; 'I descend from Alexander and Christian a.k.a. Christina Gunn Sutherland. Unfortunately their 2 sons died unmarried. The daughters 3 of whom are mentioned in the letters (see Part 3) are: Christina, Ann, Janet, plus the following: Ellen, Wilhemina, Catherine (Kate). All were born in Scotland except for the youngest son John who was born 1842 in Wentworth County, Ontario. Their son Donald was # 2 in the family born in 1829'; Bill & Sharon Gurney, e-mail to Donald Gunn.

[387]Letter or email, Betty Warrilow to Donald Gunn, 14 Aug 2008; '... you will note Alexander Sutherland. He was married to Christian (Christina) Gunn born 1802. They had 8 children. I descend from their daughter Ellen who married Hugh Gordon, their son Alex named for his grandfather Alexander Sutherland, his daughter Ellen was my mother.'

[388]Bill & Sharon Gurney, e-mail to Donald Gunn.

[389]UK Census 06 June 1841: Alexander Sutherland, cooper, 45; Christy Sutherland, 30; Christy Sutherland, 15; Donald Sutherland, 13; Ann Sutherland, 11; Jannet Sutherland. 9; Hellen Sutherland, 6; Williamina Sutherland, 4; Cathrine Sutherland, 2 and Marcus Gunn, 25. Note that census instructions for recording age were that if under 15, actual age; if over 15, record to the nearest 5 years below actual.

Sutherland (3131), and Catherine Sutherland (3133) emigrated with her parents in 1842 to Owen Sound, Canada.

Children of Ellen Sutherland (3120) and Hugh Gordon (3121) are:

35 i. Alexander GORDON (3122).

19. Janet GUNN (3113) was born in 1851 in Sydenham, Ontario.[390] She married Herbert William Jenkins (3117), son of George Jenkins (755) and Elizabeth Hopkins (3307), on 26 Dec 1876 in Owen Sound, Ontario.[391] She died on 01 May 1900 in Owen Sound, Ontario[392] and was buried in Greenwood Cemetery, Owen Sound, Ontario. She was a teacher in 1876.

Herbert William JENKINS (3117) was born on 05 Dec 1850; was 25 when married. He died on 25 Mar 1941 at age 90 and was buried in Greenwood, Owen Sound, Ontario. He was a teacher in 1876.

Children of Janet Gunn (3113) and Herbert William Jenkins (3117) were as follows:

36 i. Herbert Claude Marcus JENKINS (3160).

ii. Eva Elizabeth JENKINS (3159) was born on 03 Apr 1880 in Sydenham Twp, Grey Co., Ontario. She died on 15 Nov 1973 in Owen Sound, Ontario, at age 93. She was buried in Greenwood, Owen Sound, Ontario.

iii. Norah Blanche JENKINS (3308) was born on 24 Jan 1884 in Sydenham Twp, Grey Co., Ontario. She died on 20 Oct 1885 in Owen Sound, Ontario, at age 1 and was buried in Greenwood, Owen Sound, Ontario.

20. Margaret GUNN (3112) was born in 1852 in Sydenham, Ontario. She married James Lindsay Boyd (3116) on 21 Dec 1871. She died on 29 May 1920 in Sarawak Twp, Grey Co., Ontario.[393] She was buried in Greenwood Cemetery, Owen Sound, Ontario.

James Lindsay BOYD (3116) was born on 20 Apr 1848. He died in Dec 1918 at age 70.[394] He emigrated to Canada in 1861. He was a farmer in 1871 in Sydenham Twp, Ontario. He was buried in Greenwood Cemetery, Owen Sound, Ontario.[395]

---

390 Carol Small, e-mail to Donald Gunn, Aug 2008 and for further information on this page.

391 Carol Small, e-mail to Donald Gunn, 01 Sep 2008: 'Herbert William Jenkins, 25, teacher, England, Keppel, son of George Jenkins & Elizabeth Hopkins, married Janet Gunn, 25, Owen Sound, same, daughter of Marcus Gunn & Barbara McKay, witness John Sutherland of Sydenham & Arthur H N Jenkins of Normanby, 26 Dec 1876 at Owen Sound.'

392 Carol Small, e-mail to Donald Gunn, Aug 2008; Bill & Sharon Gurney, e-mail to Donald Gunn, 03 Oct 2008: Family of Neil McKay & Margaret Sutherland of Caithness Scotland & Ontario Canada and for further information on this page.

393 Carol Small, e-mail to Donald Gunn, Aug 2008; Bill & Sharon Gurney, e-mail to Donald Gunn, 03 Oct 2008: Family of Neil McKay & Margaret Sutherland of Caithness Scotland & Ontario Canada; *Unknown newspaper*, 'The death occurred on Saturday morning of Mrs Margaret Boyd in the Township of Sarawak. Mrs Boyd was the widow of the late James L Boyd, reeve of Sydenham for many years, and who passed away a year ago last December. Since the death of her husband, Mrs Boyd has been living with her daughter, Mrs David Riley at Presque Isle.

She was the daughter of the late Marquis and Mrs Gunn and was born on the farm on Superior Street where she lived up to the death of her husband, whom she married forty-nine years ago. She saw the country grow from a wild and tangled wilderness to a highly cultivated farming district. During her long life she endeared herself to the hearts of all she met by her quiet, motherly ways. She was a member of Knox Church, Owen Sound, and always took a deep interest in church affairs. She leaves no brothers or sisters but two sons; Marquis G of Empress, Alta., and Robert John on the Superior Street homestead, and one daughter, Mrs David Riley of Presque Isle, remain to mourn the loss...'

394 Carol Small, e-mail to Donald Gunn, Aug 2008; *Unknown newspaper*, 'The late James Lindsay Boyd was born in Ireland 76 years ago and came to this country in 1871 when a young man of 18 years, and was accompanied by his mother. Mr Boyd first settled in Derby, where he lived for ten years and then moved to Sydenham, where he took up a farm on the 12th concession, and he spent the balance of his life on this farm, with the exception of a brief period in railroading.

In the municipal life of Sydenham, Mr Boyd has played a prominent part. He always took a keen interest in the affairs of the township and for the last 16 years was a member of the township council. For three years of this he was deputy-reeve and last January he was elected to reeveship by acclamation. Not only in the township affairs was he an authority, but he was regarded as one of the best county councillors. He was well informed on all subjects and his advice was always sound.

Children of Margaret Gunn (3112) and James Lindsay Boyd (3116) were:

i. William John BOYD (3153)[396] was born on 25 Dec 1872 in Sydenham Twp, Grey Co., Ontario. He died on 18 Feb 1886 in Sydenham Twp, Grey Co., Ontario, at age 13.

ii. Barbara Jane BOYD (3152) was born on 22 Aug 1875 in Sydenham Twp, Ontario. She married David Reilly (3156) on 22 Dec 1897 in Sydenham Twp, Grey Co., Ontario. She died on 26 Aug 1973 in Greenwood, Ontario, at age 98.[397] She was buried in Aug 1973 in Greenwood Cemetery, Owen Sound, Ontario.

David REILLY (3156) was born in 1869 in Ontario. He died on 03 Apr 1924 in Owen Sound, Ontario. He was buried in Greenwood Cemetery, Owen Sound, Ontario.

37 iii. Marcus Gunn BOYD (3155).

38 iv. Robert John BOYD (3150).

v. Catherine Margaret BOYD (3154) was born on 21 Jul 1882 in Sydenham Twp, Grey Co., Ontario. She died on 30 Mar 1906 in Sydenham Twp, Grey Co., Ontario, at age 23. She was buried in Greenwood Cemetery, Owen Sound, Ontario.

On Dec 21 1871, he was married to Margaret Gunn, who survives with two sons, Robert John, on the homestead, and Marques G of Empress, Alberta, and one daughter, Mrs David Reilly of Annan. Mr Boyd was a member of Knox Church, Owen Sound and the Masonic Order. He was held in the highest esteem by hundreds of friends, not only in his own township but here in Owen Sound and elsewhere.'

395 Bill & Sharon Gurney, e-mail to Donald Gunn, 03 Oct 2008: Family of Neil McKay & Margaret Sutherland of Caithness Scotland & Ontario Canada and for further information on this page.

396 Carol Small, e-mail to Donald Gunn, Aug 2008 and for further information on this page.

397 Carol Small, e-mail to Donald Gunn, Aug 2008; *Unknown newspaper*, 'A resident of Owen Sound for 50 years, Mrs David Reilly, 98, formerly of 145-5th St, E, died Sunday in the General & Marine Hospital. Born in Sydenham Township, she was the former Barbara Jane Boyd, a daughter of the late James and Margaret Boyd. In 1897, she married David Reilly and the couple farmed at Hoath Head until 1917 when they moved to a farm in Sarawak Township. Mr Reilly died in 1923.'

Generation Four

21. Neil GUNN (3136)[398] was born at sea in 1857 on the way to Ontario, Canada. He married Catherine Cameron (3143), daughter of Alexander Cameron (3144), in 1892. He died on 22 May 1931 in Sydenham, Ontario.[399]

Catherine CAMERON (3143) was born in 1873 in Glengarry Co. Ontario. She died on 20 Apr 1928 in Sydenham, Ontario.[400] She was buried on 23 Apr 1928 in Greenwood, Ontario.

Children of Neil Gunn (3136) and Catherine Cameron (3143) were as follows:

i. Allan Alexander GUNN (3145) was born circa 1894. He married Thelma Johnson (3161), daughter of Simon Johnson (3162), circa 1920. He married Barbara Rosetta Carnahan (3267), daughter of William James Carnahan (3147) and Annie Anderson (3265), after 1927. He died on 11 Oct 1951.

Thelma JOHNSON (3161) died on 08 Jun 1927 in Sydenham, Ontario.[401]

Barbara Rosetta CARNAHAN (3267) died on 23 Nov 1979.[402]

ii. Angus William GUNN (3146) was born in 1898. He married Vera Geanetta Johnson (3258) in 1922.[403] He died on 13 Sep 1956 in Sydenham, Ontario. He had one son and two daughters.

398Carol Small, e-mail to Donald Gunn, 04 Aug 2008; 'Donald and Janet's children were Ann, Margaret, Neil, John, Donald MacKay Gunn, Barbara Janet, Jemima, William J and Angus Hector; Carol Small, e-mail to Donald Gunn, 04 Aug 2008; Donald and Janet's children were Ann, Margaret, Neil, John, Donald MacKay Gunn, Brbara Janet, Jemima, William J and Angus Hector.' She has also provided much further information for this page beyond the given footnotes.

399Carol Small, e-mail to Donald Gunn, Aug 2008; *Unknown newspaper*, 'Following an illness of about a month's duration the death occurred on Friday evening of one of Sydenham township's well known farmers in the person of Mr Neil Gunn, at the home of his son, Mr Angus Gunn, on the 10th line, some four miles from the city. His death, while not entirely unexpected, will be learned with sincere regret by a wide circle of friends and acquaintances in Owen Sound and throughout the township, where he was held in the highest esteem and respect.

The late Mr Gunn was the son of Mr. & Mrs Donald Gunn, who were among the old pioneer residents of Sydenham township. He was born in the township, and with the exception of a short time spent in Western Canada, resided there all his life. He was known as a successful farmer, a good neighbour and a man who took an interest in the welfare of those about him, although he took no part in public life. He was a Presbyterian in religion, being a member of St Andrew's church, and a Liberal in politics. He was married many years ago to Miss Catherine Cameron, daughter of the late Mr & Mrs Alexander Cameron, of Sydenham township, and she predeceased him about three years ago. He is survived by his son Angus, on the homestead, and Allan, also of Sydenham township; one brother, Angus, in the west, and one sister, Margaret of Sydenham.'

400Carol Small, e-mail to Donald Gunn, Aug 2008; *Unknown newspaper*, 'The death occurred Friday afternoon, April 20th, following an illness of about five weeks, during the last three of which she was confined to her bed, of Mrs Neil Gunn, at the home of her son, Angus Gunn, in Sydenham township, just outside the city on 8th Street East. ... The late Mrs Gunn was the daughter of the late Mr & Mrs Alexander Cameron and was born in Glengarry County and came to Sydenham township 55 years ago. Her maiden name was Catherine Cameron and she was married to Mr Neil Gunn, 36 years ago.'

401Carol Small, e-mail to Donald Gunn, Aug 2008; *Unknown newspaper*, 'A deserving tribute of honour was paid to the memory of the late Mrs Allan Gunn by the large number of friends and relatives who attended her funeral last Wednesday afternoon. Mrs Gunn, whose maiden name was Thelma Johnson, was the second daughter of Mr Simon Johnson and the late Mrs Johnson of Bognor, where she was born and where she spent most of her girlhood days.

In the death of Mrs Gunn the community has been deeply saddened but more especially in the home where the husband and two children, Donald aged five years and baby Leona aged 20 months, are left to mourn the loss of a devoted wife and mother.'

402*Unknown newspaper*, 'Mrs Barbara Gunn, at the General & Marine Hospital at R.R. No.6, Owen Sound, on Friday morning November 12, 1979. The former Barbara Rosetta Carnahan of 311 9th Street East in Owen Sound. Wife of the late Allan Alexander Gunn. Mother of Alex of R.R.4, Owen Sound, Donald and Leona, (Mrs John Wilson), both of Owen Sound. Sister of Judson, of Chatsworth and Margaret (Mrs Percy Williams) of Leith. Also survived by eight children and three great grandchildren.'

403Carol Small, e-mail to Donald Gunn, Aug 2008; *Unknown newspaper*, 'Angus William Gunn of 1312-1st Avenue west, died in the General and Marine Hospital on Thursday afternoon in his 59th year...The late Mr Gunn farmed most of his life in Sydenham township on the outskirts of the city and was employed at the creamery now operated by the Grey County Cheese Co-op. ... Mr Gunn married Vera Geanetta Johnson of Owen Sound, who survives. ... Also surviving are one son Neil of Owen Sound and two daughters, Dorothy, Mrs Norman Howell of Owen Sound and Thelma, Mrs Albert Miller of Toronto, and one grandson, Allan Gunn. Mr Gunn was predeceased by one brother, Allan Gunn, in 1951.'

Vera Geanetta JOHNSON (3258) died on 09 Oct 1980 in Owen Sound, Ontario.[404]

22. Barbara Janet GUNN (3139)[405] was born on 14 Sep 1866 in Ontario. She married William James Carnahan (3147); his third wife. She died on 27 Apr 1931 in Ontario at age 64.[406]

William James CARNAHAN (3147) was born on 18 Dec 1869. He married Cassie Anderson (3264). He married Annie Anderson (3265). He died on 24 Jun 1948 at age 78.[407]

Children of Barbara Janet Gunn (3139) and William James Carnahan (3147) were:

i. Margaret CARNAHAN (3148). She married Percy Williams (3149).

23. Jessie Barbara MILLER (284) was born in 1865 in Emerald Hill, Vic.[408] She married Charles James SWEARS (282) possibly in London in 1892.

Charles James SWEARS (282) is not listed in Vic BDMs of the period.[409]

Children of Jessie Barbara Miller (284) and Charles James Swears (282) were:

i. Hugh Miller SWEARS (286) was born after 1885. He died in 1917 in France. He attended Jesus College, Cambridge University.

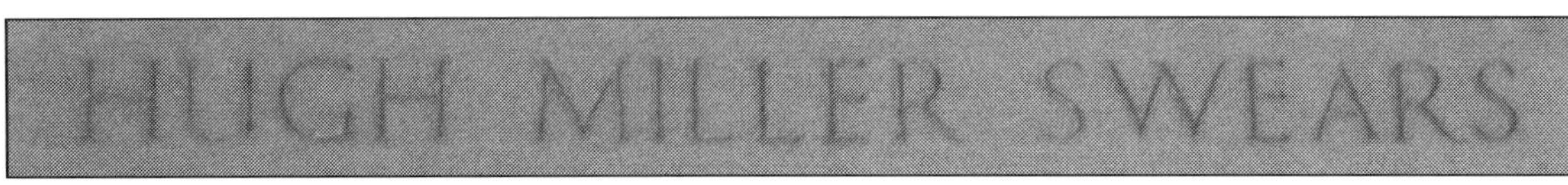

From the Jesus College Honour Board, ouside the College Chapel.

ii. Marjorie Gertrude SWEARS (287) was born 1896 / 7, London. She married the Rev. John E. C. Adams (4120) in Devon in 1926.

iii. Dorothy Catherine Swears (4129) was born in 1903.

---

404 *Unknown newspaper*, 'Mrs Vera Gunn died at Versa Care Nursing Home in Owen Sound on Thursday morning October 9, 1980, the former Vera Jeanette Johnson of Owen Sound. Wife of the late Angus William Gunn; mother of Neil of Owen Sound and Mrs Thelma Myers of Monrovia, California. ... Also survived by 2 grandsons, Allan and Robert Gunn, both of Owen Sound. Predeceased by a daughter, Mrs Dorothy Hall, 2 sisters, Mrs Elsie Javens and Mrs Thelma Gunn and 3 brothers, Melville, Herman and George.'

405 Carol Small e-mail to Donald Gunn, 04 Aug 2008 and for further information on this page; Donald and Janet's children were Ann, Margaret, Neil, John, Donald MacKay Gunn, Barbara Janet, Jemima, William J and Angus Hector.'

406 Bill & Sharon Gurney, e-mail to Donald Gunn, 12 Sep 2008 and for further information on this page; *Unknown newspaper*, 'Mrs William G Carnahan, 1863 9th Avenue East, passed away on Monday afternoon at tne Hamilton General Hospital. ... Deceased's maiden name was Barbara Janet Gunn, daughter of the late Donald and Janet Gunn, and she was born on the 10th line of Sydenham township over 64 years ago. She was married about 24 years ago to Mr William G Carnahan, who survives with two daughters, Mrs Allan Gunn, and Mrs Percy J Williams, and one son, Judson, all of Owen Sound. She also leaves one sister, Miss Margaret Gunn, of Sydenham, and two brothers, Neil Gunn of Sydenham, and Angus Gunn, in the West.'

407 *Unknown newspaper*, 'William James Carnahan, 78, a resident of Owen Sound since 1906, died in hospital Wednesday night as a result of shock received when he fell and broke his hip the day previous. A native of St Vincent Township, deceased had driven the stage between Meaford and Owen Sound for a number of years during the early part of his life. He was also manager of the Oliver Rogara Stone Co., Owen Sound, for 25 years. Thrice married, he is survived by two children of his second marriage, Judson Carnahan and Mrs Allan Gunn, both of Owen Sound, and one daughter, Mrs Percy Williams, of his third marriage. He has one sister, Mrs Bertha Medley of Owen Sound'; *Unknown newspaper*, 'William James Carnahan, a native of St Vincent and a resident of Owen Sound since 1906, died on Wednesday afternoon ... Deceased was born in St Vincent on Dec. 18 1869, a son of the late William and Nancy Londry Carnahan. ... The late Mr Carnahan was thrice married. His first wife was Cassie Anderson and to this union were born two children, ... His second wife was Annie Anderson and to this marriage were born two children, Judson Carnahan and Rosetta, Mrs Allan Gunn, both of whom survive ... Deceased's third marriage was to Barbara Gunn, who predeceased him 17 years ago. One daughter by this marriage, Margaret, Mrs Percy Williams, survives.'

408 Register of BDMs - Victoria, 1865 8468.

409 It is probable that Jessie was in England and met Charles James Swears there.

24. Katherine Margaret Mackay MILLER (285) was born in 1872 in Emerald Hill, Vic.[410] She married William Porter Vine (283), son of James John Vine (1106) and Jane McDonald (1107), in 1895 in Vic.[411]

William Porter VINE (283) was born in 1857 in Port Melbourne, Vic; age 66 at death in 1923. He died in 1923 in Prahran, Vic.[412]

Children of Katherine Margaret Mackay Miller (285) and William Porter Vine (283) all born in St Kilda, Vic, were as follows:

- i. James Miller VINE (288) was born in Dec 1896.[413] He married Rosemary Caroline Stewart (1108). He began military service on 08 Mar 1915 in St Kilda, Vic, medical student, Next of kin was his father, William P. Vine, 11 Redan Street, East St Kilda.[414] He ended military service on 21 Sep 1919 in Melbourne, Vic; awarded 1914/18 Star No.31853, British War Medal, No.9838, Victory Medal No.9749.
- ii. William Alan VINE (290) was born in Jun 1898.[415] He died on 11 Oct 1917 at age 19, killed in action. He began military service on 17 Jul 1916 in St Kilda, Vic, clerk, NOK father, William P Vine, 11 Redan Street, St Kilda, Victoria.
- iii. Catherine Noel VINE (291) was born in 1900.[416] She died in 1903 in Melbourne South, Vic.[417]
- iv. Francis Seymour VINE (292) was born in 1904.[418] He died in 1961 in Somersby, Vic.[419] He was managing director of Millers Ropes (See Part 7) until 1960.[420] He was appointed C.M.G in 1957 in Vic.
- v. Reginald Vernon VINE (694) was born in 1908.[421] He died on 21 Dec 1987 in NSW.[422]
- vi. Lesley Alison VINE (289) was born in 1914.[423]

25. John Alexander GUNN[424] (Hon.) (32) was born on 11 Feb 1860 in Buninyong, Vic.[425] He married Jessie Marie Turner (104), daughter of William Turner[426] (437) and Maria

---

410Register of BDMs - Victoria, 1872 8854.

411Register of BDMs - Victoria, 1895 880.

412Register of BDMs - Victoria, 1923 16539.

413Register of BDMs - Victoria, 1896 7042.

414Army Attestation Paper.

415Register of BDMs - Victoria, 1897 23048.

416Register of BDMs - Victoria, 1900 6741.

417Register of BDMs - Victoria, 1903 2799.

418Register of BDMs - Victoria, 1904 29047

419Register of BDMs - Victoria, 1961 1813

420See Part 7.

421Register of BDMs - Victoria, 1908 30378.

422Ryerson Index, *The Sydney Morning Herald*,, 23 Dec 1987

423Register of BDMs - Victoria, 1914 17055

424 See Part 7.

425Register of BDMs - Victoria, 1860 2643; Rookwood cemetery records.

426 William Turner was a noted banker and pamphleteer. For a time he was second in charge of the Commercial Bank of Australia in the boom years of the 1880s-1890s. His wife's brother was the Rev. Andrew Love of Geelong, sometimes Moderator of the Presbyterian Church of Victoria. The Rev Love's grand-daughter was the celebrated Australian World War One painter, Iso. Rae. William Turner's brother Joseph was a noted early photographer in Geelong and Melbourne.

Reinhardt (440), on 08 Jun 1886 in North Brighton, Vic.[427] He died on 21 Sep 1910 in Sydney, NSW, at age 50.[428] J.A. Gunn, then of Borambola Station, Wagga Wagga, purchased Lot 5 Area DN, Sec. 14[429] at the Ballarat General Cemetery where various family members are buried[430]. He was buried, in Rookwood cemetery, NSW. He was a jackaroo for Goldsborough, Mort & Co in 1878 in South Yalgogrin Station, Ardlethan, NSW.[431] He was the inventor of the first mechanical poison-bait layer, made from an old sausage machine, some cogs and a pair of wheels, which soon came into general use in various forms throughout the country between 1880 and 1885.[432] He was the manager in 1886 in South Yalgogrin Station, Ardlethan, NSW. Anthrax ravaged sheep at the Station in 1888.[433] In 1892 Yalgogrin station

---

427 Register of BDMs - Victoria, 1886 3043.

428 *Unknown newspaper*, 'The death in Randwick (Sydney) private hospital of Mrs J. M.Gunn, formerly of Wagga, and widow of the late J.A. Gunn, M.L.C., recalls the debt owing by the sheep-owners of Australia to her late husband and McGarvie Smith, who collaborated in discovering a vaccine for combating anthrax in sheep. Gunn and McGarvie Smith experimented for years before succeeding, and the benefit to the pastoral industry in Australia cannot be assessed in figures. ... He had been offered 100,000 pounds for the formula, but refused it'; Rookwood cemetery records: Gunn John Alexander, died Sydney 22 Sep 1910.

429 Ballarat Old Cemetery records.

430 From an email October 2009 form G. Jones; The inscriptions at the Ballarat Cemetery read:

1)
In loving memory
---of---
Donald Gunn (3)
Born at Brawlbin, Reay, Caithness, Scotland
28th March 1832 died 14th Feb 1901
Also his sixth son Hugh (38)
Died 24th June, aged 3 years
his beloved wife
Jane Gunn (41)
Born at Hampton Poyle, Oxford, England
18th Jan 1836, died 14th Feb 1908
and their affectionate friend
Donald Cameron

Also
Mary Jane Gunn (34)
Died 5th May 1934.

2)
In loving memory
---of---
Daniel Surman (270)
Died 21st Oct 1869 aged 62 years
Also his wife
Mary Ann Surman (271)
Died 23rd Nov 1894, aged 84 years
and their grandson
Watkins Surman (405),
Died 15th May 1875, aged 4 years.

3)
Sacred to the Memory
---of---
John Watkins Surman (118)
Died 13 Oct 1906, aged 76 years
Also his beloved wife
Jessie (120)
Died 30th May 1913, aged 79 years

431 See Part 7 for a detailed biography.

432 Rob Webster, *Bygoo and Beyond*.

433 Rob Webster, *Bygoo and Beyond*, 'one day in 1888 Gunn and his brother, Marcus Daniel Gunn, rode to a paddock on Yalgogrin where they saw hundreds of carcases of dead sheep.'

comprised 129,000 acres running 26,600 sheep, 34 horses and 41 cattle.[434] He created a double dose anthrax vaccine in Dec 1893 in NSW. He was a Justice of the Peace in 1895 in NSW. He was superintendent for all Goldsborough Mort stations in southern NSW in 1895 in NSW. In Apr 1895 John (32) entered into a partnership with John McGarvie Smith in NSW. John was commissioned as a Justice of the Peace in 1896.[435] He succeeded in developing a single dose anthrax serum in 1897 in South Yalgogrin Station, Ardlethan, NSW.

He hosted a visit by the noted British socialists and social critics Sidney and Beatrice Webb[436] in 1898 at Borambola Station, NSW. He suffered burns during bushfires in 1902. He was listed in the electoral roll in 1903 in Borambola Station, NSW.[437] He resigned from Goldsborough Mort in 1905 in NSW. He was described as a grazier, bacteriologist and station inspector in Aug 1905 in NSW. He was Chairman of the Council of Advice on Rabbit Extermination in 1908. On 21 Jul 1908 The Honourable John Gunn (32) was elected as a Member of the Legislative Council of NSW until his death on 21 Sep 1910.[438]

Jessie Marie TURNER (104) was born on 01 Jul 1862 in Beechworth, Vic.[439] She died on 05 May 1925 in Helene Pt Hospital, Randwick, NSW, at age 62. She was buried on 07 May 1925 in Rookwood cemetery, Sydney, NSW; alongside her husband. She was a dressmaker on 08 Oct 1885 in Arundel Street, Benalla, Vic.[440] She was on the electoral roll with John Alexander Gunn (Hon.) (32) in 1903 in Borambola Station, NSW.[441]

Children of John Alexander Gunn (Hon.) (32) and Jessie Marie Turner (104) were:

---

434 Rob Webster, *Bygoo and Beyond*.

435 NSW Parliament Members.

436 The Webbs established the Fabian Society and helped establish the London School of Economics and Political Science. See, as well, *The Webbs' Australian Diary 1898* edited by A.G. Austin.

437 Electoral Roll: 1903 Roll lists John Alexander Gunn, Station Manager, Marcus Daniel Gunn, Station Manager, Norman Gunn, Licensed Vaccinator, Mary Jane Gunn, Domestic Duties and Jessie Marie Gunn, Domestic Duties as residing at Borambola Station.

438 NSW Parliament Members: Life Appointment under the Constitution Act. Date of Writ of Summons 10 July 1908.

439 Rookwood cemetery records: Gunn Jessie Marie born Beechworth, Victoria 1 Jul 1862.

440 *North East Ensign*, 08 Oct 1885—'Miss Jessie Turner, wishes to inform the Ladies of Benalla that she has started DRESSMAKING, In Arundel Street - all kinds of sewing done'. Her father was working in banking at this time.

441 Electoral Roll: 1903 Roll lists John Alexander Gunn, Station Manager, Marcus Daniel Gunn, Station Manager, Norman Gunn, Licensed Vaccinator, Mary Jane Gunn, Domestic Duties and Jessie Marie Gunn, Domestic Duties as residing at Borambola Station.

Gladys Emily Gunn

i. Gladys Emily GUNN (225) was born on 31 May 1887 in Nithsdale, North Brighton, Vic[442] and was christened on 05 Jul 1887 in Nithsdale. She married Frank Lupton (224) in Vic. She died on 09 Jun 1968 in Melbourne, Vic, at age 81.[443] It appears they 'separated' after World War 2. She was not in her father's will; one notes her husband was a Catholic.

Frank LUPTON (224) 1885-1961 mainly lived in Wagga Wagga, NSW.[444]

Nithsdale, 316 St. Kilda Street, North Brighton, Victoria, Australia, 2007. Nithsdale, in the 1880s, was occupied and probably owned by Jessie Marie Turner's father, William Turner. At this time 'mothers-to-be' returned to the parental home.

---

[442] Australia Birth Index 1788-1922.

[443] Two children; Jean Frances Lupton b. 1914 (married K.B. Moore at Toorak 1939) and Ralph Skirrow Lupton d. 1959 Penrith NSW, who married twice. First to Margaret Mary Constance Unknown in Wagga Wagga in 1938, then to Eileen May Unknown in Parramatta in 1948. In 1954 he was in the Parramatta Courts (*SMH*, page 11, 9 Dec 1954). Jean Frances may have had a daughter; K. B. Moore had a daughter called Sue Moore.

[444] Australia Birth Index 1788-1922.

ii. Jessie Jean GUNN (221) was born on 05 Mar 1890 in 109 Doveton Street, Ballarat, Vic.[445] She died on 06 Jun 1891 in Yalgogrin Station, NSW, at age 1. She was buried on 07 Jun 1891 in Yalgogrin Station[446], NSW; a lonely grave.
iii. Alexander Donald GUNN (222) was born on 13 May 1892 in 32 Brougham St, Ballarat, Vic.[447] After leaving school he continued with the Cadets at Wagga Wagga.

Alexander Donald Gunn

He married Helen Ramsay[448] (226), daughter of William Ramsay[449] (514) and Caroline Maud Seaborne Robinson[450] (515), on 22 Dec 1914 in Holy Trinity Church, Kew, Vic.[451] He enlisted in the Army in Aug 1915, embarking in November. He initially joined the M.E.F and served at Heliopolis in Egypt (and elsewhere) but served in France in 1916 and was promoted to Adjutant, then Captain. He was mentioned in dispatches Jan 1918 and served to the end of the war, returning to Australia in 1919[452]. He and Helen Ramsay (226)

---

445 Register of BDMs - Victoria, 1890 9535; GEDCOM file from Alastair Gunn.

446 Burial: Ref; NSAG B7/11/131 p153.

447 Register of BDMs - Victoria, 1892 9956.

448 The musical symphonic work 'Australia' by the German composer Dr von Keussler is dedicated to her. He opened an exhibition of her paintings at the International Club in October 1935 where those in attendance included Max Meldrum. http://newspapers.nla.gov.au/ndp/del/article/11774920?searchTerm=Gunn

449 William Ramsay was a pioneer Melbourne Bookseller; see page 63 *The Early Australian Booksellers.* Interestingly 'The Argus' of 3 December 1920, page 6, lists, at the funeral of the notable banker, cultural authority and conservative historian Henry Gyles Turner, William Ramsay as a nephew, A. D. Gunn as a relative, and Gresham Robinson is placed in the 'family' list of mourners. The parents of William Ramsay were Charles Ramsay and Helen Turner; the wife of Henry Gyles Turner was Helen Ramsay. All were from London. The world of the Melbourne elite was small. Martha Turner, a sister of Henry Gyles Turner, was the Minister of the Unitarian Church in Melbourne and a notable supporter of women's causes. It is possible that she was the first female Minister of religion in the British Commonwealth. http://web.ukonline.co.uk/m.gratton/Names/Martha.htm

450 The Robinsons were very involved with education, most visibly through Gresham Robinson—Caroline's uncle—who, amongst other achievements was the foundation Principal of Essendon Grammar School in Victoria. Dr. George A. A. Robinson was heavily involved with the Williamstown Hospital and later head of the company Ramsay Surgical.

451 Register of BDMs - Victoria, 1914 9671; 'The Argus' page 1, 5 January 1915

452 Derived from the war records held by the National Archives of Australia.

were divorced in 1924; the newspaper report[453] says he was living in Sunshine as a dairy farmer at that time. It is possible that time apart, during the war, contributed to the divorce. He married Joan White Larkin (665) circa 1930 in Vic. He (probably) lived at 34 Tester Grove Caulfield in 1935. He died on 03 Nov 1956 in the Alfred Hospital, Melbourne, Vic, at age 64. He was educated between 1908 and 1910 in Geelong College, Geelong, Vic (and before that at Carlton College where his uncle, Gresham Robinson, was Headmaster).[454] He was bow of the 1st VIII in 1910 for Geelong College.[455] He was a grazier, perhaps in the sense that he helped run the farm after his father's death. He was a representative for Golden Fleece Oil Company circa 1930.[456]

Helen RAMSAY (226) was born on 25 Jan 1893 in Brighton, Vic. She died in 1966 in the Repatriation Hospital, Heidelberg, Vic.

Joan White LARKIN (665) was born on 05 Sep 1910. She died in 1980 in Vic.

iv. Angus William GUNN (223) was born on 23 May 1895 in Ballarat, Vic.[457] He was christened on 23 Jun 1895 in Elsternwick, Vic. He won the Senior Boarders' Scripture Prize at Carlton College in 1908.

Angus William Gunn[458]

[453] *The Argus*, page 12, 7 November 1924.

[454] Letter from Paul Mishura to Donald Gunn, 15 Sep 1998.

[455] Page 162, ed. B.R. Keith, *The Geelong College 1861-1961*. His brother Angus William was also Bow in 1913 and 1914.

[456] Letter, Jack Alexander Gunn to unknown recipient, 08 Mar 2001.

[457] Register of BDMs - Victoria, 1895 9056.

[458] The latter picture being from the *Sunday Times*, Perth, 24 October 1926

He married Eliza Margaret McKenzie (227), daughter of David Lowe McKenzie (2495), on 03 Apr 1919 in Randwick, NSW.[459] He died on 14 Oct 1926 in the Palace Hotel or Perth Hospital, Perth, WA, at age 31.[460] He was educated between 1909 and 1914 at Geelong College, Geelong, Vic. He was bow of 1st VIII in 1913.[461] He was the manager of the family sheep station during war between 1915 and 1918 in South Yalgogrin, near Wagga Wagga, NSW. He was an insurance agent for the Life Insurance Company of Australia in Aug 1926 in Perth, WA.

Eliza Margaret MCKENZIE (227)[462] was born in 1889 in Gundagai, NSW. She died on 29 Mar 1950 in St Vincent's Hospital, Darlinghurst, NSW. She was buried on 31 Mar 1950 in RC Section, Botany, NSW. She was a hotel manageress. Their two children have 'disappeared' from the records.

26. William Watkins GUNN (33) was born on 26 Dec 1861 in Cardigan, Nr Ballarat, Vic.[463] He married Margaret Jane Balharrie (42), daughter of John Balharrie (1314) and Jane Carmichael (1315), on 24 Jun 1891 in Bloomfield, Vic.[464] He died on 24 Jun 1935 in Crossover, Vic, at age 73.[465] He was buried on 26 Jun 1935 in Warragul Cemetery, Vic. He

---

459Alastair Gunn, 08 Apr 2005 using NSW BDM.

460*Melbourne Argus*, 15 Oct 1926 p. 8 Insurance Agent's Suicide. Shoots himself in head. Perth Thursday
Angus William Negus, a young insurance agent, committed suicide this afternoon by shooting himself in the head with a revolver. He walked across the billiard-room at the Palace Hotel into a lavatory, and a few seconds later a revolver shot was heard. He was hurried to the hospital, but died shortly after admittance. Negus, who arrived from the East about 10 months ago, was employed by the Life Insurance Company of Australia;
Melbourne Argus, 30 Oct 1926, p22 'Salesman's Suicide. Perth Friday
A verdict of suicide was given at an inquest into the death of a man who was known in Perth as Arthur William Negus, but who was afterwards found to be Angus William Gunn, formerly managing director of a large firm in Sydney which, subsequently, went into liquidation. Gunn walked into the lavatory at the Palace Hotel on October 14 and shot himself in the head with a revolver. Evidence was given that Gunn had stated he came from Sydney in consequence of domestic troubles. He seemed to think that a maintenance order was being made against him and that if his wife knew that he was in Perth she would have him imprisoned. He was a travelling salesman up to two months ago and, although ordinarily a moderate drinker, he indulged heavily at times, and had threatened to commit suicide. He admitted to a friend that he had pawned goods belonging to the firm for which he was travelling.' We have no record of his involvement with any Sydney firm; the social pages of Sydney newspapers record his wife attending events by herself.

461Page 162 ff., ed. B.R. Keith, *The Geelong College 1861-1961*.

462Certificate of Death: NSW 1950 007066.

463Register of BDMs - Victoria, 1862 467.

464Register of BDMs - Victoria, 1891 3581.

465Register of BDMs - Victoria, 1935 15057; *Unknown newspaper*, 'On the 24th June, at Crossover, William Watkins, beloved husband of Margaret Jane, and loving father of John, Jean (Mrs Milner), Violet (Mrs Wadeson), Edith (deceased), Marjorie and Allan, aged 73 years'; *The Warragul Gazette*, 'The death occurred at Crossover on Monday of William Watkins Gunn, at the age of 73 years. He commenced a sawmilling business at Crossover more than 40 years ago. He leaves a widow, two sons and three daughters'; *The Warragul Gazette*, 'W.W. Gunn Passing of a Pioneer
One of the oldest pioneers in the timber industry of Gippsland in the person of Mr W.W. Gunn, of Crossover and Noojee, passed away last week, and the 'natural' body was placed to rest in the Warragul Cemetery. At the graveside on Wednesday last a number of relatives and friends of the family assembled to pay their last respects to one who had fought a good fight and a strenuous one, in the heavily timbered country of Gippsland.
Tangible evidence of the affection and esteem felt for him was seen in the large number of beautiful wreaths which covered the casket.
At the funeral which took place at the Warragul Cemetery on Wednesday, the coffin-bearers were:- Messrs A Aldersea, J Parker, J Byrnes, N McDougall, F Young and R Holmes, several of whom were old employees of the firm. The burial service was read by the Rev. Neil McDonald, of the Presbyterian Church, and all the arrangements were entrusted to Messrs JA McGilton Pty Ltd.
The late Mr Gunn came of a real old Highland family, who emigrated to Australia in the early days. He was born in the Burrumbeet district near Ballarat and came to Gippsland in the very early days about 1884, and engaged in sawmilling in what is now known as Lionel Young's farm. He moved over to Bloomfield, now called Nilma, and later still to Crossover and Noojee. In fact, he was a pioneer of this forest country, over 50 years ago. Notwithstanding his strenuous life and the hard work of handling timber, he enjoyed splendid health for over 70 years and was never happier than when among the giant Eucalypts.

was a timber miller with Amoss as partner circa 1888 in Bloomfield (now Nilma), Vic.[466] He was a member in 1894 and 1895 of the Cricket Club, Traralgon, Vic.[467] [468] He took out a mining lease on 01 Jun 1892 with brother Donald Gunn (35), brother in law J. Balharrie (1317) and others and established a gold mining company—'The South Warragul Gold Mining Company' with plans to employ 150 miners[469]. He took out a mining right circa 1895 in Vic.[470] He was a miner in 1904.[471] He brought the first car to Crossover district in 1912 in Vic.[472] He invented a method to destroy submarines in 1915.[473]

One of the most memorable events of his life was his visit to the Old Highland homeland with the Scottish Delegation (See Part 3.) There he met his cousin, Col. Gunn, a landed proprietor by whom he was introduced to, and enjoyed the hospitality of, many of the notabilities of the North.
By his marriage with Miss Balharrie, he became associated with another well-known pioneer family of Gippsland, Cr. Balharrie being her brother. The family consists of two sons and several daughters, John Gunn being the eldest son, is now in charge of the sawmilling business.
A man of sterling qualities, strong in his convictions and of the strictest integrity, the deceased pioneer has left behind him a name and character, which will be remembered with affection, by a very large circle of friends'.

466 John William Gunn.

467 Photograph; Royal Historical Society of Victoria, Melbourne, Vic, Group of men belonging to Traralgon Cricket Club
Item No. MSPH-0498.

468 Photograph; Royal Historical Society of Victoria, Group of men belonging to Traralgon Cricket Club
Item No. MSPH-0499.

469 The Argus, 1 June 1892, page 7.

470 John William Gunn.

471 Archive CD Books, *Ballarat and District Directory 1904*, CD-ROM, 2004.

472 Dorothy Hunt, *A History of Neerim* : 'William Watkins Gunn first came to Darnum Gippsland in 1884. He married Margaret Jane Balharrie at Bloomfield in 1891. They settled in Crossover in 1895 and had six children - John, Jean, Violet, Edith, Marjorie and Marcus Allan. They all attended Crossover State School.
William built and operated successful sawmills at Crossover, Shady Creek and districts, employing many men. He built a three foot six inch tramway for transporting the sawn timber from these mills to the rail-head at Crossover.
William brought in the first car to the district in 1912.
In 1921 he took up milling at Noojee, his son John was manager.
During the First World War he invented a method for destroying submarines which was duly adopted by the British Admiralty with considerable success. He attempted to obtain recognition for this invention during a visit to England in 1928 but failed to do so. The Admiralty claimed it their right to commandeer such inventions in wartime. William also had a large interest in goldmining in Crossover and Buchan.
He died in 1945 aged 74 years.
(Typed notes written by Dorothy Margaret Jenkin (nee Milner) for *A History of Neerim*, and held by her in March 1996).

473 Gunn, William Watkins - Power of Attorney from William Watkins Gunn to The Admiralty, 17 Oct 1928;, granted to Gunning Francis Plunkett Esq dated 17 October 1928 relating to claim against the Admiralty, prepared by Galbraith & Best, Australia House, Strand W.C.2.
This Power of Attorney is made by me William Watkins Gunn of Crossover in the State of Victoria in the Commonwealth of Australia Saw Miller at present temporarily residing at the Ardmay Hotel Woburn Place in the County of London the seventeenth day of October one thousand nine hundred and twenty eight,
Whereas
(1) I have a claim for Twenty five thousand pounds against the Commissioners for executing the office of Lord High Admiral of the United Kingdom of Great Britain and Ireland (hereinafter referred to as 'the Admiralty') in respect of an award or compensation due to me in relation to my having submitted to the Admiralty during the year 1915 a method or methods for destroying or attempting to destroy submarines which were duly adopted by the Admiralty with considerable success
(2) I have for some time past been in England with a view (inter alia) of prosecuting and obtaining a settlement of my said claim but am now compelled to return to Australia
Now this deed witnesseth that I the said William Watkins Gunn hereby appoint Gunning Francis Plunkett of Australia House Strand in the said County of London (hereinafter called 'the Attorney') my true and lawful Attorney for me and in my name to do and execute all the following acts deeds and things or any of them that is to say:-
1. To demand sue for and receive from the Admiralty or from such other body liable to pay the same the said sum of twenty five thousand pounds or such other sum for compensation or otherwise as I may be entitled to in respect of my said claim.
2. Upon payment of the same to give a good receipt or discharge for the same.
3. Upon non-payment of the said claim or any part thereof or of any interest due in respect thereof to commence and prosecute all actions and proceedings and use all other expedients for obtaining payment of the same or for damages or compensation in respect thereof or in respect of any express or implied warranty relating thereto or otherwise as fully and effectually to all intents and purposes whatsoever as I myself could have done if personally present and this deed had not been made.
To settle my said claim for such amount and upon such terms and subject to such conditions in all respects as the Attorney may in his absolute discretion think fit and to settle all accounts relating to the premises and refer to arbitration or compromise any disputes actions or proceedings concerning the same and to accept and give a good discharge for any securities or other property in or towards satisfaction of the same.

William Watkins Gunn

From time to time to appoint any Attorney or Attorneys under him for any of the purposes aforesaid.
And I the said William Watkins Gunn hereby agree at all times to ratify and confirm whatsoever the said Gunning Francis Plunkett or his said Attorney or Attorneys shall lawfully do or cause to be done in the premises by virtue of this Deed.
And I declare that the power hereby created shall be irrevocable for the space of one year from the date hereof.
In witness whereof I have hereto set my hand and seal the day and year first above written.
Sealed and Delivered by the said William Watkins Gunn in the presence of: - F. Maxwell Best Solicitor Australia House Strand London; National Archives of Australia 1919/89/676
(Shown on the following page) Letter from W W Gunn, Sawmiller, Crossover 29 September 1919 to Capt. the Hon. D Finch-Knightley, Military Secretary, Gov't House
Dear Sir,
As arranged I herewith enclose copy of plans for dealing with hostile submarines which I placed before his Excellency in April 1915 after getting the best possible expert opinion available as to its feasibility, I remain Yours Faithfully, W.W.Gunn.
Letter from Official Secretary to the Governor General to Mr W.W. Gunn, Crossover dated 18 October 1919
Dear Sir,
With reference to the representation recently submitted by you verbally, on the subject of the proposals which you made in 1915 for dealing with hostile submarines, I desire to inform you that your memoranda were brought to the notice of the Commonwealth Naval authorities who stated, in July 1915, that you had been informed that in the opinion of the Naval Board there was nothing in the proposals which was not perfectly well known.
I am communicating with the Navy Department in the matter. Yours faithfully.'

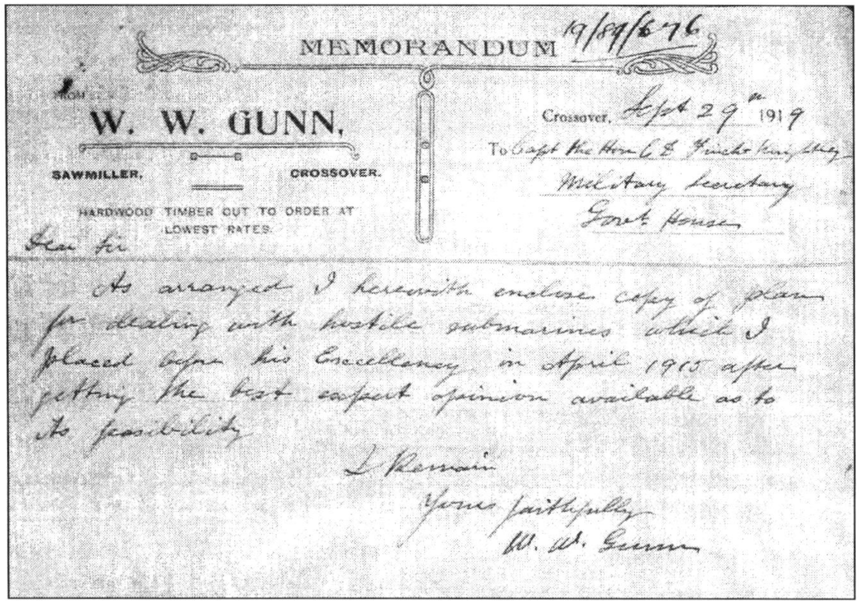
MEMORANDUM 19/89/876

From W. W. GUNN,
SAWMILLER. CROSSOVER.
HARDWOOD TIMBER CUT TO ORDER AT LOWEST RATES.

Crossover, Sept 29th 1919
To Capt the Hon C. E. [illegible]
Military Secretary
Govt House

Dear Sir

As arranged I herewith enclose copy of plan for dealing with hostile submarines which I placed before his Excellency in April 1915 after getting the best expert opinion available as to its feasibility.

I Remain
Yours faithfully
W. W. Gunn

W.W. Gunn's 1919 memorandum

William (33) took up saw milling in 1921 in Noojee, Vic.[474] [475]. He had a little local legal battle in July 1925 and won[476]. He was there when George McKenzie (3435) gave details of family genealogy to Marcus Daniel Gunn and himself both being part of the Scottish Delegation on 19 Jun 1928 in Wick Parish, Caithness.[477] He wrote to 'The Argus'[478] November 28 commending the use of hardwood cases for moving Australian apples as there was some suggestion about not using them; bad news for sawmillers! He has a personal history written by his son, John William Gunn.[479] He was interested in nature.[480] He is mentioned in *Neerim - A History*.[481] There is a Gunn Road at Crossover, presumably named after him (and / or his family).

---

474 Letter from Sylvia Bairsto to Donald Gunn, Dec 1996. Norman (Sylvia's father, Norman Gunn Padgett) worked for William Watkins Gunn at Noojee and it was from there that Norman first went to Borneo; John William Gunn.

475 http://newspapers.nla.gov.au/ndp/del/article/10523684 concerns one of WW Gunn's employees.

476 *The Argus* 23 July 1925 http://newspapers.nla.gov.au/ndp/del/article/2144683?searchTerm=Gunn

477 See Part 3. Note: It is clear that William & Marcus did not realise the change from the male to the female line with regards to the Chief of the Clan Gunn. This change has led to confusion, including the misdrawing of 'The Gunns' chart prepared after their return to Australia with copies held by many descendants. It shows all the named ancestors as being of the male line.

478 *The Argus* 30 November 1931, page 15.

479 John William Gunn, 'William Watkins Gunn – Jackaroo' on stations mainly around Ballarat eg Mt Eniur (?) and Creilaowne (?) then to Gippsland about 1888 to Bloomfield (now Nilma) timber milling with Amoss as partner. Dissolved partnership then to South of Darnum (Gainsborough).
Married Margaret Jane Balharrie.
Land boom burst about 1893 - banks closed. Found Crossover whilst on expedition for gold. Took a milling right at Crossover about 1895 or 6 - built 'Brawlbin.' Bushfires 1898, 1908. Took up Noojee milling about 1921-2. John William married Jessie Eileen Evans 1925. Burnt out 1926, 32, 39.
William brought first car to district about 1912.
Goldmine. Brother Donald went to Buchan with Ralph Milner mining - returns were good, while Ralph was in charge. Milner retired and McRae part manager and then Mackieson came in. The family members retired but WW carried on with Mackieson as manager. Quartz reef formation caolinore rich gold. Abandoned about 1917 - got down to sulphides named Mt Tara, turn right before going down to Buchan about 3-4 miles.'
(Held by Dorothy Margaret Jenkin (nee Milner) - Mar 1996).

480 See, for example http://newspapers.nla.gov.au/ndp/del/article/4108493?searchTerm=Gunn *The Argus,* 29 August 1930

481 Dorothy Hunt, *A History of Neerim.*

Margaret Jane BALHARRIE (42)[482] was born on 27 Dec 1860 in Blairgowrie, Perth, Tayside. She died on 16 May 1946 in Frankston, Vic, at age 85 from cancer. She was buried in Springvale, Vic. She arrived in Melbourne, Vic. in 1862.

Children of William Watkins Gunn (33) and Margaret Jane Balharrie (42) were:

i. John William GUNN (133) was born on 28 Feb 1895 in Lydiard St, Ballarat, Vic.[483] He was baptized on 30 Mar 1895 in Scots Church, Ballarat, Vic, register no. 26.[484] He married Jessie Eileen Evans (140) on 13 May 1925 in Vic. He died on 29 Oct 1981 in Frankston, Vic, at age 86 due to a heart issue—on the same day as his brother Marcus (136). John was an engine driver, single in 1917 in Crossover, Gippsland, Vic.[485] He began military service on 09 Nov 1917[486] in Melbourne, Vic, as a gunner, service number 39648, next of kin father, William W Gunn.[487] He was a saw miller. He began military service again on 17 March 1942 in Sale, Vic, service number V364815, next of kin Jessie Gunn.[488] He was discharged 9 October 1945 as a Lance Corporal.

Jessie Eileen EVANS (140) was born on 27 Feb 1895. She died on 03 Dec 1974 in S. Peninsula Hospital, Rosebud, Vic, at age 79. She was a school teacher (teacher record number probably being 18031).

ii. Jean Margaret GUNN (139) was born on 06 Apr 1896 in Lydiard St, Ballarat, Vic.[489] She was baptized on 04 May 1896 in Scots Church, Ballarat, Vic; Register number 50.[490] She married Harry Milner (137), son of Ralph Edwin Milner (1332) and Ellen Allinson (1333), on 19 Nov 1924 in Vic. She died on 30 Nov 1975 in Glenhuntly, Vic, at age 79 cancer. She was buried on 02 Dec 1975 in Springvale, Vic; cremated.

Harry MILNER (137) was born on 08 Nov 1891 in Buln Buln, Crossover, Vic.[491] He died on 13 Jan 1981 in Linacre Hospital, Hampton, Vic, at age 89.[492] He was cremated on 15 Jan 1981 in Springvale, Vic. He was a tram conductor, unmarried in 1915 in Buln Buln, Neerim South, Gippsland, Vic.[493] He began military service on 07 Apr 1915 in Liverpool, NSW, as a private,

---

482 *International Genealogical Index (IGI)*.

483 Register of BDMs - Victoria, 1895 567.

484 *Ballarat BDMs CD.*, CD-ROM).

485 The AIF Project.

486 The Australian Commonwealth Military Forces record reads: 'Regimental number 39648, Religion Presbyterian, Occupation Engine driver, Address Crossover, Gippsland, Victoria , Marital status Single, Age at embarkation 22, Next of kin Father, W W Gunn, Crossover, Gippsland, Victoria, Enlistment date 9 November 1917. Rank on enlistment Gunner, Unit name Field Artillery Brigade, Reinforcement 35, AWM Embarkation Roll number 13/128/2, Embarkation details Unit embarked from Sydney, New South Wales, on board SS Port Darwin on 30 April 1918, Rank from Nominal Roll Driver, Unit from Nominal Roll 6th Field Artillery Brigade, Fate Returned to Australia 23 September 1919'.

487 National Archives of Australia Series B2455, control symbol Gunn J W, barcode 4380048, born Ballarat; The AIF Project.

488 National Archives of Australia Series B884, barcode V364815, date of birth 28 Feb 1895, Ballarat.

489 Register of BDMs - Victoria, 1896 8449.

490 *Ballarat BDMs CD*.

491 Register of BDMs - Victoria, 1892 1689.

492 Register of BDMs - Victoria, 1981 01413.

493 The AIF Project.

next of kin mother, Mrs Ellen Milner, Crossover.[494] He served at Beersheba, Palestine, in 1917.

iii. Violet Helen GUNN (141) was born on 29 May 1898 in Warragul, Vic.[495] She married Reginald Thomas Wadeson (138) on 24 Apr 1924 in Vic. She died on 24 Aug 1968 in Frankston, Vic. at age 70 cancer.

Reginald Thomas WADESON (138) was born on 18 Jun 1897 in Diamond Creek, Vic.[496] He died on 21 Dec 1950 in Flinders Street Station, Melbourne, Vic, at age 53 of a heart attack.

iv. Edith Mary GUNN (134) was born on 13 Oct 1899 in Warragul, Vic.[497] She died on 16 Feb 1901 in Sandringham, Vic, at age 1 of diphtheria.[498]

v. Marjorie May GUNN (135) was born on 09 Apr 1904 in Warragul, Vic.[499] She died on 16 May 1970 in Launching Place, Vic, at age 66 of a heart attack.

vi. Marcus Allan GUNN (136) was born on 20 Jul 1906 in Brawlbin, Crossover, Vic.[500] He married Grace Frances Stephenson (142) on 18 Sep 1945 in St Paul's Cathedral, Melbourne, Vic. Licence for solemnization of marriage, no. 6297, she was born in about 1892. He died on 29 Oct 1981 in Alfred Hospital, Melbourne, Vic, at age 75 of pneumonia the same day as his brother John (133).[501] He was cremated in Springvale, Vic.[502] Grace Frances STEPHENSON (142) died in Apr 1980 in Vic.

27. Marcus Daniel GUNN[503] (36) was born on 11 May 1868 in Buninyong, Vic.[504] He married Mary Jane Chenhall (105), daughter of Nicholas Chenhall (864) and Mary J. Mills (865), on 19 May 1903 in Corowa, NSW.[505] He died on 01 Dec 1952 in South Yarra, Vic, at age 84.[506] He was present with his brother John (32) when anthrax ravaged sheep at the Station in 1888.[507] Marcus (36) was granted a licence to inoculate animals with anthrax vaccine in Aug 1894.[508] He was a temporary manager on Borambola station on 01 Apr 1902.[509] He was on the electoral roll with John Alexander Gunn (Hon.) (32) in 1903 in

---

494The AIF Project.

495Register of BDMs - Victoria, 1898 2271.

496Leoni Jenkin e-mail to Donald Gunn, 6 May 2005.

497Register of BDMs - Victoria, 1899 30631.

498Register of BDMs - Victoria, 1901 3553.

499Register of BDMs - Victoria, 1904 22056.

500Register of BDMs - Victoria, 1906 22996.

501Register of BDMs - Victoria, 1981 25078.

502*The Sun,* Melbourne, The funeral today will be private.

503See Part 3.

504Register of BDMs - Victoria, 1868 14645; "William Watkins Gunn."

505Letter or email from Ian M Gunn to Donald Gunn, Mar 1997; Register of BDMs - NSW, 1903 3446.

506*The Sun*, Wednesday 2 Dec 1953 'Mr M. Gunn, pioneer grazier, dies. Marcus Daniel Gunn of Walsh St, South Yarra, a pioneer pastoralist, died yesterday, aged 85. Mr Gunn was born at Mt Banningong Station, near Ballarat, in 1868. He contributed much to the pastoral industry. He and his brother Mr J.A. Gunn discovered and developed late last century the anti-anthrax vaccine still in use. He is survived by a daughter, Norma Caro and a son Keith Gunn. The funeral today will be private.'

507See Part 7. Rob Webster, *Bygoo and Beyond*, 'one day in 1888 Gunn and his brother, Marcus Daniel Gunn, rode to a paddock on Yalgogrin where they saw hundreds of carcases of dead sheep'.

508Letter from J. H. Todd (note Jan Todd's texts in the Bibliography) to Ian Marcus Gunn, 27 May 1990; '... your grandfather, Mark. He assisted John Gunn with the vaccinating work. By the way, did you know that he (Marcus) was granted a licence to inoculate animals with anthrax vaccine in August 1894?'

509See Part 7.

Borambola Station, NSW.[510] He was a station master.[511] He was present when George McKenzie (3435) gave details of family genealogy to William Watkins Gunn and Marcus Daniel Gunn of the Scottish Delegation on 19 Jun 1928 in Wick Parish, Caithness.[512]

Marcus Daniel Gunn

Mary CHENHALL (105)[513] was born on 08 Oct 1873 in Doma Mungi (aboriginal for 'Black Dog Creek') Chiltern, Vic.[514] She died in 1941 in Melbourne.[515]

510Electoral Roll: 1903 Roll lists John Alexander Gunn, Station Manager, Marcus Daniel Gunn, Station Manager, Norman Gunn, Licensed Vaccinator, Mary Jane Gunn, Domestic Duties and Jessie Marie Gunn, Domestic Duties as residing at Borambola Station.

511Ian M Gunn to Donald Gunn, Mar 1997.

512See Part 3. 'Genealogy given by McKenzie cousin to W.W. & M.D. Gunn, sons of Donald Gunn, June 19th 1928
Father
Donald Gunn born Brawlbin emigrated Australia, was at Burrumbeet. Died at Ballarat. Married Jane Surman.
Grandfather.
Alexander Gunn died Brawlbin married wife Gunn (Barbara).
Great Grandfather
Donald Gunn died at Brawlbin after leaving Braehour. ***[Barbara's line]***
Great Great Grandfather
John Gunn of Strathmore. ***[Barbara's line]***
Great Great Great Grandfather
Alexander Gunn of Strathmore ***[Barbara's line]***
Cousins
J D Nicholson, Minister of Strathpepper.
Alexander Gunn, Cape Wrath Land Steward Durness.
John & Alexander Miller of Wick, McKenzie, Wick
Sir John Gunn, Cardiff, brother Hector Gunn and cousin of Donald Gunn father as above.
Sir Oliver Lodge also related, probably through Cardiff Gunns.'

513Ian M. Gunn to Donald Gunn, Mar 1997.

514Register of BDMs - Victoria, 1873 22731.

515Letter or email from Jan Tracy to Donald Gunn, 20 Aug 2007.

Children of Marcus Daniel Gunn (36) and Mary Jane Chenhall (105) both born in Corowa, NSW, were as follows:

i. Keith Lindsay GUNN (121) was born in 1904.[516] He married Winifred Hardy (124), daughter of Charles Hardy (944) and Mary Alice Pownell (945), in 1939 in Vic. He died on 10 Aug 1967 in Melbourne, Vic.[517]

Winifred HARDY (124) was born on 13 Jun 1905 in Wagga Wagga, NSW. She died on 09 Jun 1984 in Healesville, Vic, at age 78.

ii. Norma Mary GUNN (125) was born on 16 Apr 1907.[518] She married Harvard Wendall Wilkinson (122) in Vic. She married George Alfred Caro (123), son of Maximilian Caro (701) and Esther Margaret Gollin (702), in 1945 in Melbourne, Vic.[519] They went on a major cruise in 1950 visiting the USA, England, South Africa and Kenya (at least). She died in Jul 1971 in Melbourne, Vic, at age 64.[520]

Harvard Wendall WILKINSON (122) died in 1962.

George Alfred CARO (123) was born on 10 May 1893 in Vic.[521] He married Alice Lilian May (871) in 1920.[522] He died in Feb 1971 in Melbourne, Vic, aged 77.[523]

28. Barbara GUNN (106) was born on 20 Jun 1870 in Burrumbeet, Vic.[524] She married Isaac Padgett (103), son of George Padgett (2330) and Martha Turner (2331), on 29 Mar 1899 at 185 Lydiard St, Ballarat, Vic.[525] She died on 17 Jul 1941 in Braemore, Werribee, Vic, at age 71.[526] She was a schoolteacher in 1898 in Mount Cole, Vic.[527] She was a schoolteacher and post mistress between 1900 and 1930 in Vic. She was given a valedictory on leaving circa 1905 in Mount Cole, Vic.[528] Barbara and Isaac Padgett lived at Braemore, Werribee South, Victoria from some time after their marriage until their deaths.[529]

---

516 Ian M. Gunn to Donald Gunn, Mar 1997 and 27 Feb 2005 and for much further information on this page; Register of BDMs - NSW, 1904 21523.

517 Ian M. Gunn to Donald Gunn, Family Group sheet Apr 1999.

518 Register of BDMs - NSW, 1907 12761.

519 Jan Tracy to Donald Gunn, 20 Aug 2007.

520 Register of BDMs - Victoria, 1971 18190; Jan Tracy to Donald Gunn, 20 Aug 2007.

521 Register of BDMs - Victoria, 1893 24158X1922; Jan Tracy to Donald Gunn, 20 Aug 2007.

522 Register of BDMs - Victoria, 1920 14780.

523 Register of BDMs - Victoria, 1971 2912; Jan Tracy to Donald Gunn, 20 Aug 2007.

524 Register of BDMs - Victoria, 1870 14268.

525 Register of BDMs - Victoria, 1899 983.

526 *Unknown newspaper*, 'On 17 July, at her residence, Braemore, Duncans Road, Werribee South, Barbara, the dearly beloved wife of the late Isaac Padgett, and loving mother of Barbara (Mrs Bence), Norman, and Jean (Mrs Gilmour) aged 71 years - mother and father reunited.
On 17 July, at her residence, Braemore, Werribee South, Barbara, relict of the late Isaac Padgett, loved mother of Barbara (Mrs Bence) Norman, and Jean (Mrs Gilmour), and loved sister of M.D., Norman and Catherine Gunn.'

527 Letter, Sylvia Bairsto to Donald Gunn, Dec 1996; 'Barbara and Isaac Padgett lived at Braemore, Werribee South, Victoria from some time after their marriage until their deaths. Son Norman (1903-1952) bought the house and farm from the estate. His family lived there through the war until selling the property in 1947. Barbara was a schoolteacher (& as such had the secondary task - unpaid - of Post Mistress) at Mount Cole before marriage. Also at Point Arlington (Portarlington) as school teacher. Isaac - dairy farmer with pure bred Friesan cattle. Grand-daughter Sylvia was born in Wellington NZ when parents were taking delivery of a bull (Ferdinand Prince Domino) for her grandfather Isaac. Later grandson Arthur Bence (1926-1994), dairy farmer, had progeny from his herd.'

528 *Unknown newspaper*, '1st July [Probably about 1905 - DG 7/97] On Thursday evening last, in the local Hall, a valedictory social was tendered to Mr & Mrs Isaac Padgett, who are leaving this district for their new home at Cressy.
The hall was tastefully decorated with ferns, heath and wattle blossom, and a large number of local residents gathered to wish Mr & Mrs Padgett au revoir.

Isaac PADGETT (103)[530] was born in 1867 in Mount Cole[531], Vic.[532] He died on 30 Sep 1937 in Braemore, Werribee, Vic.[533]

Barbara Padgett (nee Gunn) and family c.1924

Mr Padgett had for many years been our church organist, and his place will be very difficult to fill.
Mr J Tait, as chairman, spoke in the highest terms of Mr Padgett, and his words faithfully expressed the sentiments of all present. Geo. Gordon also in a very humorous speech endorsed Mr Tait's remarks, but said that the one thing against Mr Padgett, inasmuch as he had done the younger part of the population of Mount Cole an irreparable injury, by taking from them their painstaking and popular school teacher, but he would forgive him. He had much pleasure, on behalf of their numerous friends, in presenting Mrs Padgett with a small token of their regard, in the shape of a very handsome hot water kettle. ....Mrs Padgett kindly acted as accompanist (to a programme of songs and recitations) in her usual efficient manner.'

529 Letter, Sylvia Bairsto to Donald Gunn, Dec 1996.

530 Letter from Margaret Bence to Donald Gunn, 17 Aug 2005.

531 Isaac had siblings (William b. Warrenheip, 1856-1921, George b. Ballarat 1858-1865, Louisa Curson b Ararat 1861, John b. Mt Cole 1863, Emily b. Mount Cole 1865, Amy Sarah b. Ararat 1870, Samuel George b. 1872 Herbert Charles b. Warrak 1875-1949, Mark Joseph 1878-1949 and James Arthur 1880-1961. The father was George Padgett who married Martha Turner in 1855 in Vic, both buried at Warrak, Mt. Cole. George probably came from Wisbeach (Wisbech St Peters Norfolk?) in England. He had title to various blocks of land at Warrak.
See http://www.rootschat.com/forum/index.php?topic=485998.msg3442395;topicseen for a fuller discussion or *Mt. Cole – Warrak. A history and its people* compiled by M. Beattie and B. Shalders, 1990.

532 Letter, Margaret Bence to Donald Gunn, 17 Aug 2005.

533 *Unknown newspaper*, 'On the 30th September, 1937 (suddenly) at Braemore, Werribee, Isaac, loved husband of Barbara, and loving father of Barbara, Norman and Jean.'

Children of Barbara Gunn (106) and Isaac Padgett (103) were as follows:

i. Barbara Gunn PADGETT (184) was born in 1901 in Ballarat, Vic.[534] She married Ernest Arthur Bence (181), son of Richard Bence (381) and Lena Churchill (382) on 11 Apr 1925 in Vic[535]. She married Reginald Clarence Austin (182) in Vic. She died on 19 Jul 1960.[536]

Ernest Arthur BENCE (181) was born on 09 Nov 1900 in Bombay. He married Olga Maud Gillespie (2334) after 1928.[537] He was a horse trainer[538] and artist. He died in 1961.

ii. Norman Gunn PADGETT (180) was born on 01 Dec 1903 in Ballarat East, Vic.[539] In 1928 Norman went by ship from Hong Kong to Canada; he had already spent some time as a 'lumberman' in Borneo.[540] He married Marjorie Rosina Minchin (185), daughter of Corker Wright Minchin (442) and Florence Carpenter (443), on 13 Feb 1932 in Punt Rd Presbyterian Church, South Yarra, Vic.[541] In January 1939 he was a part-owner of a sawmill at Narbethong[542]. He died on 10 Dec 1952 at St Clair Station, Princhester, Qld, at age 49.[543] He was buried on 15 Dec 1952 in Rockhampton, Qld. He competed at Victorian Amateur Boxing and Wrestling Championships circa 1922 in Wirths' Olympia, Melbourne, Vic.[544] He began military service on 09 Aug 1943 in Melbourne, Vic, in the RAAF, Service No. 408148, next of kin Marjorie Padgett.[545] He ended military service on 02 Jan 1946 in Station HQ, Laverton, Vic, as a Flying Officer having being awarded the Air Force Medal. He had an interesting history working in Sarawak and North

---

534Register of BDMs - Victoria, 1901 24234.

535 Barbara Gunn Bence was divorced from Ernest Arthur Bence on the grounds of desertion reported in 'The Argus' 11 February 1939.

536 http://newspapers.nla.gov.au/ndp/del/printArticlePdf/12096145/3?print=n

537Letter, Margaret Bence to Donald Gunn, 17 Aug 2005.

538Known personally by Margaret Bence, 11 May 2005.

539*Nominal Roll WW2.*

540Canadian Passenger Lists 1865-1935, 'Empress of Russia' 22 January 1928.

541*Unknown newspaper*, 'On the 13th February, 1932, at Presbyterian Church, Punt Road, South Yarra, by the Rev. H Douglas Fearon, Marjorie Rosina, third daughter of Mr and Mrs F.J.C. Minchin, Korumburra, to Norman Gunn, only son of Mr and Mrs I Padgett, Braemore, Werribee.'

542http://newspapers.nla.gov.au/ndp/del/article/17633327?searchTerm=Gunn for the September 1 1939 newspaper report of the Coroner's finding.. http://newspapers.nla.gov.au/ndp/del/article/17600899?searchTerm=Gunn for a second report which suggests Norman Gunn Padgett was sole owner. And *The Sydney Morning Herald* 30 August 1939, page 15 and the SMH of 1 September 1939 suggests some 'interesting' aspects as to the cause of the fire. Also http://newspapers.nla.gov.au/ndp/del/article/11259427?searchTerm=Gunn

543*Unknown newspaper*, 'On 10 December (result of accident), St Clair, Rockhampton, loved husband of Marjorie, father of Sylvia, Judy and Jan, loved brother of Barbara and Jean.'

544*Unknown newspaper*, Undated; 'Victorian Amateur Championships The second series of the boxing and wrestling championships was held at Wirths' Olympia last night. Senator Walter Kingsmill presided. There were some excellent contests, particularly in the wrestling bouts. ...... Middles: W.Padgett (11.0) and P.Nelson (11.3), two magnificent specimens of Australian youth provided a stirring go. Padgett got a bar-hold at 7 minutes, and refusing to release lost his position. He won, however, comfortably. Middleweight:- F.Greatorese, 10.12, St Kilda, v MG Padgett, 11.4, Werribee. Padgett sent his opponent to the mat and applied a scissors hold, but found Greatorese too smart when down. Padgett was the aggressor, but was bleeding from the nose. Greatorese almost gained a fall with a headlock, but Padgett stood the strain and escaped. Honors were fairly even, with Padgett showing most strength. At the end of 10 minutes the verdict was a tie on points, with an order for five minutes' more wrestling. Padgett brought his opponent down with a headlock, but could not retain his hold. Greatorese was too smart on the mat. Both wrestlers were laughing during the last few minutes. Padgett then applied a scissors hold, and followed with an armlock, and secured a fall half a minute before the extra five minutes expired and won the match.'

545*Nominal Roll WW2*; National Archives of Australia RAAF service no. 408148.

Borneo.[546] In November 1952 it was reported that 'Indonesian authorities at Sourabaya are holding a 35 ft luxury yacht valued at £9,000 owned by a Queensland grazier. The owner, Mr Norman Gunn Padget 43, of St Clair Station near Rockhampton, returned to Australia by air...'[547] He died when clearing a runway for his plane to land on his property; he had flown it from Singapore to take over the property six weeks after his yacht had been seized. A burning tree fell on him.[548] He may have owned an aeroplane in New Guinea[549] 1942-1944.

Marjorie Rosina MINCHIN (185) was born on 31 Aug 1905 in WA. She died in 1999.

iii. Jean Gunn PADGETT (186) was born on 15 Jul 1913 in Vic. She married William Frederick Gilmour (Rev.) (183), son of Hugh Bicket Gilmour (588) and Hannah Cock (2969), on 17 Nov 1937 in St Thomas Presbyterian Church, Werribee, Vic.[550] She died on 25 Feb 2002 at age 88.[551] She was a school teacher.

William Frederick GILMOUR (Rev.) (183) was born on 12 Feb 1905 in Brunswick, Vic.[552] He died on 08 Oct 1996 in Geelong, Vic, at age 91.[553] He was appointed a Presbyterian Minister in 1947 for Red Cliffs, Vic [554] followed by the Minister for Surrey Hills, Vic. in 1957 and then the Minister for Coleraine, Vic. in 1961 and finally for South Yarra, Vic. in 1970.

29. Arthur Gilbert GUNN (9) was born on 19 May 1878 in Burrumbeet, Vic.[555] He married Louisa Maud Miriam Retallick (10), daughter of Edgar Retallick (100) and Louisa Miriam Hore (102), on 03 Dec 1901 in Scots Church, Lydiard St, Ballarat, Vic.[556] He died on 18 Jun 1933 in Ivanhoe, Vic, at age 55[557] and was buried on 20 Jun 1933 in Brighton cemetery, Vic. He

---

546 Letter, Sylvia Bairsto to Donald Gunn, 23 Jan 1997: 'Norman was timber miller, grazier, pilot, sea captain, engineer, etc, etc. Norman worked for William Watkins Gunn (1861-1935) at Noojee and it was from there that Norman went to Borneo (first time - he was there twice). Worked for North Borneo Timber and Trading Co on the Kinabatangan River, North Borneo. After the war Norman had a timber business based on the Baram River, Sarawak. Ed and I visited Noojee early this year and found the old railway line that served the mill. Also met (casually) a man who'd known of the Gunns and found the crossing (of river) where the road went in to the mill. I'll be looking at material held on a nearby farm (Stephen found when on holiday) I think photos, paper cuttings etc when next in Melbourne.'

547 *Sydney Morning Herald,* 17 November 1952, page 3. http://newspapers.nla.gov.au/ndp/del/search?searchTerm=Gunn&textSearchScope=full&startFrom=6500

548 *Rockhampton Morning Bulletin*, 11 December 1952, page 4.

549 http://trove.nla.gov.au/work/13569392?q=+padgett&c=picture

550 *Unknown newspaper*, 'On the 17th November, 1937, at St Thomas's Presbyterian Church, Werribee, by Rev. P W Turner and Rev. K C Wood, William Frederick, younger son of Mr and Mrs H B Gilmour, Sunbury, to Jean Gunn, younger daughter of Mrs Padgett and the late Mr I Padgett, Braemore, Werribee.'

551 Margaret Bence, 11 May 2005; Letter, Margaret Bence to Donald Gunn, 17 Aug 2005; Letter or email, Dougal Gilmour to Donald Gunn, 05 Mar 2008.

552 Register of BDMs - Victoria, 1905 1176 - father, Hugh Bicket Gilmour, mother Hannah Cock.

553 Letter or email, Dougal Gilmour to Donald Gunn, 27 May 2005.

554 *Index of Presbyterian Ministers in Victoria 1859-1977* Synod Archives, Victoria 1993, 1905, born at Ormond College; 1939, ordained; 1940, Chaplain RAAF;1947 Redcliffe; 1957, Surrey Hills; 1961 Coleraine; 1970 South Yarra.

555 Register of BDMs - Victoria, 1878 7226.

556 Register of BDMs - Victoria, 1901 7407; Certificate of Marriage, Scots Church Register No. 114 - Arthur Gilbert Gunn, 23, Warehouseman, of Clarendon Street, Ballarat, born Burrumbeet, and Louisa Maud Miriam Retallick, 26, Spinster, of Campbells Crescent, Ballarat, born Naseby, New Zealand, at Scots Church, Ballarat. Witnesses Alice Louisa Pascoe and Paul Hore.

557 *Unknown newspaper*, 'on the 18th June (suddenly), at Ivanhoe, Arthur Gilbert, dearly beloved husband of Louisa Maud Gunn, and beloved father of Malcolm, Kenneth, Angus, and Collier (deceased), late of Ballarat; Certificate of Death: 1933 4607: 18th June 1933 at Kenilworth Private Hospital, Kenilworth Parade, Ivanhoe, Shire of Heidelberg, Arthur Gilbert Gunn,

was a commercial traveller.[558] He was a warehouseman on 03 Jan 1905 in Kalgoorlie, WA, and a business manager in Jan 1916 in Ballarat, Vic.[559]

Louisa Maud Miriam RETALLICK (10)[560] was born on 21 Nov 1875 in Naseby, Otago. She was christened on 07 Jan 1877 in St George's Church, Naseby, Otago. She died on 13 Nov 1959 in Elsternwick, Vic, at age 83 and was buried in Brighton cemetery, Vic.

Arthur Gilbert Gunn and family c. 1913 / 1914

Children of Arthur Gilbert Gunn (9) and Louisa Maud Miriam Retallick (10) were as follows:

i. Malcolm Donald GUNN (11) was born on 22 Mar 1903 in Ballarat, Vic.[561] He married Audrey Marley Tyers (13), daughter of Alexander Mackenzie Tyers (15) and Mary Jane Johnston (14), on 07 Jun 1930 in the Presbyterian

---

Commercial Traveller, age 55 years, of coronary thrombosis, 1st attack 2 years ago, cardiac failure, father Donald Gunn, farmer, mother Jane Gunn formerly Surman, buried 20th June 1933 at Brighton Cemetery. Born Ballarat, 43 years in Victoria, 12 years in Western Australia. Married at age 24 years to Louisa Maud Retallack; children Malcolm Donald, 30 years, Kenneth Douglas, 28 years, Angus Norman, 21 years, Collier (Colin?), deceased.'

558Electoral Roll: Arthur Gilbert Gunn, Traveller, 85 Lyon Street South; Louisa Maud Marion Gunn, Home Duties, 85 Lyon Street South.

559Certificate of Death: of son Colin.

560Certificate of Baptism: No.89: born Nov 21st 1875, baptised Jan 7th 1877, child Louisa Maud Miriam Retallick, parents Edgar & Louisa, abode Naseby, trade miner, sponsors James Hore, Silas Hore & mother.

561Register of BDMs - Victoria, 1903 7705.

Church, Canterbury, Vic.[562] He died on 26 Oct 1961 in the Austin Hospital, Heidelberg, Vic, at age 58.[563] He was cremated in Vic.

He was educated on 20 Apr 1916 in Ballarat, Vic; Primary School Junior Swimming Certificate. He was awarded a silver medallion engraved on front MDG, on back Champion Cadet Team, 1917 M.D. Gunn. He was educated on 16 Mar 1918 in Pleasant Street School, Ballarat, Vic; Secondary School Merit Certificate. He was educated in Dec 1918 at Ballarat College, Ballarat, Vic; Secondary School School prizes 1st chemistry, eq 2nd algebra, 2nd history. He was a bank official following payment of 'the sum of Ten Pounds, being amount of deposit in terms of Probationer's Agreement' on 27 Sep 1920 in Commercial Bank of Australia Ltd, Melbourne, Vic. On 11 Mar 1924 Malcolm foiled a theft of cash from the ticket box in his charge at a local race meeting at Bunyip, Vic by chasing robbers with a drawn revolver.[564] He was later the bank manager at Kew, Swan Hill and Dandenong in Vic.

Malcolm Donald Gunn, 1933 and 1956

Audrey Marley TYERS (13)[565] was born on 12 Mar 1900 in Bendigo, Vic.[566] She died on 18 Apr 1984 in East Ringwood, Vic, at age 84.[567] She

---

562Certificate of Marriage, Malcolm Donald Gunn, Bank Officer age 27, Bachelor, born Ballarat, residence Bambra Road, Caulfield, father Arthur Gilbert Gunn, Traveller, mother Louisa Maud Miriam Retallick, married Audrey Marley Tyers, Clerk age 30, Spinster, born Bendigo, residence Burwood Avenue, Upper Hawthorn, father Alexander McKenzie Tyers, Civil Engineer, mother Mary Jane Johnston, on 7 June 1930 at the Presbyterian Church, Canterbury according to the forms of the Presbyterian Church of Australia.

563Register of BDMs - Victoria, 1961 20080.

564*The Argus* 29 April 1924 page 4; 'Peace and harmony which prevailed at a Bunyip (Victoria) race meeting were suddenly interrupted by cries of "robbery" and the spectacle of a man 6ft. 2in. in height waving a revolver in the air. The man with the revolver was Malcolm Gunn, a clerk employed by Commercial Bank at Bunyip. He had been sent to take charge of the tickets and the money, and while he was out of the ticket office for a few minutes the money was taken...'

565Bible of Mary Jane Tyers nee Johnston.

566Register of BDMs - Victoria, 1900 8588; Bible of Mary Jane Tyers.

was cremated in Springvale Crematorium, Vic. A photo of the staff of the Head Office of the Commercial Bank of Australia in Melbourne includes Audrey; it was taken on 27 Jun 1922. She was a clerk in 1924.[568] Report of the wedding was in *The Sun News-Pictorial* on 09 Jun 1930.[569]

ii. Kenneth Douglas GUNN (23) was born on 03 Jan 1905 in Kalgoorlie, WA.[570] He married Mary Fraser Staveley (46), daughter of William Stavely (663) and Emily Edith Richards (664), on 15 Nov 1932 in Holy Trinity C of E, Yackandandah, Vic; Register 1932 32.[571] He died on 30 Jul 1951 in Longreach, Qld.[572] He was buried on 03 Aug 1951 in Rockhampton, Qld; cremated. He was educated between 1915 and 1918; Pleasant Street, Ballarat.[573] He was educated in 1919; Ballarat College.[574] He was a bank manager. He began military service on 08 Jul 1940 in Caulfield, Vic, army, service number VX26787, next of kin Mary Fraser Gunn.[575] He ended military service on 06 Oct 1945 in AAPC-CPM SEC (ME) as a sergeant after total service of 1917 days, of which 792 were in Australia and 1040 overseas.[576]

---

567 Register of BDMs - Victoria, 1984 8827.

568 Electoral Roll.

569 *The Sun*, Gunn - Tyers Evening Wedding at Canterbury Presbyterian Church on Saturday, at 7 pm, the marriage of Malcom Donald Gunn and Audrey Marley Tyers was solemnised by Rev. J.A.Forrest. The church had been prettily decorated with pink flowers and asparagus fern by friends. The bride is the third daughter of Mr and Mrs A.Mackenzie Tyers, Jancourt, Burwood Avenue, Upper Hawthorn, and the bridegroom is the eldest son of Mr and Mrs Arthur Gunn, Bambra Road, Caulfield. Mr Tyers gave his daughter away.
During the signing of the register, a solo was sung by Mrs A.W. Nicholls.
Parchment tinted triple Georgette and lace formed the graceful frock worn by the bride. It almost touched the ground. A beautiful Brussels lace veil (lent by Mrs W.B. Montgomery) was mounted over tulle, and confined by orange blossom. Her bouquet was of white azaleas and maiden hair fern. Misses Gean and Joyce Tyers, as bridesmaids, wore floral poult de sole frocks, the first being in pale blue and the second in a soft shade of gold. They were made with tight-fitting bodices, and circular skirts, which fell to the ankles in uneven lines. Hats of felt to match were worn, and they carried baskets filled with flowers to tone, one being filled with pink carnations and blue delphiniums, and the other in golden yellow and orange tonings.
Mr Donald Robinson was best man, and Mr Angus Gunn (brother) the groomsman.
After the ceremony the bride's parents entertained 50 guests in their home, which was bright with flowers. Mrs Tyers wore a gown of black crepe satin, with a wrap of black moire silk and fur, and toque of Oriental ring velvet and gold tissue. Her bouquet was of Duchess of York pansies. The bridegroom's mother wore black ring velvet under her wrap of dahlia-red velvet and sable fur. Her toque was of black tulle, and her bouquet of deep pink carnations.'

570 Register of BDMs - Western Australia, 1905 1627 (or 1905 20094?); National Archives of Australia Series B883, control symbol VX26787, barcode 6227284, date of birth 03 Jan 1905, Kalgoorlie.

571 Certificate of Marriage, Kenneth Douglas Gunn, Bank Official, 27 Bachelor, born Kalgoorlie, resident at Yackandandah, WA, father Arthur Gilbert Gunn, Retired Traveller, mother Louisa Maud Miriam Retallick, married Mary Fraser Stavely, Home Duties, 27, Spinster, born Wangaratta, resident Yackandandah, father William Stavely, Station Master, mother Emily Edith Richards, according to the Rites of the Church of England.

572 Inquest, 23 Aug 1951 Longreach, Coroner P T Noone.

573 *Consolidated Index to Ballarat & District School Student Registers*, Pleasant Street - Kenneth Douglas Gunn, DOB 3 Jan 1905, No. in register 298/2086.

574 *History of Ballarat College 1864-1964*, College Register 1919 K D Gunn.

575 National Archives of Australia Series B883, control symbol VX26787, barcode 6227284; *Nominal Roll WW2*, Date of enlistment 8 Jul 1940, Caulfield, SN VX26787.

576 *Nominal Roll WW2*. We cannot make the days add up.

Kenneth Douglas Gunn 1940

Mary Fraser STAVELEY (46) was born on 01 Mar 1905 in Wangaratta, Vic. She died on 16 Dec 1966 in Heidelberg, Vic, at age 61.[577] She was cremated in Springvale, Vic.

iii. Angus Norman GUNN (24) was born on 15 Apr 1912 in the Hospital, Egan Street, Kalgoorlie, WA.[578] He married Jeanette Lottie Paton (51), daughter of Hugh Paton (472) and Ellen Lottie Davis (473), on 06 Mar 1937 in the Trinity Presbyterian Church, Camberwell, Vic.[579] He died on 26 Mar 1994 in Sutherland District Hospital, Caringbah, NSW, at age 81[580] and was buried on 29 Mar 1994 in Woronora Crematorium, Sutherland, NSW; former Australian Prime Minister Gough Whitlam was among the mourners.[581] He was a pharmacist. He was educated circa 1920 in Pleasant Street School, Ballarat, Vic.[582] He was educated in 1925 in Ballarat College, Ballarat, Vic.[583] He witnessed the marriage of Malcolm Donald Gunn (11) and Audrey Marley Tyers (13) on 07 Jun 1930 in the Presbyterian Church, Canterbury, Vic.[584]

577Register of BDMs - Victoria, 1967 497.

578Register of BDMs - Western Australia, 1912 6546; Certificate of Birth: 1912 6546: 15 April 1912, in the East Coolgardie District of Western Australia, Angus Norman Gunn, father Arthur Gilbert Gunn, Manager, age 34 born Burrumbeet, residing at Ward Street, Kalgoorlie, married Louisa Maud Miriam Retallick, age 36 born Naseby New Zealand, on 3 December 1901 at Ballarat.

579Certificate of Marriage, Trinity Presbyterian Church, Riversdale Road, Camberwell, reg A247.

580*Sydney Morning Herald*, 28 Mar 1994, 'Gunn, Angus Norman, 26 Mar 1994 at Sutherland Hospital late of Cronulla, dearly loved husband of Jeanette, loved father of Valerie, Coralie and Kenneth, cherished grandpop to his 10 grandchildren and 1 great grandchild'; Certificate of Death: NSW 1994 10745.

581*Sydney Morning Herald*, 28 Mar 1994, 'the relatives and friends of the late Angus Norman Gunn of Cronulla are invited to attend his funeral service to be conducted in the West Chapel of the Woronora Crematorium today (Tuesday 29 Mar 1984) at 11 am.'

582*Ballarat Student Registers*, Angus Gunn DOB 15 Apr 1912 School Pleasant Street No.in register 1121.

583W.G. Mein, *History of Ballarat College*, 1925 A. N. Gunn.

584Certificate of Marriage, Malcolm Donald Gunn, Bank Officer age 27, Bachelor, born Ballarat, residence Bambra Road, Caulfield, father Arthur Gilbert Gunn, Traveller, mother Louisa Maud Miriam Retallick, married Audrey Marley Tyers, Clerk age 30, Spinster, born Bendigo, residence Burwood Avenue, Upper Hawthorn, father Alexander McKenzie Tyers, Civil Engineer, mother Mary Jane Johnston, on 7 June 1930 at the Presbyterian Church, Canterbury according to the forms of the Presbyterian Church of Australia.

Angus Norman Gunn 1930

Jeanette Lottie PATON (51) was born on 05 Oct 1912 at home, 89 Broadway, Camberwell, Vic.[585] She died on 21 Jun 1998 in Bethany Nursing Home, Port Macquarie, NSW, at age 85.[586] She was cremated at Woronora Crematorium, Sutherland, NSW on 26 Jun 1998.

iv. Colin GUNN (29) was born on Sep 1915 in Ballarat, Vic [587] and died on 18 Jan 1916 in Doveton Street, Ballarat, Vic.[588] He was buried on 19 Jan 1916 in Old Cemetery Area DN Sec.14 Lot 5, Ballarat, Vic.[589]

30. John Daniel SURMAN (272) was born in 1866 in Cardigan, Vic.[590] He married Margaret Cowley (1553) in 1895. He died in 1935 in Dunolly, Vic.[591] He may have been a dentist[592] (a John Daniel Surman is registered as a dentist in Victoria in 1907 with an address of 18 Carlton Street Carlton. The 1903 and 1909 electoral rolls list John Daniel Surman a dentist, living by himself; which suggests a marital split).

Margaret COWLEY (1553) was born in 1866. She died on 17 Jul 1951 in Geelong, Vic.[593]

---

585 Certificate of Birth: Victoria 1912 26307.

586 *Sydney Morning Herald*, 23 June 1998; Certificate of Death: NSW 1998 20964.

587 Register of BDMs - Victoria, 1915 18328; Certificate of Death: Victoria, 1916 166 aged 4 months, suddenly from exhaustion and heart failure following three days of gastro-enteritis.

588 *Unknown newspaper*, gives name as Collier; both birth and death certificates, Colin. 'Collier (assumed to be an editing error); Certificate of Death: Victoria, 1916 166 aged 4 months, suddenly from exhaustion and heart failure following three days of gastro-enteritis, father Arthur Gilbert Gunn, Business Manager, mother Louisa Maud Miriam Gunn nee Retallack.'

589 Ballarat Old Cemetery records; Certificate of Death: buried 19 January at Ballarat Old Cemetery.

590 Judy Meyer, 02 Aug 2004 and much further information on this page.

591 Register of BDMs - Victoria, 1935 18026.

592 http://gazette.slv.vic.gov.au/images/1907/V/general/14.pdf

593 In the 1919 electoral roll both she and her daughter Jessie Marguerite Surman (1554) were recorded at 86 Western Beach Geelong; the mother with 'home duties' and the daughter was a 'dress maker' and they were still there with the same duties in 1924 and 1931. A Margaret Surman was 'home duties' in Geelong in Victoria Terrace in 1902 (being the only Surman); she was at Western Beach in 1914. By 1936 only Margaret Surman was at 49 The Esplanade suggesting her daughter was married by then. In 1942 she was at 38 Alexandra Avenue, Corio.

Children of John Daniel Surman (272) and Margaret Cowley (1553) were as follows:

i. Jessie Marguerite SURMAN (1554) was born in 1896 in Armadale, Vic. She married Gustav Adolf Paul Danier[594] (2866) before 1936 (probably in 1935); they lived at 49 The Esplanade. He worked for the Harbour Trust. They lived at 56 Church Street Corio Geelong in 1942. By 1949 he was a proprietor and they still lived at the same address. This was still the case in 1954.[595] Jessie died in 1955 in Geelong, Vic.

ii. Thomas William SURMAN (1555) was born in 1899 in Carlton, Vic. He died in 1965 in Melbourne, Vic.

31. Alexander Gunn SURMAN (273) was born in 1868 in Ballarat, Vic.[596] He married Esther Kirk (676) on 16 Sep 1891 in Vic.[597] He died in Dec 1909 in Ballarat.[598] and was buried on 31 Dec 1909 in New Cemetery, Ballarat.[599] He was a farmer.

Esther KIRK[600] (676) was born in 1864.[601] She died on 11 Mar 1938 in Cardigan, Vic.[602]

Children of Alexander Gunn Surman (273) and Esther Kirk (676) were as follows:

i. Jessie Beatrice SURMAN[603] (680) was born in 1892 in Ballarat, Vic.[604] She married William George Nathaniel Stephens (1556) in 1915. She died in 1954 in Caulfield, Vic.

ii. Linda Pearl SURMAN[605] (682) was born on 18 Sep 1893 in Ballarat, Vic.[606] She married W. G. Johnson. She was the postmistress at Cardigan in 1950.

iii. Eric SURMAN[607] (683) was born on 17 Feb 1895 in Haddon, nr Ballarat, Vic.[608] He married Annie Walton (1557). He died on 11 Jan 1959 in Ballarat, Vic, at age 63. He was a farmer in 1915. He began military service on 17 Feb 1915 in Ballarat, Vic, in B Coy 23rd Battalion[609] and ended military service on 23 Mar 1919 after 1361 days overseas.

---

594 The Electoral Rolls vary the sequences of both sets of first names; in the 1937 he is down as 'Gustavo'.

595 Judy Meyer; further details from the Electoral Rolls of the time.

596 Register of BDMs - Victoria, 1868 819.

597 Register of BDMs - Victoria, 1891 5725; Judy Meyer, 02 Aug 2004.

598 Register of BDMs - Victoria, 1909 11179.

599 Ballarat Old Cemetery records: Area Presbyterian, Section 7 Lot 40.

600 Esther and Stella Surman (681) are recorded as living at Cardigan with Home Duties in the 1919 electoral roll.

601 Judy Meyer, 02 Aug 2004 and for other information on this page.

602 http://newspapers.nla.gov.au/ndp/del/article/11155279?searchTerm=Adelaide+Hazel+Kelson

603 Recorded as a saleswoman at 105 Drummond Street Carlton in the 1914 electoral roll.

604 Register of BDMs - Victoria, 1892 19447.

605 Recorded at Gardenia Road Elsternwick with 'home duties' in the 1919 Electoral roll.

606 Register of BDMs - Victoria, 1893 28456.

607 Erica and Annie were recorded at Wunghnu (near Numurkah Vic) in the 1924 electoral roll. He was a farmer, she with home duties. In the 1931, 1936, 1937, 1942, 1949 and 1954 electoral rolls Eric and Annie were at 11 Webster Street Ballarat, he was a railway employee, she with home duties.

608 Register of BDMs - Victoria, 1895 3948; National Archives of Australia Series No. V361080.

609 *Attestation paper*, farmer, age 20 years, NOK Esther Surman, mother.

E. SURMAN
Tree No. 201

Eric Surman was born at Cardigan and educated at the Cardigan State School. He enlisted on 17th February, 1915, at the age of 20 years, at this time he was farming.
He sailed on the "Southland" for England as a member of the 23rd Battalion, he served in Egypt and France. During service in Flanders he was severely gassed and was evacuated to a hospital in England. After service abroad for 1361 days he returned to Australia on 14th December, 1918, and was discharged on 23rd March, 1919.

From Duty Nobly Done by the Learmonth & District Historical Society, used with permission.

Studio portrait of 902 Private (Pte) Eric Surman, 23rd Battalion, of Cardigan, Vic. Pte Surman enlisted on 17 February 1915 and embarked aboard HMAT Euripides on 10 May 1915. He returned to Australia on 14 December 1918.[610]

[610] http://cas.awm.gov.au/photograph/DA08686 Copyright expired, public domain. Darge Photographic Company.

We believe the following show, from left to right; Eric Surman (683), Geoffrey Surman (277) and perhaps the third soldier could be a Brewster. It is not James W. Surman as he enrolled later than the given date of the photo, and he is not known with a moustache.

He began military service again on 19 Mar 1942 in Ballarat, Vic, enlisted in Australian Army, Service Number V361080, next of kin Annie Surman.[611] He ended military service on 24 Apr 1943 as a private in 20 Battalion Volunteer Defence Corps.[612]

Annie WALTON (1557)[613] was born in 1897.[614] She died on 26 Jan 1965 in Ballarat, Vic.

iv. Stella SURMAN (681) was born in 1897 in Haddon, Vic.[615] She married David Draffin (2867). She died in 1968 in Ballarat, Vic.[616] She had six children.

v. Tettie SURMAN (679) was born in 1898 in Ballarat, Vic.[617] She married R. Thompson.

vi. Reginald Gunn SURMAN (678) was born on 26 Sep 1899 in Haddon, Vic.[618] He married Eva Draffin (2868) in 1928.[619] He died on 08 Aug 1943 in

611 National Archives of Australia.
612 National Archives of Australia.
613 Judy Meyer, 02 Aug 2004.
614 Judy Meyer, 02 Aug 2004 and for further information on this page.
615 Register of BDMs - Victoria, 1897 3749.
616 Register of BDMs - Victoria, 1968 7211.
617 Register of BDMs - Victoria, 1898 15908.
618 Register of BDMs - Victoria, 1899 27009; Judy Meyer, 02 Aug 2004.
619 Register of BDMs - Victoria, 1928 11857.

Ballarat, Vic, at age 43.[620] According to the electoral roll in 1931, 1936, 1937 he was a farmer at Cardigan; his wife and mother were both 'home duties'.

Eva DRAFFIN (2868) was born in 1906.[621] She died on 24 Oct 1948 in Ballarat, Vic.

vii. Margery SURMAN (687) was born on 01 Dec 1904 in Ballarat, Vic.[622] She married James Clifford Sharp (995) on 11 Mar 1931 in St Peters Anglican Church, Ballarat, Vic.[623]

32. Barbara Margaret McKay SURMAN (274) was born in 1870 in Ballarat, Vic. She married James Brewster (1559) in 1892. Various events are known concerning the family and her[624]. She died in 1928 in Morwell, Vic.

Children of Barbara Margaret McKay Surman (274) and James Brewster (1559) were as follows:

i. Renee Grace Daphne BREWSTER (1577) was born in 1893 in Learmonth, Vic. She married Percy Osborne Scouller (2869) in 1915. She died 1978 in Doncaster, Vic.

ii. James William Ashley BREWSTER (1578) was born in 1895 in Ballarat, Vic. He married Elsie May Souller (2870) in 1926. He died in 1957 in Sale, Vic.

iii. John Watkins Surman BREWSTER (1579)[625] was born in 1897 in Ballarat, Vic. He died in 1975 in Leongatha, Vic.

iv. David Baxter BREWSTER (1580) was born in 1899 in Yinnar, Vic.

v. Janet Barbara BREWSTER (1581) was born in 1902 in Yinnar, Vic.

vi. George Alan BREWSTER (1582) was born in 1904 in Yinnar, Vic. He died in 1985 in Leongatha, Vic.

vii. Hugh Gordon BREWSTER (1583) was born in 1906 in Leongatha, Vic. He died in 1976 in Leongatha, Vic.

viii. Oswald Geoffrey BREWSTER (1584) was born in 1912 in Morwell, Vic.

ix. Robert Norman BREWSTER (1585) was born in 1913 in Morwell, Vic.

---

620 Register of BDMs - Victoria, 1943 18948.

621 Ballarat Old Cemetery records: Eva Surman age 42, buried 26 Oct 1948, last residence Cardigan, widow, YOB 1906.

622 Register of BDMs - Victoria, 1905 378.

623 *Ballarat BDMs CD.*; Reg Bk 29/798

624 Barbara Brewster was at Middle Creek with Home Duties in 1909 and 1914, her husband James was a Grazier. Her brother Theodore Oswald Surman (276) signed up for the AIF from Yinnar and named her as the next of kin. On 14 November 1917 there was an advertisement in 'The Argus' newspaper saying 'Found Gold BROOCH on Flinders st station October 27 Apply Mrs Brewster Yinnar.' So Barbara Brewster obviously travelled to Melbourne at times. By 1919 also on the electoral roll were James William Ashley Brewster of Yinnar who was a farmer and John Watkins Surman Brewster of Yinnar who was a farm labourer. By 1924 there were only three on the roll; James Brewster had gone elsewhere. By 1931 John Watkins Surman Brewster has gone to Leongatha and was living in Brumley Street as a farmer. He had married Marjory Letitia 'home duties'. Oswald Geoffrey Brewster and Robert Norman Brewster both of Yinnar South are recorded as Labourers in the 1936 Electoral Roll; a James Brewster of Middle Creek was a Grazier. However the 1937 Leongatha Electoral roll is fascinating; John Watkins Surman Brewster and Marjory Letitia were still at the same address. But also on the Roll are Edith Mary Brewster and George Alan Brewster living at Cashin's loose bag via Tarwin (he was a labourer, she had home duties), Hugh Gordon Brewster and Jessie Isabella Brewster were on the Coast Road Leongatha (he as a labourer, she with home duties). So, two sons got married… Robert Norman was still in Yinnar in 1943 as a labourer. In Leongatha Edith Mary Brewster and George Alan Brewster were at Roughead Street in Leongatha, John and Marjory Brewster were at 'Neerena' via Leongatha; he was a farmer. By 1949 in Roughead Street were Edith Mary Brewster and George Alan Brewster, at Neerina were Eulalie Perry Brewster, John Watkins Surman Brewster, Marjory Letitia Brewster and Oswald Geoffrey Brewster. Robert Norman Brewster was now a farmer at Leongatha and may have had a wife Joan Alison Brewster. James Brewster of Yinnar wrote letters to the editors of various local papers.

625 Judy Meyer, 02 Aug 2004 and for further information on this page.

Pupils and teacher at the Yinnar South School, 1909[626]
Teacher Olive Drummond with pupils.

In the front row, from the left, are George Walker, Irene Keogh, Jessie Clay, ***Jean Brewster (1581)****, Ruby Marshall, Ethel Heasom and Violet Keogh. In the second row are Jessie Marshall, Percy Vagg,* ***David Brewster (1580),*** *Eric Walker,* ***Alan Brewster (1582)*** *and Jack Heasom. In the third row are ? Heasom, Edith Walker, Mary Heasom, Violet Marshall, Emily Keogh. At the back are Ian Heasom,* ***Bill Brewster (possibly 1578),*** *Gerald Keogh and Archie Vagg.*

33. James William SURMAN (275) was born in 1873 in Sago Hill, Vic.[627] He married Alice Maud Grace Curtis (677) on 21 Feb 1894 in Ballarat, Vic [628] and died on 05 Dec 1947 in Horsham, Vic.[629] He was educated in Windermere, now Cardigan, Vic. He was a teacher, spending fifty years in the Education Department of Vic[630]. He began military service when

626 http://arrowprod.lib.monash.edu.au:8080/vital/access/manager/Repository/monash:4412?expert=subject:"Brewster,+Jean" copyright expired.

627 Register of BDMs - Victoria, 1873 5211.

628 Register of BDMs - Victoria, 1894 1393; Judy Meyer, 02 Aug 2004.

629 Register of BDMs - Victoria, 1947 22836; Judy Meyer, 02 Aug 2004.

630 'The Horsham Times', Feb 19, 1937, page 1—' More Than Fifty Years A Teacher Fine Record of Mr J. Surman (Horsham) When Mr J.W. Surman leaves the Horsham State School this afternoon on his furlough prior to retirement he will have spent over 50 years as a teacher in the Education Department. Looking back over his long association with the department he told a "Times" representative on Wednesday that that teachers nowadays "are on velvet," compared with the teachers of 40 or 50 years ago. The conditions, not only from the financial viewpoint, were a great deal better, but the schools were modern and teachers in the country were able to secure board and lodging as a rule in easy distance of the school. In his young days at one place he had to travel seven miles to the school in the morning and back again at night, while at another place he walked knee deep in water to school during the winter. Mr Surmnan claims to be as old as the Educarion Act itself for he was born on the same day as it

war broke out in 1914 in Vic. He taught for some time in Gippsland and was a Presbytrerian Church Sunday school teacher and cricketer in his younger days.[631]

James W. SURMAN
Tree No. 203

James Surman went to school at Windermere, now called Cardigan. He became a teacher, and spent 50 years in the Education Department.

He enlisted when war broke out, was in active service for years, during which time he was on the ill-fated "Ballarat" when it was torpedoed. He returned to teaching. It is interesting to note that since 1854 and until 1937, there had been an unbroken line of Surmans in the teaching profession in Victoria.

From Duty Nobly Done by the Learmonth & District Historical Society, used with permission.

Alice Maud Grace CURTIS (677) was born in 1874 in Buninyong, Vic.[632] She died on 02 May 1956 in Horsham, Vic. At one point they lived at 1 Caroline Stret Horsham.

Children of James William Surman (275) and Alice Maud Grace Curtis (677) were:

i. Grace Jessie Frances SURMAN (684) was born in 1895 in Wonwondah South, Vic.[633] She died in 1895 in Mount Jeffcott, Vic, aged 3 months.[634]

---

passed. He went to school at Windermere, now called Cardigan, near Ballarat. At 12 years of age he became a paid monitor teacher under his late father, who taught at Windermere for 33½ years. In 1877 he was gazetted as a teacher and at the age of 18 years he was appointed a head teacher and was sent to Dunmunkle North, now known as the Boolite school. Water was so scarce there that it had to be obtained from crab holes in one vicinity. After a period at Daylesford, following six months at Dunmunkle North, Mr. Surman came to Laharum in 1892. The school was not on the present site then. He taught children at Laharum who now have grandchildren attendng the same school. He spent over two years at Laharum, during which time he married, and then went to Jeffcott West, and was there at the start of the drought which culminated in 1902. While at Jeffcott the weather was so hot that the temperature did not go below a 100 degrees at night for over a month. The school was on the corner of a 640 acre paddock. Prior to coming to Horsham Mr Surman then spent periods at Middle Bridge (now known as Betley), Faraday in the Castlemaine district, Blackwood North and Woolsthorpe. He was at the last named place when war broke out and he enlisted. He was on active service for two years at the great war, during which time he was on the ill-fated "Ballarat" when it was torpedoed. On his return, he went as assistant to the Camberwell school, and later to Ashby, Geelong west. In January he came to Horsham amd has been here for the past 14 years.
It is interesting to note that since the year 1854 there has been an unbroken line of Surmans in the teaching profession of Victoria. Mr Surman's son (Mr J. Surman) is at present teaching at Natimuk,

631 *The Horsham Times*, 9 December 1847, page 2. 'Obituary'.

632 Judy Meyer, 02 Aug 2004 and for further information on this page.

633 Register of BDMs - Victoria, 1895 8192.

634 Register of BDMs - Victoria, 1895 6635.

ii. Leslie Watkins SURMAN[635] (685) was born in 1896 in Horsham, Vic.[636] He died in 1939 in Scone NSW.[637] He had been a bank clerk.

iii. Hazel Marion SURMAN (686) was born on 13 May 1901 in Dunolly, Vic.[638] She married Robert Devlin (1560) in 1925.[639] She died in 1984 in Horsham, Vic. She was a schoolteacher, perhaps at Swan Hill in 1924. She had three children

iv. Harry 'Jack' SURMAN (1561) was born on 11 Dec 1917 in Horsham and died in Drouin, Vic in 2006. He was a secondary school teacher at Bairnsdale, Sale, Yallourn and elsewhere throughout Gippsland. He married and had children.

34. Geoffrey Eustace SURMAN (277) was born on 29 Jun 1878 in Sago Hill, Vic.[640] He may have been a farmer at Curyo[641] near Birchip in 1909. He married Winifred May Littlehales (458), daughter of John Littlehales (768) and Martha Young (767), on 25 Apr 1917 in St Peters Anglican, Ballarat, Vic.[642] He married Ethel Stella Todd (1552) in 1926.[643] He died in Jul 1951 in Heidelberg, Vic, at age 73 [644] and was buried on 01 Aug 1951 in the New Cemetery Area Private, Section 3 Lot 6R1, Ballarat, Vic.[645] He was a farmer, unmarried in 1914 in Cardigan, Ballarat, Vic.[646] He began military service on 25 Aug 1914 as a private, Regimental No. 129, next of kin, brother J. O. Surman, Cardigan.[647] He was a billiards professional in 1920. In 1924 he was living at 210 Sturt Street Ballarat and his profession was billiardmaker.[648]

---

635 It is possible he joined the Bank of Australasia and went to Toowoomba as a clerk by 1925 and was a bank manager at Hamilton, near Newcastle, in 1930, but by 1933 (due to the Depression?) he was at 40 Beach Road Edgecliff Woollahra in Sydney as a clerk and probably with a wife as well. Eileen Avonia Surman is 'home duties' at the same address. In 1936 and 1937 they lived at 9 Waverton Avenue in North Sydney. But by 1943 she was living by herself at 38 Gerard Street Cremorne.

636 Register of BDMs - Victoria, 1896 12223.

637 Australian Death Index 1787-1985.

638 Register of BDMs - Victoria, 1901 18594; Judy Meyer, 02 Aug 2004.

639 Judy Meyer, 02 Aug 2004 and for further information on this page,

640 Register of BDMs - Victoria, 1878 18658; Judy Meyer, 02 Aug 2004.

641 Electoral Roll 1909.

642 Register of BDMs - Victoria, 1917 2043; *Ballarat BDMs CD*, register book 18/565.

643 Register of BDMs - Victoria, 1926 572.

644 Register of BDMs - Victoria, 1951 9171.

645 Ballarat Old Cemetery records.

646 The AIF Project.

647 The AIF Project.

648 Electoral Roll 1924.

Geoffrey SURMAN
Tree No. 205

Geoffrey Surman, son of James Watkins Surman, enlisted with the 8th Battalion in 1914, and was posted overseas.

He was wounded in the Gallipoli landing and lay wounded for 13 hours. He was evacuated to Enlgand, and spent two years in hospital, returned to Australia and spent another two years in hospital before being able to walk. His name is listed on the Cardigan School Honour Board.

Being from 'Duty Nobly Done', used with permission.

Winifred May LITTLEHALES (458) was born in 1892 in Vic.[649] She died circa 20 Apr 1920 in Ballarat, Vic. She was buried on 24 Apr 1920 in New Cemetery, Ballarat, Vic.[650]

Children of Geoffrey Eustace Surman (277) and Winifred May Littlehales (458) both born in Ballarat, Vic, were:

i. Geoffrey Oswald SURMAN (4) was born in 1918.[651] He was baptized on 17 Oct 1918 in St Andrews Kirk, Ballarat, Vic.[652] He died in Mar 1921 in Sale, Vic.[653] He was buried on 31 Mar 1921 in New Cemetery Area Private Section 3 Lot 6R1, Ballarat, Vic.[654]

ii. John Watkins SURMAN (689) was born on 10 Apr 1920.[655] He was baptized on 29 Apr 1920 in St Peters Anglican, Ballarat, Vic.[656] He married Audrey Barker (1551) on 28 Jun 1947.[657] He died on 28 Sep 1996 in Brisbane, Qld, at age 76. He began military service on 01 Jul 1939 in Melbourne, Vic, enlisted, service number V29491, next of kin J. Surman.[658] He ended military service on 24 Jul 1941 as a Private, Vic.[659] He enlisted again on 22 Dec 1941 in Caulfield, Vic, service number VX66510, next of kin Geoffrey Surman.[660] He ended military service on 21 Mar 1946 as a Corporal.[661]

Ethel Stella TODD (1552) was born in 1901.

---

[649] Register of BDMs - Victoria, 1920 4167.

[650] Ballarat Old Cemetery records.

[651] Register of BDMs - Victoria, 1918 389.

[652] *Ballarat BDMs CD.*

[653] Register of BDMs - Victoria, 1921 3455.

[654] Ballarat Old Cemetery records.

[655] Register of BDMs - Victoria, 1920 8904; National Archives of Australia Series B883, control symbol VX66510, barcode 6115408, born 10 Apr 1920, Caulfield.

[656] *Ballarat BDMs CD.*

[657] Judy Meyer, 02 Aug 2004 and for further information on this page.

[658] National Archives of Australia Series B884, control symbol V29491, barcode 6621239, born 10 Apr 1920, Ballarat; *Nominal Roll WW2.*

[659] *Nominal Roll WW2.* (Were there medical issues involved here?)

[660] National Archives of Australia Series B883, control symbol VX66510, barcode 6115408, born 10 Apr 1920, Caulfield; *Nominal Roll WW2.*

[661] *Nominal Roll WW2.*

There were no children of Geoffrey Eustace Surman (277) and Ethel Stella Todd (1552). They lived at 715 Sturt Street Ballarat in the 1931 Electoral roll. In the 1936 Roll he was a billiard room proprietor (she with home duties) living at 10 Raglan Street North, Ballarat[662].

35. Alexander GORDON (3122)[663] married Elizabeth Mowat (3125).

Children of Alexander Gordon (3122) and Elizabeth Mowat (3125) are:

i. Ellen GORDON (3123) married Stanley Foster (978).

She was a nurse in 1924.[664] She lived to age 99, the oldest of seven children.[665]

36. Herbert Claude Marcus JENKINS (3160)[666] was born on 30 Nov 1877 in Keppel, Grey Co., Ontario.[667] He married Agnes Jane Brown (3290) on 02 Sep 1902 in Owen Sound, Ontario.

Agnes Jane BROWN (3290) was born in 1877.

Twin children of Herbert Claude Marcus Jenkins (3160) and Agnes Jane Brown (3290) born in Owen Sound, Ontario, were as follows:

i. Cecil Herbert JENKINS (2871) was born on 23 Oct 1903.

ii. Nora Gertrude JENKINS (3310) was born on 23 Oct 1903.

37. Marcus Gunn BOYD (3155) was born on 02 Mar 1878 in Sydenham, Grey Co., Ontario. He married Henrietta Reilly (3158) on 11 Mar 1903 in Sydenham.

Henrietta REILLY (3158) was born in 1878 in Ontario. She died on 04 Feb 1929 in Empress, Alberta.[668]

Children of Marcus Gunn Boyd (3155) and Henrietta Reilly (3158) were as follows:

i. Opal Eileen BOYD (3287) born circa 1905. She married A. K. McNeill (3289).

ii. Harold Elliott BOYD (3288) was born circa 1907.

662There are further records for Ethel Stella Surman living 13 Peel Street Prahran with home duties (no mention of a husband) in 1943 Roll but by 1949 they are both there at the same address (Geoffrey now a clerk), and she stayed there after his death in 1951 as she was in the 1954 Roll.

663Letter or email, Betty Warrilow to Donald Gunn, 14 Aug 2008; 'In the letters you will note Alexander Sutherland. He was married to Christian (Christina) Gunn born 1802. They had 8 children. I descend from their daughter Ellen who married Hugh Gordon, their son Alex named for his grandfather Alexander Sutherland, his daughter Ellen was my mother.' See Part 3. And for further information on this page.

664Letter or email, Betty Warrilow to Donald Gunn, 06 Sep 2008; 'My mother, Ellen Gordon named after her grandmother, Ellen Sutherland Gordon lived to be 99. She trained as a nurse, graduating in 1924. She was the oldest of 7 children. I was her only child born in 1929. My father Stanley Foster was a farmer. I married Percy Warrilow in 1955. We had 3 children two sons and one daughter (deceased in 1978). Our sons have presented us with 5 grandchildren, the eldest soon to be 20 and the youngest 13'.

665Letter or email, Betty Warrilow to Donald Gunn, 07 Aug 2008; 'My line -gt. Grandmother Ellen Sutherland married Hugh Gordon, their son Alexander Gordon, my grandfather, Ellen Gordon, my mother who lived to be 99. My name is Mary Elizabeth Foster Warrilow'; Letter or email, Betty Warrilow to Donald Gunn, 06 Sep 2008.

666Carol Small, e-mail to Donald Gunn, Aug 2008 and for further information on this page.

667Bill & Sharon Gurney, e-mail to Donald Gunn, 03 Oct 2008: Family of Neil McKay & Margaret Sutherland and for further information on this page.

668*Unknown newspaper*, 'Word has been received in the city of the death of a former resident of Owen Sound in the person of Henrietta Boyd, wife of Marcus G Boyd, which occurred at her late residence at Empress, Alberta, a short time ago, following a brief illness, from pleuro pneumonia. Deceased, whose maiden name was Henrietta Reilly, daughter of John and Mary J Reilly, was born in Sydenham and Owen Sound, and in 1903 was married to Mr Marcus G Boyd. They immediately went to the west and near Froude for 11 years, and went to Empress in 1913, when the town was started and have lived there ever since. ... She is survived by her husband, one daughter, Opel Eileen (Mrs A K McNeill), and one son, Harold Elliott.'

38. Robert John BOYD (3150) was born on 23 Feb 1880 in Sydenham, Grey Co., Ontario. He married Sarah Alice Cook (3157). He died on 12 Nov 1939 in Owen Sound, Ontario, at age 59 and was buried in Greenwood, Owen Sound, Ontario.

Sarah Alice COOK (3157) was born in 1887. She died on 21 May 1968.

Children of Robert John Boyd (3150) and Sarah Alice Cook (3157) were as follows:

i. James Henry Robert BOYD (3268) was born in 1910 in Sydenham, Ontario. He married Catherine Lilian Locke (3276) on 01 Oct 1927.[669] He died on 20 Oct 1952.

ii. Norman BOYD (3165)[670] was born after 1911. He married Laurene Vance (--?--) (3272). He died after 1952.

iii. Earl BOYD (3269) was born after 1911. He married Margaret Morton (3279). He died after 1952.

iv. William James BOYD (3270) was born after 1911. He died after 1952.

v. Edna BOYD (3271) was born after 1911. She married Allan Bothwell (3283).

---

669 *Unknown newspaper*, 'A well known Owen Sound contractor, R. J. Harry Boyd, was fatally injured late Friday morning when he fell about 20 feet to the ground while he was building a new roof. He died in the G and M Hospital less than three hours later. ... the late Mr Boyd was born in Sydenham township 46 years ago last March 16. He was the son of Mrs Sadie Ellis Boyd and the late Robert Boyd. Twenty five years ago October 1 he married the former Catherine Lillian Locke in Meaford. Mr Boyd is survived by his wife and mother, two children, Bobbie and Lorna, both at home, three brothers, Earle of Barrie, Norman of Sydenham and William of Owen Sound on one sister, Edna, Mrs Allen Bothwell of Annan.'

670 Carol Small, e-mail to Donald Gunn, Aug 2008 and further information on this page.

Part 3—Documents written by, or concerning, the family

Many original documents have come down though time in my branch of the family from Scotland, Canada and the early days of Ballarat; they are entered here.

Alastair J. Gunn

Generation One

Donald Gunn in Tormsdale (262)

Only a few documents[671] exist relating to the earliest period and these are, not unsurprisingly, bills. In some ways the most interesting is—

George Sutherland late Guisborne
Now in Edinburgh D[r]

1815 To John Gunn Mercht Halkirk
NovTo Bal due this date Paid £2 17.3
To Int until paid---

George Suth[d]
You will pay the
Above acct to Mr Alex[r] Gunn
Shoer Boulchork who will
Give you a receipt for the same

Don[d] Gunn

Swiney 31 May
1827

[671] It is possible that some of these documents refer to Donald Gunn (708) the Sennachie, father of Barbara Gunn (6) who married into the Tormsdale family, but given that no other documents from him are in my possession and that she predeceased her father it is considered unlikely.

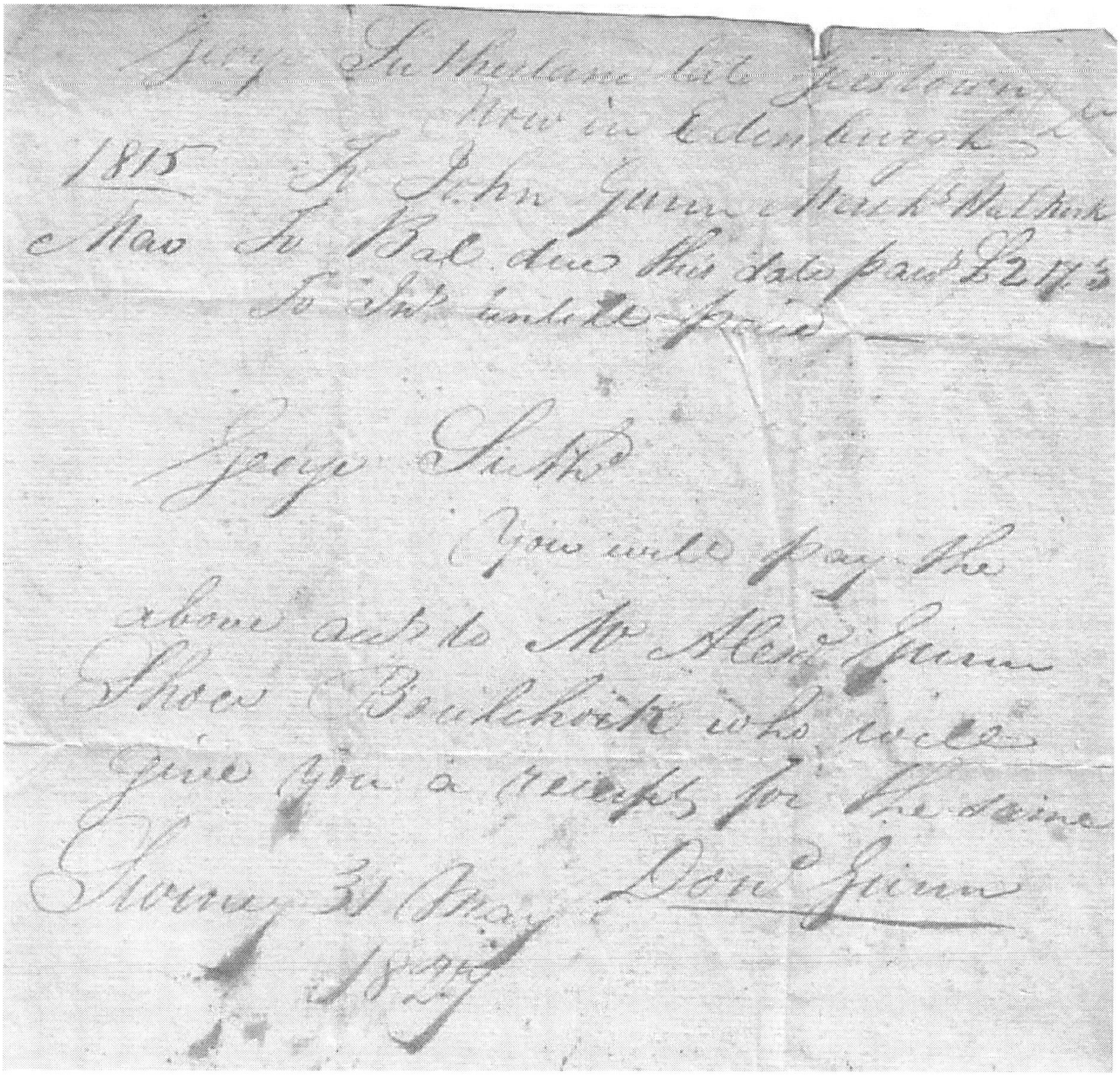
Geo. Sutherland late [illegible]
Now in Edinburgh
1815 To John Gunn [illegible]
Mar To Bal. due this date paid £2.17.3
To Int. until paid
Geo. Sutherland
You will pay the
above acct to Mr Alex Gunn
Shoe [illegible] who will
give you a receipt for the same
[illegible] 31 May Don. Gunn
1827

It was quite possible to run bills for long periods of time; the next is for the period October 10, 1832 to May 26 1834 being paid some time in 1854, as shown by the date and the fiscal stamp. The gap in time seems amazing but the blue stamp was only issued in 1853. The bill is for assorted raw materials associated with clothing / dress making—shirting, moleskin, white cotton, canvas, tweed, doeskin, black silk etc.. It was payable to MacDonald and Co. The total was for £11.10.10. Was this just to dress the family in that period or was someone a dressmaker / tailor?

Mr. Dund Gunn Breadalbane
1832
To Wm. McDonald & Co

Oct 10 To 2 yds fine Blk Venetian @ 9/- £ — 18 "
5/8 yd Canvas 5d Padding 4d 1 yd Cotton 6d — " 1 3
— 1/4 yd Blk Cotton 5 — 1 yd Skirt Lining 1/2 — 1 7
— Linen 1d — Silk & Twist — 7 Butts 2 Staytape &c 4 — 1 2
— 2 1/4 yd Doeskin & furnishings — " 10 "
— 7 yd Cotton 3/6 — 3 3/4 yd Blue Stripe 1/10 — " 5 4 1/2
— pearls 3d — 1/2 yd Drab Kersey 2/6 — 2 9
— 3/8 yd Linen 3 Silk Twist & Thd &c 4 1/2 — — 7 1/2
Do 29 — 18 yds Shirting Stripe — 6 3/4 — 10 1 1/2
14 yd White Cotton — 6 1/2 7 7
6 yds Moleskin — 1/8 — 10 "
4 yd Cotton 1/6 1 yd Canvas 7d — 2 1
1 1/2 dz pearls 7 1/2 6 C worsted 2/- — 2 7 1/2
3 5/8 yd Blue Pilot Cloth @ 6/6 1 3 7
1/4 yd Canvas 6 1/2 yd Blk Cotton 10d " 1 4
1/2 yd Saxe Tartan 2/9 1/2 yd Cotton 9 — 3 6
3/4 yd Blk Canvas 6 — 1/2 yd Linen 10d " 1 4
Silk & Twist 10d — Butts for Coat & Vest 11 — 1 9
3/4 yd Linsed 3/2 9 yd Stripe 4/6 " 7 8
24 — 4 yd Swanskin Cotton 3/ 1/2 yd Cotton 8d — 3 8
Vest pe 3/ Furnishings 1/6 — 4 6
7 yd Cotton 9 — 9 yds Sheeting 6/9 — 7 6
3 yd Twisted Cotton 1/9 4 yd other Tyck 3/9 — 3 6
2 1/4 yd Cotton Tyck 1/4 Tape &c 3d Hat & Bag 8/- 9 10
Day 7 - 3 - 4 Brot forwd £7 - 2 - 4

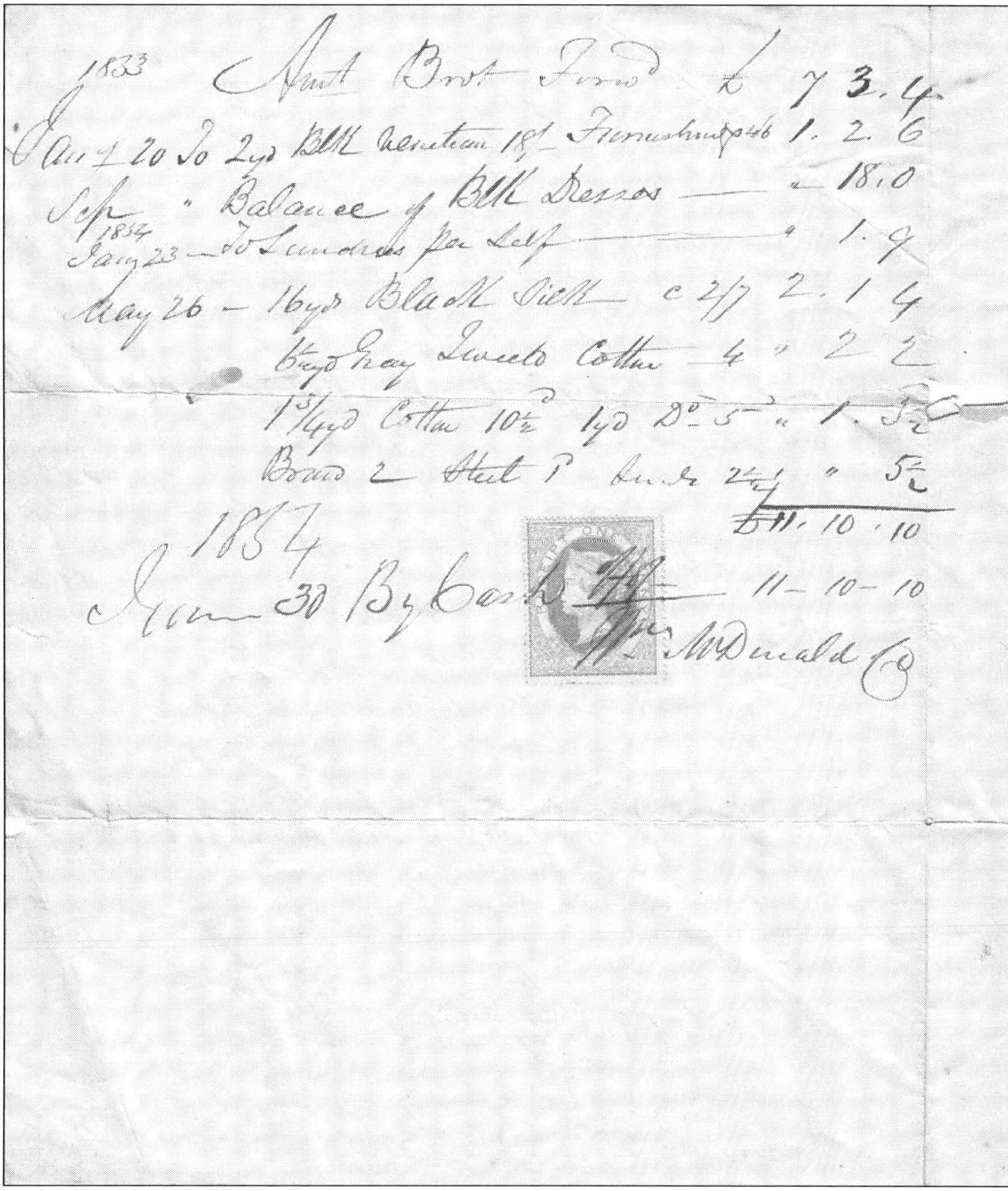
1833 Amt Brot Forwd £ 7. 3. 4
Jan 20 To 2yd Blk venetian 18/- Furnishings 46 1. 2. 6
Sep " Balance of Blk Dresses — 18.0
1834 Jany 23 To Sundries for Self — 1. 9
May 26 — 16yd Black Silk c 2/7 2. 1 4
6yd Gray Sweeds Cotton 4 " 2 2
1 3/4 yd Cotton 10½ 1yd Do 5 " 1. 3½
Board 2 Stut [illegible] " 5½
£11. 10. 10
1834
Jan 30 By Cash 11-10-10
Wm McDonald & Co

Donald's signature

But there are other essentials of life. The next bill covers the period November 30 1842 (starting paying off the previous bill) to February 13 1843 and is much less well presented (and spelt) than the previous bill. One can read across the top Donald Gunn Bralbin and various items—'January 27 Supper 1/-', 'February 4 Barrel Whiske 1/4½ d and '... sugar' in the last item. Paid by cash...

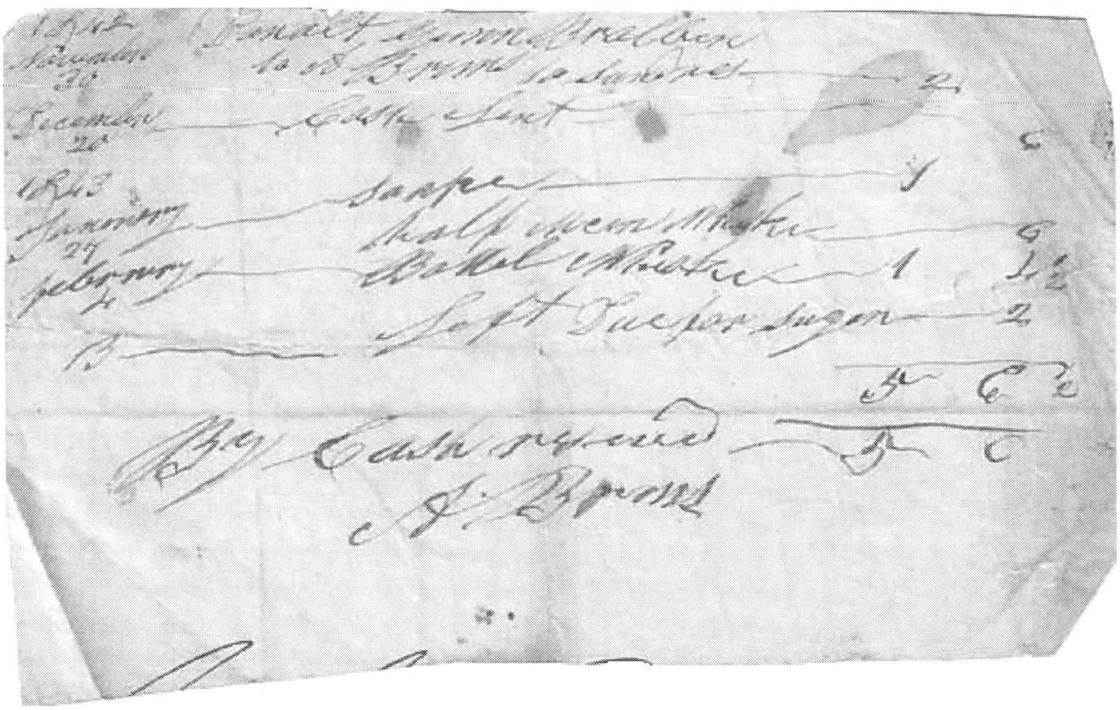

There is one final bill left concerning Donald Gunn[672] of Tormsdale (262). It has the name Donald clearly written on the other side which is also shown (the sizes are not comparative). This clearly shows Donald to be alive. Is it from the Bar of Geo. Craig?

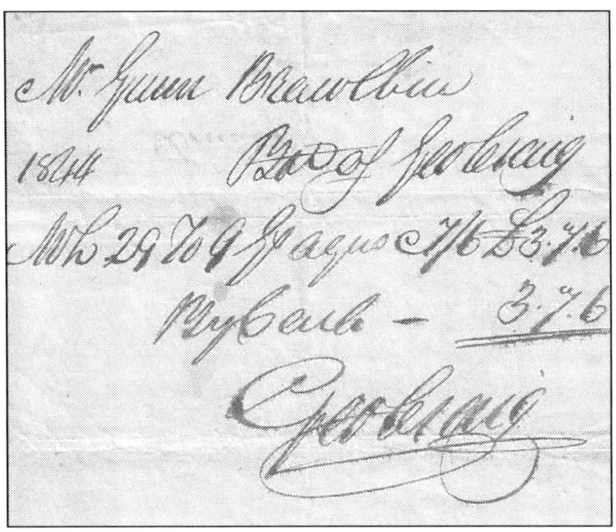
Mr Gunn Brawlbin
1844
By Cash - 3.7.6
Geo Craig

[672]To repeat an earlier point—it is possible that this refers to Donald the Sennachie who was also living at Brawlbin at this time but given that all other documents relate to the other Gunn line, this seems unlikely.

Generation Two

Concerning, in the main, the children of Donald Gunn in Tormsdale (262). Note that John was 'of Bualchork' by 1818, Alexander by 1820 and Donald by 1829.[673]

The Children

John Gunn (293)

The first son was John (293) who was born in 1783 and died in the same year or possibly 1784. This birth was in the year after Donald's (292) marriage.

John Gunn (294)

Another John (294) was born in the following year and he died in 1857. Most of his family stayed in Scotland but one of the sons—Donald (315)—emigrated to Ontario.

Hugh Gunn (295)

The third son was Hugh, see page 21 for an early document by him. He stayed in the Caithness area.

[673] E-mail from Sharon Gurney October 2009.

Alexander Gunn in Bualchork and Brawlbin (1)

The fourth son was Alexander in Bualchork and Brawlbin[674] (1) whose five children migrated to Australia. Alexander was married from Bualchork in 1829.

Alexander considered emigrating (possibly partially due to the 'Dalton Minimum', a period of lower than average global temperatures which included 1816 sometimes called 'the year without a summer'[675]) but he finally did not go, although his children did after he died. What were the conditions like at home? What can be said of Alexander?

The first document is a 'certificate in favour of Alexander Gunn' written in Halkirk on the 29th March 1817 which reads:

These certify the Bearer Alexander Gunn an unmarried young Man & Native of this Parish County of Caithness lived therein for the most part from his Infancy to this date sustain an irreproachable Character free from Scandal, Church Censure or anything else known to us that might hinder his admission into any Christian Society or Family where Providence may order his lot. In witness whereof this presentation in Name and by Appointment of the Kirk Session of Halkirk subscribed by

John Cameron Min^r
Donald Grant S. Clk.

[674] Ibidem; from the 'Will of George Gunn, merchant at Thurso who died April 2, 1821. "To Alexander Gunn in Achlibster Bualchork one pound to purchase any article he may choose in memory of a Friend." This will was made in June of 1820. George Gunn was 40 years old when he died and the son of a David Gunn and Christian Henderson.'

[675] http://en.wikipedia.org/wiki/Dalton_Minimum

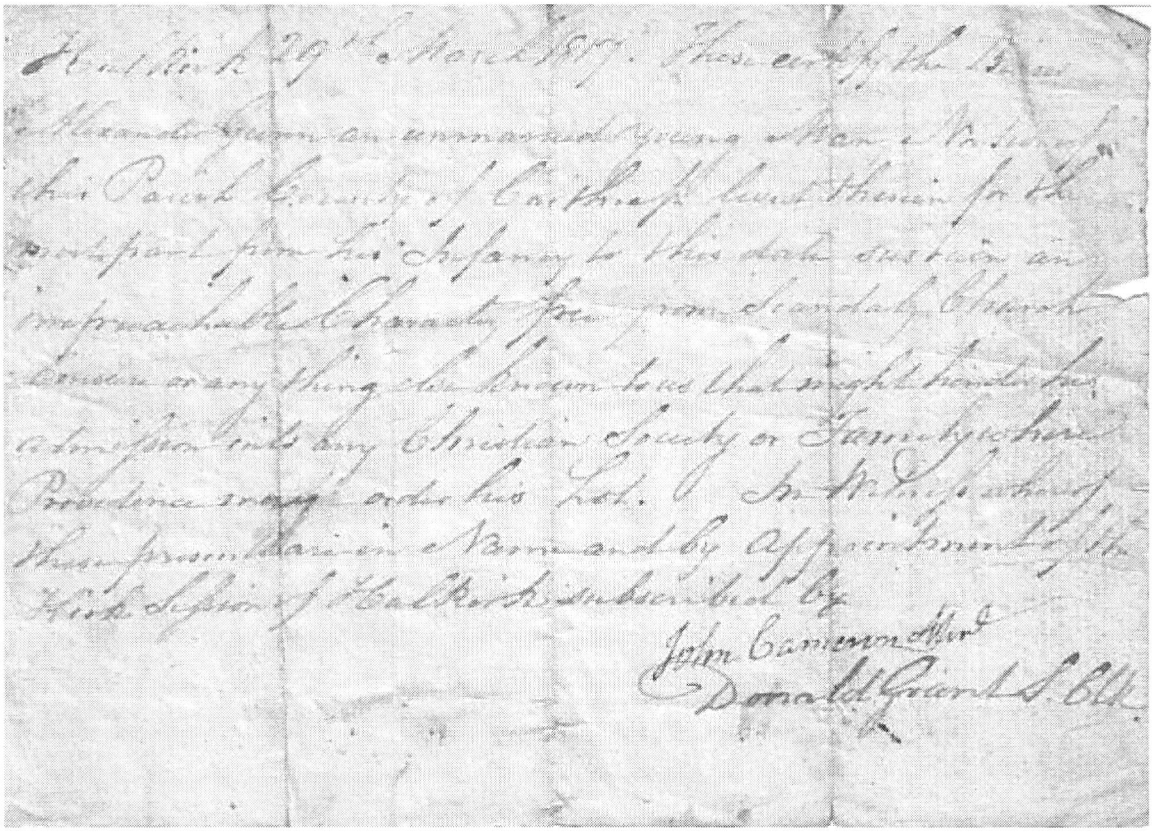
Halkirk 29th March 1817. These certify the Bearer Alexander Gunn an unmarried young Man a Native of this Parish County of Caithness lived therein for the most part from his Infancy to this date sustain an unreproachable Character free from Scandal & Church Censure or any thing else known to us that might hinder his admission into any Christian Society or Family where Providence may order his Lot. In Witness whereof these presents are in Name and by Appointment of the Kirk Session of Halkirk subscribed by

John Cameron Minr

Donald Grant S. Clk

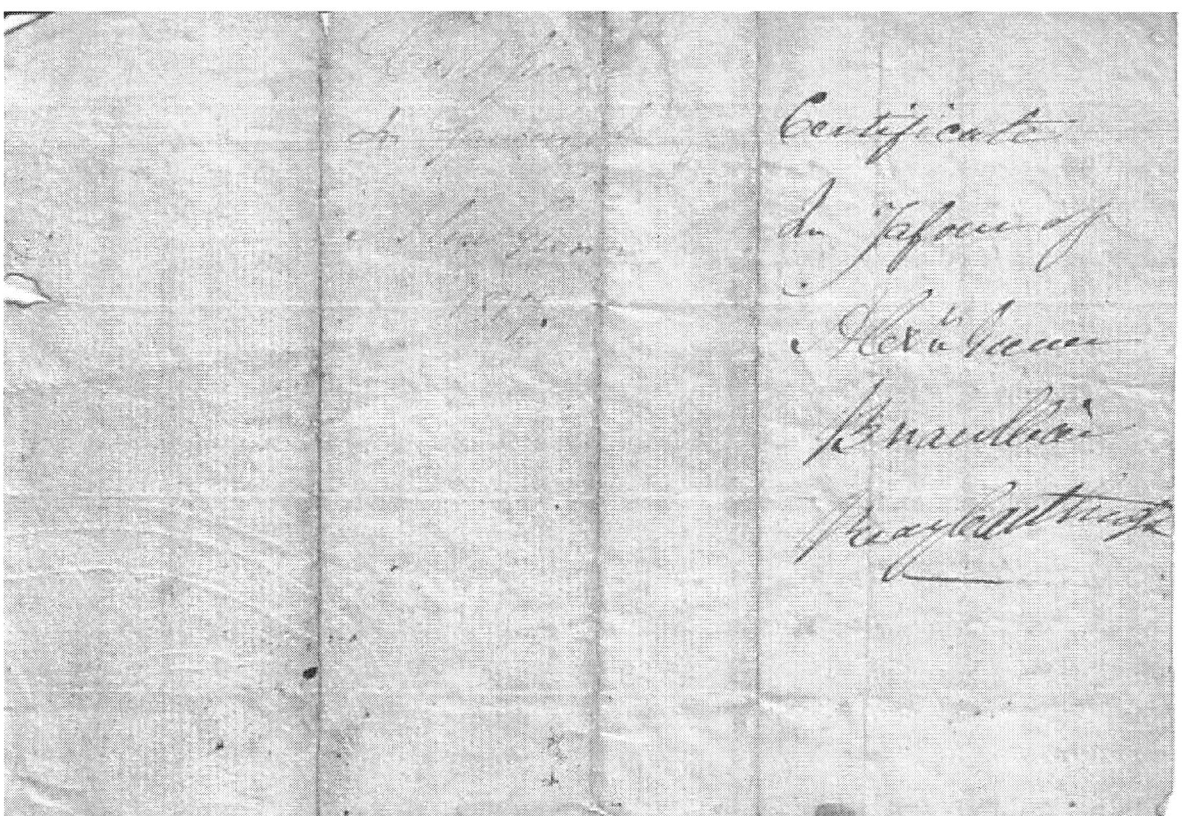
Certificate
In favour of
Alexr Gunn
Braulbin
Reay Caithness

But one has to note the quality of the Minister and the area of Halkirk; 'The Rev. John Cameron, minister of Halkirk from 1769 to 1821, was more of a man than a minister. He was lame at handling a text, it is said, but an adept with musket or shotgun, and as game was of little value to the lairds in those days, he spent a good deal of his time roaming the moor with dog and gillie. He arranged to stay at home on a certain date to marry a couple, but when the day came the minister forgot all about it, and set out on one of his hunting expeditions. In the dusk of the evening, as he was coming round the bend at Pollyhour, he observed the bedraggled marriage party returning home on the opposite side of the river, signalled to them, and tied the knot there and then, though the river Thurso in flood ran between him and them.

As might be expected in such circumstances, the Parish Church was neglected; many stayed at home or wandered in the hills on the Lord's Day, while some betook themselves to fellowship meetings. ... As Mr Cameron held the pulpit of Halkirk for well over half a century, the parish was spiritually to seed, for fellowship meetings in the uncontrolled hands of unlearned though pious men breed self-righteousness, uncharitableness, obscurantism.'[676]

It seems likely that this document of Alexander's was a preliminary to travel—perhaps the ancient equivalent of a passport? Obviously the support is from the Church but the reason for the character reference is unknown.

Below is a very early extract from the Register of Baptisms—

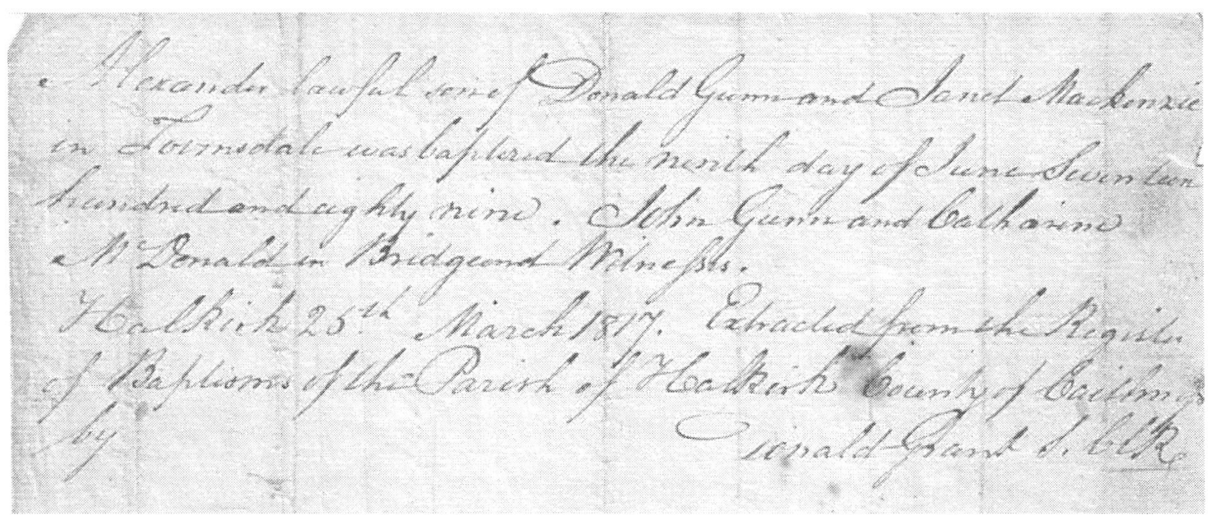
Alexander lawful son of Donald Gunn and Janet Mackenzie in Tormsdale was baptized the ninth day of June Seventeen hundred and eighty nine. John Gunn and Catharine McDonald in Bridgend Witnesses.
Halkirk 25th March 1817. Extracted from the Regist. of Baptisms of the Parish of Halkirk County of Caithness by
Donald Grant S. Clk.

Alexander lawful son of Donald Gunn and Janet Mackenzie in Tormsdale was baptized the ninth day of June Seventeen Hundred and eighty nine. John Gunn and Catherine McDonald in Bridgend Witnesses. Halkirk 25th March 1817 Extracted from the Register of Baptisms of the Parish of Halkirk County of Caithness by Donald Grant S. Clk.

[676]Drawn from that written by the Rev. A. Mackay, M.A. and Cor. Mem. S.A. Scott. at the Westerdale Manse on 21st April 1911. It appeared in the 'Ye Booke of Halkirk' (A Ross Institute Souvenir) that was issued by the Bazaar Publications Committee in 1911.

This extract is dated 25th March 1817 and, as it is by the same person (Donald Grant) as in the preceding document, it is reasonable to assume they are linked. The Christian birth extracts act to support the preceding document as well. John Gunn and Catherine M^C^Donald as witnesses are also of interest; see footnote 1, page 2.

It is obvious from the following two letters that Alexander had a desire to leave the country at this time. As Mark Rugg Gunn writes in his book *Clan Gunn* - "the land of the Gunns was cleared in stages between May 1811, the date of the first Kildonan evictions, and 1819." [677] The effect of the clearances on this family is clear when one notes the amount of emigration; as well the zeitgeist[678] could not easily be ignored.

Kildonan, 2011

[677] p.212

[678] 'It was indeed a tragic irony that some of the worst atrocities committed against the Australian Aborigines were carried out by Gaels who had left Scotland as their own traditional world of clanship and tribalism disintegrated during the Highalnd Clearances' p.289, T.M. Devine, *Scotland's Empire*.

William MacKenzie (806) (Uncle), Jamaica

It was his uncle, William MacKenzie[679] who provided firm proof of Alexander's desire to emigrate. On 12 January 1819 William wrote in response to a letter from Alexander, from Jamaica—

Dear Nephew

Your favour of date the 18 March 1818 come to my hands but owing to sickness and Deaths in my familie prevented my answering you long before this - I having a large familie to support and have met with very bad payments in my Business - and the wear while have Reduced me very much - and my health has been very bad for some years back - I observe what you say Respecting our friends at home which I am very sorry to find is so bad - but it is the ----(?) of this world

Now that you have a great wish to come - to Jamaica - but Jamaica is not the same country that it was twenty years ago when the slave trade was open, but if that you have a wish to come - you better come yourself first before that your Brother(s?) comes - as I see your being mentioning there wish to come out also - and when that you get settled then in a little time you can be able to inform them better - if that you intend to come out - come out in a Vessel Bound for Port Antonio[680] - or Morant Bay or Port Morant as Either of those places would answer with – I hope the letter that I have Received from you - his in your own hand writing - on Receipt of this write me when that I may look for you and what ship - if you can and give me all the news that you can Respecting the North - and our families - And give my Blessings to them all - and my sister Chirstie - tell her that I will write soon to her

I am my dear Nephew
yours with Esteem
William Mackenzie

Port Antonio
Portland Jamaica
14 January 1819

It is worth noting that the letter is addressed to Mr Alexander Gunn and the reference in the letter to the slave trade. Perhaps William made money from it around the turn of the century? As well, one has to note he has been in Jamaica for around twenty years. Given that the wishes are to his sister Chirstie (943) (Christian in the second letter), why not to another sister Janet (703) wife of Donald Gunn in Tormsdale (262)? Or perhaps he has just written to her as well?

[679] It is easy to find MacKenzies in Jamaica (occasionally McKinzie) but so far none have positive links to the people of this book.

[680] Port Antonio is the capital of the Portland region of Jamaica in 2009; it is on the north-east corner. Robert Burns thought about emigrating in 1786 as 'book-keeper on a Scottish-owned sugar estate in Port Antonio'. P. 250, T.M. Devine, *Scotland's Empire 1600-1815*.

Dear Nephew

Your favour of date the 18 March 1818
came to my hand — but owing to sickness
and Deaths in my family prevented my
answering you long before this —
— I have a large family to support and
have met with very bad payments in my
Business — and the war which has Reduced
me very much — and my health has been
very bad for some years back —
— I observe what you say Respecting
our friends at home which I am very
sorry to find is so bad — but its the lot
of this world —
I see that you have a great wish to
come to Jamaica — but Jamaica is not the
same country that it was twenty years ago
when the slave trade was open — but if that
you have a wish to come — you better come
yourself first before that your Brother comes
— as I see your being mentioning their wish
to come out also — then when that you get
settled — then in a little time you can be able to
inform them better — If that you intend to
come out — come out in a vessel bound for
Port Antonio — or Annotto Bay — or Port Morant
Either of those places would answer
with — I hope the letter that I have Received
from you — his in your own hand writing
— On Receipt of this write me when that I may

turn over

look for your ance which ships - if you can
And give me all the news that you can
Respecting the North - and our families -
- And give my blessings to them all -
And my Sister Christie - tell her that I will
write soon to her

I am my dear Nephew
Yours with esteem
William Mackenzie

Port Antonio
Portland Jamaica
16 January 1819

To Mr Alexander Jun

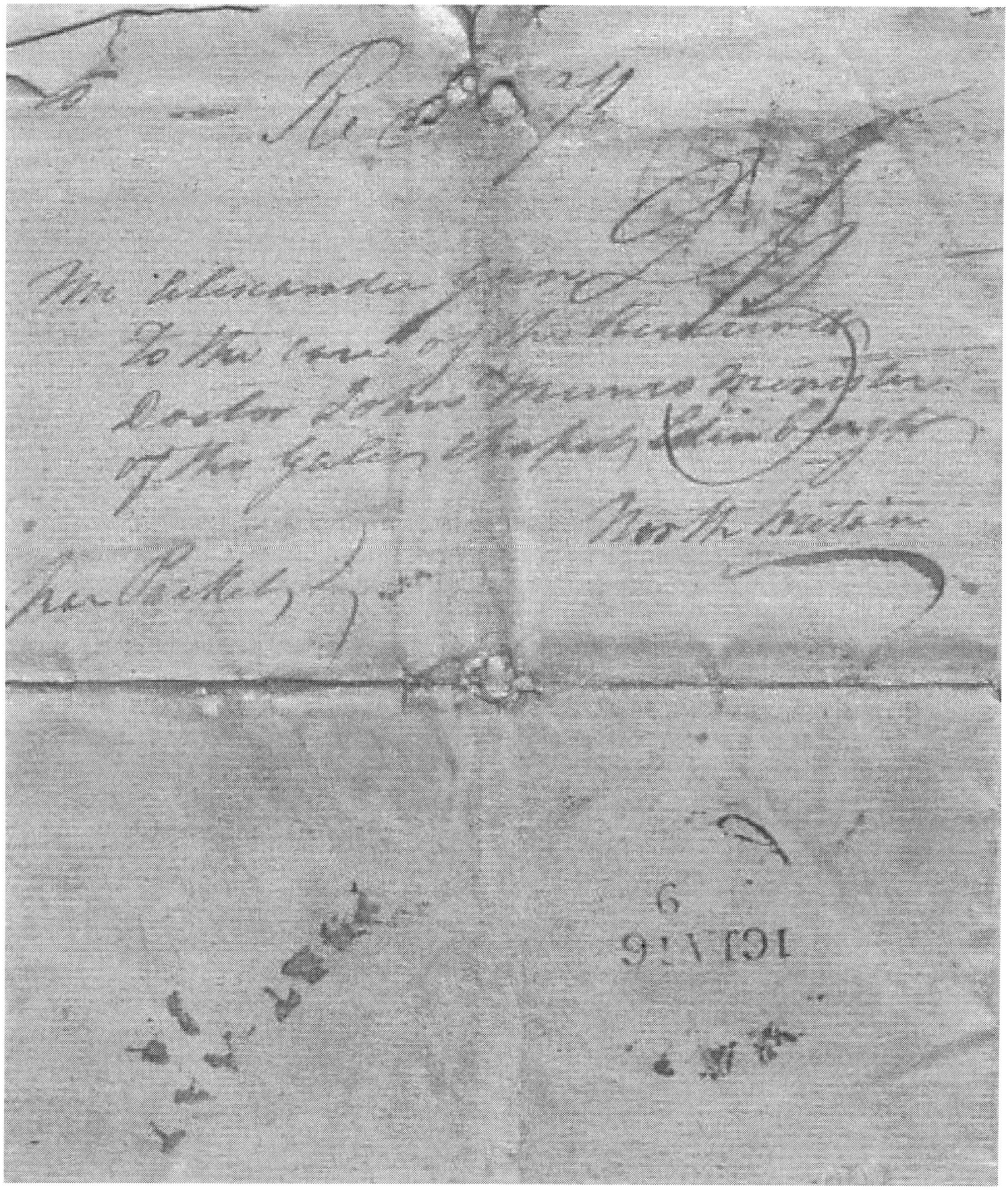

Very much not to the scale of the preceding pages

The above shows the marked section of the ‘outer’ of the letter; note the two line poor PORT ANT / JA (Port Antonio Jamaica mark), manuscript 2/3 being the cost of the letter to post (the inland UK mail rate 1812-1839 gives a cost of 1/1 for Edinburgh to London mail, so the rest must be the cost to post the letter from Jamaica to Britain), the red circular—probably British—arrival mark of MAR 4 1819, a circular date stamp mark of 16JA 9 (possibly a Jamaican transit mark as it is has the same poor quality of the Port Antonio part strike) and other marks. The letter is addressed ‘Mr Alexander Gunn to the care of the Reverend Doctor John Munro Minister of the Galic Chapel Edinburgh'. Where exactly was Alexander? Or is this merely a way to get the letter delivered by hand to Alexander in North

Scotland (it would save 4d)? Note that to send a letter to Jamaica and wait for a reply is about a year and that the British GPO ran the Jamaican external mails from 1755 to 1860.
A second and final letter exists from a member of the MacKenzie family. The letter is not by William; the endearment at the end is different as is the signature. In particular the letter from William refers to his 'sister Chirstie' and this letter refers to 'Aunt Christian'. I assume these are the same person, as such this may be written by William's wife. As well, there is a reference in this letter to 'your uncle William', written about four months after the previous letter—

Dear Nephew

your favour came to my hands sometime ago with a letter from your Aunt Christian and now will answer both in this letter -- what you say Rispecting your two young brothers I take notice of and if they have good Education as you say - will be much, in there favour in this Country, as such - if they have any wish to come to Jamaica - this will be their time. and mind that they must come out in the summer time of the year . and at the same time write me when, that I may Expect them, they must provide themselves well, with closes of every kind for the Jamaican seasons, and must Endeavour to come out in a ship Bound for Port Antonio - or Morantz bay -

- youl tell your Aunt that I am very glade, to hear from her - and that she is well - and that I will write her very soon -

- your uncle William told me that you wished much to come out yourself. therefor, the sonner that you come out, the better, being young -

-about twenty one years ago I (???) a Coffee Estate[681] Called Berriedale and sunk upon Coffee about Sixty Thousand pounds - where in I might have come home with a large Fortun. when I be gon Coffee give my best respects. to your aunts and all our friends - And with them my Dear Nephew I am yours most Respectfully

???? Mackenzie

Burriedale (?) Portland ,
Jamaica 13th April 1819

It is interesting to note that this letter is on 'Bath Superfine Paper'. This letter was addressed care of the Reverend John Munro in Merchant Street, Edinburgh but is most remarkable for the information given within. Obviously Alexander has decided not to go to Jamaica but one wonders which of his younger brother(s) were interested. £60,000 pounds buying a coffee estate in 1800 was obviously a huge amount of money; one wonders if the estate is now part of the exclusive 'Blue Mountain range' coffees of today which come from near Portland?

[681] It would be useful to know if this estate still exists.

Dear Nephew

Your favour came to my hand some time ago with a letter from your Aunt Christian and now will answer both in this letter —

— what you say respecting your two young brothers I take notice of and if they have good learning as you say — will be much in their favour in this Country, as such — if they have any wish to come to Jamaica — this will be their time — and mind that — they must come out in the summer time of the year — and at the same time write me when that I may expect them, they must provide themselves well, with Closes of every kind for the Jamaica Seasons, and must endeavour to come out in a ship Bound for Port Antonio or Morant Bay —

— You'll tell your Aunt that I am very glad to hear from her — and that she is well — and that I write with her very soon —

— Your uncle William told me that you wished much to come out yourself — therefore, the sooner that you come out, the better — being young —

— About twenty one years ago I settled a Coffee Estate Called Burnside and sunk upon Coffee about Sixty Thousand pounds — where in I might have come home with a large Fortune — when I began Coffee give my best respects to your Aunt and all our friends — and with esteem my Dear Nephew I am yours most

Respectfully

Chas Mackenzie

Burnside Portland
Jamaica 13th April 1817

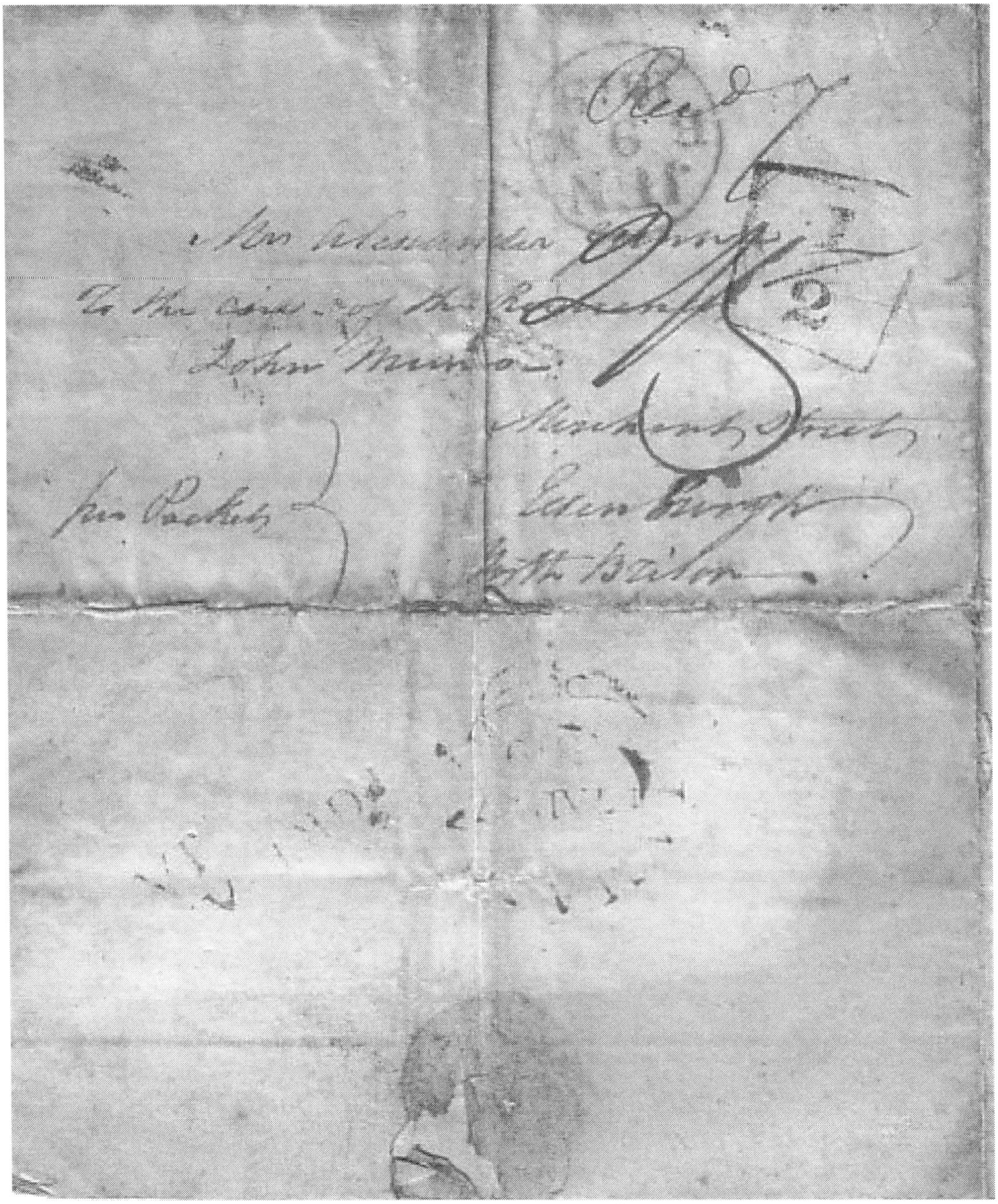

Not to scale with the letter

Note the PORT A(ntonio) JA(maica) light straight line mark, the 2/3 manuscript postage cost (and additional ½d boxed mark which was a further tax applied in Scotland on any letter carried by four wheel drive coaches), a light Jamaica 17 AP 1891 black circular mark (showing the letter took four days to just get to the main Post Office). The red June 9 1819 circular mark showing arrival again shows the time to sail across the Atlantic; not quite two months.

*****

It is not easy to unravel any career so long gone and the career of Alexander is a fine example of this problem. This is not due to a lack of information, but rather due to a plethora of information but much of it trivial. We know that he was interested in emigrating in the late 1810s but he did not go and the detail about him really commences in the 1820s (he married in 1829) when he was in his thirties.

An interesting (and amusing) letter to him is sent care of Mr Wm Brims Merchant Thurso Caithness. Fairly obviously this letter writer (Robert Hammond) is a friend and a businessman. It reflects well on Alexander—and on Robert Hammond—in terms of humour, friendship, honesty and parsimony. Alexander's father-in-law also lives close to Bualchork, one assumes. Although it is possible that the father-in-law is the person to whom the letter is sent in the first instance. The whisky sounds interesting as well… At this time Alexander is a shoe maker in Bualchork—

Edin[r] 25July 1824

Dear Sir

Your Letter I recived and Iam very sorry for what has happened to the sadles but the fault rests totally uppon your self being so cound founded hard as not to pay for a box and how the Divel do you suppose that I could afford it you not only Should pay the sadles but have a good tanned hide for carelessness and you may depend that I will give you a compleate blow up a bout them the next month when I come but Ceriously I dont know what to say a bout them I realy think by you given me a five pound note I will take them both back and run all Risque -

but without any Joke before I come to Caithness write to me what a sadler will repair them for as it will be out of my power to repair them for as it will be out of my power to repair them at that Quarter of the globe and I will Deduct that of the price or pay as a concencious man what they are worth to you and I make no doubt but we will both a gree to any thing that is reasonable and like wise advise me by post what things I may bring to pay my expences I was thinking to bring a few secondhand Sadles if I could fall in with them but it will be the latter end of August till I get a way but I will hold you at your word for bed and board and your whiskie will suffer if I am sposed and I may barter with sadles for that artickle with natives of the Island provided you will conduct me through your large forests with safety

and please give my father-in-law the pound and you and he will not fall out the price of the sadles are as follows

of two ladys sadles	£5
a hunting sadle	£1 12/-
	£6 12/-

I received the Box the fish was two dry but the whiskie was most excelent tell Mr. Gunn and I am glad to hear they got the boys clothes as for your old casks it is a great neglect of me not to send them but I will fetch them with me you will grudge the postage I know but just be content for I am that poor I cannot afford to pay your letter having lost forty pounds lately and it is most likely I will not cost you a nother before I come but neverthe less I will not grudge yours and expect you will write me immadetly and say what sort of bridles you want M[r.] C Jaims(?) is respects to you and your friends

your most obedient servant

Robt. Hammond

Edinr 25 July 1824

Dear Sir

Your Letter I received and I am
very sorry for what has happened to the
Sadles but the fault rests totally uppon
your self being so Pound-foolish and
as not to pay for a box and how the
Divel do you suppose that I could
afford it you not only should pay the
Sadles but have a good tanned hide for
Carelessness and you may depend that
I will give you a compleate blow up
a bout them the next month when I come
but Seriously I dont know what to say
a bout them I realy think by you sending
me a five pound note I will take them
both back and run all Risque —
but without any Joke before I come
to Caithness write to me what a Sadler
will repair them for. as it will be out
of my power to repair them at that
Quarter of the Globe and I will deduct

that of the price or Say as a
Concencious Man what they are worth
to you and I make no doubt but we
will both a gree to any thing that is
reasonable and like wise advise me
by post what things I may bring to
pay my expences I was thinking to bring
a few Secondhand Sadls if I could sell in
with them but it will be the latter end
of August till I get a way but I will hold
you at your word for bed and board and
your Whiskie will suffer if I am spared
and I may barter with Sadles for that
articlle with natives of the Island
provided you will conduct me through
your large forests with Safety

an please give my Father in Law the ~~other~~
pound and you and me will not fall out.
the price of the Sadls are as follows

To two Ladys Sadles	£5
a hunting Sadle	1 " 12
	£6 " 12

I received the Box of the fish was too dry
but the Whiskee was most excelent tell Mr Gunn
and I am glad to hear they got the boys both
as for your old casks it is a great neglect
of me not to send them but I will fetch them
with me   you will grudge the postage I know
but Just be content for I am that poor
I cannot afford to pay your letter having lost
forty pounds lately and it is most likely
I will cost you a nother be fore I come
but never the less I will not grudge yours
and expect you will write me Imadetly
and say what bit or bridles you want
Mrs C Joins in respects to you and
friends

Yours Mo obt Servent
R H Hammond

The relevant section of the outer of the letter; not to scale of the preceding pages.

Again the outer has the normal manuscript cross showing the postage cost and the additional ½d for post going on four wheels in Scotland at this time. Was it cheaper to direct the letter just to Thurso than all the way to Bulcork? Or was Alexander staying or working at Thurso at this time? Whether the saddles were for personal use or for sale by him is not known. At this point the answers are unknown…

Alexander is very much the businessman. There is an account (the amount was for one pound four shillings and sixpence and was settled within three months) in his hand to Mr. James McKenzie[682] 'Manager Thurso Tanyard' which was written at Boulchork on 17th October 1826 which reads:

Boulchork 17th Oct 1826

Sir

Please give the Bearer Neal McKay Olgrinbeg the half hide which he marked for himself and mark it to his own acct. and he shall pay you at the agreed time and for I action him and in so doing you will greatly oblige your obed. servt.

Alexr. Gunn

Shoemaker Boulchork

Mr and Mrs McKenzie Thurso

Tanyard

Settled

James McKenzie

---

[682] Was this McKenzie related to Alexander Gunn's mother, Janet McKenzie (703)? The tanyard was in Riverside Road, opposite what is now the Tourist Office. The land it occupied is now a public toilet.

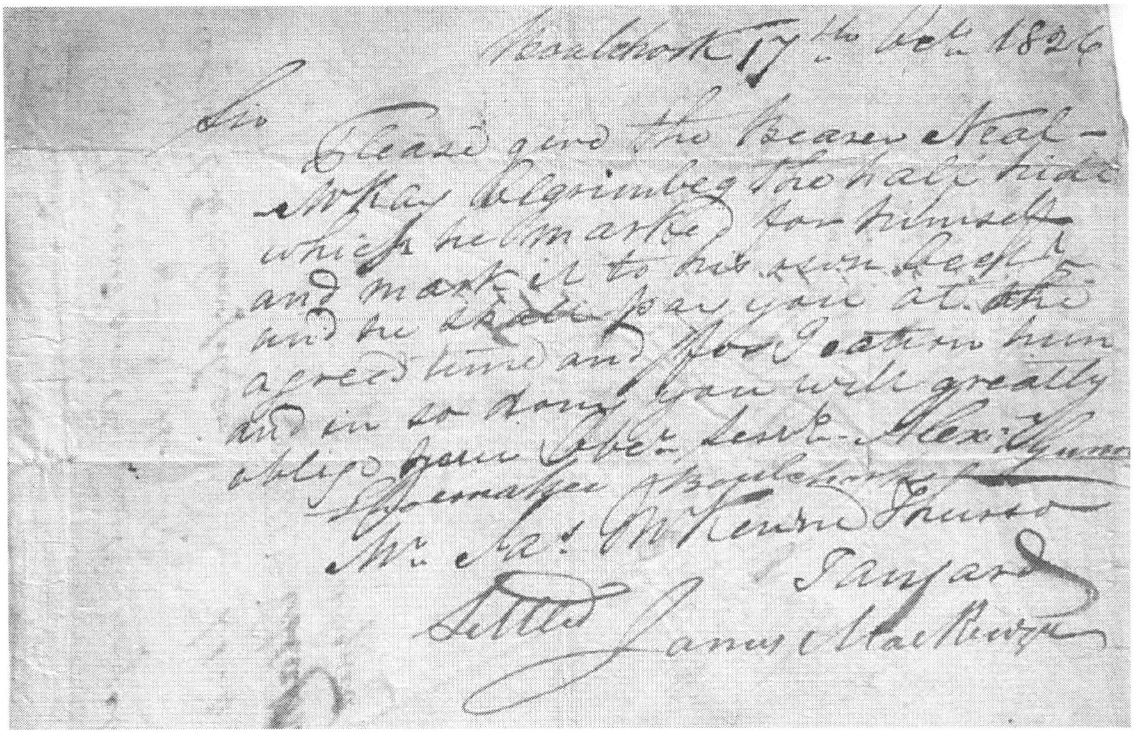

Boulchork 17th Octr 1826

Sir

Please give the bearer Neal McKay Olgrimbeg the half hide which he marked for himself and mark it to his own debt and he shall pay you at the agreed time and for paying him and in so doing you will greatly oblige your Obedt Servt Alex Gunn
Shoemaker of Boulchork

Mr. Alx. McKenzie Thurso
Tanyard

Settled James MacKenzie

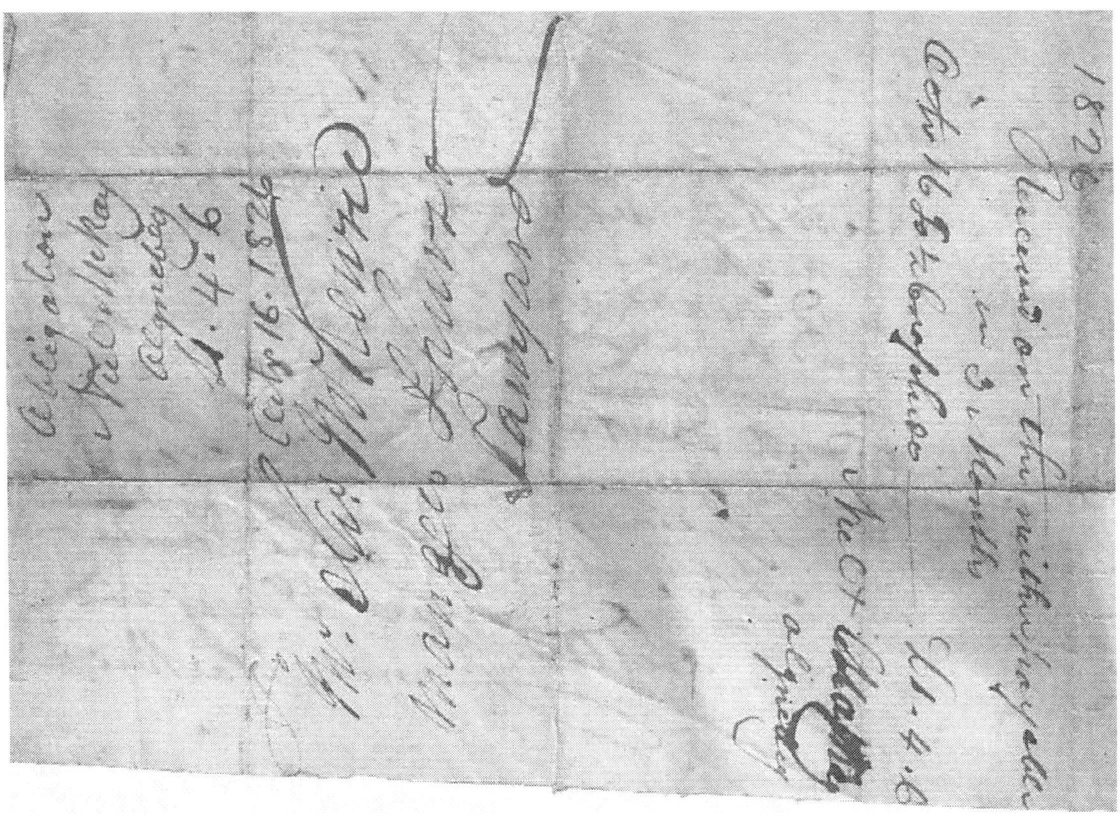

1826
Received on the within
Octr 16 £1.4.6

Obligation
Neil McKay
Olgrimbeg
£1.4.6

Octr 16 1826
Mr. Alex. McKenzie
Tanyard

The back is a little more awkward to decipher not least as the writing is at 180 degrees in parts. It basically is the recipient and address, details of the obligation to Neil McKay of Olgrinbeg and the details showing how it was paid.

But business is picking up and Alexander is busy. The next document is an account held by Mr Alexander Gunn Shoemaker Bulcork D[r] to John MDonald Merch[t] Calder for the period January1824 to October 1827. It's detailed and shows a busy business and what is needed to run that business. Alexander owed over £32 in a two year period mainly for such items as leather, tacks, material and oil—all items associated with his trade. Note the bottom lines on page two where it is pointed out that £1 paid in is not recorded by this merchant…

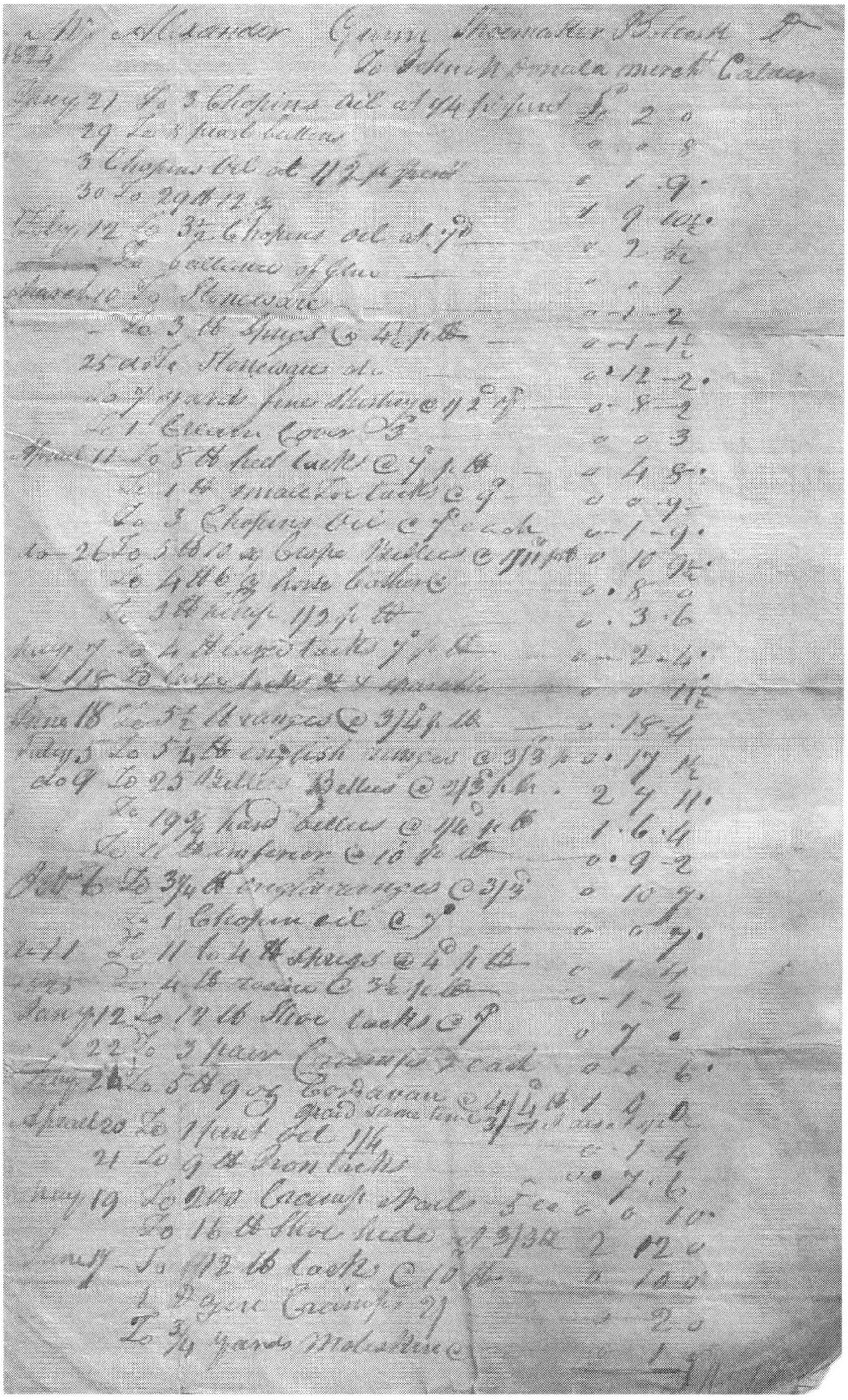
Mr Alexander Gunn Shoemaker Bulcork Dr
1824 To John McDonald Mercht Calder
Jany 21 To 3 Chopins oil at 1/4 p pint £0 2 0
29 To 8 [illegible] 0 0 8
3 Chopins oil at 1/2 p pint 0 1 9
30 To 29 lb 12 [illegible] 1 9 10½
Feby 12 To 3½ Chopins oil at 7d 0 2 0½
To ballance of Glue 0 0 1
March 10 To Stoneware 0 1 2
To 3 lb Sprigs @ 4½ p lb 0 1 1½
25 do To Stoneware do 0 12 2
To 7 yards fine Sheeting @ 1/2 [illegible] 0 8 2
To 1 Earthen Cover @ 3d 0 0 3
April 11 To 8 lb heel tacks @ 7d p lb 0 4 8
To 1 lb smaller tacks @ 9 0 0 9
To 3 Chopins Oil @ 7d each 0 1 9
do 26 To 5 lb 10 oz [illegible] Leather @ 1/11 p lb 0 10 9½
To 4 lb 6 oz horse leather 0 8 0
To 3 lb [illegible] 1/2 p lb 0 3 6
May 7 To 4 lb large tacks 7d p lb 0 2 4
[illegible] To large tacks [illegible] sparables 0 0 11½
June 18 To 5½ lb ranges @ 3/4 p lb 0 18 4
July 5 To 5¼ lb english ranges @ 3/3 p 0 17 1½
do 9 To 25 [illegible] Belles @ 2/3 p lb 2 7 11
To 19¾ hard belles @ 1/4 p lb 1 6 4
To 11 lb inferior @ 10 p lb 0 9 2
Octr 6 To 3¼ lb english ranges @ 3/3 0 10 7
To 1 Chopin oil @ 7d 0 0 7
do 11 To 11 lb 4 oz sprigs @ 4d p lb 0 1 4
[illegible] To 4 lb rosin @ 3½ p lb 0 1 2
Jany 12 To 12 lb Shoe tacks @ 7d 0 7 0
22 To 3 pair Crimps 2d each 0 0 6
Feby 24 To 5 lb 9 oz Cordavan @ 4/4 lb 1 0 0
paid same time 3/ [illegible]
April 20 To 1 pint oil 1/4 [illegible]
21 To 9 lb Iron tacks 0 1 4
0 7 6
May 19 To 200 Crimp nails 5d 0 0 10
To 16 lb Shoe hide @ 3/3 2 12 0
Jany 17 To 12 lb tacks @ 10 0 10 0
1 Dozen Crimps 2/ 0 2 0
To ¾ yards Moleskin @ 0 1 9

	Brought over amount of	£16 6 5½
	To Buttons 7	£0 0 7
	To thread 1/4 silk 6d wax 1½	0 0 11½
July 13	To 9 lb 14 oz english range @ 3/4	1 12 11
Oct 10	To 4 lb 8 oz Kip leather @ 3/3	0 14 7
	To 4 lb 8 oz english range @ 3/2	0 14 5
	To 2 lb 3 oz upper leather @ 4d	0 4 [illegible]
	To 9 oz [illegible] range @ 2	0 1 6
	To 2 lb sole backs @ 9d lb is	0 1 6
Nov 10	To 1 Chopin oil 9d	0 0 9
Dec 28	To 3 Chopins oil 1/ each	0 2 6
Jan 1827	To 6 lb rosin at 3½	0 1 9
	To 8 sheet paper @	0 0 6
Feby 14	To 3½ Dozen pair Cramp 2/	0 7 0
June 3	To 5 lb Cordovan @ 3/6 lb	0 17 6
	To 11 english range @ 3/2	1 14 10
	To 1 piece Cordovan at 6	0 0 6
Octr	To 66¼ lb english butt @ 2/6	8 6 [illegible]
Nov 16	To 1 Moleskin [illegible]	0 0 5
26	To 9 lb foreign bend @ 2/	0 18 0
		32 7 2

	By Cash in Ledger	£8 5 0	
1827	By Cash [illegible] in £ 13	7 8 0	
		Totall	15 13 0
1827		Ballance Due	£16 14 2
Octr	By Cash in full this 9 Oct 1827		15 12 7

J. McDonald

1826
Dec 1

One Pound [illegible] being paid by me and not marked in [illegible] Books which [illegible] cannot [illegible] [illegible] paid [illegible] the Balance [illegible] than £2 - [illegible]

Further large accounts exist with money going in and out; the next two sides are from James McKenzie at the Thurso Tanyard December 1827-September 1829—

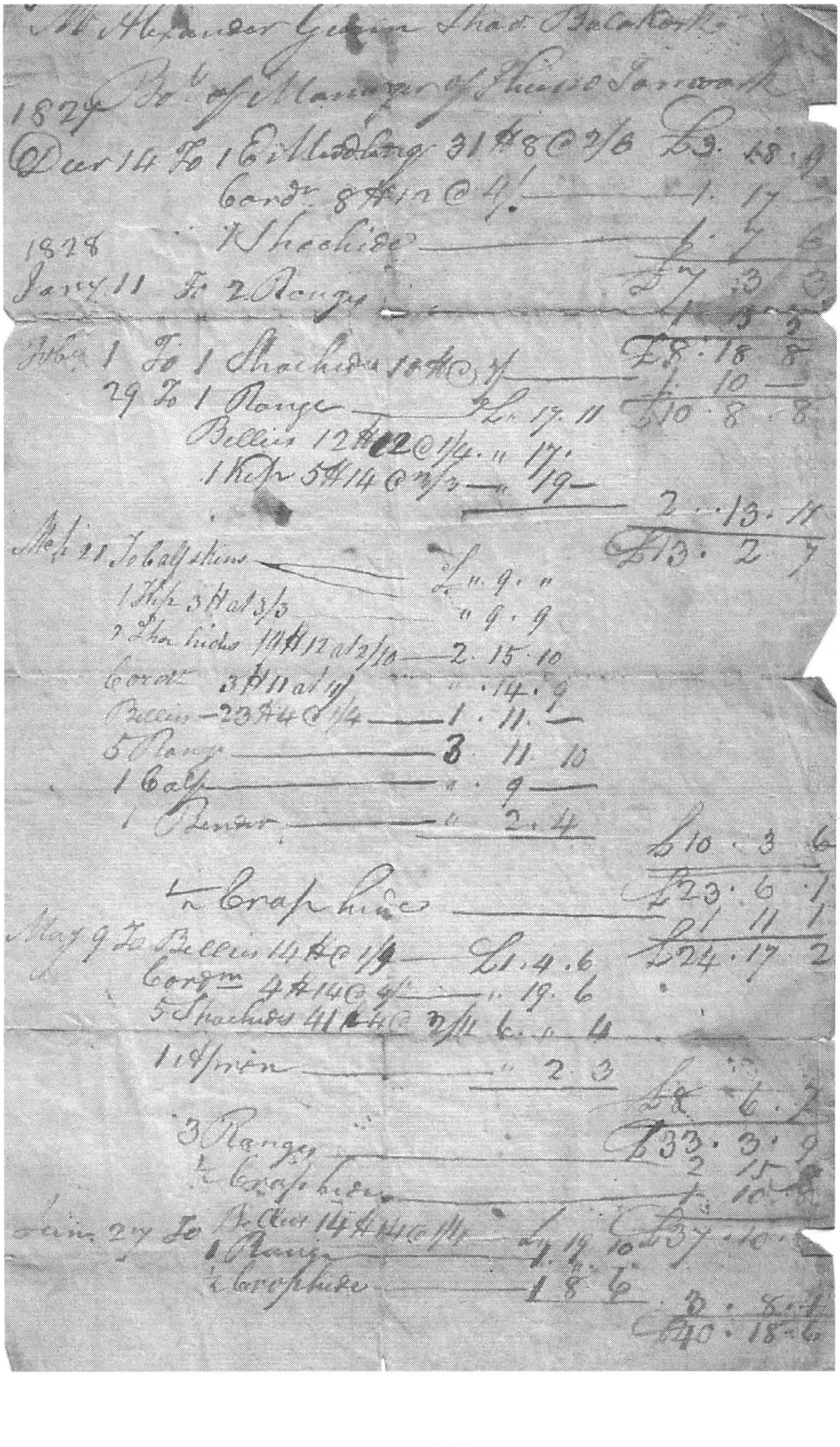

1828	Brought over		£40 . 18 . 6
July 16	To 1 Range	£1 . 1 . 2	
	1 Butt 4# @ 4	5 . 5	
	1 Benger	2 . 4	
	1 Sheehide 9# 8 @ 3	1 . 8 . 6	
			2 . 17 . 5
			£43 . 15 . 11
	2 Butts 9# @ 1/9		16 . 7
			44 . 12 . 6
	To Cordovan 3# 10 @ 4/		14 . 6
Augt 22	By Cash		£45 . 7 .
			10 . 1
	To 1 Ellastring 32# @ 2/6	£4 . .	£35 . 7 .
	1 Crophide 21# @ 4	1 . 16 . 9	
	1 Range	18 . 6	
	2 Sheehides	2 . 10	
	2 Butts 7# @ 1/9	. 12 . 3	£10 . . 6
			£45 . 7 .
Sept 15	To 1 Sheehide 10# 4 @ 3/		1 . 10 .
1829			
July 29	By Cash		22
			£24 . 18 . 3
	7 July Sheehide	11/6	
	Cordovan 1# 15	7 9	
			19 . 3
			1 . 3 . 2
Augt 29	By Cash		27 . . 8
			25 . 17 . 6
	Discount 1/7		£1 . 3 . 2
	Cash 1/		1 . 3 .

[illegible]

The sums are enormous; Alexander must be doing more than shoes[683]! He has certainly earned some money; the next document indicates he lent £50 (in three lots; £10, £20, £20) to Donald M^c^Donald Shoemaker. But was the money just £10 with an added £10 the following year which was rolled over? The amounts to be repaid were due on Nov. 2 1827, Nov. 2 1828, Nov. 2 1829. Witnesses were Sinclair Murray and John Sutherland—

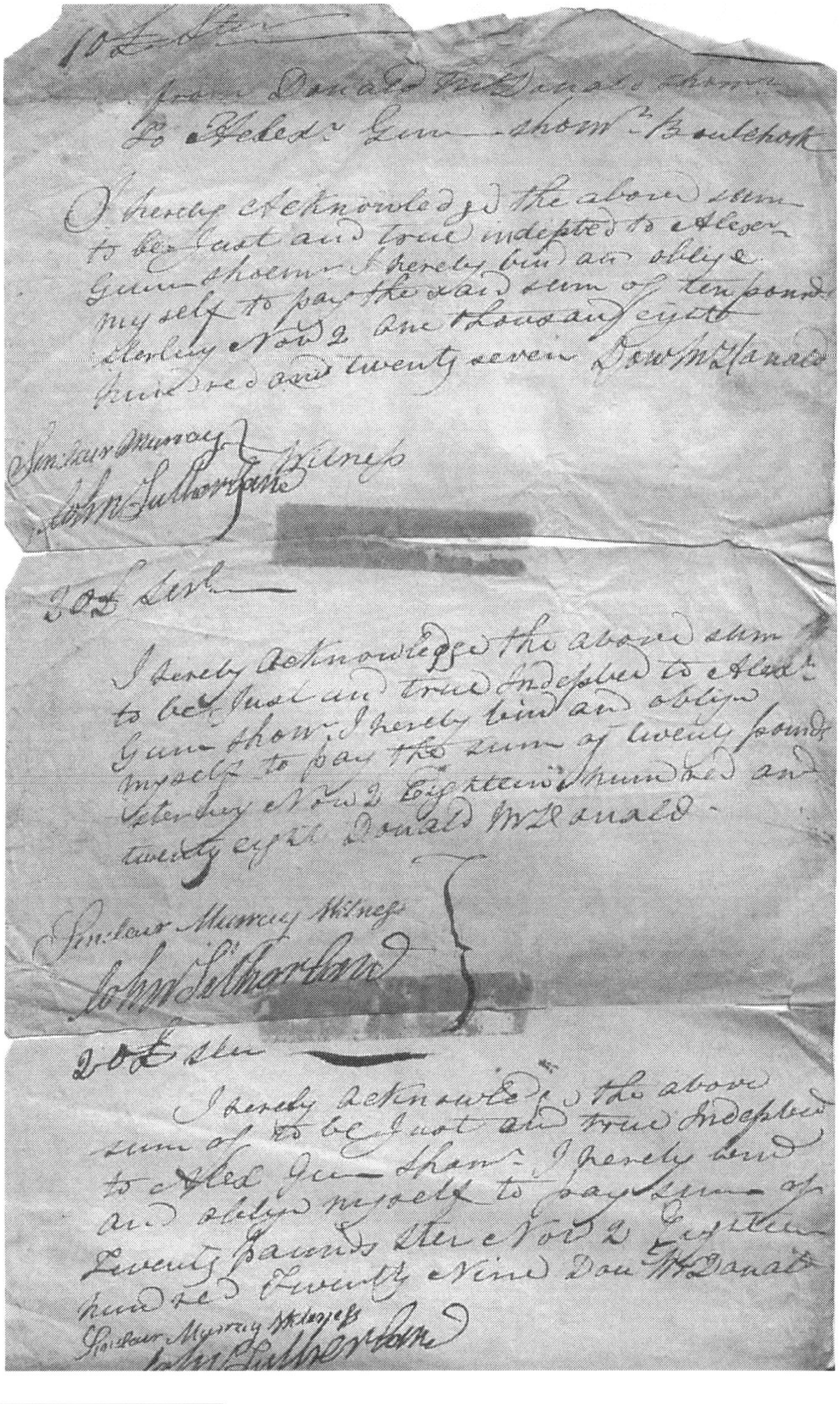
10 £ Ster

from Donald McDonald Shoemr

To Alexr Gun shoemr Boulchork

I hereby acknowledge the above sum to be just and true indepted to Alexr Gun shoemr I hereby bind and oblige myself to pay the said sum of ten pounds sterling Nov 2 One thousand eight hundred and twenty seven Don McDonald

Sinclair Murray }
John Sutherland } Witness

30 £ Ster

I hereby acknowledge the above sum to be just and true indepted to Alexr Gun shoemr I hereby bind and oblige myself to pay the sum of twenty pounds sterling Nov 2 Eighteen hundred and twenty eight Donald McDonald

Sinclair Murray Witness }
John Sutherland }

20 £ ster

I hereby acknowledge the above sum of to be just and true indepted to Alexr Gun Shoemr I hereby bind and oblige myself to pay sum of twenty pounds Ster Nov 2 Eighteen hundred and twenty nine Don McDonald

Sinclair Murray Witness
John Sutherland

---

[683]Shoemakers were viewed as one of the more literate 'upper class' tradesmen—they had the time and place to read. See http://www.electricscotland.com/history/1820/1820_rising.htm

There is an interesting receipt from 1827 which reads—

Thurso 8 Sep 1827 Recd this day from John Suth[d] Horntick(?) Dunbeath one pound Stg through the hands of Mr Alex Gunn

D Munro

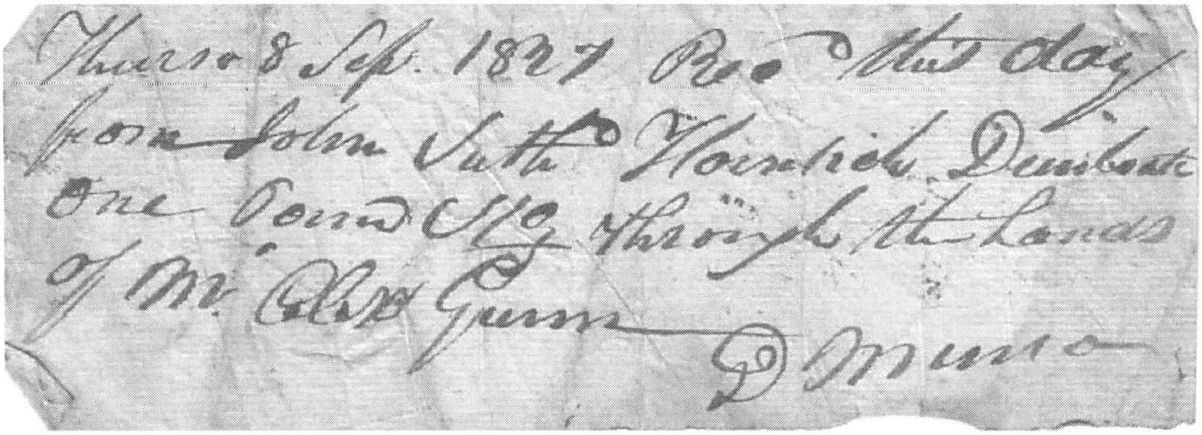

He is helping others by paying for them 'through the hands'; it shows integration into the community.

He also ran a small bill with David Henderson of Westerdale around this time—

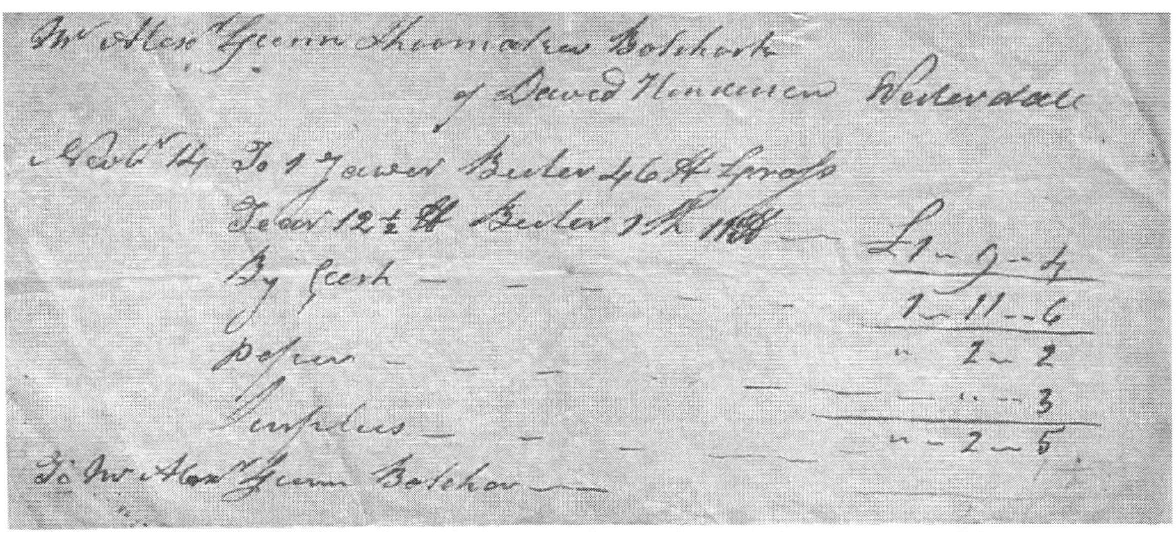

Mr Alexr Gunn Shoemaker Botchart
of David Henderson Westerdale

Feby 14 To 1 [illegible] Butter 46 lb [illegible]
[illegible] 12½ lb Butter 1st 1828 — £1-9-4
By Cash — 1-11-6
Paper — -2-2
— -3
Surplus — -2-5

To Mr Alexr Gunn Botchar

He also bought items for cash from Alex. Gillon in Edinburgh on the 16th of October 1828—

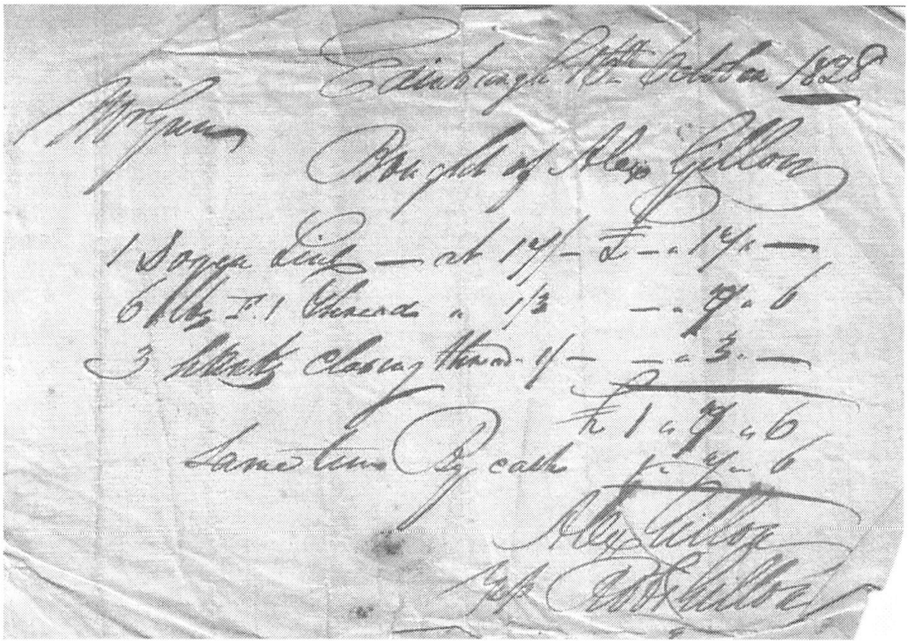
Edinburgh 16th October 1828
Mr Gunn
Bought of Alex Gillon
1 [illegible] — at 14/- £ — 14 —
6 lbs [illegible] Thread 1/3 — 7 . 6
3 [illegible] closing thread 1/- — 3 —
£1 4 6
Same time By cash 1 4 6
Alex Gillon
p. Robt Gillon

Note that it is signed by Robt Gillon on behalf of Alex Gillon.

Alexander also ran his own accounts. A note from George Gunn Mybster (March 15th 1828) reads

Mybster March 15th 1828

Sir all the grievance that I sustain by your acct to me you will come to know by comparing this to your acct which I hope you will acgree with and place the sum (?) to the credit of Mr Alexr. McLeods account and I am Sir your most obdt. Svnt.

Geo. Gunn

To Mr A Gunn Shoemaker

Bualchork

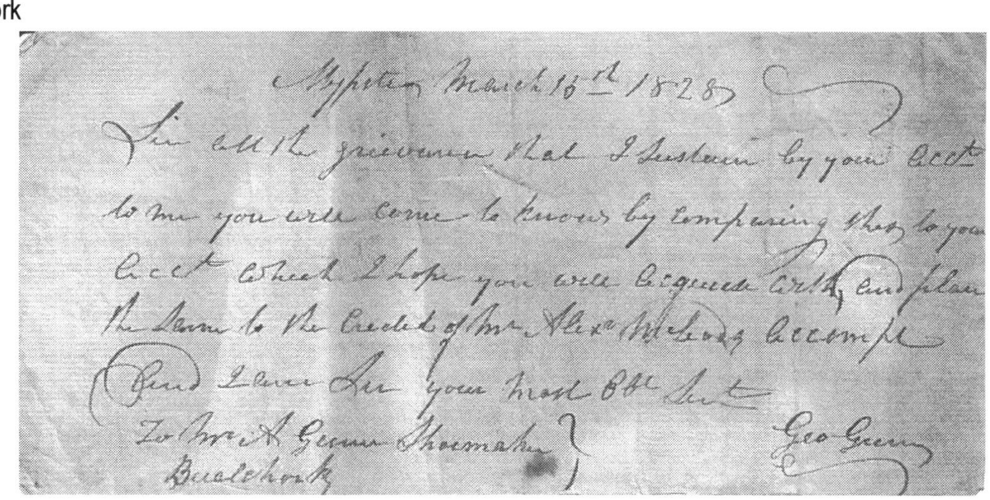
Mybster March 15th 1828
Sir all the grievance that I sustain by your Acct to me you will come to know by comparing this to your Acct which I hope you will acquiesce with and place the sum to the credit of Mr Alexr McLeods account and I am Sir your most obdt Svnt
To Mr A Gunn Shoemaker
Bualchork
Geo Gunn

The original account from Alexander does not exist but the sum that George Gunn was in credit was, in his eyes, nearly ten shillings—

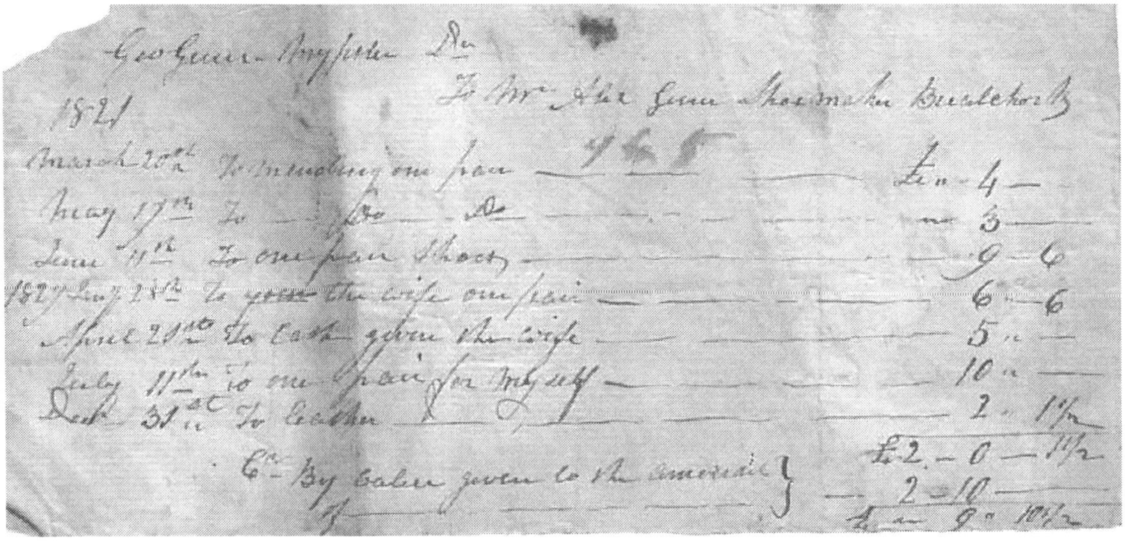
Geo Gunn Dr
To Mr Alex Gunn Shoemaker
1821
March 20th To mending one pair — £ 4 —
May 17th To Do Do — 3 —
June 4th To one pair Shoes — 9 6
1822 Aug 28th To the wife one pair — 6 6
April 21st To cash given the wife — 5 —
July 11th To one pair for myself — 10 —
Decr 31st To Leather — 2 1½
£2 — 0 — 1½
Cr By Balance given to the amount — 2 10 —
£ — 9 — 10½

A large difference from being an actual debtor and probably a good reason to close his account with Alexander if his sums were accurate!

Alexander married Barbara Gunn (Gunn is both her maiden and marred surname but of her line see Parts 4 and 5 in particular) on the 19th March 1829. She was nineteen and he was forty.

There is a second letter[684] from Robert Hammond to Alexander (care of Mr Benjamen Murray (Munro?) Inn Keeper(?) Thurso) written in Edinburgh on 6th January 1829. It begins with an account -

Mr Alex^r Gunn

Edin^r 6TH January 1829
To Robert Hammond Saddler

1828		
Dec.8	one Ladys sadle	£ 2/5/-
	8 sadles at 1/11/6	12/12/-
	one hand plate suffle(?)	14/-
	two table cloths	6/-
	Barrol	2/6
		£15-19-6

Dear Sir

I had your letter partly wrote when the goods was shipped on December last - I am sorry that I could not find the old sadle that you Bought from me owing to the person that I purchased them from making no a batement uppon the large one therefore our Bargain was with drawn but the new one you will find a Bargain at the money -I am very sory to inform you that my Brother John has nearly ruined me with Security for him the a mount being £96 I would have wrote you long a go but oweing to the state of mind that I was in made me past doing any thing - if you could send me one ankor of Whiskie A long with one for Mr Russell(?) as soon as

---

[684] See page 137 for his first letter.

possible you will oblidge me to send it by the next vessell - I trust you are in better spirits than Iam at present - you will please pay Grandfather 10/- I would have allowed more but it is realy more than I can afford - for how I am to get that money raisd I cannot tell - Mrs Hammonds Compliments to you not forgeting your Father Mother & Sisters - if you can conveneny send some of the money down it will be a favour - & best here & loose no time with the whiskie

I am
Dr sir
Yours Respectfully
Robt. Hammond

To Alex^r Gunn Esq.
of
Boulchork
Caithness

Mr Alex^r Gunn
To Robt Hammond

1828		
Dec 8	one ladys sadle	£2/10/-
	8 sadles at £1/13/-	13/8/-
		£15/18/-

Sir
I have send the sadles by the Johno Groat trust that they will please and turn out to your intire satisfaction when your further comands will oblige
Your humble servant
Robt Hammond

A fascinating letter; where is the 'whiskie' from? Who is the Grandfather? Note this issue of the need to provide money to members of the family; we are pre 'social welfare' here.

Mr Alexr Gunn Edinr 6th Jany 1829

To Robert Cramond Sadler

1828

Decr 8	One Lady's Sadle	£ 2. 5. –
" "	8 Sadles at £ 1. 11. 6	12. 12 –
" "	One hard plate Arngale	. 14 –
" "	Two Table Cloths	. 6.
" "	Barrol	2. 6
		£ 15 - 19 . 6

Dr Sir

I Recd your Letter partly wrote
when the Goods was shipped on December
last – I am sorry that I could not send
the old sadle that you bought from me
owing to the person that I purchased it
from insisting on a batement upon the
large one therefore our Bargain was
with drawn but the new one you will find
a Bargain at the money – I am very sorry
to inform you that my Brother John has
nearly ruined me with security for him the
Amount being 96 £ I would have wrote
you long a go but owing to the state
of mind that I was in made me past doing
any thing – if you could send me one Anker
of Whiskie a long with one for Mr Russell as soon
as possible you will oblige me to send it by

the next vessell — I trust you are in
better spirits than I am at present — you
will please pay Grandfather 10/ I would have
allowed more but it is realy more than
I can afford — for how I am to get that mony
raised I cannot tell — Mrs Cramonds
Compliments to you not forgeting your
Father Mother & sisters — if you can conveni
=enty send some of the mony soon it
will be a favour — & be shure & loose
no time with the Whiskee

I am
Dr Sir
yours Respectfully
Robt Cramond

To Alexr Gunn Esqr
of
Boulcouk
Caithness

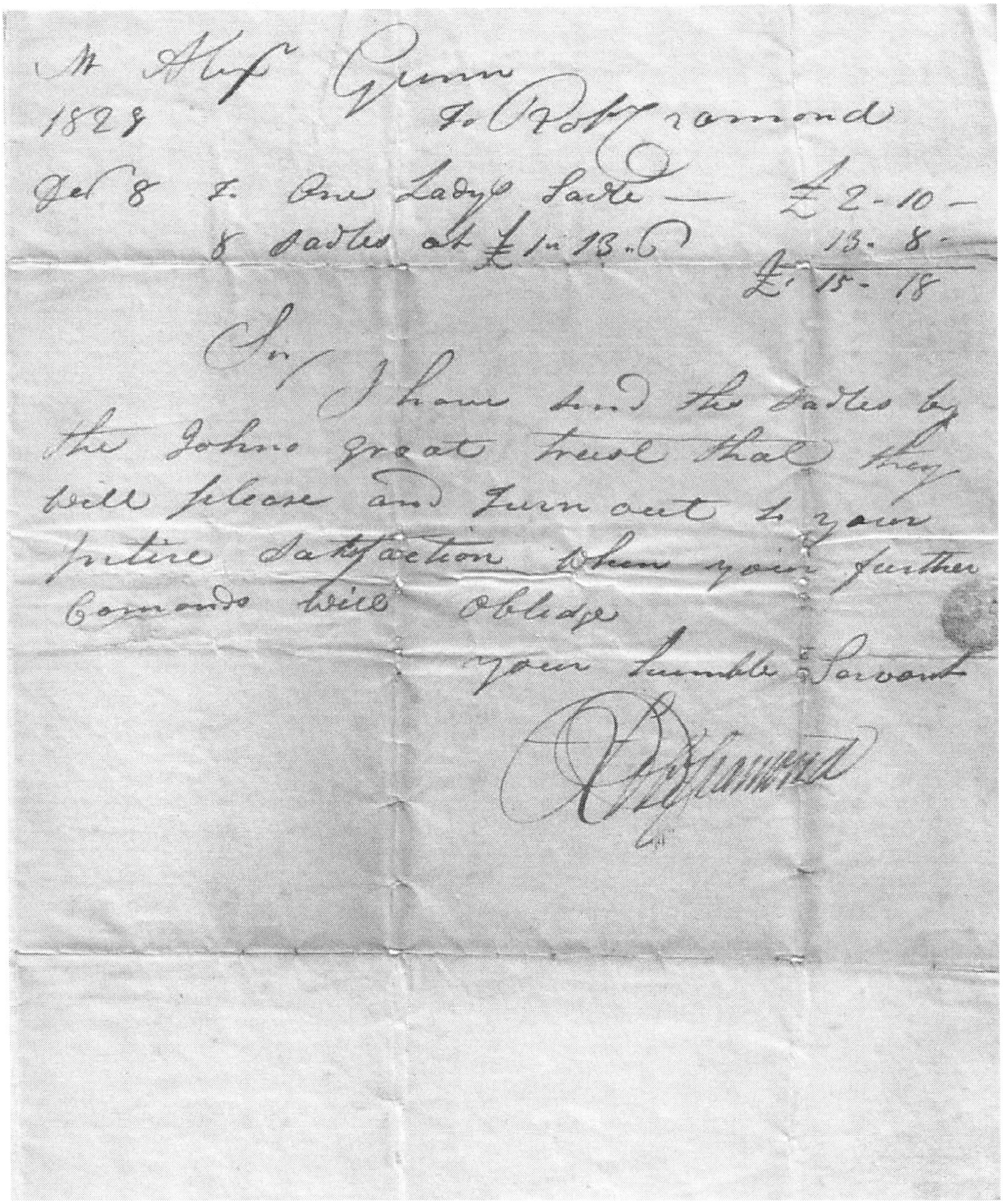

Mr Alexr Gunn
1828 To Robt Drummond

Oct 8 To One Ladys Sadle — £2-10-
8 Sadles at £1-13-6 13-8-
£15-18

Sir
I have send the Sadles by the Johns great trust that they will please and turn out to your intire Satisfaction When your further Comands will Oblidge
Your humble Servant
R Drummond

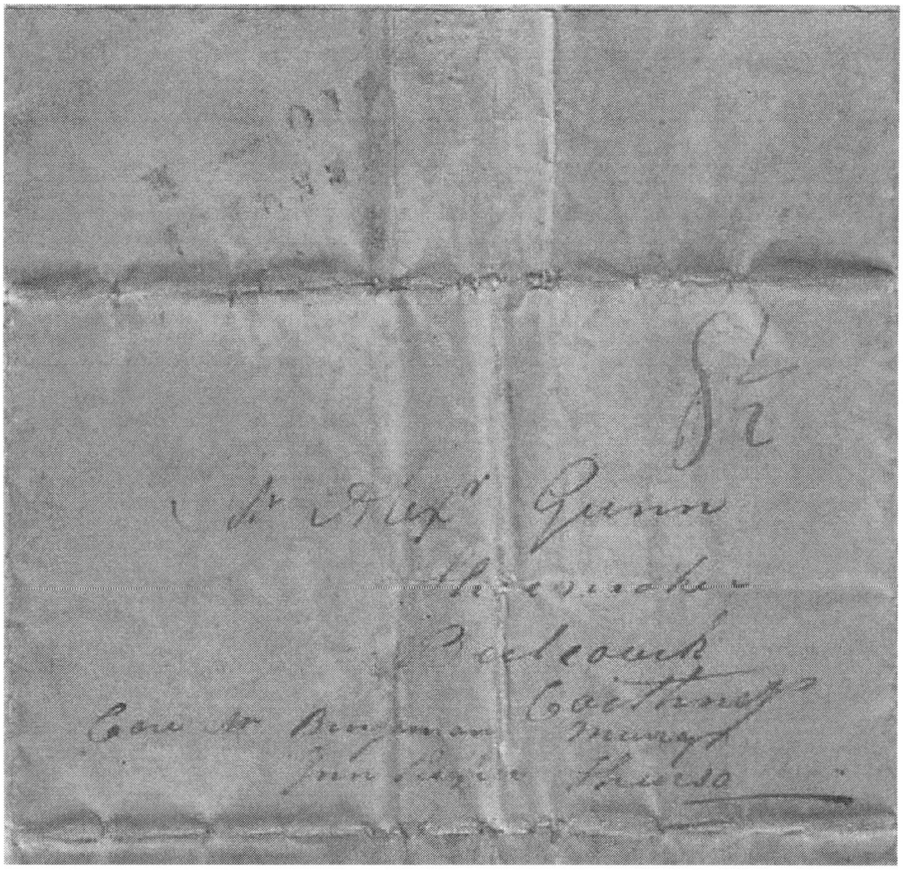
8½
Mr Alexr Gunn
Shoemaker
Bulcourk
Caithness
Care Mr Benjamen Murray
Inn Keeper Thurso

Not to scale with the preceding pages.

The letter is expensive—8½d. The address is of interest as well; Mr Alexr Gunn / Shoemaker / Bulcourk / Caithness / Care Mr Benjamen Murray / Inn Keeper / Thurso. Note the Inn Keeper; is it he who provides the whisky? Is that why the letter is sent to him, to ensure the whisky is not forgotten? At the top is a typical two line straight mark detailing distance from Edinburgh. This one is a transit mark and has the letters…ERWA ... and a mileage second line ...10-E; Erwa being part of a place name and the …10-E indicates distance from Edinburgh.

Somewhere in his life, though, remains the unusual. There is a pawn ticket 'for a silver watch Jn Otway London 1380(?)' Was 1380 a docket number? Or the year misplaced and should it be be 1830? Is this a pawn ticket? Or part payment for some bill? This document is just not able to be pinned down—

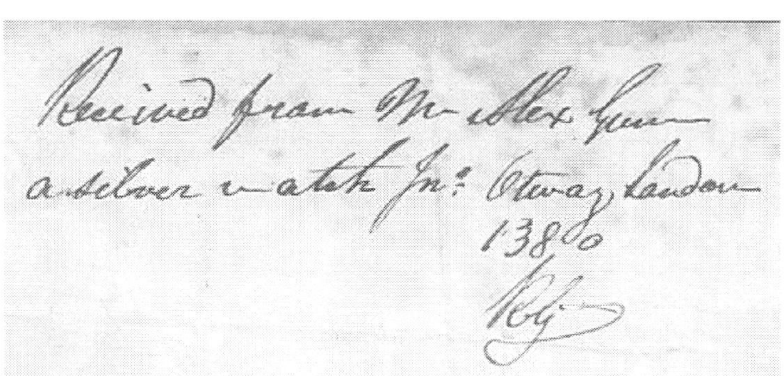
Received from Mr Alex Gunn
a silver watch Jno Otway London
1380
[illegible]

Further bills by or for Alexander exist. An interesting one (printed) is from Stark, Gunn and Co. for a variety of tacks and similar goods. They were based in Falkirk. Note that credit is now printed on the bill '6 months running'. They were to let Alexander

'know of 4 bags tacks to which our mutual friends Messrs Sutherland & Gunn Swiney (?) ordered us to send...'

One wonders why? The interplay of commerce at this time cannot be followed.

The confusion is that it is addressed to Mr A Gunn Shoemaker Bualchork care of Mr A Gunn Merchant Thurso!

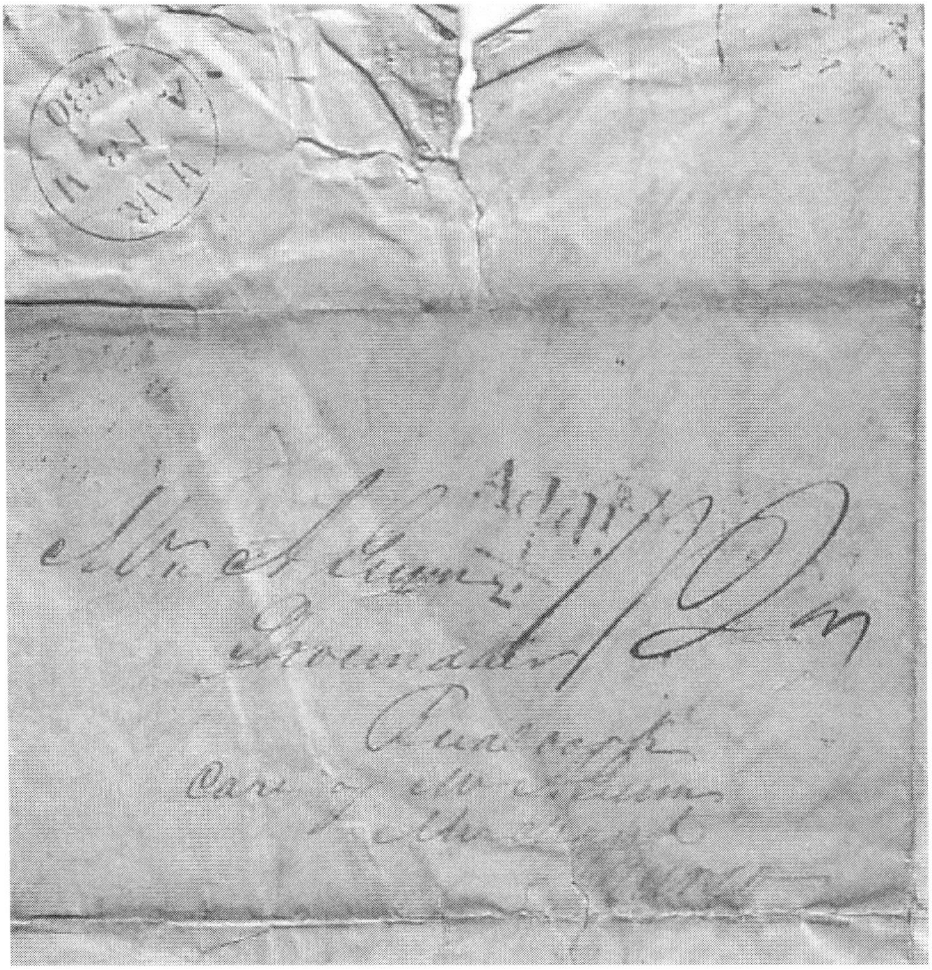

Note the manuscript cost of posting the bill—½d with the normal further ADDL ½ bill. There is a red transit circular date stamp of 18 March 1830.

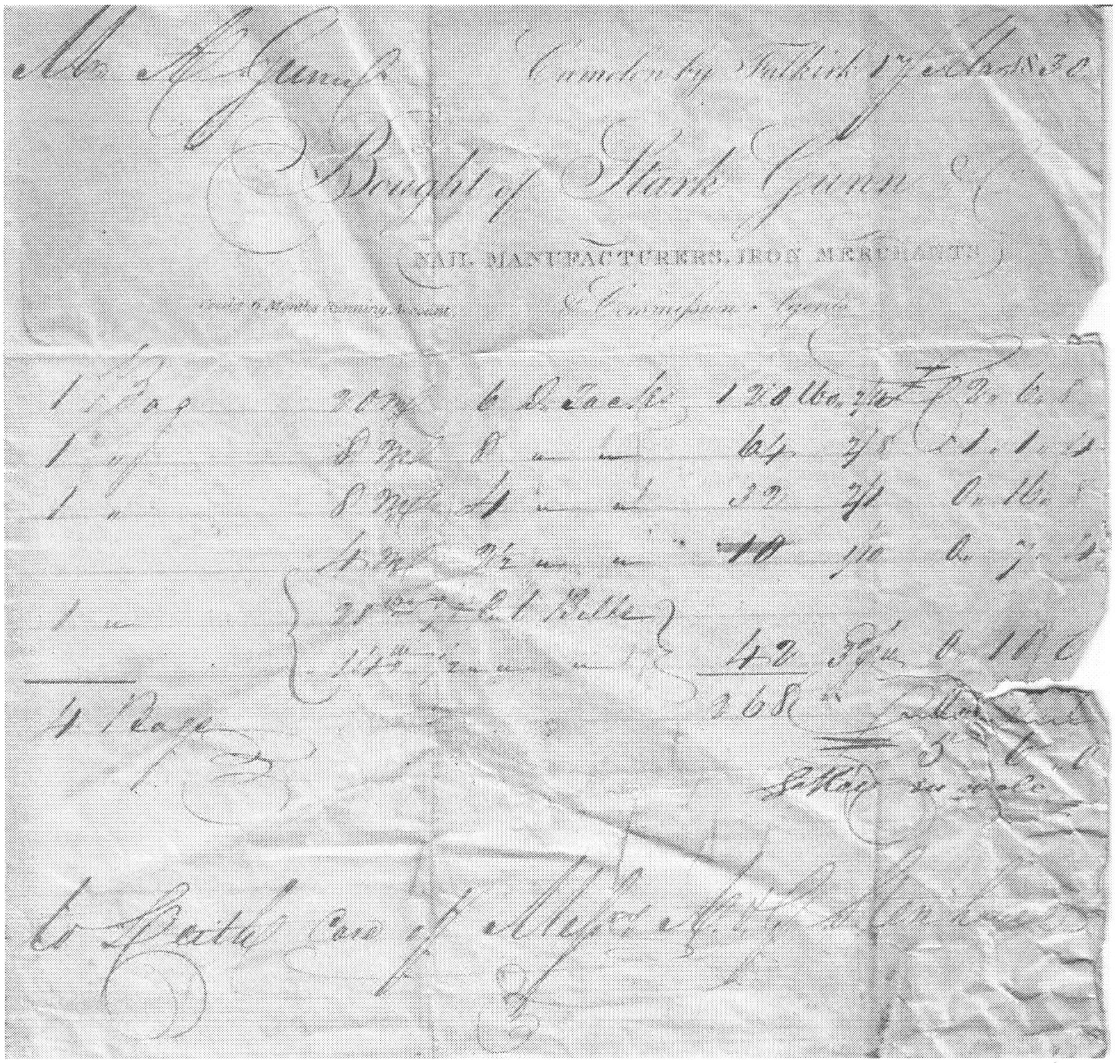

Mr A. Gunn Esq. Camelon by Falkirk 17th Jan 1830

Bought of Stark Gunn & Co.

NAIL MANUFACTURERS, IRON MERCHANTS & Commission Agents

Credit 6 Months Running Account.

1 Bag	20 M	6 D. Tacks	120 lbs	7/10	3 . 6 . 8
1 "	8 M	8 " "	64	7/8	1 . 1 . 4
1 "	8 M	4 " "	32	7/1	0 . 16 . 8
	4 M	2½ " "	10	7/10	0 . 7 . 4
1 "	28 M	[illegible]			
	14 M	" " "	42	[illegible]	0 . 18 . 0
4 Bags			268	[illegible]	5 . 6 . 0

[illegible]

to Leith care of Messrs [illegible]

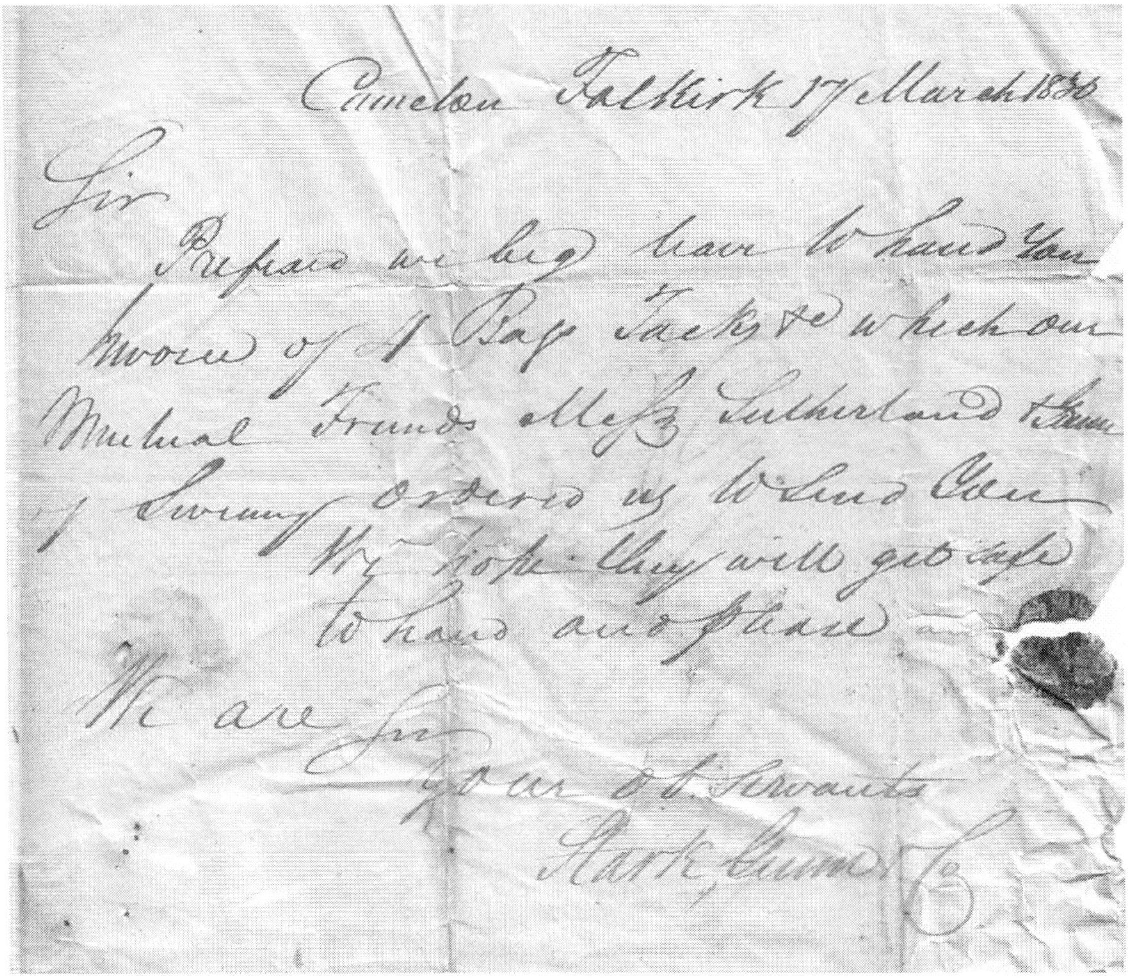

Camelon Falkirk 17 March 1830

Sir

Prefixed we beg leave to hand You
Invoice of 4 Bags Tacks &c which our
Mutual Friends Messrs Sutherland & Gunn
of Swiney ordered us to send Over
by Hope they will get safe
to hand and please

We are Sir
Your ob. Servants
Stark, Cumm[illegible] & Co

The following bill for over £35 was run up by Alexander in one day on March 25, 1830 for material for his trade (Cordwain, Shoe hides, skins etc.)!

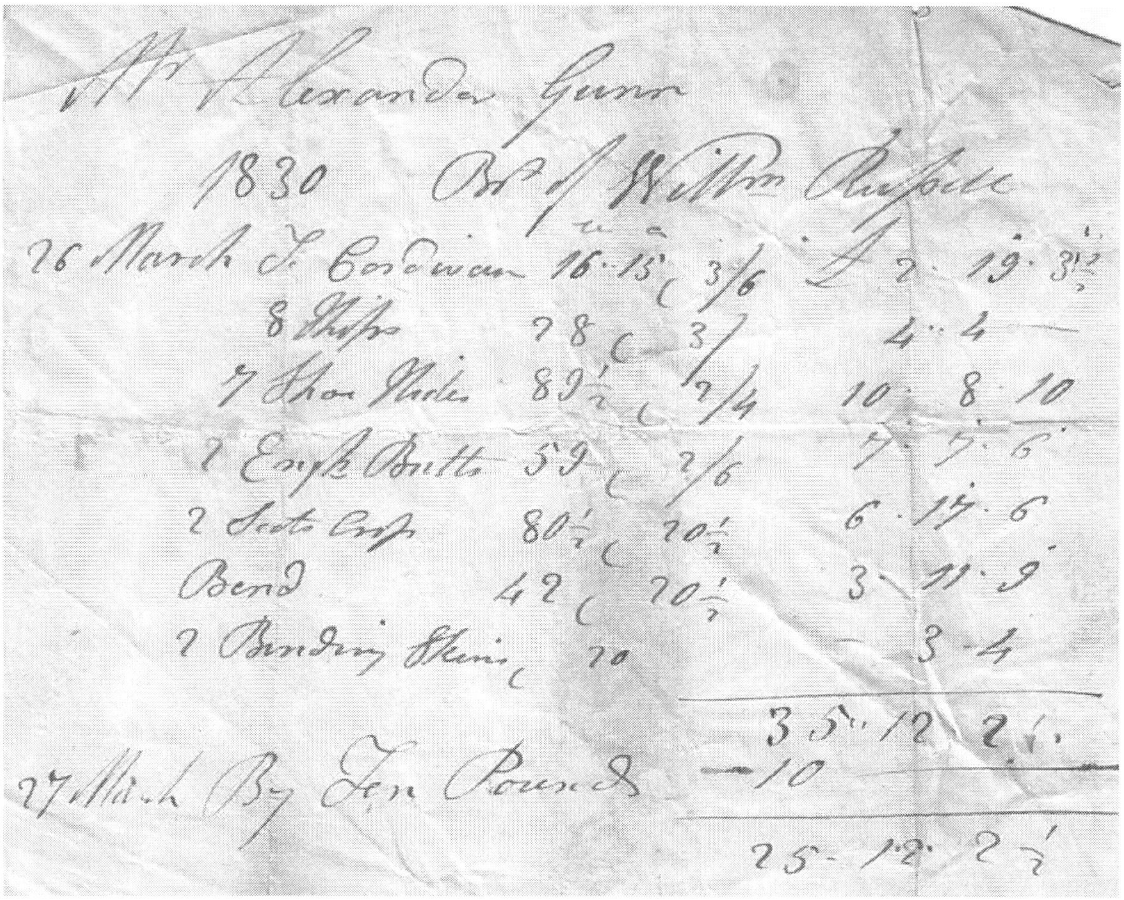

Mr Alexander Gunn

1830 Bot of Willm Russell

26 March	To Cordwain	16.15	@ 3/6	£ 2. 19. 3½
	8 Skins	28	@ 3/	4. 4 —
	7 Shoe Hides	89½	@ 2/4	10. 8. 10
	2 Engh Butts	59	@ 2/6	7. 7. 6
	2 Scots Crop	80½	@ 20½	6. 17. 6
	Bend	42	@ 20½	3. 11. 9
	2 Binding Skins		@ 20	— 3. 4
				35. 12. 2½
27 March	By Ten Pound			— 10
				25. 12. 2½

Of real interest is the following receipt showing Alexander's possession of Brawlbin—not Bualchork. It reads—

Calder 4th May 1830 Recd. from Mr Alex. Gunn Tenant Brawlbin sixteen shillings & 10 ½ being full payment of his acct till this date

Don Hamilton

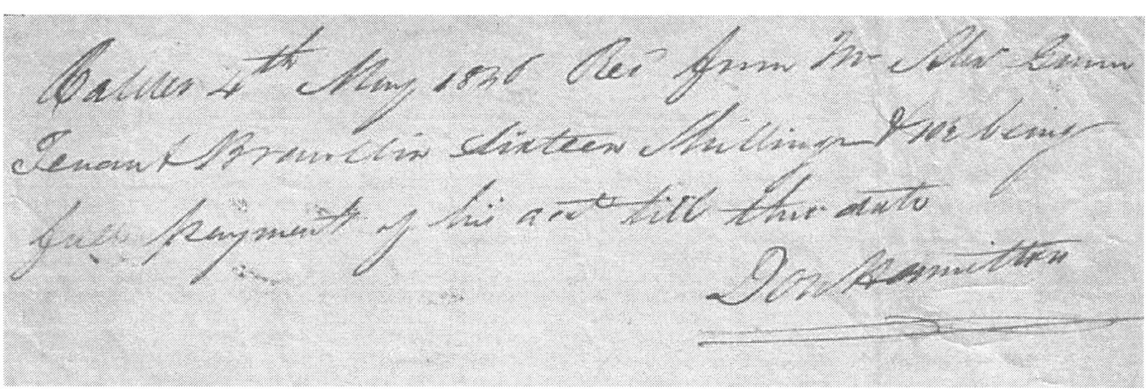

Calder 4th May 1830 Recd from Mr Alex Gunn Tenant Brawlbin Sixteen Shillings & 10½ being full payment of his acct till this date

Don Hamilton

And a further bill in favour of Alexander Gunn shoemaker at Brawlbin for October 1830—

To one pair of Shoes at

To one pair of Shoes at

Alexr Gunn Shoemaker

But this shift to Brawlbin is not known by everyone. Alexander may have been content to run up bills and have bills run up on him (seemingly typical of his society) but his citation of Peter Macdonald Tenant of (?) Blanful (?) of Shurrery before "The Honourable His Majesty's Justices of the Peace for the settling of sixteen shillings and one penny" is uncommon in his extant papers. The writ was obtained at Thurso on 11 October 1830 and the action was due to be held on the 21st of October. The summons was issued under the hand of Nile Miller clerk and served by Constable James Mackay on the twelfth 'delivering to him (McDonald) personally apprehended'. The actual cost for this service being 6/3d which is a significant percentage of the principal. (Warrant and copy 1/7d Travelling fees 4/4d -----(?) 4d).

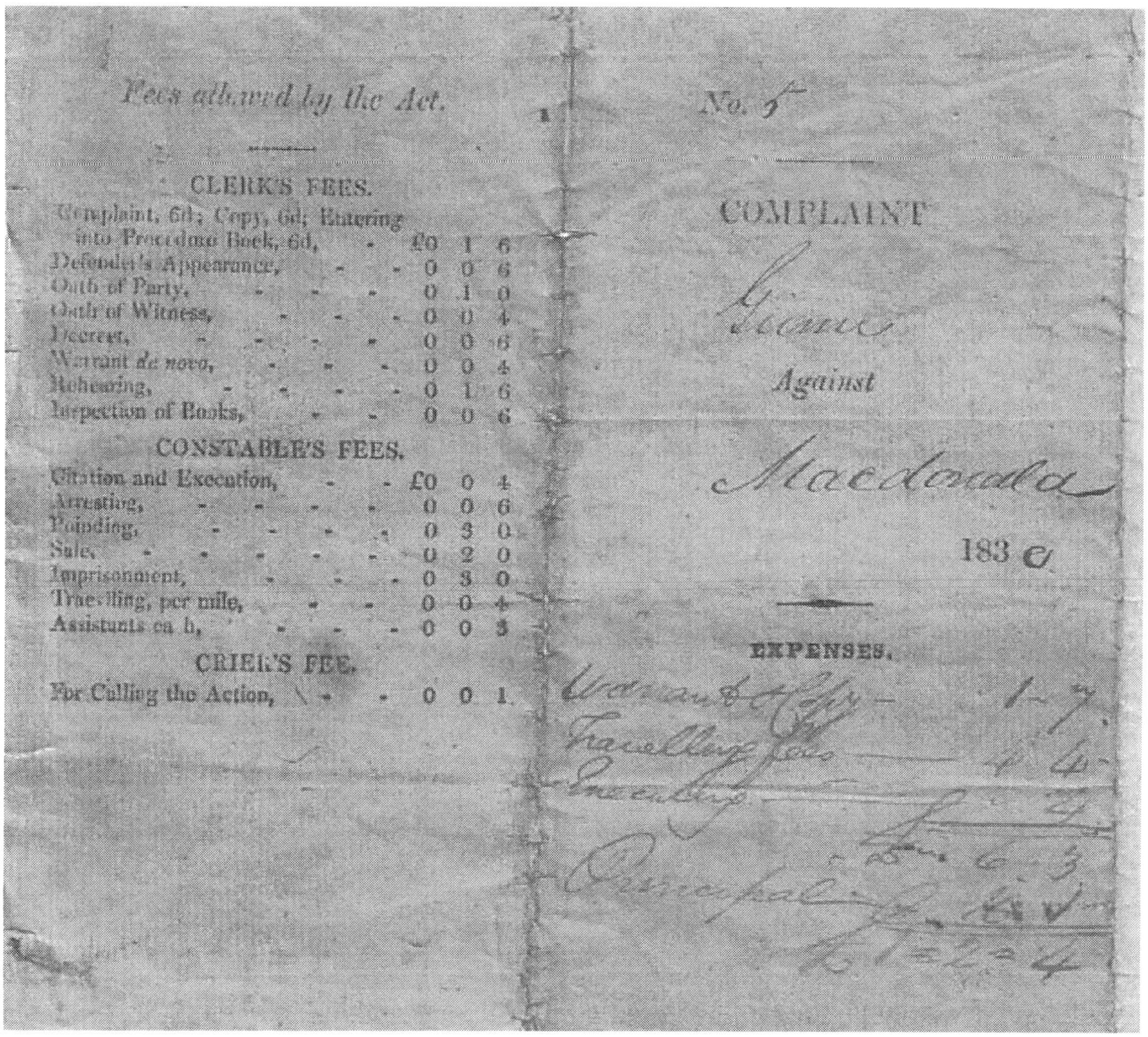

Fees allowed by the Act.

CLERK'S FEES.

Complaint, 6d; Copy, 6d; Entering into Procedure Book, 6d,	£0	1	6
Defender's Appearance,	0	0	6
Oath of Party,	0	1	0
Oath of Witness,	0	0	4
Decreet,	0	0	6
Warrant *de novo*,	0	0	4
Rehearing,	0	1	6
Inspection of Books,	0	0	6

CONSTABLE'S FEES.

Citation and Execution,	£0	0	4
Arresting,	0	0	6
Poinding,	0	3	0
Sale,	0	2	0
Imprisonment,	0	3	0
Travelling, per mile,	0	0	4
Assistants each,	0	0	3

CRIER'S FEE.

For Calling the Action,	0	0	1

No. 5

COMPLAINT

Gow

Against

Macdonald

183 0

EXPENSES.

Warrant & Copy — 1-7

Travelling fees 4-4

Principal

It is an expensive option to use the law.

UNTO THE HONOURABLE

HIS MAJESTY'S JUSTICES OF THE PEACE

For the Shire of Caithness.

COMPLAINS, Alexander Gunn Shoemaker Burloch

That Peter Macdonald Tenant Blaufal of Alness

is owing the Complainer , the sum of Sixteen Shillings and one penny Sterling per account

which he refuse to pay unless compelled: —Therefore the said Defender OUGHT and SHOULD be DECERNED and ORDAINED to make payment to the Complainer of the aforesaid sum with interest and expenses.

At Thurso the Eleventh day of October 1830

The Clerk of the Peace, for the Shire of Caithness, grants warrant for summoning the said Defender to compear before the Justices of the Peace for the said Shire, at Thurso in the Court-house there, upon Thursday the Twentyfirst day of October Current at eleven o'clock forenoon, to answer at the instance of the said Complainer ; and appoints a copy of the account pursued for, document of debt, or state of the demand, to be delivered to the Defender along with the citation; also grants warrant for citing witnesses for both parties, to compear at the same place and date, to give evidence in the said matter.

W. Miller S Clerk.

Upon the Twelfth day of October one thousand eight hundred and thirty —— years, I James Mackay Constable, summoned the above-designed Peter McDonald

to compear before his Majesty's Justices of the Peace, time and place above-mentioned, to answer at the instance of the Complainer , with certification, that he will otherwise be held as confessing the debt. This I did by delivering to him personally apprehended

a full copy of the complaint or warrant, with a short copy of citation thereto subjoined, and a copy of the ground of debt sued for

J McKay Constable.

At the day of one thousand eight hundred and thirty years, the which day his Majesty's Justices of the Peace, for the County of Caithness, found and hereby finds the above-designed

Defender , liable to the also above-designed

Pursuer , in the principal sum of

and

of expenses, as hereon indorsed, and decerned and ordained, and hereby decern and ordain instant execution by arrestment, and also execution to pass hereon by Poinding and Imprisonment, after of ten free days.—— Extracted by

Clerk.

Alexander continued to run up debts. The following is from the Edinburgh merchant William Bruce dated 7 May 1830 for items needed for his business (rosin, copper etc.)

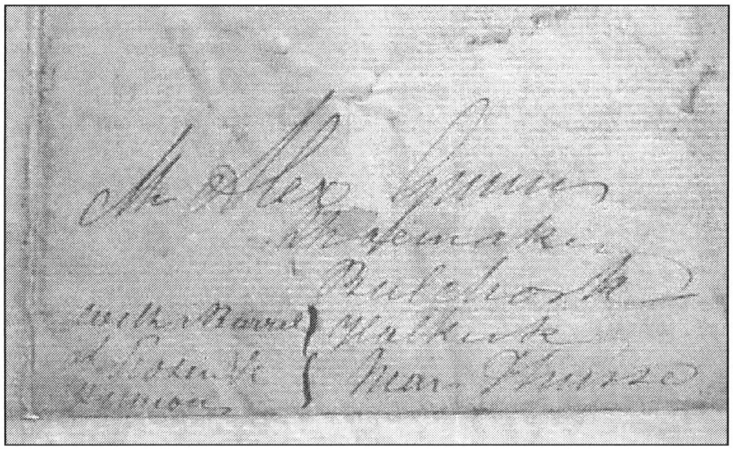
Mr Alex Gunn
Shoemaker
Bulchork
with Barrel of Rosen &c by Union } Halkirk
Near Thurso

There are no postal markings on the outside as presumably it went with the items just bought, note the above bottom left corner 'with Barrel of Rosen +c…'.

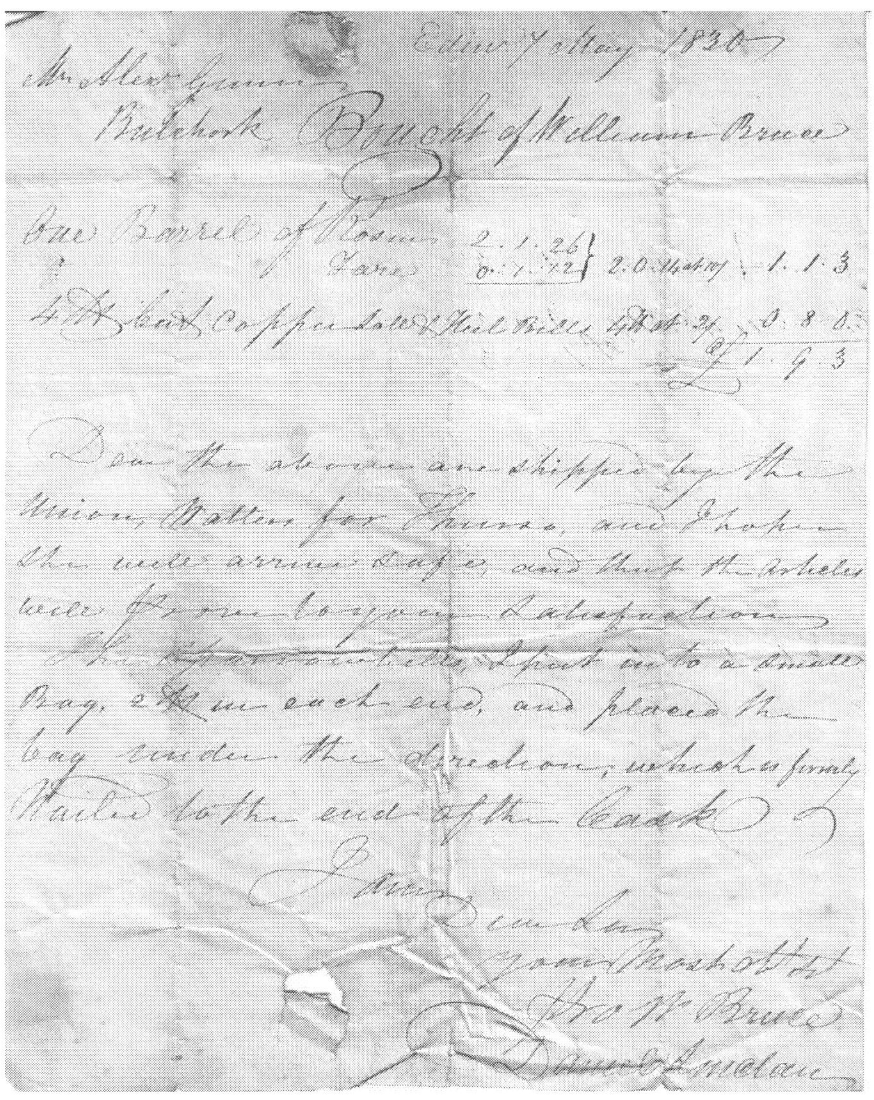
Edinr 7 May 1830

Mr Alex Gunn
Bulchork Bought of William Bruce

One Barrel of Rosin 2.1.26 }
Tare 0.1.12 } 2.0.14 at [illegible] 1.1.3
4 lb [illegible] Copper Sole & Heel Bills [illegible] 0.8.0
£1.9.3

Dear Sir the above are shipped by the Union, Watters for Thurso, and I hope she will arrive safe, and that the Articles will prove to your Satisfaction
The [illegible] I put into a small Bag, [illegible] in each end, and placed the bag under the direction, which is firmly Nailed to the end of the Cask

I am
Dear Sir
your Most obt St
Wm Bruce
[illegible]

Another printed receipt occurs at this time from William Miller Jun., Leith dated 14 May 1830. It is for freight and shore-dues from Edinburgh for a bale of lear (?), a bag of nails and one cask. The cost was two shillings. Possibly the following bill is for the carriage of the above goods....

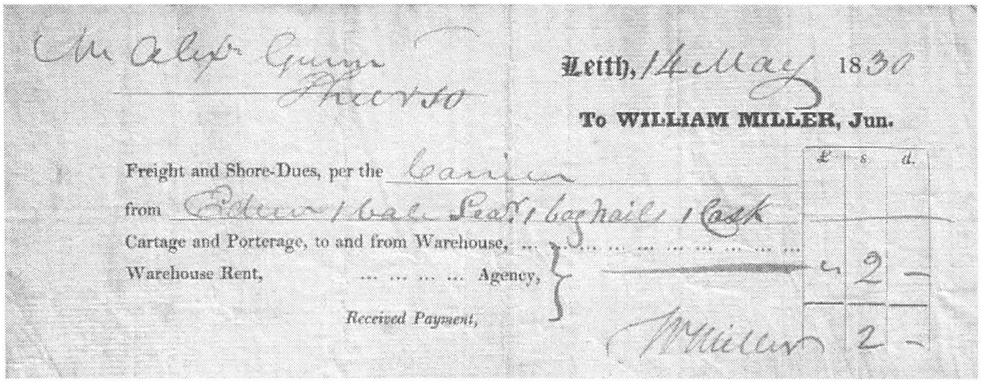
Mr Alexr Gunn
Thurso

Leith, 14 May 1830

To WILLIAM MILLER, Jun.

	£	s.	d.
Freight and Shore-Dues, per the Carrier			
from Edinr 1 bale, 1 bag nails 1 Cask			
Cartage and Porterage, to and from Warehouse,			
Warehouse Rent, ... Agency,		2	–
Received Payment, W Miller		2	–

The bills and receipts continue. There is a bill from the Commercial Banking Company of Scotland for the non-payment of a thirteen pound bill "indorsed" by Alexander made to John Gunn Lamsdale(?) on January 2 and payable three months later (it was signed by John Mackay the Bank's agent on 3 May 1831). It was addressed to the shoemaker Boulchork. It shows a manuscript 1d cost and the boxed black Thurso (origin) mark. (Only the relevant section is shown.)

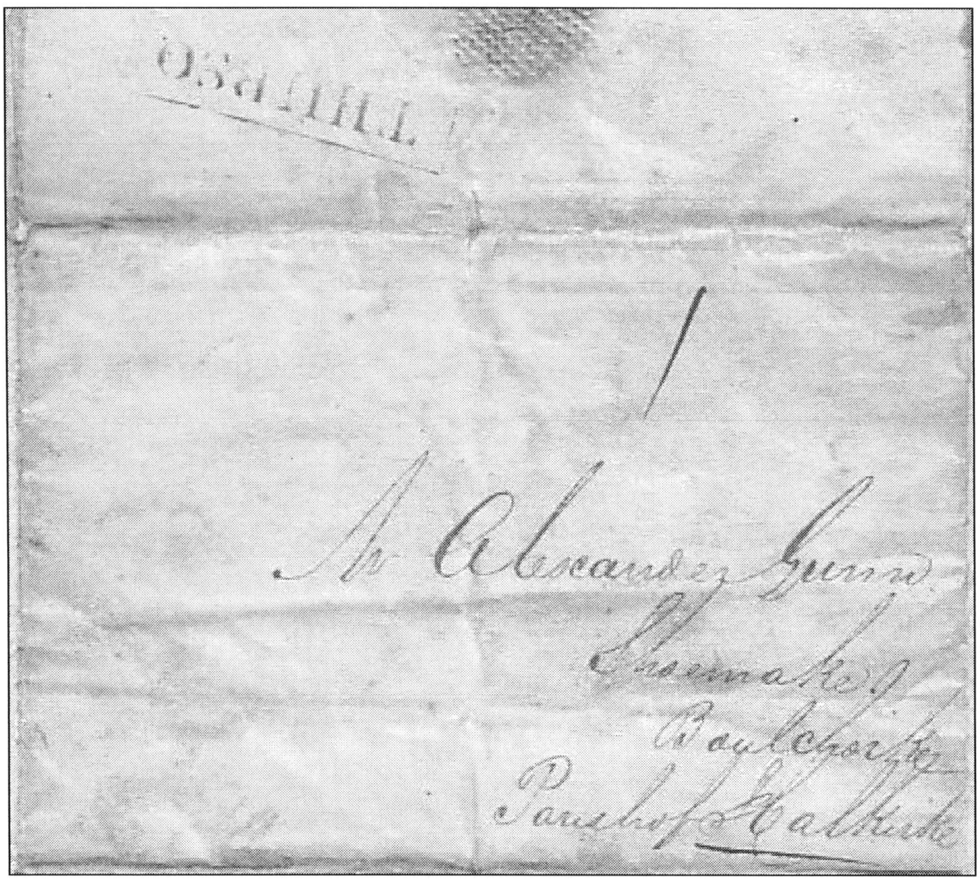

The bill is below

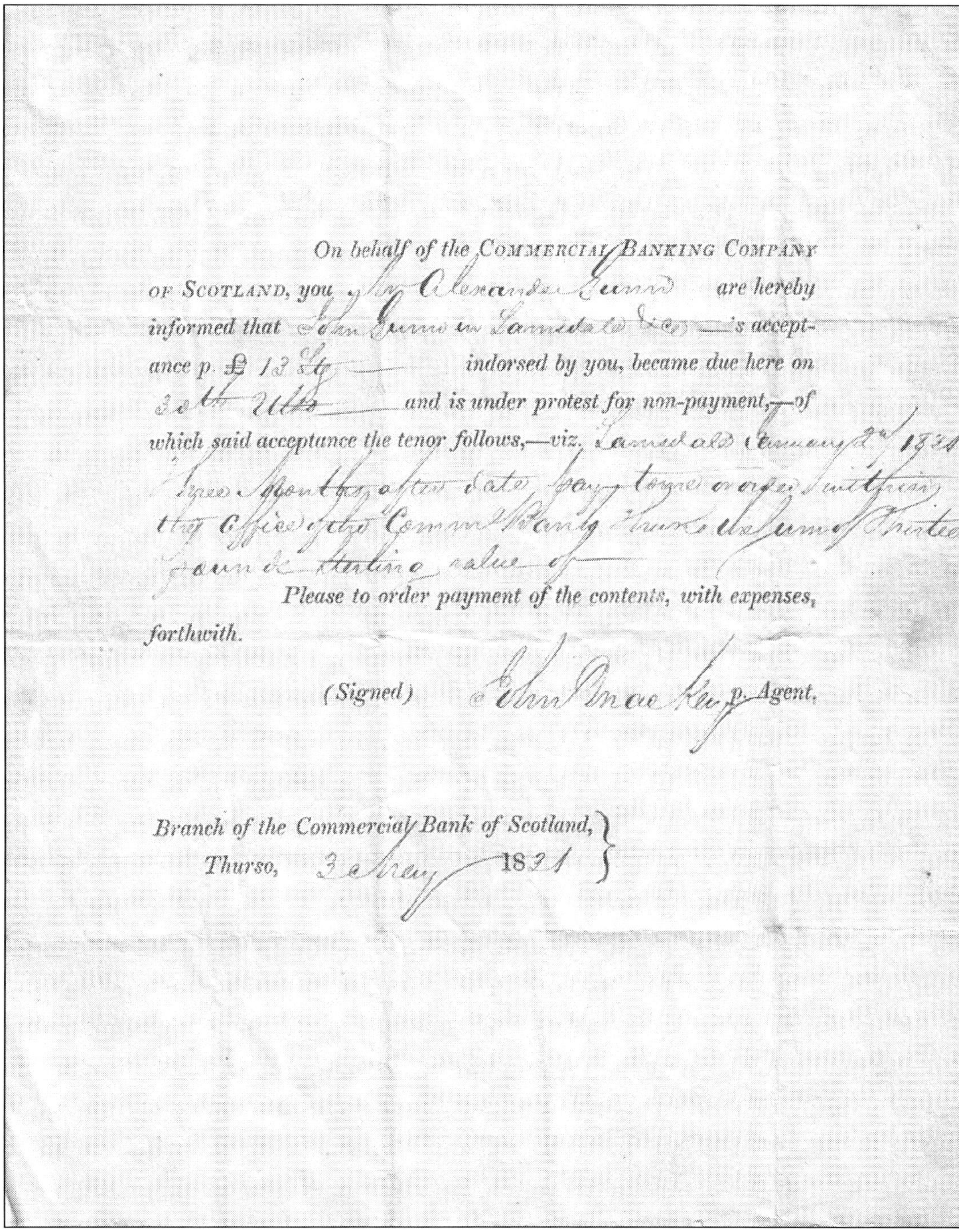

On behalf of the COMMERCIAL BANKING COMPANY OF SCOTLAND, *you* Mr Alexander Gunn *are hereby informed that* John Gunn in Lamsdale &c. *'s acceptance p.* £ 13 Stg *indorsed by you, became due here on* 30th Ulto *and is under protest for non-payment,—of which said acceptance the tenor follows,—viz.* Lamsdale January 2d 1821 Three Months after date pay to me or order within the Office of the Comml Bank Thurso the Sum of Thirteen Pounds Sterling value of

Please to order payment of the contents, with expenses, forthwith.

(Signed) John Mackay *p. Agent.*

Branch of the Commercial Bank of Scotland,
Thurso, 3 May 1821

The next unusual event is Alexander's relationship with a John Gunn, presumably not his brother. Note the double address on the following for Alexander; he is 'Shoemaker Boulcork or Brawlbin'. But the address on the front is more definite; Alexander is now 'Shoemaker Brawlbin'.

There is also a note from Dunbeath 19th Sept. 1831 which reads

Sir Give the Bearer John Keith from Boul tack of Dunbeath a pair of good shoes for which I will pay you on the little market of Dunbeuth on 12th of Nov next please send the shoes immediately

I am Sir your servant

John Gun

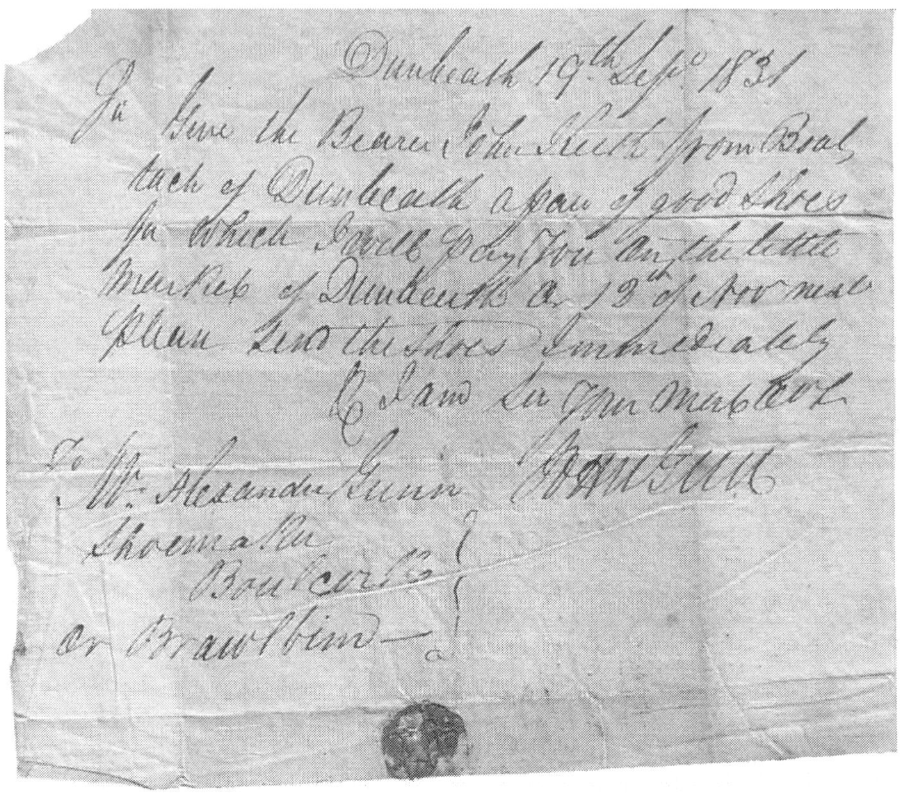

Dunbeath 19th Sept 1831

Sir Give the Bearer John Keith from Boal tack of Dunbeath a pair of good Shoes for Which I will pay You on the little Market of Dunbeuth on 12 of Nov next Please Send the Shoes Immediately

I am Sir your Servant

John Gun

To Mr Alexander Gunn

Shoemaker

Boulcork

or Brawlbin

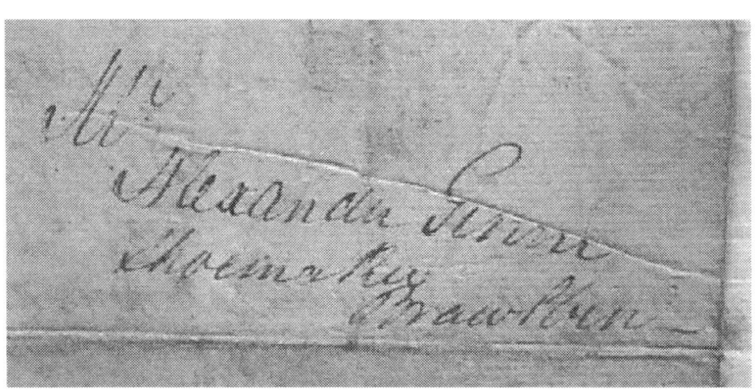

Mr

Alexander Gunn

Shoemaker

Brawlbin

Given that there are no marks on the exterior of the letter it was, presumably, hand delivered.

The next note is from John Gunn Constable, the handwriting and signature seems to be the same. It is a difficult document to read as it has been poorly 'restored'—

Upon the Sixth day of June Eighteen Hundred and thirty three years , I John Gunn Constable , by virtue of His Majesty's Justices of the Peace, their (e)nacted Decree, dated at Thurso the Twenty third day of February Eighteen Hundred and Thirty Three years. Raised at the instance of Hector Mackay Achlipester against Donald Sutherland Dalnaglaton and Peter Matheson there. I lawfully fenced(?) and arrested in the hands of Alexander Gunn Achorley and William Gunn there, and Donald Gunn Banskirke sums of (mon)ey owing by them to the aforesaid Peter Matheson or to defen(d) or to any other ... or persons for his use and behalf and all goods and effects in the custody of the said arresters belonging to the said Defendant and that to an amount or extent not exceeding the sum of Five Pounds Sterling all to remain under sure fence and some time... at the foresaid complaining instance until the said complainers be fully satisfied and paid of principal sum upon said Decree and expenses account of Law.

This I did by delivering a just copy of arrestment to Alexander Gunn personally, and by leaving a copy of said arrestment in the Key hole of the most patent door of the othe other partys dwelling house, as I could not find access therein which copy of arrestments were subscribed by me and bore the date hereof, and date of said Decree -all which is true

John Gunn Constable

Upon the Sixth day of [illegible] Eighteen Hundred and thirty three years, I John Gunn Constable, by virtue of His Majesty's Justices of the Peace their [illegible] Decreet, dated at Thurso the Twenty third day of February Eighteen Hundred and thirty three years, Raised at the instance of Hector McKay [illegible] against Donald Sutherland [illegible] and Peter Matheson there, I lawfully fenced and arrested in the hands of Alexander Gunn [illegible] William Gunn there, and Donald Gunn [illegible] [illegible]

This I did by delivering a just copy of arrestment to Alexander Gunn personally, and by leaving a copy of said arrestment in the key hole of the most patent door of the other parties' dwelling house, as I could not find access thereto; which copies of arrestments were subscribed by me and bore the date hereof, and date of said decreet — all which is truth.

John Gunn Constable

For the back, see the following. The key is at the top; 'Alex Gunn Brawlbin to John Gunn Constable'

It says' Caution Arrestment Mckay against agt Sutherland fees arresting at Brawlbin arresting Thurso & Baniskirk. The total fees came to 16/- and were mainly against Donald McKay for proccess and summons. It seems as though Alexander Gunn was involved with 'arresting at Brawlbin arresting Thurso Do Baniskirk'; was Alexander a part time policeman?

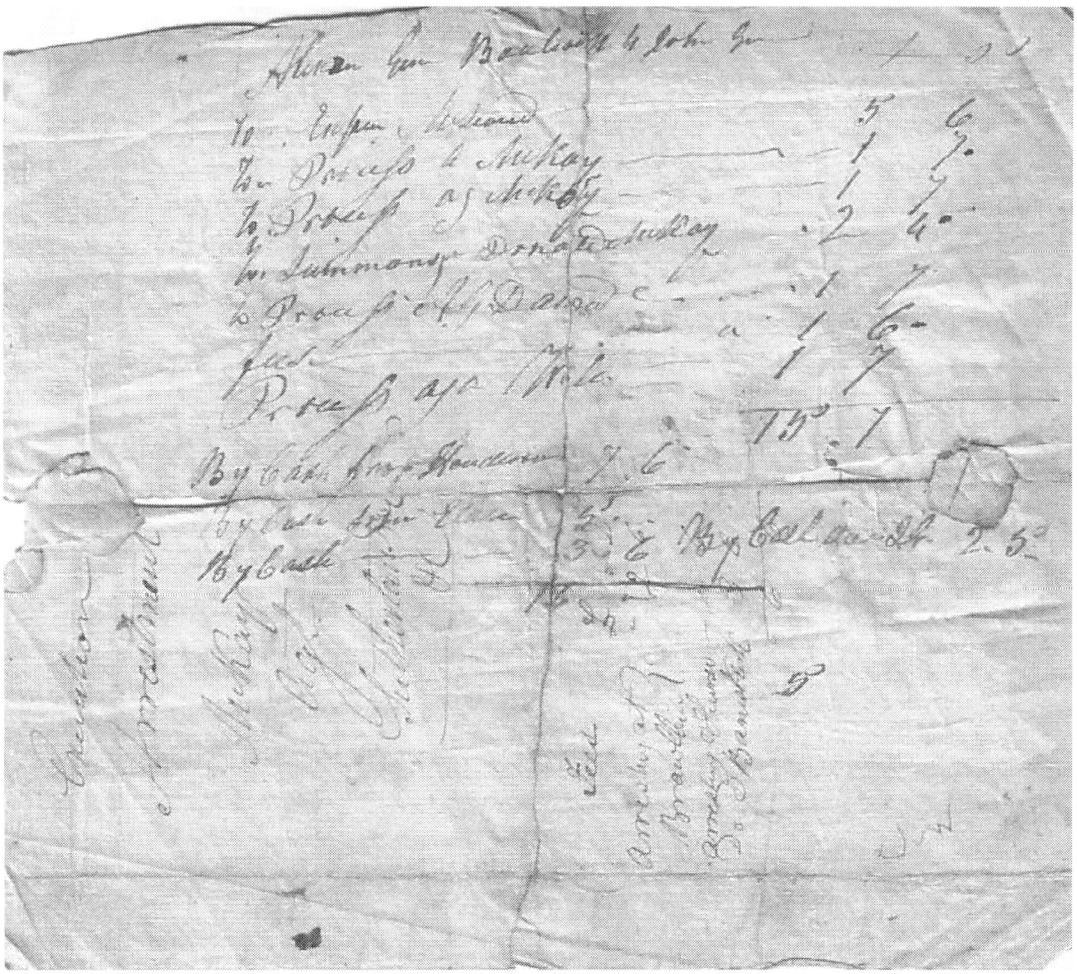

It's an interesting document…

The final document from John Gunn—'Sherriff officer Breahour' as he now describes himself—is to certify that Alexander's bill is correct. He had run a bill for £2/6/- for shoes slippers boots and 'oate meale' between 1829 and 1833. There is a later note—for 1842!—to subtract the balance of the account Alexander owed at court – 2s. 5d. The exact nature of the relationship between the two is interesting (and unclear) especially given where John Gunn lived. The 1841 census records John Gunn Sherriff at Braehour, along with his wife, probably his father and four children. Areas such as Braehour should be considered as estates with various houses; the 1841 census records 40 occupied houses and 172 adults for Brawlbin.

The most important letter of this time is the tenancy letter for the sixteen acre farm of Brawlbin (there were 'perennial springs, remarkable for the purity and lightness of their waters…rather of a whitish colour' in the Brawlbin area[685]) made with James Sinclair Esq. of Forss[686] for a fourteen year period.

---

[685] P.15, The New Statistical Account of Scotland Vol. XV

[686] http://www.electricscotland.com/history/nation/sinclair.htm accesssed 8 November 2009; 'In Caithness-shire are also the Sinclairs of Forss, an estate acquired from the Earl of Sutherland in 1560, the representative of which family, James Sinclair, Esq. of Forss, advocate, succeeded his father in 1822; the Sinclairs of Lybster; the Sinclairs of Freswick; and other families of the

Forss House 2011

Given that he is 'of Brawlbin' by late summer 1831 it is surprising that it takes this long for a permanent lease to be made. Was he earlier on a short term lease to prove his worth? The lease reads:

Forss 30 June 1834

Sir,

I make offer of sixteen pounds stg. of yearly Rent payable in equal parts at Martinmas and Whitsunday after Entry for the place occupied presently by me on a lease of fourteen years from Whitsunday last. I bind myself to cultivate the farm in a proper manner and in a regular rotation of six crops, viz: Turnip or Fallow, Bear with grass seeds, Hay, pasture for one or two years followed by one or two white Crops - And bind myself to pay an additional Rent of ten shillings per acre for every acre not so cropped during the first ten years of the lease And forty shillings for every acre not so cropped during the last four years and left on this rotation at the end of the lease.

I bind myself to leave all the dung made on the farm after laying down the last Crop but one to the incoming tenant as also one tenth of the Ground in Labor for fallow or Green Crops with liberty to plough the same at Martinmas before any out going for which measure I am to receive payment according to a valuation made by Sir now mutually chosen

I bind myself to consume all the straw and Chaff on the farm And it is understood that I am to receive the Hay or first Crop of the Ground or Grass of the first year at my out going with liberty to cut the same and ferry it away or stack it in a Convenient place while it is sold

name.' Also see J.T. Calder's *The History of Caithness*. For a full history of the Sinclairs of Forss see http://www.fionamsinclair.co.uk/genealogy/Caithness/Forss.htm and note that at least one of them was killed in the well known Gunn / Sinclair feud of the late 1500s. James Sinclair of Forss's third son was George William Sinclair 1831-1876 who was buried at Mt. Koroit cemetery in rural Victoria, Australia.

I am to receive valuation at the end of the lease for the mason work of such of the houses as shall be rebuilt by me according to the aware of two men mutually chosen-

I am also to receive payments according to a valuation made as above for such stone fences as I may build between the arable land and the hill and leave in Good Repair the Same having been first approved of and lined off by the proprietor

I am your obtst

Alexr. Gunn

Sir

I agree to and accept of the foregoing offer on condition that no houses are to be rebuilt or erected by you except such as are indispensably neccessary for the farm. And shall have first been approved of by me.Also that you are expressly prohibited from assigning or subletting that you agree to pay one half the expenses of a regular Tarh (tenant?) when called upon so to do

I am Sir yours

Ja^{s} Sinclair

To Alexander Gunn
Tenant Brawlbin

It is an interesting and complex agreement which provided a base for Alexander and Barbara for the rest of their lives.

Fass 7th June 18[illegible]

James Simlan Esqr
of Fass

Sir,

I make offer of sixteen pounds Stg. of yearly Rent payable in equal parts at Martinmas and Whitsunday after Entry for the place occupied presently by me on a Lease of fourteen years from Whitsunday last. I bind myself to Cultivate the Farm in a proper manner and in a regular rotation of six Crops Viz. Turnip or Fallow, Bear with Grass seeds, Hay, Pasture for one or two years followed by one or two White Crops. And bind myself to pay an additional Rent of ten shillings per acre for every acre not so Cropped during the first ten years of the Lease and forty shillings for every acre not so Cropped during the last four years and left in the rotation at the end of the Lease. —

I bind myself to leave all the dung made on the Farm after laying down the last Crop but one to the incoming tenant As also one sixth of the Ground in Labour for fallow or Green Crop with liberty to plough the same at Martinmas before my out going for which manure I am to receive payment according to a Valuation made by two Men Mutualy Chosen —

I bind myself to Consume all the straw and Chaff on the Farm and it is understood that I am to receive the Hay or first Crop of the Ground in Grass of the first year at my out going with the liberty to Cut the same and Carry it away or Stack it in a Convenient place until it is Sold —

I am to receive at the end of the Lease Valuation for the Mason work of such of the houses as shall be rebuilt by me ~~at the end of the lease~~ according to the award of two Men Mutually Chosen — —

I am also to receive payment according to a Valuation made as above for such Stone fences as I may build between the arable land and the Hill and leave in Good Repair the same having been first approved of and lined off by the proprietor —

I am Sir your most Obt.

Alexr. Gunn

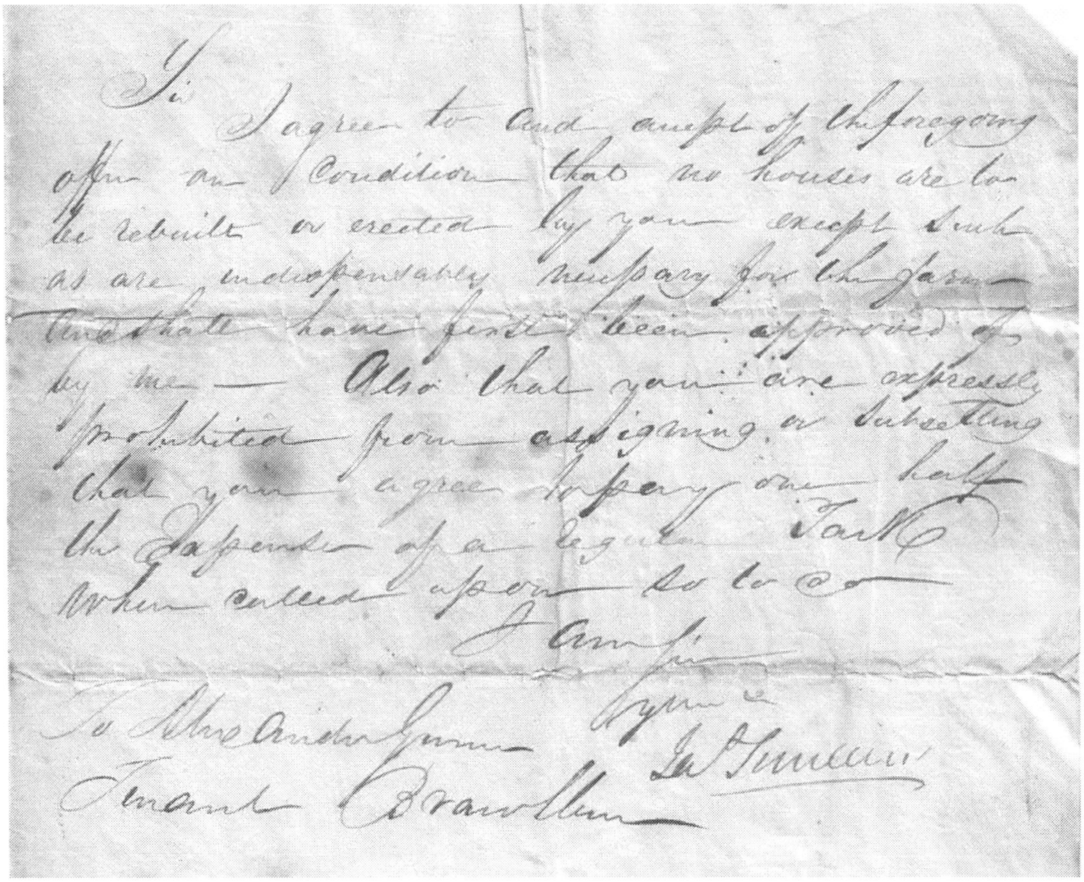

Sir
I agree to and accept of the foregoing offer on Condition that no houses are to be rebuilt or erected by you except such as are indispensably necessary for the farm and that have first been approved of by me — Also that you are expressly prohibited from assigning or subsetting that you agree to pay one half the Expense of a regular Fank when called upon so to do

I am Sir
Yours
Ja[illegible]

To Mr Alexander Gunn
Tenant Brawlbin

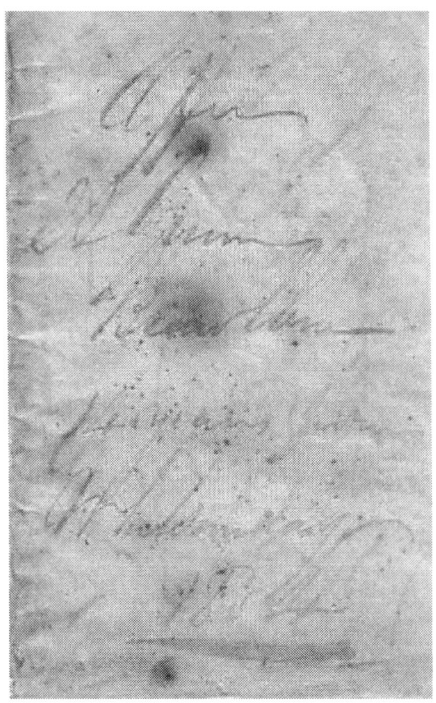

Offer
A Gunn
Brawlbin

Larger than actual size

And the outside reads something like;'… Gunn Brawlbin 14+ years lease .. (signature) 1834'.

There is a final receipt for this period from Robert Mackay for seven pounds sixteen shillings and 9d

Mr Alexr Gunn
Sir
I hereby acknowledge to have Received from you the sum of seven pounds sixteen shillings Stg being amount in full due me for the wool of the Rams(?) left in my possession in Brawlbin and now -------(?) by you for which I shall I grant you a stamp Receipt when a stamp can be got.
Brawlbin 15 Decr 1834 Robert Mackay

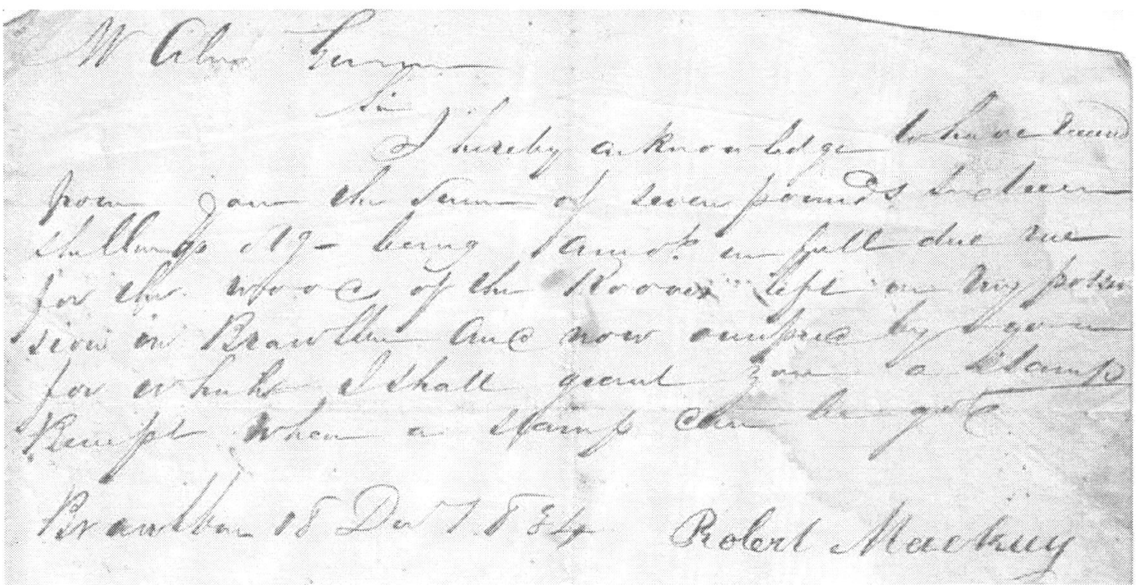
Mr Alexr Gunn
Sir
I hereby acknowledge to have Received
from you the sum of seven pounds sixteen
shillings Stg being amount in full due me
for the wool of the Rams left in my posses
sion in Brawlbin and now [illegible] by you
for which I shall grant you a stamp
Receipt when a stamp can be got
Brawlbin 15 Decr 1834 Robert Mackay

Were these goods related to the lease acquisition? At this point it is impossible to tell.

There is a limited statement of account made by Alexander from May 1838 to Nov 1838.

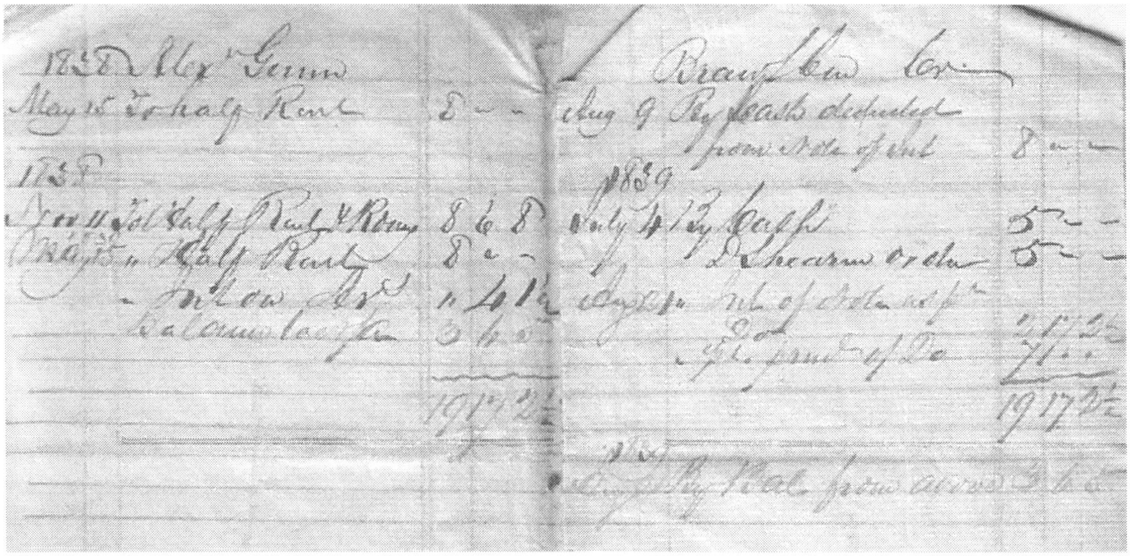

He paid the rent in roughly half yearly amounts. Mainly this was in cash 'deducted from role of int.'

The 1830s though was not just about money and land—this was when his five children were born. First there was Catherine (1830-1912) then Donald (1832-1901) then Janet Macleod (1834-1913) then John (1836-c.1856 who died without issue) and William (1839-d. after 1863, who also died without issue). He was also religious at least to a degree. He kept a family Bible which he used to record the details about the family—

Alexr Gunn was born 1789
and died on the 29th March 1847
My wife Barbra Gunn born April 17 1810
Died on the 28th. February 1844
My Daughter Kitty Born May 13 1830
Dito Donald Gunn Born March 28 1832
Dito Jannet Gunn Born May 8th 1834
Dito John Gunn Born February 12th 1836
William Gunn Born January 10th 1839

See page 27 for the original document.

The receipts continue for the 1840s. Firstly there are payments for the relief of the poor.

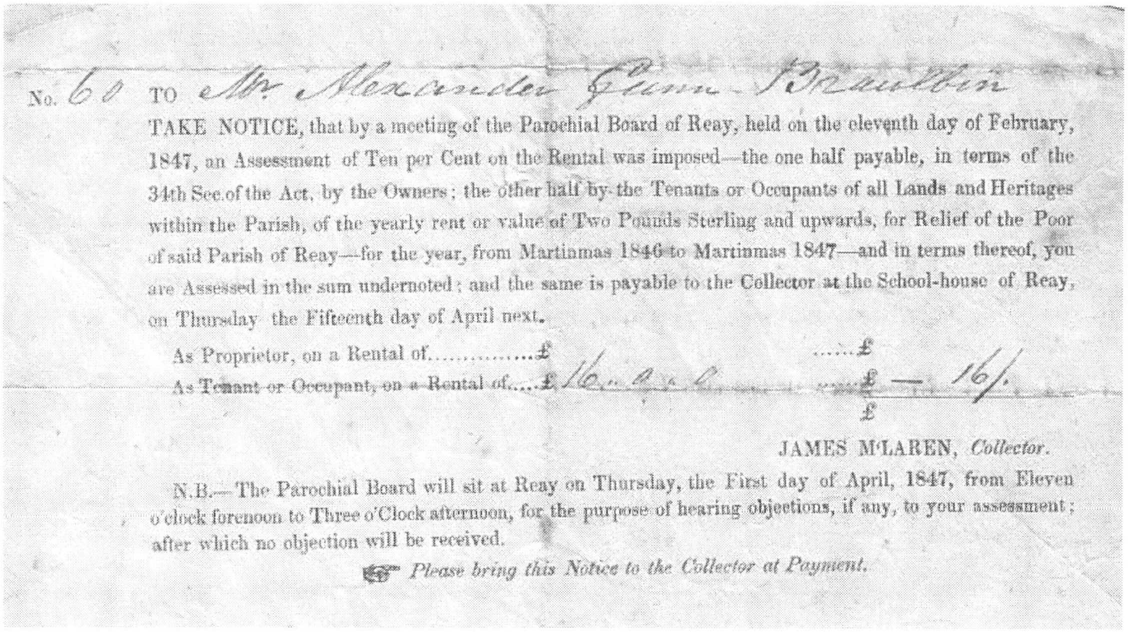

No. 60 TO Mr Alexander Gunn - Brawlbin

TAKE NOTICE, that by a meeting of the Parochial Board of Reay, held on the eleventh day of February, 1847, an Assessment of Ten per Cent on the Rental was imposed—the one half payable, in terms of the 34th Sec. of the Act, by the Owners; the other half by the Tenants or Occupants of all Lands and Heritages within the Parish, of the yearly rent or value of Two Pounds Sterling and upwards, for Relief of the Poor of said Parish of Reay—for the year, from Martinmas 1846 to Martinmas 1847—and in terms thereof, you are Assessed in the sum undernoted; and the same is payable to the Collector at the School-house of Reay, on Thursday the Fifteenth day of April next.

As Proprietor, on a Rental of.............£ ......£

As Tenant or Occupant, on a Rental of.....£16 " 0 " 0 ......£ — 16/.

£

JAMES M'LAREN, *Collector.*

N.B.—The Parochial Board will sit at Reay on Thursday, the First day of April, 1847, from Eleven o'clock forenoon to Three o'Clock afternoon, for the purpose of hearing objections, if any, to your assessment; after which no objection will be received.

☞ *Please bring this Notice to the Collector at Payment.*

The 1847 official notice for the 'Relief of the Poor'.

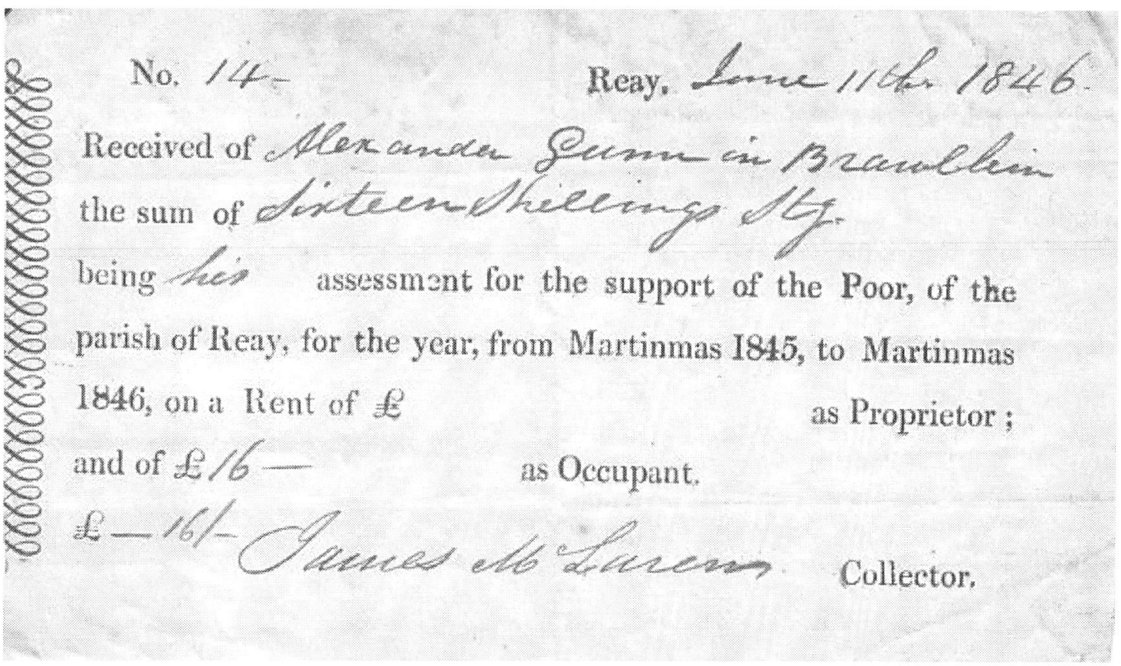

No. 14 - Reay, June 11th 1846.

Received of Alexander Gunn in Brawlbin

the sum of Sixteen Shillings Stg.

being his assessment for the support of the Poor, of the parish of Reay, for the year, from Martinmas 1845, to Martinmas 1846, on a Rent of £ as Proprietor; and of £16 — as Occupant.

£ — 16/- James McLaren Collector.

The 1846 receipt for the 'Relief of the Poor'.

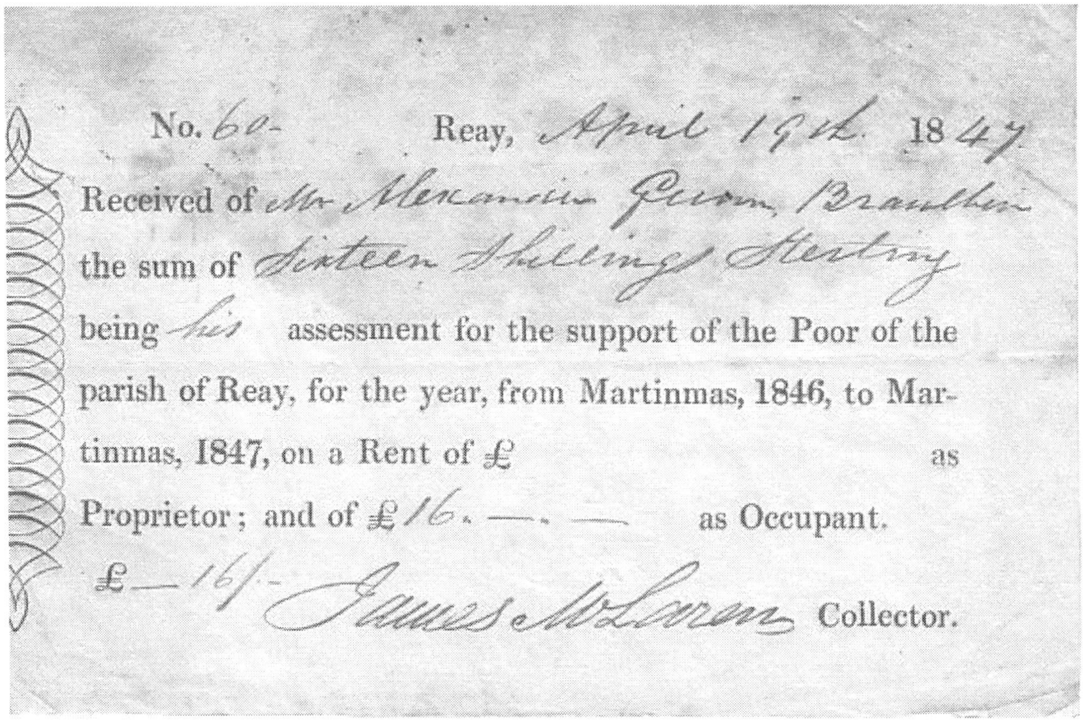

No. 60- Reay, April 19th 1847

Received of Mr Alexander Gunn, Braulbin

the sum of Sixteen Shillings Sterling

being his assessment for the support of the Poor of the parish of Reay, for the year, from Martinmas, 1846, to Martinmas, 1847, on a Rent of £ as Proprietor; and of £16. —. — as Occupant.

£—16/- James McLaren Collector.

The 1847 receipt for the 'Relief of the Poor'.

Presumably other receipts / bills for this purpose existed.

Then there were the rental payments (note the impressed rental stamps on the left hand side with a 'tax' rate of 3d for payments under £10)

Thurso 1 July 1840 Received from Alexander Gunn in Braulbin Eight Pounds Sterling as the half Rent payable by him at the term of Whitsunday last.

[illegible]

1 July 1840

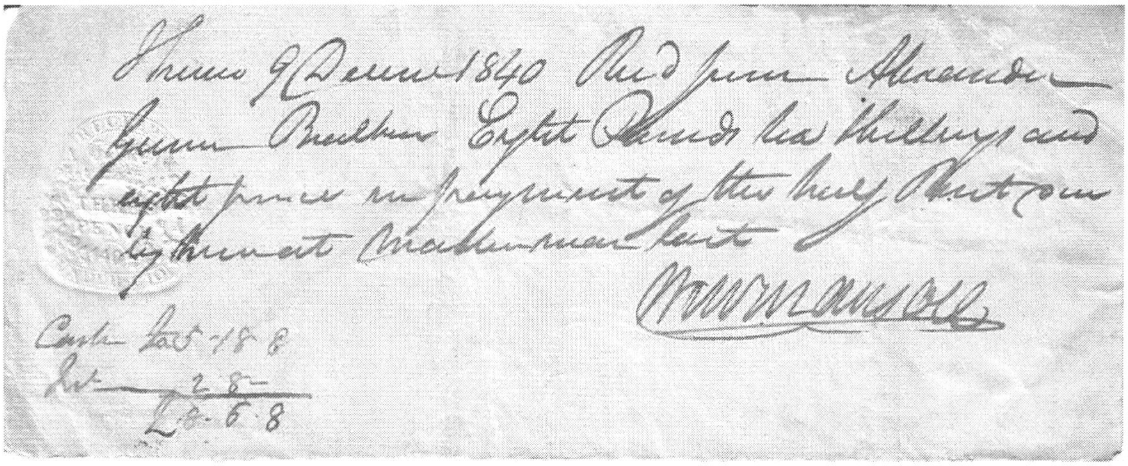

Thurso 9 Decr 1840 Recd from Alexander Gunn Brawlbin Eight Pounds six shillings and eight pence in payment of the half Rent due at Martinmas last

Wm Manson

Cash £5.18.8
Int 2.8
£8.6.8

9 December 1840

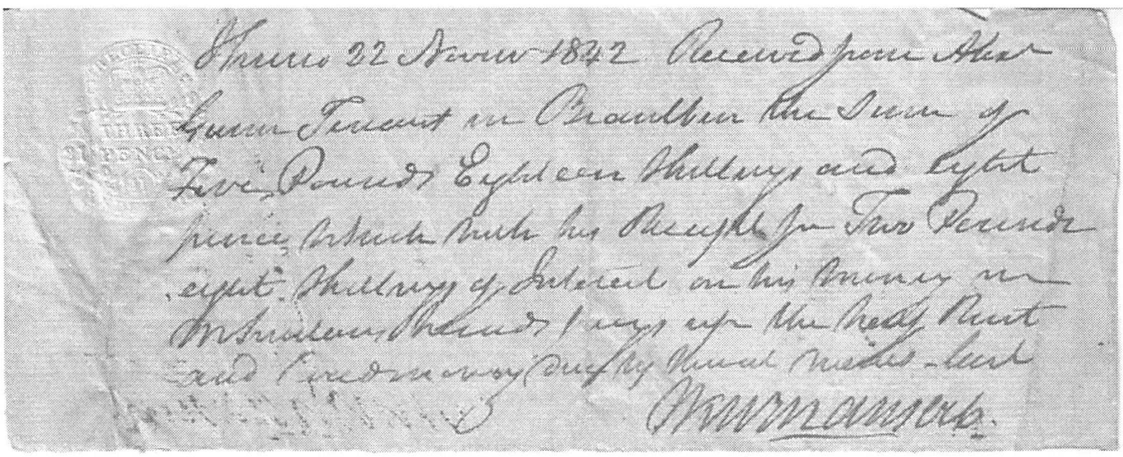

Thurso 22 Novr 1842 Received from Alexr Gunn Tenant in Brawlbin the Sum of Five Pounds Eighteen Shillings and eight pence which with his Receipt for Two Pounds eight Shillings of Interest on his money in Mr Sinclair's hands makes up the half Rent and Peat money due by him at Martinmas last

Wm Manson

22 November(?) 1842

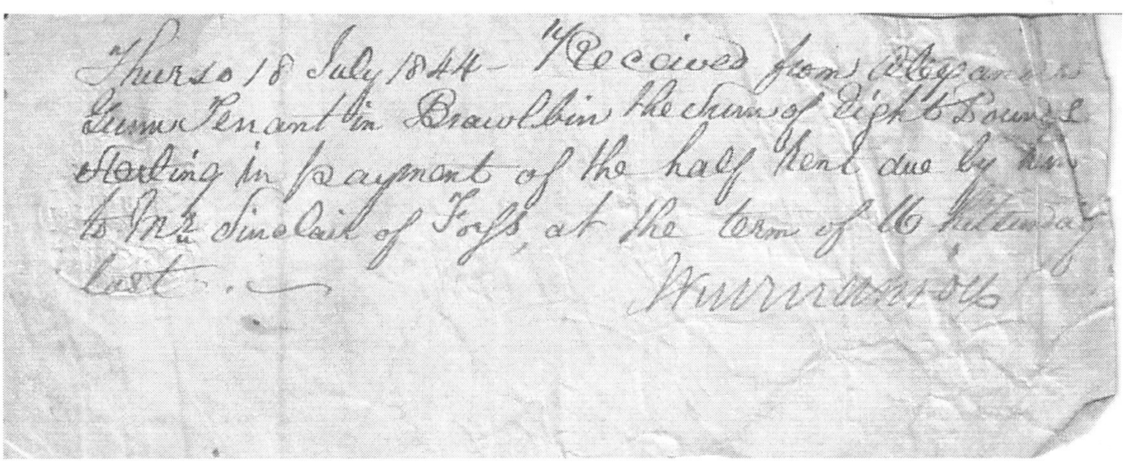

Thurso 18 July 1844 Received from Alexander Gunn Tenant in Brawlbin the sum of Eight Pounds Sterling in payment of the half Rent due by him to Mr Sinclair of Forss at the term of Whitsunday last.

Wm Manson

18 July 1844

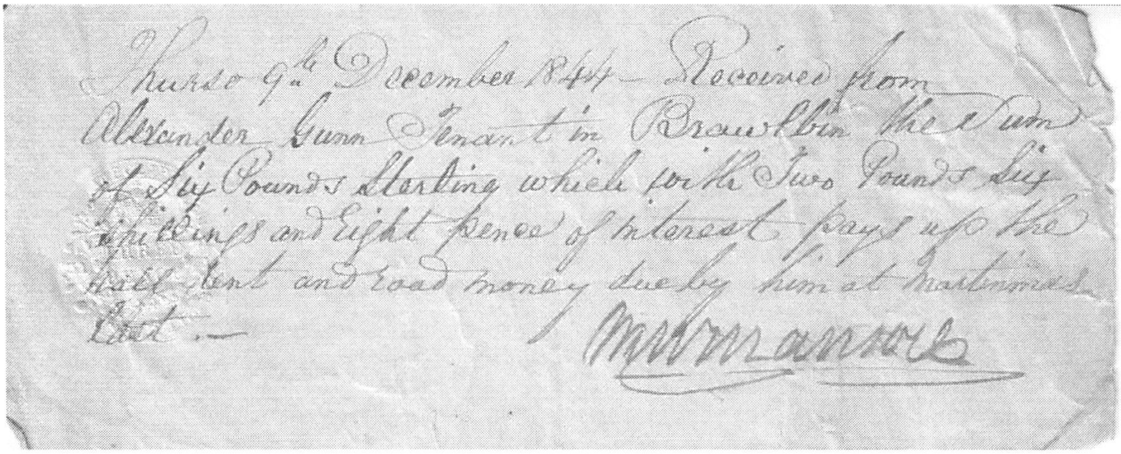

Thurso 9th December 1844 – Received from Alexander Gunn Tenant in Brawlbin the sum of Six Pounds Sterling which with Two Pounds Six shillings and Eight pence of interest pays up the half rent and road money due by him at Martinmas last —

9 December 1844

But the most fascinating is the below receipt—

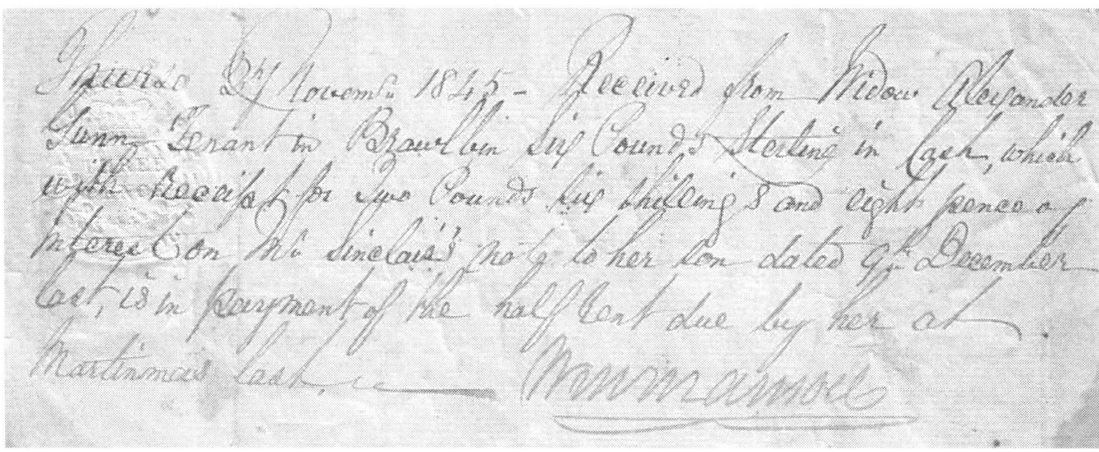

Thurso 27 Novemr 1845 – Received from Widow Alexander Gunn Tenant in Brawlbin Six Pounds Sterling in Cash, which with Receipt for Two Pounds Six shillings and eight pence of interest on Mr Sinclair's No 9 to her son dated 9th December last, is in payment of the half rent due by her at Martinmas last, —

It is dated 27(?) November 1845 and it is to the 'Widow Alexander Gunn' and makes reference to 'her son'—this clearly implies that Alexander has died. But the family Bible on page 27 (rarely are such things wrong) records his death as March 1847! Both can not be right! It seems likely that the above is 'wrong' as other later receipts for Alexander exist.

Alexander was still running accounts with a variety of places and times; assorted further bills are shown—

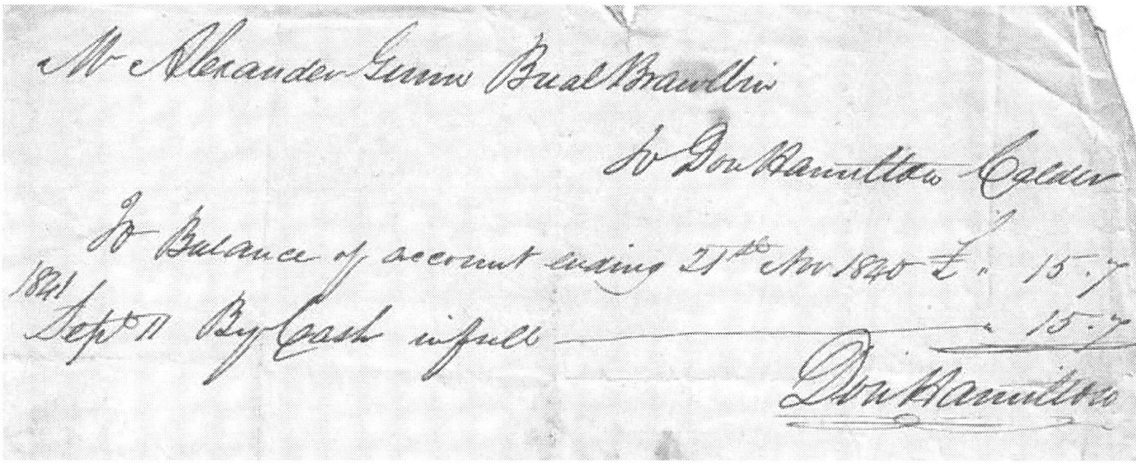
Mr Alexander Gunn Brealbrandhu

To Don Hamilton Calder

To Balance of account ending 21st Nov 1840 £ . 15 . 7
1841 Sept 11 By Cash in full — . 15 . 7

Don Hamilton

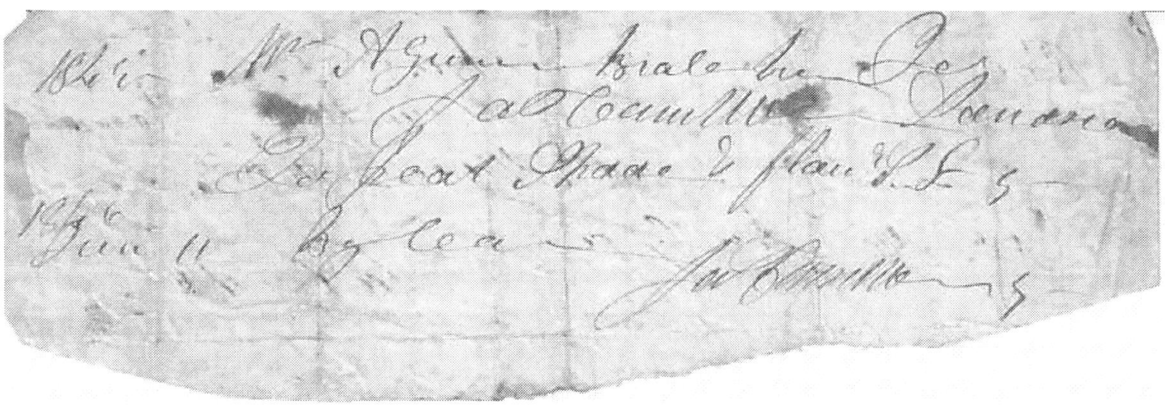
1846 Mr A Gunn Brale... Dr

To Jas Hamilton [illegible]

To [illegible] Spade & [illegible] £ 5

1846 June 11 By Cash

Jas Hamilton 5

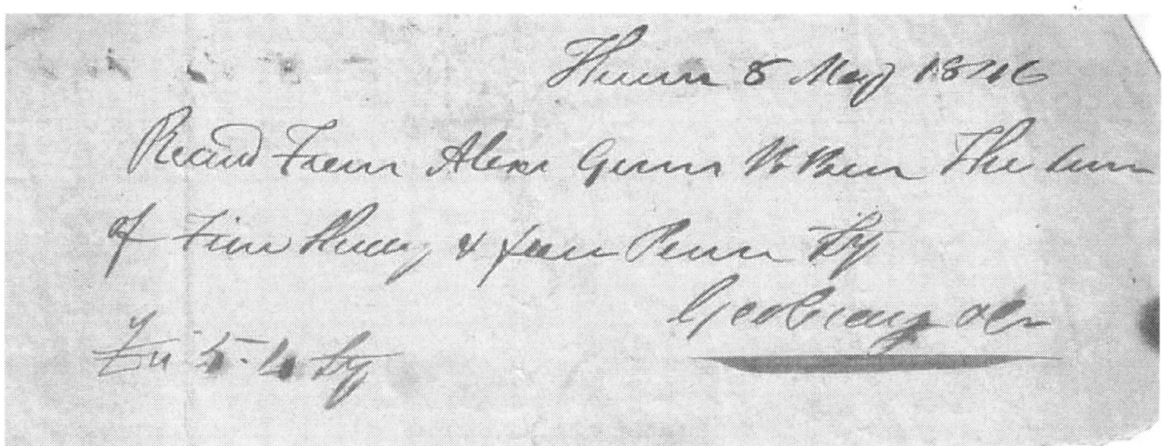
Thurso 8 May 1846

Recd from Alexr Gunn the sum

of Five Shillings & four pence Stg

Geo Craig

£0 5.4 Stg

1845 November 1 Mr Alexr Gunn farmer Brawl Bin
to Wm Campbell B Smith

	mounting a Cart 26 lb at 5d	10 8
	repairing old mounting	2 6
	ringing 2 wheels	2
	1 new shackle of my own	3
April 24 1846	1 new shoe and 2 removed	1 3
		18 5
	Paid by Cash in full Wm Campbell	18 6

Mr Alexr Gunn

1846 To Donald Hamilton

Feby 29	To Goods pr acct	£ 16 = 4
April 2	By Cash	16 4

Donald Hamilton

Thurso 21 May 1847

Received from Mr Alexr Gunn B.B.

3½ Gallon a [illegible] 10/- Geo Craig & Co

There were more detailed accounts held as well—

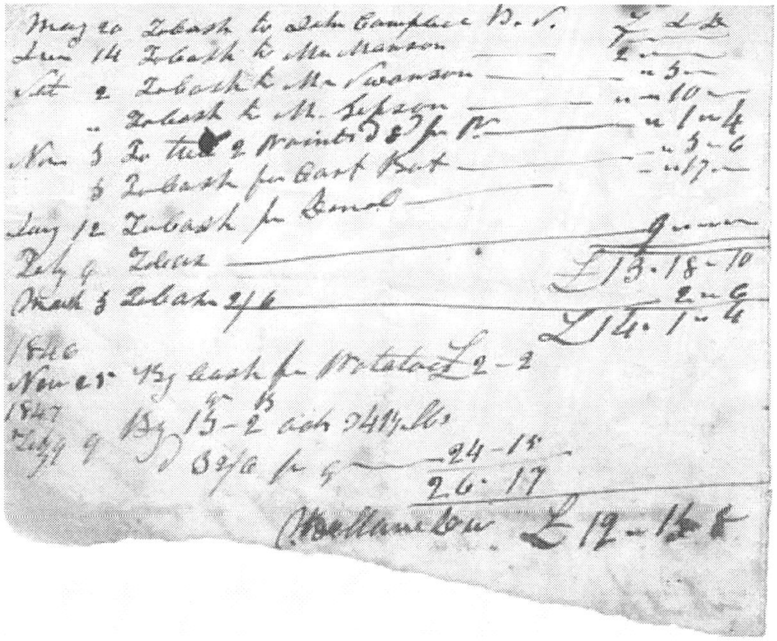

May 20 To cash to John Campbell B.S. — £ s d
Jun 14 To cash to Mr Manson — 2 —
Oct 2 To cash to Mr Swanson — 5 —
" To cash to M. [illegible] — 10 —
" To [illegible] 2 printed [illegible] — 1 – 4
Nov 3 To [illegible] — 5 – 6
3 To cash for Cart [illegible] — 17 —
Jany 12 To cash for [illegible]
Feby 9 To [illegible] — £13 – 18 – 10
March 3 To cash 2/6 — 2 – 6
£14 – 1 – 4
1846 Nov 25 By cash for Potatoes £2 – 2
1847 Feby 9 By 15 – 2 [illegible] lbs 32/6 [illegible] — 24 – 18
26 – 17
Ballance Due £12 – 4 – 8

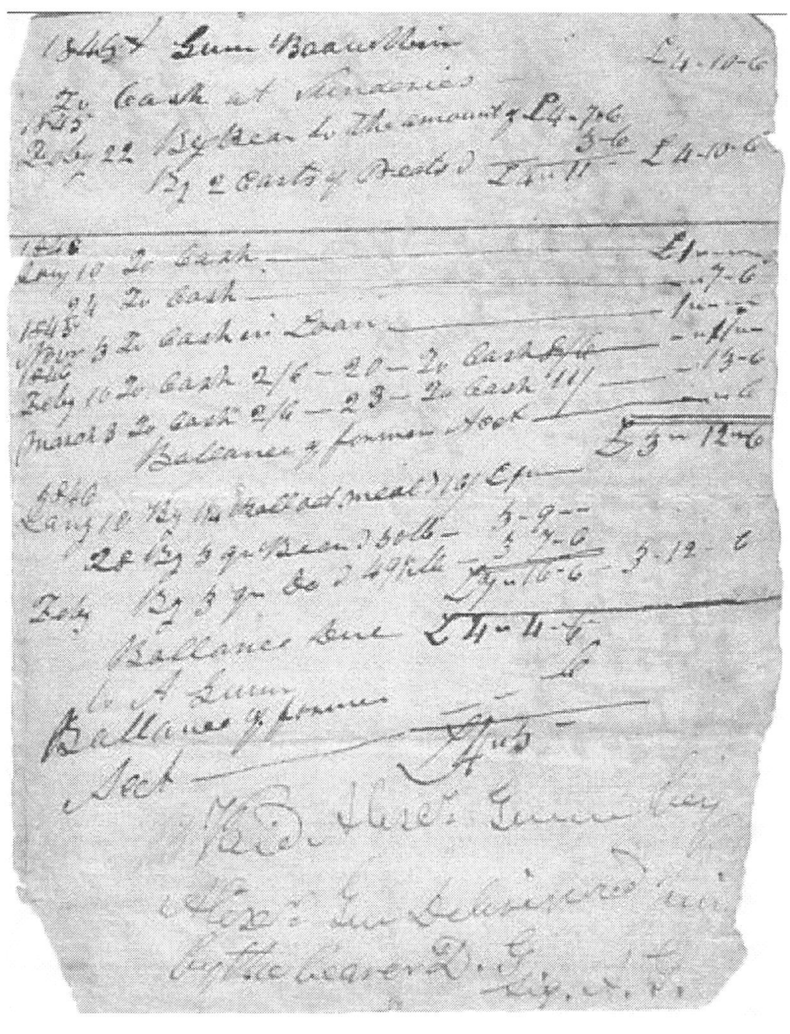

1847 Gunn [illegible] £4 – 10 – 6
To Cash at [illegible]
1845 Feby 22 By Bear to the amount of £4 – 7 – 6
By 2 Carts of [illegible] 3 – 6 £4 – 11 £4 – 10 – 6
1846 Jany 10 To Cash — £1 —
24 To Cash — 7 – 6
1845 Nov 3 To Cash in Loan — 1 —
1846 Feby 10 To Cash 2/6 – 20 – To Cash [illegible] — 13 – 6
March 3 To Cash 2/6 – 23 – To Cash [illegible] — 6
Ballance of former Acct £3 – 12 – 6
1846 Jany 10 By [illegible] meal [illegible]
28 By [illegible] Bear [illegible] — 3 – 9 —
Feby By [illegible] — 3 – 7 – 6 — 3 – 12 – 6
£7 – 16 – 6
Ballance Due £4 – 4 – 6
to A Gunn
Ballance of former Acct £4 – 4 – 6
[illegible]

Alexander died in 1847; Barbara had predeceased him in 1844. The eldest child was Catherine who, in 1847 was around seventeen years of age. The eldest son was Donald and he was approximately 15 years old.

A late bill to Alexander ('+ son') was bill No. 712 from the Inland Revenue (Stamps and Taxes), Thurso 1 February 1850. It demanded payment 9/4d under schedule A. This was roughly two years after Alexander's death.

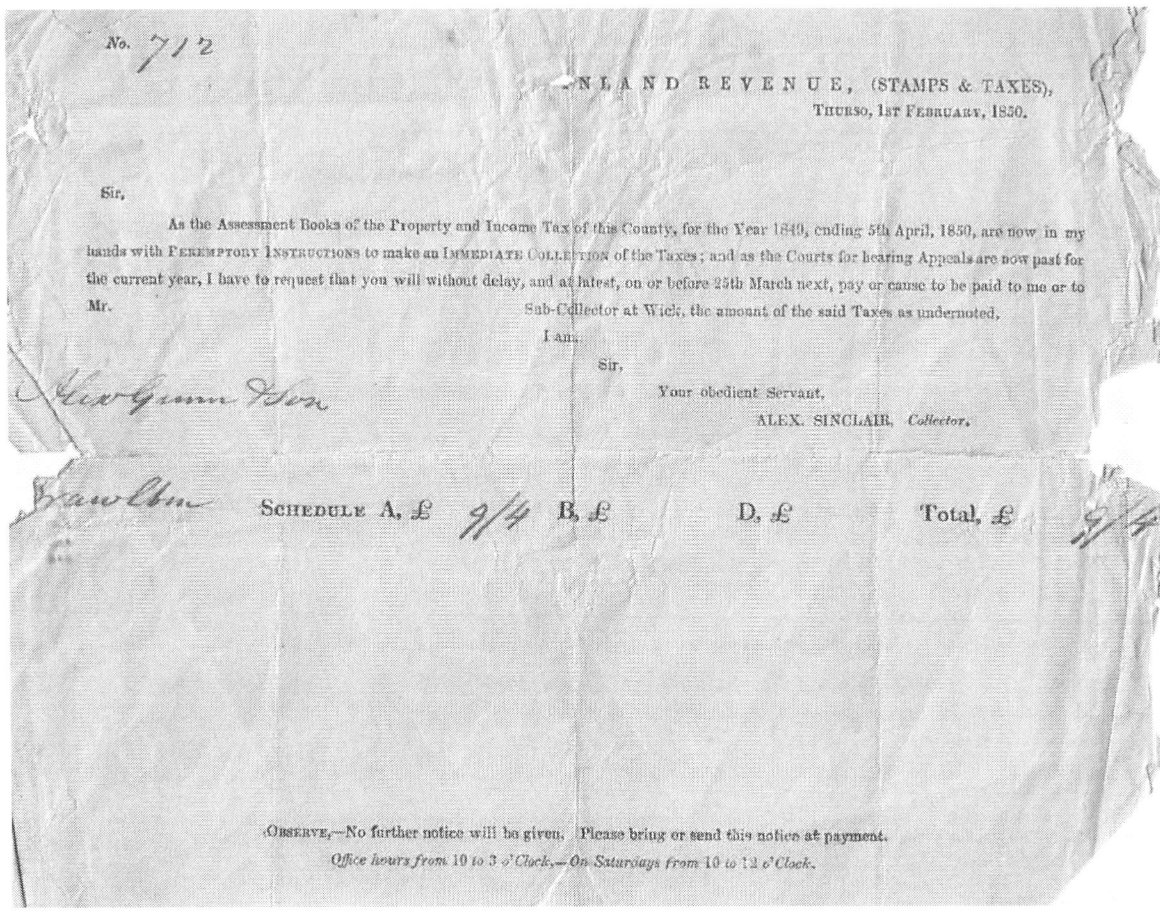

No. 712

INLAND REVENUE, (STAMPS & TAXES),
THURSO, 1ST FEBRUARY, 1850.

Sir,

As the Assessment Books of the Property and Income Tax of this County, for the Year 1849, ending 5th April, 1850, are now in my hands with PEREMPTORY INSTRUCTIONS to make an IMMEDIATE COLLECTION of the Taxes; and as the Courts for hearing Appeals are now past for the current year, I have to request that you will without delay, and at latest, on or before 25th March next, pay or cause to be paid to me or to Mr. Sub-Collector at Wick, the amount of the said Taxes as undernoted.

I am,
Sir,
Your obedient Servant,
ALEX. SINCLAIR, *Collector*.

Alex Gunn & Son
Brawlbin

SCHEDULE A, £ 9/4 B, £ D, £ Total, £ 9/4

OBSERVE,—No further notice will be given. Please bring or send this notice at payment.
Office hours from 10 to 3 o'Clock,—On Saturdays from 10 to 12 o'Clock.

The one following reads--

Thurso 13 April 1850

Received from Mr Gunn Brawlbin the

Sum of nine shillings + to a/c

Geo Craig & Co

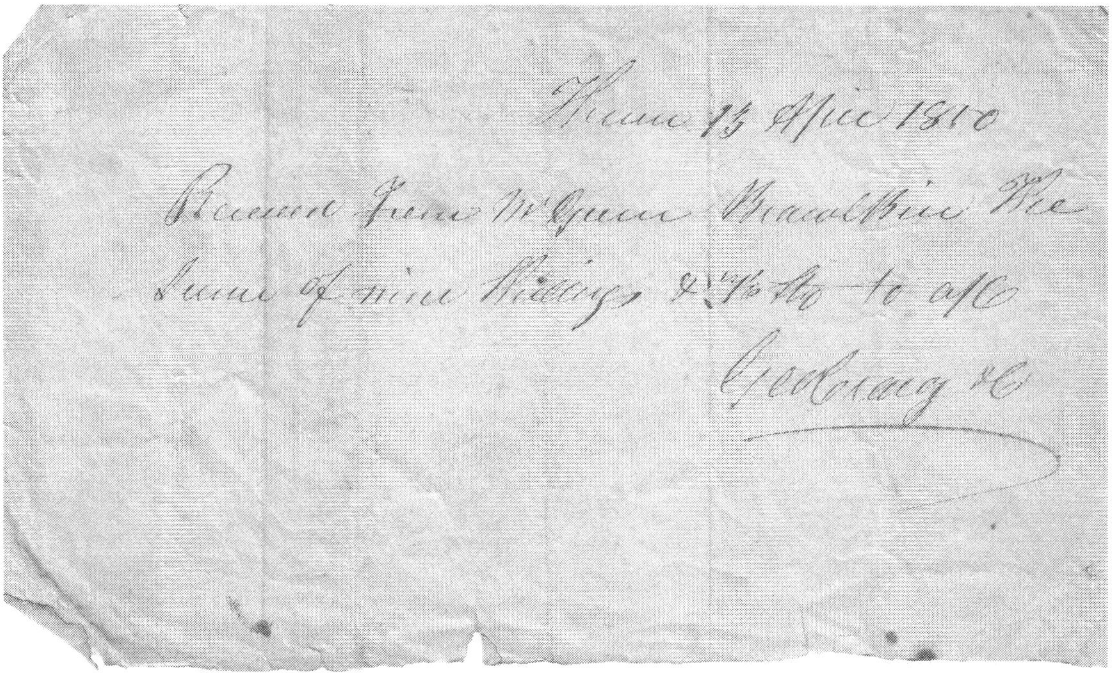

Thurso 13 April 1850

Received from Mr Gunn Brawlbin the Sum of nine shillings & Stg to a/c

Geo Craig & Co

This was not the last gasp—his son Donald cleared the following account with Geo. Craig and Co.of the 18/6d owing on the 26 April 1851 over three years after Alexander's death!

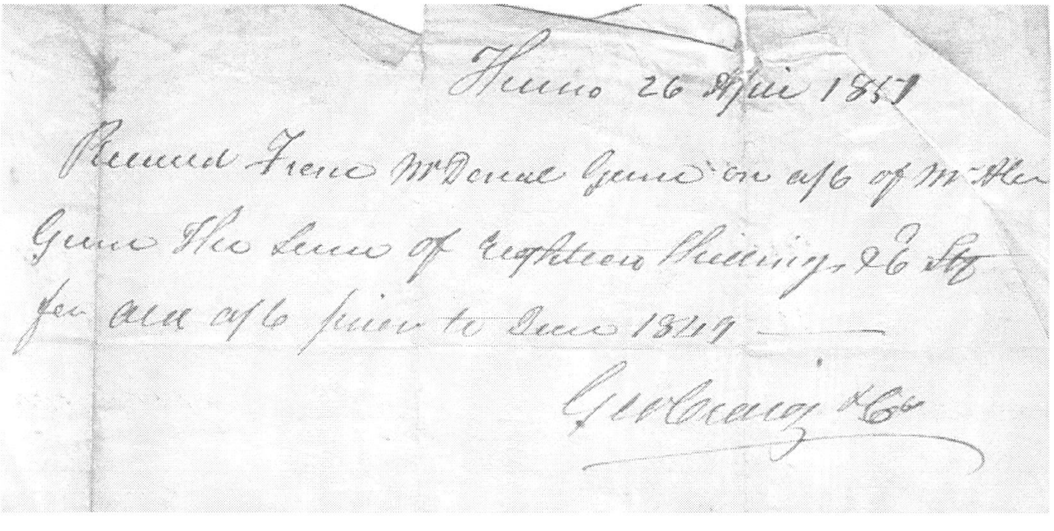

Thurso 26 April 1851

Received from Mr Donald Gunn on a/c of Mr Alex Gunn the Sum of eighteen shillings & 6 Stg for all a/c prior to Dec 1849

Geo Craig & Co

The family would have been in an awkward position; they were very young to be left without parents.

*****

George Gunn (804)

The fifth son was George (804) whose descendants remained Scottish.

Donald Gunn (296)

The sixth son was Donald (296) whose descendants were mainly Scottish or Welsh. The most notable of their children was Sir John Gunn of Tormsdale (3250). See Part 7.

William Gunn (297), Jamaica[687]?

There is a tradition of emigration and it begins with Donald Gunn (262) of Tormsdale's wife, Janet McKenzie (703), more accurately with her brother William who had been In Jamaica for some time by 1819. Letters addressed to Alexander from William McKenzie are on page 130 and the following pages. The following, we suspect, to be written by William Gunn.

Golden State September 4th 1819-

My Dear Parents

I have arived here on July 14th and we had avery good Passage of six weeks and three days Sailing to Kingstown and I was fourteen days there along with the rest of the Passsenters which was about ten; and Eight of them fell sick in the Course of three days after Coming there and died before I left them which left me verry sorry to see them buried there. But Blessed be God for it. I never had yet as much as asore head since I came here, and the Place that I am in just now its avery good place(/) but avery unhealthy Place there Died here the last year Seven White People what we Call buckies Herd this his the unhealthiest time here becuse sometimes it is so verry hot here that the sweeting will be Pouring down from your body in to your shoes and Perhaps in an hours time it will rain sometimes Continues for amonth and there is not adrop...rain but what is as if ...Jamaica his nothing Besides what you are hearing of it A Man that behaves himself oberly and keeps himself in a gentlemans way will get Employment and good wages of about 80£ currency but then Every thing is very Dear here which takes away the wages for instance you will not get abreakfast here under ten shillings dinner twice that And anights lodging without ten and apair of shoes will Cost £1.10 the cheapest and then where is the wages and that Pair will keep only a Month when it burns and wastes away and Clothes likewise But if I was as well acquaint with Jamaica as I am just now I would been better aforded for it For the best Gentleman here wears only a tartan Coat and Every thing Else according to the sun. My Dear brother; Alexr.was wishing to come here but I am afraid that he would not live long here but however if has gone to school as he was saying to ... he would do here but a man without School . Need ... once here. But I am determined....

So, we believe this to be addressed to Donald Gunn (262) and his wife Janet (703) and we believe that the Alexander discusssed is Alexander (1). Why? Firstly given the letters by William Mackenzie and his wife (probably) we see that Alexander was clearly thinking of emigrating at one point and this letter supports it.

---

[687] But also see page 269 for further references to the area of the Golden Estate.

Golden Vale September 4th 1819

My Dear Parents

I have arrived here on July 14th and we had a very good Passage of six weeks and three days Sailing to Kingston and I was fourteen days there along with the rest of the Passengers which was about Ten and Eight of them fell sick in the Course of three days after Coming there and died before I left them which left me Very sorry to see them buried there — But Blessed be God for it. I never had yet as much as a sore head since I came here, and the Place that I am in just now is a very good place but a very unhealthy place there Died here the last year Seven White People what we call buckras — And this his the unhealthiest time here because Sometimes it is so Verry hot here that the sweating will be flowing down from your body into your shoes and Perhaps in an hours time it will rain sometimes Continues for a month and there is not a drop [illegible] but what is

[illegible]

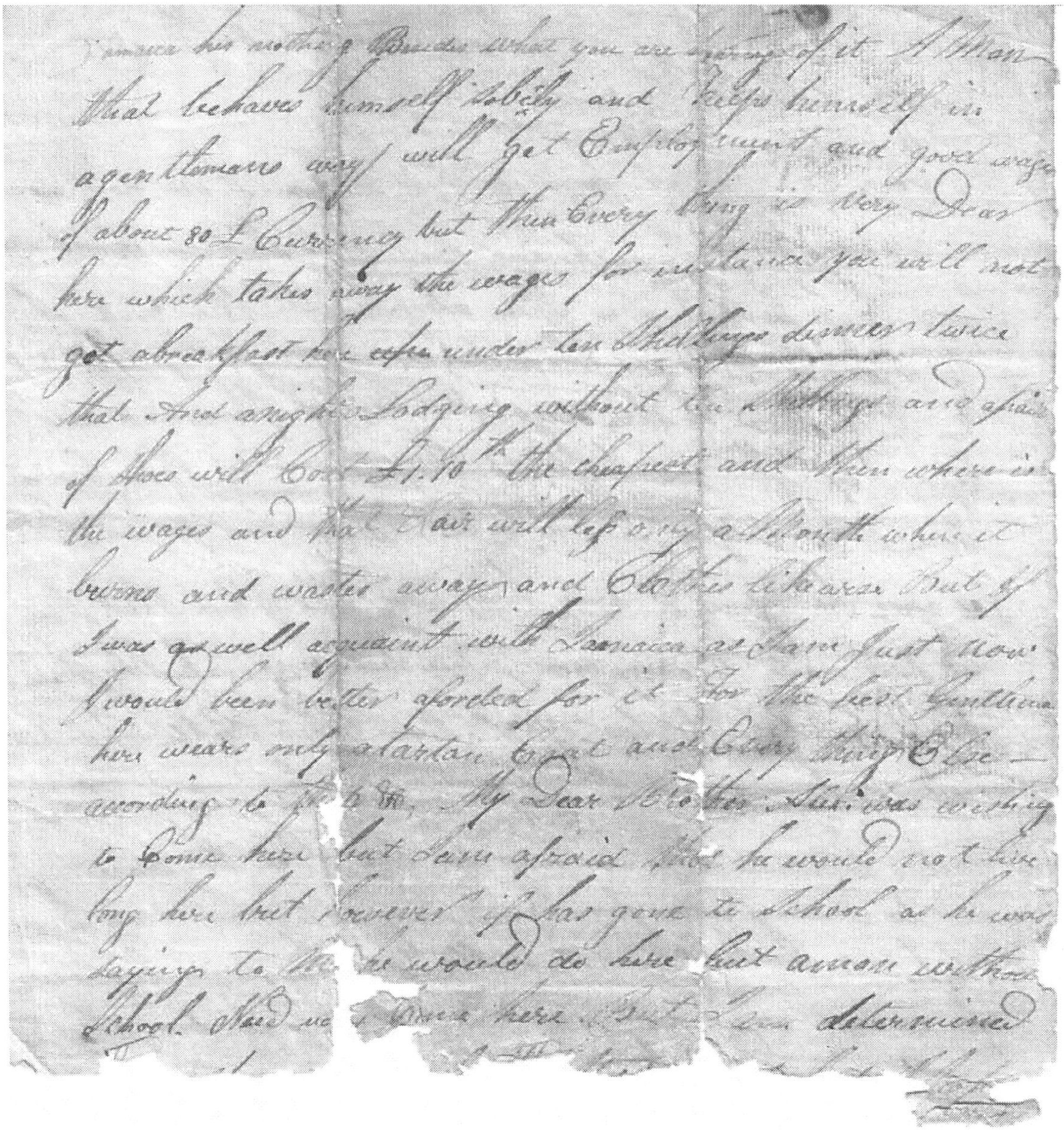

Jamaica has nothing Besides what you are [illegible] of it A Man
that behaves himself Soberly and keeps himself in
a gentlemans way will get Employment and good wages
of about 80 £ Currency but then Every thing is very Dear
here which takes away the wages for instance you will not
get a breakfast here less under ten Shillings dinner twice
that And a nights Lodging without ten Shillings and a pair
of Shoes will Cost £1.10th the cheapest and then where is
the wages and that air will [illegible] a Month when it
burns and wastes away and Clothes likewise But if
I was as well aquaint with Jamaica as I am just now
I would been better aprovided for it For the best Gentlemen
here wears only a tartan Coat and Every thing Else —
according to [illegible] My Dear Brother [illegible] was wishing
to Come here but I am afraid that he would not live
long here but however if has gone to School as he was
saying to [illegible] he would do here but a man without
School Need not Come here But I am determined

There is also a small booklet in which William recorded (in now faded light pencil) some early dates and some thoughts about the greatness of man and basic algebra.

The light pencil signature of William Gunn Brawlbin being one of three in the small booklet.

Also recorded were the marriage dates for George Dunbar and William Brims (see page 137) who were both married on the 24 December 1852. This is annoying as one assumes that William Gunn stayed in Jamaica. The notebook is held by a descendant of Donald Gunn who emigrated to Australia. The writing about the marriages is similar to William's, but so was all handwriting at this time... Perhaps William left the notebook when he left home and someone else later used it.

The most obviously useful part of this notebook is the confirmation of birth and death dates—

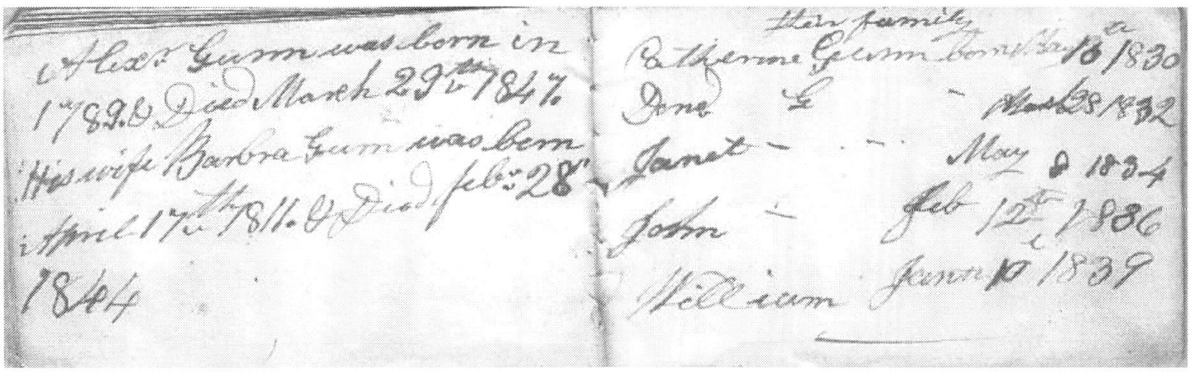
Alexr Gunn was born in
1788 & Died March 29th 1847.
His wife Barbra Gum was born
April 17th 1811 & Died feb 28th
1844
their family
Catherine Gunn born Sept 18 1830
Jane — March 28 1832
Janet — May 8 1834
John — feb 12th 1836
William June 10 1839

It is the only one in ink. It also spells Barbara inaccurately. It does not look like the light pencil writing associated with William (nor is it as fluent as the letter on the preceding pages).

So, William disappears from view but perhaps somewhere in Jamaica there are Gunns (and Mackenzies)...

Christian Gunn (602)

The eighth child was the first (and only known) girl. She was named Christian Gunn (602) and married Alexander Sutherland (3119) of Inshag. They emigrated, with their children, to Ontario see page 33 onwards.

Marcus Gunn (298), Canada

The youngest child, Marcus (298) (b.1805) emigrated to Canada. Although Marcus was a successful cattle dealer in 'Bulcork' in October 1829 the conditions at the time seem less than ideal and this may have influenced him. A letter to him is below (possibly from his nephew John Munro (3166))—

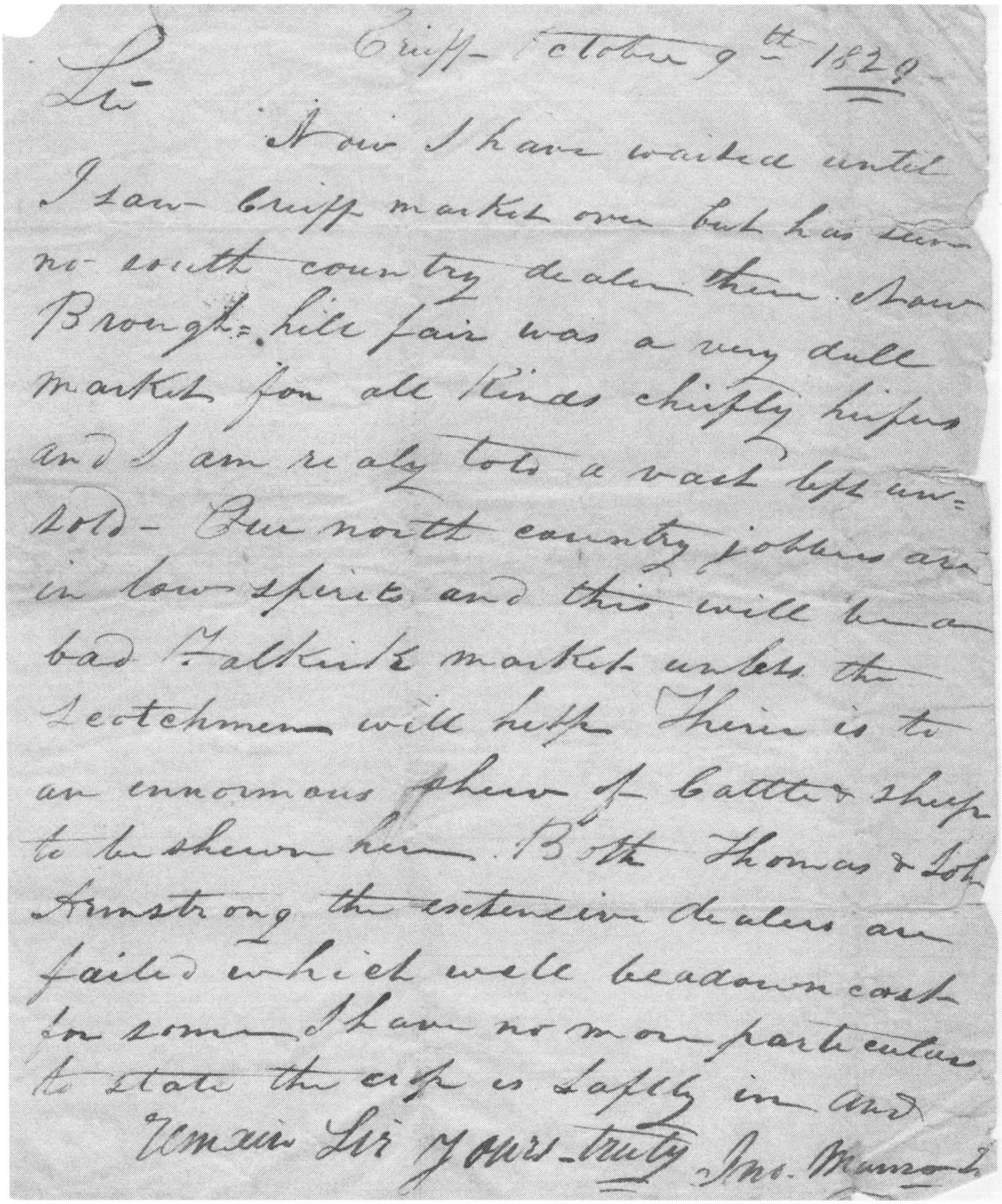

Crieff October 9th 1829

Sir

Now I have waited until I saw Crieff market over but has seen no south country dealer there. Now Brough=hill fair was a very dull market for all kinds chiefly heifers and I am realy tols a vast left un=sold - Our north country jobbers are in low spirits and this will be a bad Falkirk market unless the Scotchmen will help. There is to an ennormous shew of Cattle & sheep to be shewn here. Both Thomas & John Armstrong the extensive dealers are failed which will bea down cast for some. I have no more particulars to state the crop is safely in and

remain Sir yours truly Jno. Munro

The letter reads—

Crieff October 9th 1829

Sir

Now I have waited until I saw Criff market over but has seen no south country dealer there. Now Brough hill fair was a very dull market for all kinds chiefly heifers and I am really told a vast left unsold. Our north country jobless are in low spirits and this will be a bad Falkirk[688] market unless the Scotchmen will help Their is to an ennormous show of Cattle & sheep to be shown here. Both Thomas and John Armstrong the extensive dealers are failed which will be a down cash for some I have no more particulars to state the crop is safely in and

remain Sir yours truly Jno. Munro (?)

Here one can see some of the problems of the community, namely financial stress and the consequent community unsureness. The life of the highlanders at this time is too well known to need much restatement; but the clearances and mass emigration had begun. The few roads of the time were also of a poor kind.

The front cover of the letter is shown—

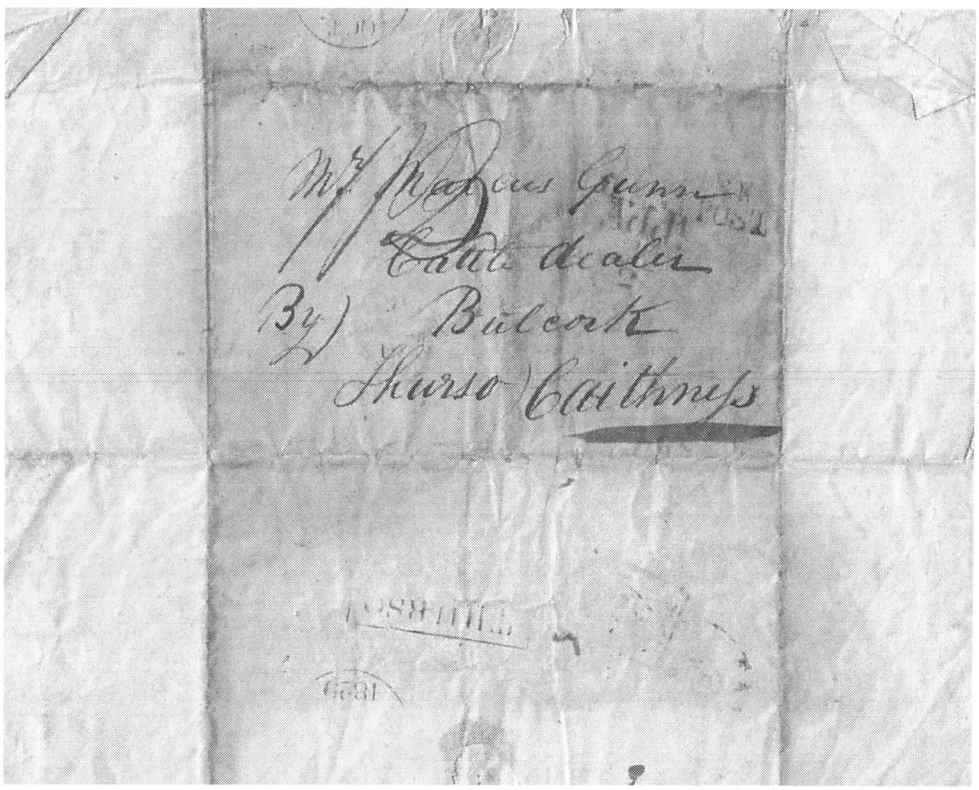

It is to Mr Marcus Gunn Cattle Dealer Bulcork Thurso Caithness. It has assorted other postal marks; a poor 'Penny Post' mark, a typical 'ADDL ½d' mark (being a further charge if the letter was carried by four wheeled coach in Scotland at this time) a manuscript mark and, most interestingly a red 'top half' Thurso mark towards the bottom. This mark is earlier than anything recorded in Auckland's *Postal Markings of Scotland to 1840*[689].

---

[688] 'The greatest market in Scotland was at Falkirk' p.61. Iain Sutherland, *Caithness 1770 to 1832.*

[689] 2nd edition edited by Ron Stables.

The next letter by Marcus (298) is from 'Owens Sound Upper Canada North America' via the 'St. Vinsint' post office. Some bits are missing from the letter as the original shows. It reads—

Bradford 27 September 1842

Dear John

I take the opportunity of writing you this few lines stating that I am in good health at present which I hope will find you in same, for the which I had reason to be thankful to the Almighty. We have had a long passage of eight weeks and 4 days to Quebec for we had to stop 4 days at the Grosse Isle (to get our clothes washed) at the Quarantine Ground for we had Sicknes on Board and one death, and their was 24 in number of our passengers kept at the Quarantein in the hospital and the ship and the rest forwarded to Quebec and arrived on a saturday morning after Breakfast we went a shore and saw a sight which I never saw an equal that Is the ports and Barracks. Their is 3 regiments their at present. The Pidoo(?) passengers was landed at Quebec and a great many of the rest which applied to the government for forwarding to Montrial gratis. My Comrade and me and a few more of us was allowed by the Captain to wait a board the ship to Montrial and took us their gratis, for my part I could not express the kindness with which he treated me and my partner, that is Osborn Sinclair it was in the second cabon we had our births in when the sickness began the birth below ours their was a wife and 3 Children and the woman and one her children got sick and so very sick that we could get no rest by being in the Birth above for two or three nights. I came in conversation one morning with the Captain and asked me how the woman and the boy was which I told him to be same way, only I told the Captain that we would not sleep in the same place that night should we sleep on dake the which he answered me imediately that he had an empty Birth and that he would make me and my partner welcome for the use of it to the Journeys end which we felt it very comfortable for when we all came to the quarantine all the chaff Beds was enptied and thrown away, and then had nothing to ly on but the bear deals., we had reason to be thankfull to the Almighty for that was the woman that died that was in the birth below us, The Captain has been very kind he ordered a Coffin to be made and sailed as near as possible to land an got her buried. When we got to Montrial my partner and me parted. he waited at Montrial and I assure you we was sorry in parting with each other for he was such an agreeable fine lad we messed together all three together Mr McLennan him and me and we had a midaged woman from Inverness which was an acquaintance of Mr McLennan. I took no kind of Beef neither Ham or mutton not a day ... Broth or fryed Ham to our din ... same to Montrial their was a few ... took a steam boat to Toronto ... but I found the Captain very kind ... bed from him in the cabin gratis ... beatiful country the very first hous ... of America we thought a great deal as the farther we went on the prettier it was. As we was coming we was enquiring about their crops which is very good in General, which I hope to hear from you about your Harvest and crops. I have no more particular news to mention but give my best respects Mr James Henderson and and both Mrs Henderson and likewise give my Best respects to Donald Sutherland Thurso and David Gunn wife & family. Likewise give my compliments to Chirsty McLeod and to the Revd. Rob Rose McKay likewise give my compliments to my brothers and families and to all the neighbours that enquires about me, and Especially to my Brother that I resided with wife and family and my dear little Johnie above all the rest and give my compliments to Donald *(of Tormsdale 262)* father (?) wife and mother & family, give my Compliments to your father and mother Brother and sisters not forgetting yourself. mind write as soon as possible with all the news you can from the old country and how the price of cattle came and the price of the meal.

I have no more to say at present But remains yours truly
Marcus Gunn.

(address—see the top of the page)

Bradford 27 Sept 1842

Dear John

I take the opportunity of writing you this few lines stating that I am in good health at present which I hope will find you in same, for the which I had reason to be thankful to the Almighty. We have had a long passage of eight weeks & 4 days to Quebec for we had to stop 4 days at the Grosse Isle at the Quarantine Ground for we had Sickness on Board and one death, and their was 24 in number of our passengers kept at the Quarantine in the hospital and the ship and the rest forwarded to Quebec and arrived on a saturday morning after Breakfast we went a shore and saw a sight which I never saw an equal that is the forts and Barracks their is 3 Regiments their at present, The Pilot Passengers was landed at Quebec and a great many of the rest which applied to the government for forwarding to Montrial gratis my Comrade and me and a few more of us was allowed by the Captain to wait a board the ship to Montrial and took us their gratis, for my part I could not express the kindness with which he treated me and my partner that is Osborn Sinclair it was in the second sabon we had our births in when the sickness began the birth below ours their was a wife and 3 Children and the woman and one

× to get our clothes washed

her children got sick and so very sick that we could get no rest by being in the Birth above for two or three nights, I came in conversation one morning with the Captain and asked me how the woman and the boy was which I told him to be same way, only I told the Capten that we would not sleep in the same place that night should we sleep on deake the which he answered me imediately that he had an empty Birth and that he would make me and my partner welcome for the rest of the Journeys end which we felt it very comfortable for when we all came to the quarantine all the chaff Beds was emptied and thrown away, and then had nothing to ly on but the bear deals, but we had reason to be thankfull to the Almighty for that was the woman that died that was in the birth below us, The Captain has been very kind he ordered a Coffin to be made and sailed as near as possible to land an got her buried. When we got to Montrial my partner and me parted. he waited at Montrial and I assure you we was sorry in parting with each other for he was such an agreable fine lad we Messed together all three together Mr. McLennan him and me and we had a Midaged woman from Inverness which was an acquantance of Mr McLennan I took no kind of Beef neither Ham

or mutton But I was not a day wi[...]
Broth or some fryed Ham to our din[...]
came to montreal their was a few
took a steam boat to Toronto st[...]
but I found the Captain very kind
bed from him in the cabin gratis, [...]
beatiful countrie the very first Hous[...]
of America we thought a great deal [...] the farms
we went on the pretter it was. as we was coming
we was enquiring about their crops which is very
good in General, which I hope to hear from you
about your Harvest and crops, I have no more
particular news to mention but Give my best respects
Mr James Henderson and and both Mrs Henderson
and likewise Give my Best respect to Donald
Sutherland Thurso and David Gunn wife &
family likewise give my compliments to
Christy McLeod and to the Revd Mr Rob Rose
McKay likewise give my Compliments to
my Brothers and families and to all the
neighbours that enquires about me, and
Especialy to my Brother that I resided with wife
and family and my dear little Johnie above all the[...]
and give my Compliments to Donald [illegible] wife
and mother & family, give my Compliments to your
father and mother Brother and sisters not forget
ting yourself. mind write as soon as possible with all
the news you can from the old country and how the price of
cattle came on and the price of the meal
Adress to Marcus Gunn { I have no more to say at present
Owen Sound. { But Remains yours truly
St Vincent Post Office upper Canada North America
Marcus Gunn

Addressed—
to John McKay Achlipster
Parish of Halkirk
County of Caithness
North Britain

There is a light, part inked BROADFORD circular postal mark under the manuscript Sept 30/44; the date being a manuscript addition to it. Note the cost—1 shilling and 2 pence; expensive.

The recipient is John McKay (3467), a son-in-law of the Sennachie. He wrote letters to Donald in Australia, see page 281 (and elsewhere).

The next letter by Marcus was written at Owens Sound on 3 November 1845 to his brother Alexander (1) (who married Barbara Gunn (6) and whose children emigrated to Australia) and reads:

Dear Brother

I find my myself under the Obligation of writing you these few lines to let you know that I enjoy my Health better than when I parted with you which I have reason to be thankfull to the most High, that we are spared in the land of the living, and on the ground of hope, which I hope will find you in the usual state of Health that I got an acount the last time I got an account from Caithness. I am to state to you the number of weeks that we took on our passage which I understand has been told you before but how ever I am to state it in your own letter since I left Thurso we had been 8 weeks and four days to Quebec, which I was kindly treated by our Captain both myself and my Comrade about 4 weeks sailing sickness happened to break out on the ... in the Birth Below where we were sleeping in so much that I could not get any sleep in the night time and after making an aplication to the Captain I and my comrade was ordered in to the Cabin with our Bed Clothes and was their till we came to Quebec and got along with him from Quebec to Montreal without charging for our Birth in the Cabin of the Extra passage to Montreal. When we came to Montreal their was different steamers the one in oposition to the other espesially their agents acting for them with handbills, the which I had a number of them before I left the ship, the which I came in conversation with the first of the agents that spoke to me and enquired of him about Hugh Gunn the Butcher that was at Thurso and told me to have known him well and went along with me where he was and a few more and after treating us kindly advised me to go by this agents steamer which he thought to be the safest and cheapest for it was to Carry us to Toronto without touching at Kingston and told me that he would call upon me aboard the steamer before we would sail and stood to his promise supose I did not happen to be a board at the time, however I felt his kindness in a manner that I got my luggage, and a bed in the Cabin gratis only 8 shillings of passage money, the which the rest had to pay for their luggage and Births and passage, I have not settled myself ... any land as yet or do not mean to do this season I work still upon my trade and with the same man. Alex Suther (Sutherland?) wife and family is all well and is working considerably well on his new farm and has a good deal of Cattle one yoke of good Oxen two young sheers and four cows in Calf and two Calfes, and I have bought myself two good Heifar Calves which if theywill be wintered well and attended regularly in giving them salt will be bulled the first season, Should A man be ever so poor if he is a well doing man and industrious and gets a lot of land a cow and a yoke of oxen he will soon have a good stock for their is not a farrow cow to be seen in this country or a two year old heifar without bulld about a months ago I have seen the two Campbells from Brubster and two Campbells from Spary (?) and Donald McKay from Grimby(?) and they have bought a 100 acres the piece of land as beautiful land as I have ever seen with good spring creeks and likewise I have seen John Gunn ...hour and is likewise settle upon a lo... of 100 acres, likewise Donald Munro's widow from Harpisdale (?) and her son is in the neighbourhood here and are quiet well and George Ba... from Thurary (?) as in the neighbourhood and a great deal of the Scotch which may be called the scotch Line and Angus Bain has ... arried to Georges wifes sister servant... from 3 1/2 to 4 dollars per month and her servant gets æ gets from 10 to 12 dollars per D and 1/2 a dollar when employed by the day that is 2 shilling sterling and John my brother I would not advise him to come unless his own mind would lead him but one thing aman that could come himself and family to this part of the country he would do well for their is chances going here now in the way of Grants which I am afraid will not continue long, please give my kind compliments to widow Sinclair and family to Margaret Sutherland and sister and your father Finlay wife and family. To John Gunn and sister and Robart Mckay and John Bain Calder (?) wife family and well wishers not forgetting yourself and family and enquirers

Dear Brother I remain yours with respect

Marcus Gunn

PS Alex. Sutherland wife and family Join in sending their kind Compliments to you and your family now as soon as this comes to your hand you shall write me an answer imediately with all the news you possibly can from that part of the country I beg to be excused for delaying so long in writing to you, but it was proposed by the free church presbytery of Hamilton that the Sacrrament of the Lords Super would be held in this township which did not come to pass and that was the reason of my delaying so long that I might have something more to state , I remain yours truly Marcus Gunn

Direct to the care of Mr Telfer, Land agent, Lower Jour..., St. Vincent Post Office, Ca … merica.

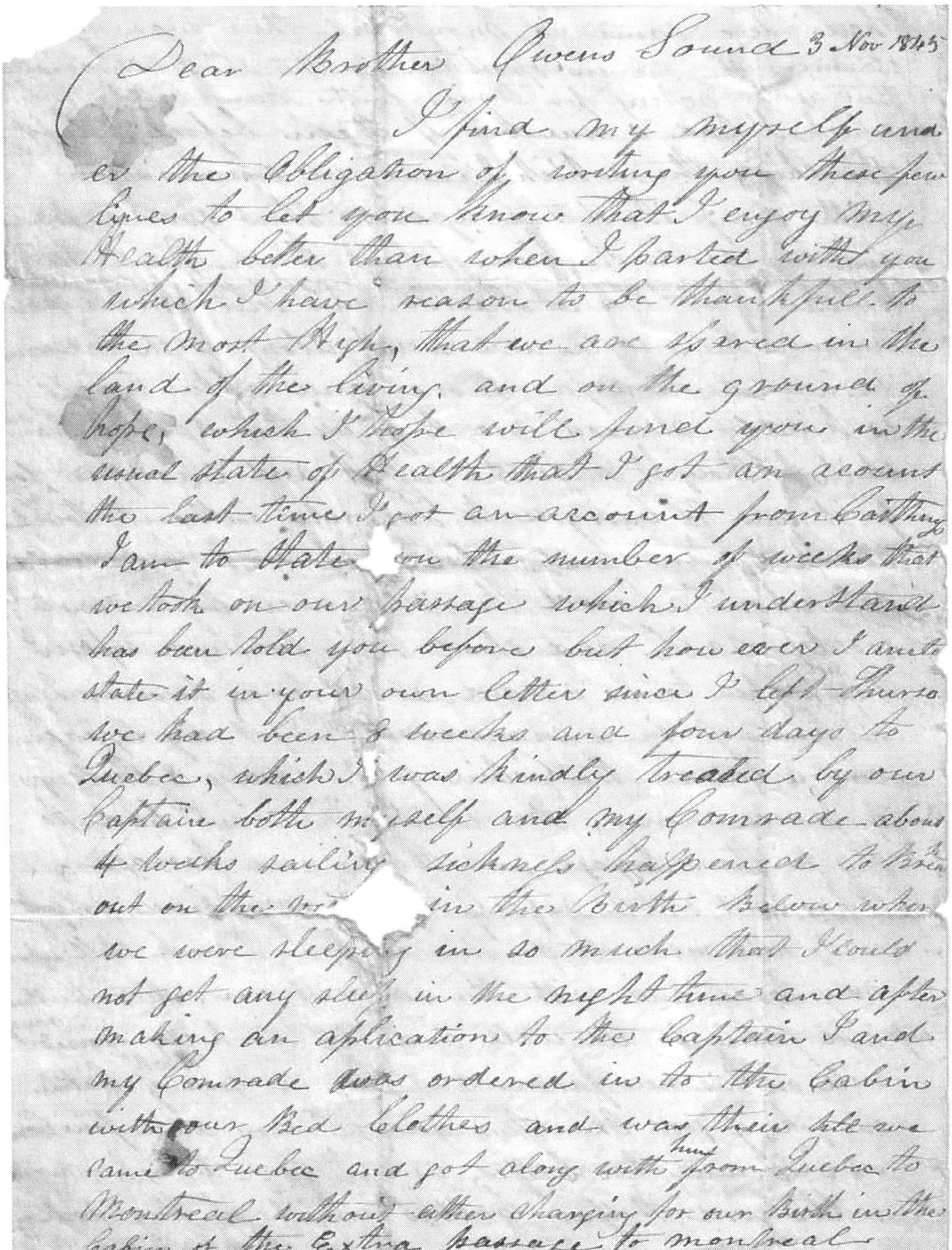
Dear Brother Owens Sound 3 Nov 1845
I find my myself und
er the Obligation of writing you these few
lines to let you know that I enjoy my
Health better than when I parted with you
which I have reason to be thankfull to
the Most High, that we are spared in the
land of the living and on the ground of
hope, which I hope will find you in the
usual state of Health that I got an acount
the last time I got an account from Caithn[illegible]
I am to state [illegible] on the number of weeks that
we took on our passage which I understand
has been told you before but how ever I am to
state it in your own letter since I left Thurso
we had been 8 weeks and four days to
Quebec, which I was kindly treated by our
Captain both myself and my Comrade about
4 weeks sailing sickness happened to brea[illegible]
out on the [illegible] in the Birth below wher
we were sleeping in so much that I could
not get any sleep in the night time and after
making an aplication to the Captain I and
my Comrade was ordered in to the Cabin
with our Bed Clothes and was their tile we
came to Quebec and got along with him from Quebec to
Montreal without either charging for our birth in the
cabin or the Extra passage to montreal

When we came to montreal their was differint
steamers the one in oposition to the other especially
their agents acting for them with hand bills, the
which I had a number of them before I left
the ship, the which I came in conversation
with the first of the agents that spoke to me
and enquered of him ofabout Hugh Gunn the
Butcher that was at Thurso and told me to have
known him well and went along with me where
he was and a few more and after treating
us kindly advised me to go by this agents steamer
which he thought to be the safest and Cheapest for
for it was to Carry us to Toronto without touching
at Kingston and toled [illegible] that he would
call upon me aboard the steamer before we
would sail and stood to his promise supose I
did not happen to be aboard at the time, however I fer
his kindness in a manner that I got my loggage
and a bed in the Cabin gratis only 8 shilings
of passage money, the which the rest had to
pay for their loggage and Berths and passage,
I have not settled myself [illegible] any land as yet
or do not mean to do this season I work still upon
my trade and with the same man, Alex Guthrie
wife and family is all well and is working considerably
well on his new farm and has a good deal of Cattle
one yoke of good Oxen two young Steers and four Cows
in Calf and two Calfes, and I have bought mysel
of two good Helfar Calbes which if they will

be wintered well and attended regularly in
giving them salt will be bulld the first season,
should the man be ever so poor if he is a well
doing man and industrious and gets a lot of land
a cow and a yoke of oxen he will soon have a
good stock for their is not a farrow cow to be seen
in this country or a two year old Heifer without a
bulld about a month ago I have seen the two Cam
pbells from Brubster and two Campbels from
Apary and Donald McKay from Clyniber and
they have bought a 100 acres the piece of land
as beautiful land as I have ever seen with
good spring creeks and likewise I have seen
John Gunn [illegible] hour and is likewise to
settle upon a lo[t] of 100 acres, likewise Donald
Munro, widow from Harpsdale and her son is
in the neighbourhood here and are quite well
and George Ba[in] from Thuravy is in the neig
hbourhood and a great deal of the Scotch which
may be called the scotch Line and Angus
Bain has [m]arried to Georges wifes sister
Servant [illegible] from [illegible] 1/2 to 4 dollars per m[onth]
and Men servants gets from 10 to 12 dollars per [illegible]
and 1/2 a dollar when Employed by the day
that is 2 Shilling Sterling, and John my Brother [I would]
not advice him to come unless his own mind would
lead him but one thing a man that could come him
and family to this part of the country he would [do]
well for their is chances going here now in way of Grant
which I am afraid will not continue long. Please give my
kind compliments to Widow Sinclair and family
to Margaret Sutherland and sister and your father in law
wife and family. To John Gunn and sister and Robert
McKay and John Bain [illegible] wife and family and well wishes
not forgetting yourself and family and inquirers

Dear Brother I remain yours with respect
Marcus Gun[n]

the news you possibly can from that part of
the country. I beg to be excused for delaying so
long in writing to you, but it was proposed by the free
Church Presbetry at Hamilton, that the Sacrament
of the Lords Supper would be held in this Township
which did not come to pass and that was the
reason of my delaying so long that I might have
some thing more to state, I remain yours truly
Marcus Gunn

Direct Marcus Gunn
to the care of Mr Telfer
land agent Owen Sound

P.S.
Alex Sutherland wife and family Joins
in sending their kind Compliments to you and your
family now as soon as this comes to your hand
you shall write me an answer imediately with all

The letter was addressed to Mr Alexander Gunn / Farmer Brawlbin Parish Reay / to the care of William Macdonald / Merchant Thurso / Caithness / North Britain. The postal marks are of interest. The letter was written 2 November 1845; it goes through Richmond Hill in Canada with a manuscript date in a blue ring on 15 November 1845 and has a red UK arrival mark of December 17, 1845.

The next extant letter by Marcus is to his brother Alexander (1);

Sydenham 14 July 1846

My dear beloved Brother,

I sit down with pleasure to write an answer to your letter of the 8 Jan which came to hand in the latter end of Feb and now I am to let you know about my friends here that we enjoy our usual health thanks be to the Almighty God for it, in whose hands is our moving our life and our being. But now I suppose you will be surprised for my delaying in writing you But my reason of delaying was to give you as proper an account of the plase as I could, and you wished me to mention what preacher we have got. their is not any as yet stationed in this place, But the Presbybrty of Hamilton, I mean of the free church are now and then, and the Sacrament of the Lords Supper was administered in this place By two ministers Belonging to the free church. The ones name was McSmelly (?) from Orkny which preached in english and the others name was Mr Meldrum from Lochabar or their Abouts, the which account I give of them both that they took Caithness again in my view, which often is in regard of that, but I have to state about them both that I heard nothing like them since I left their, But their be a whole line of Highland Scotch here that keeps a meeting every Sabbath between themselves but all connected with the free church, which I attend regular myself that is if I can for it is upon the same line or conception (concession?) that my lot is only my clearing is upon the rear of the ... for the man that I bought the right of it was their ... gan (one word) to clear because it was nearer to the village. But their is the same convenience on both ends to build and clear which I mean to do if spared in health, But I mean first to clear 10 or 12 acres on the rear and fence it in, and then clear and settle upon the front, for their is two beautiful spring creeks one on the rear and one on the front which does not dry a day in the year which is a great object in this country, and both free from swamps the which very few of this country creeks is, I have cleared the one on the rear this year free from having any wood in it. I can go to the town from this end of the lot in ¾ of an hour. It is on the same ...(?) now with Sutherlands but is 3½ miles nearer the town than his, my lot is the next to the town reserve, their was 4 lines (?) of grants surveyed last harvest, a line in each township which was given out by Billoting the same as the milittia and after that, was oblidged to put Blanks in along with the tickets (*to the side*—owing to the number of men there for Grants), which I had no chance of getting any but I bought a ticket from a partner I had working in the same shop but it was about 9½ miles from the village but thought it too far away but preserved it all the time till I got a chance at this one I have got upon which was between 4 or 5 acres cleared and a neat Shanty built upon it and I bought the crops and cooking utensils and what furniture belonged to him Which cost me High for every acre that is cleared in this country is woth four pounds for the choping and clearing of it. I have been working all the summer and the most of the Spring on the place. I have got 6 Bushels of wheat in the ground and near two bushels of oats and ½ of Bear merely for a trial and some Indian corn and 9 Bushels of potatoes and some turnips which appears to be a fair crop all through and likewise Alex. Sutherland has got a perty large clearing and likewise his crop is promising to be a fair crop and one of his little girls Jannet is keeping house for me and Chirsty His daughter is serving in the village in the house that I had been working in this six or seven months and gets 4 dollars a month. That is the rate of 12 currency a year and her occupation is ... and dressing and Ann his second daughter is engaged in the village since a month or two and gets 7/6 per month but I suppose they will require them themselves for the harvest. But Sutherland poor man lost one of his oxen this spring in the Bush it is supposed that he has been carried away and killed which is a great loss to him and to me likewise for I will not get a pair of oxen to log a day without 5/ a day and a labouring man 2/6 a day and Board, the which I had a good number of them since I commenced,

I am sorry to learn from my brother Donald letter that you are still in poor state of Health, But I was glad to learn from your own letter, that you had no servant in the house but Angus's Keith and that your family did wonderfully and were a blessing to you, the which news I hope to find in your next. Alexr Sutherland wife and family and I join

in sending our kind Compliments you and family and all enquiring friends and acquaintances, for I have no room to mention them seperately,
Dear Alexander I remain your sincere

and loving Brother

Marcus Gunn

My Dear Friend, *(to Mr Robert Sinclair, Brawlbin)*

I am to write this few lines to let you know that I enjoy my usual Health which I hope will find you in the same manner of Health for the which we should be thankful. Now I'll let you know a little about our new settlement which is but a young one, the Village or township Owen Sound their is double the quantity of Houses their more than when I came here. Their was only two merchant shops their and one shoemakers shop and one ainer (tanner?), now there are seven merchant shops and 4 shoemaker shops and two tanners and two taverns and one Bakers Shop and every thing is getting ...nderfully. We ..pe to have aminister Belonging to the ... church Settle ...mong us soon and again when I came there was but two scooners upon the Lake But now their is two small Propellas or Steamers which is a great advantage to emigrants to this part of the country, the price of wheat in this settlement from 4/ to 5/-per Bushel flour 4½ dollars to 5½ per Barrel, Bear 3/ per bushel, salt 1/9 to 2/3 per Bushel, potatoes 1/3 to 2/ per Bushel, pork 6d to 7½. per lb., Beef 2½. per lb., Eggs 7½ . to 8. per doz., Butter 7½ to 10d. per lb.
And to all enquiring friends acquaintances and well wishers not forgeting yourself
I am yours with respect
Marcus Gunn
To Mr Robert Sincliar
Brawlbin
please make Alexr. my Brother give my respect to John my Brother wife and family and likewise to Hugh wife and family and that they need not be offended for me not writing them
I am -----(?) respect----(?) M

I have seen John Gunn Brayhour he is quiet well in health and the McKays or Bains from Thurary and many more from that parish which is in the same township with me and are well in health as far as I know, please give my compliments to your Brother (s?) Mother and Sister and to your friends in that town and to the Revd. R Mckay

*****

The people in the above two paragraphs are Alexander Gunn (1), John Gunn (294) Hugh Gunn (295) and probably John Gunn 'Brayhour' (3406).

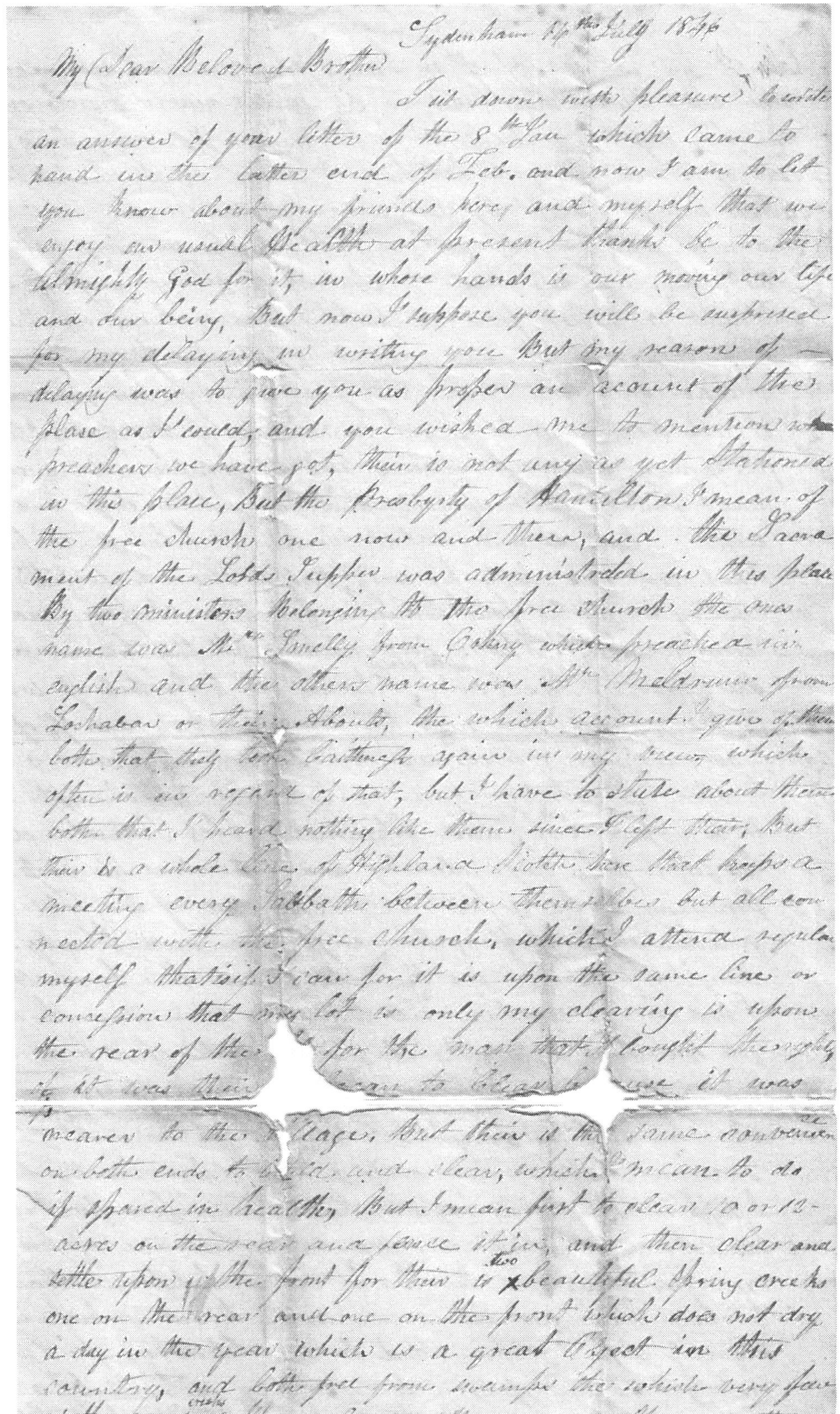

Sydenham 14th July 1844

My Dear Beloved Brother

I sit down with pleasure to write
an answer of your letter of the 8th Jan which came to
hand in the latter end of Feb. and now I am to let
you know about my friends here and myself that we
enjoy our usual health at present thanks be to the
Almighty God for it, in whose hands is our moving our life
and our being, But now I suppose you will be surprised
for my delaying in writing you But my reason of
delaying was to give you as proper an acount of the
plase as I could, and you wished me to mention wh
preachers we have got, their is not any as yet Stationed
in this place, But the Presbyrty of Hamilton I mean of
the free church one now and then, and the Sacra
ment of the Lords Supper was administrded in this place
By two ministers Belonging to the free church the ones
name was Mr Tamelly from Coburg which preached in
english and the others name was Mr Mcldrum from
Lochaber or their Abouts, the which account I give of them
both that they look Earthness again in my view, which
often is in regard of that, but I have to state about them
both that I heard nothing like them since I left their, But
their is a whole line of Highland Scotch here that keeps a
meeting every Sabbath between themselves but all con
nected with the free church, which I attend regular
myself thatis if I can for it is upon the same line or
concession that my lot is only my clearing is upon
the rear of the [illegible] for the man that I bought the right
of it was their [illegible] to clear [illegible] it was
nearer to the [illegible]llage, But their is the same convenience
on both ends to [illegible] and clear, which I mean to do
if spared in health, But I mean first to clear 10 or 12
acres on the rear and fence it in, and then clear and
settle upon the front for their is two beautiful Spring creeks
one on the rear and one on the front which does not dry
a day in the year which is a great Object in this
country, and both free from swamps the which very few
of this country is, I have cleared the one on the rear this
year free from ~~[illegible]~~ having any wood in it I can go to the town from this

This letter is scanned in two parts as it is approximately 13 inches / 330 mm in length.

End of the lot in 3/4 of an hour, it is on the same Conces
sion with Sutherlands but is 3 1/2 miles nearer the town
than his, my lot is the next to the town Reserve, their was
4 lines of grants surveyed last harvest a line [in] each township
which was given out by billeting the same as the [Highlands?]
and after that was obliged to put blanks in along with
the tickets, which I had no chance of getting any but
I bought x a ticket from a partner I had working in the
same shop but it was about 9 1/2 miles from the
village but thought it too far away but preserved
it all the time till I got a chance of this one I have
got. upon which was between 4 or 5 acres cleared and
a neat Shanty built upon it and I bought the crops and
cooking utensils and what furniture belonged to him
Which cost me Kife for every [acre] that is cleared in this
country is worth four pounds for the chopping and
clearing of it. I have been working all this Summer and
the most of the Spring [on the place] I have got 6 Bushels of wheat
in the ground and near two Bushels of oats and 1/2 of
Bear merely for a trial and some Indian corn and 9
Bushels of potatoes and some turnips which appears
to be a fair crop [all through] and likewise Alex Sutherland
has got a pretty large clearing and likewise his crop is
promising to be a fair crop and one of his little
girls Janet is keeping house for me and Chirsty his
daughter is serving in the village in the house that
I had been working in this six or seven months and
gets 4 dollars a month that is the rate of 12 currency
a year [illegible] supplation in [illegible] and dressing and
[illegible]
Ann his second daughter is engaged in the village
since a month or two and gets 7/6 per month but
I suppose they will require them themselves for the
harvest, Bill. Sutherland poor man lost one of his
oxen this spring in the Bush it is supposed that
he has been carried away and killed which is
a great loss to him and to me likewise for I will
not get a pair of oxen to log a day without 5/ a day
and a labouring man 2/6 per day [and Board] the which I had
a good number of them since I commenced,

x Along with the numbers of men there for grants

I am sorry to learn from My Brother Donald letter
that you are still in a poor State of Health, But I
was glad to learn from your own letter that you had
no servant in the House but Anguis Keith, and that
your family did wonderfuley and were a blessing to
you, the which news I hope to find in your next
Alexr Sutherland wife and family and I Join
in sending our kind Compliments you and
family and all Enquiring friends and Acquain-
-tances, for I have got no room to mention them
seperately,

Dear Alexander I remain your sincere
and loving Brother
Marcus Gunn

My Dear friend
I take to write this few lines
to let you know that I enjoy my usual Health which
I hope will find you in the same manner of Health
for the which we should be thankful, now I [illegible]
let you know a little about our new settlement
which is but a young one, the Vilage or town [illegible]
Owen Sound their is double the Quantity of Houses
their more than when I came here their was only
two marchant shops their and one shoemaker
shop and one [illegible], now their is seven merchant
shops and 4 shoemaker shops and two tanners
and two tavern[illegible] and one baker shop and every
thing is getting [illegible]nderfully, we [illegible] to have a minister
belonging to [illegible] church settl[illegible] among us soon
and again wh[illegible]n I came there was but two Schooners
upon the Lake But now their is two small
Propellas or Steamers which is a great advantage
to emigrants to this part of the Country, the price of wheat in this settlement from 4/ to 5/ per Bushel
flour 4½ to 5½ Dollars per Barrel Bear 3/ per Bushel salt
1/9 to 2/3 per Bushel potatoes 1/3 to 3/ per Bushel
Pork 6d to 7½ per lb Beef 2½ per lb Eggs 7½ to 8 p Doz
Butter 7½ to 10d per lb

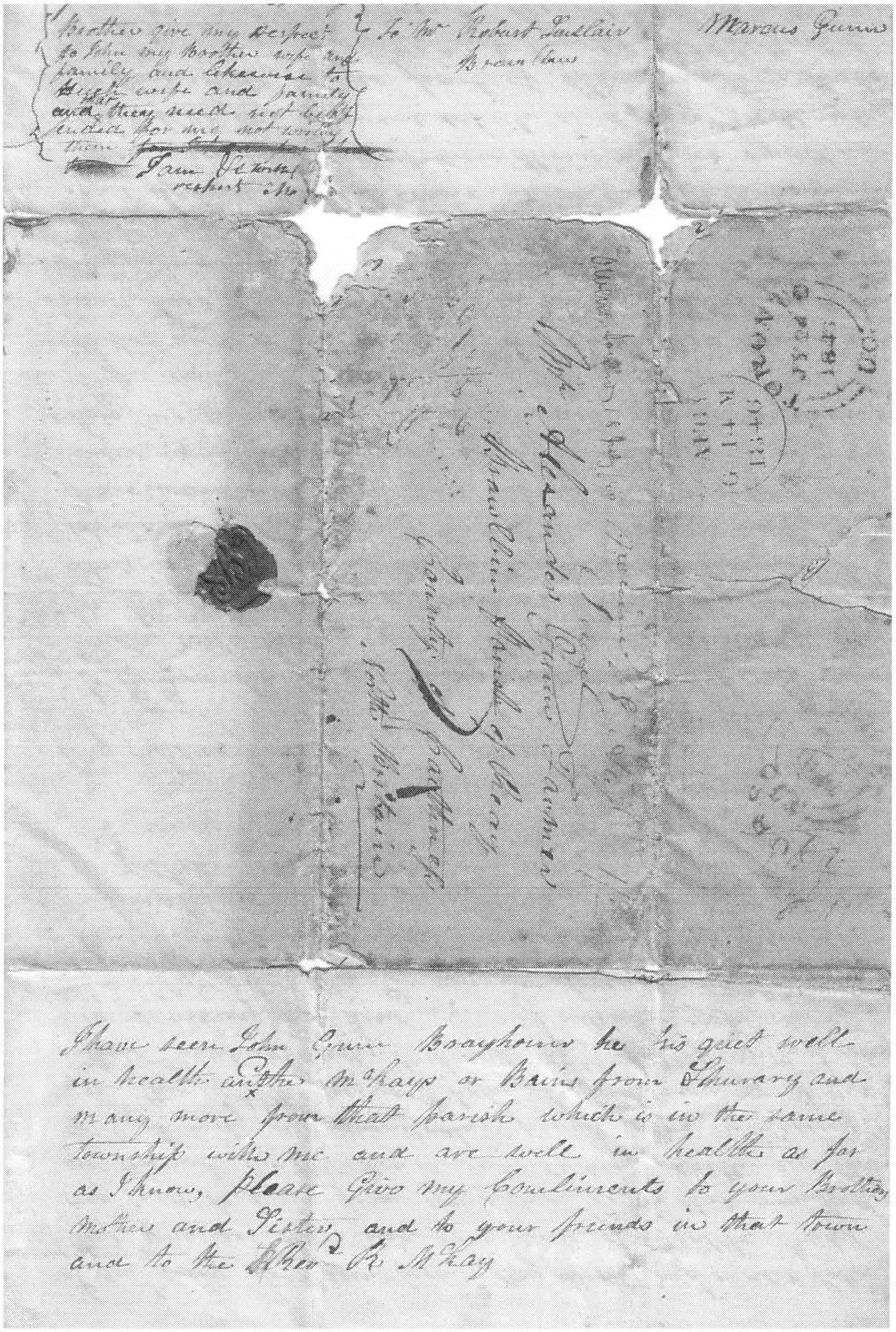

brother give my respect
to John my brother wife and
family and likewise to
Hugh wife and family
and that they need not be offended
for me not writing
them [illegible]

I am with respect etc.

To Mr Robert Sinclair
Braehour

Marcus Gunn

I have seen John Gunn Brayhouse he is quiet well
in health and the McKays or Bains from Thurary and
many more from that parish which is in the same
township with me and are well in health as far
as I know, please Give my Compliments to your Brother
Mother and Sister, and to your friends in that town
and to the Rev. R McKay

The trials of the journey are visible. Marcus now settles into the Canadian wilderness. The vision of a little Scotland in early Canada and of the increasing prosperity of Marcus and the township provide a vivid glimpse of early Canada.

Generation Three

Janet 'MacLeod' Gunn (120)

Back in Scotland, however…

AN UNKNOWN

(W)ick Wednesday 4th Octr. 1849

Dear Madam,

The reason of my long silence will now appear and I hope plead it's own excuse for I have several times attempted to convey in words the sentiments of my heart but agitations &c has compell'd me to silence .... not in what light it may be could(?)...only if I can form any notion of my ....heart from the impression made by your many acciable accomplishments and either my happiness or condolence in this world is a great measure depends on your answer; and I confidently rely that the generosity of you(r) nat(ure) is a sufficient impediment to the ....tarting any cruel objections ....instances are pretty independent......try character hitherto unblemished of ... you shall hgave the (?) undoubted proof ......if it is to your satisfaction I shall not only consider myself as extremely happy to be permitted to pay my addresses to you; but should ... love be returned shuld make it the ....le study of my future life provide the happy ..... of her ....(?) I prefer to all others in the .... I shall wait for your answer with utmost impatience and awe,

Madam,

Your sincere admirer

Robert McKay

and in a different hand

p.s A from Atitude recure... this missive comprising a concise sumimons (?), and satiasfactory answers to the forecceeding queries in the care of Mr Gordon Sutherland Cooper Luisburgh Wick will met due attention a hearty and welcom'd acceptance by

..............................ry 4/479 2 Ocl

What a letter—to whom was it addressed? Was it to Donald's elder sister Catherine? Perhaps. Or to his younger sister Janet? She was fifteen so may have been too young to marry. But it is probably to her as other letters by her exist and no documents are held for Catherine. And is the letter deliberately burnt by the recipient who then changed her mind?

(2,) Wednesday 4th Oct. 1869

Dear Madam,

The reason of my long silence since
now appears and I hope plead its own excuse for
[illegible] several [illegible] attempted to convey in words
the sentiments of my [illegible] agitation has
compelled me to [illegible] not in what
light it may [illegible] if I can form
any notion of [illegible] from the impor[illegible]
ssion [illegible] amiable accom-
plishments. And all my happiness and condole[illegible]
in this world in a great measure depends on
your answer; and I confidently hope that
the generosity of your [illegible] a sufficient
impediment to [illegible] any
[illegible] objections. [illegible]
pretty independent [illegible] my character hitherto
unblemished of which you shall have the most
undoubted proof [illegible] if it is to your satisfaction
I shall not only consider myself as extremely
happy to be permitted to pay my addresses
to you; but should [illegible] love be returned

this let[illegible] , it [illegible] instruction for my future
life [illegible] the [illegible] [illegible]
to see others in the [illegible] . I shall wait for
your answer with the utmost impatience.
I am ever,
Madame,
[illegible] sincere admirer
Robert [illegible]

P.S. A [illegible] Recruit[illegible] this Mission comprising a concise
luminous, and satisfactory answers to the preceding queries
to the care of Mr. Gordon [illegible] Cooper [illegible]
will meet due attent[illegible] a hearty and welcome acceptance
by [illegible]
[illegible] 414 [illegible] 2d [illegible]

Donald Gunn in Brawlbin and Ballarat (3) and his brother John Gunn (12)

One has to note Donald's home life; his grandfather Donald of Tormsdale (262) died circa 1844, we do not know the death date for his grandmother Janet (703) but his father Alexander in Bualchork and Brawlbin (1) died in 1847 at Brawlbin and his mother Barbara Gunn (6)—see sections 4, 5 and 6—had predeceased her husband dying in 1844. This left Donald being in some ways the man of the family (and certainly 'head' according to the 1841 census) when only 15/16, although his grandfather on his Mother's side—Donald the Sennachie—was alive, he was 77, and so may have provided advice but unlikely to be doing hard labour. His older sister Catherine would have been about 17. How did he—and the rest of the family—cope? They certainly continued with their tenant farm but it must have been a mighty effort.

The bills continue but are now in Donald Gunn's name (and see pages 46 onwards) although he is still 'Junior', perhaps in deference to his grandfather or perhaps merely a reflection of his youth—

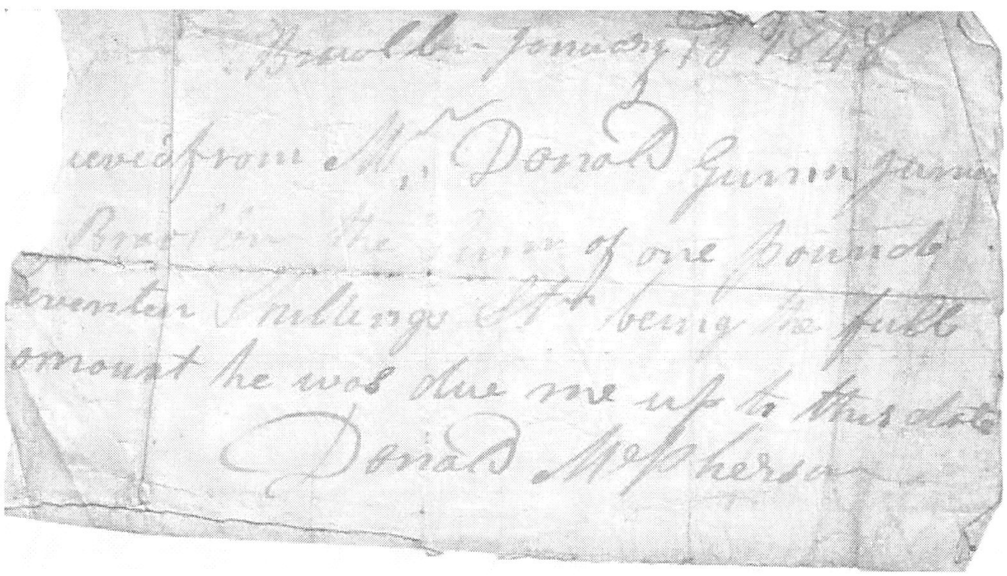
Brawlbin January 13 1848
ceived from Mr Donald Gunn Junr
Brawl the sum of one pound
seventeen shillings Stg being the full
amount he was due me up to this date
Donald McPherson

January 13 1848 receipt for £1/ 17 / 0 written at Brawlbin.

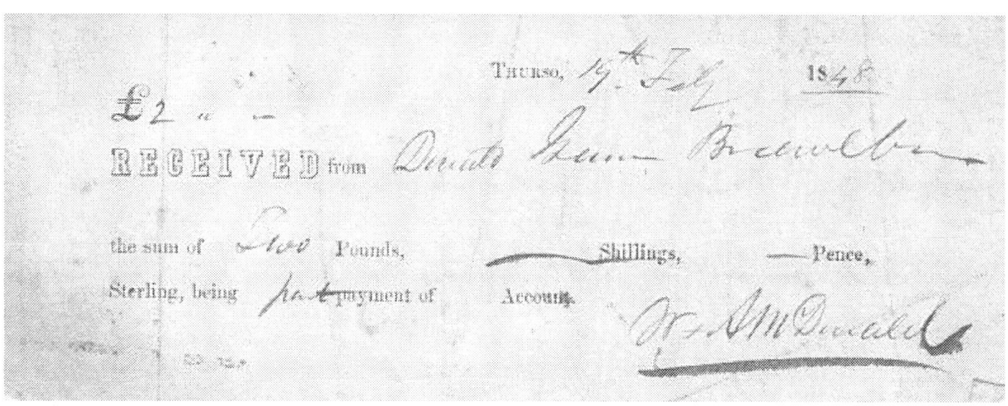
Thurso, 19th Feby 1848
£2 " –
RECEIVED from Donald Gunn Brawlbin
the sum of Two Pounds, — Shillings, — Pence,
Sterling, being part payment of Account.
W. & A. McDonald

19th February 1848 receipt for £2 being part payment to McDonald of Thurso.

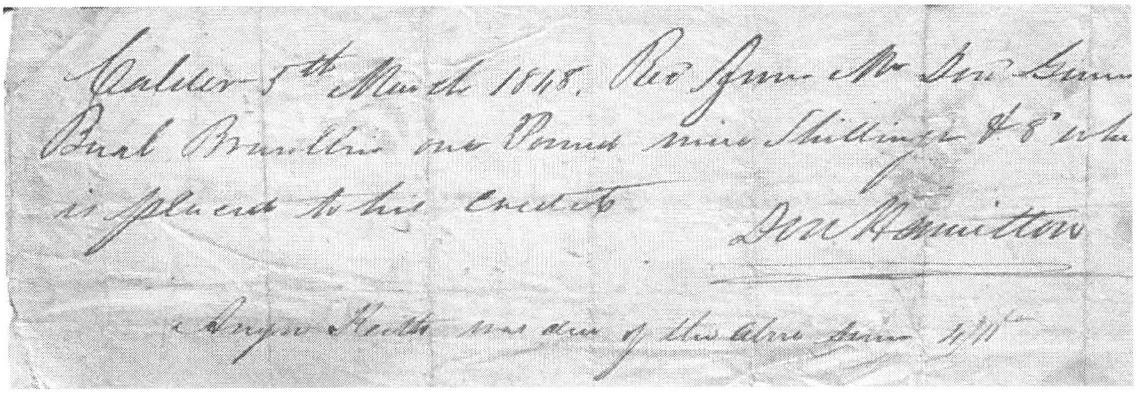

Calder 5th March 1848. Recd from Mr Don Gunn
Beal Brawlbin one Pound nine Shillings & 8d which
is placed to his Credit
Don Hamilton

Angus Keith was due of the above sum 4/11

5th March 1848 receipt from Calder but owed to Don Hamilton. Angus Keith was due part of the sum. An Angus Keith was in Alexander's household in the 1841 census, aged 30, as a male servant. It is possible that the above applied to him.

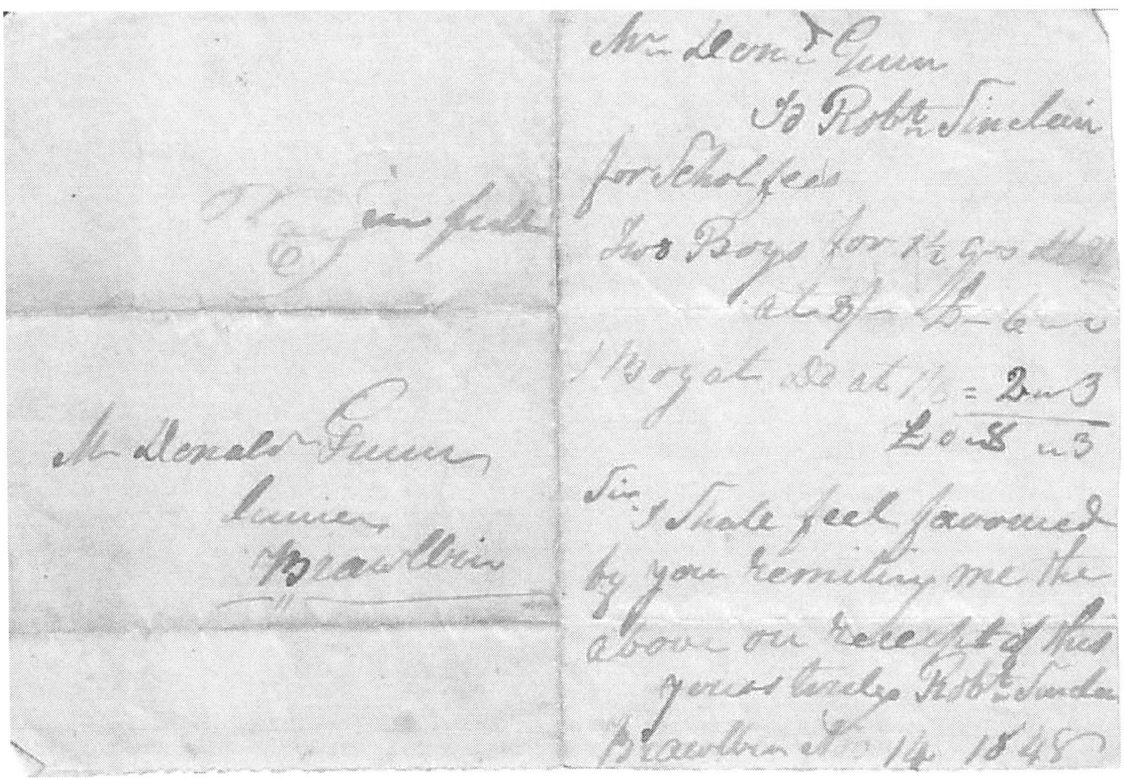

Mr Donald Gunn
Lower
Brawlbin

Mr Don Gunn
To Robt Sinclair
for School fees
Two Boys for 1½ yrs
at 8/- £0-6-0
1 Boy at do at 1/6 = 2-3
£0-8-3
Sir I shall feel favoured
by you remitting me the
above on receipt of this
yours truly Robt Sinclair
Brawlbin ... 14 1848

The above is a fascinating bill from Robt Sinclair for school fees for three children being in total for the sum of 8/3d. One assumes the teacher had not previously pressed the account as Donald's father had died in 1847. What is interesting here is that it is for two boys for one and a half years; and one boy for a shorter time. Presumably the two full time students were Donald's younger brothers—John (12) and William (220)—and the student who finished early may well have been Donald. As head of the family there would have been more important matters to attend to than school, such as earning some money. Janet (120) and Catherine (119), being female, were less likely to be formally educated.

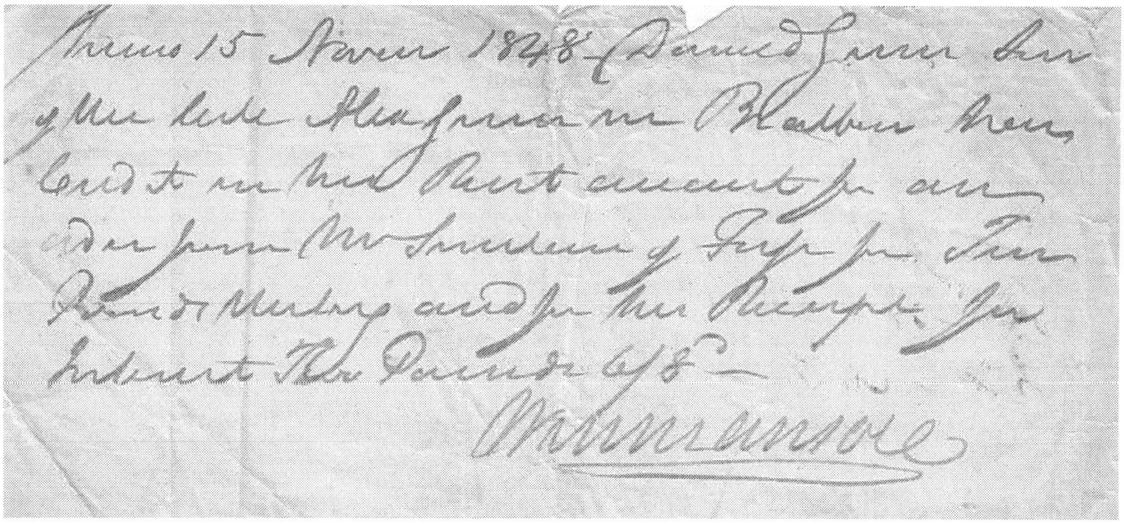

An 1848 tenancy account.

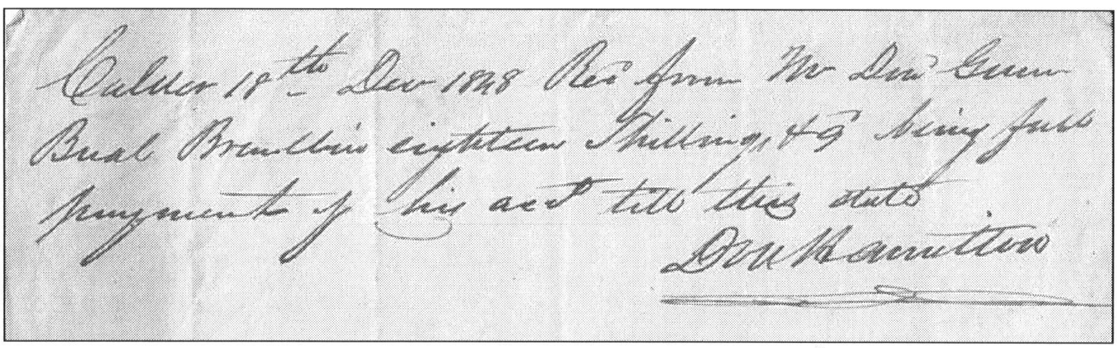

Calder 18th Dec 1848 Recd from Mr [illegible]
[illegible] eighteen Shillings & 9d being full
payment of his acct till this date
Don Hamilton

A further account from Don Hamilton in Calder is dated 18th December 1848.

No. 56 Reay January 1. 1849

To Mr Donald Gunn Junr. Braalbin

TAKE NOTICE that, by a Meeting of the PAROCHIAL BOARD of REAY, held on the Second day of November, 1848, an ASSESSMENT of Eight ℔ Cent. on the present Rental was imposed,—one half payable, in terms of the 34th Sec. of the Act, by the Owners,—the other half by the Tenants or Occupants of all Lands and Heritages within the Parish, of the yearly Rent or value of Two Pounds Sterling and upwards, for the Half-year from Martinmas, 1848, to Whitsunday, 1849, for RELIEF of the POOR of said PARISH of REAY;—and in terms thereof, you are ASSESSED in the Sum undernoted,—and the same is payable to the Collector, at the School-House of Reay, precisely, on Wednesday, the Seventh of February, 1849.

As Proprietor, on a Rental of £ .... £

As Tenant or Occupant, on a Rental of £16 .... £ — 6/4¼

£

James McLaren, Collector.

N.B.—The Parochial Board will sit at Reay, on Tuesday, the Sixth day of February next, from Twelve o'clock noon to Three o'clock afternoon, for the purpose of HEARING OBJECTIONS, if any, to your Assessment,—after which no Objections will be received.

☞ Please bring this Notice to the Collector, at Payment.

The official notice from Reay January 1, 1849 for poor relief; so the tenancy had passed to Donald. He had taken on the responsibility of family head.

Mr Donald Gunn farmer Braalbin

1851 To Donald Munro Wright Thurso

March 1	To 2 old fillies & a board 9 feet 1/	—	1	6
April 6	a pair of Cart wheels 40/ a new reak 1/	2	1	9
		£2	3	3

By Cash in full

Donald Munro

An 1851 bill from Donald Munro Wright in Thurso.

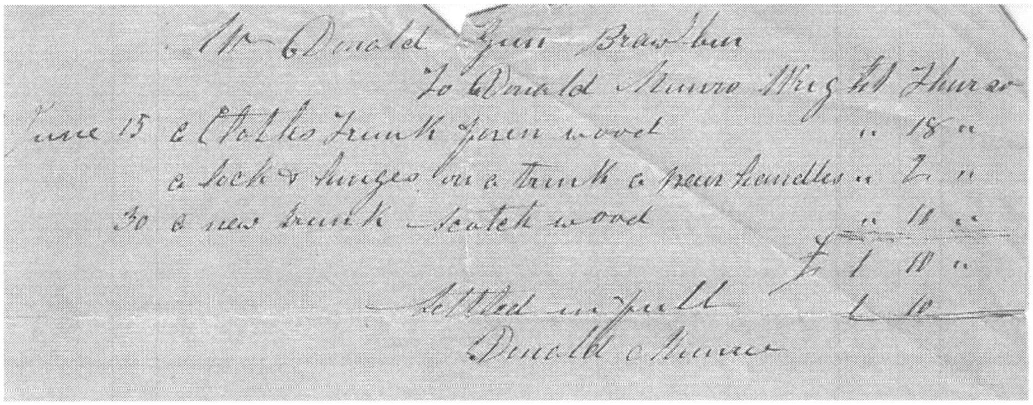

Mr Donald Gunn Brawlbin
To Donald Munro Wright Thurso
June 15 a Clothes trunk green wood .. 18 ..
a lock & hinges on a trunk a pair handles .. 2 ..
30 a new trunk scotch wood .. 11 ..
£1 11 ..
Settled in full £1 10
Donald Munro

A further, but undated, bill from Donald Munro Wright in Thurso.

Life, though, was not all comfortable; someone at Brawlbin had been quite severely ill in 1852. There is a bill from James Mill(?) 'surgeon Thurso' dated March 19 1852 which was for 'advice and prescribing for you from 16 January' and was for 7/6d and the cost of the medicine was 8/1d.This fairly considerable bill was settled on 24 Feb 1854.

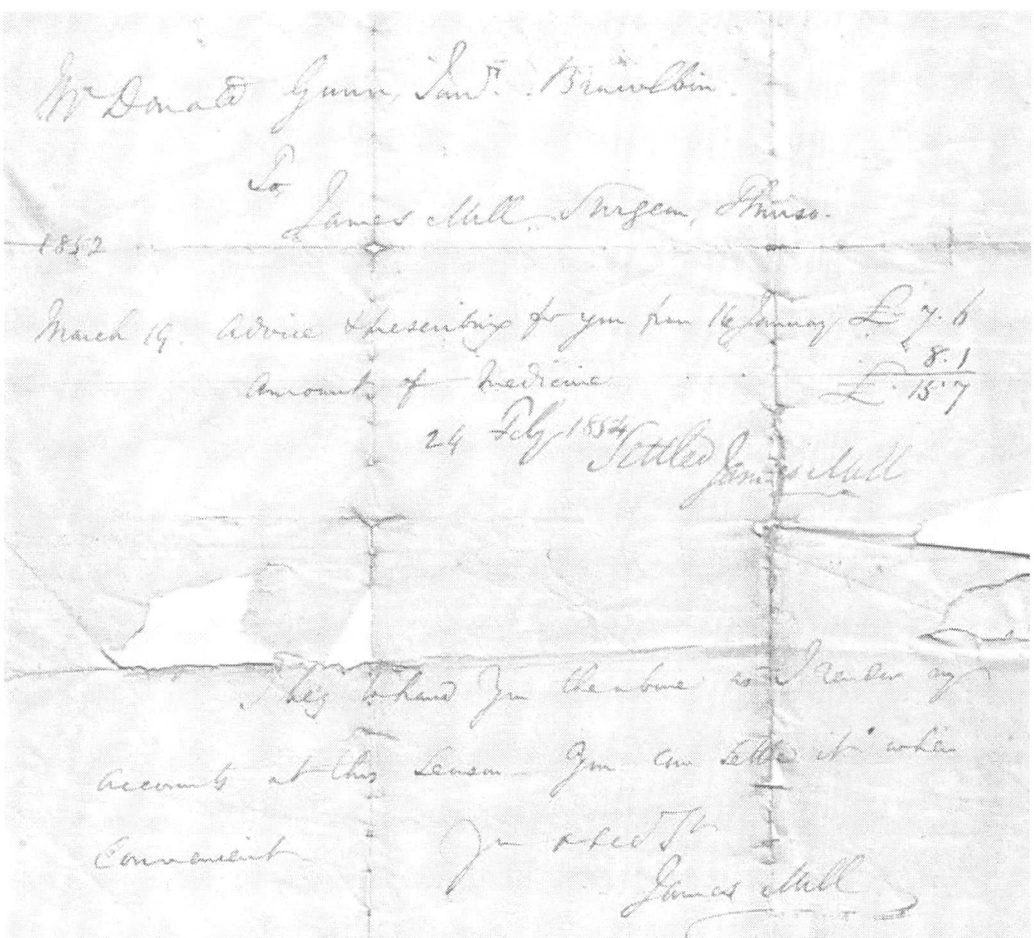

Mr Donald Gunn Junr. Brawlbin
To
James Mill, Surgeon, Thurso.
1852
March 19. Advice & prescribing for you from 16 January £ 7.6
Amount of Medicine 8.1
£ 15.7
24 Feby 1854 Settled James Mill
I beg to hand you the above as I render my accounts at this season you can settle it when convenient
Yours respy
James Mill

It raises questions about problems of health in the Highlands and may provide some explanation as to motivation for emigration. Donald at this stage is described (although still 'Junior') as 'farmer, Brawlbin' on the outer of the bill.

Mr. Donald Gunn Junr

This is in contrast with the next bill - one dated May 23 1853 and made out to Donald by a John Gunn. John was owed £2/1/3 for four and a half gallons of 'aqua' (presumably not water but whisky) and six bottles of porter and Donald paid on the 27th. The bill was written in Thurso.

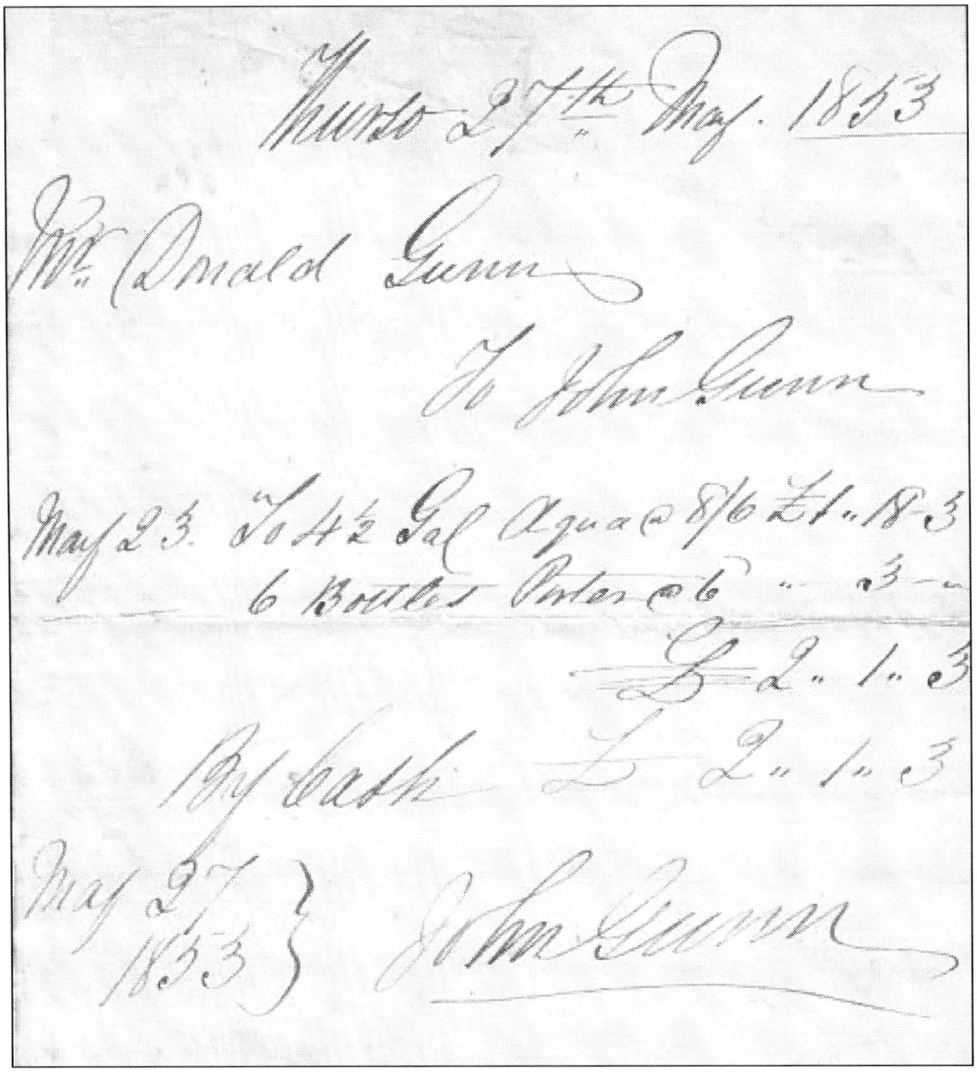
Thurso 27th May. 1853

Mr. Donald Gunn

To John Gunn

May 23. To 4½ Gal Aqua @ 8/6 £1..18..3
6 Bottles Porter @ 6 .. 3 ..
£2..1..3

By Cash £2..1..3

May 27 1853 } John Gunn

The excise certificate relating to this transcation is perhaps the following—

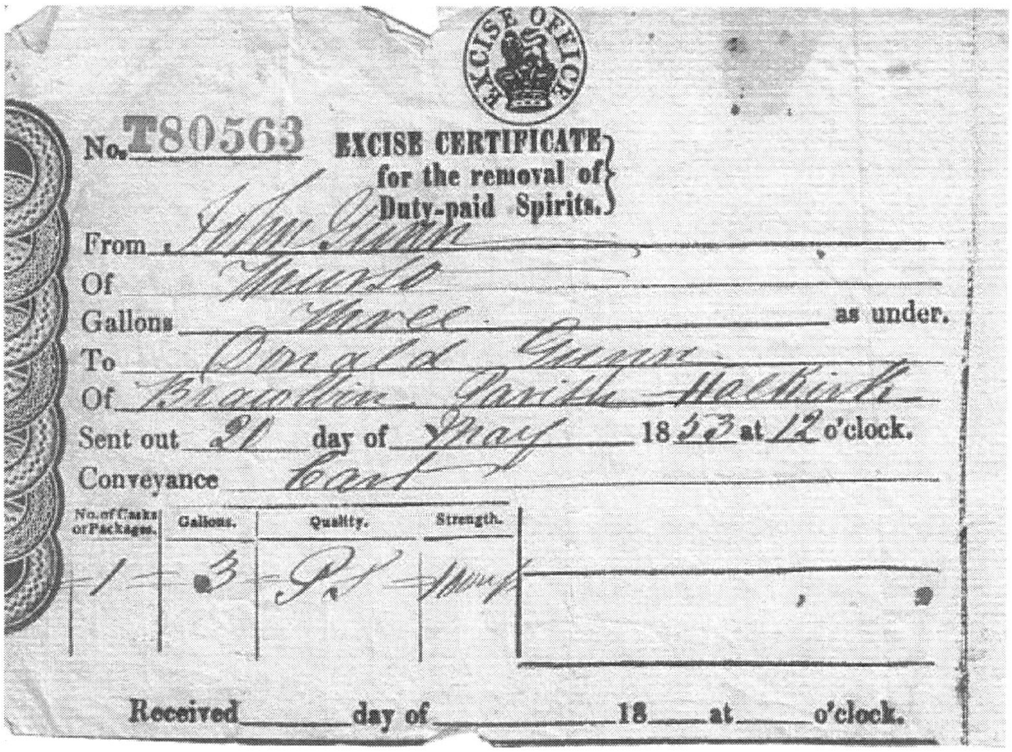

EXCISE OFFICE

No. T80563 EXCISE CERTIFICATE for the removal of Duty-paid Spirits.

From John Gunn

Of Thurso

Gallons Three as under.

To Donald Gunn

Of Brawlbin Parish Halkirk

Sent out 21 day of May 1853 at 12 o'clock.

Conveyance Cart

No. of Casks or Packages.	Gallons.	Quality.	Strength.
1	3	P.S.	[illegible]

Received ____ day of ____ 18__ at ____ o'clock.

It seems an impressive amount for one young family…

Another account exists from Donald McPherson which was begun on September 15 1851 and ran till June 29 1853. This bill includes debts from Donald, William, Katherine and John. Donald paid £2 of the £4/11/7d owing. Again Donald was paying debts accrued on behalf of the whole family; one assumes as the main adult he was responsible for these debts (presumably all goods bought were for the good of the family). Donald though did not pay it all off at one go; on June 29 1853 he paid £2 leaving a balance of £2 11/ 7d to pay.

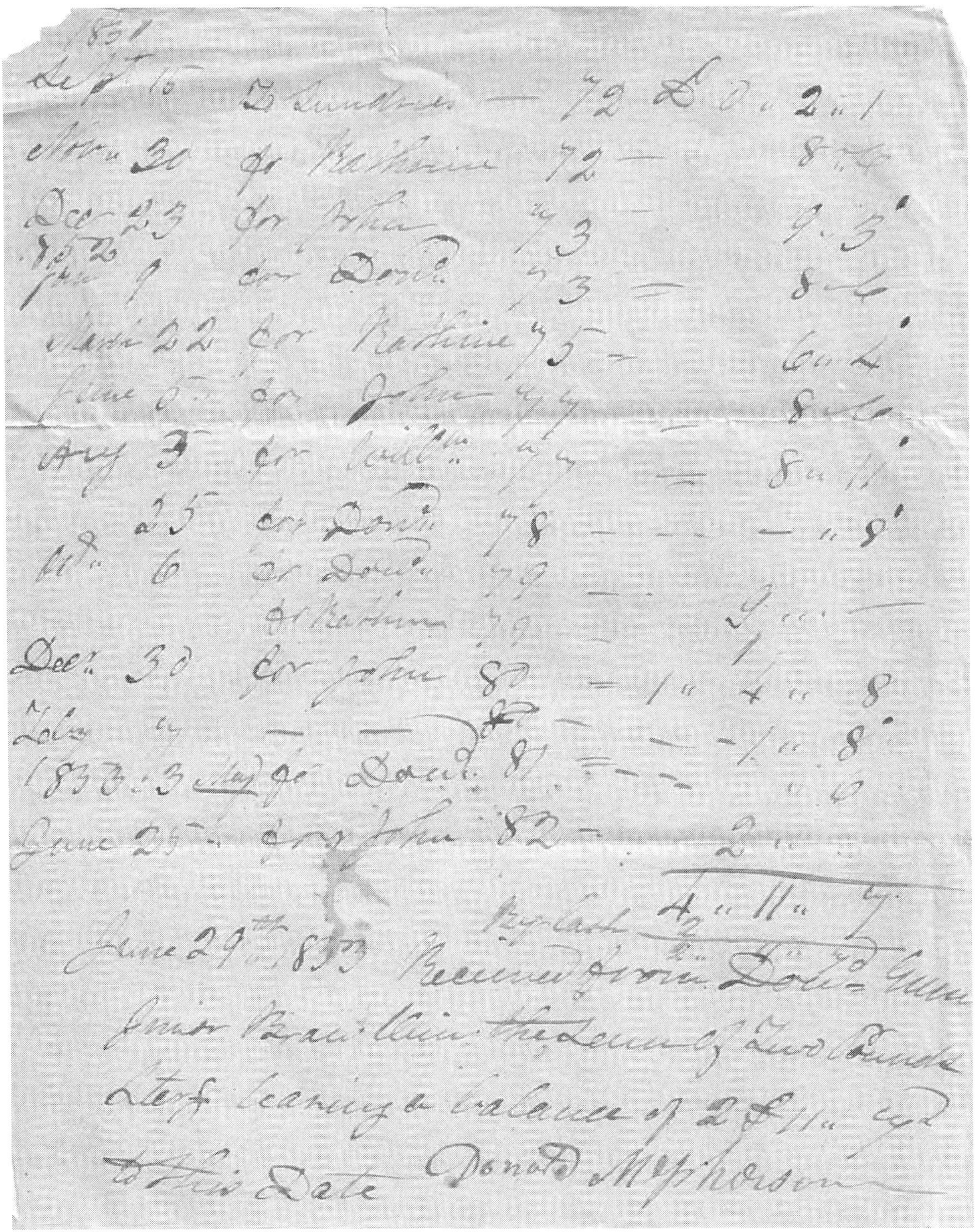
1851
Sept 16 To Sundries — 72 £0 „ 2 „ 1
Nov„ 30 for Katherine 72 — 8 „ 4
Dec 23 for John 73 — 9 „ 3
1852 Jan 1 for Donld 73 — 8 „ 4
March 22 for Katherine 75 — 6 „ 4
June 5 for John 77 — 8 „ 6
Aug 3 for Willm 77 — 8 „ 11
25 for Donld 78 — „ 8
Nov 6 for Donld 79 —
for Kathrn 79 — 9 „ —
Dec 30 for John 80 — 1 „ 4 „ 8
Feby 4 — — do — — 1 „ 8
1853: 3 May for Donld 81 — „ 6
June 25 for John 82 — 2 „
4 „ 11 „ 7
By cash 2
2 „ 11 „ 7
June 29th 1853 Received from Donld [illegible] Junior [illegible] the sum of Two Pounds Sterg leaving a balance of 2£ 11„ 7d to this Date Donald McPherson

What is one to make of the following document?

When this you see remember
me, and keep me in your mind.
Let all the world say what thay
may, Speak of me as you find

Round as the ring that has no
end, so is my love to you my
friend, your love may fail but
mine shall never, till our too
hands be clasped together,

Mr Donald Gunn
Farmer Bual
Bralbin
By Thurso
Caithness

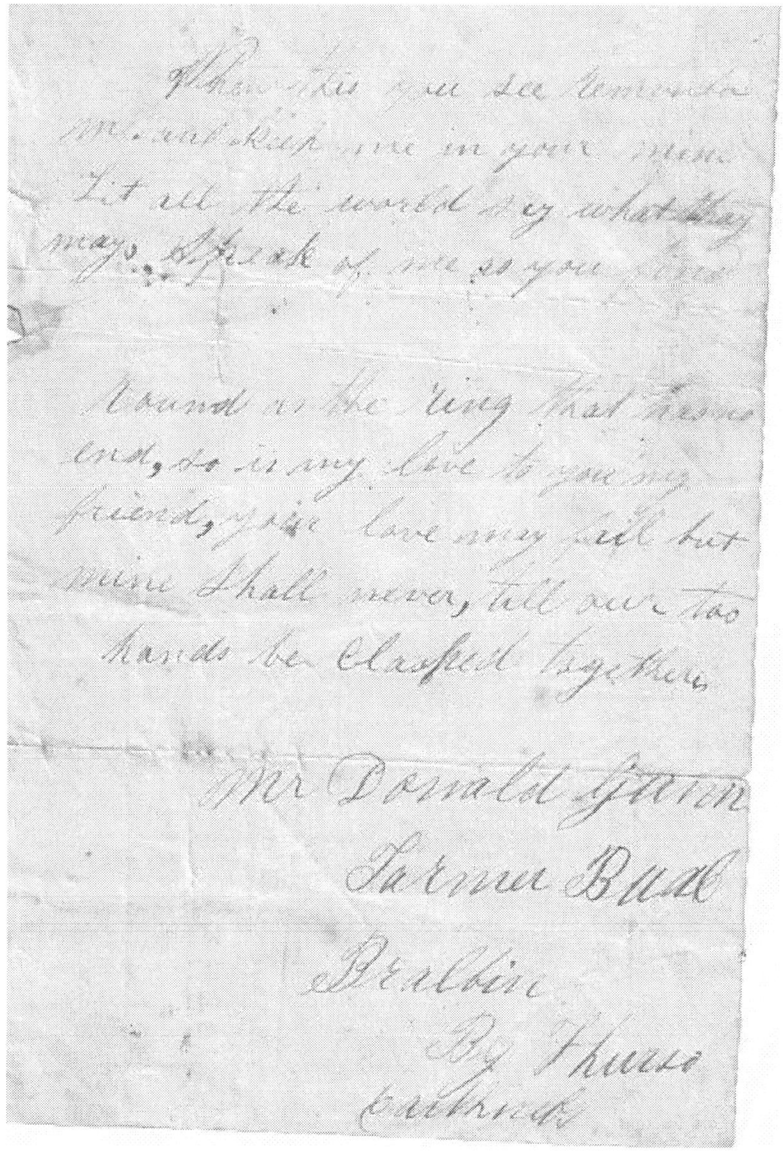
When this you see remember
me and keep me in your mind
Let all the world say what thay
may, Speak of me as you find

Round as the ring that has no
end, so is my love to you my
friend, your love may fail but
mine shall never, till our too
hands be Clasped together,

Mr Donald Gunn
Farmer Bual
Bralbin
By Thurso
Caithness

Donald clearly had a sweetheart who wrote the poem; obviously Donald did not write it otherwise the address would not be required. It is a complete message so it is sent to reflect the feeling of the sender.

Who was the sender? Is the third last line an indication of Donald's rejection? Was it perhaps an indication reflecting why he may leave Scotland?

Donald had made up his mind to emigrate and it's not surprising given the Scottish mood of the time and the circumstances in which the family was in. A letter to him reads:

Edinburgh April 25th 1853

My Dear friend,

I received your receipts from which I am glad to learn that you are enjoying good health further I learn that you have made up your mind fully for emigrating which I expect that you will find it to equal your most sanguine expectations for you will have 100 chances there of doing well to every one in Scotland. Their has come some very uncuriging letters here of late but principally from the part of the community that can neither work nor wants and one may rely that it is a failing with human nature that one will not speak well of a place where they do not succeed well. I would not hesitate one day about going were it not on my mother's account for in my own line at present the trade is uncommonly brisk and workman not to be got at any money.

In accordance to your request I have been enquiring after Government emigration but I have been informed that their is none for Scotland at the present time Their has a company started here of late to take in 2000 deposits at 10/6d each to be alotted to 80 20 being sent out free and 60 assisted their is a good many that hesitaten in sacrifising their money for their is only 80 chances out of the 2000 but still their is a good many that has suscribed already

In regard to Murdoch Campbells enquiry about the egg trade I do not think that he would be much the gainer by sending them here at present for the provision merchants are retailing them at 6d per dozen only had he opened a correspondence here in the beginning of winter he would have done very well for at the chrismas many they were buying them in at 2/- per dozen and could not get as many as they required at that. I have nothing important to communicate at present only I hope to be favoured with a note from your hand as soon as convenient meantime I remain yours faithfully

William McPherson

To Mr D Gunn

Odenburgh April 25th 1858

My Dear friend

I received your receipts from which I am glad to learn that you are enjoying good health further I learn that you have made up your mind fully for emigrating which I expect that you will find it to equal your most sanguine expectations for you will have 100 chances there of doing well to every one in Scotland There has come some very unencourageing letters here of late but principally from that part of the community that can neither work nor want

and one may rely that is is a
feeling with human nature
that one will not speak well
of a place where they do not succeed well. I would not hesitate one day about going were
it not on my brothers account
for in my own line at present
the trade is uncommonly brisk
and workmen not to be got at
any money

In accordance to your request I
have been enquiring after Government emigration but I have
been informed that their is none
for Scotland at the present time
their has a company started here of
late to take in 2000 depositors at

10/6 each to be allotted to 80
as being sent out free and 60
assisted their is a good many
that hesitate in sacrificing
their money for their is only 80
chances out of the 2000 but
still their is a good many that
has suscribed already

In regard to Murdoch Campbell's
enquiry about the egg trade I
do not think that he would be
much the gainer by sending
them here at present for the
Provision merchants are retailing
them at 6d per dozen only had
he opened a correspondence here
in the beginning of winter
he would have done very well

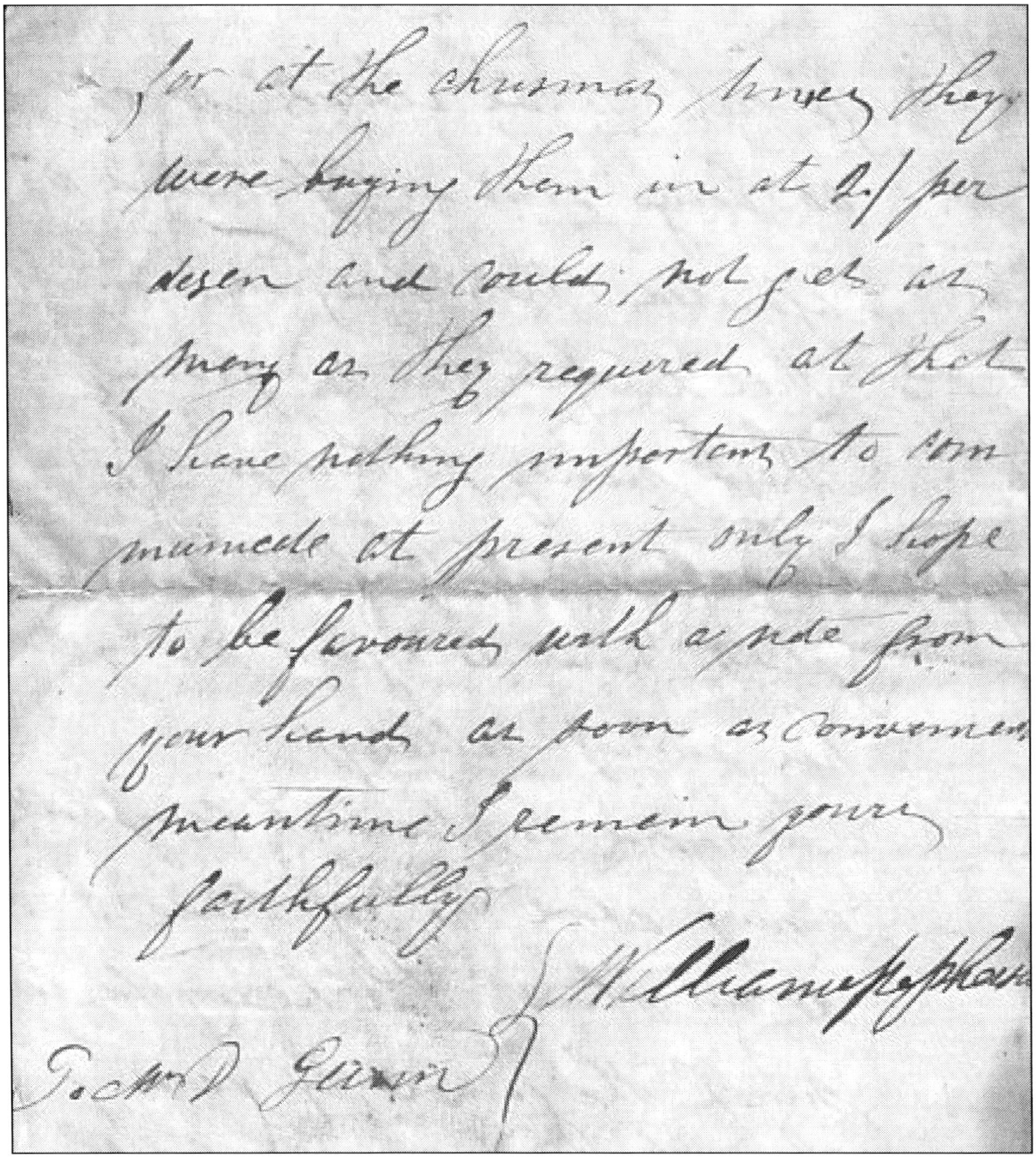

for at the christmas times they
were buying them in at 2/ per
dozen and could not get as
many as they required at that
I have nothing important to com
municate at present only I hope
to be favoured with a note from
your hand as soon as convenient
meantime I remain yours
faithfully
William McPherson

To Mr D Fraser

Donald has very clearly made up his mind to leave.

The next two documents that exist—in chronological order—are from the 'Colonial Land and Emigration Office, Park Street, Westminster.' They provide an insight into the distinct bureacratic mind of the time:

XXVI

Preliminary form 24 May 1853
25412

Donald Gunn

I am directed by the Colonial Land and Emigration Commissioners to acknowledge the receipt of your Letter of the 6th Inst. and in reply, to enclose a preliminary form to be filled up by persons wishing to ascertain whether they are likely to be put on the List of Candidates for a Passage, before going to the trouble and expense of filling up the regular Form of Application.

It is to be distinctly understood, that if the regular form be afterwards issued, the Commissioners do not thereby in any way pledge themselves to accept the Applicants, although eligible, who must not therefore leave their employment, or make any preparation for departure, unless called on by the Secretary to pay the deposit required by the regulations.

I am
Your obedient Servant

John Gliddon (?)
per Secretary

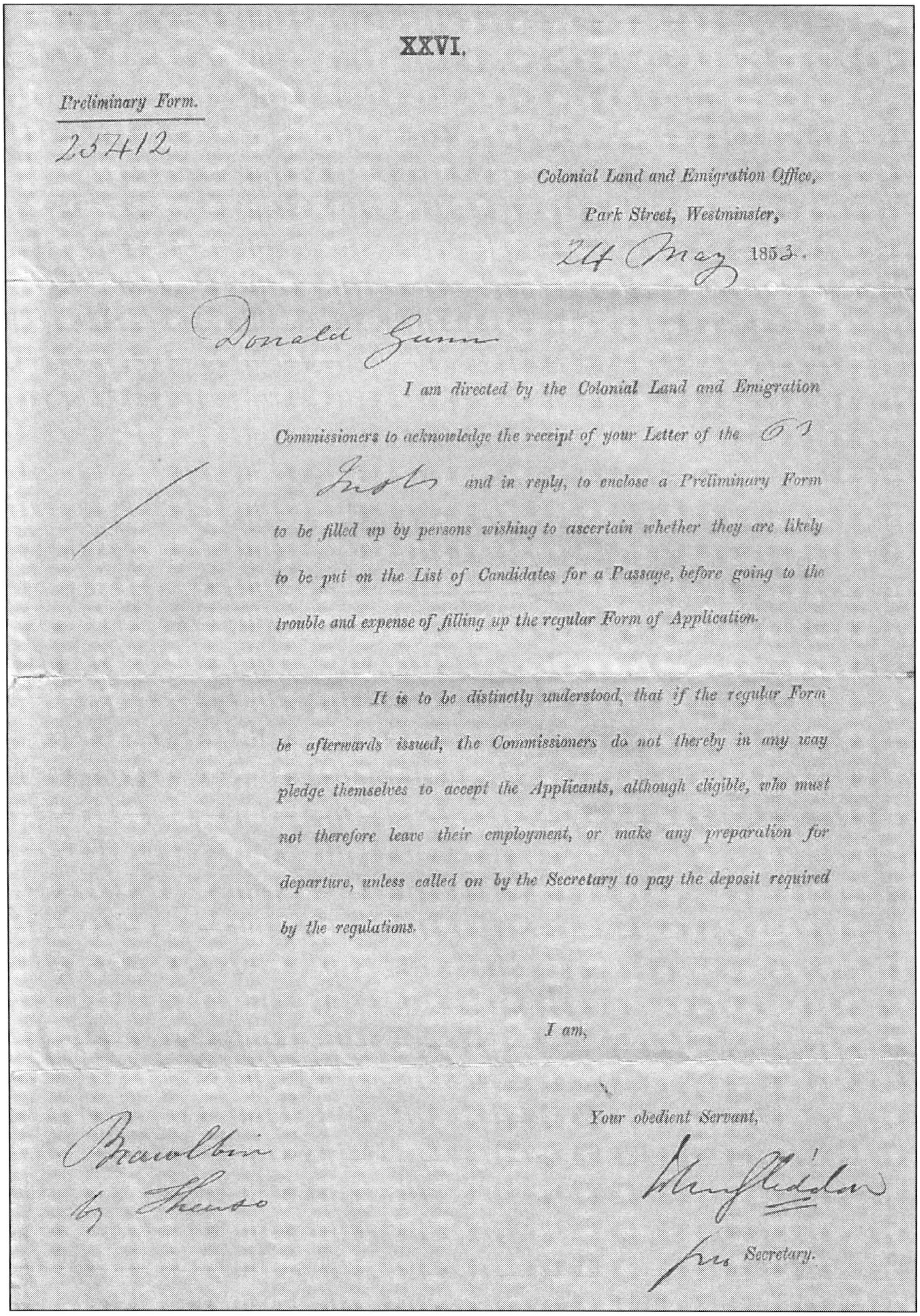

XXVI.

Preliminary Form.

23412

Colonial Land and Emigration Office,
Park Street, Westminster,
24 May 1853.

Donald Gunn

I am directed by the Colonial Land and Emigration Commissioners to acknowledge the receipt of your Letter of the 6th Inst *and in reply, to enclose a Preliminary Form to be filled up by persons wishing to ascertain whether they are likely to be put on the List of Candidates for a Passage, before going to the trouble and expense of filling up the regular Form of Application.*

It is to be distinctly understood, that if the regular Form be afterwards issued, the Commissioners do not thereby in any way pledge themselves to accept the Applicants, although eligible, who must not therefore leave their employment, or make any preparation for departure, unless called on by the Secretary to pay the deposit required by the regulations.

I am,

Your obedient Servant,

[illegible]

for *Secretary.*

Braulbin
by Thurso

Donald was not to have success this way.

The next letter from the same office was 30 June 1853. (Around this time John—Donald's younger brother—was emigrating.) It says:

IV

Donald Gunn

With reference to your application for a Passage to Australia, I am directed by the Colonial Land and Emigration Commissioners to state that they regret that they are unable to meet your wishes, as more than the due proportion of persons having already been selected from Scotland in the present Emigration, the Commissioners can only now take from that part of the United Kingdom Single Women, being Farm and Domestic Servants, and families of which at least two-thirds are females.

I am
Your obedient Servant
John Gliddon (?)
per Secretary

The official assisted passage seems to not have worked. Presumably Donald was to pay his own way.

IV.

Colonial Land and Emigration Office,
8, Park Street, Westminster,
30 June 1853

32234

Donald Gunn

With reference to your application for a Passage to Australia, I am directed by the Colonial Land and Emigration Commissioners to state that they regret that they are unable to meet your wishes, as more than the due proportion of persons having already been selected from ~~Ireland~~ Scotland in the present Emigration, the Commissioners can only now take from that part of the United Kingdom Single Women, being Farm and Domestic Servants, and Families of which at least two-thirds are Females.

I am,

Your obedient Servant,

John Gliddon
per Secretary.

Braalbin
Thurso

Working out methods of emigration though was not his sole concern—extended family life was to continue. This letter is, presumably, to Donald as it is held by his family. What is annoying is an inability to pin all the people down on the family tree; where known ID numbers have been inserted—

Edinburgh 5th october 1853

Dear Friend

I reseived your letter on the 3 instintent which I was glad to understand that you was in good health at the time Dear Friend I am to tell you som of Margret Sinclair tale conserning your aunt Margaret (880) + your uncel Alex (572) I hope you will be cind enough to ask your aunt whither they were in good terms ore not when She left Caithness hir language was discreasful to be heard concerning both of your Aunts but I hope you you will be kind enougug to write me and tell me some things concerning there corespondance + then I will tell you in my next letter hir language Dear Sir I am to tell you of hir career in this world She is in Daniel Gunns house since a Months She left Rodric Mcdonald + she is at law with him at present I do not know what is she to do, she is in a bad state at present but still she canot keep hir Long I did not speak a word to hir Since long I would be very sorry to let eny of their names to be taken in vane so I + hir hir had a black day Dear Friend, I am to apply for the County Police as the Superintendent is living on my Beat. So I am sure to get on bu if our wages will get up as we ar thinking I will be as good where I am Dear sir be sure + write me as soon as this comes to your hand and tell me what your aunt says concerning Margret Sinclair as I think whin I was at home thay were in good terms but still you will ask hir what was between them indeed I was not well pleased at hir language + tell me who is comming on the coast at present is John McKay (3467) comming yet ore cuming Dear friend give my best respict to your aunt Margret + to your sister Jinat[690] + to your Brother tell me is he in Thurso as yet Dear Friend Iam to go to Dundee the first cheap excursion I had a letter telling that your aunt had a young son I wonder much that you never told me of your aunts Death I had ben Drinking with William Mcpherson last Sunday + he was telling me that he had a letter from you at your arrival at orkney be sure + write me as soon as this comes to your hand I remain yours faithfull

Robert Gunn

No2 Ashley Buildings

Edinburgh

See pages 379 and 380.

[690] Janet MacLeod Gunn (120)

Edinburgh 5th october
1853

Dear Friend I received
your letter on the
3 instintent which I was glad to under
stand that you was in good heal
th at the time Dear Friend
I am to tell you som of
Margret Sinclair talk concerning
your aunt Margret & your
uncal Alex I hope you will
be kind enough to ask your aunt
whither they were in good terms
or not when ~~they~~ She left
Caithness hir language
was disgreasful to be heard
concerning both of your
aunts but I hope you

you will be kind enougug to write me and tell me some things concerning these corespondance & then I will tell you in ~~your~~ my next letter her language Dear Sir j am to tell you of her ~~[illegible]~~ career in this world She is in Daniel Gunn's house since 4 Months She left Rodric Mcdonald & she is at law with him at present I do not know what is she to do. she is in a bad sate at present but still she canot keep her long I did not speak a word to her since long. I would be very sorry to let eny of their names to be taken in vane so G & her her hat of black clay

Dear Friend I am to aply
for the county Police as
the Superintendent is living
on my Beat so I am sure
to get on bar if our wages
will get up as we ar thinking
I will be as good where I am
Dear Sir be sure & write
me as soon as this comes
to your hand and tell me what
your aunt says concerning Margret
Sinclair as I think when I was
at home thay were in good terms
but still you will ask her what
was between them indeed I was
not well pleased at her language
tell me who is comming on the
coast at present is John
Mckay comming yet or Cumming
Dear frien give my best respect
to your aunt Margret & to your

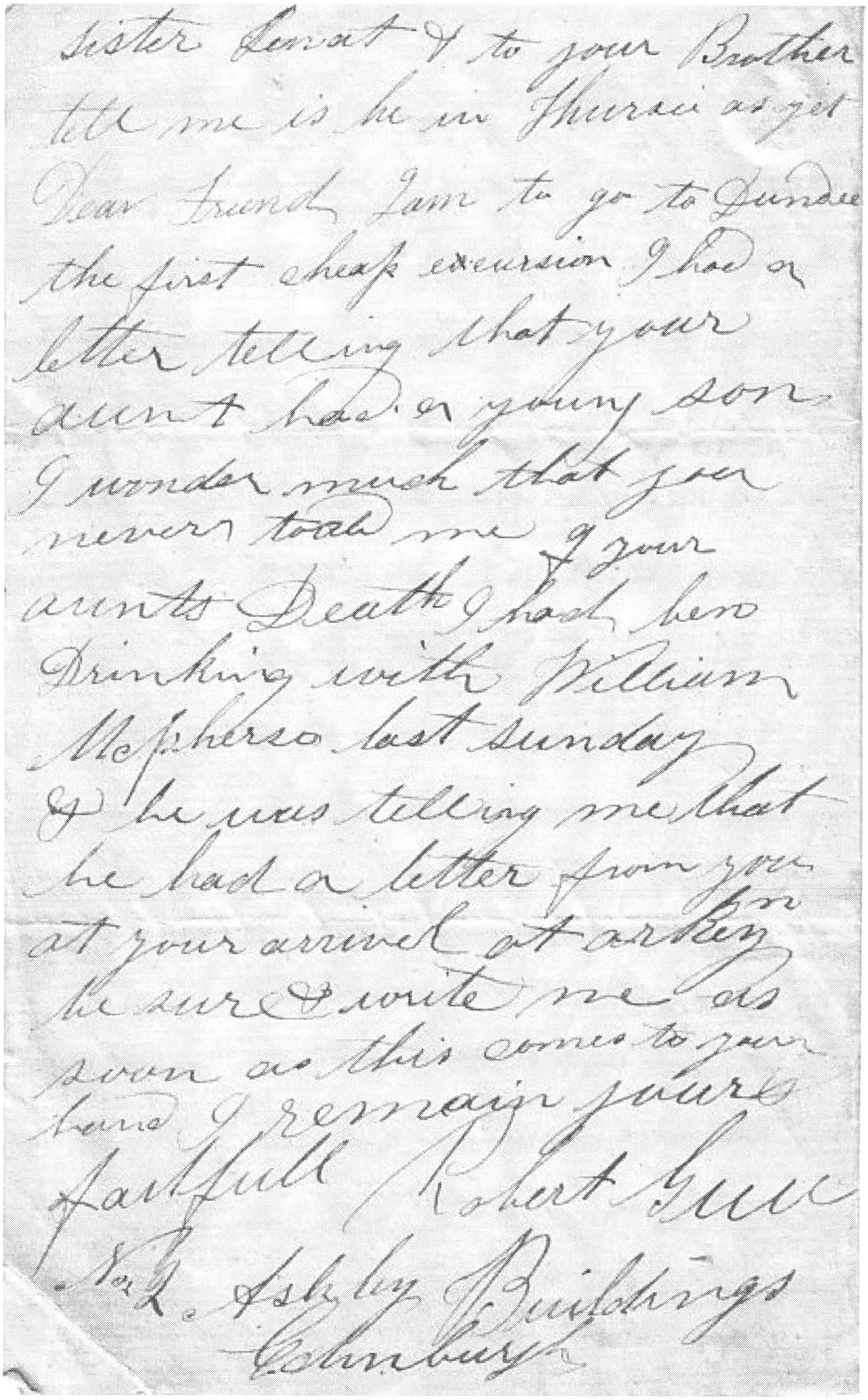
sister Janet & to your Brother
tell me is he in Thurso as yet
Dear friend I am to go to Dundee
the first cheap excursion I had a
letter telling that your
aunt had a young son
I wonder much that you
never told me of your
aunts Death I had been
Drinking with William
Mcpherso last Sunday
& he was telling me that
he had a letter from you
at your arrival at Orkney for
be sure & write me as
soon as this comes to your
hand I remain yours
faithfull Robert Gunn
No 2 Ashley Buildings
Canbury

The recipient, presumably Donald, had been to the Orkneys and family fighting was occurring at this time. It did not, though, deter Donald from his emigration plans; it may, in fact, have encouraged him.

Donald was planning to leave and his brother John's emigration may have helped. Donald was getting his certificates of character organized—

This is to certify that the Bearer hereof Donald Gunn is about twenty-two years of age Born of Respectable parents in Brawlbin parish of Reay in the County of Caithness North Britain is of an irreproable Character and a good Scholar of Sober and Steady habits and I have reason to believe that he will give every Satisfaction in whatever capacity providence is pleased to cast his lot and as such I hesitate not in recommending him to all whom it may Concern

Given under my hand at the Manse of Shebster this 29 day of June 1854
Finlay Cook Minr of Reay Free Church

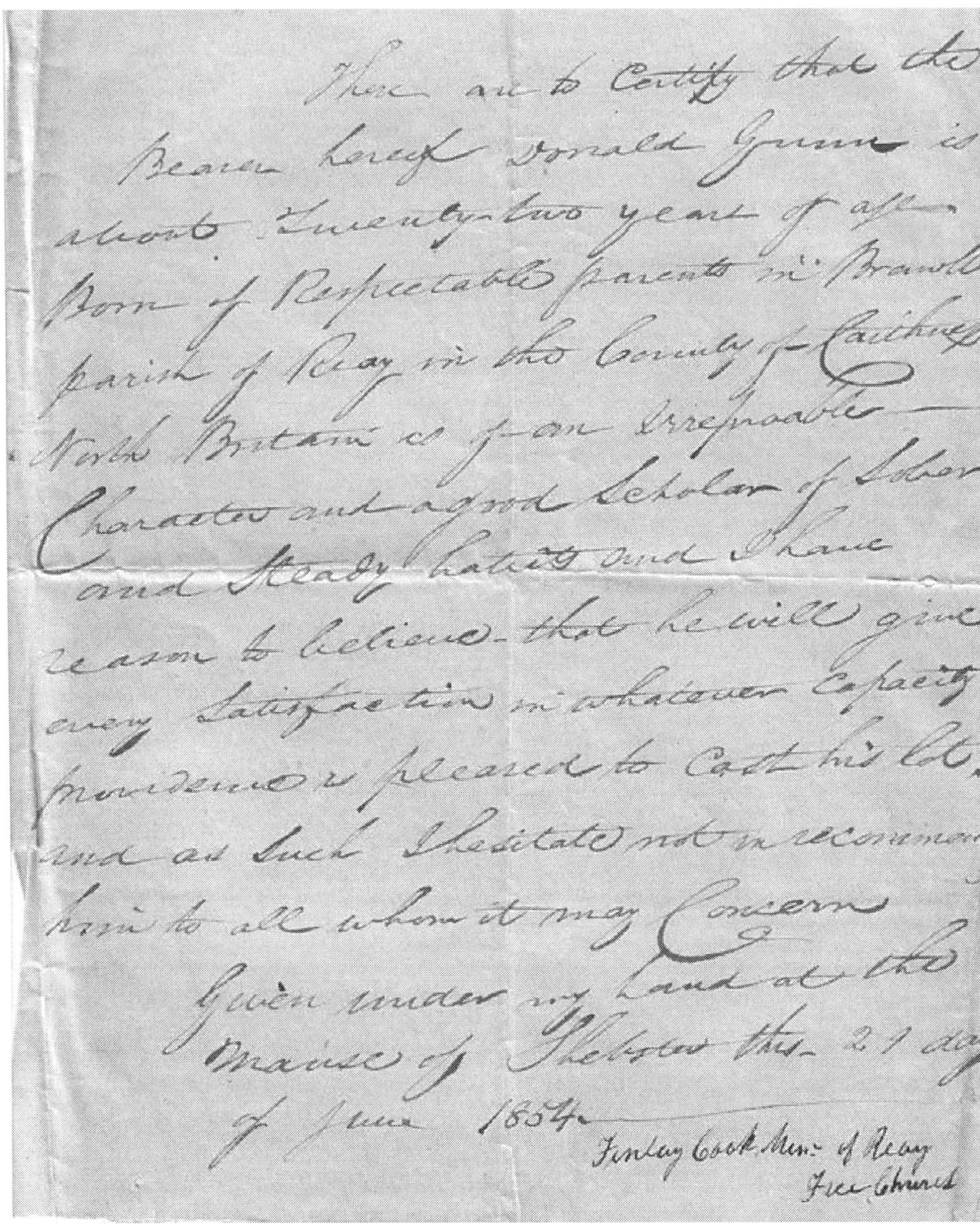
These are to Certify that the Bearer hereof Donald Gunn is about Twenty-two years of age Born of Respectable parents in Brawlbin parish of Reay in the County of Caithness North Britain is of an irreproable Character and a good Scholar of Sober and Steady habits and I have reason to believe that he will give every Satisfaction in whatever Capacity providence is pleased to Cast his lot, and as such I hesitate not in recommending him to all whom it may Concern

Given under my hand at the Manse of Shebster this 29 day of June 1854

Finlay Cook Minr of Reay Free Church

and a second exists—

Thurso 3 July 1854

A Rudge Esq

My Dear Sir

This shall be presented to you by a friend of mine who goes out to try his fortunes at the diggings[691] you may recall (?) of something (?) of his people "the Gunns of brawlbin They are an exceedingly industrious persevearing and -------- family and -------- myself shall as credit anyone that may befriend them

From our acquaintance in the days of "Lang Syne" I have presumed to give him this note of introduction wellknowing your kindness and good feeling for all Caithness people with best wishes I am

My Dear Sir

Yours very Truly

D Campbell

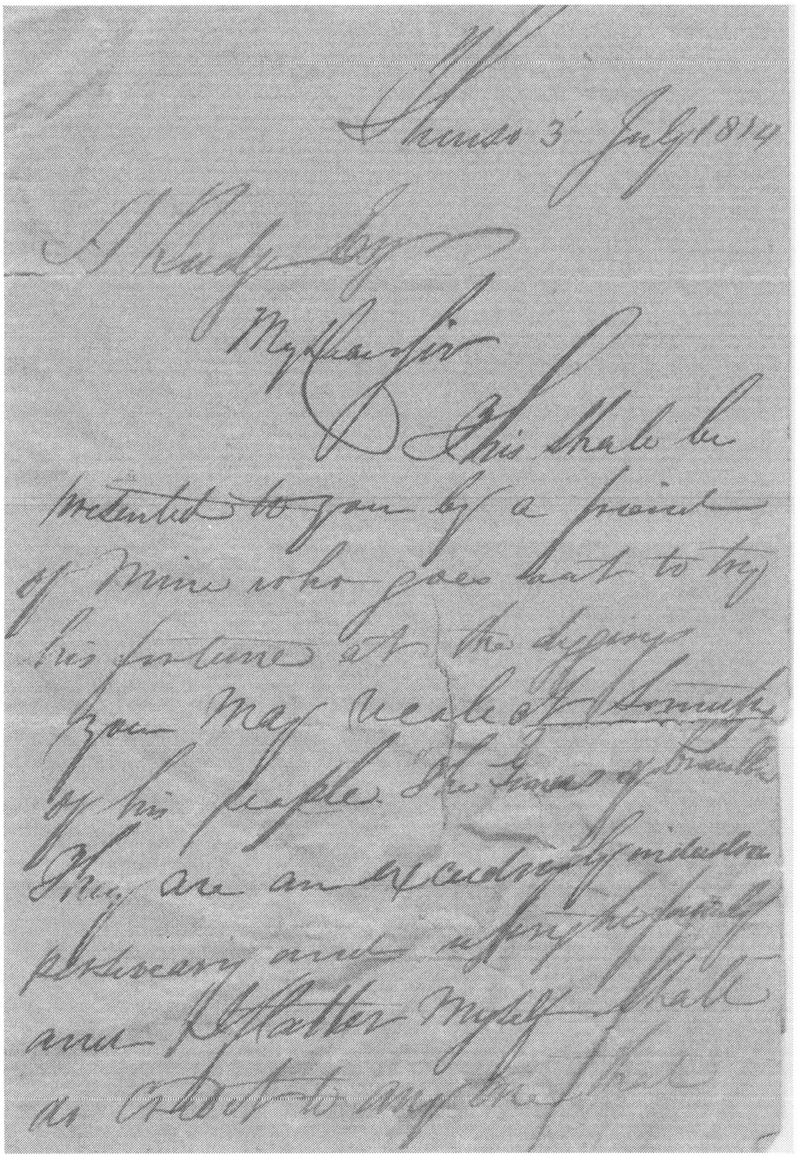

Thurso 3 July 1854

A Rudge Esq

My Dear Sir

This shall be presented to you by a friend of mine who goes out to try his fortune at the diggings you may recall of something of his people The Gunns of Brawlbin They are an exceedingly industrious persevering and [illegible] family and I flatter myself shall as credit to any one that

---

691 This alludes to the gold mines / gold rush of Victoria at this time.

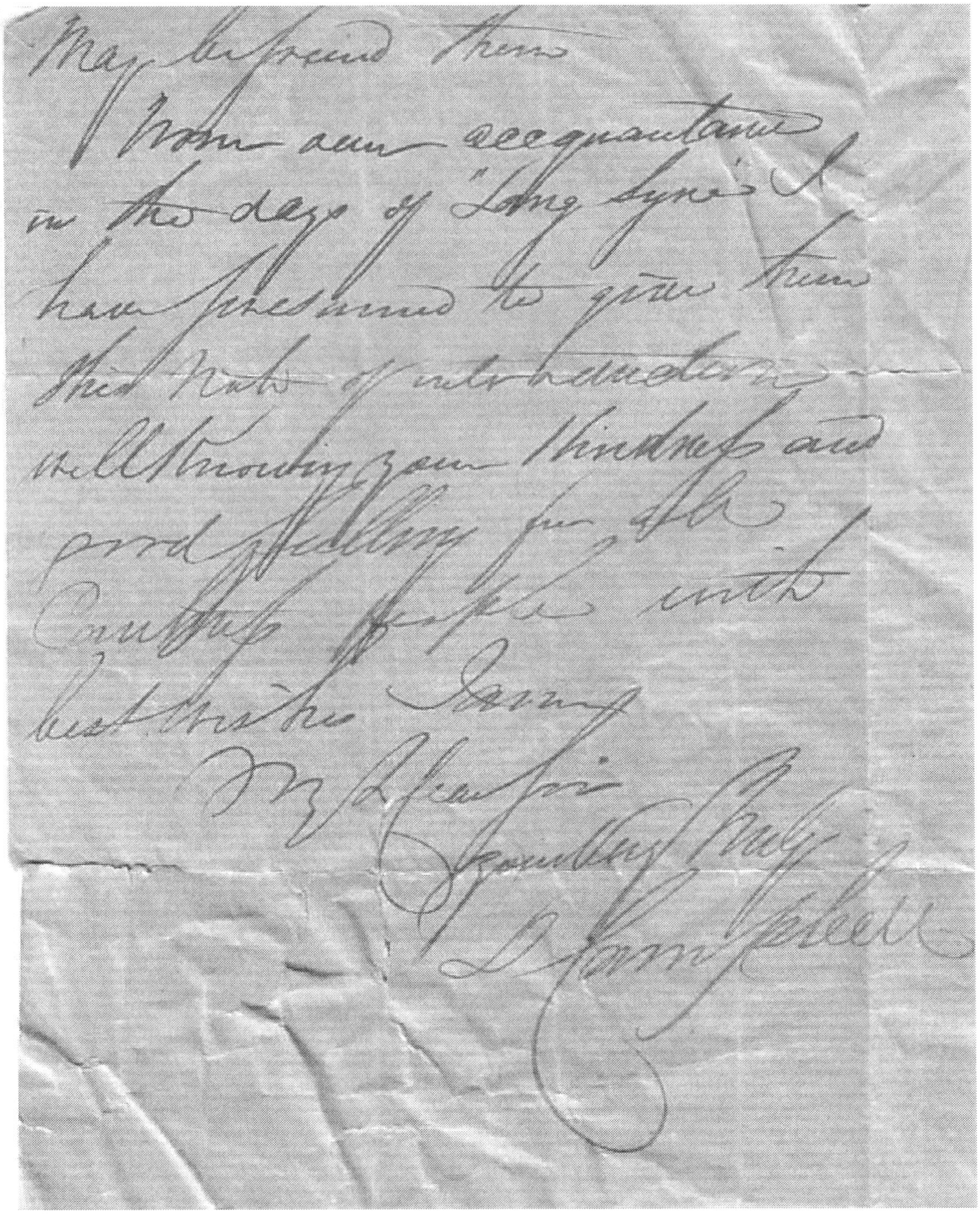

May befriend them
From our acquaintance
in the days of "Long Syne" I
have presumed to give them
this Note of introduction
well knowing your kindness and
good feeling for the
Country folks with
best wishes I am
My Dear Sir
Yours very truly

After some years of trying Donald is obviously ready to go.

An excellent summary of what the trip was like at the time was recorded by Donald's younger brother John when he went out a year earlier to Australia…

John Gunn 1836-c.1857 (12)

There are two interesting accounts from John—the first is a letter written in Glasgow (in transit to Australia) and the second is written in reflection after the voyage. They provide a detailed account of the voyage that emigrants to Australia experienced. His journey was approximately one year before Donald's. John went from Scotland in 1853. He writes of the trip from the Highlands to Glasgow. It shows, understandably, strong family feeling—

No 6 Anderson Key
July 14

Dear Brother
I write you these few lines to let you know that we have arrived here at Glasgow safe last night about 8 oclock and we remained last night aboard the steamer and we now lodge at the place above mentioned and our luggage is in A store near the place we lodge better than half A mile from shore we pay 1/6 A night for every bed we occupy but we are to sleep three of us in every bed so that will make it cheaper for us. we will get a vessel for Liverpool no sooner than saturday so that will leave us two Days and two nights here. And I am further to inform you that the sea did not agree with me very well. the first day they called first at Tongue then at Scourie(?) then at Stornoway then at Portree then at Tobermory then at Oban then at Greenock and the next place was Glasgow and all the way from Oban to Greenock was but a river hardly five chain breadth which was the beautifullest sight I saw since I left home but I might have seen more places than I did, but I was very sick all the way till we came to Stornaway when the lad Brotchie shoemaker from Thurso came and helped me out when I soon recovered. A matter I thought Till then would never occur, you would never beleive the sight you would get if you were here one hour of time between Carts Coaches Carriages boats steamboats & ships railways and all and last of all wandering scoundrels of thiefs which should be first because the are the more numerous as they go here in bands. I am to say no more at present as I am to write Catherine[692] tomorrow when I hope I shall have a little more time as you would not believe the trouble we had in taking Care of our luggage on board and ashore. Give my best respects to all friends and enquirers and tell them all that I am now at Glasgow quite safe and sound

I remain your affectionate
Brother
John Gunn

[692] Presumably Catherine Gunn (119), the oldest sibling.

No 6 Anderson Ky
July 14

Dear Brother

I write you these few
lines to let you know that we
have arrived here at Glasgow safe
last night about 8 oclock and
we remained last night aboard
the steamer and we now lodge
at the place above mentioned
and our luggage is in A store
near the place we lodge better
than half A mile from shore
we pay 1/6 A night for every
bed we occupy but we are to
sleep three of us in every bed
so that will make it cheap
-er for us we will get
a vessel for Liverpool no

Sooner than saturday so
that will leave us two
Days and two nights here
And I am further to in-
form you that the sea
did not agree with me
very well the first day
they called first at Tongue
then at Scourie then at
Stornoway then at Portree
then at Tobermory then at
Oban then at Greenock and
the next place was Glasgow and
all the way from Oban to
Greenock was but a river
hardly five chain breadth
which was the beautifulest
sight I saw since I left home

but I might have seen more
places than I did, but I
was very sick all the way
till we came to Stornoway
when the lad Brotchie shoemaker from thurso came and
helped me out when I soon
recovered A matter I thought
till then would never occur,
you would never believe the
sight you would get if you
were here one hour of time
between Carts Coaches Carriages
boats Steamboats & Ships
Railways and all and last
of all wandering scoundrels
of thiefs which should be
first because the are more

numerous as they go here in
bands I am to say no more
at present as I am to write
Catherine tomorrow when
I hope I shall have a
little more time as you
would not believe the
trouble we had in taking
care of our luggage on board
and ashore. Give my best
respects to all friends and
enquirers and tell them
all that I am now at Glasgow
quite safe and sound
I remain your affectionate
Brother
John Gunn

The more fascinating account is the one John wrote to an uncle dated 25 Oct 1853, describing the trip to Australia

Notes taken on my journey to Australia
from Caithness

Monday July 11th Took steamer from Scrabster (?) Roads to Glasgow and arrived there on Wednesday the 13th about 7 in the afternoon. I remained in Glasgow till 6 o'clock P.M. on Saturday when I took a steamer to Liverpool and arrived there about 8 o'clock P.M. on Sunday. Remained on shore until Thursday following when I embarked on Board the ship Tasmania[693] which was then hauled out of the Docks and lying in the River Mersey. The ship lay here again until Wednesday the 27th July when she weighed anchor and was tugged out of the Harbour by two steam boats the last of which left the following morning at Holy-Head when we were left to beat up the English Channell - it was a fine day + we were in high spirits. On the 29th it commenced to blow right ahead and a great many of the Passengers sea sick I myself was very sick for some days. For the four following days we were beating up the English channel the wind always blowing ahead until on Tuesday the 2nd Augt when we neared the Bay of Biscay and it fell calm and continued so all day but on the 3rd a smart breeze sprung up which carried us along at a beautiful rate and from this to the 9th we had splendid weather and all passengers were again well. there are a great many Highland people on Board and we had Music and Dancing every good evening in which I joined considering it best for the health to take a little exercise. On Tuesday the 9th the wind shifted a little ahead of us. Today we saw the Island of Porto Santo which belongs to the Portuguese. It is a wild (mild?) looking spot we saw two small boats as if they were fishing between us and the shore. 10th and 11th Very calm and doing little progress. On the 12 we came in sight of the Island of Medeira and passed about 8 miles to the east of it. 13 we had little wind but on Sunday the 14th we had a .... breeze. There were a great many fishes seen today and although it was Sunday the sailors and Passengers some of which I am sorry to say were Scotch tried with hook and spear to catch some. They did catch five of them and immediately gutted and Boiled and ate them. They were called Albacors and weighed about 30lbs each. However I did not touch them. On Monday the 15th we had a nice Breeze of Fair Wind nothing between 9 and 10 knots an hour. Passed the barque Jane of Aberdeen bound for Melbourne in Lat 31 N. On 16th the splendid screw steam ship Sidney passed us. She sailed from London on the 4th Augt and was bound for Sidney and passed steaming under a cloud of Canvas about 3 O'Clock in the afternoon. On Wednesday the 17th we entered the Tropics about 11 O'Clock am. It is now getting very warm. 17th and 18th. Good Breeze of fair wind several ships in Company but we left them all in a short time. 19th. Very Calm and at night it was the most beautiful sight I ever saw there was several ships in view and the sea was as smooth as glass. Saturday the 20th. Steward was today put in irons in consequence of his refusing to execute certain orders of the Commander. On the 21st, 22nd + 23rd we had fair wind and going very well. On the 24th it rained heavily for the first time since we left Liverpool and the passengers were eagerly engaged in catching as much of it as they could for washing with it. A child died today of the measles and committed to a watery grave about 4 O'Clock in the afternoon by the Carpenter after a funeral sermon was read by the surgeon. Immediately afterwards the passengers sang a hymn. On the 25th it was very blowy with some flashes of Lightning in the evening. It is now very warm + I can scarcely sleep in my berth with my clothes at all on me. We walk the Deck with nothing but our trowsers and shirt on and still it is very oppressing the heat. I can scarcely bear to put my naked hand on any article exposed to the sun about 12 noon. The sun is now over our heads. Friday the 26th. Very calm with some showers of rain. 27th High winds not at all favourable. On the 28th, 29th, 30th we had very good weather but the heat very great and suffering a great deal from thirst the water very bad and not drinkable

[693] An interesting vessel; the only 'Tasmania' found was wrecked in July 1853! See http://freepages.genealogy.rootsweb.ancestry.com/~nzbound/tasmania.htm

without vinegar or something to take away the taste and smell. We are all divided in 6 messes + take a day about in cleaning the berths and cooking for each mess. On Wednesday the 31st we were all ordered by the Captain on Deck from 10 to 12 noon to allow the 'tween Decks' to be aired. 1st 2nd + 3rd very varyarorable (?) weather but on the 4th we fell in with the Trade winds which are favorable. Monday 5th September. Splendid breeze going 10 + eleven knots an hour. Tuesday 6th. Blowing very strong but wind very favorable going at the rate of 14 Knots an hour and continued this way for some days but on the 12th we were oblged to go under double reefed top sails. I should have observed that that we crossed the line on the 3rd and the event was celebrated by the usual custom of shaving among the crew and passengers. 13th 14th and 15th Weather milder though the swell of the sea and the rocking of the ship made it almost impossible to walk the Decks. 16th Good weather and going well the weather is now getting colder. 17th Still good weather. 18th It commenced to blow against us and continued so for two days a tremendous quantity of sea fowl observed such as Cape Pidgeons and Albatrosses some of the latter measure from wing to wing the length of from 8 to ten feet. On the 20th we passed the Cape of Good Hope at a distance of 800 miles from it to the south. From this to the 1st of October we have very changeable and rough weather which made it very difficult to write. On the 2nd October the wind changed in our favour and we run by log the great distance of 340 miles in 24 hours but shipped several seas which washed all the decks. 3rd + 4th Very heavy sea with strong wind. Lost our main top stansail. Wednesday 5th Our our miser top Gallant yard gave way and broke through the middle. The carpenters were immediately engaged in maKing a new one and were helped by some Carpenters and Joiners on Board. Thursday 6th Heavy sea, ship labouring much shipping heavy seas. We got our yard rigged early in the morning but about 12 noon a sea struck the ship lurching her in such a manner as to break her miser mast into three pieces + Down came itself yards and sails bringing down with it in its course our Maintop gallant and Royal yards. Nothing could exceed our Consternation + surprise when we saw our ship so suddenly disabled. All hands were immediately engaged in clearing the deck and the carpenters got such help from the Passengers that the ship was soon put to rights. 7th 8 9 + 10th Got fair wind and going very well 11th Blowing rather strong. 12th Saw a ship bound to Melbourne with Passengers 115 days out we soon left sight of her she sailed from London. 13th and 14th Fair wind + going well. 15th Passengers today collected a subscription among them for to present the Captain on their arrival at Melbourne with some token of their respect. 16th Wind rather contrary but still on the right course. 17th + 18th Fair wind. 19 + 20 Fair wind and drawing near land. 21st This morning early the ....(?) was that the land was in sight and everybody was on Deck. 22nd Coasting along the Australian shore. 23rd Early this morning came in sight of Port Phillip Light House. We then got a Pilot and sailed up the straits for Melbourne where we arrived and cast Anchor three miles from the town at 2 O'Clock in the afternoon. The Custom House Officers came immediately on Board with the Inspector. We lay at Anchor here all night and next morning and this morning Tuesday the 25th. There was steam boats come to fetch us ashore. Melbourne is a strange Place. Two men was hanged yesterday and other two are to be hanged today. Wages is very good yet. I did not get any job yet but I expect to get one soon. This is now a sketch of the Passage and I hasten to inform you of my safe arrival Dear Uncle. There was no sickness on Board but 7 children died of the measles +c and we had three Births. We arrived 2 hours after the Gildfinder (?) who sailed from Liverpool 5 days before us. McWilliamson's (?) little Neil died also on the voyage. I will write you again soon with all the news.

I am My Dear Uncle
your affect nephew
John Gunn 25th Oct 1853

(I was not a day sick since I left home but a little sea sick at first.) Passage 88 days. *(to the side)*

Notes taken on my Journey to Australia from Caithness

Monday
1853 July 11th took Steamer from Scrabster Roads to Glasgow and arrived there
on Wednesday the 13th about 7 in the afternoon - I remained in Glasgow
till 6 O'Clock P.M. on Saturday when I took a Steamer to Liverpool
and arrived there about 8 O'Clock P.M. on Sunday - Remained on Shore until
Thursday following when I embarked on Board the Ship Tasmania
which was then hauled out of the Docks and lying in the River Mersey
The ship lay here again until Wednesday the 27th July when she weighed
Anchor and was tugged out of the Harbour by two steamboats the
last of which left the following morning at Holy-head when we
were left to beat up the English Channell - It was a fine day &
all were in high spirits - On the 29th it commenced to blow rather a breeze
and a great many of the Passengers were sick I myself was very sick
for some days - For the four following days we were beating up the English
Channell the wind always blowing ahead until on Tuesday the 2nd
Augt. when we neared the Bay of Biscay and it fell calm and
calmer we all day - but on the 3rd a sweet breeze sprung up which
carried us along at a beautiful rate and from this to the 9th we had
splendid weather and all passengers were again well - there are a great
many Highland people on Board and we had Music and Dancing
every good evening in which I joined considering it best for
the health to take a little exercise - on Tuesday the 9th the wind
shifted a little ahead of us - today we saw the Island of Porto Santo
which belongs to the Portuguese - It is a bold looking spot - we saw
two small boats as if they were fishing between us and the shore
10th & 11th very Calm and very little progress until 12 we came in sight of
the Island of Madeira and passed about [illegible] miles to the Great [illegible]
[illegible] of little wind but on Sunday the 14th we [illegible]
There were a great many fishes seen today and although it was Sunday
the sailors and Passengers some of which I am sorry to say were not [illegible]
tried with hook and spear to catch some - They did catch two of them
and immediately gutted and Boiled and ate them - They were called Dolphins
and weighed about 30 lbs each - However I did not touch them

On Monday the 15th we had a nice breeze of fair wind making between 9 & 10
knots an hour. Passed the Brig Jane of Aberdeen bound for Melbourne in Lat.
31 North. On 16th the splendid screw Steam ship Sidney passed us. She sailed
from ~~Southampton~~ London on the 4th Augt and was bound for Sidney and passed steaming under a cloud
of Canvass about 3 O'Clock in the afternoon. On Wednesday the 17th
we entered the Tropics about 11 O'Clock A.M. It is now getting very warm
17th & 18th Good Breeze of fair wind several ships in Company but we left
them all in a short time. 19th very Calm and at night it was the
most beautiful sight I ever saw. There was several ships in view and
the sea was as smooth as glass. Saturday the 20th. Steward was turned
put in Irons in consequence of his refusing to execute certain orders of
the Commander. On the 21st 22 & 23rd we had fair wind and going very
well. On the 24th it rained heavily for the first time since we left
Liverpool and the passengers were eagerly engaged in catching as
much of it as they could for washing with it. A child died today
of the measles and committed to a watery grave about 4 O'Clock
in the afternoon by the Carpenter after a funeral sermon was
read by the surgeon. Immediately afterwards the Passengers sung
a hymn. On the 25th it was very blowing with some flashes of
Lightning in the evening. It is now very warm & I can scarcely stay
in my berth with any clothes at all on me. We walk the Deck
with nothing but our trousers and shirt on and still it is
very oppressing the heat. I can scarcely bear to put my
naked hand on any article exposed to the sun about 12
noon. The sun is now over our heads. Sunday the 26th very calm
with some showers of rain. 27th Very winds not at all favorable
On the 28th 29th 30th we had very good weather but the heat very
great and suffering a great deal from thirst. The water very
bad and not drinkable without vinegar or something to take
away the taste and smell. We are all divided in 6 messes &
take a day about in cleaning the berths and cooking for each
mess. On Wednesday the 1st We were all ordered by
the Captain on Deck from 10 till 12 noon to allow the tween
Decks to be aired. 1st 2 & 3 very unfavorable weather but on the
4th we fell in with the Trade winds which are favorable

Monday 5th of September Splendid breeze going 10 or Eleven Knots an hour Tuesday 6th Blowing very strong but wind very favorable going at the rate of 14 Knots an hour and continued this way for some days but on the 12th we were obliged to go under double reefed topsails I should have observed that that we crossed the line on the 3rd and the event was celebrated by the usual custom of shaving among the crew and passengers - 13th, 14th & 15th Weather milder though the swell of the sea and the rolling of the ship made it almost impossible to walk the Deck. 16th Good weather and going well the weather [illegible] 17th Still good [illegible] commenced to blow against us and continued so for two days a tremendous quantity of sea fowl observed such as Cape Pigeon & Albatrosses some of the latter measuring from tip to tip the length of from 8 to ten feet On the 20th we passed the Cape of Good Hope at a distance of 800 miles from it to the south. From this to the 1st October we had very changeable and rough weather which made it very difficult to write. On the 2nd October the wind changed in our favour and we ran by log the great distance of 340 miles in 24 hours but shipped several seas which washed all the decks. [illegible] 4th very heavy sea with strong wind [illegible] top [illegible] Wednesday 5th Our the Mizen top gallant yard gave way and broke through the middle - The Carpenters were immediately engaged in making a new one and were helped by some Carpenters and Joiners on Board. Thursday 6th Heavy sea ship labouring much shipping heavy seas. We got our yard rigged early in the morning but about 12 noon a sea struck the ship [illegible] her in such a manner as to break our Mizen Mast into three pieces & down came its yards and sails bringing along with it in its course our Maintop gallant and Royal yards. Nothing could exceed our consternation & surprise when we saw our ship so suddenly disabled. All hands were immediately engaged in clearing the deck and the carpenters got 6

such

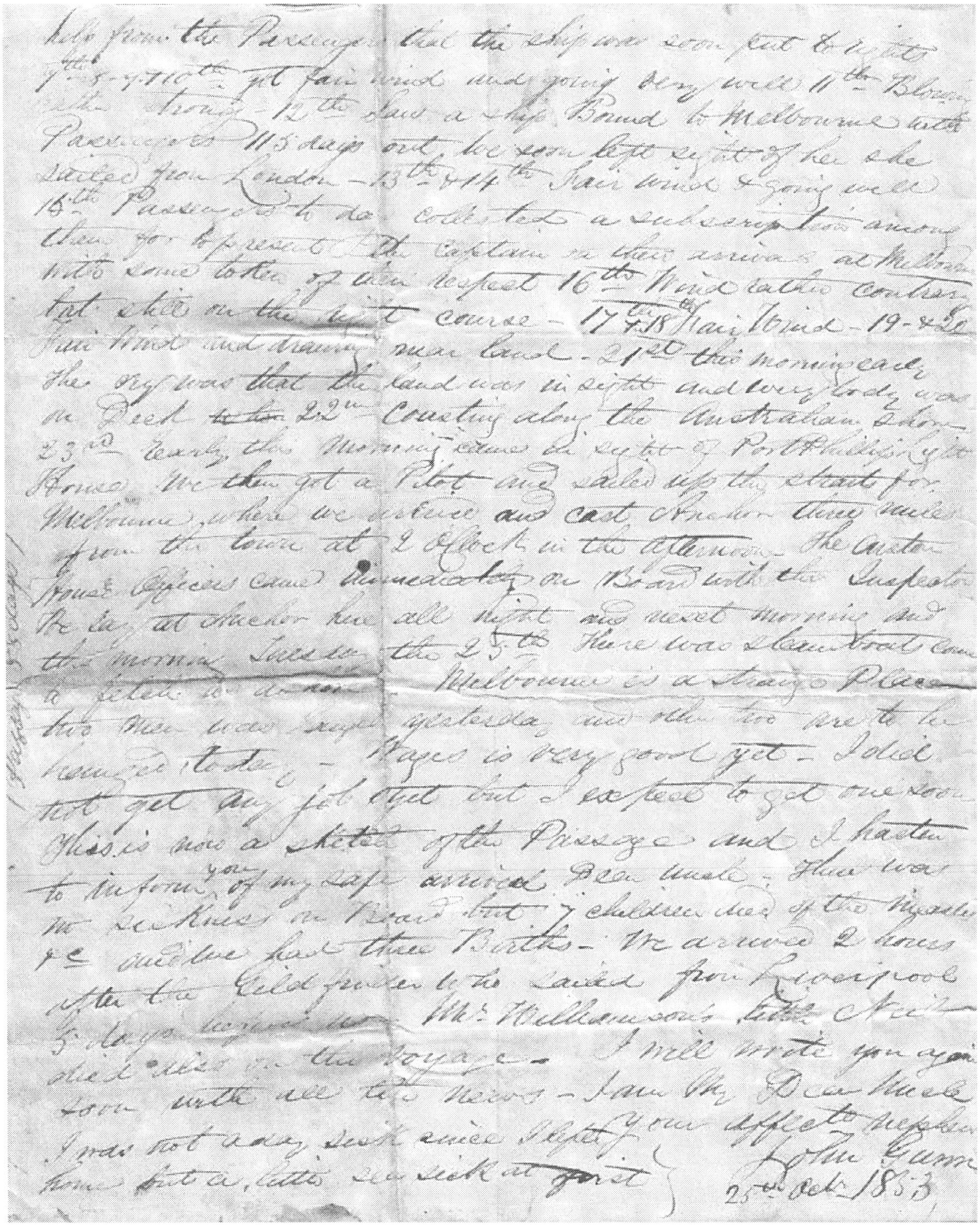

help from the Passengers that the ship was soon put to rights
7th-8-9 & 10th got fair wind and going very well 11th Blowing
rather strong - 12th saw a ship Bound to Melbourne with
Passengers 115 days out, we soon left sight of her she
sailed from London - 13th & 14th Fair wind & going well
15th Passengers to do collected a subscription among
them for to present the captain on their arrival at Melbourne
with some token of their respect 16th Wind rather contrary
but still on the right course - 17th & 18th Fair Wind - 19 & 20
Fair Wind and drawing near land - 21st this morning early
the cry was that the land was in sight and every body was
on Deck ~~to the~~ 22nd Coasting along the Australian shore
23rd Early this morning came in sight of Port Phillip Light
House We then got a Pilot and sailed up the strait for
Melbourne where we arrived and cast Anchor three miles
from the town at 2 O'clock in the afternoon - The Custom
House Officers came immediately on Board with the Inspector
We lay at Anchor here all night and next morning and
this morning Tuesday the 25th There was steamboat came
a [illegible] Melbourne is a strange Place
two men was hanged yesterday and other two are to be
hanged today - Wages is very good yet - I did
not get any job yet but I expect to get one soon
This is now a sketch of the Passage and I hasten
to inform you of my safe arrival Dear Uncle - There was
no sickness on Board but 7 children died of the Measles
&c and we had three Births - We arrived 2 hours
after the Gold [illegible] & she sailed from Liverpool
5 days [illegible] Mr Williamson's [illegible]
died [illegible] on the voyage - I will write you again
soon with all the News - I am My Dear Uncle
I was not a day sick since I left your affect. nephew
home but a little sea sick at first John Gunn
25th Oct 1853

It is conceivable that this account matches the envelope shown at the start of Part 4; that envelope is to an uncle, and the size of the folds in the letter match the envelope. John probably died at Port Melbourne in Dec. 1854, by family repute he was waiting for the boat on which his brother Donald and sister Caroline arrived.

Donald Gunn in Brawlbin and Ballarat (3) Australia, his sister Janet Gunn (120), his brother William Gunn (220), and relatives John Gunn in Durness (878) and Donald Gunn (976) Governor of the Dundee Poorhouse

It is not clear the date that Donald came to Australia; he and Catherine were both in Australia by June 1856. It is probable that it was in late 1854. Janet arrived in 1864. Donald settled at Buninyong, near Ballarat, in Victoria, which was near the gold diggings.

Many letters were written by and to the Australian Gunns that very clearly show the strength of the connections with their family in Scotland. The letter below is the first of several 'Durness' letters which appear over some years; the next remaining is written in 1863. Unusually this letter is addressed to both Donald and Catherine.The author is John Gunn (878), who was Donald and Catherine's Uncle. That is, John Gunn was the oldest child of Donald Gunn the Sennachie (708) and Catherine Gunn of Osclay (3423). Donald's mother Barbara was the second child of this family. John Gunn was a factor for the Duke of Sutherland for many years.

Durness Oct 3 1856

My Dear Don^d^. + Caithrine

your letter of the 18th June I rec^d^ by which I was glad to to hear you are both well in health - I should have written you some time ago but had nothing new to inform you all our friends is in good Health. I was down 3 weeks ago Grandfather[694] is fading fast getting very weak but is going about every day - Don^d^ + Lexy[695] was home seeing them - Don^d^ has got to be Master of a Poor House in Dundee Salary about £90 which was very lucky for him as the Trade he had was not doing much - John Campbell Inverary(?) got married lately to a Daughter of Angus in Achboune(?) Achloane Forsie a wittlass young girl - yourself will recolect her they are not well pleased at him Droving did no good this year Hugh M^c^Kenzie[696] did not go out this year till the last Kyle Market he had 25 head lost 10/ each and expences others lost more there hardly was any Drovers going this year except P- Campbell + John M^c^Kay + the Co - Grandfather sold his own to P- Campbell they were very good he got £4- 10 all told from Certainty Campbell lost on them - a pound the head Sheep is a little back the small that familes (?) is a drag 5/ each and no demand - we had a very wet Sumer Shearing only commenced 10 days ago there is a very weighty crop crop, straw will be plenty + much need as it is very few tenant that got their Cattle sold. the Herring Fishing was not good. they are selling @ 32/ per Barrel just now when I wrote you last I think I told you that John[697] was in Morayshire Teaching a school he came home at the Term Mr Traill got him appointed to the Excise a fortnight before he was the Age his Commission was here a few days before he came home he got his Instructions learnt in Thurso he is now at the Guston(?) Distellary and will be there till the Winter is over supose I had three sons I could get them appointed to the excise here through the Dukes Interest. Traill was aware of that + that what made him be so pointed in trying his endeavour I told him if he did and find it convinient that I would get him another ways - since Novr last the standard of learning for the Excise his his raised 3 times more than formerly 9 tried it in Caithness since the new act + none passed but John, one

---

694 Donald Gunn the Sennachie (708).

695 Donald Gunn (976) Governor of the Dundee Poorhouse and Alexandrina, second youngest daughter of Donald (708) (Sennachie); see page 281. She was the youngest child of eight.

696 Conceivably Hugh McKenzie (3433) who married Jean / Jane Gunn (941), Donald and Catherine's aunt, the youngest child of Donald Gunn (Sennachie) (708) and Catherine Gunn of Osclay (3423).

697 Presumably his son John (1122) 1827-1861.

in three that passed in the Kingdom since the new act came in operation the salary at present is £100 a year but as the standard of education is raised so high they expect the salary will be raised John comes every Saturday night to his Grandfather - James in Osclay got married since a month to a young Scalpay - By a letter from John to day he told me Will and Janet got your order for £10 I have got nothing more to tell you that I can mind on(?) the Tullochs + Margret Gunn cast out to a great extent - Tulloch is going to ----(?) the stock at term and pay himself (?) she says their is nothing due but I doubt he will let her know otherways—Don[d]— is a favourite -----? he was over several times when

and the rest of the letter is lost.

Dunnet Oct 3 1856

My Dear Donl & Catherine

Your letter of the 18th June
I recd by which I was glad to hear you are
both well in health. I should have
written you some time ago but had
nothing new to inform you all our
friends is in good health I was
down a week ago Grandfather is
failing fast getting very weak but
is going about every day. Donl &
Percy was home seeing them. Don
has got to be Master of a Poor House
in Dundee Salary about £90
which was very lucky for him
as the Trade he had was not
doing much. John Campbell
Lerrary got married lately to a
Daughter of Angus [illegible]

A. Mc Loane Forsie a little young
girl - yourself will recollect her
they are not well pleased at him
Droving did no good this year Hugh
McKenzie did not good this year
till the last Kyle Market he
had 25 head lost 10/ each and
expenses others lost more than
hardly was any Drovers going
this year except P. Campbell &
John McKay & the Co - Grandfather
sold his vein to P. Campbell they
were very good he got £6-10 an
told from certainty Campbell lost
on them a pound the head
Sheep is a little back the small
that Lambs is a drug 6/ each and
no demand we had a very wet sum
er Shearing only commenced 10 days
ago there is a very weighty crop

Crop & Straw will be plenty & much
need as it is very few Tenant that
got their cattle sold the Herring
Fishing was not good - They are
selling @ 32/ per Barrel just now
when I wrote you last I think I told you
that John was in Monaghan Teaching
a school he came home at the Term
Mr Traill got him appointed to the
Excise a fortnight before he was
the Age his Commission was here
a few days before he came home he
got his Instructions learnt in three
weeks he is now at the Leith Distillery
and will be there till the Winter is
over suppose I had three sons I could
get them appointed to the Excise here
through the Dukes Interest - Traill
was aware of that & that is what made
him be so pointed in keeping his endeav
our I told him if he did not find it con
venient that I would get him another
ways - since I've lost the Standard
of learning for the Excise his

his raised 3 times more than formerly
9. tried it in Caithness since the new
act & none passed but John & one in three
that passed in the Kingdom since the
new Act came in operation the Salary
at present is £100 a year but as the
standard of education is raised so high
they expect the Salary will be raised
John comes every Saturday night to his
Grandfather James in Oscley got
married since a month to young
Scalfray [illegible] I got a letter from John to
day he [illegible] me Nell & Janet got your
order for £10 I have got nothing more
to tell you that I can mind in the
Tulloch & Margaret been cast out
to a great extent Tulloch is going
to Roust the Stock at Ferm and pay
himself he says there is nothing else
but I doubt he will be better known
otherways Janet is a favourite now
he was over several times when

Further 'Durness' letters start on page 281.

The following documents show that Donald was at 'Buninyong S(t)ation' by 1857. The record of cattle killed and sheep sold for the Buninyong farm show a deal of activity. In 1857 Dec. 7-12 seventeen cattle were killed, Dec.14-19 thirteen cattle were killed and one hundred and seventy-four sheep were sold, Dec. 21-26 fourteen cattle were killed (including three on Christmas day) and one hundred and fourteen sheep sold, between the 26th and the 2nd of January 1858 eleven cattle were killed and one hundred and fifty eight sheep sold and the following week 2-9 January a further eleven cattle were killed and one hundred and thirty five sheep sold. There is reference after this to the 'doorkey Churnside' in February. (The relationship he had with the Chirnsides is unclear but of interest given the importance of the Chirnside family, if it is the well-known rural Chirnsides.) The first five days of February saw seventeen cattle killed possibly for that family.

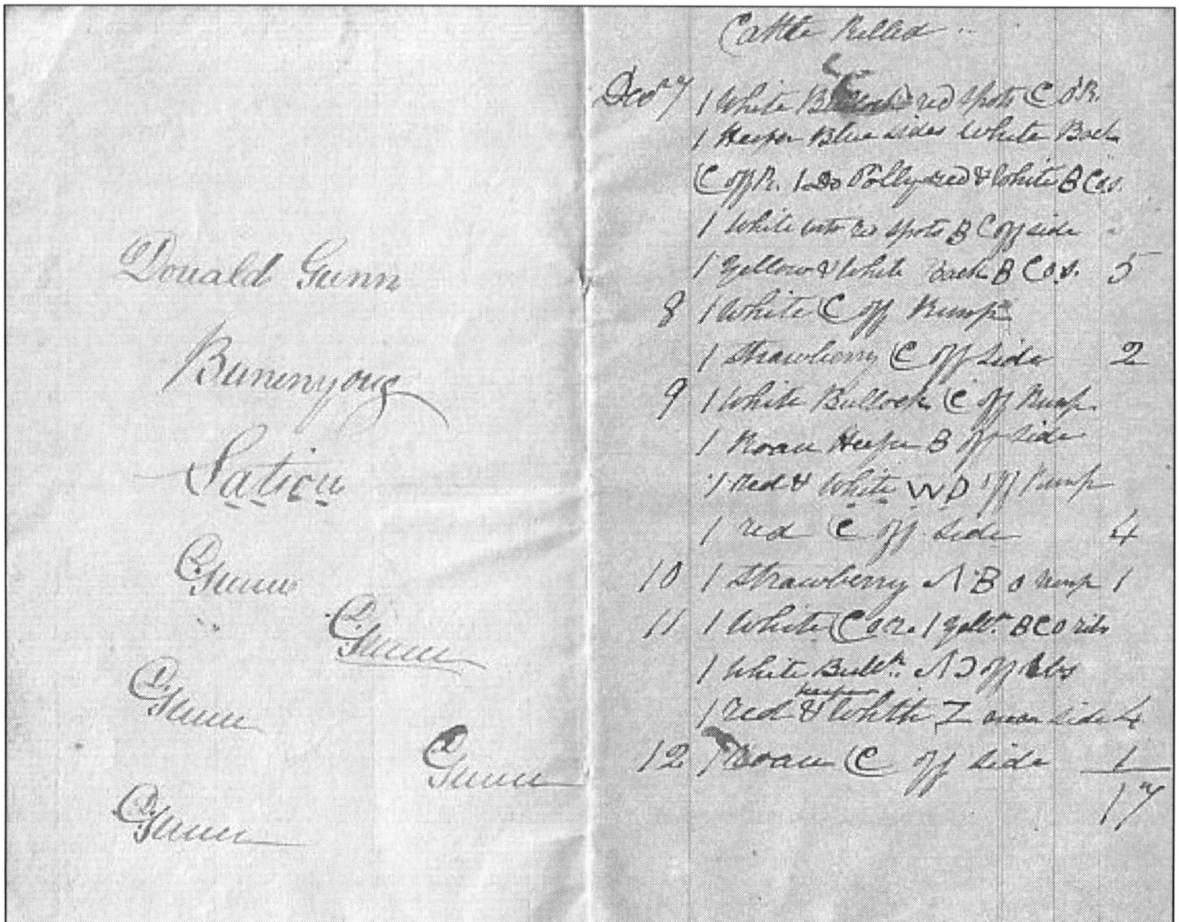
Donald Gunn
Buninyong
Sation
C Gunn
C Gunn
C Gunn
C Gunn
C Gunn

Cattle killed

Dec 7 1 White [illegible] red spots C [illegible]
1 Heifer Blue sides White Back
C [illegible] 1 Do [illegible] & White B [illegible]
1 White [illegible] spots B C off side
1 Yellow & White back B C [illegible] 5
8 1 White C off Rump
1 Strawberry C off side 2
9 1 White Bullock C off Rump
1 Roan Heifer B off side
1 Red & White WD off Rump
1 red C off side 4
10 1 Strawberry [illegible] B [illegible] Rump 1
11 1 White C [illegible] 1 [illegible] B C [illegible]
1 White Bull [illegible] off [illegible]
1 Red & White Heifer Z [illegible] side 4
12 1 Roan C off side 1
17

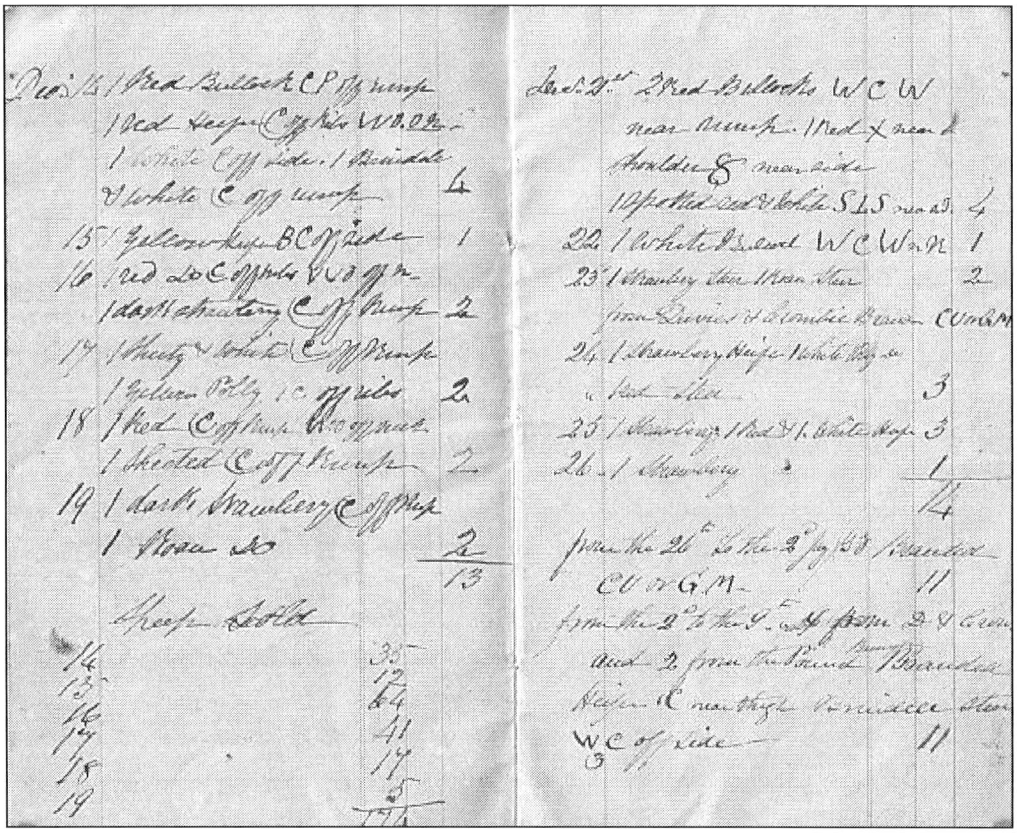

Dec 14 1 Red Bullock C P off rump
1 Red Heifer C off hip W.O. off n
1 White C off side. 1 Brindle
& white C off rump 4
15 1 Yellow Heifer B C off side 1
16 1 Red do C off hip W O off n
1 dark strawberry C off rump 2
17 1 Rusty & white C off rump
1 Yellow Polly I C off side 2
18 1 Red C off rump W O off neck
1 Skewbald C off rump 2
19 1 dark Strawberry C off rump
1 Roan do 2
13

Sheep sold

14 35
15 12
16 64
17 41
18 17
19 5
174

Jan 2nd 2 Red Bullocks W C W
near rump. 1 Red X near
shoulder & near side
1 Spotted red & white S L S near s. 4
22 1 White Steer W C W n R 1
23 1 Strawberry steer 1 Roan steer 2
from Davies & Crombie Brown C W n M
24 1 Strawberry Heifer 1 White Heifer
Red steer 3
25 1 Strawberry 1 Red & 1 White Heifer 3
26 1 Strawberry 1
14

from the 26th to the 2nd Jany 38 Branded
C W or G M 11
from the 2nd to the 9th off from D & Crom
and 2 from the Pound Brindle
Heifer C near thigh Brindle Steer
W C off side 11
3

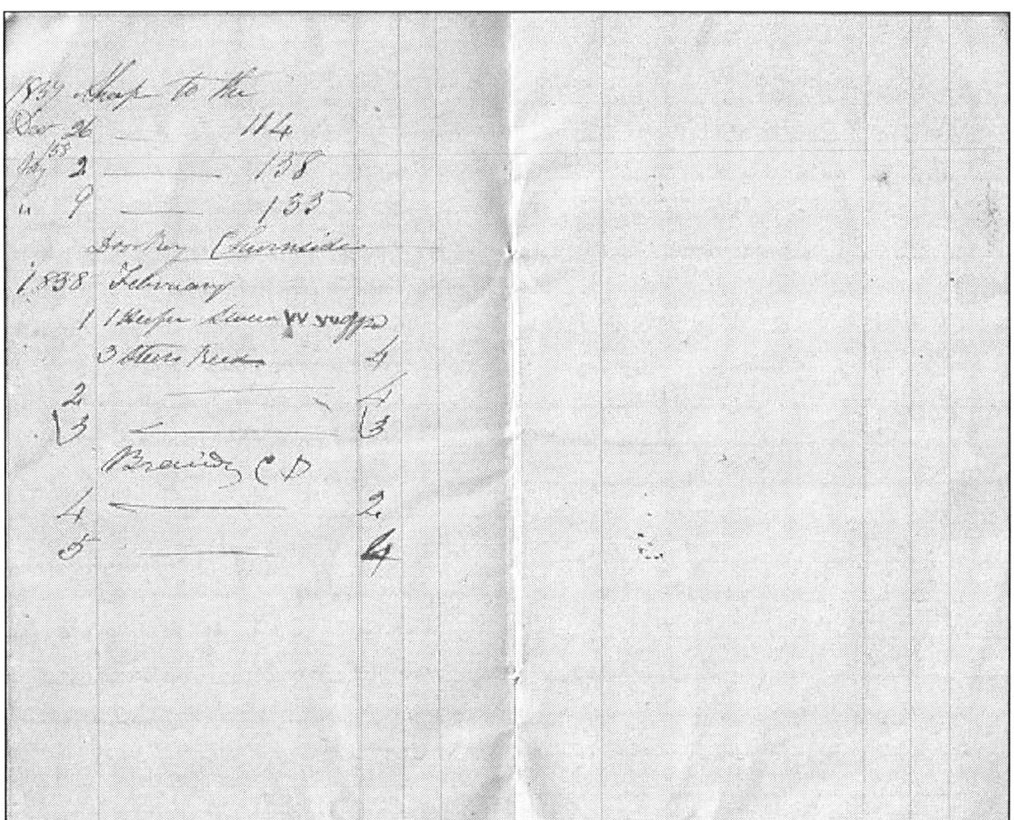

1837 Sheep to the
Dec 26 114
Jany 38 2 138
" 9 153
Docking Churnside
1838 February
1 1 Heifer Brown W X off
3 Steers Red 4
2 1
3 3
Brindle C D
4 2
5 4

All the detail concerning the brands on the animals killed, and with no obvious Gunn initials, suggest that at this stage Donald was possibly running an abattoir or butchery, and not a farm. In particular I cannot otherwise think why he killed two animals from the pound at Buninyong (in the period 26th December to 2nd January 1858) unless he had official approval to so do and therefore presumably been operating for some time.

Donald seems to be succesful which is perhaps why he decided to buy a further farm at Cardigan, near Ballarat as well. Below is a draft of a partnership agreement with John Watkins Surman who was his 'double' brother in law but the document does not provide a date to show when this was written. (John Watkins Surman married Donald's sister Janet Macleod Gunn (120) on 12 May 1864; Donald married Jane Surman (41) (John Watkins Surman's sister) on the 25 March 1859.) One notes the assumption that the Cardigan farm will have a manager, as though both partners already have enough to do. It also makes sense if one looks at the draft of the partnership agreement with the 'neither partner to give up present occupation' statement.

The crossings out on the draft have not been replicated below—

Donald Gunn -
John Wtk. Surman –

Partnership   Term General
A farm at Cardigan bought for about £250 in the name of Gunn
- Each to put in £
- Farm to be worked + held in Equal shares -
- Neither party to give up present occupation -
- Manager to be paid £   a week -
- at end or completion of partnership of partnership, which may be upon giving   months notice - one party to buy out the other upon terms of arbitration to be determined by 2 arbitrators or -------(?)
- All earnings of either party to go to Partnership acct.
- All differences as to working +c to be decided by arbitration

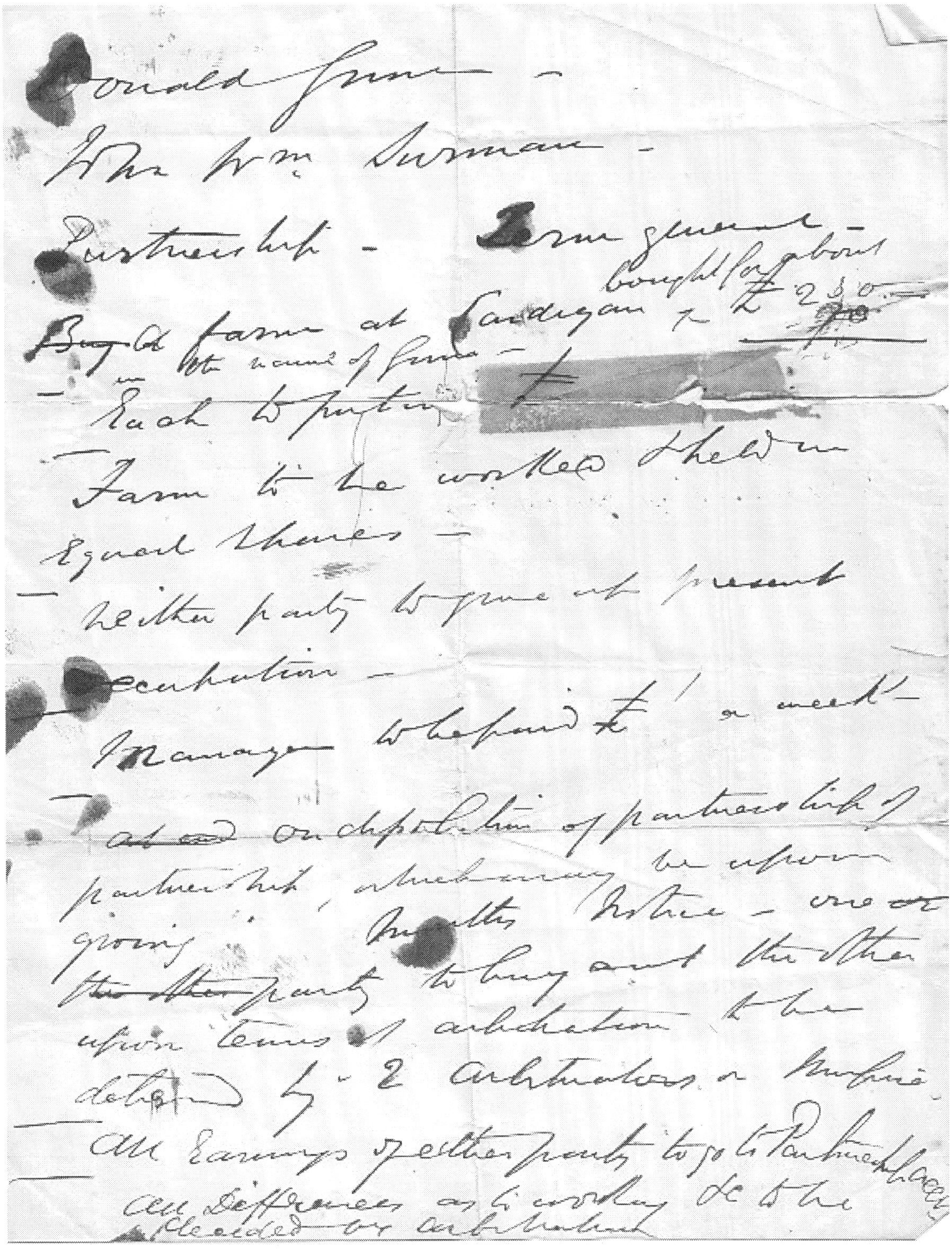
Donald Gunn –
John Wm Surman –
Partnership – Term general –
bought for about
Buy A farm at Cardigan for £230
in the name of Gunn –
Each to pay in £
Farm to be worked & held in
Equal shares –
Neither party to give up present
occupation –
Manager to be paid £1 a week –
on dissolution of partnership / partnership which may be upon
giving 3 months Notice – one or the other party to buy out the other
upon terms of arbitration to be
determined by 2 arbitrators or umpire
All Earnings of either party to go to Partnership a/c
All Differences as to working &c to be
decided by arbitration

This represents a fair amount of money—but why into the Gunn name and not the Surmans[698]? It is only a draft partnership agreement and it leaves questions unanswered. Donald remained very much in touch with home. The following is from his sister—

[698]Possibly because Donald is already operating a successful farm and John Watkins Surman's profession is 'teacher' on his marriage certificate. John Watkins Surman's father (Daniel) was a farmer. The Surmans came from Wokingham in Wiltshire.

Brawlbin

1st Sep 1858

my Dear Brother

I know not how to appolagise for not writing you before now but I was delaying to se if I could tell you what time the tartan would be ready it will not be long yours of June 13 I got on Agt 16 + one from Mrs[699] my sister I was very very happy to learn by them that you were all well as this leaves us all at present wich is the Greatest blessing that can be stowed on us we have our bear (?) cut our oats will be reddy soon the potates is very bad this year never worse the last Muir and Marie (?) was very bad + so was Falkirk the poor Drover (?) is not doing much this year your friend Mcpherson took betack(?) out to see him I supose he is making ready for going he did not write me + I will not write him you know we have not A fireside of our own as we used to have I do not know if I will see any one to take your box if not I will get it properly adresd

we have not got a minister yet it will not be easy to please them after haiving such A Godly man the sacrment of the Lords supper was kept some since 2 weeks there is nothing new that I can write you my father and mother is keepping well + all our friends as far as I can learn of was in Lybster for herrings last week we had to stop 4 days before we Got there there is A very poor fishing this year I have nothing of any importance to write you at present I hope you will not be appauled at me for asking A ring of you the one that will be big enough for my one little finger will do as A plain one for my Aunt she does not know that I am asking them she thought to much of you to scend her money+(?) times hers may be A large larger(?) than mien you will not let her know that I asked them as we asked my sister for them + she did not send them I did not care for my own part but my Aunt was so --------(?) she seeaid not let me tell you of it be surly do not say that I asked them for she might think I was writing you against (?) your sister family it is not a plain one I want

yours things will not be ready for 2 or 3 weeks yet I will write William then and enclosed to you it is 2 oclock I am sleepey

JG

It is interesting to note that Janet's writing and spelling is poor. The key point is that she was living at Brawlbin, which is the home of her mother Barbara, and her grandparents were still alive. Donald Gunn (Sennachie) died in 1861. Was she providing 'care'? And she refers to her mother and father and her aunt—and these are also Donald's. I think the terms are used loosely and refer to her grandparents and aunt. The discussion about the rings is interesting; does she want a memory of Donald or just want some wealth to show off with as they feel the Millers (see Part7) and Donald have done well?

[699] Catherine Gunn (119) who married James Miller (117), in 1857, at Buninyong.

Braalbane

1st Sep 1858

My Dear Brother

I know not how to apologise for not writing you before now but I was delaying to see if I could tell you what time the Tartan would be ready it will not be long yours of June 13 I got on Agt 16 & one from P/O my sister I was very very happy to hear by them that you were

your things will not [illegible] the [illegible]
for 2 or 3 weeks [illegible]
[illegible] there [illegible]
[illegible]

all well as this leaves
us all at present which
is the greatest blessing
that can bestowed over
we have our bear cut our
oats will be reddy soon
the patates is very bad
this year never warse
the last Muir ord mart
was very bad & so was
Falkirk the poor Drove
is not doing much this
year your friend Mcpherso
took hetack out to see him
I supose he is making
ready for going he did not
write me & I will not write
him you know

we have not A fireside
of our own as we used to
have I do not know if
I will see any one to take
your box if not I will
get it properly repaired

we have not got A mi-
-ster yet it will not be
easy to please them after
having such A godly
man the sacrement of the
Lords supper was kept since
2 weeks there is nothing
new that I can write
you my father & mother
is keeping well & all our
friends as far as I can

heard I was in [illegible] for
[illegible] last week we had
to stuck 4 days thar we
gat there there is a very
[illegible] you
I have nathing of any
importance to writ you
at present I hope you
will not be offended at me
for asking a thing of you
the one that wite [illegible]
daughter give me a little
longer all to see it plain and
for my Aunt she does not
know that I am asking the
she thought to much of
you to send her money 2
times hers may be a lone
larger than mein your
will not let her know

This letter's issues are supported by tthe next surviving letter to Donald which was commenced twenty-three days later—

Brawlbin
Sept 24
1858

dear brother Donald

I am forwarding your box there is ten yds tartan 6 pairs stockings 1 pair of mitten wich less than we thought to have but our harvest came on so soon that we have nomo to send poor william or Mr Miller or sister Cath you would not have got it at all if it were not my aunt as we sold all our own wooll before we knew of it + there is no old wife now to spin it Mrs Willson is very poorly it is not a nice pattern the measurement wrong in it but it can not be helped now I am very sory I can not send any thing to the rest I do not see any one that will bring it I hope your stockings will not be mended till I come there is a little yearn in your box yor sister

Sept 27

I did not get to the town when I thought + I am afraid your box will be late but I cannot help it you will give Cathren the worsted for 2 pairs to Mr Miller it is not ---(?) the value of them that we send it if she will not have time I will do it for her when I come I recived a letter from her husband today I will her write by the next mail when you make your suit you will bind it with black binding I have nothing strange to inform you at present hoping this to find you all well when you recive this be sure you will thank my aunt for it I did not hear A word from McPherson since long Bill is angry with you for writing him you will excuse the style of writing ----(?) hoping to hear from you soon I remain your affecn

Sister Jessie Gunn

I have recived A number of letters and do not know what is my nice s maner I have sent her A mens parker today JG

Possibly the material was sent over in response to news about the wedding. Note that by this early time Janet had definitely made up her mind to emigrate to Australia and that William is referred to as 'poor William'—he may have died in 1860. Also of interest is that Janet refers to herself as Jessie, and the conditions in which she lives.

Branthin

Sep 12th
1853

dear brother David
I am forw-
-arding your box there
is ten yds tarton 6 pairs
stockings 1 pair of mitten
much less than we thought
to have but one harvest
came on so soon that
we have nothing to
send poor william or
Mr miller or sister catherine
you would not have
got it at all if it were

not my aunt as we
sold all our own wool
before we knew of it &
there is no old wife now
to spin it mrs willson
is very poorly it is not
A nice pattern the weave
went wrong in it but
it cannot be helped now
I am very sorry I can
not send any thing to
the rest I do not see
any one that will bring
it I hope your stakings
will not be mended
till I come there is A
little yearn in your
box for sister

Sept 27

I did not
get to the town when
I thought I am afraid your
box will be late but I cannot
help it you will give Catherine
the market for 2 pairs to
Mrs Miller it is not for
the value of them that we want
it if she will not have them
I will do it for her when I
come I received a letter
from your husband today
I will write her by the next
mail when you make
your suit you will bind
it with black binding I have
nothing strange to inform you
at present hoping this to find
you all well

when you receive this be sure
you will thank my aunt for
it I did not hear a word
from McPherson since long
Bell is angry with
you for writing to me
you will receive the style
of writing you hoping to
hear from you soon
I remain your affec
Sister [illegible]

I have received a number
of letters and he not know
what is my nice name
I have sent two B
newspaper to day [illegible]

William Gunn (3175) of Bualchork

The next existing letter to Donald was one from his cousins in Scotland[700]. Note the time delay in answering. The prevarication over emigration is also worth noting. It reads—

Bualinkaid,
Westerdale,
Thurso. N.B[701].
11 October. 1858.

My dear Cousin, — It is now considerably above a twelvemonth since I received your full, interesting, and very acceptable letter; and I can assure you I never in my life felt myself more at a loss for what to say than I do at this moment in endeavouring to apologise for the awkward and to myself unaccountable delay in writing you in return. Thus I certainly passed a -----(?) that my own mind and conscience did not upbraid me for the oversight. And from my friends who happened lately to ----(?) acquainted with the true state of matters I had to submit to a storm of reproof and remonstrained. The fact has been that I have been -----(?) since delaying the thing from day to day for the want of interesting materials, and in the hope that I would by and bye get something worth writing about; but lam at this moment as poor in such matters as Ihave for many a day ----(?) — but the thing must be delayed no longer.

We all sympathised with you in the deep ordeal through which you came upon and after your arrival in the colony. We all felt that the stroke of your dear brother's death was peculiarly heavy. We cherish the hope that through divine provd he was not altogether unprepared for the great change; and although he is out of sight - he should not be out of mind - for being dead he yet speaketh, and says to one and all of us "be ye also ready". This is an event that will most certainly and may very suddenly come to us. And O my dear friend who can describe its importance — it stands on the verge of two worlds, it seals our doom for ----(?) or for woe for ever. There is only one change in this world which can, in inportance, be compared with it. That from poverty to plenty - from adversity to purposity - from sickness to health - from a low state to a high one - or vice versa - for a moment cannot. There is only one change that can and that is conversion. Of the importance of this change it is ----(?) needless to say much to one who had your early training from those who are no more - a training which Ihope you will never forget - even amidst the cares, the toils, the changes, the novelty of a colonial life. We could not also but sympathise with you in the sicknesses and ----(?) wh. you met, and thank divine providence for watching over you and bringing you so far safe through the ----(?). And further we congratulate you on the measure of success that has been vouchsafed yourself and also your sister. "In all your ways acknowledge Him, and He shall direct your paths". Prov. III. 6.

There is not much important news either of a general or a local character with which perhaps you are not already more or less acquainted. If you get the public news of the home country you would have seen the many and just commercial failures that took place both in America and Britain - failures perhaps unprecedented

---

[700] We believe this probably to be William Gunn (3175). Why? It needs to be by a relative, aged at least twenty when writing ie born before 1838, and died after 1858. Westerdale is in Halkirk Parish. Only one relative recorded seems to fit. William Gunn (3175) of Bualchork, born 1822 in Bualchork, Halkirk Parish, died 1899, and first cousin of William. His father George (804) was Alexander's (1) younger, and closest, brother. The letter has a religious slant—and William (3175) of Bualchork was a minister of the Free Church of Scotland who never married. He was 36 when the letter was written. And the letter is definitely that of a Minister.

[701] N.B. is 'North Britain' a geographic term used for some time after the (never fully completed) Union of Scotland and England (Scotland always retained some independent powers most noticeably in Education and the Law). S.B. did not exist.

in the annals of commerce - that arose in many cases through swindling, since all were attended with reckless speculatives. These failures swallowed up many ----(?) pirel (?) ruin.(?) They were the means, or rather I should say a means, sidewith of bringing in the remarkable revival of religion which has been going on for the last twelvemonth nearly over all the length and breadth of the United States of America. Men worked them to ---- feel(?) that they aquired a better portion as immortal beings than money, + to put the question "what shall we do to be saved?" - the most important of all questions - but in Britain it has as yet produced no such results. Of the just rebellion in India, and our quarrel with China, you will I suppose get the news before ouselves. There is great loss of life, but it is hoped it may turn to good account by opening up the way to commerce, civilization, and the gospel. You have doubtless heard of the great enterprise of laying a submarine telegraph between Europe and America. It was working satisfactorily at first, but through some cause or other - not known as yet - it does not now work. There are apprehensions of it proving a failure for the present; but there is little doubt it will ultimately be accomplished: + when it will what a wonder of science - perhaps the greatest the world has ever seen. There is one other wonder which in this hemisphere is at present attracting the attention of millions, and that is a splendid comet which appeared to the naked eye first in the northern hemisphere near the ----(?) (Will Major), and is now visible in the Western sky. It is now at its nearest approach to this Earth - but 100,000,000 of miles away accrd^g to Astronomers, - ----(?) to needs (?) in its motion southward. In appearent(?) like it is not so large as Venus, but its magnificent tail which is said to be 15,000,000 of miles long, is what makes it so prominent + striking. It is said to take two hundred years on its revolution. How great are the works of God!

Many local changes have no doubt taken place since you left, but Imay leave it in better hands to give an account of them. Imay mention however that several of the Golden Estate[702] tenents have been obliged to yeild. Among them Hamilton of Cerasaid (?) has been obliged to assign this farm is now in the hands of Sandy McDonald, late merchant, Thurso. Sandy Micklejohn also was obliged to yeild to the pressure of the times, + is now Iunderstand on his way to Australia to join Donald Williamson + his other friends. By the bye, are you within sight of them? Your Uncle I understand, is getting on well in Braehour. The other Sandy Gunn - his cousin again - has lost both his wife and two of his sons since you left. The youngest son died of consumption some two or three years ago. The other, James, died very suddenly six or seven weeks ago. He became minister of the parish church of Uig in Lewis last year, + got married to a daughter of McLaren the parish Schoolmaster of Reay. Your sister, Janet Father + Mother + other friends were quite well when Iheard last. Our Uncle John died in Summer 1857.

As regards our own family Ihave little to say. Age and its attendant infirmities of course creep over my father + mother. We hear often from Hugh; he is quite well + seems to be happy. The times then have changed much especially since the monetary crisis. One of my sisters is in the South, + all the rest together with my younger brothers are all at home. One or two of them have for some time been speaking of Emigrating to Australia. Our parents - + especially our mother, is not in favour of such a step:- and indeed it is a very unlikely one unless there was some respectable family going whom they might hapily accompany. Please to say what you would advise in regard to such a step; tell me candidly. As regards myself I am still very much in the same mind as well as in the same circumstances. Since I wrote you I was for 6 months assisting Mr. McKay, Bruan, who was struck with a paralytic stroke, but is able to do duty with help. Just now Iam in the West Highlands in a place called Lochalsh. I have no immediate view of a settlement – + for any thing I know Imay see you in Australia yet. There is a great dearth of preachers there as I hier; but I question very much whether the encouragement is good(?), + whether the field is so very desirable as it is represented to be. Iwanted very much some news from you on this point. Some reliable information which I could trust. Take, for

---

[702]Also see references to William Gunn, page 186.

example, Geelong[703] - whose minister Isee died lately - or any other place with which you are well acquainted. How is the minister remunerated - what salary - what manse + church accommodation - what kind of congregations? +c +c. Do the colonists keep good faith in keeping their promises in such cases? Is the work very laborious? What are the greatest discouragements? Does the gospel seem really to prosper? - + such other information as may seem most important. Ifeel my constitution would not stand there(?) What is Mr. Sutherland from Reay doing there? Idon't think he is engaged in a work of preaching at all. What is Mr. Ross from Olrig doing? Still teaching? I suppose this is a line of life that pays will there. Do you know anything about New Zealand as a field of Emigration? What do you say about getting out by Government - is this a safer or ----(?) way of emigrating than on an independent footing? Isuppose they are in that case under the contral of certain parties there till the passage money is paid. But I must conclude.

My fathers people all join in sending yourself, sister + brother William our best regards; + they all join in asking forgiveness for my negligence - of which I must say I am myself unworthy - and to express the hope that you will have the goodness to write soon stating how your brother arrived. Your affectionate cousin

William Gunn

Mr. Donald Gunn, Buninyong, Australia.

It is not clear, but it does suggest that John died on Donald's arrival, but we can not prove it. ('We all sympathised with you in the deep ordeal through which you came upon and after your arrival in the colony. We all felt that the stroke of your dear brother's death was peculiarly heavy'). The reference to the Golden Estate (Jamaica) is interesting, supporting the idea that William Gunn (297) would not have been alone if he had emigrated there[704].

---

[703] Ironically at this time in Geelong the Rev Andrew Love was the main Presbyterian Minister (and sometime Moderator of the Presbyterian Church of Victoria). He served in Geelong from 1843 to 1867 when he died. The Rev Love was the Uncle of Donald Gunn's son's wife (the son being John Alexander Gunn, the wife being Jessie Maria Turner). Jessie's father William (a Scot from the lowlands of Dumfries and Galloway) taught at the local primary school in Ballarat at an early stage of his career. One wonders if he had kept in touch with a fellow Scot as otherwise the Turners and Gunns lived many miles apart.

[704] It is a well known migration trail; see http://www.ijsl.stir.ac.uk/issue4/livesay.htm for the pro-slavery view. Or Karras, Alan L., *Sojourners in the Sun: Scottish Migrants in Jamaica and the Chesapeake, 1740-1800,* (Ithaca: Cornell University Press, 1992).

Bushinbrid,
Westdale,
Thurs. N.B.
11 October, 1858.

My dear Cousin, — It is now considerably above a twelvemonth since I received your full, interesting, and very acceptable letter; and I can assure you I never in my life felt myself more at a loss for what to say than I do at this moment in endeavouring to apologize for the extreme and to myself unaccountable delay in writing you in return. There scarcely passed a week in that my own mind and conscience did not upbraid me for the neglect. And from my friends who happened lately to become acquainted with the true state of matters I had to submit to a storm of reproof and remonstrance. The fact has been that I have been from time to time delaying the thing from day to day for the want of interesting materials, and in the hope that something by and bye [illegible] worth writing about; but I am at this moment as poor in such matters as I have for many a day been — but the thing must be delayed no longer.

We all sympathised with you in the deep ordeal through which you came upon and after your arrival in the Colony. We all felt that the stroke of your dear brother's death was peculiarly heavy. We cherish the hope that through divine grace he was not altogether unprepared for the great change; and although he is out of sight he should not be out of mind — for being dead he yet speaketh, and says to one and all of us "be ye also ready." This is an event that will most certainly and may very suddenly come to us. And O my dear friend who can describe its importance — it stands on the verge of two worlds, it seals our doom for weal or for woe for ever. There is only one change in this world which can in importance be compared with it. That from poverty to plenty — from adversity to prosperity — from sickness to health — from a low state to a high one — or vice versa — for a moment cannot. There is only one change that can, and that is conversion. Of the importance

of this change it is almost needless to say much to one who had your early training from those who are no more — a training which I hope you will never forget — even amidst the cares, the toils, the changes, the novelty of a colonial life.
We could not also but sympathise with you in the dangers and losses wh.
you met, and thank divine providence for watching over you and bringing you so far safe through the [illegible] — And further we congratulate you on the measure of success that has been vouchsafed yourself
and also your sister. "In all your ways acknowledge Him, and He shall
direct your paths." — Prov. III. 6.

There is not much important news either of a general or local character with which perhaps you are not already more or less acquainted.
If you get the public news of the home country you would have seen
the many and great commercial failures that took place both in America and Britain — failures perhaps unprecedented in the annals of commerce — they arose in many cases through swindling, & in all were attended
with reckless speculation — These failures have [illegible] up many in temporal ruin — They were the means, or rather [illegible] a means [illegible]
with, of bringing in the remarkable revival of religion which has been
going on for the last twelve month nearly over all the length and breadth
of the United States of America — Men were led there to see & feel that they required a better portion as immortal beings than money, & to put the question
"What shall we do to be saved?" — the most important of all questions — But
in Britain it has not as yet produced no such results. Of the great rebellion in India, and our quarrel with China you will suppose get the
news before ourselves. There is great loss of life, but it is hoped it may [illegible]
to good account by opening up the way to Commerce, civilization, and the gospel — You have doubtless heard of the great Enterprise of laying a submarine telegraph between Europe and America — It was working satisfactorily at first, but through some cause or other — not known as yet — it
has not now [illegible]. There are apprehensions of its proving a failure
for the present; but there is little doubt it will ultimately be accomplished. &
when it will, what a wonder of science — perhaps the greatest the world
has ever seen — There is one other wonder which in this hemisphere is at-

present attracting the attention of millions, and that is a splendid comet which
appeared to the naked eye first in the southern hemisphere. [illegible] the place
(Wells [illegible]), and is now visible in the western sky. It is now at its
nearest approach to the Earth — but 10000000 of miles away, and to Astronomers — begins to recede in its motion southward. In appearance it
is not so large as Venus, but its magnificent tail, which is said to be 15,
[illegible] of miles long, is what makes it so prominent [illegible]. It is said to take
three hundred years in its revolution. How great are the works of God!

Many [illegible] changes have no doubt taken place since you left, but I may
leave it to [illegible] to give an account of them. I may mention [illegible]
that several of the [illegible] Estate tenants have been obliged to [illegible]. Among them
Hamilton [illegible] has been obliged to resign the farm, is now in the hands
of Sandy McDonald, late merchant [illegible]. Sandy [illegible] who was obliged
to yield to the pressure of the times, is now [illegible] on his way to Australia
to join Donald [illegible] & other friends. By the bye, are you [illegible]
of [illegible]? Your uncle [illegible] is getting on well in [illegible].
The other Sandy [illegible] — his cousin again — has lost both his wife and two of
his sons since you left. The youngest son died of consumption some two
or three years ago. The other [illegible] died very suddenly [illegible] weeks ago.
He became minister of the [illegible] church of [illegible] last year, & got married to a daughter of McLaren the parish schoolmaster of [illegible]. Your sister, [illegible]
[illegible] brother & other friends were quite well when I heard last. [illegible]

As regards our own family there is little to say. Age and its attendant infirmities of course [illegible] on my father & mother. [illegible] of the Free Kirk, the
is quite well [illegible]. The times there have changed much [illegible]
since this [illegible] crisis. One young sister is in the South, & all the rest together with my younger brother are all at home. One or two of them have for
some time been speaking of emigrating to Australia. Our parents & especially
our mother is not in favour of such a step; and indeed it is very unlikely
one unless there was some respectable family going whom they might safely accompany. I have to say, what you would advise in regard to such a step, [illegible]
candidly. As regards myself I am still very much in the same mind as [illegible]
the same circumstances. [illegible] some years for [illegible]
[illegible] who was struck with a paralytic stroke, but is able to [illegible]
[illegible] and now lives in the West Highlands in a place called [illegible]. There
he [illegible] the [illegible] of a [illegible] [illegible] any thing [illegible]
[illegible] in Australia yet. There is a great [illegible] approaching [illegible]

[illegible]; but I question very much whether the encouragement is good, & whether the field is so very desirable as it is represented to be. I wanted very much some news from you on this point — some reliable information which I could trust — Take, for example, Geelong — whose minister I see died lately — or any other place with which you are well acquainted — How is the minister [illegible] — What salary — what manse & church accommodation — What kind of congregations? &c &c. Do the colonists keep good faith in keeping their promises in such cases? Is there much any [illegible] What are the greatest discouragements? Does the Gospel seem [illegible] to prosper? — Such other information as may seem most important. I fear my constitution would not stand there — What is [illegible] doing there? I don't think he is engaged in the work of preaching at all. What is Mr Ross [illegible] doing? Still teaching? I suppose this is a line of life that pays well there. Do you know any thing about New Zealand as a field of Emigration? What do you say about getting out by Government — is this a safe or better way of emigrating than as an independent party? I suppose they are in that case under the control of certain parties there till the passage money is paid — But I must conclude.

My father's people all join in kindly [illegible] yourself, sister & brother & William are [illegible]; & they all join in asking forgiveness for my negligence — of which I must say I am myself [illegible] — And I express the hope that you will take the pen to write soon stating how [illegible] your brother William. — Your affectionate cousin

William Gunn.

Mr. Donald Gunn. [illegible]

The Highland Society of Buninyong[705]

Donald was not just a worker—he participated fully in that which he believed in. Walter Withers was to write in his *The History of Ballarat from the First Pastoral Settlement To The Present Time* (published in 1887) that—

The Caledonian Society was formed in November, 1858, and the first sports were held on New Year's Day, 1859, on what is now known as the Eastern Oval. Mr Hugh Gray was the first president, and with him as judges on that day were Charles Roy, Donald M'Donald and Donald Gunn...There had been two annual gatherings before this ...The Buninyong Highland Society was formed about this time also...[706]

Donald was very involved—his love for his homeland is obvious. Both these societies predate the Melbourne society (established in 1861) and the Victorian society (established 1864). What is now the Royal Caledonian Society of Melbourne was established in 1858.[707]

The Standing Rules of the Buninyong Highland Sciety[708] make for interesting reading.

STANDING RULES
OF THE
HIGHLAND SOCIETY BUNINYONG

Rule 1st. It is imperative that Forty Pounds Sterling (£40) (the directors having power to add thereto) be secured out of the funds of the Society at the begining of every year for the next Anniversary.

" 2nd. That this money be paid in prizes, as the directors shall see most fit for the promotion of their anniversary meeting.

" 3rd. That the anniversary shall be held on the 1st January, (New Years Day) unless that such day happens to be Sunday, in which case the following Monday to be appropriated for the Gathering.

" 4th. That any Funds available to the Society after the appropriation of the aforesaid sum be applied to Charitable purposes alone.

" 5th. Any Member of the Society in distress through sickness, or accident presenting his case to the directors, shall upon their being satisfied that he is a deserving object, receive such releif as his case requires or the funds of the Society permit.

" 6th. In case of there being no available funds, and a member applying for assistance, that the directors be empowered to call a Meeting of the Members in order that steps may be taken to afford immediate releif.

---

705 http://home.vicnet.net.au/~buninhis/newsletters/feb_06.html for a full history of the Society.

706 The previous footnote has the first gathering of the Society 1 January 1858.

707 http://www.scotsofaus.org.au/scottishcaledonian-societies/royalcaledonian/

708 See http://home.vicnet.net.au/~buninhis/ February 2006 for discussion about the society and the games over time.

" 7th. That at the decease of any member of this Society, Five pounds Sterling (£5) be given to defray expenses.
" 8th. That at the decease of any member of this society, Fifteen Pounds Sterling (£15) be paid to his widow, or lawful children (Funds being available for this purpose).

" 9th. That if the deceased leave no widow or lawful children that the aforesaid sum be placed in the funds of the Society.

" 10th. Any member who has not paid into the Society for nine clear months, shall forfeit all right and claim to all or any of the benefits set down in the foregoing rules.

" 11th. That these rules cannot be revised excepting at the first general meeting of the members in each year, any member wishing to alter any of these rules must send in notice in writing to the Secretary on or before the first day of December, (preeceding).

(Sgd. D.Gunn)

List of Members for the H.S.

Donald Stewart
Hugh A. McMillan
Donald Gunn
Dugald Cambell
Thomas J. Finlay
Charles Lameret
James McCrew
T.C. McDonald
John Connell
John Kennedy
Eneas Cameron
McLenan
McInnis

Standing Rules
of the
Highland Society Braidwood

Rule 1st It is imperative that Forty Pounds Stg (£40) (the directors having power to add thereto) be secured out of the funds of the society at the beginning of every year for the next Anniversary.

2nd That this money be paid in prizes, as the directors shall see most fit for the promotion of their anniversary meeting.

3 That the anniversary shall be held on the 1st January (New years day) unless that such day happens to be Sunday, in which case the following Monday to be appropriated for the Gathering.

4th That any Funds available to the society after the appropriation of the aforesaid sum be applied to Charitable purposes alone.

5 Any member of the Society in distress through sickness or accident presenting his case to the directors, shall upon their being satisfied that he is a deserving object, receive such relief as his case requires or the funds of the society permit.

6 In Case of there being no available funds, and a member

applying for assistance. that the directors be empow-
-ered to call a meeting of the members in order that steps
may be taken to afford immediate relief. ——

7th That at the decease of any member of this Society Five
Pounds Ster (£5) shall be given to defray funeral
expenses. ——

8th That at the decease of any member of this Society
Fifteen Pounds Stg (£15) be paid to his widow, or lawful Children (Funds being available for this purpose.

9 That if the deceased leave no widow, or lawful children that the aforesaid sum be placed in the funds
of the Society. ——

10th Any member who has not paid in to the Society for
nine clear months shall forfeit all right and claim
to all or any of the benefits set down in the foregoing rules. ——

11th That these rules cannot be revised excepting at the
first general meeting of the members in each year
any member wishing to alter any of these rules must
send in notice in writing to the Secretary on or before the first day of December (preceding). ——

D. Green

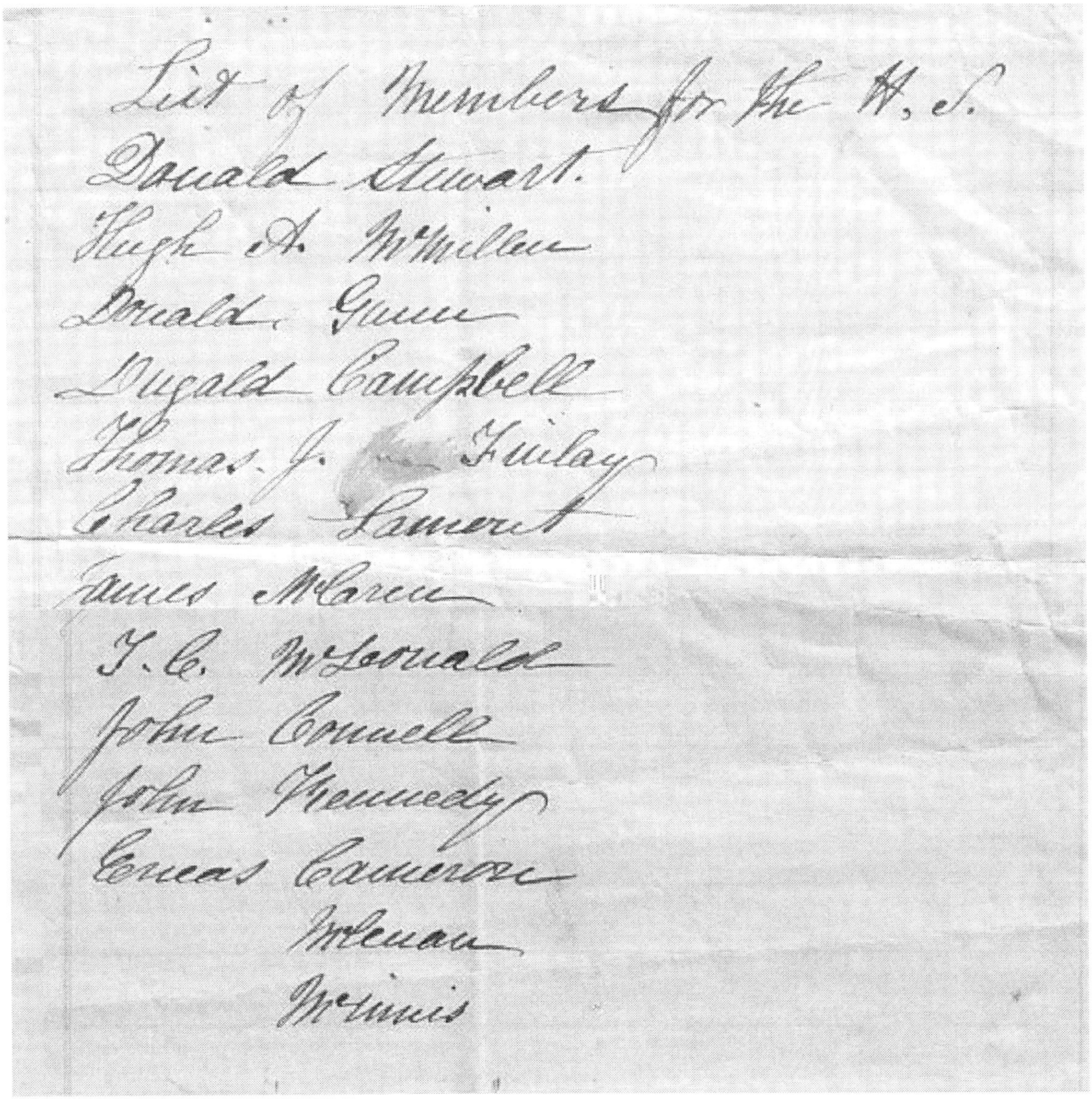
List of Members for the H. S.
Donald Stewart.
Hugh A. McMillan
Donald Gunn
Dugald Campbell
Thomas J. Finlay
Charles Lamont
James McLaren
J. C. McDonald
John Connell
John Kennedy
Eneas Cameron
McLenan
McInnis

Of course one must not forget the medal he was awarded by the Highland society and his work with the council. See page 48.

Life though was certainly altering for Donald—

(Presbyterian) Dond. Gunn Born March 28th 1832
at Brawlbin Reay Caithness Scotland

(Protestant) Jane Surman Born 18th Jany 1836
at Hampton Poyle Oxford England

Married at Buninyong Victoria
25th March 1859, (By the Revd. J. Hastie)

John Alexander Gunn born at
Buninyong 11th Feby. 1860

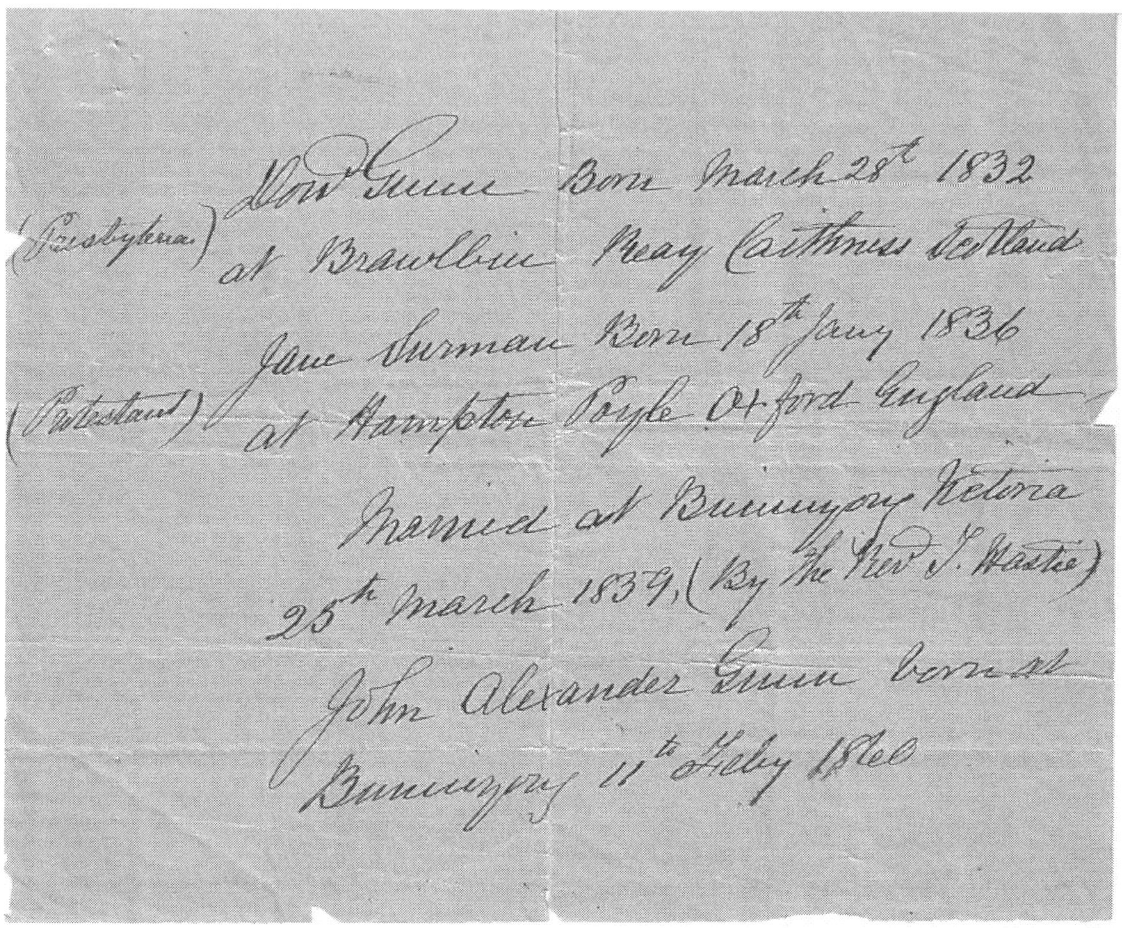
Dond Gunn Born March 28th 1832
(Presbyterian) at Brawlbin Reay Caithness Scotland
Jane Surman Born 18th Jany 1836
(Protestant) at Hampton Poyle Oxford England
Married at Buninyong Victoria
25th March 1859, (By the Revd J. Hastie)
John Alexander Gunn born at
Buninyong 11th Feby 1860

Regrettably it is impossible to know who wrote the above document.

Donald married at the age of 27 and the first of his ten children came very quickly.

Letters to William Gunn (220) (Australia) and Donald Gunn (3) (Australia) from Uncle Donald Gunn (976) Governor of the Dundee Poorhouse, Uncle John Gunn (878) (overseer) in Durness and John Mackay (3467) husband of an Aunt—a family mess, centring on Janet (120)

To slightly backtrack—a letter to William (220) (one of Donald's younger brothers) exists from the Dundee Poorhouse[709] [710]; other letters show a signature of D. Gunn. The author is Donald Gunn (976) who married Alexandrina Gunn (554) who was the daughter of Donald (708) (Sennachie). As such Alexandrina was the aunt of William Gunn (220) and Donald Gunn (3). It is noteworthy how they don't want Donald and William's sister Janet to go to Australia as she is obviously looking after Donald the Sennachie and his wife (especially Donald (708) who died in 1861) and so others would be inconvenienced if Janet left. As well, the writer notes how well the Gunns in Australia are doing but makes the comment that New Zealand is better and would William find out for him just in case he decides to go; not the most subtle of letter writers and self-interested. The zeitgeist is definitely for emigration, and at the very least one thinks about going—

[709]'On 26 August 1856 a Mr & Mrs Gunn accepted the positions of Governor and Matron of the Poorhouse (Dundee Poorhouse East). Mr Gunn's salary was £79 per year, his wife's £25 per year plus "the usual rations of the house". Mr Gunn's previous occupation was that of wine and spirit merchant.' From http://www.fdca.org.uk/FDCADundeeEastPoorhouse.html accessed November 19, 2009. 'He was in that post until about 1878'; from an email from R. Cullen, Dundee City Archives to Alastair Gunn 19 November , 2009.

[710]From an email from the Gurneys November 23 to Don Gunn—"1. Lexy (Alexandrina) Gunn, daughter of Donald Gunn and Catherine Gunn, was born in 1825 in Halkirk Parish, Caithness, was christened on 12 Jul 1825 in Halkirk Parish, Caithness, and died in 1876 in St. Andrew, Dundee, Angus at age 51. Lexy married Donald Gunn, son of Alexander Gunn and Sarah Sutherland, on 26 Apr 1852 in Reay, Caithness, Scotland. Donald was born about 1818 in Halkirk Parish, Caithness and died on 13 May 1879 in St. Andrew, Dundee, Angus about age 61.
Death Notes: Death certified by John Gunn, MBCM (son) General Notes: Donald's Grandfather was Murdoch Gunn
Donald's will was proven in 1886 in Dundee...."At Dundee the ninth day of December, eight hundred and eighty six...appeared Alexander Matthewson, Tea Merchant Union St. Dundee one of the Executors nominated by the said deceased Donald Gunn....in favour of the Deponent and George Lloyd Alison Wine Merchant Dundee the now only surviving and acting Executors of the said deceased.
1861 Census Dundee, Angus, The Poor House of Dundee
Donald Gunn Head age 43 born Halkirk House Governor
Alexandrina Gunn Mat. age 35 born Halkirk Matron
Daniel A. Gunn son age 7 born Dundee
Margaret Gunn dau. age 3 born Dundee
Catherine Gunn dau. age 7m born Dundee
1871 Census Dundee, Angus, Dundee Poor House & Lunatic Asylum
Donald Gunn head age 53 born Halkirk Governor
Alexandrina Gunn wife age 44 born Halkirk
John Gunn son age 17 born Dundee Apprentice Druggist
Daniel A. Gunn son age 16 born Dundee Apprentice Merch. Clerk
Margaret Gunn dau. age 12 born Dundee Scholar
Catherine Gunn dau. age 10 born Dundee Scholar
Wilhelmina Gunn dau. age 5 born Dundee Scholar
Robertina Gunn niece age 18 born Dundee Matron's Asst.
(Robertina was the daughter of Alexander Gunn and Mary Campbell)
1881 Census St. Andrew, Dundee, Angus, 13 King Street
John Gunn Head age 27 born Dundee General Medical Pract MBRCM Glasgow
Kate Gunn sister age 20 born Dundee
Wilhelmina Gunn sister age 15 born Dundee

Dundee Poorhouse[711]
10th Feby. 1859

My Dear William

I should have written you long ago which certainly I intended doing but it so happened this last three months that I have always been so busy, and some how or other I have been invariably to late for the mail. However I will be firm to day therefore let me say something altho I am realy at a loss for any news that can be of much Interest to you.

We hear occationaly from home. We had a letter last night and I am glad to say they are all in their usual state. Poor Grandfather[712] is holding out wonderfully he is still able to move about a little. And retains his faculties wonderfully Janet was at school in town for a while poor Janet is not injoy very good health. She tells you wanted her out, I do not think You should drag her for a time yet when she can be so very well at home as she is at present. I am realy glad and it says a very great deal for you all that you are so mindful of her. And so long as her Grandfather + Grandmother is living she may say that she has a comfortable home and besides if Marg$^{t.}$ will get married[713] as I believe she will without delay what in the harm of goodness shall become of the old people without anyone to look to them. I hope you will bear this in view. We are truly glad to learn that you are all doing verey well. I am sure you are far better than ever you could be in Caithness.

We are still here living (?) as usual we have got a great many alterations made in the place since you saw. I have got nearly all the improvements made I asked for. The last four months I dare say there has upwards of £800 been laid out on the place and now it is beginning to have some appearance. We have had a fine Committee this last year and every thing went on pleasantly. Next month a new committee will be elected so we do not know but they may again be as bad. However for support I cannot stand any of their nonsense if they were inclined to batle with me.

I have still have some Kind of hanKering idea about Australia, I would like a more settled and quieter mode of living than this and besides the duties here hang as a heavy burden continualy on the mind, and must ultimately tell upon our frames. However in the mean time their thousands worse off than us. If events be our lot to go to your distant clime I think I would rather go to New Zealand don't you think it is a better country than Australia. Please let me know your opinion. Their are a great many Scotch going from here and the Highland districts here about, to New Zel. Be sure and write us as early as you can and give us all the information in your power. Let us know particularly how you are getting on yourself and wat you are doing and what Donald is doing and how poor[714] Catherine is, I suppose we must call her Mrs. Miller now, and quite right too. Pls let us know how Mr.+Mrs. Miller and the letter from Lady –(?). We are all well thank God for it. The children are thriving well John[715] speaks often about his dear Cousin and asks when he is to come home to see him he is going to school and learns well he is wonderfully intelligent child Daniel[716] is a real highland stump and a pie...

---

711 Now called the Dundee East Poorhouse.

712 The use of 'grandfather' here seems awkward but its next use reveals what is meant; he is speaking of Janet's relationship to these people not of his relationship with his parents in law.

713 Margaret Gunn (880) married John Mackay (3467) in 1860. She was an older sister of Donald's (Dundee Poorhouse) (976) wife Alexandrina (554).

714 Why poor? Her husband was wealthy and she lived a long time. Was it a health issue?

715 John Gunn (Dr.) (3575) b. 1854 Dundee.

716 Daniel Alexander Gunn (3576) b.1855 Dundee.

Dundee Poor House
10th Feby 1857

My Dear William

I should have written you long ago which certainly I intended doing but it so happened for last three months that I have always been so busy, and some how or other I have been invariably too late for the Mail. However I will be in time to day therefore let me say something altho I am really at a loss for any news that can be of much Interest to you

We hear occasionally from home we had a letter last night and I am glad to say they are all in their usual state. Poor Grandfather is holding out wonderfully he is still able to move about a little, and retains his faculties wonderfully Janet was at School in town for a while I poor Janet is not enjoying very good health She tells you wanted her out, I do not think you should drag her

for a time yet when ~~when~~ she can
be so very well at home as she is at
present. I am realy glad and it says
a very great deal for you all that
you are so mindfule of her, and
so long as her Grandfather & Grandmother
is living she may see that she has a
comfortable home and besides if Mary
will get married as I belive she
will without delay what is the mayor
of goodness shall becom of the
old people without any one to
look to them. I hope you will
have this in view. We are truly
glad to learn that you are all doing
~~so~~ very well. I am sure you are
far better than ever you could
be in Caithness.

We are still here living
as usual we have got a great many
alteration made in the place since
you saw. I have got nearly all
the improvements made I asked

for the last four months I dare say there has upwards of £800 been laid out on the place and now it is beginning to have some appearance We have had a fine Committee the last year and every thing went on pleasantly. Next month a new Committee will be elected so we do not know but they may again be as bad. However for my part I can not stand any of that nonsense, if they were inclined to trifle with me.

I have still some kind of wandering idea about Australia I would like a more settled and [illegible] mode of living than this and besides the duties here hang as a heavy burden continually on the mind and must ultimately tell upon our frames. However in the mean time there thousands worse off than us — If it were to be our lot to go to your distant clime I think I should rather go to New Zealand don't you think it is a better

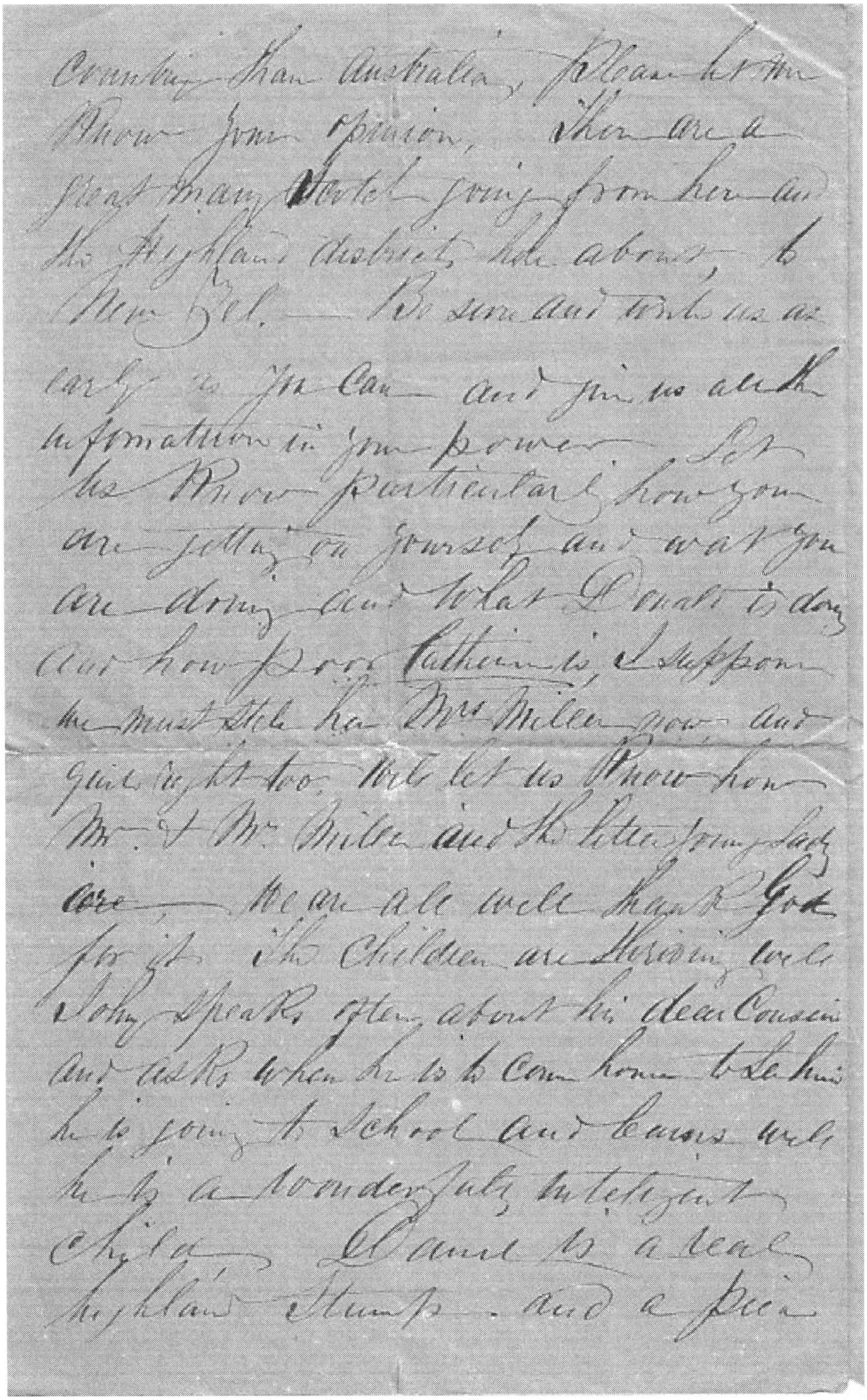
Country than Australia, please let me
know your opinion. There are a
great many Scotch going from here and
the Highland district, like above, to
New Zel. — Be sure and write us as
early as you can and give us all the
information in your power. Let
us know particularly how you
are getting on yourself and what you
are doing and what Donald is doing
and how poor Catherine is, I suppose
she must still be Mrs Miller now and
quite right too. Let us know how
Mr & Mrs Miller and the little young lady
are — We are all well thank God
for it. The Children are thriving well
John speaks often about his dear Cousin
and asks when he is to come home to see him
he is going to School and learns well
he is a wonderfully intelligent
child — Daniel is a real
Highland stump and a fine

The rest is lost…

This letter showed that a lot of the family was in Australia by now. John had died in 1854 (having arrived in October 1853) probably from sunstroke—got reputedly on waiting for the boat to arrive with Donald and Catherine. (They arrived probably in December 1854; certainly between October 1854 and June 1856.) Donald, Catherine and William were out by the time of this letter and they were trying to get Janet out and would succeed. William arrived before September 1858, possibly on the 'Donald McKay' in September 1857. Janet arrived January 1864 and married on the 12th May 1864 at the 'residence of the bride, Cardigan'—presumably the farm bought in common with the Surmans earlier—John Watkins Surman, a teacher aged 33. He, like his sister, was born at Hampton Poyle in England. Their parents were Daniel Surman and Mary Ann Watkins (271). The Minister at this wedding was Archibald Crawford—the Presybeterian Minister at Burrumbeet—it is number 2 in the Ballarat register.)

Another letter exists from the Dundee Poorhouse—

Dundee Poorhouse
7th Nov. 1859

My Dear Donald,

I have been duly favoured with your letter of 14th May for which I beg to thank you, I need not tell you how happy we are to hear of your success in life. We heartily wish every blessing to attend yourself and your good Lady[717] and may you prove a mutual blessing and comfort to one another through life.

I am glad to be able to tell you that we are all well and comfortable. And as yet we have no reason to grumble with our lot in the world. We have a heavy charge consequently enough to keep us from idleness however we are pretty well remunerated, such as remuneration goes in this County, about £200 a year. And I believe we can have the satisfaction of knowing that our services are valued. Still I have not given up the idea yet of going to Australia some day, if spared, permit heartily to thank you for your sensable and very kind letter, th° it was long in coming, and especially for your proffered kindness in providing a home for us on our arrival, which certainly of itself would be no small boon for a man with a small family. However if we go I hope it would not be with the intention of being a burden to anyone. Still I am sensable how much one needs a friend on their arrival and perhaps at all times. And I believe there is no one that could better value it than myself.

I have certainly to appologise for being so long in answering your letter but my reason for that is that owing to some circumstance over which I had no controll and my wife and family being at home in Caithneys for some time I could not have got to Aberdeen to look for the the stone you wanted and without going personaly it was of no use. However I have got at last and I have gone over with Mr Cormack every yard in Aberdeen, but of course there is nothing cheap and at the same time handsome to be got of the sort. However they are cheaper than with you and there is another advantage here you can have "pick and choice" such as would be suitable for your purpose can be got for £7 to £14. I would recommend to you one about £10 or £12 which will be about a ton weight. I saw two, and only two, at this price and weight that pleased me among the many hundreds I saw. And inded they were very pretty the one was Aberdeen and the other Peterhead granite the--? and ----? are thoroughly polished and some has a small marjin round the edge unpolished and improves the look. From the little description I have given you will be able to say which you think you will take one or not, I am told these £10 stones five years ago sold as high as £24. The lettering is from 1½ d. to ?d. per letter, add to this the freightage and you know the price of your stone. if you should think of taking one write on receipt inclosing the

[717] Donald having married in late March 1859.

inscription, but should not be nonsensealy long. And I will undertake to do the thing as well as it can be done, and as cheap, but I would not advise you to take one dearer than I have said or above a ton weight say whether Aberdeen or Peterhead Granite whether you would like it polished altogether or with the Marjin unpolished.

In regard to Janet we realy do not think she should go in the mean time she is very well where she is and can not be more comfortable her Grandfather and GMother are very much attached to her and she is very kind and attending to them And it is not likely that Grandfather will be long spared and I understand that Aunt Marg^{t} [718] is to get married this winter And if she leaves them what in the name of goodness will be come of the old people they cannot do alone So I think she should remain for at least this year yet where she is And I am glad to think that she has been injoying good health since she was out here in summer Remember us with Kindest manner to Mrs Miller and her worthy husband

(unsigned)

*****

"The Poorhouse is situated in an open and healthy part of the town at the back of Stobswell Feus. It is 210 feet long and 55 feet in width and is three stories high. Airing yards are used to separate male and female inmates. Two acres of ground is available for inmates to supply vegetables for the Poorhouse."

Dundee Perth & Cupar Advertiser[719]

On 26 August 1856 a Mr & Mrs Gunn accepted the positions of Governor and Matron of the Poorhouse. Mr Gunn's salary was £79 a year, his wife's £25 per year plus "the usual rations of the house".

http://www.fdca.org.uk/FDCADundeeEastPoorhouse.html

[718] Margaret Gunn (880) married John Mackay (3467) in 1860. She was an older sister of Donald's (Dundee Poorhouse) (976) wife Alexandrina (554).

[719] http://www.bairdnet.com/fife/poor.html

Dundee Poor House
7th Nov. 1859

My Dear Donald

I have been duly favoured with your letter of 14th May for which I beg to thank you. I need not tell you how happy we are to hear of your success in life. We heartily wish every blessing to attend yourself and your good Lady and may you prove a mutual blessing and comfort to one another through life.

I am glad to be able to tell you that we are all well and comfortable, and as yet we have no reason to grumble with our lot in the world, we have a heavy charge consequently enough to keep us from idleness however we are pretty well remunerated, such as remuneration goes in this County, about £200 a year and I believe we can have the satisfaction of knowing that our services are valued. Still I have not given up the idea yet of going to Australia some day if spared. I must heartly to thank you for your sensable and very kind letter tho, it was long a coming and especialy for your proffered kindness in providing a home for us on our arival which certainly of itself would be no small boon for a man with a small family — However if we go I hope it would not be with the intention of being a burden to any one. Still I am sensable how much one needs a friend on their arrival and perhaps at all times, and I believe there is no one that could better value it than myself.

I have certainly to appologize for being so long in answering your letter but my reason for that is that owing to some circumstan over which I had no controle and my wife and family being at home in Caithness for some time I could not have got to Aberdeen to look for the the stone you wanted and without going personaly it was of no use. However I have got it last and I have gone over with McCormack every yard in Aberdeen but of course there is nothing

cheap and at the same time handsome to
be got of the sort, & when they are cheaper
than with you and there is another advantage
here you can have "pick and choose" such
as would be suitable for your purpose can
be got from £7 to £24. I would recommend
to you one about £10 or £12 which will be
about a ton weight. I saw two, and only two,
at this price and weight that pleased me
among the many hundreds I saw and
indeed they were very pretty, the one was
Aberdeen and the other Peterhead granite
the face and edges are thoroughly polished
and some of them have a small margin
round the edge unpolished and improves
the look. From the little discription I have
given you will be able to say whether you think
you will take one or not. I am told that
£10 stones five years ago sold as high
as £24 — The lettering is from 1d to 2d
per letter, add to this the freightage
and you know the price of your
stone. If you should think of taking
one write me on receipt inclosing
the inscription, but should not be unreasonably
long and I will undertake

to do the thing as well as it can be
done and as cheap but I would not
advise you to take one dearer than I have
said or about a ton weight say whether
Aberdeen or Peterhead Granite whether
you would like it polished altogether
or with the Margin unpolished

In regard to Janet we really do
not think that she should go in the mean
time she is very well where she is and can
not be more comfortable her Grandfather
and G Mother are very much attached to
her and she is very kind and atten
tive to them and it is not likely
that Grandfather will be long spared
and I understand that Aunt Mary
is to get married this winter and
if she leaves them what in the name of
Goodness will become of the old people
they cannot do alone so I think she
should remain for at least this season
yet where she is and I am glad
to think that she has been enjoying
good health since she was out here
in summer Remember us in the
kindest manner to Mrs Miller
and her worthy husband,

Lucky Janet—what a thrilling prospect for her! It is, though, the traditional view on the prospects for the last unmarried female. Was the stone discussed possibly for a memorial (given 'pretty', 'polished' and 'designed for lettering); perhaps for John? Caithness stone was a major export at this time and so it was quite viable to send to Australia.

Another letter to Donald from the Governor of the Dundee Poorhouse (his Aunt's husband) some years later raised some major complications about the family's affairs which are carried over in the next few letters. It is impossible now to know whom to believe, but Janet finally went to Australia—

Dundee Poorhouse
24th Oct 1863

My Dear Friend

I wrote you a month ago from London when I was up there with poor Jessie. I put them[720] on Board the "Chatsworth" on 30th Sept. And they sailed the following morning. Jessie was in excellent health then indeed better than I have seen her since she came to Dundee we was a week in London owing to the ship not sailing at the stated time. We had four lettters from Jessie since then they they ---? very stormy weather for the first few days and they had to put in at Deal near Dover. She was not very well then her old complaint returning upon her but this we expected as the result of her excitement caused by parting with her friends poor thing I cannot tell you how we felt on receiving her letters but we could nothing for her then, but I can assure you did we think she would have been so ill she would not have left here this season And perhaps next year we would have have accompanied her. However we hope once she was at sea that a few days would have made a great change with her. She has been much attached to us + the children And this has made the parting mood difficult for her + us And of our Boys "Daniel" has been so much attached to her that he had been confined to bed for a few days after she left in consequence of the state he has put himself in by his crying - And can assure you we all feel lonely without her, if we knew of this so much before she left She (?) might not express ---(?) this year. We have been a while in London as I have already said and of course we spent our time to the best advantage I was willing that she could see as much of London as she could for the short time she had to be their - I had tried to make her as comfortable as I could about the ship and also tried to make as many friends for her as I could be fore she left And in so doing I did not spare any expenses that I considered necessary. And all now that we can do is to remember her continually before ------? of Grace this we are endeavouring to do tho' unworthily. And we hope tho God's --? grace who is rich in mercy will preserve her in His good providence. And bring her in safety to the desired haven. We committ her to his own care? and day + night we are trying to remember her as a footstool of God?

We hope she shall soon arrive safely with you and we have no doubt but you will be kind + good to her No doubt owing to her being absent from you for so long a time it is necessary that you should be doubly so as she is very sensitive. But we have no doubt but she shall soon feel herself at home And where could she be more so than in her own family? than is a while now since you could hardly say she was at home but I have no doubt you will be all very kind to her of this I am sure. And I beleive alsho she has not much to say there are few

[720] People travelling together are normally put on the same page on the passenger list. Janet is on page 6, the last page. The other names are Donald Campbell 20, Collins family, Jane Cornelius 20, Elliz. Hack, Richard Hander, Catherine James 23, Robert Jamieson 23, Rosannah May, William Mills 20, Joseph Wilks 20 and Will family. Donald Campbell (3514) is a grandson of Donald the Sennachie and a son of Alexandrina Gunn's (the wife of Donald Gunn Dundee Poorhouse (976)) sister May. He is definitely the person meant, as indicated by the end of the letter. They were 'unassisted passengers'; they paid their own way.

creatures more affectionate than herself And if we were differently situated I believe her Aunt would not willingly have parted with her And she feels the -----(loss)? of her -----(kind)? now

My Dear Sir Regarding the inquiry you were making Regarding your Grandfathers Affairs - I can give you but little information. As they have never condesended to write us or give us any information nor did we condescend to ask them anything about it. - Alex^r [721]. has never mentioned us tho there were a sale of what was the proceeds of it till about the time that Janet came how he wrote me asking me to become security for him with the Bank for £700 John McKay[722] of course going in for Another £700. I did not answer his letter nor till he wrote on the third stating that he had made use of my name at the Bank and that it was excepted. Then I wrote him and of course not a pleasant one In a former letter he says "I require this in consequence of my fathers Death whilst he was alive he was my security " now as I wrote him in return , tho' his father was dead he has taken nothing with him And the -----? has turned in upwards of £600 as I was told and not a farthing of that was put in the Bank where it should have been put till every one should have got their own share Alexr. has got the whole of it as far as I know Of course John will expect to share the spoil with him but still that was not sufficient for them but he would like to write me in Bills and Security However I wrote him at the last. He wrote me in reply and it is like it is the last he will write at least for a while - Now in respect of their treatment of Janet, I have never said anything to you before now about it, but since you ask me I must tell you now that it was desidedly very bad - They sent her away without, as far as I know, a single penny ----? in her pocket now tho' she had not her mother's share in the house as she had ----? there were no other claim but the laborious and ---full + filial manner in which she attended her Grandfather for the few months he was under his illness when there was no other one to do it One would think they would have treated her otherwise But no, she must go without a penny and that was not the worst of it, poor Mary[723] is abusing her to this day And Marys husband poor fool has writen me when Janet left them And if he had any sense at all he would be ashamed of himself, writing such abominable stuff A man that has a family of his own. However he was much mistaken if he thought we would turn out our Janet because they they did not like her. We have made her as welcome as one of our children And she would also ---? Her that with us And as I already have said I wrote Alexr. in return but I don't expect to hear so soon from him again. The whole cause of this has been jealousy on their part, because it was not one of their family that was in the House with their Grandmother. Of course Mary was at the root of it And I believe John with his greed was not behind. Neither of the two spock to Janet before parting or bad her goodby What think you of that And still John would have the impudence to say that if his daughter were going to Australia she would be more welcome with you than your own sister. I wonder what shall we get next from them I am glad that poor Jessie is away from them and you know of all this she was -----? than sooner I daresay they are blaming Jessie for Grandmother going to live with Margt. but has she not done what was right were could she be better than with her own daughter I would not mention these things but that I am in duty bound to do so as you might suppose there was bleam attached to Janet in these things but honestly and candidly as far as we can see there was none whatsoever but they have not used her well. Of course her aunt was kind to her as you would expect. If they had even given her a ten pound note before she left and sent her away kindly as they should I would have been well enough pleased. John and Alex^r. was very gracious at that time but warn you that they have not settled the affairs yet And before they do you will find they will not be so friendly they will not care for one another more than they did for Janet before she left. If they had behaved well to Janet I dare say I would have been tempted to go on for Alex^r. but never again Alexr. sent through a check for £3/10 (+6/ for something that was sold in the R----? belonging to your father) this was for her half years wages as any common servant of course Janet would not take it or send him a receipt. However I took it for her knowing it would do her more

---

[721] Alexander Gunn (572) was Donald's uncle and a child of Donald Gunn (Sennachie 708).

[722] John MacKay (3467) was the husband of Margaret Gunn, Donald's aunt and a child of Donald Gunn (Sennachie) (708).

[723] Mary Innes Campbell (1128), wife of Alexander Gunn (572).

good to her in her own pocket than in Alex[r] - I sent him his receipt and a few remarks not very complimentary to him .

Now my dear Sir I have given you an outline of the most I know about the matter. Of course I cannot but exonerate Janet and blame them. And I hope you will not be led asside by any thing they may say to the contrary. As for my own part I don't believe much in heirship and if they were doing to her what they should I would never had ask any thing about it . And even as they have done I will not And I donot think that you will go to Law with them either especially as the Old woman is living still I think it would be right that you should let them know that there conduct did not meet your approval. They have much need of bringing them to their senses and I cannot I am sorry to say exonerate Grandmother more than her two sons. She never gave as much as a shilling to Donald Campbell[724] when he left- to bad. Poor Jessie I hope will soon be with you and she will let you know all these things better than I can. Be sure and do not take my name into it unless it be necessary. I have no doubt DCampbell will do well He is a good worker and a qutie lad, but a real Campbell. He carries his stick in the one hand and the Bagpipes under the other I will write you again first mail We will now be thinking every ----? a month till we hear of their safe arrival. May the Lord be with them and protect them is our sincere prayer ---? unto soon. Our love to Dear William he will be glad to see his sister . Our warmest love to you all without exception excuse haste I have not time to raed this take it as it is

I remain
My Dear Sir
Yours truely
DGunn

to DGunn esq.
Blenheim Farm, Cardigan Victoria

It is worth noting the address; this may be the farm mentioned on page 256.

[724] Donald Campbell being John Gunn's (Durness) (3505) brother-in-law.

Dundee Poorhouse
24th Oct 1863

My Dear Friend

I wrote you a month ago from London when I was up there with poor Jessie. I put them on Board the Chatsworth on 30th Sept and they sailed the following morning. Jessie was in excellent health then indeed better than I have seen her since she came to Dundee. We were a week in London owing to the Ship not sailing at the stated time. We had four letters from Jessie since then they have had very stormy weather for the first few days and they had to put in at Deal near Dover she was not very well then her old complaint returning upon her but this we expected as the result of her excitement caused by parting with her friends poor thing. I cannot tell you how we felt on receiving her letters

but we could do n[illegible] then but
I can assure you did we think she
would have been so ill she would not have
left here this season, and perhaps next
year we would have accompanied her
However we hope once she was at sea
that a few days would have made
a great change with her. She has
been much attached to us & the children
and that has made the parting more difficult
for her & us. One of our Boys "Daniel"
has taken so much attached to her that he
had been confined to bed for a few days
after she left in consequence of the state
he has put himself in by crying — And
I assure you we all feel lonely without
her, if we knew of this so well before she
left, you might not expect her this
year. — We have been a while in London as
I have already said and of course we spent
our time to the best advantage. I was willing
that she would see as much of London
as they could for the short time you had to
be there — I have tried to make her as comfortable
as I could aboard the ship and also tried
to make as many friends for her as I

Could be for the best. And in so doing I
did not spare any expense that I considered
necessary. And all now that we can do
is to remember her continually before a throne
of Grace. This we are endeavouring to do tho'
unworthily. And we hope the God of all Grace
who is rich in mercy will preserve her in
His good providence and bring her in safe
to the desired haven. We commit her to his own
care. And day & night we are trying to remem
ber her at a footstool of Grace.

We hope she shall soon arrive safe
with you and we have no doubt but you
will be kind & good to her. No doubt owing
to her being absent from you for so long a time
it is necessary that you should be doubly so
as she is very sensitive. But we have no doubt
but she shall soon feel herself at home. And when
and she be more so than her own family & friends
a while now since you could hardly say she
was at home. But I have no doubt you
will be always kind to her. of this I
am sure. And I believe although she has not
much to say there are few Creatures more
affectionate than herself. And if we
were differently situated I believe her Aunty
would not willingly have parted with her
And she feels the loss of her keenly now

My Dear Sir Regarding the inquiry you were making
regarding your Grandfather affairs - I can give you
but little information, as they have never conde
scended to write us or give us any information
nor did we condescend to ask them any thing
about it — Alexr has never mentioned us that
there was a sale or what was the proceeds of
it till about the time that Sandy came here he
wrote me asking me to become security for him
with the Bank for £700, John McKay
of course going in for another £700. I did not
answer his letter nor till he wrote me the third
stating that he had made use of my name off
the Bank and that it was excepted then
I wrote him and of course not a pleasant
one In a former letter he says "I require this in
consequence of my father's Death whilst he
was alive he was my security" Now as
I wrote him in return, tho' the father was dead
he has taken nothing with him and the Crop has
turned in upwards of £600 as I was
told and not a farthing of that was put
into the Bank where it should have been put
till every one should have got their own share
Alexr has got the whole of it as far as I
know. Of course John will expect to
share the spoil with him but states that
was not sufficient for them but he
would like to use the name in Bills
and security,

However I wrote him at the ~~time~~ last
He wrote me in reply and it is the letter
it is the last he will write me at least
for a while — Now in respect of the
treatment of Janet, I have never said any
thing to you before now about it but since
you ask me I must tell you now that
it was decidedly very bad — They sent her
away without as far as I know a single
penny piece in her pocket now tho' she had
not her mother's share in the house as she had
tho there was no other claim but the laborious and
faithful & filial manner in which she attended
her Grandfather for the few months he was under
his illness when there was no other one to do it
one would think they would have treated her otherwise
But no, she must go without a penny and
that was not the worst of it, poor Mary
is abusing her to this day and Mary's husband
poor fool has written me when Janet left them
and if he had any sense at all he would be a-
shamed of himself writing such abominable
stuff a man that has a family of his own,
However he was much mistaken if he thought
we were to turn out our Janet because they
did not like her she has made her as welcome
as one of our own children and she would
always be that with us and as I

have already seen I wrote Alexr in return
but I don't expect to hear so soon from him
again. The whole cause of this has been
Jealousy on their part. because it was not
one of their family that was in the House with
their Grandmother. Of course Mary was at the
root of it and I believe John with his greed
was not behind. Neither of the two spoke to
Janet before parting or bad her good by
what think you of that and Stilt John
would have the impudence to say that if his daughter
were going to Australia she would be more welcome
with you than your own sister, I wonder what
shall we get next from them. I am glad that poor
Sophy is away from them and if she knew of all
this she was from them sooner. I daresay they
are blaming Sophy for Grandmother going to live
with Mary, but has she not done what was
right were could she be better than with her
own daughter. I would not mention these
things but that I am in duty bound to do so
as you might suppose there was blame attached
to Janet in these things. but honestly and candidly
as far as we can see there were none who ought
but they have not used her well. Of course her
Aunt was kind to her as you would expect,
If they had even given her a few pound note
before she left, and sent her away kindly
as they should I would have been well and pleased.
John and Alexr was very

will go to Law with them either especially
when the Old woman is living still I think
it would be right that you should let
them Know that their conduct did
not meet your approval. They have need
need of bringing them to their senses, and
I cannot I am sorry to say exonerate your
mother more than her two sons. She never
gave as much as a shilling to Donald
Campbell when he left to have. Poor
Lippen I hope will soon be with you and
she will let you Know all these things
better than I can. Be sure and do
not make my name into it unless it
be necessary. I have no doubt D Campbell
will do well he is a good worker and a
quiet lad, but a real Campbell. He carries his
stick in the one hand and the Bagpipes
under the other. I will write you again by
first mail. We will now be the [illegible] one
week a month till we hear of their safe
arrival. May the Lord be with them and protect them is our sincere prayer. Please give
love. Our Love to Dear William he will be glad
to see his sister. Our warmest love to you all
without exception. Excuse haste. I have no
time to read this. take it as it is

I remain My Dear Sir yours truly
L Gunn

To A. Gunn Esq.
Blenheim Farm, Cardigan Victoria

The next 'Durness' letter is below. To restate; it is to Donald from his Uncle John (who was the oldest child of the family, Donald's mother Barbara being the second eldest)—

Durness Nov 13 1863

Dear Donald,

I believe am due you a letter. But I expect you will hear on on the way for me. I have nothing particular to inform you. We are all in health expecting this will find you + your family the same not forgetting Caithrine + family + William when I write you I consider it the same as if I wrote to them, and I expect they will Recept of it the same thing - I was down in Caithness for ten days in Sept - all our friends there is in their usual health, Mother[725] is wonderfull and appears to make herself at home, No doubt I feel seeing her there, when I consider on the past - seeing how ma + all of us have scattered so far from one another + from her, But these things must be + is the case I may say with the most of families. As I told you already I would rather see mother where she was - But she is far more comfortable in every way + cheaper in Newton, and do you know there never was a more kinder friend than Peggy + John, if possible John is before our sister - Forss is always inquiring about mother and could learn of him that he would rather she had remained. Their is a large Crop over the whole Kingdom this year Corn of all kinds uncommon cheap the 4th loaf selling just now in some places as low as 4d. Oatmeal 12/- how well that pays - there was not such a Crop of Potatoes since they faild first I could by them just now at 8/- per Bll no disease appeared this year. I see in the south the Rents are coming down. And in Caithneys I can assure you matters with the farmers are not in a thriving way they had thrice very bad crops. this is a good crop - But will turn to no money owing to the little price Cattle of all kind kept up the price this year at the last two markets I never saw them higher nothing worth telling under £5. But the Drovers barely kept them moving at the last two markets. But John McKay[726] + D. Munro did a little by the summer markets. If John was free of the farm how comfortable he could be, it is a beast of a farm and the proprieter will lay no money out to try it - It will be enough for the Crop on the average of years to pay the servants
In this County the sheep farmers are ---(?) owing to that America War and not the least sign of it coming to an end - they got from 31/ to 35/ this year for their local wool and those that held on as yet is to get more - I got the former price for my own bundle I am down of shearing this -----? day I sheared 104 - But I sent 20 of that down to Caithneys pay for Turnips which all bring up in March. Alexr is fighting away the best he can - he is a purty honest man and if he had a good subject to work on he would do well By his Grace he can put the highlands from him in the first term which he will do because they are not worth having for nothing for sheep. And their name has gone so far that it will be difficult for the Laird to get anyone to -----? them. It was a black day for him that he ever took them.

Every one that goes to Australia goes under the expectation that they will make riches + then come home which is the case with some and I will expect that you will be one of them as you are only yet a young man and no man ever left the North but would wish to come back again in his old days. I wonder how money can be made from farming when labour of every kind is so high - your mother no mentions to me about any of our acquaintances their and likely you must know a great many of them in that quarter + perhaps some from here as their is several of them their not far from you. I had a letter from Will. Gunn and he is doing well by the sheep - I must conclude I am Dear Friend yours truely + Dearly

Mr Don^d Gunn) John Gunn Australia)

---

[725] 'Mother' is Catherine Gunn of Osclay (3423) c1781-1870, wife of Donald Gunn the Sennachie. Her husband had died in 1861 at Brawlbin.

[726] Presumably John Mackay (3467) husband of Margaret Gunn, (880) Donald's aunt on his mother's side and previously mentioned.

Durness Novr 13 – 1863

Dear Donald

I believe am due you a letter. But I expect you will have one on the way for me. I have nothing particular to inform you. We are all in health expecting this will find you & your family the same not forgetting Catherine & family & William when I write you I consider it the same as if I wrote to them, and I expect they will Receipt of it the same thing —

I was down in Caithness for ten days in Sept — all our friends there is in their usual health Mother is wonderfull and appears to make herself at home, no doubt I feel seeing her there, when I consider on the past — seeing how me & all of us have scattered so far from one another & from her, But these things must

must be & is the case I may say
with the most of families - As I told
you already I would rather see Mother
where she was - But she is far more
comfortable in every way & cheaper
in Newton and as you know there
never was a more kinder pair than
Peggy & John if possible John is before
our Sister - Fass is always inquiring
about Mother and could learn by him
that he would rather she had re
= married - There is a large crop over
the whole kingdom this year Corn
of all kinds uncommon cheap the 4 lb
loaf selling Just now in some places
as low as 4d Oat meal @ 12/ how
will that pay - There was not such
a crop of Potatoes since they failed first
I could buy them just now at 8/ the
Boll no decease appeared this year
I think the south the Rents are
coming down - And in Kaithness
I can assure you Mother with the far
= mers are not in a thriving way they
had three very bad crops - This is
a good crop - But will turn to no
money owing to the little price

Cattle of all kind kept up thier
price this year at the last two
markets I never saw them higher
nothing worth telling under £6 - But
the Drovers barely kept them many
at the last two markets - But John
McKay & D. Munro did a little by the
former markets - If John was free
of the Farm have comfortable he
could keep it is a beast of a Farm
and the proprietor will lay no money
out to dry it - It will be enough for
the best on the average of years to
pay the servants -
In this County the sheep Farmers
are crying owing to that America
War and not the least sign of it
coming to an end - they got from
31/ to 35/ this year for their laid
Wool and those that held on
as yet is to get more - I got the
former price for my own pickle
I am done of smearing this some
day I smeared 104 - But I sent
20 of that down to Caithness for
for Turnip - what all being up in
a march - Alexr is fighting away

the best he can — he is a worthy
honest man and if he had a good
subject to work on he would do well
By his Grace he can put the highlands
farm on the first term which he
will do because they are not worth
money for nothing for sheep and their
name has gone so far that it will
be difficult for the Laird to get any one
to take them — It was a black day for him
that he ever took them

Every one that goes to Australia goes
under the expectation that they will
make riches & then come home which
is the case with some and I expect
that you will be one of them as you are
only yet a young man and no man
ever left the north but would wish to
come back again in his old days — I
wonder how many can be making by
farming when labour of every kind is so
high — you make no mention to me
about any of our acquaintances there and
likely you must know a great many
of them in that quarter & perhaps some
from here as there is several of them
there not far from you — I had a letter
from Will Gunn he is doing well by the
sheep — I must conclude — I am

Dear Sir most yours truly
& dearly
[illegible]

Mr Donl Gunn
Australia

The actual background of the letter is light brown.

The letters were to continue to Donald from Scotland. They continue to show the extended family pressure he was under—one only wishes that the letters he wrote were available. They remain as interesting fragments of a life and one must remember that his own life near Ballarat was prospering but at the same time that he was dealing with the pressures exerted by an extended family.

The next letter from Dundee was approximately two months later.

Dundee Poorhouse
25th Dec 1863.

My Dear Sir,

I duly received your letter of 21st Oct. And I need not tell you that we were all glad to learn that you are well. Before you get this I fain hope poor Jessie will be with you we have not heard from her since they left the English coast of course she has nor had any opportunity. We shall be very anxious about her til we hear of her safe arrival. May the Lord protect her is our earnest prayer.

I am glad to tell you that we are all well. My wife has got an addition to her family a fine Boy on the 5th of this month. They are both doing well and Aunt Margt. has also been safely delivered of a Boy[727] on the 14th. of this month.You will be glad to hear of this and I am sure Jessie will.

I am glad you think the Reaper will please. I hope it will give you satisfaction when you try it, but don't be surprised tho' you don't get it to work altogether as you would wish at first, while you understand it as little is the thing that makes a difference on the working of these machines. but I am convinced from what I saw of them at work that when you handle them properly adjusted , they will make beautiful work. However we shall soon hear what your opinion of it will be. I have only sent you one since as I would like to know how these plese before I send more or if you would have improvements or alterations made on it to suit your soils.

I beg to thank you for the cash you sent me. I have just look at the check just now. I see it is for £35. Now it is clear you have made a mistake or else I have made a mistake in stating you what it cost me for by looking to my Cash Book I find I only paid £31.9.2 for the machine that is including freight, insurance Yes surely I never could have made such a gross mistake as this, be kind enough and look at my old letters and see. I will send you receiptsusual mail. I am close upon mail time now. Please sell the other one as you can dont keep it on hand sticking for a long(?) price. We all join in our love to each and all of yours

I am
My Dear Sir,
Yours Truely
DGunn

Obviously the emotions of the previous letter needed to be kept in check—the return to the formality is obvious. It is interesting as it clearly shows Donald's strong financial position as he is now importing machinery from Scotland.

[727] D. Gunn's wife having Frances Molison Gunn (1137) and Aunt Margt. having Hector MacKay (3468).

Dundee Poorhouse
25th Dec 186[illegible]

My Dear Sir

I duly received your letter of 21st Oct. and I need not tell you that we are all glad to learn that you are well. Before you get this I am hope poor Jessy will be with you. We have not heard from her since they left the English Coast of course she has not had any opportunity. We shall be very anxious about her till we hear of her safe arrival. May the Lord protect her is our earnest prayer.

I am glad to tell you

that we are all well
My wife has got an addition
to her family (a fine Boy)
on the 5th of this month
they are both doing well
and Aunt Margt. has also
been safely delivered of a Boy
on the 14th of this month
You will be glad to hear
of this and I am sure
Jessie will —
I am glad you think
the Reaper will please I hope
it will give you satisfaction
when you try it, but dont
be surprised tho' you dont

get it to work altogether
as you would wish at
first. while you understand
it as little is the thing that
makes a differen in the working
of these Machines. but I am
convinced from what I seen of them at
work that when you have them
properly adjusted, they will
make beautiful work
However we shall soon hear
what your opinion of it
will be. I have only
sent you one Shear
as I would like to know
how these please before ~~you~~
I send more or if you
would have any improvements

an alteration made on
it to suit your sort.

I beg to thank you
for the Cash you sent me
I have just look at the Check
just now I see it is for £35–
now it is clear you have made
a mistake or else I have made
a mistake in stating you what
it cost me for by looking to
my Cash Book I find I only
paid £31. 9. 2 for the machine
that is including freight insurance
&c. Surely I never could have made
such a gross mistake as this be
kind enough and look at my old letter
and see. I will send you receipts by coming
mail. I am close upon mail time now
please sell the other one as you can don't
keep it on hand sticking for a long time
we all join in our love to each an
all of you.

I am My Dear Sir
Your truly
L. Munn

The next letter is from John MacKay (3467) in Newton. John had married Margaret Gunn (880) who was the youngest sister of Barbara Gunn, and so the Aunt of Donald. In the letter starting on page 294 he was described with disapproval by Donald Gunn (Dundee Poorhouse)—

Newton 4 Jany 1864

My Dear Sir

I write you this few lines to inform you that we are all well at present thank God which I hope will find you all in like manner I am glad to tell you my wife presented us with a fine little boy on the 14th of last month + I am glad to say the Mother + Infant are doing well as yet the infant's name are Hector[728] I am glad say Granmother are very well she had not a sore head since she came here but always sorrowing after Janet I have aften seen her sheding tears whenever a letter came from Dundee during the time Janet were there now she will be asking if there came any word of the vessels arrival in Austulia poor woman She was very much attached to poor Janet and indeed not her alone but the whole of us were much cast down at her departure I hope providence were kind to her by the voyage and since and we fain hope she is safly arrived by this time, we had a very late harvest in caithness this season the grain are light as it kept green only weighing an average about 36lb. per bushel and selling at 18/ per Standard 40lb per bushel now you may see the price of grain will not amount to much we have agreat quantity of straw + corn but still it will not turn out to much as the price are low and quality light droving did well the begining of the season but it fell off at the bak --- (?) we had four bad Seasons for lean stock and four bad croaps which leaves many hard up in this country. I am very sure that farms can be easily got in this country soon I am informed that the messengers are every other day at your friends the Sinclairs in Brawlbin I know that they had been highpoticated over and over I am aware of £200 of borrowed money they have besides, all they have will not pay the half of their dept. I am told many more are hard up in this country we had a very open winter as yet but very wet with high winds but no snow at all yet, we have had six days of very hard frost the last week, our friend at Breahour had been visited by Scarler Feaver Robertina[729] his youngest Daughter got unwell Thursday last + Doctor Mill had been sent for + I am glad to say as I had a letter to day She is on the recovery but it will be awonder if the malady will not spread in the locality, for it is very prevelent in the country just now and amongst children in particular it is proving fatal in every case almost May the Lord Rebuke the malady, I had a letter from Durness from John they are all well Saturday last I had an other from Dundee by the same post they are all well. Mrs. Gunn has got another son a few days previous to our infant. Mother + infant are doing well which is acause of thankfulness.

I will now conclude by offering our united respects to Mrs Gunn family + self Remember us Mr. William + Mrs + Mr Miller + family. I am to write two or three words to poor Jessie + may every Spiritual + temporal Blessing attend you

+ I am my DSir
Yours very truly
John MacKay

D.Gunn Esq
Blenheim Farm

Now this provides an alternative to the view put forward by Donald (Dundee Poorhouse)— obviously John sees nothing hugely wrong with his relationship with Donald. He may be

[728]Hector Mackay 1863-1892 (3468)

[729]Presumably Robertina Gunn (1134) 1852-1872, youngest child of Alexander Gunn (572) and Mary Innes Campbell (1128). Alexander Gunn being Donald Gunn's (3) uncle.

tactless in pointing out the problems of the Sinclairs but he obviously does not have the depth of feeling of Donald (Poorhouse). Certainly one suspects that Janet had a hard life—the expectations placed on her seem horrendous—and she does not seem to have been fairly treated when she left but it seems possible that there may have been faults of omission which perhaps contributed to the problem from both sides. One wonders about the 'illness' she had…

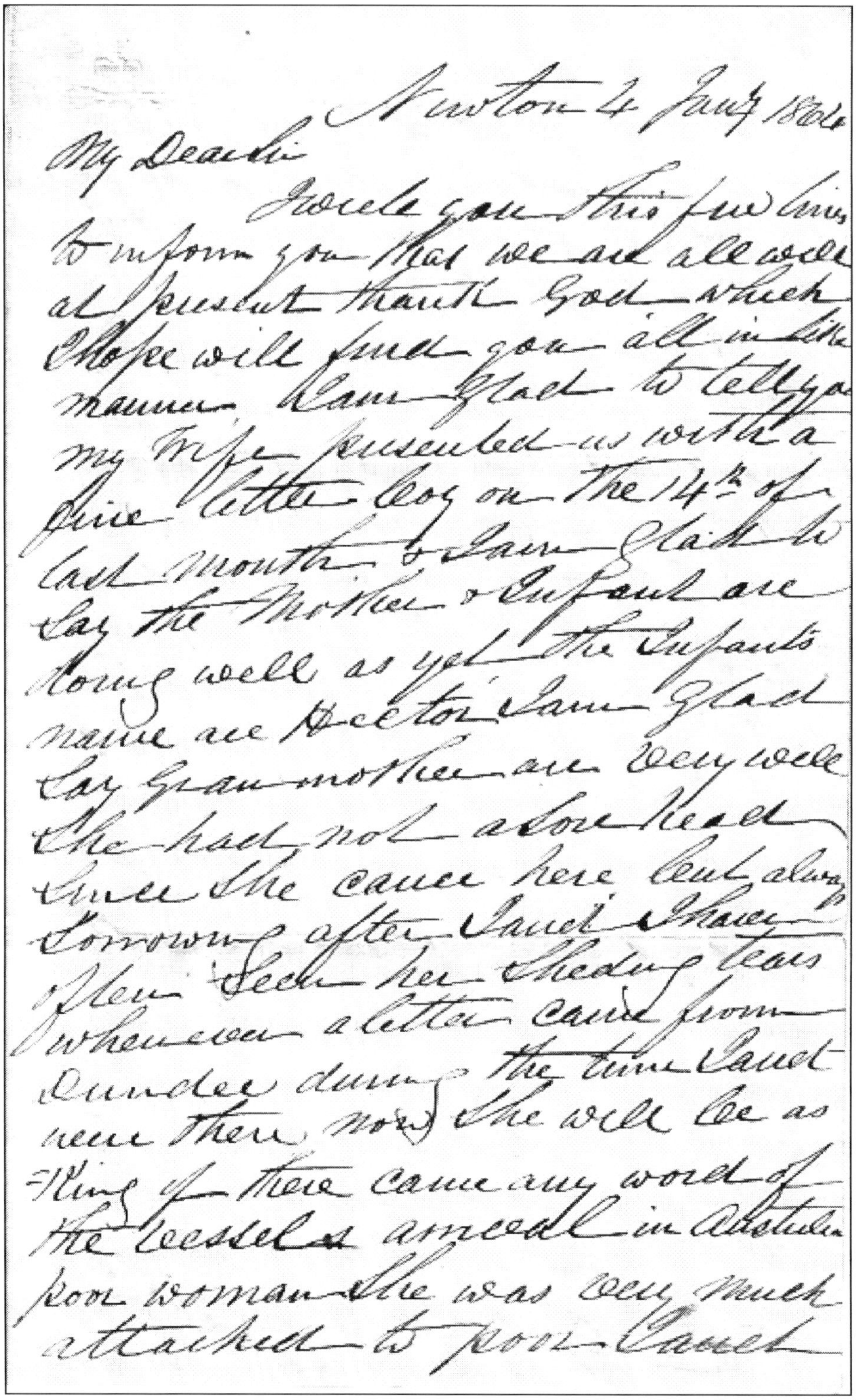
Newton 4 Jany 186[illegible]

My Dear Sir

I write you this few lines to inform you that we are all well at present thank God which I hope will find you all in like manner. I am glad to tell you my wife presented us with a fine little boy on the 14th of last month & I am glad to say the Mother & Infant are doing well as yet the Infant's name are Hector I am glad to say Granmother are very well she had not a sore head since she came here but always sorrowing after Janet I have often seen her sheding tears whenever a letter came from Dundee during the time Janet were there now she will be as [illegible] if there came any word of the vessels arrival in Australia poor woman she was very much attached to poor Janet

and indeed not her alone
but the whole of us were much
cast down at her departure,
I hope providence were kind to her
by the voyage and since and we
again hope she is safely arrived
by this time, we had a very late
harvest in caithness this season the
grain are light as it kept green
only weighing in average about 36
lb. per bushel & selling at 18/ per
Qr, standard 40 lb per bushel
now you may see the price of grain
will not amount to much, we
have a great quantity of straw
& corn but still it will not turn
out to much as the price are low
and quality light, droving did
well the beginning of the season
but it fell off at the back end
we had four bad seasons for
lean stock and four bad
crops which leaves many hard
ups in this county. I am very
sure that farms can be easily got
in this country soon, I am infor
med that the messengers are

every other day at your home the Sinclairs in Bradolbin I know that they had been high =poticated over and over I am aware of £200 of borrowed money they have besides, all they have will not pay the half of their debt. I am told many a one are hard up in this country we had a very op en winter as yet but very wet with high winds but no snow at all yet, we have had six days of very hard frost the last week, our friend at Breakon had been visited by Scarlet Fever Robertina his youngest Daughter got unwell thursday last & Doctor Mill had been sent for & I am Glad to say as I had a letter to day She is on the recovery but it will be a wonder if the Malady will not Spread in the

locality, for it is very prevalent
in this country just now and
amongst Children in particular
it is proving fatal in every case
almost. May the Lord Rebuke
the Malady. I had a letter from
Durness from John they are all
well Saturday last. I had an
other from Dundee by the same
post they are all well. Mrs Gunn
has got another son a few days
previous to our Infant Mother
& Infant are doing well, which
is a cause of thankfulness.
I will now conclude by offering our
united respects to Mrs Gunn family
& self. Remember us to Mr William &
Mrs & Mr Miller & family. I am
to write two or three words to poor
Jessie & may every Spiritual &
temporal Blessing attend you
& Lexie My D Sir
Yours Very truly
D. Gunn Esq
Blenheim &c. John MacKay

The next letter is is a black bordered 'mourning' letter from the Uncle John 'Durness'—

Durness Feby 12 1864

Dear Donald,

your letter of the 25th Nov came to hand on the 21 of Jany at 6 oclock P.M. and on the very minute it came in, my Dear Donald[730] had breathed his last. - yourself can imagine our feelings as it is beyond describing - my case is a sad one now left with five helpless Lasies + a little Boy four year old. I was afraid of his health for the last three years he was growing so fast and had not the strong appearance that he had a Boy - But for the last 12 month he was not a day confined and I suppose I was apart of him it never entered my mind that he would be taken from us - at this time he was quite well + had full charge of the Parish school, till the first day of Jany he felt himself not well weighty but no pain, thought it was only a cold. But on the 8th had to take'n his Bed. But till the 14 we expected their was nothing serious. But myself saw then plainly that he would not get ---- (?) the rest had hopes to the last. It is trying trying - his complaint would be about the heart - he had no pain + not so much as a movement in his breath. I went with his remains to Dirlot which no doubt was a foolish plan but by the manner + the attachment of his Grandfather to him, and also that I Knew if he had outlived me that he would make the attempt we left here at 9 oclock on Tuesday morning the 26th reached Reay at 3 oclock next morning and left at 8 oclock - was joined by people all the way - there would be close to 20 Gigs and often 30 riders by the time we reached the Bridge of Dale - then we were met by a -------(?) of people who took it on their shoulder till they reached Dirlot and for a wonder himself will be the only one of my family whose remains will go there. It is sad sad and mournfull for me. It is impossible for you to form an Idea of my feelings. if the almighty will be pleased to keep me in my senses It will be a good thing for my poor family - as they have now to look to now but myself and am getting well advanced in years + not very strong - you will say which is very true that my troubles not more than your own was - But only you had the youth and was restored to good health - should I have 50 sons at most be a chance in 200 if 1 any of them would have all his good qualities. He would not taste spirits would not go in to any other house would not say or hear a bad word was not a Sabath absent from Church for years - I would travel far + near before I would get a poor Lad of his standing + age that was respected so much with all classes + getting more so every day. for the last 12 month was received + kept for nights in all the best houses far + near in this side of the County He had a fine appearance warm + homely in his ways - I thought when I got myself situated in a way that I could live very comfortable and independent + nothing to do and my family within the reach of good schools that was all right. But see where I am now - the same as if I never had any and far worse - in your letter you spoke that his views were too high for Australia. he never told me what they were as I was against him speaking about it Knowing that he was not yet to work - what led him to think of it was from the tone of your own letters, seeing that you was proposing to advance so much to other of his friends to bring them there. But once he got your letter he never mentioned about Australia But applied to Mr Tach (?) for a situation the Duke is above asking anything from government But Mr Tach (?) + the County Member one Dundas applied to the government in ------(?) which I knew Mr Tach (?) would do willingly and by their letters I could see they found it very difficult to get the appointment. But on the day week before he died a letter came telling that the Treasury had accepted his name on their list and that he might look for his appointment in a month or two at the farthest to be a Clerk in the Customs £70 for the first year + a rise of £10 every year he would be in the service ----- (?) ------- (?) -- (?) 50 years in it and after the first ten years he could compete for any of the highest Branches in the service. I only waited one night down in Newton mother is looking as well + living like as she did 4 years ago - suppose I was a night their then + ma did not speak being both so much overcome It was this day two week that I came home was not out of Bed since till this day that I

[730] Donald Gunn (1116)

have tried to write you I may say that I have none now to write to but yourself - I think I could remain in Bed all my lifetime now. But reason tells me that will not do that I must join the world and has more need than ever before. For the last year whenever I would see his back I would bring my father in mind I must conclude trusting + wishing that you may never feel as I do and ever will do more

With kind regards to wife +
family Brother + Sister
John Gunn

Mr Dond. Gunn
Blenhaer Farm
Victoria

John Gunn's grave at Balnakeil, near Durness. His family is also buried there.

Inverness Feby 12 1864

Dear Donald

your letter of the 25th Novr came to hand on the 2t of Jany at 6 oclock P. M. and on the very minute it came in, my Dear Donald had breathed his last — yourself can imagine our feelings as it is beyond describing — my case is a sad one now left with four helpless Ladies & a little Boy four year old I was afraid of his health for the last three years he was growing so fast and had not the strong appearance that he had a Boy — But for the last 12 month he was not a day confined and suppose I was afraid of him it never entered my mind that he would be taken from us — at this time he was quite well & had full charge of the Parish school, till the first day of Jany he felt himself not well slightly but no pain, thought it was only a a cold - But on the 8th I had to take his Bed - But till the 14 we expected there was nothing serious - But myself saw then plainly that he would not get round the rest had hopes to the last - It is trying trying - his complaint would be about the heart - he had no pain & not so much as a movement in his breath - I went with his remains to Duthil which no doubt was a foolish plan - but by the name & the attachment of his Grandfather to him, and also that I knew if he had outlived me that he would make the attempt we left here at 9 o'clock on Tuesday morning the 26th reached P[illegible] at 3 o'clock next morning and left at 8 o'clock - was joined by people all the way - there would be close on 20 gigs and often 30 riders by the time we reached the Bridge of Dol - there we were met by a large lot of people - who took it on their shoulders till they reached Duthil, and for a wonder himself will be the only one of my family whose remains will go there - It is sad sad and mournful for me - It is impossible for you to form an Idea of my feelings - if the almighty will be pleased to keep me in my senses it will be a good thing for my poor family - as they have none to look to now but myself and am getting well advanced in years & not very strong - you will say which is very true that my troubles not more than your own was - But only you

you had the youth and was restored to good
health — should I have 60 sons it ~~would~~ be chosen
in 200 if I any of them would have all his good qual
:ities — He would not taste spirits would not go in
to any other house — would not say or hear a bad
word was not a sabath absent from Church
for years — I would travel far & near before I
would get a poor Lad of his standing & age
that was ~~of~~ respected so much with all class
& getting more so every day — for the last 12 month
was received & kept for nights in all the best
houses far & near in this side of the County
he had a fine appearance warm & homely in
his ways — I thought when I got myself
~~myself situated~~ in a
situated ~~when I get~~ comfortable and
way that I could live very
independent & nothing to do and my family
within the reach of good schools that
was all right — But see where I am
now — the same as if I never had any and
far worse — In your letter you spoke that his
views were too high for Australia — he never
told me what they were as I was against
him speaking about it knowing that he
was not fit to work — what led him
to think of it was from the tone of your
own letters, seeing that you was proposing
to advance so much to others of his friends
to bring them there — But once he got your
letter he never mentioned about Australia
But applied to Mr. Foot for a situation

the Deathe is above asking any thing from gover
-ment - But Mr Doak & the County member
one Dundas applied to the government in earnest
which I knew Mr Doak would do willingly by
and by their letters I could see they found it
very difficult to get the appointment But
on the day week before he died a letter
came telling that the Treasury had accept
-ed his name on their list and that he
might look for his appointment in a month
or two at the farthest - to be a Clerk in the
Customs £70 for the first year & a rise of £10
every year he would be in the service & should
he be 50 years in it and after the first ten
years he could compete for any of the highest
Branches in the service - I only waited one
night down in Newton mother is looking as well
& living like as she did 4 years ago - suppose I
was a night there She & me did not speak being
both so much overcome It was this day two week
that I came home was not out of Bed since till
this day that I have tried to write you I may
say that I have none news to write to but
yourself - I think I could remain in Bed all
my life time more - But reason tells me that
will not do that I must face the world and
has more need than ever before - For the last
year whenever I would see his back I want
keep my father in mind I must conclude trusting
& wishing that you may never feel as I do and
never will do more - With kind regards to Wife &
Family Brother & sister

Mr Donald Gunn
Blenheim Farm
Victoria

[illegible]

What may have been a continuation of the letter (same paper, written in response to Donald, not addressed and only initials at the end) follows and provides an interesting insight on the family—

In your letter you mention that Janet left the County penyless which was a great shame after all the money you sent her, so it was if such was the case which I cannot see though, no doubt money found is very easy parted with by some, But I never thought that she was one of those that would part with it in that way - during my fathers lfetime I never knew or inquired what she got I took it for granted that she lived their as one of the family and during the time she was with mother it was proposed that she would get regular wages which would be the legal way in a general concern. I may mention that when my father died his effects had got into a very small compass his money all spent except the £100 that Forss had which he made over to me + Alexr.[731] two years before his death along with the watch as either of us never got a shilling out of the house He wished to make more over to us - which both of us objected. the Farm stock had fallen off in quanity + quality to the one half of which you saw it - and to give you an idea of it their was 8 stuks (?) at the sale and I would far rather that day that they had cut there thirots before the sale than strangers to see them - I have not seen the like of them except with the Sinclairs that was in Framside which you will mind the Horses was worth nothing old + useless except one mare - I mention this things to show you how fast things will go to wreck when there is no proper man to manage were it not for the crop fallow break + clover it was very little money the stock did considering what you and me saw it at one time - By Law my mother was only entitled to one third of effects which would not support her many years - therefore Alexr. proposed that the whole of the money would be lodged together and her to get her living out of the face (?) of it and after her day if there was a balance let it be equally divided. To these proposals I readily agreed + took it for granted that there was none of her family but would do the same and am sure you on the first. Knowing how industrious she was - it would be very ungratefull + low of us if we would act otherways - The two years she was in the room at Brawlbin her expenses came to about £30 a year but in Newton I expect it will not come to the half of that thanks to Peggy + John McKay? for that as their is not a more kinder pair in the County and if they had a paying Farm am sure it would be very little they would allow her to spend - I was much for mother leaving Brawlbin + Forss is still displeased but it is better that I can see that she did leave as she would have soon go through her means however saving she might be, + besides she gets her health far better in Newton.

There was some difference or coolness between Alexr. + Janet but how it was is more than I can tell neither did I wish to know and should you or me know it It would be our wisdom to overlook it as we must take it for granted that always in cases of this kind that there will be faults on both sides - therefore the less we hear or know of it the better - you may hear her side from herself and even then it is your wisdom to take no notice of it as the less we inquire into matters of this kind the better, Alexr. has his faults and who is without them. But there is one thing to be said about him which is a credit to himself + friends that his Policy in all things is truth + honesty towards all men there is not another of his standing in the County that is respected more than him for his principles - in fact were it not his truth + honesty he would not get through as he is doing - they are his principall support - It is very easy for a person when he is Known to be independent to get friends that will crow very Kindly to him + ready to assist him But as the word says a friend in need is the friend indeed and it would be natural that Alexr. would have more concern for her welfare than others and also natural that she would overlook his faults In Feby last year Janet wrote me that she was to leave for Australia in a few weeks - I wrote her back that I approved very much of her going But that I thought that she should wait till the first of sumer - she wrote me back that she could not therefore I went down about the middle of march + rough weather it was.

[731] Alexander Gunn (572) 1814-1900, being another of Donald's uncles.

But my reaching Brawlbin where I expected to spend the night - I found the door closed + was told that they left that day Bag + Baggage for Newton which effected me very much and I found Alexdr. not less affected and holding out that he was not aware of their removing that till after they left which did not look very well whether it was him or her that had the blame I cannot tell. But as I have said already likely that their would be blame on both sides. And on my going to Newton next day - I must say that I spoke rather angry to Janet for the way they acted and also puting John McKay to much trouble in getting a house for them not having a warning till a day or two before their coming - If they had waited till the first of sumer it have been more suitable. I must say that Alexdr. is uncommonolly Kind towards his mother which herself always tells. To show you how little some will do unless they can see that they are to be repaid when your father died my father spoke to Dond. Boulchork (?) + George Bralead as they were both then in a good way with their families whole + laying by a little money - that they would give a little help to defray the funeral expenses - not a shilling would either of them give. I never could look at that two men since but with hatered . And many was the pounds that your father helped them both and was the means of setting the whole of them on their feet

I am sorry that Hector Gunn is not more fortunate with you - I had always a good opinion of him for being a good Kind hearted fellow the best of the lot by far unless he changed. I have no doubt but you will be Kind to him as I think he would be the same to you if he had the means.

I have given you a long scrol here of things that is not worth reading. But when you read it Burn it dont show it to any other,

They have a large crop in Caithness this year but the price is only 17/ for oats it turns to very little money as the oats are very light. All those that has nothing to depend on but their corn (?) farms are in a miserable standing - there is plenty of farms open but not one offering for them. The Sinclairs are hanging (?) together as yet and I believe that is all. Their credit is gone they have a large crop this year but they have not a single sheep they have their turnips let - their is no rot among the sheep in Caithness this year but for the last two years it carried away the half of them. I have a score of wether 1 (7?) bags myself of turnip and ---------?

This has been a very fine winter without any snow but plenty of frost - I must conclude and were it not yourself it is me that is not in the turn for writing being in such a confused state I suppose was the means of my writing this long scrol as am sure if I was away farming that I would never think of it .

Am I not to be pitied with my poor helpless family

J- G-

D.G.

Obviously this was written in a state of stress but one wonders the result on Donald. Here he is, as pointed out in the letter, a young man establishing himself and many members of his family in a new country yet the enormous pressures and expectations placed on him by the old world are large. The problems with his sister Janet, his Uncles John and Alexander and his grandmother are obvious—and all this to be dealt with from the other side of the world! His life was not an easy one…

In your letter you mention that I and left the County penniless which was a great shame after all the money you sent her, so it was if such was the case which I cannot see through, no doubt money found is very easy parted with by some, But I never thought that she was one of those that would part with it in that way — during my fathers life time I never knew or inquired what she got I took it for granted that she lived there as one of the family — and during the time she was with mother it was proposed that she would get regular wages which would be the legal way in a general concern — I may mention that when my father died his effects had got into a very small compass his money all spent except the £100 that Jess had which he made over to me & almost two years before his death along with the ward as either of us never got a shilling out of the house — he wished to make over to us — which both of us objected, the Farm stock had fallen off in quantity & quality to the one half of what you saw it — and to give you an idea of it there was 8 stirks at the sale and I would fain rather that day that they had cut their throats before the sale than strangers to see them — I have not seen the like of them except with the Sinclairs that was in Fromside which you will mind the horses was worth nothing old & useless except one mare — I mention these things to show you how fast things will go to wreck when there is no proper man to manage — were it not for the crop fallow break & clover it was very little money the stock did considering what you & me saw it at one time — By Law my mother was only entitled to one third of the effects — which would not support her many years — therefore Alex proposed that the whole of the money would be lodged together and her to get her living out of the face of it and after her day if there was a balance let it be equally divided

To these proposals I readily agreed & took it for granted that there was none of her family but would do the same and am sure you in the first knowing how industrious she was. It would be very ungrateful & low of us if we would act otherways - the two years she was in the room at Brouther her expenses came to about £20 a year but in Newton I expect it will not exceed the half of that - thanks to Peggy & John Orthy for that as there is not a more kinder pair in the County and if they had a paying Farm and were so it would be very little they would allow her to spend - I was vexed for mother leaving Brouther & Tras is still displeased but it is better. I can see that she did leave as she would have savings through her means however saving she might be, & besides she gets her health far better in Newton

There was some difference & coolness between Alex & Janet but how it was is more than I can tell neither did I wish to know and should you or me know it - It would be our wisdom to overlook it as we must take it for granted that always in cases of this kind that there will be faults on both sides - therefore the less we hear or know of it the better - you may hear her side from herself and even then it is your wisdom to take no notice of it, as the less we inquire into matters of this kind the better, Alex has his faults and who is without them But there is one thing to be said about him which is a credit to himself & friends that his Policy in all things is truth & honesty towards all men there is not another of his standing in the County that is so respected more than him for these principles - in fact were it not his truth & honesty he would not get through as he is doing - they are his principall support - It is very easy for a person when he is known to be independent to get friends that will crow very kindly to him & ready to assist him But as the word says the friend in need is the friend indeed - and it would be natural that Alex would have more concern for her welfare than others and also natural that she would overlook his faults

In Feby last year Janet wrote me that she was
to leave for Australia in a few weeks - I wrote
her back that I approved very much of her going
But that I thought she should wait till the
first of summer - she wrote me back that she
could not - therefore I went down about the
middle of march & rough weather it was - But
on reaching Broxburn where I expected to spend
the night - I found the door closed & was told
that they left that day Bag & Baggage which
too which effected me very much and I found
Alexr not less effected, and holding out that
he was not aware of their removing that till
after they left which did not look very well
whether it was him or her that had the blame
I cannot tell - But as I have said already likely
there would be blame on both sides - and on my
going to Newton next day - I must say that I spoke
rather angry to Janet for the way they had acted
and also putting John Milloy to much trouble in
seeking a house for them not having a warning
till a day or two before their coming - If they had
waited till the first of summer it have been
more suitable - I must say that Alexr is uncommonly kind towards his mother which himself
will always tell - To show you how little some will
do unless they can see that they are to be repaid
when your father died - my father spoke to Donald
Boulshalk & George Boulcod as they were both then
in a good way with their families whole & laying
by a little money - that they would give a little help
to defray the funeral expenses - not a shilling would
either of them give - I never could look at that
two men since but with hatred - and many was
the favours that your father helped them both and was
the means of setting the whole of them on their feet

I am sorry that Mister Green is not more fortunate
with you - I had always a good opinion of him
for being a good kind hearted fellow the best of
the lot by far unless he changed - I have no doubt
but you will be kind to him as I think he would
be the same to you if he had the means -

I have given you a long scroll here of things that
is not worth reading - But when you read it
Burn it dont show it to any other,

They have a large crop in Caithness this year but the
price is only 17/ for oats it leaves very little money as
the oats are very light - all those that has nothing to
depend on but their own farms are in a miserable
standing - There is plenty of farms open but not one
offering for them - The Sinclairs are hanging
together as yet and I believe that is all - their
credit is gone - they have a large crop this year but
they have not a single sheep - they have their Turnips
let - There is no rot among the sheep in Caithness
this year but for the last two years it carried away
the half of them - I have a score of wether hogs
myself at Turnips in Olgrinmore

This has been a very fine winter without any
snow but plenty of frost - I must conclude and
mind it not yourself it is ~~not~~ me that is
not in the humor for writing being in such a
confused state I suppose was the means of my
writing this long scroll as [illegible] if I was in my
former way that I would never think of it.

Am I not to be pitied with my poor helpless family

Yours [illegible] —

D. G.

The next letter is from 'Dundee' and shows that Donald has suggested legal action against his Uncle Alexander (572) and John Mackay (880).

Dundee Poorhouse
25th. April 1864

Mr D + Wm Gunn
My dear Friends

Being in a hurry at the time of the last mail I was not able to write you and I put it off till this mail in the hope that I would have abundance of time but alas; I have never much of it to spare in these times.

We received your letter of 25th. Jany we are glad to learn that you are all well and extremely glad to learn of Poor Jessie safe arrival; for this we desire to be thankfull to the giver of all good. We have had many an uneasy hour thinking of her since she left so you may easily imagine how happy we are to hear of her landing safely in the bosom of her family, where I have no doubt she will be treated with much kindness. She says herself in her letter that she could not express how kind Mrs. Gunn was to her as well as the whole of you this is no more than we could express of Mrs. Gunn

In your note you said you were to threaten John + Alexr.[732] with prosecution for the manner in which they have treated Jessie I am no ways surprised at that. It is right that you should demand astatement of the affairs which is clearly not in a satisfactory state nor easy for them to give - I beleive the money of the sale is in Alexander's hands but what right has he to it more than the rest of the family - However if he had treated her as he ought I would be the last in the world to dispute with him on this point - But you know I have often prayed ---(?) -- (?) --------(?) your sister at home as long as the old man was living. And she has done well there and has treated her Grandfather better than any of them could have done And I naturally expected that they would not have forgot that to her, but that was not the case. It is not only that they sent her away empty handed which they have no right to do, but Alexr. was <u>kind</u> enough to send his <u>venom</u> here after her because he was fool enough to think that we were to be led by him. Tho they had not given her any thing in the shape of money they might have given her their blessing and parted with her in kindness.

But with all this farther than calling them to give account of their stewardship I would not do any thing in this matter. You will do very well without it And I believe they will need it all. I do not believe much in heirship myself - When I left Caithness myself I had only £3 in my pocket I had just what paid my first weeks lodging in London after arriving ----(?) ------(?) of --- (?) I left plenty behind - but where is it to day. I am sure I am better of than than those that got the whole of it. Ill <u>gotten geans</u> will never thrive, just lit it go Alexr. will need it all, and my wife all of us do without it. It is Gods blessing that alone maketh rich.

In regard of my account which you wished to get do not trouble yourself about it. I never kept an account of it nor did I ever intend to charge you. If you now not this , unable to look to her. She and have been as ----(?) with us as any of our own children, indeed I believe we could have made little difference on her and I have no doubt but you both will be kind to my child if any of them will ever come your way which is hard to say in the mean time we shall say no more about the account but let me beg you will not consider yourselves in the least indebted to me . All that we have done for her we have done for her own sake and would do more for her if it was necessary. Our Love to Mrs Gunn and Mrs Miller not forgetting your goodselves. Write as often as you can

I am
My Dear Friend
Yours truly
DGunn

to Messrs D + W Gunn / Blenheim, Cardigan Melbourne

---

[732] Capt. Alexander Gunn is normally highly respected; this is an unsual suggestion that he had another side to him.

Oneida Poorhouse
28th April 1864

Mr. D & Wm Guinn

My dear Friends

Being in a hurry at the time of the last mail I was not able to write you and I put it off till this mail in the hope that I would have abundance of time but alas! I have never much of it to spare in these times.

We received your letter of 25th Jany and we are glad to learn that you are all well. And extremely glad to learn of Poor Sophy's safe arrival; for this we desire to be thankful to the giver of all good. We have had many an uneasy hour thinking of her since she left so you may easily imagine how happy we are to hear of her landing safely in the bosom of her family, where I have no doubt she will be treated with much kindness. She says herself

in her letter that she could not
express how kind Mrs. Gunn was to her, as
well as the whole of you this is no more
than we could expect of Mrs. Gunn,

In your note you said you was
to threaten John & Alexr. with prosecution
for the manner in which they had treated Sophia
I am no ways surprised at that. It is right
that you should demand a statement of the affair
which is clearly not in a satisfactory state nor easy
for them to give — I believe the money of the sale is
is in Alexander's hands — but what right has
he to it more than the rest of the family —
However if he had treated her as he ought
I would be the last in this world to dispute
with him on this point — But you know
I have often prayed of you to leave your
sister at home as long as the old man
was living. And she has done well
there and has treated her grandfather
better than any of them could have done
And I naturally expected that they would
not have forgot that to her, but

go Alone: will need it all, and may with
all of us do without it. It is God's blessing that alone maketh rich.

In regard of my account which
you wished to get, do not trouble yourself
about it. I never kept an account of it
nor did I ever intend to charge you. If you
were not there, or able to look to her, she would
have been as welcome with us as any of our
own children, indeed I believe we could have
made little difference on her and I have
no doubt but you both will be kind
to my child if any of them will ever
come your way which is hard to say.
In the mean time we shall say no more
about the account but let me beg
you will not consider yourselves in the
least indebted to me, all that we have done
for her we have done for her own sake
and would do more for her if it was
necessary. Our love to Mrs [illegible]
and Mrs [illegible] not forgetting yourselves
write as often as you can

I am
My Dear Friend
Yours truly
[illegible]

to Messrs D & W Gunn
[illegible] [illegible] [illegible]

At which point Durness, Dundee, Alexander and the rest of the world disappears from the written records—what is left is now Australian. Obviously this is a messy way to end a family history. It is hard to know the truth of the matter but it reveals interesting lights about many characters and it is central to this story.

*****

There is one more note written in 1864—an odd one but it shows a different side to life;

Melbourne 15th June, 64

My Dear Sir,

I think when coming away Mr Gunn said he would be from home this week, and desired me to send an outline of the bill for the first Lecture to you. Herewith you will receive the same Make any alterations you may think proper.

McMeakin / Mr Muckin (?) is well and leaves us on Friday for Ballarat. Remind him of the Lecture on Sabbath that he may intimate the same

With kind regards to Mrs ? +yourself Remain---? in ---?

Archd. Crawford

Now, Archibald Crawford was the Presbyterian Minister of the time at Ballarat. And this may be he. But whose lectures; and are the prices the figures shown in the following second scan a large amount of money? To whom was the letter addressed? It's kept in the family papers so it may be to Donald, but that's guesswork….

Melbourne, 15th June, 64.
My Dear Sir,
I ~~think~~ when coming away Mr Gunn said he would be from home ~~this~~ week, and desired me to send an outline of the bill for the first Lecture to you. Herewith you will receive the same. Make any

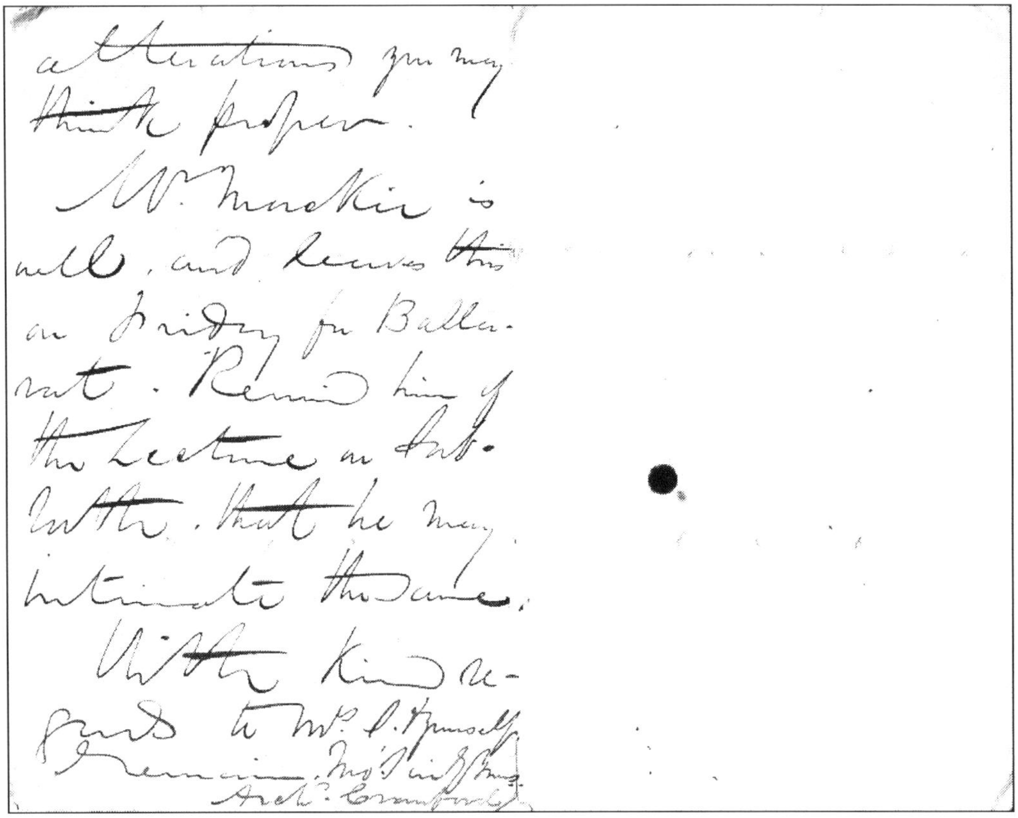
alterations you may
think proper.
Mr Mackie is
well, and leaves this
on Friday for Balla-
rat. Remind him of
the Lecture on Sab-
bath, that he may
intimate the same.
With kind re-
gards to Mrs C. & yourself
I remain, My dear Sir, Yours
Archd. Crawford

It provides a noticeable variation on the problems from Scotland.

*****

To a large extent though Donald's time was about to be taken up by other activites—he had brought his family in from Scotland but was now going to start a tradition in public life that his eldest son would follow. Donald is recorded as the rated owner of Burrumbeet from 1865 to 1886. He became a Councillor of the Shire of Ballarat (for the South Riding) on 30 August 1865 and continued sitting until 10 June, 1867. He rejoined the Council on the 15 August 1870 and continued until 12 October 1874, being President of the Shire from 11 November 1872 until 12 October 1874.

Donald was a busy man—one assumes his business was prospering. His family was growing, as although he married comparatively late, he had ten children between 1860 and 1880. These were, in order, John Alexander, William Watkins, Mary Jane, Donald, Marcus Daniel, Barbara, Norman, Hugh, Arthur Gilbert and Catherine Alexandrina. The first was born at Buninyong, the next two at Cardigan and the rest were born at Burrumbeet.

Jane Gunn (41)

Delightfully there is a letter written by Jane (41) (Donald's wife) late in her life in 1897 from Ballarat. It is to Alick (Alexander Donald Gunn, the elder son of John Alexander Gunn (32) and hence her eldest grandson.) He is four at the time and living in 'outback' New South Wales, at Ardlethan, near Wagga Wagga—

185 Lydiard St
1. 1. 97

My Dear Little Alick

I am writing you my first letter in the New Year I cannot tell you how pleased I was to get a letter from you and such a nicely written one I am so glad you are coming down to see me as you were quite a small boy when here last and cannot remember being down I suppose. I was wishing to see you all very much tell mamma she is very good to bring you. Norman said you had such hot weather it is quite cool here to day we are almost wanting a fire. Arthur is gone to Gippsland to see Uncle Will I don't know how he will get on as he has a lame leg. It is nearly well now though. His bicycle threw him he might bettter have ridden a horse. Wish them all a happy new year for me and with much love to my dear litlle boy

I am
Ever yr loving grandma
Jane Gunn

It is a delightful memory of a female who played a very important part in the history of our Australian Gunn family. It is interesting to note the address; they now live in central Ballarat city. (Barbara Gunn (106) was married from the address in 1899, so it obviously had some permanence.)

185 Lydiard St
1.1.97

My dear little Alick
I am writing you my first letter in the New Year I cannot tell you how pleased I was to get a letter from you and such a nicely written one I am so glad you are coming down to see me as you were quite a small boy when here last and cannot remember being down I suppose. I was wishing to see you all very much tell mamma she is very good to bring you. Norman said you had such hot weather it is quite cool here to day we are almost wanting a fire. Arthur is gone to Gippsland to see uncle Will I don't know how he will get on as he has a lame leg. It is nearly well now though. His bicycle threw him he might better have ridden a horse. Wish them all a happy New Year for me and with much love to my dear little boy

I am
Ever yr loving grandma
Jane Gunn

'Statement by Mr McKenzie[733] taken down verbatim by William W. (33) + Marcus D. Gunn (36)[734] sons of Donald Gunn late of Bralbin + Australia. June 20th 1928'

We are providing two versions here; one is from the original notes and one, slightly different, being a transcription by Barabara Gunn Padgett which may be based on a later, more fluent copy. Or she may have just embellished the originals.

1

These notes, written on paper from the Station Hotel, Wick in June 1928, were given to Sylvia Bairsto nee Padgett, daughter of Norman Gunn Padgett, by her aunt Barbara Gunn Padgett who, on 16 February 2011, passed them to Donald Gunn son of Malcolm Gunn, he being a male descendant of that family and currently writing about the family.

The following are transcriptions of the original hand written texts.

Pages 1 and 2 Statement by Mr McKenzie, taken down verbatim by William W and Mark D Gunn at Wick June 19th 1928.

Father
Donald Gunn, born at Bralbin lived there until he left for Australia
Grandfather *[Donald's father – DG]*
Alexander Gunn married wife Gunn, also lived at Bralbin.
G. Grandfather *[Barbara's grandfather, not Donald's – DG]*
Donald Gunn died at Bralbin.
This Donald Gunn came to Braehour from Strathmore under following circumstances. Lady Guthrie was raising men for service in Ireland putting down Irish Rebellion ?? at the time of a big war?? Although there were a large number of young men none would go unless Donald Gunn went. She came to Donald Gunn and asked him to go he asked her what he would get if he went. She promised anything he wanted he said if he got the lease of Braehour at a fixed rent he would go but it must be in writing. On these conditions he went to Ireland was there 7 years & got Braehour on his return. She never expected him to return & did not expect to have to keep her promise. When he came home he applied to her for the farm. She refused to give it. Before he left he gave her letters promising the farm & also his money to Henderson of "Hemmskel." *[name hard to read]*. When refused the farm he went to Henderson who was a banker & Sheriff in Thurso. He told him (H) how it stood. Henderson told him to fetch him the letter. When he saw the letter he said "It is all right Donald, I will get you the farm", & he did so.
Donald Gunn stayed at Braehour a good many years then went to Brawlbin. When at Brawlbin he had to pay £50 a year to get a vote. Died at Brawlbin 94 years of age.
Mrs Surman nee Jessie Gunn Father's sister, lived with him there. He died before she left also William Father's brother. John went out first he came down to meet Father & Aunt Kate (Mrs James Miller) got sunstroke & was dead before they landed at Port Melbourne.
Donald Gunn (father) was at Brawlbin until they left Scotland. The old family burying ground was at Dirlot.

[733] The genealogy he offers is awkward and suffers from the blurring of Alexander Gunn's tree with Barbara Gunn's tree. The only real option for this Mr McKenzie is that he is George McKenzie (3435), see page 384.

[734] William Watkins Gunn and Marcus Daniel Gunn visited Caithness as members of the 'Australian Scottish Delegation Tour of the Motherland 1928'. It had a major White Horse Distillers link. http://www.nla.gov.au/apps/doview/nla.aus-vn4903185-p provides a photographic record of the event.

P3. Genealogy given by McKenzie cousin *[82 y. o. George McKenzie, first cousin once removed to William & Marcus – DG]* to W.W. & M.D. Gunn, sons of Donald Gunn, June 19th 1928
Father
Donald Gunn born Brawlbin emigrated Australia, was at Burrumbeet. Died at Ballarat. Married Jane Surman.
Grandfather.
Alexander Gunn died Brawlbin married wife Gunn (Barbara).
Great Grandfather
Donald Gunn died at Brawlbin after leaving Braehour. *[Barbara's line – DG]*
Great Great Grandfather
John Gunn of Strathmore. *[Barbara's line – DG]*
Great Great Great Grandfather
Alexander Gunn of Strathmore *[Barbara's line – DG]*
Cousins
J D Nicholson, Minister at Strathpepper.
Alexander Gunn, Cape Wrath Land Steward Durness.
John & Alexander Miller of Wick, McKenzie, Wick
Sir John Gunn, Cardiff, brother Hector Gunn and cousin of Donald Gunn father as above.
Sir Oliver Lodge also related, probably through Cardiff Gunns.

P4. Transcription on tombstone – family burying ground Dirlot, copied June 20th/1928 – Erected By
Donald Gunn in memory of his father John Gunn ?? who departed this life 9th March 1852 aged 80 years & his mother elizabeth Gunn ?? who departed this life 4th March 1850 aged 82 years & also his some John who departed this life 4th April 1847 aged 8 years & of his daughter Isabella who departed this life 29th March 11865 aged 390 years.
Donald Gunn Halsary died 1st April 1885 aged 85 years.

In addition to this stone there are several partially undecipherable two: bearing the letter DG & several with the name Gunn but not decipherable. *[this text has all been crossed through – DG]*

This inscription was taken from the 2nd burying ground also called (Dirlot). This may refer to the John Gunn son of Alexander who is buried in the proper family burying ground (Dirlot) 1½ miles past Westerdale visited by us June 21st/28.

P5. Dirlot Cemetery from Wick Caithness go 1 ½ miles past Westerdale first track on left.
Copy on stone
Here lies the corpse of Alexander Gunn sometime tenant in Dalnaglaton who died on 22 June 176(2)5 aged 77 years & Janet McKloud his spouse & the burial place of George, John & Aneas his children.
Note
W.W Gunn & M. D. Gunn visited this cemetery June 21st 1928.

Approaching Dirlot Cemetery, 2011

Dirlot Cemetery, 2011

Dirlot Cemetery, 2011

Looking back at Dirlot Cemetery, 2011

Donald Gunn father of above born at Bralbin lived there until he left for Australia was at Buninyong Cardigan Burrumbeet Breadalbane + Ballarat died at Ballarat. Alexander Gunn (Grandfather) also lived at Bralbin. G.Grandfather Donald Gunn died at Bralbin This Donald Gunn came to Braehour under the following circumstances. Lady Guthrie was raising men for sevice in Ireland putting down an Irish rebellion at the time of a big war!! Although there were a large number of young men in the district none of them would go unless Donald Gunn went. She came to Donald Gunn + asked him to go. he asked her what he would get if he went + she promised anything he wanted He said if he got the lease of Braehour [735]at a fixed rent he would go but it must be writing. On these conditions he went to Ireland was away 7 years + got Braehour on his return. She never expected him to return + did not expect to have to keep her promise When he came home he applied to her for the farm + she refused to give it it Before he left he gave her letter promising the farm + also the his money to Henderson of Stemmskel (?) When refused the farm he went to Henderson who was a banker + sherriff in Thurso told him how it stood + Henderson after seeing the papers said "It's alright Donald" + got him the farm. Donald Gunn stayed at Braehour a number of years then went to Bralbin He had to pay £50 a year to get a vote died at Bralbin aged 94 years. Mrs Surman (nee Janet Gunn) fathers sister lived with him there after her father died he died (Grandfather) before she left Scotland also her brother William. John another brother went out first he came out to meet father + Aunt Kate got sunstroke + was dead before they landed at Port Melbourne. Father (Donald Gunn) was at Bralbin until they left Scotland. The old family burying ground was at Dirlot Marcus + I saw and photographed one on June 20th but it was wrong and photographed another on 21st June

Genealogy given by Mr McKenzie cousin to W.W + M.D. Gunn sons of Donald Gunn June 19th 1928 Donald Gunn born Bralbin emigrated to Australia lived at Burrumbeet he died at Ballarat married Jane Surman. Alexander Gunn (Grandfather) died at Bralbin married Barbara Gunn. Donald Gunn great grandfather died at Bralbin after leaving Braehour. John Gunn of Strathmore (great great grandfather)
Cousins : - J.D.Nicholson Minister Strathpepper Alexander Gunn Cape Wrath Land Steward Durness John + Alexander Miller + George McKenzie East Banks Wick Alexander Miller Grain Merchant Willow Bank Wick Sir John Gunn Cardiff brother Hector Gunn + cousin of Donald Gunn (father)
Sir Oliver Lodge's son married Sir John Gunn's daughter Inscription on Tombstone Drilot near Strathmore Lodge visited by W.W. + M.D. Gunn June 20th 1928 The proper burying ground was Drilot visited 1 1/2 miles past Westerdale first track to the left by us in company of Mr A. Miller June 21 1928 Erected by Donald Gunn in memory of his father John Gunn who departed this life 9th March 1852 aged 80 years + his mother Elizabeth Gunn who departed this life 4th March 1850 aged 82 years aslo his son John who departed this life 4th April 1847 aged 8 years + his daughter Isabella who departed this life March 29th 1865 aged 30 years Donald Gunn Halsay died 1st April 1885 aged 85 years two other stones bearing D.G. + several with name Gunn were undecipherable

[735]See Mark Rugg Gunn's *History of the Clan Gunn*, p.206.

Dirlot Cemetery From Wick Caithness Scotland go 1 ½ mls past Westerdale first track to left

Copy of the words on the stone

Here lies the corpses of Alexander Gunn sometime tenant of Dalniglaton who died 21st June 1765 aged 77 years + Janet McKloud his spouse + the burial place of George John + Aneas Gunn his children (note) John was probably buried at cemetery near Strathmore house 4 mls futher on

D.G.

This stone was bought here by Donald Gunn of Cairnmuck who was in his Majesty's service to the memory of Donald Gunn his father Jan 9th 1726 + first wife not decipherable + afterwards espoused to Christina Mclara.

William Gunn (Waranga Park) was cousin to my great (Grandmother?) He was Messenger at Arms at Wick Two young men comitted a crime + a tinker named Cluny(?) was had up for stealing . William Gunn was taking the 3 of them to Inverness stopped the other side of Helmsdale for night at inn putting the two prisoners + the tinker in an upstairs room while he + some more were drinking downstairs The tinker told the other two if they wanted to go he would take the handcuffs off as he was too old to go himself so he took their handcuffs off They opened the window jumped out + got away William Gunn was held responsible + had to resign. then went to Australia where he stayed with a man named Mackay who left him the place when he died.

From family papers held at one time by Barbara Gunn Padgett (Austin) (184)

We suspect the last paragraph is an addition by Barbara Gunn Padgett, added when transcribing the original notes. It was attached with a family tree which follows with further additions, probably by the below Barbara. It is assumed that this is a copy written by her as other documents in her handwriting are held. The original document's whereabouts is not known. The document provides some tantalizing scraps of history; some of which may, of course, be mythology. We have not, in this case, provided scans of the original as it is but a modern transcript. However we do show the tree, for bits of it are of interest although much is confused.

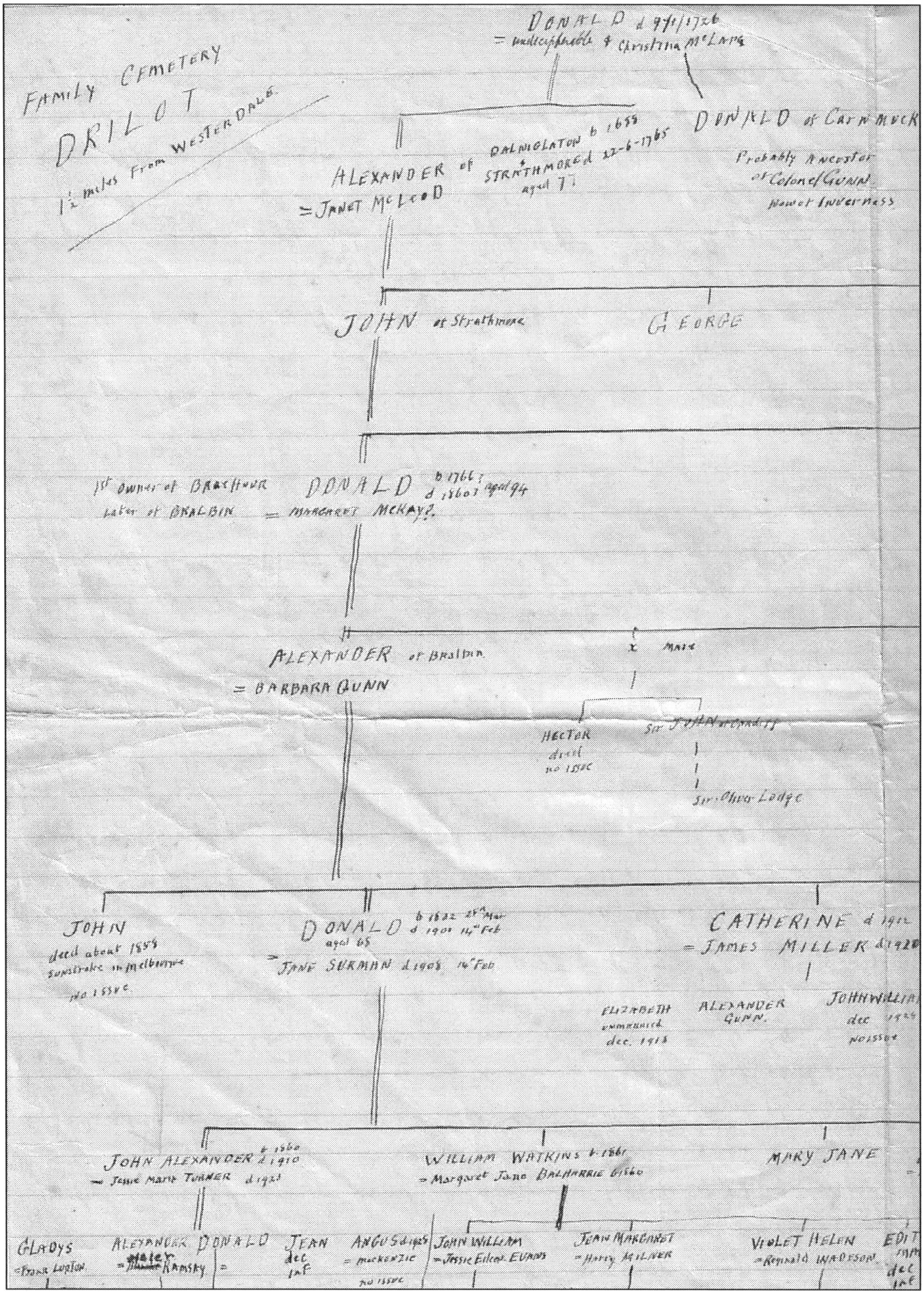
FAMILY CEMETERY
DRILOT
1½ miles from WESTERDALE
DONALD d 9/1/1726
= undecipherable & Christina McLane
ALEXANDER of DALNIGLATON b 1655
STRATHMORE d 22-6-1765
aged 77
= JANET McLEOD
DONALD of CARNMUCK
Probably Ancestor of Colonel GUNN now of Inverness
JOHN of Strathmore
GEORGE
1st owner of BRACHOUR
later of BRALBIN
DONALD b 1766
d 1860 aged 94
= MARGARET MCKAY?
ALEXANDER of Bralbin
= BARBARA GUNN
x
HECTOR
died
no issue
Sir JOHN
Sir Oliver Lodge
JOHN
died about 1858
sunstroke in Melbourne
no issue
DONALD b 1822 25th Mar
d 1901 14th Feb
aged 65
= JANE SURMAN d 1908 14th Feb
CATHERINE d 1912
= JAMES MILLER
ELIZABETH
unmarried
dec. 1918
ALEXANDER GUNN
JOHN WILLIAM
dec
no issue
JOHN ALEXANDER b 1860
d 1910
= Jessie Marie TURNER d 1923
WILLIAM WATKINS b 1861
= Margaret Jane BALHARRIE b 1860
MARY JANE
GLADYS
= Frank Lupton
ALEXANDER
DONALD
JEAN
dec
inf
ANGUS
= mckenzie
no issue
JOHN WILLIAM
= Jessie Eileen EVANS
JEAN MARGARET
= Harry MILNER
VIOLET HELEN
= Reginald WADESON
EDIT
dec
inf

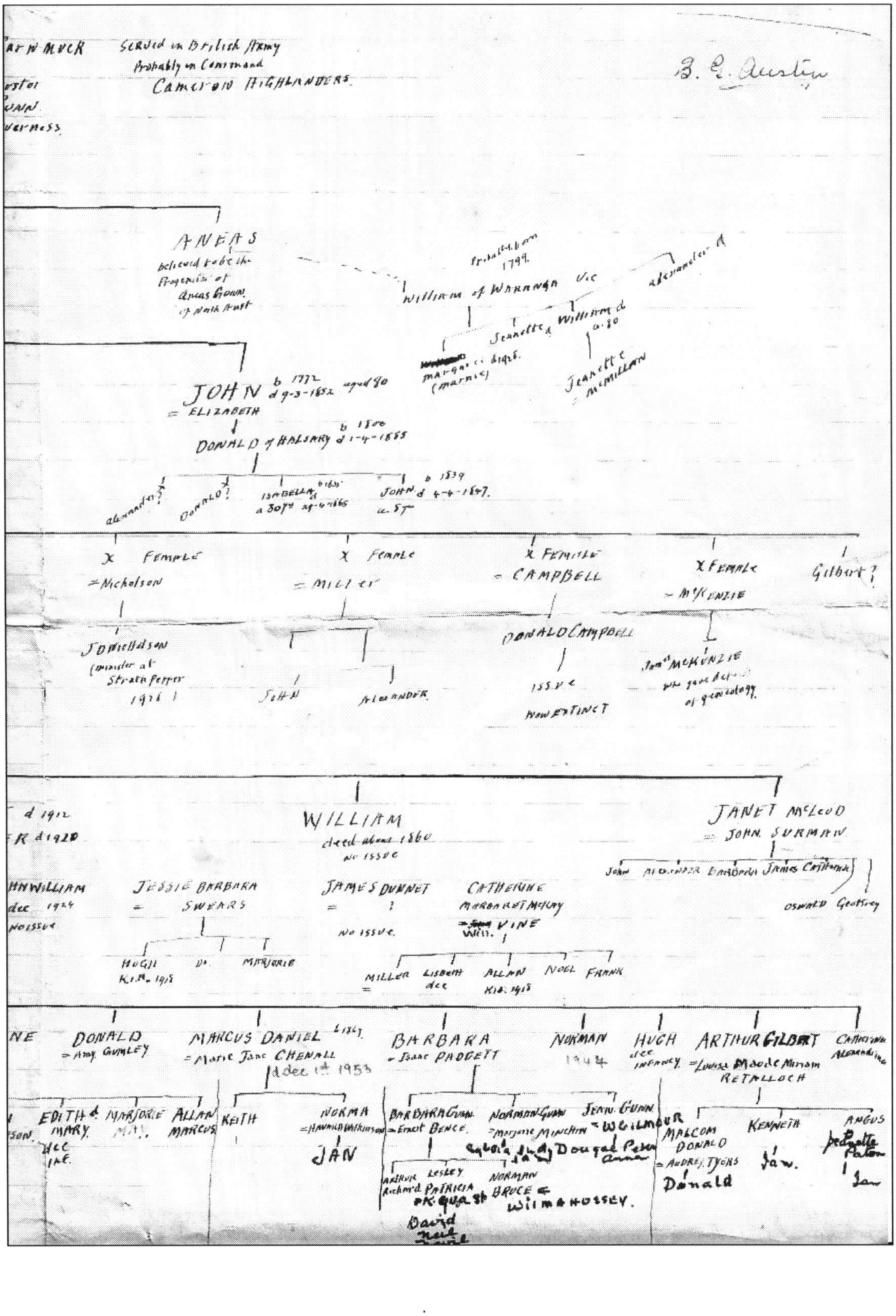
Served in British Army
Probably in Command
Cameron Highlanders
B. C. Austin
ANEAS
believed to be the Progenitor of Aneas Gunn of North Aust
William of Warnnga Vic
JOHN b 1772 d 9-3-1852 aged 80
= ELIZABETH
DONALD of HALSARY b 1800 d 1-4-1865
X FEMALE = Nicholson
X FEMALE = MILLER
X FEMALE = CAMPBELL
X FEMALE = McKENZIE
Gilbert ?
DONALD CAMPBELL
ISSUE
NOW EXTINCT
JOHN
ALEXANDER
WILLIAM
JANET McLEOD
= JOHN SURMAN
JESSIE BARBARA = SWEARS
JAMES DUNNET
NO ISSUE
CATHERINE
HUGH K.I.A. 1915
MARJORIE
MILLER
ALLAN
NOEL
FRANK
OSWALD
DONALD = Amy GUMLEY
MARCUS DANIEL = Marie Jane CHENALL
BARBARA = Isaac PADGETT
NORMAN
HUGH
ARTHUR GILBERT
= Louisa Maude Miriam RETALLOCH
EDITH MARY
MARJORIE
ALLAN MARCUS
KEITH
NORMA
JAN
BARBARA GUNN = Ernest BENCE
NORMAN GUNN
JEAN GUNN
= W. GILMOUR
MALCOM DONALD
= AUDREY TYCHS
Donald
KENNETH
ANGUS
David

Part 4—John Gunn in Dalnaha, Strathmore & Braehour (707); a genetic descendant chart

This line has clear links to the Chief line of the Clan Gunn and via it to other family trees in Scotland and Europe. However these links are, overall, beyond the scope of this book.

Braehour farmhouse

(The year is given on the back. The identification of 'Braehour Wick Scotland 7000 acres owned by James Miller' is in Barbara Gunn Padgett's handwriting and it would make sense if she was given a copy of such a photo when transcribing the previous documents. It is certainly probable this photo was taken on William Watkins and Marcus Daniel Gunn's trip in 1928. It may be a 1956 reprint.)

Braehour farmhouse, 2011

Probably the most important person here is Barbara Gunn. The critical point is her position as eldest daughter of Donald Gunn (Sennachie 1770-1861) and Catherine Gunn (1781-1870) who were married in 1807. Donald had a brother John (1772-1862) who went to Canada and is already mentioned and another brother William whose son Donald went to Canada. Donald the Sennachie's father was John in Dalna / Dalnaha, Strathmore and Braehour (d.1810 who married Marjory ('May') Dunbar of Hempriggs in 1745). His father was Alexander of Dalnaglaton and Strathmore d. 1765 who married Janet McLeod. Alexander's father was John Gunn of Knockfinn. John Gunn's father was George of Achintoul. George's father was John Gunn b.1601 and his second wife Catherine Sinclair (m. 1641); this John Gunn was the 5th Mackeamish of Kilearnan and Navidale. John Gunn's father was the 4th Mackeamish, Alexander, son of William Gunn, the 3rd Mackeamish. John had a brother George (Borobol) who was the ancestor of the Georgeson sept. Alexander Gunn's father was William Gun[736]. (William 'mor'; big.) He was the son of Alexander Gun (Kilearnan), the 2nd Mackeamish and Barbara Mackay. Alexander Gun's father was William mac Sheumais mhic Crunar of Kilearnan Gun. His father was James Sheumis mac Crunar Gun d 1496. His father was James Gun. The father of James Gun was Thomas Gun. His father was Magnus ('George') Gun d. 1464, Crowner of Caithness[737]. See Appendices 4, 5 and 6.

*****

An envelope to Barbara's brother Alexander[738] (572) exists, sent from Melbourne. It is unclear who sent the message but it is possibly from John who died in 1856.

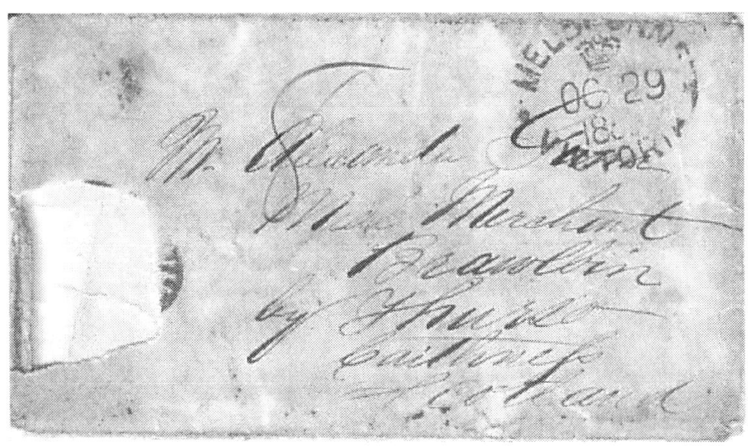

There are two poor red backmarks on the reverse, dated Febrary 1854—it is not clear where the marks were applied but they indicate a travel time of at least four months.

---

[736] It is suggested in an 1860s family tree held by one of the authors that from William Bheg comes a line leading to the Rev Peter Gunn of Melbourne and, more importantly perhaps, his son Aeneas. His 'Under a Regent Moon' exploring early attempts to live in the Kimberley region of WA is worthy of note. His wife, Mrs Aeneas Gunn, is the well-known author of 'We of the Never-Never' and 'The Little Black Princess'; the former of these books was also adapted into a film in 1982.

[737] Being based on *Burke's Peerage, Baronetage & Knightage, 107th edition Volume 2,* page 1705 ff. and http://thepeerage.com/p42862.htm\#i428614 provides further Gunn genealogy. Continual male line descendants from John in Dalna / Dalnaha, Strathmore and Braehour have a good claim to be Chief of the Clan Gunn.

[738] The 1851 census confirms that Alexander was a corn merchant—' Brawlbin, Reay, Caithness: Alexander Gunn corn merchant born Braehour age 36, Mary aka Margaret Campbell born Reay age 36, Williamina age 8, Barbara age 6, Peter age 4, Catherine age 2'. He is often referred to as 'Captain Alexander'.

Descendants of John Gunn in Dalnaha, Strathmore & Braehour (707)

John GUNN in Dalnaha, Strathmore & Braehour (707), b. 1722 Halkirk Parish, Caithness, d. 1810 Halkirk Parish, Caithness
+**Marjory DUNBAR of Rowens**[739] (706), b. circa 1728, m. 1745 Watten Parish, Caithness

- **Alexander GUNN** (3712), b. circa 1747 Caithness
- **Jean GUNN** (3690), b. say 1749 Caithness
  +**John MACGREGOR** (3691), m. 1769 Wick Parish, Caithness
  - **Marjory MACGREGOR** (3692), chr. 1770 Caithness
  - **Donald MACGREGOR** (3693), chr. 1774 Caithness
  - **Alexander MACGREGOR** (3694), chr. 1776 Caithness
  - **John MACGREGOR** (3695), chr. 1778 Caithness
- **Angus GUNN in Braehour** (3592), b. circa 1750
  +**Elizabeth MATHESON** (3702), m. 1782 Halkirk Parish, Caithness
  - **John GUNN** (3593), b. circa 1785
  - **Catherine GUNN** (3703), b. 1789 Latheron Parish, Caithness, d. 1872 Wick, Wick Parish, Caithness
    +**David NICHOLSON** (3704), b. circa 1796 Bower Parish, Orkney Islands, m. 1819 Sanday, Orkney Islands
  - **Margaret GUNN** (3705), b. 1790, d. 1861 Bardnaclaven, Thurso Parish, Caithness
    +**John HENDERSON** (3706), b. circa 1780 Halkirk Parish, Caithness, m. 1812 Halkirk Parish, Caithness
    - **John HENDERSON** (3707), b. circa 1815
  - **Jean GUNN** (3708), b. 1792 Halkirk Parish, Caithness, d. 1868 Rosskeen, Dalmore Parish, Ross & Cromarty
    +**William SUTHERLAND** (3709), m. 1814 Reay Parish, Caithness, d. before 1841
  - **William GUNN** (3710), b. circa 1801, d. 1870 Braehungie, Latheron Parish, Caithness
  - **Angus GUNN** (3711), b. 1805 Reay Parish, Caithness
- **George GUNN in Braehour** (879), b. circa 1757 Halkirk Parish, Caithness, d. 1842 Braehour, Halkirk Parish, Caithness
  +**Margaret GUNN** (3519), m. circa 1783
  - **William GUNN** (3512), b. before 1787
  - **Alexander GUNN of Dalnaha & Banniskirk** (3508), b. 1788 Halkirk Parish, Caithness, d. 1875 Thurso, Thurso Parish, Caithness
    +**Ann WATERS of Dalnaha** (3520), m. 1814 Halkirk Parish, Caithness, d. before 1888
    - **John GUNN** (3523), b. 1815 Halkirk Parish, Caithness, d. 1874 Cramond, Cramond Parish, Lothian
    - **George GUNN** (3524), b. 1818 Halkirk Parish, Caithness, d. 1881 Craigcrook, Cramond Parish, Edinburgh
      +**Margaret ABERDEEN** (3537), b. circa 1822 Edinburgh, Midlothian, m. 1853 Barony, Lanarkshire, d. 1895 Cramond Bridge, Dalmeny Parish, Linlithgow
      - **Marion Aberdeen GUNN** (3538), b. 1854 Barony, Lanarkshire, d. 1919 Cramond Parish, Lothian
      - **Ann Waters GUNN** (3539), b. 1856 Cramond, West Lothian
      - **Margaret Aberdeen GUNN** (3540), b. 1858 Cramond, West Lothian
      - **David Waters GUNN** (3541), b. 1860 Cramond, West Lothian
    - **Janet GUNN** (3525), b. circa 1821 Halkirk Parish, Caithness
      +**George MACKAY** (3542), b. circa 1815 Tongue, Sutherland, m. 1845 Halkirk Parish, Caithness
      - **John MACKAY** (3543), b. circa 1847 Tongue, Sutherland
      - **Ann MACKAY** (3544), b. circa 1848 Tongue, Sutherland
      - **Barbara MACKAY** (3545), b. 1849 Thurso Parish, Caithness
      - **Alexander MACKAY** (3546), b. 1851 Halkirk Parish, Caithness
      - **George MACKAY** (3547), b. 1855 Thurso Parish, Caithness

---

[739] From a November Gurney email 14.11.2009 we 'have come to a firm conclusion that Marjory (or the shorthand, May) is the right way to refer to your ancestor, Marjory (Dunbar) Gunn. She is Marjory in the Watten Parish Register (Marriage) and Marjory in another Watten document .... Thereafter she is referred to as May (sons Donald and John Death registrations). Alexander Gunn (Braehour) also has her recorded as May Dunbar on his Genealogical tree-"May, daughter of Alexander Dunbar of Rowens". Rowens is about 7 kilometres south of Loch Watten about 1 kilometre to the west of the very secondary road north from West Clyth. Camster Burn is known also as Rowens Burn, being part of the Wick river basin, which also includes Loch Hempriggs. She has been referred to in some old documents as 'of Hempriggs'. The Dunbar of Hempriggs family were very well known; see http://www.laird.org.uk/Caithness/Ackergill-Hempriggs.htm for details. Hempriggs means hemp ridge! But the Dunbars are well researched— http://www.fionamsinclair.co.uk/genealogy/Caithness/Hempriggs.htm --for example and she does not appear. Why? Illegitimate, perhaps? Too lowly a marriage? Both? Neither?

| | | ├── **Margaret MACKAY** (3550), b. 1857 Reay Parish, Caithness
| | | ├── **David James MACKAY** (3548), b. 1859 Thurso Parish, Caithness
| | | ├── **Charles Robert MACKAY** (3549), b. 1862 Thurso Parish, Caithness, d. 1864 Thurso Parish, Caithness
| | | └── **Charles Robert MACKAY** (3551), b. 1864 Thurso Parish, Caithness
| | ├── **James GUNN (Rev.)** (3687), b. 1822 Halkirk Parish, Caithness, d. 1858
| | ├── **Margaret GUNN** (3527), b. 1828 Caithness
| | ├── **Bell GUNN** (3529), b. circa 1830 Caithness
| | ├── **David Waters GUNN** (3530), b. 1832 Latheron Parish, Caithness, d. 1856 Cramond Parish, Edinburgh
| | └── **Agnes/Aneasina GUNN** (3528), b. 1833 Latheron Parish, Caithness, d. 1888 Lanarkshire
| | +**James MARSHALL** (3941), b. circa 1831, m. 1859, d. 1879
| | └── **Anna MARSHALL** (3948), b. 1860
| | +**Annie James PORTEOUS** (3521), b. circa 1819 Edinburgh, Midlothian, m. 1867 Thurso, Thurso Parish, Caithness
| ├── **Angus GUNN** (3509), b. 1790 Halkirk Parish, Caithness
| ├── **Marjory GUNN** (3510), b. 1798 Halkirk Parish, Caithness
| └── **John GUNN** (3511), b. 1803 Halkirk Parish, Caithness, d. 1855 Thurso Parish, Caithness
| +**Margaret MACKENZIE** (3522), b. circa 1811, m. 1832 Braehour, Halkirk Parish, Caithness
| ├── **Aeneas (Angus) GUNN** (3531), b. circa 1834 Halkirk Parish, Caithness
| ├── **Colin GUNN** (3532), b. 1835 Halkirk Parish, Caithness, d. 1851 Halkirk Parish, Caithness
| ├── **George GUNN** (3533), b. 1838 Halkirk Parish, Caithness, d. 1859 Brims, Thurso Parish, Caithness
| ├── **Margaret GUNN** (3534), b. 1838 Halkirk Parish, Caithness
| ├── **Barbara GUNN** (3535), b. circa 1840 Halkirk Parish, Caithness
| └── **John GUNN** (3536), b. circa 1844 Halkirk Parish, Caithness
├── **William GUNN in Braehour** (2500), b. 1750 Latheron Parish, Caithness, d. circa 1812 Caithness
| +**Janet SINCLAIR** (896), b. circa 1780 Halkirk Parish, Caithness, d. 1870 Braehour, Halkirk Parish, Caithness
| ├── **Donald GUNN (Hon.) of Manitoba** (372), b. 1797 Halkirk Parish, Caithness, d. 1878 St Andrew, Little Britain, Manitoba
| | +**Margaret SWAIN** (923), b. 1802 York Factory, Rupertsland, Manitoba, m. 1819, d. 1870 Little Britain, Manitoba
| | ├── **William Henry GUNN** (2547), b. 1820 York Factory, Rupertsland, Manitoba, d. 1842 Red River Settlement, Manitoba
| | | +**Isabella ROSS** (2548), b. 1820 Oregon Territory, m. 1841 Red River Settlement, Manitoba, d. 1865 St Johns, Red River Settlement, Manitoba
| | | └── **Henrietta GUNN** (2633), b. 1841, d. 1869 Pembina, North Dakota
| | ├── **James GUNN** (2549), b. 1824 St Andrews, Manitoba, d. 1905 St Andrews, Manitoba
| | | +**Mary DONALD** (2550), chr. 1825, m. circa 1862, d. 1890
| | | └── **Margaret Ann GUNN** (2635), b. 1864 Kildonan, Rupertsland, Manitoba
| | ├── **John GUNN (Hon.) of Manitoba** (2551), b. 1826 St Andrews, Manitoba, d. 1898 St Andrews, Manitoba
| | | +**Emma GARRIOCH** (2552), b. 1824 St Johns, Red River Settlement, Manitoba, m. 1855 Winnipeg, Manitoba, d. 1922 St Boniface, Manitoba
| | | ├── **Margaret Jane GUNN** (2574), b. 1855 Kildonan, Manitoba, d. 1927 Fairford, Manitoba
| | | ├── **William Reginald GUNN** (2626), b. 1857 Kildonan, Manitoba, d. 1910 Melfort, Saskatchewan
| | | ├── **Donald John GUNN** (2682), b. 1859 St Andrews, Manitoba, d. after 1901 Calgary, Alberta
| | | ├── **John James GUNN** (2628), b. 1861 Kildonan, Manitoba, d. 1907 Selkirk, Manitoba
| | | ├── **Emma Ann GUNN** (2629), b. 1862 St Andrews, Manitoba, d. 1950 Selkirk, Manitoba
| | | ├── **Mary GUNN** (2630), b. 1865 Selkirk, Manitoba, d. 1948 St Andrews, Manitoba
| | | ├── **Henry George GUNN (Rev.)** (2631), b. 1866 Selkirk, Manitoba, d. 1945 Lockport, Manitoba
| | | └── **Gilbert Garrioch GUNN** (2632), b. 1868 Kildonan, Manitoba, d. 1933 Selkirk, Manitoba
| | ├── **Alexander GUNN** (2531), b. 1829 St Andrews, Manitoba, d. 1902 Little Britain, Manitoba
| | | +**Angelique MACKENZIE** (2532), b. 1832, m. 1854 Kildonan, Rupertsland, Manitoba, d. 1905 Little Britain, Manitoba
| | | ├── **Benjamin McKenzie GUNN** (2602), b. 1855 St Andrews, Manitoba, d. 1930 St Andrews, Manitoba
| | | ├── **Eliza Margaret GUNN** (2604), b. 1857 St Andrews, Manitoba
| | | ├── **Lucy GUNN** (2605), b. 1858 St Andrews, Manitoba, d. 1878

Colin Roderick GUNN (2606), b. 1863 St Andrews, Manitoba
Alexander James GUNN (2607), b. 1865 St Andrews, Manitoba, d. 1865 St Andrews, Manitoba
Donald GUNN (2608), b. 1867 St Andrews, Manitoba, d. 1962
Alexander William Montgomery Muckle GUNN (2533), b. 1873 St Andrews, Manitoba, d. 1952 Selkirk, Manitoba
Matilda GUNN (2553), b. 1831 St Andrews, Manitoba
+**John ATKINSON** (2554), b. 1825, m. 1860 St Andrews, Manitoba
George GUNN (2555), b. 1833 St Andrews, Manitoba, d. 1901 Swift Current, Saskatchewan
+**Eliza WINECHILD** (3445), m. circa 1870 Red River Settlement, Manitoba
Donald Edward GUNN (2621), b. 1877 Mire Creek, North West Territory, d. 1954 Shaunavon, Saskatchewan
Eliza Margaret GUNN (2622), b. 1879 Dark Sand Hills, North West Territory, d. 1883 Red Deer River, North West Territory
Catherine Jane GUNN (2620), b. 1882 Parkberg, North West Territory, d. 1910
Nancy GUNN (2624), b. 1872 Fort Garry, Manitoba, d. 1959 Maple Creek, Saskatchewan
+**Eliza OTTERSKIN** (2556), m. after 1873 Fort Qu'appelle, Saskatchewan, d. 1917
Max GUNN (2623)
William James GUNN (2625), b. 1890 Maple Creek, Saskatchewan, d. 1989 Swift Current, Saskatchewan
Jane GUNN (2557), b. 1835 St Andrews, Manitoba, d. 1844 St Andrews, Manitoba
Margaret GUNN (2558), b. 1838 St Andrews, Manitoba, d. after 1881
+**William TAYLOR** (2559), m. 1856 Kildonan, Rupertsland, Manitoba
Elizabeth Mary TAYLOR (2603), b. 1857
Donald GUNN (2560), b. 1840 St Andrews, Manitoba, d. 1927 Devils Lake, Saskatchewan
+**Caroline BELLENDINE** (2561), b. 1846 Grand Rapids, Manitoba, m. 1867, d. 1878
Donald James GUNN (2610), b. 1868 St Andrews, Manitoba, d. 1917 Lintlaw, Saskatchewan
George GUNN (2687), b. 1870 St Andrews, Manitoba, d. 1943 Preeceville, Saskatchewan
Annabelle Ellen GUNN (2612), b. 1871 Little Britain, Manitoba, d. 1959 Preeceville, Manitoba
William Henry GUNN (2614), b. 1874 Little Britain, Manitoba, d. 1906 Canora Area, Saskatchewan
Margaret Francis GUNN (2615), b. 1876 Little Britain, Manitoba, d. 1964 Preeceville, Manitoba
Unnamed GUNN (2688), b. 1878 Little Britain, Manitoba, d. 1878 Little Britain, Manitoba
+**Sarah FIDLER** (2581), b. 1851 Rupertsland, Manitoba, m. 1881 St Pauls, Manitoba, d. 1897 Devils Lake, Saskatchewan
Unnamed GUNN (2689), b. 1882 Fort Qu'appelle, Saskatchewan, d. 1882 Fort Qu'appelle, Saskatchewan
John Alexander GUNN (2582), b. 1883 Fort Qu'appelle, Saskatchewan, d. 1947 Fort San, Saskatchewan
Amelia Mary GUNN (2586), b. 1885 Fort Qu'appelle, Saskatchewan
Robert GUNN (2562), b. 1842 St Andrews, Manitoba, d. 1843 St Andrews, Manitoba
Janet GUNN (2563), b. 1846 St Andrews, Manitoba, d. 1930 Muckle's Creek, Manitoba
+**Alexander Montgomery MUCKLE** (2564), b. 1844 Quebec City, Quebec, d. 1908 Clandeboye, Manitoba
Anna Hollins MUCKLE (3367)
Monty MUCKLE (3368)
Alexander Montgomery MUCKLE (3365)
Robert James Tennant MUCKLE (3003), b. 1875
Leticia Margaret MUCKLE (2609), b. 1877, d. 1914
William GUNN (2565), b. 1848 St Andrews, Manitoba, d. 1917 Shaunavon, Saskatchewan
+**Catherine Ann MOWAT** (2566), b. 1857 Kildonan, Manitoba, m. 1876 Little Britain, Manitoba, d. 1950 Shaunavon, Saskatchewan
Donald Edward GUNN (2616), b. 1877 St Andrews, Manitoba, d. 1954 Shaunavon, Saskatchewan
Mary Jane GUNN (2683), b. 1879 St Andrews, Manitoba, d. 1881 St Andrews, Manitoba
James GUNN (2684), b. 1881 St Andrews, Manitoba, d. 1882 St Andrews, Manitoba

Janet GUNN (2685), b. 1884 St Andrews, Manitoba, d. 1886 St Andrews, Manitoba
Isabella Catherine GUNN (2686), b. 1886 St Andrews, Manitoba, d. 1887 St Andrews, Manitoba
William GUNN (2619), b. 1888 St Andrews, Manitoba, d. 1969 Shaunavon, Saskatchewan
Alexander Montgomery GUNN (2617), b. 1891 Selkirk, Saskatchewan, d. 1959 Shaunavon, Saskatchewan
Victor John GUNN (2618), b. 1897 Gunview, Saskatchewan
John GUNN of Braehour & Ontario (3406), b. 1801 Halkirk Parish, Caithness, d. 1887 Ontario
Marjory GUNN (2527), b. 1803 Braehour, Halkirk Parish, Caithness, d. 1873 Percy Township, Northumberland County, Ontario
+**Peter MCDONALD** (3564), b. 1802, m. 1825 Reay Parish, Caithness, d. Ontario
Janet MCDONALD (3565), b. 1826 Reay Parish, Caithness
Murdoch MCDONALD (3566), b. 1830 Reay Parish, Caithness, d. 1905 Percy Township, Northumberland County, Ontario
+**Annie MCMULLIN** (3567), b. circa 1850 Ontario, m. 1872 Osclay, Peterboro, Ontario
Martha A. MCDONALD (3611), b. 1844 Percy Township, Northumberland County, Ontario
Peter MCDONALD (3607), b. 1873 Rawdon Township, Northumberland County, Ontario, d. 1946 Percy Township, Northumberland County, Ontario
Eleanor MCDONALD (3609), b. 1877 Percy Township, Northumberland County, Ontario
Abraham MCDONALD (3610), b. 1878 Percy Township, Northumberland County, Ontario, d. 1908 Percy Township, Northumberland County, Ontario
Henry MCDONALD (3568), b. 1833 Reay Parish, Caithness, d. 1869 Percy Township, Northumberland County, Ontario
William MCDONALD (2303), b. 1836 Reay Parish, Caithness
John MCDONALD (3569), b. circa 1844 Upper Canada
Jane MCDONALD (3513), b. circa 1845 Upper Canada, d. 1916 Percy Township, Northumberland County, Ontario
+**unknown spouse**
Mary MCDONALD (3606), b. 1862, d. 1876
William GUNN of Waranga (374), b. 1804 Halkirk Parish, Caithness, d. 1888 Waranga, Vic
+**Cecilia CORMACK** (375), b. 1819 Wick Parish, Caithness, m. 1850 Aberdeen, Grampian, d. 1906 Rushworth, Vic
Margaret Elizabeth GUNN (376), b. 1850 Caithness, d. 1929 Hawthorn, Vic
Janet GUNN (900), b. 1852 Wick Parish, Caithness, d. 1888 Waranga, Vic
+**Alfred COLLIER** (901), m. 1887 Melbourne, Vic
William GUNN (377), b. 1853 Wick Parish, Caithness, d. 1921 Rushworth, Vic
+**Julia Janet INGRAM** (903), b. 1860 Rockford, Vic, m. 1889 South Melbourne, Vic, d. 1957 Murchison, Vic
William Ingram GUNN (389), b. 1890 Rushworth, Vic, d. 1891 Rushworth, Vic
Janettie GUNN (2494), b. 1894 Rushworth, Vic, d. 1992 Mooroopna, Vic
William GUNN (909), b. 1896, d. 1896
Elizabeth GUNN (384), b. 1859 Rushworth, Vic
+**Alexander INGRAM** (905), m. 1888
Cecelia Catherine INGRAM (386), b. 1890 Rushworth, Vic, d. 1976
Marie Elizabeth Gunn INGRAM (914), b. 1898 Rushworth, Vic, d. 1957
Alexander GUNN (906), b. 1861 Rushworth, Vic, d. 1915 Rushworth, Vic
Cecilia Jane GUNN (907), b. 1863 Rushworth, Vic, d. 1864 Waranga, Vic
Janet GUNN (927), b. 1807 Halkirk Parish, Caithness, d. 1879
Alexander GUNN (926), b. circa 1810 Halkirk Parish, Caithness, d. 1871
Jane GUNN (3407), b. 1813 Halkirk Parish, Caithness
John GUNN (3360), b. 1766 Dalnaglaton, Halkirk Parish, Caithness, d. 1855 Bualintagle, Halkirk Parish, Caithness
+**Barbara GUNN** (3446), m. circa 1790, d. before 1855
Margaret GUNN (3448), b. before 1805, d. before 1855
John GUNN (3447), b. before 1820, d. before 1855
Donald GUNN (the Sennachie) of Braehour & Brawlbin (708), b. circa 1769 Caithness, d. 1861 Brawlbin, Reay Parish, Caithness

+**Catherine GUNN of Osclay** (3423), b. circa 1781 Latheron Parish, Caithness, d. 1870 Newton, Watten Parish, Caithness

- **John GUNN in Durness** (878), b. 1808 Halkirk Parish, Caithness, d. 1885 Durness Parish, Sutherland
  +**Catherine GUNN in Campster** (1120), b. circa 1817 Reay Parish, Caithness, m. 1836 Caithness, d. 1871 Sutherland
  - **John GUNN** (1122), chr. 1837 Lamesdale, Reay Parish, Caithness, d. 1861 Comber, County Down
  - **Margaret GUNN** (1123), b. 1841 Carriside, Reay Parish, Caithness, d. 1892 Durness Parish, Sutherland
    +**Torquil NICHOLSON** (1127), b. circa 1844 Snizort, Inverness, m. 1870 Edinburgh, Edinburgh Parish, Midlothian
    - **John NICHOLSON (Rev)** (3928), b. 1873 Durness, Sutherland
    - **Donald NICHOLSON (Rev)** (3929), b. 1877 Durness, Sutherland
  - **Donald GUNN** (1116), b. 1844 Brawlbin, Reay Parish, Caithness, d. 1864 Durness, Sutherland
  - **Barbara GUNN** (1124), chr. 1847 Carriside, Reay Parish, Caithness, d. 1905
  - **Catherine GUNN** (1125), b. 1849 Carriside, Reay Parish, Caithness, d. 1907
  - **Johan GUNN**[740] (1126), b. 1855 Reay Parish, Caithness, d. 1868
  - **Alexander GUNN in Sangomore** (887), b. 1859 Sangomore, Durness Parish, Sutherland, d. 1945 Sangomore, Durness Parish, Sutherland
    +**Georgina MACKAY** (2749), b. circa 1857 Durness, Sutherland, m. circa 1885 Durness Parish, Sutherland
    - **Catherine GUNN** (3353), b. 1888 Durness, Sutherland, d. 1930
    - **Marianne GUNN** (3355), b. circa 1890, d. circa 1891
    - **John Alexander GUNN** (3354), b. 1890 Durness Parish, Sutherland, d. 1890
    - **Andrew Mackay GUNN** (888), b. 1894 Durness Parish, Sutherland, d. 1970
    - **Donaldina GUNN** (3358), b. 1896 Durness, Sutherland, d. 1974
    - **Marion Ellen GUNN** (3359), b. 1899 Durness, Sutherland, d. 1975
  - **Williamina GUNN** (889), b. 1859 Durness Parish, Sutherland, d. 1951
    +**George CAMPBELL** (890), b. circa 1860, m. circa 1885
    - **Catherine CAMPBELL** (891), b. circa 1888
- **Barbara GUNN of Braehour** (6), b. 1810 Halkirk Parish, Caithness, d. 1844 Brawlbin, Reay Parish, Caithness
  +**Alexander GUNN of Bualchork and Brawlbin** (1), b. 1789 Halkirk Parish, Caithness, m. 1829 Halkirk Parish, Caithness, d. 1847 Brawlbin, Reay Parish, Caithness
  - **Catherine GUNN** (119), b. 1830 Reay Parish, Caithness, d. 1912 Vic
    +**James MILLER** (117), b. 1826 Wick Parish, Caithness, m. 1857 Buninyong, Vic, d. 1918 Vic
    - **Elizabeth MILLER** (278), b. 1858 Geelong, Vic, d. 1918 Vic
    - **Alexander Gunn MILLER** (279), b. 1860 Geelong, Vic, d. 1938 Apollo Bay, Vic
    - **John William Gunn MILLER** (280), b. 1862 Geelong, Vic, d. 1925 St Kilda, Vic
    - **Jessie Barbara MILLER** (284), b. 1865 Emerald Hill, Vic, d. 1936 Totnes, Devonshire
    - **James Dunnet MILLER** (281), b. 1868 Emerald Hill, Vic, d. 1933 Heidelberg, Vic
    - **Katherine Margaret Mackay MILLER** (285), b. 1872 Emerald Hill, Vic, d. 1951 Sydney, NSW
  - **Donald GUNN of Brawlbin & Ballarat** (3), b. 1832 Brawlbin, Reay Parish, Caithness, d. 1901 Ballarat, Vic
    +**Jane SURMAN** (41), b. 1836 Hampton Poyle, Oxfordshire, m. 1859 Buninyong, Vic, d. 1908 Ballarat, Vic
    - **John Alexander GUNN (Hon.)** (32), b. 1860 Buninyong, Vic, d. 1910 Sydney, NSW
    - **William Watkins GUNN** (33), b. 1861 Nr Ballarat, Vic, d. 1935 Crossover, Vic
    - **Mary Jane GUNN** (34), b. 1864 Cardigan Nr Ballarat, Vic, d. 1934 Werribee, Vic
    - **Donald GUNN** (35), b. 1865 Burrumbeet, Vic, d. 1933 Crossover, Vic
    - **Marcus Daniel GUNN** (36), b. 1868 Buninyong, Vic, d. 1952 South Yarra, Vic
    - **Barbara GUNN** (106), b. 1870 Burrumbeet, Vic, d. 1941 Werribee, Vic
    - **Norman GUNN** (37), b. 1872 Burrumbeet, Vic, d. 1944 Williamstown, Vic
    - **Hugh GUNN** (38), b. 1875 Burrumbeet, Vic, d. 1879 Burrumbeet, Vic
    - **Arthur Gilbert GUNN** (9), b. 1878 Burrumbeet, Vic, d. 1933 Ivanhoe, Vic
    - **Catherine Alexandrina GUNN** (39), b. 1880 Burrumbeet, Vic, d. 1960 Ormond, Vic
  - **Janet 'Mcleod' GUNN** (120), b. 1834 Brawlbin, Reay Parish, Caithness, d. 1913 Cardigan, Vic

[740] We suspect Johan to be a daughter.

+**John Watkins SURMAN** (118), b. 1831 Hampton Poyle, Oxfordshire, m. 1864 Cardigan, Vic, d. 1906 Ballarat, Vic

- **Baby SURMAN** (1550), b. 1865 Ballarat, Vic, d. 1865 Ballarat, Vic
- **John Daniel SURMAN** (272), b. 1866 Cardigan, Vic, d. 1935 Dunolly, Vic
- **Alexander Gunn SURMAN** (273), b. 1868 Ballarat, Vic, d. 1909 Ballarat, Vic
- **Barbara Margaret McKay SURMAN** (274), b. 1870 Ballarat, Vic, d. 1928 Morwell, Vic
- **Watkins SURMAN** (405), b. 1871 Sago Hill/Cardigan, Vic, d. 1875 Cardigan, Vic
- **James William SURMAN** (275), b. 1873 Sago Hill, Vic, d. 1947 Horsham, Vic
- **Irene Marian Catherine SURMAN** (693), b. 1874 Sago Hill, Vic, d. 1940 Melbourne, Vic
- **Theodore Oswald SURMAN** (276), b. 1876 Cardigan, Vic, d. 1918 Melbourne South, Vic
- **Geoffrey Eustace SURMAN** (277), b. 1878 Sago Hill, Vic, d. 1951 Heidelberg, Vic

John GUNN (12), b. 1836 Reay Parish, Caithness, d. circa 1854 Port Melbourne, Vic

William GUNN (220), b. 1839 Reay Parish, Caithness, d. after 1864 Vic

Mary (May) GUNN (487), chr. 1812 Halkirk Parish, Caithness, d. 1853 Halkirk Parish, Caithness

+**John CAMPBELL** (3505), b. circa 1815 Reay, Caithness, m. circa 1837 Caithness

- **Johan CAMPBELL**[741] (3570), b. 1838 Thurso, Thurso Parish, Caithness
- **Donald CAMPBELL** (3514), b. 1840 Thurso, Thurso Parish, Caithness
- **William CAMPBELL** (3515), b. 1843 Halkirk Parish, Caithness, d. 1873 Halkirk Parish, Caithness
- **John CAMPBELL** (3571), b. circa 1850 Halkirk Parish, Caithness, d. 1851 Halkirk Parish, Caithness

Alexander GUNN (Capt.) of Braehour & Newton (572), chr. 1814 Halkirk Parish, Caithness, d. 1900 Thurso, Thurso Parish, Caithness

+**Mary Innes CAMPBELL** (1128), b. 1808 Reay Parish, Caithness, m. 1841 Caithness, d. 1864 Braehour, Halkirk Parish, Caithness

- **Catherine GUNN** (1129), b. 1842 Reay Parish, Caithness, d. before 1849
- **Williamina GUNN** (1130), b. 1843 Reay Parish, Caithness, d. 1909 Lanarkshire
  +**James D CLARKE** (3411), m. 1875 Braehour, Halkirk Parish, Caithness, d. before 1881
  - **William CLARK** (3453), b. 1877 Hamilton, Lanarkshire
  - **Alexander Gunn CLARK** (3454), b. 1878 Hamilton, Lanarkshire
  - **Mary Campbell CLARK** (3455), b. 1880 Hamilton, Lanarkshire
- **Barbara GUNN** (1131), b. 1844 Reay Parish, Caithness, d. 1879 Glasgow, Lanarkshire
- **Peter GUNN** (1132), b. 1846 Reay Parish, Caithness
- **Catherine GUNN** (1133), b. 1849 Reay Parish, Caithness, d. 1929 Edinburgh, Midlothian
  +**John SCOTT** (3450), b. circa 1848 Forfarshire, m. 1873 Inverness
  - **Robertina G SCOTT** (3458), b. 1874 Cupar, Angus, d. 1944 Inverness
  - **John SCOTT** (3460), b. 1876 Dalry, Ayrshire
  - **Alexander S SCOTT** (3461), b. 1878 Hamilton, Lanarkshire
  - **Charles SCOTT** (3462), b. 1880 Hamilton, Lanarkshire
  - **William SCOTT** (3463), b. 1882 Falkirk, Stirlingshire
  - **Patrick S SCOTT** (3464), b. 1885 Perthshire
  - **Walter SCOTT** (3465), b. 1887 Ayrshire
- **Robertina GUNN** (1134), b. 1852 Reay Parish, Caithness, d. 1872

Margaret GUNN (880), b. 1819 Caithness, d. 1888 Newton, Watten Parish, Caithness

+**John MACKAY** (3467), b. circa 1815 Halkirk Parish, Caithness, m. 1860 Brawlbin, Reay Parish, Caithness, d. 1865 Newton, Watten Parish, Caithness

- **Hector MACKAY** (3468), b. 1863 Watten Parish, Caithness, d. 1892 Halkirk Parish, Caithness
  +**Mary Ann MACKINNON** (3469), b. circa 1861 Watten Parish, Caithness, m. circa 1888, d. 1946 Watten Parish, Caithness

Alexandrina (Lexy) GUNN of Braehour (554), b. 1825 Halkirk Parish, Caithness, d. 1876 Dundee, Angus

+**Donald GUNN of Brawlbin & Dundee** (976), b. circa 1818 Brawlbin, Halkirk Parish, Caithness, m. 1852 Brawlbin, Reay Parish, Caithness, d. 1879 Dundee, Angus

- **John St Clair GUNN (Dr)** (3575), b. 1854 Dundee, Angus, d. 1907 Kaikoura, Marlborough
  +**Hester EASTON** (3713), b. circa 1867, m. circa 1890, d. 1939 Kaikoura

---

[741] The name is recorded as Johan in one source.

├── **Agnes Loeda GUNN** (3715), b. 1893
├── **Alexandrina Margaret GUNN** (3717), b. 1896, d. 1967
└── **Donald St Clair GUNN** (3719), b. 1899, d. 1973
├── **Daniel Alexander GUNN** (3576), b. 1855 Dundee, Angus, d. circa 1890
├── **Margaret GUNN** (3577), b. 1859 Dundee, Angus, d. 1881 Dundee, St Andrew Parish, Angus
├── **Catherine GUNN** (3578), b. 1860 Dundee, Angus
+**Peter MUNRO** (3714), b. circa 1866, m. 1887 Perthshire
└── **Peter Lascelles MUNRO** (3722), b. 1889 Kansas, d. 1918 Fouilloy, Somme
├── **Francis Molison GUNN** (1137), b. 1863 Dundee, Angus, d. 1864 Dundee, Angus
├── **Williamina GUNN** (3579), b. 1865 Dundee, Angus, d. Omaha, Nebraska
+**Thomas H ARTHUR** (3581), b. 1866 Angus, m. 1885 Aberdeen
├── **Thomas Hutton ARTHUR** (3582), b. 1885 St Andrew, Angus
├── **Sturrock ARTHUR** (3583), b. 1888 Kansas
├── **Douglas ARTHUR** (3584), b. 1891 Nebraska
├── **Stanley ARTHUR** (3585), b. 1894 Nebraska
└── **Stewart ARTHUR** (3586), b. 1899 Nebraska
├── **Francis Molison GUNN** (1138), b. 1867 Dundee, Angus, d. before 1871 Dundee, Angus
└── **Alexander GUNN** (1139), b. 1868 Dundee, Angus, d. 1868 Dundee, Angus
├── **Jean (Jane) GUNN** (941), b. 1816 Braehour, Halkirk Parish, Caithness, d. 1910 Killimister, Wick Parish, Caithness
+**Hugh MACKENZIE** (3433), b. circa 1802 Farr, Sutherland, m. 1840 Reay Parish, Caithness, d. 1870 Winless, Caithness
├── **Donald MACKENZIE** (3434), chr. 1841 Reay Parish, Caithness, d. 1915 Bonar Bridge, Sutherland
├── **Catherine MACKENZIE** (3437), chr. 1843 Reay Parish, Caithness, d. before 1848 Reay Parish, Caithness
├── **Barbara MACKENZIE** (3438), b. 1845 Reay Parish, Caithness, d. 1926 Killimister, Wick Parish, Caithness
├── **George MACKENZIE** (3435), b. 1846 Reay Parish, Caithness
+**Margaret (--?--)** (3441), b. circa 1846 Wick Parish, Caithness, m. 1892 Wick Parish, Caithness
├── **Catherine MACKENZIE** (3439), b. circa 1848 Reay Parish, Caithness, d. 1924 Wick Parish, Caithness
├── **Jessie/Janet MACKENZIE** (3440), b. 1850 Reay Parish, Caithness, d. 1926 Wick Parish, Caithness
├── **William MACKENZIE** (3400), b. 1853 Reay Parish, Caithness, d. 1902 Cradock
├── **Hugh MACKENZIE** (3401), b. 1855 Reay Parish, Caithness, d. 1868 Stemster, Latheron Parish, Caithness
└── **Alexander MACKENZIE** (3436), b. 1856 Reay Parish, Caithness, d. 1860 Brawlbin, Reay Parish, Caithness
└── **William GUNN** (3696), b. 1818, d. 1838

Part 5—The Descendants of John Gunn in Dalnaha, Strathmore & Braehour (707); a journal with details

Dalnaha, near Halkirk, is close to Tormsdale; and is 'A township comprising one roofed building, two partially roofed long buildings, three unroofed buildings and an enclosure are depicted on the 1st edition of the OS 6-inch map (Caithness 1876, sheet xxvii). One roofed and three unroofed buildings, two unroofed structures and an enclosure are shown on the current edition of the OS 1:10,560 map (1962).'
http://www.scotlandsplaces.gov.uk/search_item/index.php?service=RCAHMS&id=7614

Generation One

1. John GUNN in Dalnaha, Strathmore and Braehour (707) was born in 1722 in Halkirk Parish, Caithness.[742] He married Marjory Dunbar of Rowens (706), daughter of Alexander Dunbar of Rowens (798), on 02 Jul 1745 in Watten Parish, Caithness.[743] He died in 1810 in Halkirk Parish, Caithness[744] and was buried in 1810 in Dirlot, Caithness.[745]

John was a farmer.[746] He was a deponent, age 81, at the Gunn Succession hearing in 1803 in Wick.[747] See next page.

Marjory DUNBAR of Rowens (706) was born circa 1728. She was also known as May Gunn (706).

Children of John Gunn (707) and Marjory Dunbar (706) were as follows:

i. Alexander GUNN (3712) was born circa 1747 in Caithness.
He was the eldest son, a soldier who died wihout issue.[748]

2 ii. Jean GUNN (3690).

3 iii. Angus GUNN in Braehour (3592).

4 iv. George GUNN in Braehour (879).

5 v. William GUNN in Braehour (2500).

6 vi. John GUNN (3360).

7 vii. Donald GUNN (the Sennachie) of Braehour and Brawlbin (708).

---

742 *Burke's Peerage and Gentry 107th Edition*, 2009).

743 *The Church of Jesus Christ of Latter-day Saints*, CD-ROM , Marriage of John Gunn and Marjory Dunbar 2 Jul 1745 at Watten, Caithness;
Letter from Colin Gunn, Clan Gunn genealogist, to Donald Gunn, Jan 1988: Alexander Gunn was the third recorded child of Donald Gunn, Tormsdale, and Janet McKenzie, married Halkirk parish, banns 1829 Halkirk, death 1847, 1841 census, Reay parish approx. 50 years.
Barbara was the eldest daughter of Donald Gunn in Braehour, and later Brawlbyn. He was known as the Seanachy. Her dates are: baptised 30 Mar 1810 Halkirk, banns 1829 Halkirk.
Donald, Barbara's father, was the 3rd son of John Gunn in Dalnaha, Halkirk parish (aka John in Strathmore). His wife was Mary aka Marjory Dunbar. Donald would seem to have been baptised 26 years after his parents' banns were called. I do not regard this as a problem.
John in Dalnaha's father was Alexander Gunn of Dalnagaton, Halkirk, baptised 1688, died June 1765, married to Janet McLeod.
'These men were McHamishes, directly descended from the early chiefs of Clan Gunn.'

744 Michael J Gunn, "Descent of the Gunns", John in Braehour, d 1810; Bill and Sharon Gurney, e-mail message to Donald Gunn.

745 Dirlot cemetery tombstone: Dirlot cemetery is reached along a track which starts 1.3 miles towards Dirlot from Westerdale Post Office. Turn left along the track past sandpit for 0.4 miles. Open first gate on right past the first house on the right. Cemetery is 50 metres out of sight into paddock.
HERE LIES THE CORPS OF ALEXANDER GUNN SOMETIME TENENT IN DALNIGLATON WHO DIED THE 29 JUNE 1765 AGED 77 YEARS and JANET McKLOUD HIS SPOUSE THE BURIAL PLACE OF GEORGE, JOHN and AENEAS GUNNS HIS CHILDREN. See page 343.

746 Certificate of Death, John Gunn age 89 Dalnaglaton, parents John Gunn, farmer, deceased and Mary Gunn, maiden name Dunbar, deceased, wife Barbara Gunn, children John, dec. 35, Margaret, dec. 55. Died April 18, 1855 at Bualintagle, burial Dirlot. Informant Alex. Gunn, nephew.

747 Chart from Colin Gunn, Clan Gunn Genealogist, as drawn for M J Gunn by Hugh Peskett; *Burke's Peerage*.

748 Thomas Sinclair, *The Gunns* 1890, Supplement 15 has John Gunn, Braehour, had a son Alexander, the eldest, a soldier who died without issue, and further mentions John's other sons, John, Donald of Braehour, the Sennachie, and William who was named after his uncle, the father of the Hon. Donald, but he died young.

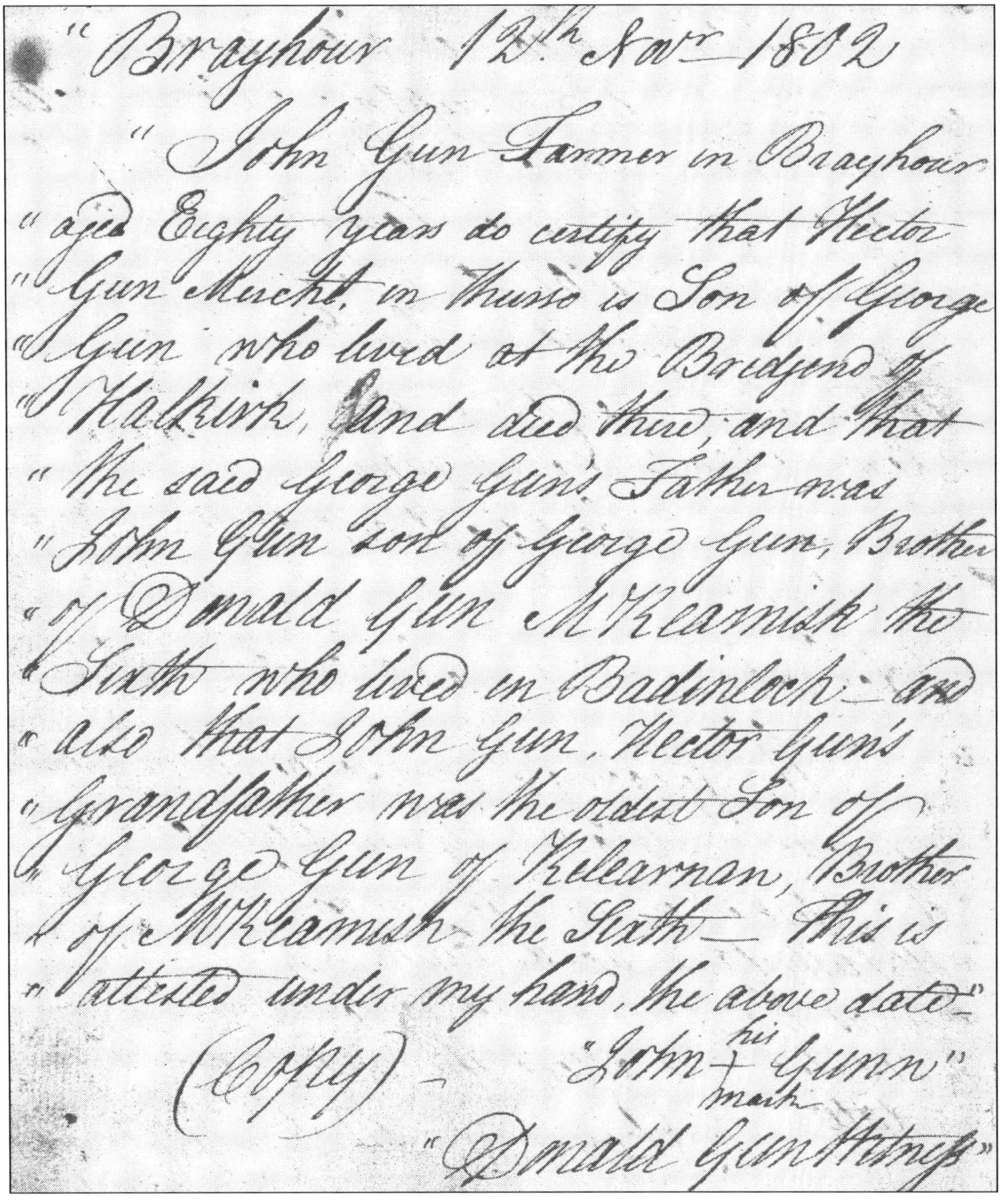
"Brayhour 12th Novr 1802
"John Gun Farmer in Brayhour
"aged Eighty years do certify that Hector
"Gun Mercht in Thurso is Son of George
"Gun who lived at the Bridgend of
"Halkirk, and died there, and that
"the said George Gun's Father was
"John Gun son of George Gun, Brother
"of Donald Gun McKeamish the
"Sixth who lived in Badinloch — and
"also that John Gun, Hector Gun's
"Grandfather was the oldest Son of
"George Gun of Kilearnan, Brother
"of McKeamish the Sixth — This is
"attested under my hand, the above date"
(Copy) — "John his mark Gunn"
"Donald Gun Witness"

John Gunn Farmer in Brayhour aged eighty years do certify that Hector Gunn Mercht in Thurso is Son of George Gun who lived at the Bridgend of Halkirk, and died there, and that the said George Gun's father was John Gun son of George Gun, Brother of Donald Gun McKeamish the sixth who lived at Badinloch – and also that John John Gun, Hector Gun's Grandfather was the oldest Son of George Gun of Kilearnan, Brother of McKeamish the Sixth – This is attested under my hand, the above date (Copy) John (his mark) Gunn Donald Gunn witness.

It is probable that John Gunn's views at the Gunn succession hearing in 1803 are reflected by the above document. This issue is also picked up in Thomas Sinclair's history.

Generation Two

2. Jean GUNN (3690)[749] was born around 1749 in Caithness. She married John Macgregor (3691) on 11 May 1769 in Wick Parish, Caithness.

Children of Jean Gunn (3690) and John Macgregor (3691) all born in Caithness were as follows:

i. Marjory MACGREGOR (3692) was christened in 1770.
ii. Donald MACGREGOR (3693) was christened in 1774.
iii. Alexander MACGREGOR (3694) was christened in 1776.
iv. John MACGREGOR (3695) was christened in 1778.

3. Angus GUNN in Braehour (3592) was born circa 1750.[750] He married Elizabeth Matheson (3702) on 12 Dec 1782 in Halkirk Parish, Caithness.

He was a farmer in Abbot and later Dalnaclatton in Caithness.[751] In 12 Dec 1782 he lived in Dalnaglaton, Caithness.

Elizabeth MATHESON (3702) lived in Latheron Parish, Caithness; before marriage.

Children of Angus Gunn in Braehour (3592) and Elizabeth Matheson (3702) were as follows:

i. John GUNN (3593) was born circa 1785. He died in India.
He was recorded by Capt Alex. Gunn. He was a soldier in the 78th Regiment. He had 1 son and 2 daughters, believed in India.

ii. Catherine GUNN (3703) was born in 1789 in Latheron Parish, Caithness. She married David Nicholson (3704) on 23 Apr 1819 in Sanday, Orkney Islands. She died on 03 Jun 1872 in Coachroad, Wick, Wick Parish, Caithness, aged 83.
David NICHOLSON (3704) was born circa 1796 in Bower Parish, Orkney Islands. He was a farm manager.

8 iii. Margaret GUNN (3705).

iv. Jean GUNN (3708) was born in 1792 in Halkirk Parish, Caithness. She married William Sutherland (3709) on 04 Mar 1814 in Reay Parish, Caithness. She died on 02 May 1868 in Rosskeen, Dalmore Parish, Ross and Cromarty, at age 76.
She was also known as Jane GUNN (3708).
William SUTHERLAND (3709) died before 1841. He was a merchant.

v. William GUNN (3710) was born circa 1801. He died on 10 Aug 1870 in Braehungie, Latheron Parish, Caithness, at age 69.

vi. Angus GUNN (3711) was born on 19 May 1805 in Reay Parish, Caithness.
He had three sons, names unknown.

4. George GUNN in Braehour (879) was born circa 1757 in Halkirk Parish, Caithness.[752] He married Margaret Gunn (3519) circa 1783. He died on 07 Oct 1842 in Braehour, Halkirk Parish, Caithness, age 85.[753]

---

749 Bill and Sharon Gurney, e-mail to Donald Gunn, 30 Oct 2009

750 Bill and Sharon Gurney, e-mail to Donald Gunn, 01 Apr 2009: Family of John Gunn and Marjory Dunbar.

751 Bill and Sharon Gurney, e-mail to Donald Gunn, 15 Nov 2009: The Family of Angus Gunn and Elizabeth Matheson.

He was a tacksman. He appeared on the census of 06 Jun 1841 in the household of his brother Donald (708) and Catherine Gunn of Osclay (3423) in Brawlbin, Reay Parish, Caithness.[754] He appeared on the census of 06 Jun 1841 in Braehour, Halkirk Parish, Caithness.[755]

Children of George Gunn in Braehour (879) and Margaret Gunn (3519) were as follows:

i. William GUNN (3512) was born before 1787.[756]

He was mentioned in a family tree prepared by Capt Alexander Gunn of Braehour. William apparently lived in Dundee and had a son Robert Gunn of Edinburgh. No birth record has been found.

9 ii. Alexander GUNN of Dalnaha and Banniskirk (3508).

iii. Angus GUNN (3509) was born in 1790 in Halkirk Parish, Caithness. He was christened on 07 Dec 1790 in Halkirk Parish, Caithness.[757]

iv. Marjory GUNN (3510) was born in 1798 in Halkirk Parish, Caithness. She was christened on 19 Dec 1798 in Halkirk Parish, Caithness.

10 v. John GUNN (3511).

5. William GUNN in Braehour (2500)[758] was born in 1760 in Latheron Parish, Caithness.[759] He married Janet Sinclair (896), daughter of John Sinclair of Reay (2885) and Janet Gunn of Dalnaglaton (3425), on 26 Mar 1800 in Caithness.[760] He died circa 1812 in Caithness; as recorded in Capt. Alexander's genealogy chart. He died before 1841 in Caithness not recorded in 1841 census; wife Janet and children John, Janet and Alexander were.

He was a tenant farmer in the strath of Braeholm.[761]

Janet SINCLAIR (896)[762] was born circa 1780 in Halkirk Parish, Caithness.[763] She died on 25 Jan 1870 in Braehour, Halkirk Parish, Caithness, reported by Alexander Gunn, nephew.[764] She appeared on the census of 06 Jun 1841 in Braehour, Halkirk Parish, Caithness.[765]

---

752 Bill and Sharon Gurney, e-mail to Donald Gunn.

753 *John O'Groat Journal*, 24 Jan 1861, 14 Oct 1842: At Braehour, Parish of Halkirk, on the 7th Inst., Mr George Gunn, tacksman, age 85.

754 UK Census 06 June 1841: District of Brawlbin lying in the south part of the Parish of Reay. Each person who abode in each house on night of 6 June 1841: Donald Gunn 72 farmer; Kathrine Gunn 60; Alexander Gunn 26; Mary Gunn 26; Margaret Gunn 22; Alexandrina Gunn 18; all born in Caithness; together with George Gunn 80 servant, George Gunn servant 22 and three other servants. Note: Census instructions for recording age were that if under 15, actual age; if over 15, record to the nearest 5 years below. The summary notes that there were 40 occupied houses, 2 uninhabited houses, 78 males and 94 females comprising 40 families in the Brawlbin District.

755 UK Census 06 June 1841: District of Braehour, Parish of Halkirk.

756 Bill and Sharon Gurney, e-mail to Donald Gunn, 12 Feb 2009: George Gunn is named as a son of John Gunn and Marjory Dunbar by Alexander Gunn (Capt.) in the family chart I mentioned. There is also another reference to him in article ten of the Sinclair Supplements, 1902. Sinclair quotes "Sexagenarian" who "published several years ago" the following "...Donald was the fourth son of John, Dalnaha. George Gunn Cramond Bridge by Edinburgh, and Angus and John Gunn both in Queensland, Australia*are the grandsons of George Gunn, Braehour, third son of John, Dalnaha....". Death Notice: John O'Groat Journal, Oct. 14, 1842...."At Braehour, Parish of Halkirk, on the 7th Inst. Mr. George Gunn, tacksman, age 85." George was enumerated twice in the 1841 census. Once with Donald and family and once as an 85 year old with his son John and family in Braehour.* His recorded children were Alexander, Angus, Marjory, John and a William who is named in Alexander Gunn's chart. I think the young George with Donald in 1841 was the son of Alexander Gunn. John and Angus Gunn of Queensland were the sons of John. This is the family that we have been working on. Capt. Alexander Gunn also records a son Angus for John Gunn/Marjorie D.

757 Bill and Sharon Gurney, e-mail to Donald Gunn, 03 Apr 2009: The Family of George Gunn and Margaret Gunn.

758 Letter from Colin Gunn, Jan 1998: Donald, Barbara's father, was the third son of John Gunn in Dalnaha, Halkirk parish (aka John in Strathmore).

759 Debbie Kuzub, "Family of Donald Gunn of Canada", 07 Feb 2006 e-mail

760 Bill and Sharon Gurney, e-mail to Donald Gunn, 23 Oct 2008: Families of William Gunn and Janet Sinclair.

761 Gunn, Donald by L G Thomas, online http://www.biographi.ca/en/ShowBio.asp?BioId=39136andquery=.

Children of William Gunn in Braehour (2500) and Janet Sinclair (896) were as follows:

11 i. Donald GUNN (Hon.) of Manitoba (372).

ii. John GUNN of Braehour and Ontario (3406) was born in 1801 in Halkirk Parish, Caithness. He was christened on 02 Mar 1801 in Halkirk Parish, Caithness.[766] He died on 18 Nov 1887 in Ontario age 86, unmarried.[767] He was buried in 1887 in Chatsworth United Church, Holland Township, Grey County, Ontario.

He appeared on the census of 06 Jun 1841 in the household of his mother Janet (896) in Braehour, Halkirk Parish, Caithness. His birth and christening details are correct, but other details may refer to a different John Gunn.

12 iii. Marjory GUNN (2527).

13 iv. William GUNN of Waranga (374).

v. Janet GUNN (927) was born in 1807 in Halkirk Parish, Caithness. She was christened on 22 Oct 1807 in Halkirk Parish, Caithness.[768] She died on 09 Mar 1879 informant was Alex. Gunn, cousin.

She appeared on the census of 06 Jun 1841 in the household of her mother Janet (896) in Braehour, Halkirk Parish, Caithness.

vi. Alexander GUNN (926) was born circa 1810 in Halkirk Parish, Caithness.[769] He died on 31 May 1871 informant Alex. Gunn, cousin.

He appeared on the census of 06 Jun 1841 in the household of his mother Janet (896) in Braehour, Halkirk Parish, Caithness.

vii. Jane GUNN (3407) was born in 1813 in Halkirk Parish, Caithness. She was christened on 14 Jul 1813 in Halkirk Parish, Caithness.[770]

6. John GUNN (3360) was born in 1766 in Dalnaglaton, Halkirk Parish, Caithness. He married Barbara Gunn (3446) circa 1790.[771] He died on 18 Apr 1855 in Bualintagle, Halkirk Parish, Caithness. He was buried in Dirlot, Caithness.

Barbara GUNN (3446) died before 1855.[772]

Children of John Gunn (3360) and Barbara Gunn (3446) were as follows:

i. Margaret GUNN (3448) was born before 1805. She died before 1855.[773]

ii. John GUNN (3447) was born circa 1820. He died before 1855 age 35.

762Two letters from William Gunn of Waranga's granddaughter Janettie McMillanin April and October 1974 are reproduced in full in Part 7 and are not further referenced here.

763Debbie Kuzub, "Donald Gunn of Canada;" Bill and Sharon Gurney, e-mail to Donald Gunn, 23 Oct 2008:

764Bill and Sharon Gurney, e-mail to Donald Gunn, 23 Oct 2008: Families of William Gunn and Janet Sinclair.

765UK Census 06 June 1841: Janet Gunn 55; John Gunn, 35; Janet Gunn, 25; Alexander Gunn, 25 farmer.

766Caroline Armstrong, Descendants of Donald Gunn, e-mail message to Donald Gunn, 20 Mar 2006.

767Bill and Sharon Gurney, e-mail to Donald Gunn, 08 Nov 2008.

768Caroline Armstrong, e-mail to Donald Gunn, 20 Mar 2006.

769Debbie Kuzub, "Donald Gunn of Canada;" Bill and Sharon Gurney, e-mail to Donald Gunn, 23 Oct 2008: Families of William Gunn and Janet Sinclair.

770Caroline Armstrong, e-mail to Donald Gunn.

771Certificate of Death: John Gunn age 89 Dalnaglaton, parents John Gunn, farmer, deceased and Mary Gunn, maiden name Dunbar, deceased, wife Barbara Gunn, children John, dec. 35, Margaret, dec. 55. Died April 18, 1855 at Bualintagle, burial Dirlot. Informant Alex. Gunn, nephew.

772Bill and Sharon Gurney, e-mail to Donald Gunn.

773Certificate of Death: John Gunn age 89 Dalnaglaton, parents John Gunn, farmer, deceased and Mary Gunn, maiden name Dunbar, deceased, wife Barbara Gunn, children John, dec. 35, Margaret, dec. 55. Died April 18, 1855 at Bualintagle, burial Dirlot. Informant Alex. Gunn, nephew.

7. Donald GUNN (the Sennachie) of Braehour and Brawlbin (708)[774] was born circa 1769 in Caithness.[775] He was christened in 1771 in Caithness.[776] He married Catherine Gunn of Osclay (3423), daughter of Alexander Gunn of Osclay (3424) and Barbara Weir (Wheir) (797), on 03 Mar 1807 in Halkirk Parish, Caithness.[777] He died on 03 Jan 1861 in Brawlbin, Reay Parish, Caithness of a fractured neck.[778] He was buried in Caithness.

Donald began military service in 1797 with the Rothesay and Caithness Fencible Regiment.[779] He ended military service in 1802 with the Rothesay and Caithness Fencible Regiment. He lived in Braehour, Halkirk Parish, Caithness.[780] He was a farmer. He and Catherine Gunn of Osclay (3423) appeared on the census of 06 Jun 1841 in Brawlbin, Reay Parish, Caithness,[781] and again on the census of 30 Mar 1851 in Brawlbin.[782]

Catherine GUNN of Osclay (3423) was born circa 1781 in Latheron Parish, Caithness. She died on 24 Oct 1870 in Newton, Watten Parish, Caithness.[783]

Children of Donald Gunn (the Sennachie) of Braehour and Brawlbin (708) and Catherine Gunn of Osclay (3423) were as follows:

14 i. John GUNN in Durness (878).
15 ii. Barbara GUNN of Braehour (6).
16 iii. Mary (May) GUNN (487).
17 iv. Alexander GUNN (Capt.) of Braehour and Newton (572).
18 v. Margaret GUNN (880).
19 vi. Alexandrina (Lexy) GUNN of Braehour (554).
20 vii. Jean (Jane) GUNN (941).
viii. William GUNN (3696) was born in 1818. He died in 1838.

---

774 Letter from Colin Gunn, Jan 1998 - ... Donald Gunn in Braehour, and later Brawlbin. He was known as the Seanachy;

775 Michael J Gunn, "Descent of the Gunns", Donald Gunn of Brawlbin and Braehour b 1767 d 1861.

776 Letter from Colin Gunn, Jan 1998 - Donald would seem to have been baptised 26 years after his parents banns were called. I do not regard this as a problem.

777 *LDS Church*, Marriage of Donald Gunn and Catharine Gunn, 3 Mar 1807, Halkirk.

778 *John O'Groat Journal*, 24 Jan 1861, of the late Mr Donald Gunn, tacksman, Brawlbin, who died on the 3d inst; Bill and Sharon Gurney, e-mail to Donald Gunn, 09 Feb 2009; The Descendants of Donald Gunn.

779 The plan of raising Fencible Corps in the Highlands was first proposed and carried into effect by Mr Pitt (afterwards the Earl of Chatham), in the year 1759. During the three preceding years both the fleets and armies of Great Britain had suffered reverses, and to retrieve the national character great efforts were necessary. In England county militia regiments were raised for internal defence in the absence of the regular army; but it was not deemed prudent to extend the system to Scotland, the inhabitants of which, it was supposed, could not yet be safely entrusted with arms. Groundless as the reasons for this caution undoubtedly were in regard to the Lowlands, it would certainly have been hazardous at a time when the Stuarts and their adherents were still plotting a restoration to have armed the clans. An exception, however, was made in favour of the people of Argyll and Sutherland, and accordingly letters of service were issued to the Duke of Argyll, then the most influential and powerful nobleman in Scotland, and the Earl of Sutherland to raise, each of them, a Fencible regiment within his district. Unlike the militia regiments which were raised by ballot, the Fencibles were to be raised by the ordinary mode of recruiting, and like the regiments of the line, the officers were to be appointed and their commissions signed by the king. The same system was followed at different periods down to the year 1799, the last of the Fencible regiments having been raised in that year. http://www.coghlan.co.uk/fencibles.htm

780 WW and MD Gunn: William Watkins and Marcus Daniel Gunn, sons of Donald Gunn in Brawlbin and Ballarat, visited Caithness in 1928 as members of the Scottish Delegation. See page 338.

781 UK Census 06 June 1841.

782 Census 30 March 1851: Reay Parish, Brawlbin: Donald Gunn 80 farmer, 60 acres, b Halkirk; Catherine Gunn 68, b Latheron; Margaret Gunn dau 30, b Halkirk, housemaid; Alexandrina Gunn dau 28, b Halkirk, housemaid; George Gunn 28, b Halkirk, servant; George Dunbar 30, b Halkirk, servant; Mary Gunn 16 b Reay herd; Margaret Sutherland 24, b Halkirk, outdoor servant.

783 Bill and Sharon Gurney, e-mail to Donald Gunn, 09 Feb 2009: The Descendants of Donald Gunn.

8. Margaret GUNN (3705)[784] was born in 1790. She married John Henderson (3706) on 14 Feb 1812 in Halkirk Parish, Caithness. She died on 06 Aug 1861 in Bardnaclaven, Thurso Parish, Caithness, of bronchitis and dropsy aged 71.

John HENDERSON (3706) was born circa 1780 in Halkirk Parish, Caithness. He was an agriculural labourer in 1841 in Badachlaven, Thurso Parish, Caithness. He was a farmer in 1851 in Newlands, Thurso Parish, Caithness.

Children of Margaret Gunn (3705) and John Henderson (3706) were:

i. John HENDERSON (3707) was born circa 1815.

He was the informant at the death aged 71 of Margaret Gunn (3705) of bronchitis and dropsy on 06 Aug 1861 in Bardnaclaven, Thurso Parish, Caithness.

9. Alexander GUNN of Dalnaha and Banniskirk (3508) was born in 1788 in Halkirk Parish, Caithness. He was christened on 07 Dec 1788 in Dalnaha, Halkirk Parish, Caithness.[785] He married Ann Waters of Dalnaha (3520) on 03 Jun 1814 in Halkirk Parish, Caithness.[786] He married Annie James Porteous (3521) on 12 Aug 1867 in 1 High Street, Thurso, Thurso Parish, Caithness.[787] He died on 06 Apr 1875 in Shore Street, Thurso, Thurso Parish, Caithness, at age 87.[788]

He was a farmer in 1841.[789] He and Ann Waters of Dalnaha (3520) appeared on the census of 06 Jun 1841 in Milton, Halkirk Parish, Caithness. He was a coal merchant in 1861.[790] He appeared on the census of 30 Mar 1861 in Shore Street, Thurso Parish, Caithness. He and Annie James Porteous (3521) appeared on the census of 03 Apr 1871 in Shore Street, Thurso Parish, Caithness.[791]

Ann WATERS of Dalnaha (3520) died before 1867.

Children of Alexander Gunn of Dalnaha and Banniskirk (3508) and Ann Waters of Dalnaha (3520) were as follows:

i. John GUNN (3523) was born in 1815 in Halkirk Parish, Caithness.[792] He was christened on 24 Aug 1815 in Halkirk Parish, Caithness. He died in 1874 in Cramond Kirk, Cramond, Cramond Parish, Lothian, age 67.[793]

21 ii. George GUNN (3524).

22 iii. Janet GUNN (3525).

---

784 Bill and Sharon Gurney, e-mail to Donald Gunn, 15 Nov 2009: The Family of Angus Gunn and Elizabeth Matheson.

785 Bill and Sharon Gurney, e-mail to Donald Gunn, 03 Apr 2009: The Family of George Gunn and Margaret Gunn.

786 Alexander Gunn of Banniskirk married Ann Waters of Dalnaha on June 3, 1814 in Halkirk Parish.

787 Unknown short register title, Alexander Gunn, son of George Gunn and Margaret Gunn, widower, age 77, coal merchant, res. Thurso married Annie James Porteous, age 50, spinster on the twenty first day of August 1867 at 1 High Street, Thurso after Banns according to the forms of the Free Church of Scotland. Witnesses, George Mackay and James Crament.

788 Bill and Sharon Gurney, e-mail to Donald Gunn, 03 Apr 2009: The Family of George Gunn and Margaret Gunn.

789 UK Census 06 June 1841: Milton, Halkirk: Alexander Gunn farmer 45; Anne Gun 45; George Gun 20; Janet Gun 15; James Gun 15; Margaret Gun 12; Bell Gun 10; Aeneasina Gun 8; David 7.

790 UK Census 30 March 1861: Shore Street, Parish of Thurso: Alexander Gunn age 70 born Halkirk, coal merchant.

791 UK Census 1871: Shore Street, Parish of Thurso, Breck House: Alexander Gunn, head, age 75, born Halkirk coal merchant; Annie Gunn, wife, age 49, born Edinburgh.

792 Bill and Sharon Gurney, e-mail to Donald Gunn, 03 Apr 2009: The Family of George Gunn and Margaret Gunn.

793 Gravestone Photographic Resource, online http://www.gravestonephotos.com/public/findfamily.php?name=Gunn.

iv. James GUNN (Rev.) (3687) was born in 1822 in Halkirk Parish, Caithness. He died in 1858 age 36.

He was a minister in Uig parish.[794] He appeared on the census of 06 Jun 1841 in the household of his parents Alexander (3508) and Ann (3520) in Milton, Halkirk Parish, Caithness.[795]

v. Margaret GUNN (3527) was born in 1828 in Caithness. She was christened on 23 May 1828 in Latheron Parish, Caithness.

She appeared on the census of 06 Jun 1841 in the household of her parents Alexander (3508) and Ann (3520) in Milton, Halkirk Parish, Caithness.

vi. Bell GUNN (3529) was born circa 1830 in Caithness.

She appeared on the census of 06 Jun 1841 in the household of her parents Alexander (3508) and Ann (3520) in Milton, Halkirk Parish, Caithness.

vii. David Waters GUNN (3530) was born on 17 Dec 1832 in Latheron Parish, Caithness. He was christened on 11 Apr 1833 in Latheron Parish, Caithness. He died in 1856 in Cramond Parish, Edinburgh.[796] He was buried in Cramond Kirk, Cramond Parish, Lothian.[797]

He appeared on the census of 06 Jun 1841 in the household of his parents Alexander (3508) and Ann (3520) in Milton, Halkirk Parish, Caithness.[798]

23 viii. Agnes/Aneasina GUNN (3528).

Annie James PORTEOUS (3521) was born circa 1819 in Edinburgh, Midlothian.[799] She appeared on the census of 03 Apr 1881 in Shore Street, Thurso Parish, Caithness.[800] She appeared on the census of 1891 in Cowgate, Thurso Parish, Caithness.[801]

There were no children of Alexander Gunn of Dalnaha and Banniskirk (3508) and Annie James Porteous (3521).

10. John GUNN (3511) was born in 1803 in Halkirk Parish, Caithness.[802] He was christened on 03 Oct 1803 in Halkirk Parish, Caithness.[803] He married Margaret Mackenzie

---

794Bill and Sharon Gurney, e-mail to Donald Gunn, 04 Oct 2009.

795UK Census 06 June 1841: Milton, Halkirk: Alexander Gunn farmer 45; Anne Gun 45; George Gun 20; Janet Gun 15; James Gun 15; Margaret Gun 12; Bell Gun 10; Aeneasina Gun 8; David 7.

796Gillian Bartlett email to Donald Gunn, Aug 2010; Certificate of Death: 1856 deaths in the Parish of Cramond in the County of Edinburgh, David Gunn, single, student of Divinity, on April third 1856 age 21 years, father Alexander Gunn, farmer, mother Ann Gunn, maiden name Waters, buried April 5th at the Church Yard of Cramond, informant George Gunn, brother.

797Gravestone Photographic Resource, online http://www.gravestonephotos.com/public/findfamily.php?name=Gunn.

798UK Census 06 June 1841: Milton, Halkirk: Alexander Gunn farmer 45; Anne Gun 45; George Gun 20; Janet Gun 15; James Gun 15; Margaret Gun 12; Bell Gun 10; Aeneasina Gun 8; David 7.

799Bill and Sharon Gurney, e-mail to Donald Gunn, 03 Apr 2009: The Family of George Gunn and Margaret Gunn; Census 1871: Shore Street, Parish of Thurso, Breck House: Alexander Gunn, head, age 75, born Halkirk coal merchant; Annie Gunn, wife, age 49, born Edinburgh.

800Census 1881: Shore Street, Thurso: Ann Gunn widow age 55 born Edinburgh.

801Census 1891: Cowgate, Thurso: Ann Gunn, head, age 63, living on own means, born Edinburgh.

802Bill and Sharon Gurney, e-mail to Donald Gunn, 12 Feb 2009: George Gunn is named as a son of John Gunn and Marjory Dunbar by Alexander Gunn (Capt.) in the family chart I mentioned. There is also another reference to him in article ten of the Sinclair Supplements, 1902. Sinclair quotes "Sexagenarian" who "published several years ago" the following "...Donald was the fourth son of John, Dalnaha. George Gunn Cramond Bridge by Edinburgh, and Angus and John Gunn both in Queensland, Australia*are the grandsons of Geroge Gunn, Braehour, third son of John, Dalnaha....". Death Notice: John O'Groat Journal, Oct. 14, 1842...."At Braehour, Parish of Halkirk, on the 7th Inst. Mr. George Gunn, tacksman, age 85." George was enumerated twice in the 1841 census. Once with Donald and family and once as an 85 year old with his son John and family in Braehour.*His recorded children were Alexander, Angus, Marjory, John and a William who is named in Alexander Gunn's chart. I think the young George with Donald in 1841 was the son of Alexander Gunn. John and Angus Gunn of Queensland were the sons of John. This is the family that we have been working on. Capt. Alexander Gunn also records a son Angus for John Gunn/Marjorie D. We haven't

(3522) on 06 Sep 1832 in Braehour, Halkirk Parish, Caithness. He died on 09 Feb 1855 in Thurso Parish, Caithness, at age 52. He was buried in Dirlot, Caithness.

Margaret MACKENZIE (3522) was born circa 1811.

Children of John Gunn (3511) and Margaret Mackenzie (3522) all born in Halkirk Parish, Caithness, were as follows:

i. Aeneas (Angus) GUNN (3531) was born circa 1834. He was christened on 02 Nov 1834 in Halkirk Parish, Caithness.

He and John Gunn (3536) emigrated say 1860 to Queensland..

ii. Colin GUNN (3532) was born on 20 Aug 1835. He died in 1851 in Halkirk Parish, Caithness, at age 16.

iii. George GUNN (3533) was born on 29 Aug 1838. He was christened on 05 Oct 1838 in Halkirk Parish, Caithness. He died on 14 Jul 1859 in Brims, Thurso Parish, Caithness, at age 20 at age 21. He was buried in Dirlot, Caithness.

George and Margaret were twins.

iv. Margaret GUNN (3534) was born on 29 Aug 1838. She was christened on 05 Oct 1838 in Halkirk Parish, Caithness.

George and Margaret were twins.

v. Barbara GUNN (3535) was born circa 1840.

vi. John GUNN (3536) was born circa 1844.

He and Aeneas (Angus) Gunn (3531) emigrated say 1860 to Queensland.

11. Donald GUNN (Hon.) of Manitoba (372)[804] was born in Sep 1797 in Halkirk Parish, Caithness.[805] He was christened on 10 Jun 1798 in Halkirk Parish, Caithness.[806] He married

---

tried to find him yet.; Bill and Sharon Gurney, e-mail to Donald Gunn, 03 Apr 2009: The Family of George Gunn and Margaret Gunn.

803 Bill and Sharon Gurney, e-mail to Donald Gunn, 03 Apr 2009: The Family of George Gunn and Margaret Gunn.

804 Letter from Janettie McMillan to Donald Gunn, 24 Apr 1974; See Part 7. The Scottish Way of Birth and Death, online http://www.gla.ac.uk/departments/scottishwayofbirthanddeath/, Illegitimate births were very common in certain parts of Scotland in the mid-nineteenth century, particularly in the North East and the South West. Many working people did not regard this as a problem, in spite of lectures from their parish ministers; Letter from Janettie McMillan to Donald Gunn, 24 Apr 1974.

"Donald Gunn of Canada," L G Thomas, GUNN, DONALD, educator, scientist, historian, and politician; b. at Halkirk, Caithness-shire, Scotland, September 1797, youngest son of William Gunn, a tenant farmer in the strath of Braeholme; d. at St Andrews, Man., 30 Nov. 1878.

Donald Gunn was educated in the parish school of Halkirk. In 1813 he entered the service of the Hudson's Bay Company and spent ten years at York Factory, Severn Fort, and Oxford House successively, earning promotion to lesser postmaster. In 1819 he married Margaret, eldest daughter of James Swain, a company officer; between 1822 and 1849 they had seven sons and two daughters. In 1823, his services not being required after the union of the HBC and the North West Company, he settled at Red River in "Little Britain," later the parish of St Andrews. His farm prospered and after ten years the assistance of his growing family enabled him to take charge for the next 18 years of the Church Missionary Society's parish school. He also acted later in his substantial stone house as custodian and librarian of the only public collection of books in Red River.

A critic of the company and a leader of the settlers in the demand for a greater degree of self-government, Gunn was never appointed to the Council of Assiniboia, but he early became a magistrate and president of the Court of Petty Sessions in his district. He served as foreman of the jury at the trial of Pierre-Guillaume Sayer in 1849. In 1870 he was chosen as delegate from St Andrews to the provisional assembly, although he was an advocate of the entry of the northwest into confederation. The Gunns seem to have been on friendly terms with John Christian Schultz* and his wife. Subsequent to the establishment of Manitoba as a province, Gunn was appointed police magistrate, justice of the peace, postmaster, and inspector of fisheries. On 10 March 1871 he was appointed to the Legislative Council of Manitoba and remained a member until its abolition, which he supported, in 1876.

Gunn played an important part not only in public affairs but also in the cultural and intellectual life of Red River. As an outspoken opponent of the HBC and as a leading Presbyterian layman, he was frequently involved in controversy with the authorities of the colony. Nevertheless he retained the respect of the majority and the personal esteem of many. He was a member of the Council of the Institute of Rupert's Land of 1862. His interest in natural history was reflected in his experiments with new methods of tillage and new strains of wheat and led to his long-standing connection with the Smithsonian Institution, of which he was one of the earliest meteorological correspondents. He earned a tribute from its secretary for the reliability of his observations of the weather and the importance of the objects he contributed in nearly every branch of natural history as well as archaeology and ethnology. In

Margaret Swain (923), daughter of James Swain (904) and Mary (--?--) (902), in 1819; "a la facon du pays" (in the way of the country) a half-breed wife.[807] He married Margaret Swain (923), daughter of James Swain (904) and Mary (--?--) (902), on 17 Jan 1826 in Manitoba; they weren't married in the church until 1826, when they already had three children.[808] He died on 30 Nov 1878 in St Andrew, Little Britain, Manitoba, at age 81.[809]

His life is summarised in Mark Rugg Gunn's History of the Clan Gunn.[810] He was an educator, scientist, historian, politician and farmer. His life is summarised in the *Dictionary of Canadian Biography*.[811] He was the subject of an article in the St Clement's History Book.[812]

1866 he made a special exploration for the Smithsonian of the region west of Lake Winnipeg to collect skins and birds' eggs, "among the latter several previously entirely unknown in museums."
Gunn disputes with Alexander Ross* the title of father of the history of Canada's prairie west. As an historian he was primarily concerned to provide for his readers all the available information. At the same time he by no means ignored the historian's duty of critical evaluation of his sources. An eye-witness of many of the events described in his posthumously published *History of Manitoba*, he was aware of the danger of "depending for our knowledge of past events on the special pleading of others." Though his history is essentially a narrative of events he did not avoid problems of interpretation. His sympathies clearly lie with the settlers rather than with the HBC. A staunch Presbyterian and an elder of his Kirk, he was not illiberal in religious outlook, though often critical of the Anglican and Roman Catholic clergy of the colony. His attitude to those he saw as representative of an unjust order, from Lord Selkirk [Douglas*] to Bishop David Anderson*, was tinged with an acerbity by no means characteristic of the relations with others of this genial and humorous man. L. G. Thomas
Smithsonian Institution, *Annual report, 1878* (Washington), 63–64. Donald Gunn, "Indian remains near Red River settlement, Hudson's bay territory," Smithsonian Institution, *Annual report, 1867* (Washington), 399–100; "Notes of an egging expedition to Shoal lake, west of lake Winnipeg. Made under the direction of the Smithsonian Institution in 1867 . . . ," Smithsonian Institution, *Annual report, 1867* (Washington), 427–32. Donald Gunn and C. R. Tuttle, *History of Manitoba from the earliest settlement to 1835 by the late Hon. Donald Gunn, and from the admission of the province into the Dominion by Charles R. Tuttle* (Ottawa, 1880). Begg, *Hist. of North-West*, I, 393ff., 450; II, 35. Morton, *Manitoba, a history*; unknown repository, unknown repository address; Debbie Kuzub, "Donald Gunn of Canada."

806Caroline Armstrong, e-mail to Donald Gunn.

807http://www.biographi.ca/en/ShowBio.asp?BioId=39136andquery=; Debbie Kuzub, "Donald Gunn of Canada".

808Debbie Kuzub, e-mail to Donald Gunn, Hon. Donald and Margaret were married "a la facon du pays" in the way of the country (she was a half breed, and given to Donald by her father) in 1819. They weren't married in the church until 1826, when they already had three children; Certificate of Birth, The Diocese of Rupert's Land, Donald Gunn of unstated age, born Kaithness, Scotland residing at Red River Settlement, married Margaret Swain of unstated age and place of birth, residing at Red River Settlement, on 17 January 1826, solemnized by The Reverend David T Jones, Chaplain to the H H B Company.

809 Debbie Kuzub, "Donald Gunn of Canada."

810Mark Rugg Gunn, *History of the Clan Gunn* (Glasgow: Alex. MacLaren and Sons, c1986), ' Donald Gunn was the eldest son of William in Braehour (son of John, son of Alexander, son of George, son of Alexander MacHamish) and left his home near Halkirk in 1813 at the age of 16 to serve as a labourer in the Hudson's Bay Company. He had had the merest rudiments of an education, his native tongue was Gaelic and he could read and to some extent write English. The next 10 years were spent in the arctic wastes of the Severn district, reading what books were available and taking every opportunity to increase his learning. He was early promoted to the position of master of an outpost, but when the North-West and Hudson's Bay Companies united in 1821, he decided to leave and settled in the Red River region. He married Margaret, daughter of James Swain, the Hudson's Bay officer of the York district in 1819. For a time he ran a farm, but in 1833 he took charge of the Parish school which had been established by the Church of England, and became librarian to the region. During this time he was described as the keenest student of them all, for he set himself to master Latin, Greek and mathematics and laid the foundations of that scientific knowledge which was to stand him in good stead later when he became a correspondent of the Smithsonian Institution, Washington. The secretary of that Institute, writing after Donald's death remarked that 'his long continued observations of the weather were among the most reliable of those within its archives. His contributions of objects of natural history were still of more important, embracing as they did nearly every branch in the various classes of the animal and vegetable kingdoms, and numerous collections in ornithology and ethnology' 'The Red River colony was still under the auspices of the Hudson's Bay Company who may have been paternal whilst the colony was small, but became despotic ..., the council of Assiniboia was inaugurated, but all the officers were appointed by the Company and the people began to demand a say in the management of their affairs. Meetings were held and petition after petition was drafted to the Canadian and Imperial Governments requesting a change. In this agitation Donald played a leading part, always advocating union with Canada as the colony's most desirable destiny. He held the position of magistrate and President of the Court of Petty Sessions in the district, and when the province of Manitoba became a reality he took his seat as 'Honourable' in the Upper House of legislature. He died at St. Andrews on the Red River in November 1873, his book 'The History of Manitoba' was published two years after his death and is still considered to be among the best. His life history makes a remarkable true-life success story; the small fair-haired and blue-eyed boy who went from the Strath of Braehour to learn English at Halkirk school and emigrated as an unskilled labourer to the northern wastes of Canada at the age of 16, becomes by sheer hard work and devotion to learning the leading citizen of the new province of Manitoba and the author of its standard history. They must have been a gifted family for his elder brother who migrated to Australia likewise achieved success and became one of the largest wool-growers and sheep farmers in Australia.'

811Unknown author, *Dictionary of Canadian Biography*, Gunn Donald: See Part 7

812Caroline Armstrong, e-mail to Donald Gunn, Taken from the St. Clements Centennial History Book

He was educated in Parish School, Halkirk Parish, Caithness.[813] He emigrated in 1813 to Canada, initially the Badger River Post near York Factory, in the service of the Hudson's Bay Company, per ship *Eddystone* in company wtih three other ships, one being *The Prince of Wales,* carrying the Red River Settlers.[814] He lived in 1822 in Little Britain, later known as the Parish of St Andrews, Winnipeg, Manitoba. Donald (372) was appointed to the Legislative Council of Manitoba and remained a member until its abolition in 1878 on 10 Mar 1871. He appeared at court on 14 Oct 1920 Family dispute on the land the Hon Donald settled in 1820 was resolved in an out-of-court settlement.[815]

Margaret SWAIN (923)[816] was born on 02 Apr 1802 in York Factory, Rupertsland, Manitoba. She died on 28 Nov 1870 in Little Britain, Manitoba, at age 68.[817] Her father was a factor in the Hudson Bay Co.

John Gunn was the son of the Hon. Donald Gunn who had come to Canada via Churchill in 1813 while in the employ of the Hudson's Bay Company. After severing his connections with the honorable Company, he purchased a homestead, Lot 163, Parish of St. Andrew's, on the east side of the Red River of considerable acreage. Donald was married to Margaret Swain, the daughter of James Swain.

The Hon. Donald Gunn had 12 children: William born in 1822, James born in 1824, John born in 1827, Alexander born in 1829, Mathilda born in 1831, George G born in 1832, Jane born in 1836, Margaret born in 1838, Donald Jr. born in 1840, Robert born in 1842, Janet born in 1846, and William (2nd) born in 1848.

John, the third child of Donald and Margaret Gunn grew up and married Emma Garrioch in 1855. They had eight children: Margaret Jane, Reginald, Donald J, John James, Gilbert Garrioch, Henry George, Emma Ann and Mary.

The original Gunn homestead was deeded over to son John as he reached manhood and had made plans for his marriage. This lot is right at the property spanning where the Lockport Bridge now stands. The Hon. Donald Gunn along with John also purchased Lot 167 where they built a fairly large Water-Gist-Mill not far from the junction of Gunn's Creek with the Red River on the east side. It was two stories high and built entirely by Manitoba materials and labour in the early 1850s.

John was educated by his father and took an active part in politics in the years surrounding 1870 thereafter. He was a returned Member of the Local Legislature for St. Andrews North at the 1874 election and the following. He was always a staunch opponent of liquor traffic and spent considerable time trying to combat it in the parishes along the Red River. John Gunn died Sat. Sept. 10, 1898, at the age of 71 years and 1 month. He had been ill for most of that spring and summer. His wife Emma (Garrioch) died in the year 1921.

813Many details on the family of Donald Gunn and margaret Swain are drawn from emails titled 'Donald Gunn of Canada' from Debbie Kuzub, Commissioner of the Central Canada Branch of the Clan Gunn Society of North America, and a descendant of the Hon Donald Gunn of Manitoba. Donald Gunn, online http://www.biographi.ca/en/ShowBio.asp?BioId=39136andquery=.

814Debbie Kuzub, e-mail to Donald Gunn, 09 Jan 2006: was just 16 on arrival in Canada, the group he arrived was the 'Pilgrim Fathers of the North-West', later known as the Selkirk Settlers.

815Caroline Armstrong, e-mail to Donald Gunn, SETTLE LAND IN 1820; SETTLE SUIT IN 1920 (FREE PRESS) OCT. 14, 1920 Legal Argument over Donald Gunn Homestead is Finally Adjusted

When Donald Gunn, one of Manitoba's first settlers, took up a homestead near Lockport in 1820, he had no idea that his heirs would be disputing over it a century later. But strange and unforseen things may happen within a hundred years and for a long time past the soil there Donald tilled in all the hardship of a pioneer life had been the centre of much family controversy and legal argument.

Not the least strange part of the story of the old Gunn homestead is the fact that after years of dispute, settlement was finally reached in the year of the centenary anniversary. The land was first broken in 1820 and the heirs settled their disputes over it in 1920. The last event took place yesterday in the King's Bench Court. Donald Gunn is a well known figure in the history of Manitoba. He was one of the earliest settlers with Lord Selkirk and is famous as the first historian of this part of the country. He took out his homestead at the time of the arrival of John West. When he died Donald Gunn left his homestead to his son John.

John died many years ago, leaving a widow and five children. His widow, Emma, who came from the old Garrioch family is still alive at the age of 97 years. When John Gunn died he left the homestead to his son James on the condition that the latter would maintain his mother as long as she lived.

In 1907, John James Gunn was gored to death by a bull. His property, including the old homestead, was left to his widow, Eleanor, as he had no children. After the death of her husband, Eleanor Gunn sold all the cattle and farm implements and supported herself by teaching school. She retained the old homestead but did not work it. The old widow, Emma, who was to have been supported by the son who was killed lived on the land, with her two daughters, Emma Ann and Mary. Her sons Gilbert and George gave assistance in maintaining their mother.

For years there were family disputes as what should be done with the old homestead. Eleanor still retained it but could not follow out the will by maintaining her mother-in-law as she had to support herself. The sons and daughters of the Gunn family supported their mother. They desired possession of the homestead. At various times the parties concerned in the case tried to reach an amicable settlement of the question but nothing resulted.

J. B. Hugg, K. G. and W. A. Johnston for the Gunn family brought the matter to court before Mr. Justice Curran, and asked for possession of the homestead, acted for the case. T. Hunt, K. G. acted for Mrs. Eleanor Gunn in the case.

After considerable discussion the controversy of years was brought to an end yesterday and arrangements were made for a settlement out of court. The homestead is to go to the family and Eleanor Gunn will be awarded $2,500.

816Debbie Kuzub, e-mail to Donald Gunn, 19 Jun 2007.

Children of Donald Gunn (Hon.) of Manitoba (372) and Margaret Swain (923) were as follows:

24 i. William Henry GUNN (2547).
25 ii. James GUNN (2549).
26 iii. John GUNN (Hon.) of Manitoba (2551).
27 iv. Alexander GUNN (2531).
v. Matilda GUNN (2553) was born on 20 Nov 1831 in Lot 163, St Andrews, Manitoba. She married John Atkinson (2554) on 29 Mar 1860 in St Andrews, Manitoba.
John ATKINSON (2554) was born in 1825.
28 vi. George GUNN (2555).
vii. Jane GUNN (2557) was born on 24 Nov 1835 in Lot 163, St Andrews, Manitoba. She died on 01 Nov 1844 in St Andrews, Manitoba, at age 8.
29 viii. Margaret GUNN (2558).
30 ix. Donald GUNN (2560).
x. Robert GUNN (2562) was born on 08 May 1842 in Lot 163, St Andrews, Manitoba. He died on 02 Nov 1843 in St Andrews, Manitoba, at age 1.
31 xi. Janet GUNN (2563).
32 xii. William GUNN (2565).

12. Marjory GUNN (2527) was born in 1803 in Braehour, Halkirk Parish, Caithness.[818] She was christened on 10 Mar 1803 in Braehour, Halkirk Parish, Caithness.[819] She married Peter McDonald (3564) on 14 Apr 1825 in Reay Parish, Caithness. She is believed to have died between 1871 and 1881 on 28 Jun 1873 in Percy Township, in Percy Township, Northumberland County, Ontario.[820] She was buried in 1874 in Warkworth, Percy Township, Northumberland County, Ontario.

She and Peter McDonald (3564) emigrated between 1836 and 1841 to Canada. She and Peter McDonald (3564) lived in Lot 20, Con. 6, Percy Township, Northumberland County, Ontario.

Peter MCDONALD (3564) was born in 1802. He died in Ontario. He was a farmer.

Children of Marjory Gunn (2527) and Peter McDonald (3564) were as follows:

i. Janet MCDONALD (3565) was born in 1826 in Reay Parish, Caithness. She was christened on 10 Mar 1826 in Reay Parish, Caithness.

---

[817]Debbie Kuzub, "Donald Gunn of Canada;" Caroline Armstrong, e-mail to Donald Gunn, Script Affidavate for Margaret Swain SWAIN, Margaret; Filed: The Honorable Donald GUNN; St. Andrew; Lisgar; farmer, for my deceased wife; b. 2 April 1802, NW; d 28 Nov 1870; James SWAIN (Englishman) was father; (Indian) was mother, Heirs: the deponent and her children: James; John; Alexander; George; Donald; William GUNN; Matilda, wife of John ATKINSON, Margaret, wife of John DRANE; Janet, wife of A. M. MUCKLE, all living; and the grandchildren of my son William Henry, his daughter, who married Frank Larned HUNT, said grandchildren being William Gunn HUNT and Winifred HUNT. My said son William was my oldest son and died in May 1842. English; Donald GUNN; 29 July 1875; John GUNN, farmer, Thomas TRUTHWAITE, farmer. Under the law of England which provided at death of said intestate her sole heir was James GUNN the oldest son subject to husband's life. 15 Nov 1880.
Scrip affidavit for Gunn, Margaret Deceased wife of Donald Gunn born: April 2, 1802; father: James Swain (English); mother: Indian; died: November 28, 1870; heirs: her children: James; John; Alexander; George, Donald; William, who died: May 1842; Matilda, wife of John Atkinson; Margaret, wife of John Drane; Janet, wife of A.M. Mickle; grandchildren of her son William through his daughter who married Frank Hunt; said grandchildren being Wm. Hunt and Winifred Hunt; claim no: 3039; date of issue: 1880.

[818]Bill and Sharon Gurney, e-mail to Donald Gunn, 23 Oct 2008: Families of William Gunn and Janet Sinclair; Bill and Sharon Gurney, e-mail to Donald Gunn, 23 Apr 2009: Family of Marjory Gunn and Peter McDonald.

[819]Caroline Armstrong, e-mail to Donald Gunn, 20 Mar 2006; Bill and Sharon Gurney, e-mail to Donald Gunn, 23 Apr 2009: Family of Marjory Gunn and Peter McDonald.

[820]Bill and Sharon Gurney, e-mail to Donald Gunn, 23 Apr 2009: Family of Marjory Gunn and Peter McDonald.

ii. Murdoch MCDONALD (3566).
iii. Henry MCDONALD (3568) was born in 1833 in Reay Parish, Caithness. He was christened on 29 Aug 1833 in Reay Parish, Caithness. He died on 26 Jan 1869 in Percy Township, Northumberland County, Ontario. He was buried in Warkworth, Percy Township, Northumberland County, Ontario.
iv. William MCDONALD (2303) was born in 1836 in Reay Parish, Caithness. He was christened on 07 Jul 1836 in Reay Parish, Caithness.
v. John MCDONALD (3569) was born circa 1844 in Upper Canada.
vi. Jane MCDONALD (3513).

13. William GUNN of Waranga (374)[821] was born in 1804 in Halkirk Parish, Caithness; granddaughter Janettie McMillan gives age as 84 at death in 1888. He was christened on 28 Apr 1805.[822] He married Cecilia Cormack (375), daughter of Alexander Cormack (928) and Elizabeth (--?--) (929), on 26 Jul 1850 in Aberdeen, Grampian.[823] He died in Oct 1888 in Waranga, Vic.[824] His estate was applied for probate on 20 Dec 1888 in the Supreme Court, Vic.[825]

He was promoted from sheriff-officer to messenger-at-arms on 10 Nov 1837 in Caithness.[826] He was Messenger at Arms on 06 Jun 1841 in Wick Parish, Caithness.[827] He lived on 06 Jun 1841 in Bridge Street, Wick Parish, Caithness.[828] He appeared on the census of 30 Mar 1851 in Wick Parish, Caithness.[829] He emigrated in 1853 and settled at Waranga, near Rushworth by the Goulburn River in Northern Victoria. Gold was found on the property in 1853.[830] The possible origin of the name Waranga was detailed in an article in the Melbourne Argus in July 1927.[831] . He was a farmer of 51 840 acres in 1856 in Waranga Park, Vic.[832] He

---

821 See Part 7 for a biography of William Gunn of Waranga.

822 Caroline Armstrong, e-mail to Donald Gunn, 20 Mar 2006.

823 Much of the detail regarding William of Waranga and his decendants is derived from letters written by his grand daughter Janettie McMillan to Donald Gunn. These are reproduced in full in Part 7.

824 Register of BDMs - Victoria, 1888 15610 father William Gunn, mother Janet Sinclair, age 84; *The Melbourne Argus*, 26 Oct 1888 p1: Deaths GUNN.—At his residence, Waranga-park, Rushworth, William Gunn, aged 84 years. Friends please accept this intimation; Letters from Janettie McMillan to Donald Gunn, 17 Oct 1974 and 24 Apr 1974.

825 *Melbourne Argus*, 20 Dec 1888 p3: NOTICE is hereby given that after the expiration of fourteen days from the publication hereof application will be made to the Supreme Court of the Colony of Victoria in its Probate jurisdiction, that PROBATE of the WILL of WILLIAM GUNN, late of Waranga, County of Rodney, in the colony of Victoria grazier, deceased, may be granted to William Gunn (the younger) and Alexander Gunn, both of Waranga aforesaid, landowners, sons of the said deceased, the executors named in and appointed by the said will. Dated this eighteenth day of December, 1888. BROMFIELD and FEDDEN, High Street, Rushworth, Proctors for the said executors.

826 *John O'Groat Journal*, 24 Jan 1861, Law and Order: Friday, November 10, 1837. Caithness. Mr William Gunn, sheriff-officer, promoted to messenger-at-arms.

827 WW and MD Gunn: William Gunn (Waranga Park) was cousin to my great (grandmother?). He was Messenger at Arms at Wick. Two young men committed a crime and a tinker named Cluny who was had up for stealing was with them. William Gunn was taking the three of them to Inverness and stopped the other side of Helmsdale for the night at an inn, putting the two prisoners and the tinker in an upstairs room while he and some more were drinking downstairs. The tinker told the other two if they wanted to go he would take the handcuffs off as he was too old to go himself, so he took their handcuffs off and they opened the window, jumped out and got away. William Gunn was held responsible and had to resign. He then went to Australia where he stayed with a man named Mackay who left him the place where he died; UK Census 06 June 1841. See **page XXX**

828 UK Census 06 June 1841.

829 Census 30 March 1851: William Gunn born Halkirk age 42, messenger at arms; Cecilia Gunn born Wick age 31; Margaret Elizabeth Gunn born Wick age 5 mo.

830 Caroline Armstrong, e-mail to Donald Gunn, 20 Mar 2006.

831 *Melbourne Argus*, 01 Jul 1927 p10: THE NAME WARANGA Concerning the meaning of the name Waranga, a woman living in the district says that it was named Waranga Park when the late William Gunn, the second owner of the run settled there in the early fitties, and the basin was long known as Gunn's Swamp. The son of the first owner explained that the meaning ol Waranga was water- this information being got from a tnbe of blacks who had a camp on the opposite side of the swamps from the Gunns'

was added to the roll of Magistrates for the Colony on 16 Oct 1863 in Waranga Park, Rushworth, Vic.[833] He was issued with a Licence for 8 800 sheep under The Scab Act, with no fine imposed on 07 Jan 1874 in Waranga Park, Vic.[834] He was granted a licence to transfer the mining lease of Sandhurst, lease no. 1976 to W. Gunn on 14 Feb 1874 in Vic. He was granted confirmation of a grazing licence for 18 970 acres at an annual rent of £64/5/- on 09 Jan 1888 in Waranga Park, Vic.[835] Waranga Park was sold by auction on 14 Sep 1953.

Cecilia CORMACK (375)[836] was born in 1819 in Wick Parish, Caithness. She died in 1906 in Rushworth, Vic. She appeared on the census of 30 Mar 1851 in the household of William Gunn of Waranga (374) in Wick Parish, Caithness.[837] She emigrated in 1857 to Melbourne with son William, leaving daughters Margaret and Janet with relatives in Scotland until 1874.[838] As of 1859, she was also known as Cecilia Cormick (375) birth registrations for children Elizabeth and Alexander record name as Cecilia Cormick. She wrote to her husband's niece Janet Muckle in Canada on 06 Oct 1893.

Children of William Gunn of Waranga (374) and Cecilia Cormack (375) were as follows:

i. Margaret Elizabeth GUNN (376) was born in Oct 1850 in Caithness; was 5 mo. at time of 1851 census. She died in 1929 in Hawthorn, Vic.[839]

She was also known as Marnie (376). She appeared on the census of 30 Mar 1851 in the household of her parents William (374) in Wick Parish, Caithness. She appeared on the census of 30 Mar 1861 in the household of her uncle and aunt James Cormack (3409) and Margaret (--?--) (3410) in Wick Parish, Caithness.[840] She and Janet Gunn (900) emigrated in 1874 to Melbourne.

ii. Janet GUNN (900) was born in 1852 in Wick Parish, Caithness. She married Alfred Collier (901) in 1887 in Melbourne, Vic.[841] She died in 1888 in Waranga, Vic, no issue.[842]

She appeared on the census of 30 Mar 1861 in the household of her uncle and aunt James Cormack (3409) and Margaret (--?--) (3410) in Wick Parish, Caithness. She and Margaret Elizabeth Gunn (376) emigrated in 1874 to Melbourne.[843]

---

homestead, the site of which is now 13 ft under water. For long after the blacks disappeared their camp was known locallv as 'the blackfellows' camp.' One thing noticeable in aboriginal dialects is that the names of things much in use, as water would be, are generally short, either one or two syllables. In the locality named, Katyin, or some word like it, is generally the aboriginal name for water.

832 Letter, Edith Christoe to Donald Gunn, 29 Nov 2005; Caroline Armstrong, e-mail to Donald Gunn, 20 Mar 2006.

833 *Melbourne Argus*, 17 Oct 1863 p6: THE GAZETTE Appointments To be added to the roll of Magistrates of the Colony:- William Gunn Esq, Waranga Park, Rushworth.

834 *Victoria Government Gazette*), 1874.

835 *Victoria Government Gazette*, 1888.

836 Register of BDMs - Victoria, 1906 14767.

837 Census 30 March 1851: William Gunn born Halkirk age 42, messenger at arms; Cecilia Gunn born Wick age 31; Margaret Elizabeth Gunn born Wick age 5 mo.

838 Caroline Armstrong, e-mail to Donald Gunn, 20 March 2006; In 1857 Cecelia came out to Australia bringing her son William but leaving the two daughters Margaret and Janet with relatives in Scotland until 1874.

839 Register of BDMs - Victoria, 1929 9879.

840 Census 30 March 1861: James Cormack; Margaret Cormack; Margaret Gunn, born Wick age 10 niece; Janet Gunn, born Wick age 8 niece.

841 Register of BDMs - Victoria, 1887 5980.

842 Register of BDMs - Victoria, 1888 3593.

843 Caroline Armstrong, e-mail to Donald Gunn, 20 March 2006 In 1857 Cecelia came out to Australia bringing her son William but leaving the two daughters Margaret and Janet with relatives in Scotland until 1874.

Alfred COLLIER (901) was a bank manager in 1887 in Rushworth, Vic.

35 iii. William GUNN (377).

36 iv. Elizabeth GUNN (384).

v. Alexander GUNN (906) was born in 1861 in Rushworth, Vic.[844] He died on 31 Aug 1915 in Rushworth, Vic, unmarried, no issue, following injury sustained after being thrown from a gig.[845]

He and William Gunn (377) were named as Lessees in Arrears under Sec 20 of the Land Act 1869, of lease no. 2970 Waranga and no. 2730 Murchison on 01 Apr 1888 in Rushworth, Vic. He was a beneficiary of the estate of William Gunn of Waranga (374) on 20 Dec 1888 in Supreme Court, Vic.[846]

vi. Cecilia Jane GUNN (907) was born in 1863 in Rushworth, Vic. She died in 1864 in Waranga, Vic.[847]

14. John GUNN in Durness (878); 5 daughters and 1 son living after death of son Donald on 21 Jan 1864[848] was born in 1808 in Halkirk Parish, Caithness.[849] He married Catherine Gunn in Campster (1120), daughter of John Gunn in Dyke (1121) and Catherine Gunn (3192), on 08 Jun 1836 in Caithness.[850] He died between 10 Jan 1885 and 1885 in Durness Parish, Sutherland, age 77.[851] He was buried in the Old Cemetery, Balnakeil, Durness Parish, Sutherland.

---

[844] Register of BDMs - Victoria, 1861 9208; Letter from Janettie McMillan to Donald Gunn, 24 Apr 1974 aged 54 when died.

[845] Register of BDMs - Victoria, 1915 11067; *Melbourne Argus*, 03 Sep 1915: Gunn - on the 31st August, at Waranga Park, (result of accident) Alexander (Tal), yougest son of the late Wiliam Gunn, aged 54 years; *The Melbourne Age*, 31 Aug 1915: A serious accident happened to Mr Alexander Gunn, of Waranga Park, Waranga, on Friday. While driving to Rushworth in company with his niece, the horse suddenly propped, and Mr Gunn was thrown out of the gig on the hard metal roadway, sustaining serious injury to the head, and he has not regained consciousness. The horse bolted, and Miss Gunn was also thrown out and injured.

[846] *Melbourne Argus*, 20 Dec 1888 p3: NOTICE is hereby given that after the expiration of fourteen days from the publication hereof application will be made to the Supreme Court of the Colony of Victoria in its Probate jurisdiction, that PROBATE of the WILL of WILLIAM GUNN, late of Waranga, County of Rodney, in the colony of Victoria grazier, deceased, may be granted to William Gunn (the younger) and Alexander Gunn, both of Waranga aforesaid, landowners, sons of the said deceased, the executors named in and appointed by the said will. Dated this eighteenth day of December, 1888. BROMFIELD andFEDDEN, High Street, Rushworth, Proctors for the said executors.

[847] Register of BDMs - Victoria, 1864 4666; Letter from Janettie McMillan to Donald Gunn, 24 Apr 1974.

[848] Chart from Colin Gunn.

[849] Chart from Colin Gunn: eldest son; Michael J Gunn, "Descent of the Gunns", Descent of the Gunns of Dalnaglaton and Braehour.

[850] Parish Register - Death, Wick Parish Register - 1835(6) - Marriage: John Gunn, farmer in Brawlbin, Parish of Reay; Catherine Gunn in Campster; witnesses Alexander Gunn, farmer, Brawlbin for the man; Donald Gunn, farmer, Brawlbin for the son; Michael J Gunn, "Descent of the Gunns", Descent of the Gunns of Dalnaglaton and Braehour.

[851] Chart from Colin Gunn; Michael J Gunn, "Descent of the Gunns", Descent of the Gunns of Dalnaglaton and Braehour; Balnakeil Cemetery : Text reads: In loving memory of John Gunn Land Steward Durness who died 10th Jany 1885 aged 77 years. Also Catherine Gunn his Spouse who died 14th Octr 1871 aged 55 years. Also their Sons John Gunn Inland Revenue Officer who died at Comber Ireland 9th January 1861 aged 23 years and interred there. Donald Gunn Teacher who died 21st Jany 1864 aged 20 years. Also their Daughters Johan [Gunn] who died 11th Octr 1868 aged 13 years. Barbara [Gunn] who died 3rd Novr 1905 aged 58 years. Catherine [Gunn] who died 3rd April 1907 aged 56 Erected by their Son Alexander [Gunn].

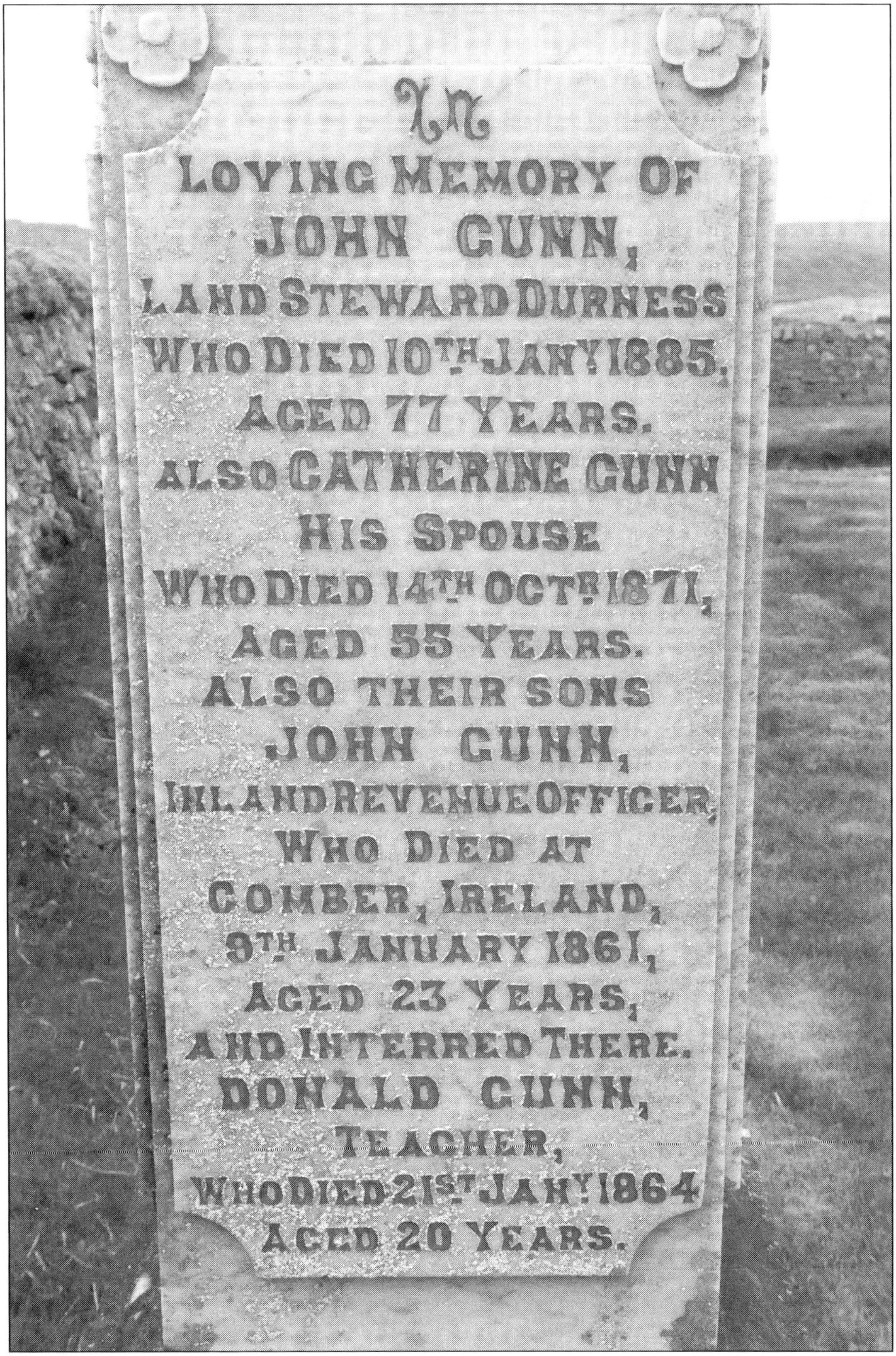

Part of the memorial to John Gunn and his family at the Old Cemetery at Balnakeil, near Durness, 2011.

He was the Land Steward, Durness. He and Catherine Gunn in Campster (1120) appeared on the Census dated 30 Mar 1851.[852] He wrote to nephew Donald and niece Catherine in Australia on 03 Apr 1856 and again on 13 Nov 1863. He wrote to nephew Donald in Australia on 12 Feb 1864.

Catherine GUNN in Campster (1120)[853] was born circa 1817 in Reay Parish, Caithness.[854] She died on 14 Oct 1871 in Durness, Sutherland, age 55, informant was son-in-law Torquil Nicholson.[855]

The Old Cemetery at Balnakeil, near Durness, 2011; the Gunn monument is on the right.

Children of John Gunn in Durness (878) and Catherine Gunn in Campster (1120) were

i. John GUNN (1122) was born in 1837 in Lamesdale, Reay Parish, Caithness and christened on 20 Jun 1837 in Lamesdale. He died on 09 Jan 1861 in Comber, County Down, at age 23.[856] He was an inland revenue officer.

852Census 30 March 1851: John Gunn born Reay age 46, Catherine Gunn born Reay age 34, Margaret born Reay age 10, Donald born Reay age 6.

853Bill and Sharon Gurney, e-mail to Donald Gunn, 21 Sep 2008.

854Michael J Gunn, "Descent of the Gunns", Descent of the Gunns of Dalnaglaton and Braehour.

855Bill and Sharon Gurney, e-mail to Donald Gunn, 21 Sep 2008; Balnakeil Cemetery: Text reads: In loving memory of John Gunn Land Steward Durness who died 10th Jany 1885 aged 77 years. Also Catherine Gunn his Spouse who died 14th Octr 1871 aged 55 years. Also their Sons John Gunn Inland Revenue Officer who died at Comber Ireland 9th January 1861 aged 23 years and interred there. Donald Gunn Teacher who died 21st Jany 1864 aged 20 years. Also their Daughters Johan [Gunn] who died 11th Octr 1868 aged 13 years. Barbara [Gunn] who died 3rd Novr 1905 aged 58 years. Catherine [Gunn] who died 3rd April 1907 aged 56 Erected by their Son Alexander [Gunn].

856Michael J Gunn, "Descent of the Gunns;" *John O'Groat Journal*, 24 Jan 1861, At Combes, Co. Down, Ireland, on the 9th inst., Mr John Gunn, Inland Revenue Officer, son of John Gunn Durness, Sutherlandshire, and grandson of the late Mr Donald Gunn, tacksman, Brawlbin, who died on the 3d inst; Balnakeil Cemetery: Text reads: In loving memory of John Gunn Land Steward

37 ii. Margaret GUNN (1123).

iii. Donald GUNN (1116) was born in 1844 in Brawlbin, Reay Parish, Caithness. He was christened on 16 Jan 1844 in Brawlbin, Reay Parish, Caithness. He died on 21 Jan 1864 in Durness, Sutherland, age 20 years. He was buried on 27 Jan 1864 in Dirlot, Caithness, and his body was carried to Dirlot from Durness to be buried beside his grandfather.

He was a teacher.[857] He appeared on the 1851 Census.[858] He had to raise a 4 year old son and 5 lassies after son Donald's death in Feb 1864.

iv. Barbara GUNN (1124) was born in 1847 in Carriside, Reay Parish, Caithness.[859] She was christened on 28 Jan 1847 in Carriside, Reay Parish, Caithness. She died on 03 Nov 1905 at age 58 age 58 years.

v. Catherine GUNN (1125) was born on 31 Oct 1849 in Carriside, Reay Parish, Caithness. She was christened on 02 Nov 1849 in Carriside, Reay Parish, Caithness.[860] She died on 03 Apr 1907 at age 57 age 56.

She lived with her brother Alexander and family in Durness in 1891 and 1901.

vi. Johan GUNN (1126) was born on 19 Jan 1855 in Reay Parish, Caithness. She died on 11 Oct 1868 at age 13 age 13 years.

She was a teacher.

38 vii. Alexander GUNN in Sangomore (887).

39 viii. Williamina GUNN (889).

15. Barbara GUNN of Braehour (6)[861] was christened on 30 Mar 1810 in Halkirk Parish, Caithness, but her husband's family bible records birth date as 17 Apr 1810.[862] She married Alexander Gunn of Bualchork and Brawlbin (1), son of Donald Gunn in Tormsdale (262) and Janet MacKenzie of Dunbeath (703), on 19 Mar 1829 in Halkirk Parish, Caithness.[863] She died on 28 Feb 1844 in Brawlbin, Reay Parish, Caithness, at age 33.[864]

Durness who died 10th Jany 1885 aged 77 years. Also Catherine Gunn his Spouse who died 14th Octr 1871 aged 55 years. Also their Sons John Gunn Inland Revenue Officer who died at Comber Ireland 9th January 1861 aged 23 years and interred there. Donald Gunn Teacher who died 21st Jany 1864 aged 20 years. Also their Daughters Johan [Gunn] who died 11th Octr 1868 aged 13 years. Barbara [Gunn] who died 3rd Novr 1905 aged 58 years. Catherine [Gunn] who died 3rd April 1907 aged 56 Erected by their Son Alexander [Gunn].

857 Balnakeil Cemetery: Text reads: In loving memory of John Gunn Land Steward Durness who died 10th Jany 1885 aged 77 years. Also Catherine Gunn his Spouse who died 14th Octr 1871 aged 55 years. Also their Sons John Gunn Inland Revenue Officer who died at Comber Ireland 9th January 1861 aged 23 years and interred there. Donald Gunn Teacher who died 21st Jany 1864 aged 20 years. Also their Daughters Johan [Gunn] who died 11th Octr 1868 aged 13 years. Barbara [Gunn] who died 3rd Novr 1905 aged 58 years. Catherine [Gunn] who died 3rd April 1907 aged 56 Erected by their Son Alexander [Gunn].

858 UK Census 30 March 1851: John Gunn born Reay age 46, Catherine Gunn born Reay age 34, Margaret born Reay age 10, Donald born Reay age 6.

859 Bill and Sharon Gurney, e-mail to Donald Gunn, 13 Sep 2008.

860 Bill and Sharon Gurney, e-mail to Donald Gunn, 27 Jul 2010, Descendants of Alexander Gunn and Barbara Weir.

861 *LDS Church*, Christenings of children of Donald Gunn and Catherine Gunn: Barbara 1810, Mary 1812, Alexander 1814, Jean 1816, Lexy (Alexandrina) 1825; Clan Gunn Parish Records held at the Clan Gunn Heritage Centre, Latheron.

862 *Bible of Alexander Gunn*: my wife, Barbra Gunn born April 17 1810. Letter from Colin Gunn, Jan 1998; Parish Register - BaptismHalkirk Parish Register. 1810 Gunn Barbara lawful daughter of Donald Gunn and Catherine Gunn in Braehour was baptised 30th March. Elizabeth Tait there and Donald Murray, Olgrinmore Witnesses.

863 *LDS Church*, Marriage, Alexander Gunn, Barbara Gunn, 19 Mar 1829, Halkirk, Caithness; Clan Gunn Parish Records: Marriages 1829 - Alexander of Bualchork married Barbara Gunn of Braehour.

864 *Bible of Alexander Gunn*: died on the 28th February 1844; Bill and Sharon Gurney, e-mail to Donald Gunn, 09 Feb 2009; The Descendants of Donald Gunn.

She and Alexander Gunn of Bualchork and Brawlbin (1) appeared on the census of 06 Jun 1841 in Brawlbin, Reay Parish, Caithness. Angus Keith age 30 male servant, was also listed in the household.[865]

Alexander GUNN of Bualchork and Brawlbin (1) was born on 04 Jun 1789 in Halkirk Parish, Caithness.[866] He was christened on 09 Jun 1789 in Halkirk Parish,[867] and died on 29 Mar 1847 in Brawlbin, Reay Parish, at age 57.[868] Bualchork is no longer recorded, even in ordnance survey maps, but a location, Bullechach, is close to Tormsdale, Dirlot and Braehour, and is probably Alexander's birth location.

Bullechach farm, 2011

Alexander (1) thought of emigrating to Jamaica in 1819. Alexander (1) was a shoemaker. He was a manager of the Loyal and United Benevolent Society of the Clan Gunn when it was formed on 18 Dec 1821 in Thurso Parish, Caithness.[869] He was a farmer after 1828 in Brawlbin, Reay Parish, Caithness. He entered into a 14 year lease of Brawlbin farm for £16/a

---

865UK Census 06 June 1841: District of Brawlbin lying in the south part of the Parish of Reay. Each person who abode in each house on night of 6 June 1841: Alexander Gunn 50 farmer; Barbara Gunn 30; Kathrine Gunn 11; Donald Gunn 9; John Gunn 5; Janet Gunn 7; William Gunn 2; all born in Caithness. Note: Census instructions for recording age were that if under 15, actual age; if over 15, record to the nearest 5 years below actual ie Alexander Gunn was between 50 and 55 and Barbara between 30 and 35 on 6 June 1841. Birth years are thus Alexander 1786-1791 and Barbara 1806-1811.

866*LDS Church*, christenings at Halkirk, Caithness, of children born to Donald Gunn and Janet McKenzie: John 18 Jan 1783 and Hugh 7 Jan 1787, with Alexander 9 Jun 1789, Donald 19 Mar 1796, William 12 Mar 1799, Christian 30 Jan 1802, Marcus 9 Aug 1805 further described as born at Halkirk; *Bible of Alexander Gunn*: Alexr Gunn was born 1789 and died on 29 Mar 1847; Chart from Colin Gunn.

867Parish Register: Alexander lawful son of Donald Gunn and Janet Mackenzie in Tormsdale was baptised the ninth day of June seventeen hundred and eighty nine. John Gunn and Catherine McDonald in Bridgend, Witnesses. Halkirk 25th March 1817. Extracted from the Register of Baptisms of the Parish of Halkirk, County of Caithness, by Donald Grant, S.Clk.

868*Bible of Alexander Gunn*: Alexr Gunn was born 1789 and died on 29 Mar 1847.

869Thomas Sinclair, *The Gunns*, p174; The Loyal and United Benevolent Society of the Clan Gunn, instituted at Thurso, 18th December, 1821. Alexander Gunn, shoemaker in Bualkork is named as one of the Society's managers.

on 30 Jun 1834. He witnessed the marriage of John Gunn in Durness (878) and Catherine Gunn in Campster (1120) on 08 Jun 1836 in Caithness.[870]

Children of Barbara Gunn of Braehour (6) and Alexander Gunn of Bualchork and Brawlbin (1) were (but see Part 3 and Part 7):

40 i. Catherine GUNN (119).

41 ii. Donald Gunn in Brawlbin and Ballarat (3).

42 iii. Janet Mcleod GUNN (120).

iv. John GUNN (12)[871] was born on 12 Feb 1836 in Reay Parish, Caithness.[872] He was christened on 20 Feb 1836 in Reay Parish, Caithness. He died circa Dec 1854 in Port Melbourne, Vic.

He appeared on the 1841 Census of Brawlbin, Reay Parish, Caithness, in the household of his parents Alexander Gunn of Bualchork and Brawlbin (1) and Barbara Gunn of Braehour (6), and on the 1851 Census in the household of his brother Donald (3). He left Caithness by steamer for Glasgow, thence Liverpool on 11 Jul 1853.[873] On 21 Jul 1853 he emigrated rom Liverpool, Merseyside, per sailing ship Tasmania, 1195 t, for voyage to Australia. He arrived in Melbourne, Vic, listed in the ship's manifest as John Gum, aged 24 on 25 Oct 1853.

v. William GUNN (220) was born on 10 Jan 1839 in Reay Parish, Caithness. He died after 15 Jun 1864 in Vic being the date of a letter written in Melbourne referring to him. He may have died in 1873. Alastair Gunn cites this as possible.

He appeared on the 1841 Census of Brawlbin, Reay Parish, Caithness, in the household of his parents Alexander Gunn of Bualchork and Brawlbin (1) and Barbara Gunn of Braehour (6). He appeared on the 1851 Census of Brawlbin, Reay Parish, Caithness, in the household of Donald Gunn in Brawlbin and Ballarat (3). He probably emigrated on 01 Jul 1857 in the Donald McKay 2560 ton register carrying 595 passengers from Liverpool to Melbourne, Vic, arriving in Sep 1857. This is the only shipping record of a William Gunn aged around 18 to travel to Melbourne between late '54 and late '58.[874] Letter from Janet to Donald dated 11 Oct 1858 sends regards to William. He was the recipient of a letter from Donald Gunn of Brawlbin and Dundee (976) written on 01 Feb 1859, and another written on 25 Apr 1864.

---

[870] Parish Register, Wick Parish - 1835(6) - Marriage: John Gunn, farmer in Brawlbin, Parish of Reay; Catherine Gunn in Campster; witnesses Alexander Gunn, farmer, Brawlbin for the man; Donald Gunn, farmer, Brawlbin for the son; Michael J Gunn, "Descent of the Gunns", Descent of the Gunns of Dalnaglaton and Braehour.

[871] *LDS Church*, Christenings of children of Barbara Gunn, father Alexander Gunn Catherine, 18 May 1830, Halkirk; Donald, 9 Jun 1832, Reay; Janet, 19 Aug 1834, Reay; John, 29 Feb 1836, Reay.

[872] Clan Gunn Parish Records: Births 1836 John Gunn, parents Alexander, Brawlbin - Barbara; UK Census 06 June 1841.
UK Census 30 March 1851: County of Caithness, Parish of Reay. Residents at Brawlbinn. Donald Gunn head, unmarried 19, farmer, 16 acres, born Halkirk; Katherine Gunn sister, unmarried 20, general service, born Reay; Janet Gunn sister, unmarried 17, scholar, born Reay; John Gunn brother, unmarried 15, scholar born Reay; William Gunn brother, unmarried 12, scholar born Reay. *Bible of Alexander Gunn*: John Gunn born 12 February 1836.

[873] See Part 3, page 237 for letters from John to brother Donald, the first undated, the second dated 25 Oct 1853:

[874] Immigration to Victoria, British Ports 1852-1859, the only shipping record of a William Gunn aged around 18 to travel to Melbourne between late '54 and late '58 was per the Donald McKay of 2560 ton register carrying 595 passengers. He was recorded as a labourer and travelled alone. There is a further record of a William Gunn aged 21 arriving on the Delgany in Dec '54. There are no possible corrupted names on this passenger list, National Archives, UK.

16. Mary (May) GUNN (487)[875] was born in 1812 in Halkirk Parish, Caithness.[876] She was christened on 07 Feb 1812 in Halkirk Parish, Caithness. She married John Campbell (3505) circa 1837 in Caithness.[877] She died on 13 Sep 1853 in Halkirk Parish, Caithness, at age 41 and was buried in Dorrery, Halkirk Parish, Caithness.

She was also known as Marjory (487). She appeared on the census of 06 Jun 1841 in the household of her parents Donald (708) and Catherine (3423) in Brawlbin, Reay Parish, Caithness.

John CAMPBELL (3505) was born circa 1815 in Reay, Caithness.[878] He married Margaret Angus (3572) circa 1855 after the death of his first wife and they had at least eight children by 1870.[879]

Children of Mary (May) Gunn (487) and John Campbell (3505) were as follows:

i. Johan CAMPBELL (3570) was born in 1838 in Thurso, Thurso Parish, Caithness. He was christened on 18 Jan 1838 in Thurso.

ii. Donald CAMPBELL (3514) was born on 18 Dec 1840 in Thurso, Thurso Parish, Caithness. He was christened on 03 Jan 1841 in Thurso.

He arrived in Melbourne, Vic, aboard the Chatsworth with his cousin Janet MacLeod Gunn (120) on 16 Jan 1864.

iii. William CAMPBELL (3515) was born on 08 Nov 1843 in Halkirk Parish, Caithness. He was christened on 22 Nov 1843 in Thurso. He died on 09 Jan 1873 in Halkirk Parish, Caithness, at age 29. He was buried in Dorrery, Halkirk Parish, Caithness.

iv. John CAMPBELL (3571) was born circa 1850 in Halkirk Parish, Caithness. He died in 1851 in Halkirk Parish, Caithness. He was buried in Dorrery, Halkirk Parish, Caithness.

17. Alexander GUNN (Capt.) of Braehour and Newton (572) was born in 1814 in Braehour, Halkirk Parish, Caithness.[880] He was christened on 23 Apr 1814 in Halkirk Parish, Caithness. He married Mary Innes Campbell (1128), daughter of Peter Campbell (1135) and Catherine Innes (1136), in Apr 1841 in Caithness.[881] A genealogist, he died on 03 Jan 1900 in Thurso, Thurso Parish, Caithness, at age 85 informant at death was niece Jessie Mackenzie of Killimister, Wick.[882]

He appeared on the census of 06 Jun 1841 in the household of his parents Donald (708) and Catherine (3423) in Brawlbin, Reay Parish, Caithness.[883] He was a corn merchant in

---

875 *LDS Church*, Christenings of children of Donald Gunn and Catherine Gunn: Barbara 1810, Mary 1812, Alexander 1814, Jean 1816, Lexy (Alexandrina) 1825.

876 Bill and Sharon Gurney, e-mail to Donald Gunn, 27 Jul 2010, Descendants of Alexander Gunn and Barbara Weir.

877 Bill and Sharon Gurney, e-mail to Donald Gunn, 09 Feb 2009; The Descendants of Donald Gunn.

878 Bill and Sharon Gurney, e-mail to Donald Gunn, 09 Feb 2009; The Descendants of Donald Gunn.

879 Details of the family of Mary (May) Gunn and John Campbell are mostly drawn from an email from Bill and Sharon Gurney to Donald Gunn, 23 Apr 2009: Family of May Gunn and John Campbell.

880 Census 30 March 1851: Alexander Gunn born Braehour age 39, Mary aka Margaret Campbell born Reay age 36, Williamina age 8, Barbara age 6, Peter age 4, Catherine age 2; Chart from Colin Gunn.

881 Details of the family of Alexander Gunn and Mary Campbell are largely drawn from an email from Bill and Sharon Gurney to Donald Gunn, 07 Jan 2009; *John O'Groat Journal*, 24 Jan 1861, Friday 16 Apr 1841; Gunn, Alexander: Brawlbin to Mary Campbell: Reay.

882 Chart from Colin Gunn.

883 UK Census 06 June 1841: District of Brawlbin lying in the south part of the Parish of Reay. Each person who abode in each house on night of 6 June 1841: Donald Gunn 72 farmer; Kathrine Gunn 60; Alexander Gunn 26; Mary Gunn 26; Margaret Gunn 22;

1851. He and Mary Innes Campbell (1128) appeared on the census of 30 Mar 1851 in Brawlbin, Reay Parish.[884] He witnessed the marriage of John Mackay (3467) and Margaret Gunn (880) on 14 Feb 1860 in Brawlbin, Reay Parish.[885] He was a farmer of 600 acres in 1861. He was the informant at the death of Donald Gunn (the Sennachie) of Braehour and Brawlbin (708) on 03 Jan 1861 in Brawlbin, Reay Parish, Caithness; fractured neck.[886] He and Mary Innes Campbell (1128) appeared on the census of 30 Mar 1861 in Halkirk Parish, Caithness.[887] He was the informant at the death of Mary Innes Campbell (1128) on 05 Sep 1864 in Braehour, Halkirk Parish, Caithness. He was the informant at the death of Catherine Gunn of Osclay (3423) on 24 Oct 1870 in Newton, Watten Parish, Caithness.[888] He appeared on the census of 1871 in Braehour, Halkirk Parish.[889] He appeared on the census of 1881 in Bridge Street, Halkirk, Halkirk Parish.[890] He appeared on the census of 1891 in the household of his nephew Hector Mackay (3468) and Mary Ann MacKinnon (3469) in Newton, Watten Parish.[891]

Mary Innes CAMPBELL (1128) was born in 1808 in Reay Parish, Caithness. She was christened on 12 Dec 1808 in Reay Parish, Caithness. She died on 05 Sep 1864 in Braehour, Halkirk Parish, Caithness. She was also known as Margaret (1128).

Children of Alexander Gunn (Capt.) of Braehour and Newton (572) and Mary Innes Campbell (1128) all born in Reay Parish, Caithness, were:

i. Catherine GUNN (1129) was christened on 08 Feb 1842 in Reay Parish, Caithness and died before 1849.

ii. Williamina GUNN (1130).

iii. Barbara GUNN (1131) was born in 1844 and christened on 30 Nov 1844 in Reay Parish, Caithness. She died on 13 Feb 1879 in 109 Lowan Street, Glasgow, Lanarkshire.

She appeared on the census of 30 Mar 1851 in the household of Alexander Gunn (Capt.) of Braehour and Newton (572) and Mary Innes Campbell (1128) in Brawlbin, Reay Parish, Caithness.[892] She appeared on the census of 30 Mar 1861 in the household of her parents Alexander (572) and Mary (1128) in

---

Alexandrina Gunn 18; all born in Caithness; together with George Gunn 80 servant, George Gunn servant 22 and three other servants. Note: Census instructions for recording age were that if under 15, actual age; if over 15, record to the nearest 5 years below.

884 UK Census 30 March 1851: Brawlbin, Reay, Caithness: Alexander Gunn corn merchant born Braehour age 36, Mary aka Margaret Campbell born Reay age 36, Williamina age 8, Barbara age 6, Peter age 4, Catherine age 2.

885 Bill and Sharon Gurney, e-mail to Donald Gunn, 08 Jan 2009; unknown title, John Mackay, age 45, Achalibster, Parish of Halkirk, farmer, bachelor, son of Hector Mackay, farmer, deceased, and Janet Mackay, deceased married Margaret Gunn, age 37, Brawlbin, Parish of Reay, spinster, daughter of Donald Gunn, farmer and Catherine Gunn on 14th of February 1860 at Brawlbin. Marriage (after Banns) was solemnized to the Forms of the Free Chuch of Scotland. Witnesses were A. Gunn and Hugh Donaldson. (signed) David Ferguson, Minister.

886 *John O'Groat Journal*, 24 Jan 1861, of the late Mr Donald Gunn, tacksman, Brawlbin, who died on the 3d inst; Bill and Sharon Gurney, e-mail to Donald Gunn, 09 Feb 2009; The Descendants of Donald Gunn.

887 UK Census 30 March 1861: Alexr Gunn 46 farmer 600 acres; Mary Gunn 48; Williamina Gunn 17; Barbara Gunn 15; Peter Gunn 13; Catherine Gunn 11; Robertina Gunn 9.

888 Bill and Sharon Gurney, e-mail to Donald Gunn, 09 Feb 2009; The Descendants of Donald Gunn.

889 UK Census 1871: Alexr Gunn 56 farmer 600 acres; Williamina Gunn 26; 3 servants.

890 UK Census 1881: Alexr Gunn 66 widower retired farmer; Catherine Campbell 35 general servant.

891 UK Census 1891: Hector McKay 27 farmer; Mary A McKay 30; Alexander Gunn 76 uncle retired farmer; John McKinnon 18 visitor; 3 servants.

892 UK Census 30 March 1851: Brawlbin, Reay, Caithness: Alexander Gunn corn merchant born Braehour age 36, Mary aka Margaret Campbell born Reay age 36, Williamina age 8, Barbara age 6, Peter age 4, Catherine age 2.

Halkirk Parish, Caithness.[893] She witnessed the marriage of John Scott (3450) and Catherine Gunn (1133) on 18 Jun 1873 in Inverness.[894] Her usual residence was in Braehour, Halkirk Parish, Caithness.

iv. Peter GUNN (1132) was born in 1846. He was christened on 10 Sep 1846 in Reay Parish, Caithness.

He appeared on the census of 30 Mar 1851 in the household of Alexander Gunn (Capt.) of Braehour and Newton (572) and Mary Innes Campbell (1128) in Brawlbin, Reay Parish, Caithness. He emigrated to Australia, date unknown, and possibly lived in Wagga Wagga, NSW. He appeared on the census of 30 Mar 1861 in the household of his parents Alexander (572) and Mary (1128) in Halkirk Parish, Caithness.

v. Catherine Innes GUNN (1133), married John Scott and had seven children.

vi. Robertina GUNN (1134) was born in 1852. She was christened on 16 Apr 1852 in Reay Parish, Caithness. She died in 1872.

She was working in the poorhouse while living with her aunt Alexandrina Gunn in 1871 in Dundee, Angus. She appeared on the 1871 Census of Dundee Poor House and Lunatic Asylum, Dundee, Angus, in the household of her uncle Donald Gunn of Brawlbin and Dundee (976) and aunt Alexandrina (Lexy) Gunn of Braehour (554).[895]

18. Margaret GUNN (880) was born in 1819 in Caithness. She married John Mackay (3467), son of Hector Mackay (3470) and Janet (--?--) (3471), on 14 Feb 1860 in Brawlbin, Reay Parish, Caithness. She died in 1888 in Newton, Watten Parish, Caithness. She was buried in Dirlot, Caithness.

She appeared on the census of 06 Jun 1841 in the household of her parents Donald (708) and Catherine (3423) in Brawlbin, Reay Parish, Caithness. She appeared on the census of 30 Mar 1851 in the household of her parents Donald (708) and Catherine (3423) in Brawlbin, Reay Parish, Caithness.[896] She appeared on the census of 1871 in Newton, Watten Parish, Caithness.[897] She appeared on the census of 1881 in Newton, Watten Parish, Caithness.[898]

John MACKAY (3467) was born circa 1815 in Halkirk Parish, Caithness. He died on 20 Aug 1865 in Newton, Watten Parish, Caithness. He was a farmer of 200 acres in 1860 in Achalibster, Halkirk Parish, Caithness. He was a farmer of 200 acres in 1861 in Newton,

---

[893]UK Census 30 March 1861: Alexr Gunn 46 farmer 600 acres; Mary Gunn 48; Williamina Gunn 17; Barbara Gunn 15; Peter Gunn 13; Catherine Gunn 11; Robertina Gunn 9.

[894]Unknown translator, John Scott, contractor, age 25, Angus, married Catherine Gunn age 24, Braehour in the Parish of Halkirk on 18 June 1873 in Inverness. Witnesses were William Scott and Barbara Gunn.

[895]Bill and Sharon Gurney, e-mail to Donald Gunn, 23 Nov 2009: Family of Alexandrina and Donald Gunn; Census 1871: Donald Gunn head age 53 born Halkirk Governor; Alexandrina Gunn wife age 44 born Halkirk;John Gunn son age 17 Apprentice Druggist; Daniel A Gunn son age16 born Dundee Apprentice Merch. Clerk; Margaret Gunn dau. age 12 born Dundee Scholar; Catherine Gunn dau. age 10 born Dundee Scholar; Wilhelmina Gunn dau. age 5 born Dundee Scholar; Robertina Gunn niece age 18 born Dundee Matron's Asst.

[896]UK Census 30 March 1851: Reay Parish, Brawlbin: Donald Gunn 80 farmer, 60 acres, b Halkirk; Catherine Gunn 68, b Latheron; Margaret Gunn dau 30, b Halkirk, housemaid; Alexandrina Gunn dau 28, b Halkirk, housemaid; George Gunn 28, b Halkirk, servant; George Dunbar 30, b Halkirk, servant; Mary Gunn 16 b Reay herd; Margaret Sutherland 24, b Halkirk, outdoor servant.

[897]UK Census 1871: Margaret McKay, head age 51, born Halkirk, farmer of 240 ac,; Hector McKay, son age 7, born Watten scholar.

[898]UK Census 1881: Margaret McKay, head age 60, born Halkirk, farmer of 240 acres.; Hector McKay, son age 17 born Watten; plus several servants and boarders.

Watten Parish, Caithness. He appeared on the census of 30 Mar 1861 in Newton, Watten Parish, Caithness.[899] He wrote to Donald Gunn in Australia, the nephew of his wife on 04 Jan 1864.[900] He wrote again to Donald in Australia on 25 Apr 1864.

Children of Margaret Gunn (880) and John Mackay (3467) were:

i. Hector MACKAY (3468) was born on 14 Dec 1863 in Watten Parish, Caithness.[901] He married Mary Ann MacKinnon (3469), daughter of Donald MacKinnon (3472) and Margaret Robertson (3473), circa 1888. He died on 09 Aug 1892 in Halkirk Parish, Caithness, at age 28 and was buried in Dirlot, Caithness.

He appeared on the census of 1871 in the household of his mother Margaret (880) in Newton, Watten Parish, Caithness.[902] He appeared on the census of 1881 in the household of his mother Margaret (880) in Newton, Watten Parish, Caithness.[903] He and Mary Ann MacKinnon (3469) appeared on the census of 1891 in Newton, Watten Parish, Caithness.[904]

Mary Ann MACKINNON (3469) was born circa 1861 in Watten Parish, Caithness.[905] She died on 27 Dec 1946 in Watten and was buried in Watten, with her parents and brother George.

19. Alexandrina (Lexy) GUNN of Braehour (554) was born in 1825 in Halkirk Parish, Caithness. She was christened on 12 Jul 1825 in Halkirk Parish, Caithness.[906] She married Donald Gunn of Brawlbin and Dundee (976), son of Alexander Gunn (3573) and Sarah Sutherland (3574), on 26 Apr 1852 in Brawlbin, Reay Parish, Caithness.[907] She died in 1876 in St Andrew, Dundee, Angus.

She appeared on the census of 06 Jun 1841 in the household of her parents Donald (708) and Catherine (3423) in Brawlbin, Reay Parish, Caithness. She appeared on the census of 30 Mar 1851 in the household of her parents Donald (708) and Catherine (3423) in Brawlbin, Reay Parish, Caithness.[908] She and Donald Gunn of Brawlbin and Dundee (976) appeared on the 1861 Census of The Poor House of Dundee, Dundee, Angus, dated 1861.[909] She and Donald

---

[899]UK Census 30 March 1861: John McKay, head, married age 46, born Halkirk, farmer of 200 ac.; John McLeod, nephew, single age 23, born Halkirk, ploughman.

[900]See Part 3.

[901]Bill and Sharon Gurney, e-mail to Donald Gunn, 08 Jan 2009.

[902]UK Census 1871: Margaret McKay, head age 51, born Halkirk, farmer of 240 ac,; Hector McKay, son age 7, born Watten scholar.

[903]UK Census 1881: Margaret McKay, head age 60, born Halkirk, farmer of 240 acres.; Hector McKay, son age 17 born Watten; plus several servants and boarders.

[904]UK Census 1891: Hector McKay 27 farmer; Mary A McKay 30; Alexander Gunn 76 uncle retired farmer; John McKinnon 18 visitor; 3 servants.

[905]Bill and Sharon Gurney, e-mail to Donald Gunn, 08 Jan 2009.

[906]*International Genealogical Index (IGI).*

[907]Clan Gunn Parish Records and for elsewhere on this page.

[908]Census 30 March 1851: Reay Parish, Brawlbin: Donald Gunn 80 farmer, 60 acres, b Halkirk; Catherine Gunn 68, b Latheron; Margaret Gunn dau 30, b Halkirk, housemaid; Alexandrina Gunn dau 28, b Halkirk, housemaid; George Gunn 28, b Halkirk, servant; George Dunbar 30, b Halkirk, servant; Mary Gunn 16 b Reay herd; Margaret Sutherland 24, b Halkirk, outdoor servant.

[909]Bill and Sharon Gurney, e-mail to Donald Gunn, 23 Nov 2009: Family of Alexandrina and Donald Gunn; Census 30 March 1861: Donald Gunn head age 43 born Halkirk House Governor; Alexandrina Gunn Mat. age 35 born Halkirk Matron; Daniel A Gunn son age 7 born Dundee; Margaret Gunn dau. age 3 born Dundee; Catherine Gunn dau. age 7m born Dundee.

Gunn of Brawlbin and Dundee (976) appeared on the 1871 Census of Dundee Poor House and Lunatic Asylum, Dundee, Angus.[910]

Donald GUNN of Brawlbin and Dundee (976) was born c. 1818 in Brawlbin, Halkirk Parish, Caithness.[911] He died on 13 May 1879 in St Andrew, Dundee, Angus.[912] He was a wine and spirit merchant.[913] He was the Manager at a salary of £79 per year and his wife £25 per year on 26 Aug 1856 in The Poor House, Dundee, Angus. He wrote to nephew William in Australia on 01 Feb 1859[914] and to nephew Donald in Australia on 07 Nov 1859. He wrote to nephew Donald in Australia again on 24 Oct 1863 and on 25 Dec 1863. He wrote to nephews Donald and William in Australia on 25 Apr 1864. He left a will which was proved on 09 Dec 1886 in Dundee, Alexander Matthewson, Tea Merchant Union St, Dundee one of the Executors nominated by the said deceased Donald Gunn ... in favour of the Deponent and George Alison Wine Merchant Dundee the now only surviving and acting Executors of the said deceased.

Children of Alexandrina (Lexy) Gunn of Braehour (554) and Donald Gunn of Brawlbin and Dundee (976) all born in Dundee, Angus, were as follows:

45 i. John St Clair GUNN (Dr) (3575).

ii. Daniel Alexander GUNN (3576) was born on 09 Feb 1855.[915] He died circa 1890 according to Capt Alex. Gunn of Braehour.

He appeared on the 1861 Census[916] and on the 1871 Census.[917]

iii. Margaret GUNN (3577) was born in 1859.[918] She died on 07 Mar 1881 in Dundee, St Andrew Parish, Angus.

She appeared on the 1861 and 1871 Censuses.

46 iv. Catherine GUNN (3578).

v. Francis Molison GUNN (1137) was born on 05 Dec 1863. He died in Feb 1864 in Dundee, Angus.

47 vi. Williamina GUNN (3579).

vii. Francis Molison GUNN (1138) was born on 03 Aug 1867. He died before 1871 in Dundee, Angus.

viii. Alexander GUNN (1139) was born on 20 Sep 1868. He died in 1868 in Dundee, Angus, aged 2½ months.

---

910 Bill and Sharon Gurney, e-mail to Donald Gunn, 23 Nov 2009: Family of Alexandrina and Donald Gunn; Census 1871: Donald Gunn head age 53 born Halkirk Governor; Alexandrina Gunn wife age 44 born Halkirk;John Gunn son age 17 Apprentice Druggist; Daniel A Gunn son age16 born Dundee Apprentice Merch. Clerk; Margaret Gunn dau. age 12 born Dundee Scholar; Catherine Gunn dau. age 10 born Dundee Scholar; Wilhelmina Gunn dau. age 5 born Dundee Scholar; Robertina Gunn niece age 18 born Dundee Matron's Asst.

911 Bill and Sharon Gurney, e-mail to Donald Gunn, 23 Nov 2009: Family of Alexandrina and Donald Gunn.

912 Bill and Sharon Gurney, e-mail to Donald Gunn, 09 Feb 2009; The Descendants of Donald Gunn.

913 Dundee Poor House, online http://www.fdca.org.uk/FDCADundeeEastPoorhouse.html, 'On 26 August 1856 a Mr and Mrs Gunn accepted the positions of Governor and Matron of the Poorhouse. Mr Gunn's salary was £79 per year, his wife's £25 per year plus "the usual rations of the house". It should be noted that Mr Gunn's previous occupation was that of wine and spirit merchant.'

914 See Part 3.

915 Bill and Sharon Gurney, e-mail to Donald Gunn, 23 Apr 2009: Family of Alexandrina Gunn and Donald Gunn.

916 Bill and Sharon Gurney, e-mail to Donald Gunn, 23 Nov 2009: Family of Alexandrina and Donald Gunn; UK Census 30 March 1861: Donald Gunn head age 43 born Halkirk House Governor; Alexandrina Gunn Mat. age 35 born Halkirk Matron; Daniel A Gunn son age 7 born Dundee; Margaret Gunn dau. age 3 born Dundee; Catherine Gunn dau. age 7m born Dundee.

917 UK Census 1871: Donald Gunn head age 53 born Halkirk Governor; Alexandrina Gunn wife age 44 born Halkirk;John Gunn son age 17 Apprentice Druggist; Daniel A Gunn son age16 born Dundee Apprentice Merch. Clerk; Margaret Gunn dau. age 12 born Dundee Scholar; Catherine Gunn dau. age 10 born Dundee Scholar; Wilhelmina Gunn dau. age 5 born Dundee Scholar; Robertina Gunn niece age 18 born Dundee Matron's Asst.

918 Bill and Sharon Gurney, e-mail to Donald Gunn, 23 Apr 2009: Family of Alexandrina Gunn and Donald Gunn.

20. Jean (Jane) GUNN (941)[919] was born in 1816 in Braehour, Halkirk Parish, Caithness.[920] She was christened on 27 Jul 1816 in Halkirk Parish.[921] She married Hugh Mackenzie (3433) on 18 Dec 1840 in Reay Parish, Caithness.[922] She died on 10 Aug 1910 in Killimister, Wick Parish, Caithness, informant was son George McKenzie. She was buried in Dirlot, Caithness. She appeared on the census of 1881 in Killimister, Wick Parish, Caithness.[923] She was a farmer of 35 acres in 1881. She appeared on the census of 1891 [924] and 1901[925] in Killimister, Wick Parish, Caithness.

The Dirlot gravestone for Hugh Mackenie and Jane Gunn, 2011

---

[919] *LDS Church*, Christenings of children of Donald Gunn and Catherine Gunn: Barbara 1810, Mary 1812, Alexander 1814, Jean 1816, Lexy (Alexandrina?) 1825.

[920] Dirlot cemetery tombstone: Hugh McKenzie, dealer farmer born Aultnaharrow, Strathnaver died Ha' of Winless 11.5.1870 70, wife Jane Gunn born Braehour died Killimister Wick 10.8.1910 95 children Alex died Brawlbin 13.2 186? 2, Hugh died Cradock Africa 13.10.1902, 50, Donald I.R. Officer died Bonar Bridge 27.11.1915 75, Barbara died Killimister 26.1.1926 75, Catherine died Wick 28.3.1924 75 Janet died at East Banks 30.11.1926 Aged 76.

[921] Details of the family of Jane Gunn and Hugh McKenzie are mostly drawn from an email from Bill and Sharon Gurney to Donald Gunn, 01 Dec 2008: Family of Jane Gunn and Hugh McKenzie.

[922] *John O'Groat Journal*, 24 Jan 1861, Fri 01 Jan 1841; Mackenzie, Hugh: farmer to Jane Gunn, Braalbin.

[923] Census 1881: Jane Gunn head, widow age 65, born Halkirk farmer 35 acres; George McKenzie son age 35 born Reay; Barbara McKenzie duaghter age 33 born Reay; Janet McKenzie daughter age 28 born Reay.

[924] UK Census 1891: Jane MacKenzie, head widow age 75 farmer; Barbara MacKenzie, dau. age 44 born Reay gen. servant; Catherine MacKenzie dau. age 38 born Reay gen. servant; Jessie MacKenzie, dau. age 38 born Reay gen.servant; George MacKenzie son age 33 (sic) born Latheron farm servant.

[925] UK Census 1901: Jane MacKenzie mother age 86 born Reay; Jessie MacKenzie head; Barbara MacKenzie sister; Catherine MacKenzie sister.

Hugh MACKENZIE (3433) was born circa 1802 in Farr, Sutherland. He died on 11 May 1870 in Winless, Caithness.[926] He was buried in Dirlot, Caithness.[927] He appeared on the census of 30 Mar 1851 in Brawlbin, Reay Parish, Caithness, a cattle dealer. He appeared on the census of 30 Mar 1861 in Brawlbin, Reay Parish, Caithness, a cattle dealer.

Children of Jean (Jane) Gunn (941) and Hugh Mackenzie (3433) all born in Reay Parish, Caithness, were as follows:

i. Donald MACKENZIE (3434) was christened on 09 Aug 1841. He died on 27 Nov 1915 in Bonar Bridge, Sutherland, age 74.

He was an inland revenue officer in 1901 in Sutherland.

ii. Catherine MACKENZIE (3437) was christened on 30 Aug 1843. She died before 1848 in Reay Parish, Caithness.

iii. Barbara MACKENZIE (3438) was born in 1845. She died on 26 Jan 1926 in Killimister, Wick Parish, Caithness. She was buried in Dirlot, Caithness.

She appeared on the census of 1881 in the household of her mother Jean (941) in Killimister, Wick Parish, Caithness.[928] She appeared on the censuses of 1891 and 1901in the household of her mother Jean (941) in Killimister, Wick Parish, Caithness.[929] [930]

iv. George MACKENZIE (3435) was born in 1846.[931] He married Margaret (--?--) (3441) in 1892 in Wick Parish, Caithness.

He was a farmer. He appeared on the censuses of 1881 and 1891 in the household of his mother Jean (941) in Killimister, Wick Parish, Caithness. He and Margaret (--?--) (3441) appeared on the census of 1901 in Wick Parish, Caithness.[932] He was the informant at the death of Jean (Jane) Gunn (941) on 10 Aug 1910 in Killimister, Wick Parish, informat was son George McKenzie. He gave details of family genealogy to William Watkins Gunn and Marcus Daniel Gunn of the Scottish Delegation on 19 Jun 1928 in Wick Parish, Caithness.[933]

Margaret (--?--) (3441) was born circa 1846 in Wick Parish, Caithness.

v. Catherine MACKENZIE (3439)was born circa 1848. She died on 28 Mar 1924 in Wick Parish, Caithness. She was buried in Dirlot, Caithness.

She appeared on the censuses of 1891 and 1901 in the household of her mother Jean (941) in Killimister, Wick Parish, Caithness.

---

926 Bill and Sharon Gurney, e-mail to Donald Gunn, 01 Dec 2008: Family of Jane Gunn and Hugh McKenzie and for elsewhere on this page.

927 Dirlot cemetery tombstone: Hugh McKenzie, dealer farmer born Aultnaharrow, Strathnaver died Ha' of Winless 11.5.1870 70, wife Jane Gunn born Braehour died Killimister Wick 10.8.1910 95 children Alex died Brawlbin 13.2 186? 2, Hugh died Cradock Africa 13.10.1902, 50, Donald I.R. Officer died Bonar Bridge 27.11.1915 75, Barbara died Killimister 26.1.1926 75, Catherine died Wick 28.3.1924 75 Janet died Wick 30.11.1926 76.

928 Census 1881: Jane Gunn head, widow age 65, born Halkirk farmer 35 acres; George McKenzie son age 35 born Reay; Barbara McKenzie duaghter age 33 born Reay; Janet McKenzie daughter age 28 born Reay.

929 Census 1891: Jane MacKenzie, head widow age 75 farmer; Barbara MacKenzie, dau. age 44 born Reay gen. servant; Catherine MacKenzie dau. age 38 born Reay gen. servant; Jessie MacKenzie, dau. age 38 born Reay gen.servant; George MacKenzie son age 33 (sic) born Latheron farm servant.

930 Census 1901: Jane MacKenzie mother age 86 born Reay; Jessie MacKenzie head; Barbara MacKenzie sister; Catherine MacKenzie sister.

931 Bill and Sharon Gurney, e-mail to Donald Gunn, 01 Dec 2008: Family of Jane Gunn and Hugh McKenzie.

932 Census 1901: George McKenzie, head age 55, born Reay, retired farmer; Margaret McKenzie, wife age 55 born Wick.

933 See page 338 for complete text.

vi. Jessie/Janet MACKENZIE (3440) was born in 1850. She died on 13 Nov 1926 in Wick Parish, Caithness. She was buried in Dirlot, Caithness.

She appeared on the censuses of 1881 and 1891 in the household of her mother Jean (941) in Killimister, Wick Parish, Caithness.[934] She appeared on the census of 1901 in the household of her mother Jean (941) in Killimister, Wick Parish, Caithness, farm house.[935]

vii. William MACKENZIE (3400) was born in 1853. He died on 13 Oct 1902 in Cradock.

He was a government inspector of works.

viii. Hugh MACKENZIE (3401) was born on 03 Jun 1855. He died on 28 Apr 1868 in Stemster, Latheron Parish, Caithness, at age 12.

ix. Alexander MACKENZIE (3436) was born on 23 Oct 1856. He died on 13 Feb 1860 in Brawlbin, Reay Parish, Caithness, at age 3.

934Census 1891: Jane MacKenzie, head widow age 75 farmer; Barbara MacKenzie, dau. age 44 born Reay gen. servant; Catherine MacKenzie dau. age 38 born Reay gen. servant; Jessie MacKenzie, dau. age 38 born Reay gen.servant; George MacKenzie son age 33 (sic) born Latheron farm servant.

935Census 1901: Jane MacKenzie mother age 86 born Reay; Jessie MacKenzie head; Barbara MacKenzie sister; Catherine MacKenzie sister.

Generation Four

21. George GUNN (3524) was born in 1818 in Halkirk Parish, Caithness. He was christened on 24 Feb 1818 in Halkirk Parish, Caithness. He married Margaret Aberdeen (3537), daughter of Marion Smith (3944), on 15 Mar 1853 in Barony, Lanarkshire. He died on 19 Nov 1881 in Craigcrook, Cramond Parish, Edinburgh.[936] He was buried in Cramond Kirk, Cramond Parish, Lothian.[937]

He appeared on the census of 06 Jun 1841 in the household of his parents Alexander (3508) and Ann (3520) in Milton, Halkirk Parish, Caithness.[938] He was the informant at the death of David Waters Gunn (3530) in 1856 in Cramond Parish, Edinburgh.[939]

Margaret ABERDEEN (3537)[940] was born circa 1822 in St Cuthberts, Edinburgh, Midlothian.[941] She died on 23 Jul 1895 in Cramond Bridge, Dalmeny Parish, Linlithgow, at age about 73.[942] She was buried in Cramond Kirk, Cramond Parish, Lothian.[943]

Children of George Gunn (3524) and Margaret Aberdeen (3537) were as follows:

i. Marion Aberdeen GUNN (3538) was born on 13 May 1854 in Barony, Lanarkshire. She died in 1919 in Cramond Parish, Lothian. She was buried in Cramond Kirk, Cramond Parish, Lothian.

ii. Ann Waters GUNN (3539) was born on 16 Jun 1856 in Cramond, West Lothian.

iii. Margaret Aberdeen GUNN (3540) was born on 16 Jan 1858 in Cramond, West Lothian.

iv. David Waters GUNN (3541) was born on 30 Jul 1860 in Cramond, West Lothian.

22. Janet GUNN (3525) was born circa 1821 in Halkirk Parish, Caithness. She married George Mackay (3542) on 10 Dec 1845 in Halkirk Parish, Caithness.

She appeared on the census of 06 Jun 1841 in the household of her parents Alexander (3508) and Ann (3520) in Milton, Halkirk Parish, Caithness.

George MACKAY (3542) was born circa 1815 in Tongue, Sutherland.

---

[936]Parish Register, George Gunn, hotelkeeper and farmer, married to Margaret Aberdeen, died November nineteenth,1881 in Craigcrook, Parish of Cramond, age 63 years. Father was Alexander Gunn, mother was Ann Waters. Died from disease of the heart. Informant at death was David W. Gunn, son.

[937]Gravestone Photographic Resource, online http://www.gravestonephotos.com/public/findfamily.php?name=Gunn.

[938]UK Census 06 June 1841: Milton, Halkirk: Alexander Gunn farmer 45; Anne Gun 45; George Gun 20; Janet Gun 15; James Gun 15; Margaret Gun 12; Bell Gun 10; Aeneasina Gun 8; David 7.

[939]Gillian Bartlett email to Donald Gunn, Aug 2010; Certificate of Death: 1856 deaths in the Parish of Cramond in the County of Edinburgh, David Gunn, single, student of Divinity, on April third 1856 age 21 years, father Alexander Gunn, farmer, mother Ann Gunn, maiden name Waters, buried April 5th at the Church Yard of Cramond, informant George Gunn, brother.

[940]Gravestone Photographic Resource, online http://www.gravestonephotos.com/public/findfamily.php?name=Gunn, George Gunn grave monument details:
George Gunn age 63 buried 1881
Margaret Aberdeen Gunn b1822 buried 1895, wife of George Gunn
Marion Aberdeen Gunn buried 1919, daughter of George Gunn
Marion Smith 83 buried 1871, mother-in-law of George Gunn
David Waters Gunn 23, buried 1856, brother of George Gunn
John Gunn 67 buried 1874, brother of George Gunn.

[941]Bill and Sharon Gurney, e-mail to Donald Gunn, 03 Apr 2009: The Family of George Gunn and Margaret Gunn.

[942]Parish Register, Margaret Gunn, hotel keeper, widow of George Gunn, hotel keper, died July 23, 1895 at Cramond Bridge, parish of Dalmeny, age 73 years from hepatitis. Informant at death was son David W Gunn, farmer, Craigcrook, Blackhall, Midlothian.

[943]Gravestone Photographic Resource, online http://www.gravestonephotos.com/public/findfamily.php?name=Gunn.

Children of Janet Gunn (3525) and George Mackay (3542) were as follows:

i. John MACKAY (3543) was born circa 1847 in Tongue, Sutherland.

ii. Ann MACKAY (3544) was born circa 1848 in Tongue, Sutherland.

iii. Barbara MACKAY (3545) was born on 25 Dec 1849 in Thurso Parish, Caithness. She was christened on 07 Jan 1850 in Thurso Parish, Caithness.

iv. Alexander MACKAY (3546) was born on 24 Nov 1851 in Halkirk Parish, Caithness. He was christened on 05 Dec 1851 in Thurso Parish, Caithness.

v. George MACKAY (3547) was born on 06 Aug 1855 in Thurso Parish, Caithness.

vi. Margaret MACKAY (3550) was born on 25 Jul 1857 in Reay Parish, Caithness.

vii. David James MACKAY (3548) was born on 31 Jul 1859 in Thurso Parish, Caithness.[944]

viii. Charles Robert MACKAY (3549) was born on 13 Feb 1862 in Thurso Parish, Caithness. He died on 24 Jan 1864 in Thurso Parish, Caithness, at age 1.

ix. Charles Robert MACKAY (3551) was born on 06 Jun 1864 in Thurso Parish, Caithness.

23. Agnes/Aneasina GUNN (3528) was born in 1833 in Latheron Parish, Caithness. She married James Marshall (3941), son of Alexander Marshall (3945) and Jane McLellan (3947), on 06 Jun 1859.[945] She died on 17 Apr 1888 in Lanarkshire.[946]

She appeared on the census of 06 Jun 1841 in the household of her parents Alexander (3508) and Ann (3520) in Milton, Halkirk Parish, Caithness.[947] She and James Marshall (3941) appeared on the 1861 Census of Argyllshire dated 1861.[948] She was the informant at the death of James Marshall (3941) in 1879.

James MARSHALL (3941) was born circa 1831. He died in 1879. He was a county police constable in 1861 and a sheriff officer in 1879.

Children of Agnes/Aneasina Gunn (3528) and James Marshall (3941) were:

i. Anna MARSHALL (3948) was born in 1860.

944Bill and Sharon Gurney, e-mail to Donald Gunn, 03 Apr 2009: The Family of George Gunn and Margaret Gunn.

945Gillian Bartlett email to Donald Gunn, Aug 2010: My mother's ggrandfather was an Alexander Marshall whose brother James Marshall married Agnes Gunn. Agnes was born at Latheron, Caithness, 1834. Her parents were Alexander Gunn and Ann Waters, married in 1814; Gillian Bartlett email to Donald Gunn, Aug 2010: Agnes Gunn, George Gunn's sister, married James Marshall in 1859. He was a brother of Mum's great grandmother Ann Marshall; Certificate of Marriage, 1859 Marriages in the District of St George in the City of Edinburgh, on the sixth day of June 1859 at Edinburgh, James Marshall age 28, residing at Innellan (?), county constable, bachelor, father Alexander Marshall teacher, mother Jane Marshall, maiden name McLellan, to A Gunn age 25, residing at Thurso, spinster,father Alexander Gunn, corn merchant.

946Gillian Bartlett email to Donald Gunn, Aug 2010; Certificate of Death: 1888 Deaths in the District of ??? in the County of Lanark, Agnes Marshall, widow of James Marshall, died April seventeenth, 34 (?) years, father Alexander Gunn, farmer (deceased), mother Anna Gunn M.S, waters (deceased), buried April 18th at ??

947UK Census 06 June 1841: Milton, Halkirk: Alexander Gunn farmer 45; Anne Gun 45; George Gun 20; Janet Gun 15; James Gun 15; Margaret Gun 12; Bell Gun 10; Aeneasina Gun 8; David 7.

948Census 30 March 1861: 1861: Cairn's Land, Dunoon and Kilmun, Argyll: James Marshall 29, county police constable; wife Agnes 25 b Latheron, Caithness; Anna, dau 1; Jane mother 65; father teaching Abertarff.

24. William Henry GUNN (2547)[949] was born on 31 Aug 1820 in Badgers River, York Factory, Rupertsland, Manitoba. He married Isabella Ross (2548) on 04 Feb 1841 in St Johns Anglican Church, Red River Settlement, Manitoba.[950] He died on 06 May 1842 in Red River Settlement, Manitoba, at age 21.

Isabella ROSS (2548) was born in 1820 in Oregon Territory. She died on 18 Feb 1865 in St Johns, Red River Settlement, Manitoba.

Children of William Henry Gunn (2547) and Isabella Ross (2548) were:

i. Henrietta GUNN (2633) was born in 1841. She married Frank Larned Hunt (2634). She died on 15 Apr 1869 in Pembina, North Dakota.

25. James GUNN (2549) was born on 06 Jan 1824 in Lot 163, St Andrews, Manitoba. He married Mary Donald (2550) circa 1862. He died on 27 Jan 1905 in St Andrews, Manitoba, at age 81.

He was a farmer in 1875.[951]

Mary DONALD (2550) was christened on 12 Jan 1825. She died on 07 Apr 1890 at age 65. She had a script application on 28 Jul 1875 in St Andrews, Manitoba.[952]

Children of James Gunn (2549) and Mary Donald (2550) were:

i. Margaret Ann GUNN (2635) was born on 03 Sep 1864 in Kildonan, Rupertsland, Manitoba. She married James Young (2636).

26. John GUNN (Hon.) of Manitoba (2551) was born on 08 Aug 1826 in Lot 163, St Andrews, Manitoba. He married Emma Garrioch (2552) on 02 Feb 1855 in Kildonan Presbyterian Church, Winnipeg, Manitoba. He died on 08 Sep 1898 in St Andrews, Manitoba, at age 72.

He was the subject of a 1965 press article regarding his conduct following rejection of a proposed marriage in Sep 1853.[953] He was the subject of an article in the St Clement's

---

949Many details on the family of Donald Gunn and Margaret Swain are drawn from emails titled 'Donald Gunn of Canada' from Debbie Kuzub, Commissioner of the Central Canada Branch of the Clan Gunn Society of North America, and a descendant of the Hon Donald Gunn of Manitoba.

950Caroline Armstrong, e-mail to Donald Gunn.

951Caroline Armstrong, e-mail to Donald Gunn, James had a script application: on July 28, 1875 at St. Andrews, Manitoba, Canada, Canada,; James Gunn; St. Andrews; farmer; HB Head: myself, wife and one child; Born: January 06, 1824; Father: Donald Gunn (Scotch)[was]; Mother: Margaret Gunn (HB) [was]; English; James Gunn; July 28, 1875; John Gunn; St. Andrew; farmer; Donald Gunn: farmer.

952Caroline Armstrong, e-mail to Donald Gunn, Mary Donald (Gunn) had a script application: on July 28, 1875 at St. Andrews, Lisgar, Manitoba, Canada, : Mary Gunn (Donald); St. Andrews; Lisgar; wife of James Gunn; HB Head: myself, husband and child; Born: January 12, 1818; NW; Father: William Donald (HB)[was]; Mother: Anne Donald (HB)[was]; English; Mary Gunn (x); July 28, 1875; John Gunn; St. Andrew; farmer; Donald Gunn; farmer. C-14928 (ibid.).

953Caroline Armstrong, e-mail to Donald Gunn, Article taken from *Free Press* Sept. 11, 1965
HENRIETTA ROSS'S REJECTED SUITOR
Mary Mindless tells of a love triangle that rocked the Settlement in 1853

There may be some rejected lovers who agree that: "Tis better to have loved and lost Than never to have loved at all" but John Gunn wasn't one of them.

When John lost Henrietta Ross to Rev. John Black, he proclaimed to the entire Red River Settlement that he had been cruelly deceived. Within three months he proposed to four other girls, all of whom turned him down. And, in his vindictiveness, he almost succeeded in splitting the congregation of the Little Britian Church.

This tempest was stirred up in 1853. John Gunn, who farmed on the east bank of the Red River just above St. Andrew's Rapids, had long admired the dark-eyed, black-haired Henrietta. Finally, he asked her to marry him.

It is possible that Henrietta would have become his bride but for one thing: she had fallen in love with John Black, the young Presbyterian minister, who had come to Red River two years earlier. However, she may have been afraid that the well-educated, serious-minded Scot might not consider a Metis girl to be a suitable wife for a minister. For, although Henrietta's father, Alexander Ross, was also a Scottish, and a prominent man in the settlement, her mother was an Indian.

Centenary Historical Book.[954] An obituary was published on 10 Sep 1898 in an unknown paper[955] and in Sep 1898 in an unknown paper.[956] Family dispute on the land the Hon. Donald settled in 1820 was resolved in an out-of-court settlement on 14 Oct 1920.

While we do not know exactly what reply Henrietta made to John Gunn's proposal, it seems that she gave him reason to believe that he had been accepted. He sent off a happy letter to her brother, James, who was studying at the University of Toronto, announcing that he would soon become his brother-in-law.

But then Rev. John Black also decided to ask for Henrietta's hand in marriage. He first approached her father, who apparently assured him that the girl had not been spoken for. Probably Alexander had his daughter's happiness in mind; but, in addition, he undoubtedly knew a good match when it presented itself. Thus encouraged, John Black proposed -- and this time Henrietta said yes, and meant it.

Poor John Gunn soon learned that he had been thrown over. His pride wounded, he received the news with very poor grace. The story of how badly he reacted is told in a number of letters which may be found in the Ross collection in the Manitoba Archives.

In November, 1853, Henrietta's oldest brother, William, informed James in Toronto that: "We have not seen John Gunn. The cause -- he wrote a most shameful letter to Henrietta. I wrote an appropriate reply..."

About a month later Gunn himself supplied James with his version of the affair. He described William's letter as "an insult" and added that in answer he had given him "as good a drubbing as he ever got in black and white."

According to Gunn, Henrietta had "torn (his) tenderest feelings, and now enjoyed the fruits of her villainy and deceit." John Black heard of his claims and went down to St. Andrew's to see him.

So -- "I told him all, and gave up all and every claim I had to her person. I told him to go home and marry her but that I could never meet her as a friend, nor any of the family."

Then, continued Gunn, two days later William visited him "to try to renew the friendship that had been broken. But he made a real humbug of it..."

Gunn added that all the Scottish people in the settlement were opposed to the marriage of Henrietta and the minister, and that many would never set foot in the church again. (He referred to the old "meeting house," the first Little Britain church, which stood on the Red's west bank on land belonging to his father, Donald Gunn.)

Meanwhile, William sent James a somewhat different account of the quarrel. On December 19 he wrote: " Mr. Black is to marry Henrietta the day after tomorrow.... I daresay John Gunn has given you a fearful account of our doings. He tried to raise people to oppose Black. They even tried to shut the meeting house at Donald Gunn's."

The wedding was quieter than most in Kildonan, where feasting and dancing often continued for several days. The Rev. Mr. Black was against drinking and dancing, and tried to stamp them out among his parishioners.

A few weeks later William wrote further: "John Gunn is notorious. Old Gunn is as bad if not worse. They begun abuse Mr. Black, then turned to Henrietta and every member of the family not excepting you. When they found they could not prevent the marriage, John thought he would get married for spite. He asked Sally McDermot, Bella Cloustone, Jane McKenzie and Jane Cloustone in the course of three months. He was refused..."

References to the quarrel are found in several later letters. John was not a man to forget a grudge. Eventually, however, he cooled down and was again on reasonably good terms with the Rosses and Mr. Black.

In the end he married Emma Garrioch and the couple raised a family of eight children on his farm in what is now the Lockport area. His house was close to a lovely stream, known as Gunn's Creek, which flowed into the Red. There he built a large water mill with great oaken wheels measuring 16 feet across. Visitor's to Lockport may still see the wheels in that vicinity.

954Caroline Armstrong, e-mail to Donald Gunn, Taken from the St. Clements Centennial History Book

John Gunn was the son of the Hon. Donald Gunn who had come to Canada via Churchill in 1813 while in the employ of the Hudson's Bay Company. After severing his connections with the honorable Company, he purchased a homestead on the east side of the Red River of considerable acreage. The original Donald Gunn homestead was on Lot 163, Parish of St. Andrew's, on the east side of the Red River. Donald was married to Margaret Swain, the daughter of James Swain.

The Hon. Donald Gunn had 12 children: William born in 1822, James born in 1824, John born in 1827, Alexander born in 1829, Mathilda born in 1831, George G born in 1832, Jane born in 1836, Margaret born in 1838, Donald Jr. born in 1840, Robert born in 1842, Janet born in 1846, and William (2nd) born in 1848.

John, the third child of Donald and Margaret Gunn grew up and married Emma Garrioch in 1855. They had eight children: Margaret Jane, Reginald, Donald J, John James, Gilbert Garrioch, Henry George, Emma Ann and Mary.

The original Gunn homestead, Lot 163, was deeded over to son John as he reached manhood and had made plans for his marriage. This lot is right at the property spanning where the Lockport Bridge now stands. The Hon. Donald Gunn along with John also purchased Lot 167 where they built a fairly large Water-Gist-Mill not far from the junction of Gunn's Creek with the Red River on the east side. It was two stories high and built entirely by Manitoba materials and labour in the early 1850's.

John was educated by his father and took an active part in politics in the years surrounding 1870 thereafter. He was a returned Member of the Local Legislature for St. Andrews North at the 1874 election and the following. He was always a staunch opponent of liquor traffic and spent considerable time trying to combat it in the parishes, along the Red River. John Gunn died Sat. Sept. 10, 1898, at the age of 71 years and 1 month. He had been ill for most of that spring and summer. His wife Emma (Garrioch) died in the year 1921.

955Caroline Armstrong, e-mail to Donald Gunn, OBITUARY 1898 JOHN GUNN, EX-M.P.P. OF GONOR

On Saturday last, the 10th just., John Gunn of Gonor, passed quietly away at the old homestead, aged 72 years and one month. He had been more or less an invalid for some years back, and with him is buried much interesting but unwritten history of the Little Britain settlement and of many historical incidents of the Red River settlement, Hudson's Bay Company and Northwest Trading Company's struggles for priority of trading privileges. Mr. Gunn was the son of the Hon. Donald Gunn, who came here when but 16 years old, working for the Hudson's Bay Co. for a few years at Fort York and Churchill, then coming on to Assiniboia and settling at Little Britain on the east side of the river in 1824. It was in a house but a few rods from the site of the -present-homestead that the deceased was born in August, 1826. He received a good education from his father who for a time had to undertake the duties of teacher for children of other settlers and being fond of reading was always well informed on the questions of the day. Those were stirring times and Mr. Gunn took an active part with the "free traders" against the Hudson's Bay Co. and was a participant in some of the struggles against the constabulary of the Company where seizures were being made.

He took an active part in politics in the latter years of the Hudson's Bay Co's rule and for many years after the entrance of the Northwest into the Dominion, was twice elected to the legislature for the constituency of St. Andrew's North, first in 1874 and again at the general election following, however, he was defeated in a three cornered fight with the Hon. J. W. Sifton and Mr. E. H. G. G. Hay, the latter gentleman being elected.

Mr. Gunn was a vigorous campaigner in those days and was seldom absent from a political platform in his neighborhood, either in Dominion or local politics; reveling less on diplomatic wiles in his arguments than on blunt and vigorous presentation of facts. He was always a heavy hitter on the platform and shoulder to shoulder with the late Sir John Schultz, in his contests in Lisgar, took the brunt of many a fierce assault when that gentleman was still a mark for the bitter animosity engendered by his course in the fight for confederation.

He was also an uncompromising opponent of the liquor traffic, and whenever an opportunity occurred spent neither time nor labor in fighting it; often sacrificing popularity and even more substantial interest in the struggle.

In 1855 he was married to Miss Emma Garrioch, daughter of Wm. Garrioch of the Hudson's Bay Co's service. Their family consisted of eight children, of which the eldest, John J., remains at the homestead. The others are the Rev. H. G. Gunn, of Jamestown, Dakota; Donald Gunn, Contractor, of Calgary; W. R. Gunn, Barrister, Prince Albert; Gilbert G. Gunn, of Little Britain; Mrs. Jos. Johnston, of Cook's Creek, and two unmarried daughter Miss Emma and Miss Mary Gunn. The funeral took place from his late residence on Tuesday last followed by a large concourse of friends and relatives to the Little Britain Cemetery. The Rev. H. G. Gunn, owing to the train being late, arrived at the grave just as the remains were being lowered to its last resting place. The other two sons, Donald and W. R. Gunn were unable to be present. The services were conducted by the Rev. Mr. Peacock assisted by Mr. Cocks. The bearers were A. R. Lillie, G. T. Sutherland, J. H. Gunn, Mayor Colcleugh and Councillor Ross. Mrs. Gunn has the sympathy of her many friends in the loss of her beloved partner.

[956]Caroline Armstrong, e-mail to Donald Gunn, INTERESTING SKETCH OF THE EARLY SETTLER WHO HAS RECENTLY PASSED AWAY

There appears today a cut of the late Mr. John Gunn, of Gonor, whose death was briefly noticed in the issue of the 14th inst. By the death of Mr. Gunn is again reduced the already small number of those who can speak from memory of the interesting and often curious incidents of the early settlement of the Red River Valley. Having always taken a keen and active interest in anything of a public nature, and being blessed with a good memory, he was a perfect storehouse of information in regard to the early settlement of the country, the manners and customs of past days, the causes of friction and the struggles between the Hudson's Bay Company and the settlers, and all such matters; matters which, when disposed of in a sentence or paragraph attract but little notice; but when recounted at length by one who was a participant or a witness of them, assume an interest too intensely real to be easily forgotten.

It seems common-place enough, for instance, to read of the precautions taken by the H.B. Company to safeguard its interests in this country, but when listening to Mr. Gunn as he told of carrying letters twenty miles to Fort Garry that the man in charge there might read them and decide whether or not they contained anything likely to injure the company before accepting them for transfer abroad; the thing took on a very different hue. And so with the grim struggle for existence pure and simple which in those far back times had so often to be faced, when the supply of food was prospective and consisted of a flint-lock gun and a net.

As stated in the issue of the 14th, Mr. Gunn's father was the late Hon. Donald Gunn. His mother was Margaret Swain, daughter of Mr. James Swain, an officer of the Hudson's Bay Company, for a long time in charge of York Factory and the district of which it was the centre, the same mentioned in the company's deed to Lord Selkirk as one of a number who were to give his lordship peaceable possession of the territory of Assiniboia. This couple, together with a Mr. John McDonald and his wife, another Miss Swain, settled at what was afterward known as Little Britain in the year 1824, and were the first settlers at that place. These were joined within the next few years by four other men, like themselves retired servants of the H. B. Company, making six in all, three of whom were Scotch and the other three English. The spot where these people settled was not on the west side of the river, as is generally supposed, but on the heavily wooded eastern bank, the other side being at that time a treeless waste known as Prairie la Biche. No fewer than four of these men were married to daughters of Mr. Swain already referred to; and of the six no fewer than four were drafted away to become school teachers as the country filled up and the establishment of schools took place, Mr. Gunn being one of the number. At this place the subject of this sketch was the first white child born, the date being August 08, 1826.

He received his education from his father, and at the age of 19 himself assumed the duties of teacher at St. John's where he remained for two years. He used to tell that while there he had for a few days among his pupils an embryo premier, in the person of John Norquay, still too young for anything but mischief making, and a curly headed chubby urchin -- as one can very well believe.

On quitting school teaching he took a trip to St. Paul, Minnesota, in the company of a large party of "free traders," and the accounts he used to give of the encounters of that party with the officers of the company, who, under the leadership of Cuthbert Grant, warden of the plains, pursued them all the way to Two Rivers, in Minnesota, was one of many such that he could tell, all admirably illustrative of the real life of those peculiar times.

On his return he settled down of the original site of Little Britain (the first settlers having in the meantime moved to the other side of the river), where he remained till his death. Very naturally he took a lively interest in the efforts of the people of the Red River Settlement to throw off the yoke of Hudson's Bay Company rule and secure annexation to Canada, his father being, as has been said, "the literary man of the movement." And when in 1870 those efforts were crowned with success and government by the people became an established fact, he at once entered into the field of provincial politics, being a candidate in the first general elections; and until recent years, when failing health began to tell on his robust frame, was ever an active and vigorous participant in the political life of the province. He was twice elected to the legislature, first in 1874 and again in 1878, on both occasions for the old parish of St. Andrew's north. He served as a school trustee for about twenty continuously ever since the formation of the province. He espoused warmly every interest of the people, and being a ready and forcible speaker was seldom missed from a platform where any question of public moment was being discussed. He was but little of a partisan, and except as a private citizen and as a member of the legislature, to follow his own judgement rather than that of a party. Personally, Mr. Gunn was a man of genial and kindly disposition, one of nature's gentlemen, honored and beloved by all who knew him. He was, both in public and private life, a man of stainless integrity and benevolence, cheerfully suffering disadvantage himself rather than infringe upon the

Emma GARRIOCH (2552)[957] was born on 20 Jul 1824 in St Johns, Red River Settlement, Manitoba. She died on 28 Feb 1922 in St Boniface, Manitoba, at age 97. She quoted uncomplimentarily in letters to relatives in Oct 1899.[958] An obituary was published on 01 Mar 1922 in an unknown paper.[959]

Children of John Gunn (Hon.) of Manitoba (2551) and Emma Garrioch (2552) were:

i. Margaret Jane GUNN (2574) was born on 24 Nov 1855 in Kildonan, Manitoba. She married Joseph William Johnstone (2575). She died on 21 Apr 1927 in Fairford, Manitoba, at age 71.

Joseph William JOHNSTONE (2575) was born in 1855. He died on 20 Nov 1899.

ii. William Reginald GUNN (2626)[960] was born on 03 Sep 1857 in Kildonan, Manitoba. He died on 18 Nov 1910 in Melfort, Saskatchewan, at age 53.

iii. Donald John GUNN (2682) was born on 12 Jun 1859 in St Andrews, Manitoba. He died after 1901 in Calgary, Alberta.

iv. John James GUNN (2628) was born on 21 Apr 1861 in Kildonan, Manitoba. He married Eleanor Flannigan (994). He died on 22 Sep 1907 in Selkirk, Manitoba, at age 46.

Eleanor FLANNIGAN (994) was born in Bloomfield, Ontario.

v. Emma Ann GUNN (2629) was born on 12 Oct 1862 in St Andrews, Manitoba. She died on 05 Aug 1950 in Selkirk, Manitoba, at age 87.

An obituary was published on 14 Aug 1950 in the Winnipeg Tribune.[961] She was the subject of an article in the St Clement's Centennial Record.[962]

---

rights of others. It is by these rare and enduring personal qualities, rather than what he accomplished of a public nature, that those who were nearest to him and knew him best shall remember him.

957 Debbie Kuzub, "Donald Gunn of Canada."

958 Caroline Armstrong, e-mail to Donald Gunn, Note on Emma Garrioch Gunn taken from Joyce Anaka's Family History Book in a letter Janet Muckle wrote to her brother Donald. "It would seem that Janet Muckle got along well with all the family, and usually had good things to say about them, but at times her sister-in-law Emma, John's wife, sorely tried her patience! In a letter of Oct. 2nd, 1898 she writes: "I was up to see our brother John just three weeks before he died and had a good long talk with him. He said he would not live very long. He had his will made and was quite resigned... I did not go up to the funeral, neither did Willie. I did not feel like going so far and it would have done no good anyway. I tell you they found fault and criticized my dress, and everything else, and I said if they all died I would never go up to see one of them, but since then I took some of it back as John is a splendid fellow (Note: her nephew John), and Mary not bad." ...

"After Minnie went to stay with her Aunt Janet, Janet took her, in Oct 1899, to, as she put it: "see them all at Sandy's, John's and Jamie's and to see the church yard, old home and everything. Emma wants her for a week or two, they were so kind to her." About ten years later, in a letter to her brother, Janet said of her sister-in-law: "I had a lovely visit at Aunt Emma's with Mrs. McNabb in January. Emma Sr. is as bright and nice as can be. Old age has softened the acerbity of her temper, and she is so jolly and kind, even forgets to say 'You are so ugly.'"

959 Caroline Armstrong, e-mail to Donald Gunn, Mrs. Emma Garrioch Gunn who died this morning at 7:30 at the family residence, Lockport. Mrs. Gunn was 96 years, 7 months and 4 days old. She was connected with several of the outstanding families of the old Red River settlement and was the eighth child of William Garrioch, of Middlechurch and formerly of St. John's parish, at which latter place she was born July 24, 1824. Her mother was Nancy Cook, daughter of William Henning Cook, chief factor and former govenor of the Hudson's Bay Company. Mr Cook was one of those who, on his retirement from the company's service, decided to cast his lot in with the Red River settlement, locating at Middlechurch and taking an active and influential part in the affairs of the settlement, becoming a member of the council of Assininboia and holding other important offices. Mr. Garrioch, the late Mrs. Gunn's father, whose home at Middlechurch was known as Orkney Cottage in commemoration of his own Orkney home across the seas, was also a man who commanded the respect and approval of his neighbors to a marked degree.
The deceased Mrs. Gunn was married to John Gunn, fourth son of Hon. Donald Gunn, of Little Britain, well known as one of Manitoba's earliest historians and whose name is connected with the history of the country in various other ways. He pre-deceased his wife some 28 years. Upon her marriage Mrs. Gunn went to the present Lockport to reside and upon the same homestead that she went to as a bride 67 years ago she remained until her death. Of this marriage there were born 8 children, the eldest son being W. R. Gunn, M.A. who died a few years ago at Melfort, Sask. The living survivors of the family are Mrs. Kemper Garrioch, of Fairford; the Misses Emma A, and Mary Gunn, living at home; G. G. Gunn, of Lockport, and Rev. H. G. Gunn.
The funeral will be held from the family residence at Lockport to Little Britain Cemetery.

960 Many details on the family are drawn from emails from Debbie Kuzub, Commissioner of the Central Canada Branch of the Clan Gunn Society of North America, and a descendant of the Hon Donald Gunn of Manitoba.

vi. Mary GUNN (2630) was born on 05 May 1865 in Selkirk, Manitoba. She died in Nov 1948 in St Andrews, Manitoba, at age 83.

vii. Henry George GUNN (Rev.) (2631) was born on 14 Jan 1866 in Selkirk, Manitoba. He died on 20 Dec 1945 in Lockport, Manitoba, at age 79.

viii. Gilbert Garrioch GUNN (2632) was born on 12 Jul 1868 in Kildonan, Manitoba. He died on 17 Mar 1933 in Selkirk, Manitoba, at age 64.

27. Alexander GUNN (2531) was born on 10 Feb 1829 in Lot 163, St Andrews, Manitoba. He married Angelique MacKenzie (2532) on 08 Mar 1854 in Kildonan, Rupertsland, Manitoba. He died on 25 Aug 1902 in Little Britain, Manitoba, at age 73.

Angelique MACKENZIE (2532) was born on 06 Oct 1832. She died in 1905 in Little Britain, Manitoba.

Children of Alexander Gunn (2531) and Angelique MacKenzie (2532) all born in Lot 127, St Andrews, Manitoba, were as follows:

i. Benjamin McKenzie GUNN (2602) was born on 24 Dec 1855. He married Elizabeth Mary Taylor (2603), daughter of William Taylor (2559) and Margaret Gunn (2558). He died on 14 Apr 1930 in St Andrews, Manitoba, at age 74.

Elizabeth Mary TAYLOR (2603) was born on 22 Jan 1857.

---

961 Caroline Armstrong, e-mail to Donald Gunn, COPIED FROM WINNIPEG TRIBUNE AUGUST 14, 1950
Emma Gunn, 87, Granddaughter of Historian, Dies.
Special to the Winnipeg Tribune
SELKIRK, August 14-- The funeral service for Miss Emma Ann Gunn, 87, a pioneer resident of the St. Andrews district, who died August 05 at Selkirk General Hospital, was held Wednesday in Little Britain United Church, Little Britain. Burial was in the family plot in the churchyard cemetery. Langrill's Funeral Home was in charge of arrangement. Rev. J.A. McConnell officiated. Pall-bearers were William Mowatt, William Weddell, Peter and Stephen Pawluk, Michael Fyramchuk and Stephen Hopaluk.
Born at St. Andrews, Miss Gunn had lived all her life in the district. She was the daughter of the late John Gunn and Emma Garrioch, and grand-daughter of the late Hon. Donald Gunn, member of the first legislature in Manitoba and well-known historian.
Miss Gunn attended school at Little Britain, this first school being a commercial school for the children of Hudson's Bay Company officials, where her grandfather taught for 10 years.
She taught Sunday School at Little Britain Presbyterian Church for many years and was a lifelong member of the church, taking and active part in women's organizations until a few years ago.
At one time her family owned property north and south along the Red River at Lockport, while her grandfather, who had also came from Caithness, Scotland, owned a considerable stretch of land on the west side of the Red River at Little Britain.
Four brothers predeceased her, Reginald, a lawyer at Prince Albert; John J., who farmed at Lockport, and wrote "Echoes of the Red"; Rev George Gunn, of Lockport, who did newspaper work and wrote poetry; and Gilbert.
Two sisters, Margaret and Mary, also predeceased her. She is survived by three nephews, Charles Johnston, Clandeboye; Campbell Johnston, Mafeking; and Dale Johnston, Lockport; and two nieces, Mrs. Harold Ozouf, Clandeboye; and Mrs. Eva Garrioch, Saskatoon.

962 Caroline Armstrong, e-mail to Donald Gunn, TAKEN FROM THE EAST SIDE OF THE RED A CENTENNIAL PROJECT OF THE RURAL MUNICIPALITY OF ST. CLEMENTS
EMMA ANN GUNN
Emma was the daughter of John Gunn and Emma Garrioch. She was born in about the year 1862 and got most of her early education at the school for the children of the Hudson's Bay Company where her grandfather, the late Hon. Donald Gunn taught school for about a decade.
Emma was a devout church goer and attended the Little Britain Presbyterian Church. She taught Sunday School and was a Life Member of the Church.
Emma had two sisters, Margaret Jane and Mary as well as five brothers: Reginald, Donald J., John James, Gilbert Garrioch and Henry George.
Emma lived most all of her life on the east side of the Red River on Lot 163 in the Gonor area. The last years were spent with her sister Mary Gunn. Miss Emma never married and spent most of her life caring for her family and the homestead. Emma was a grand cook and had great love for animals and the land.
All of her family predeceased her. Emma passed away in the year 1949 and is buried in the Little Britain Cemetery in the Gunn family plot.
It is rumored widely that Emma, in her younger years, had fallen in love with a young gentleman from England, visiting Canada and connected with the Diplomatic Corp. The story goes that they hit it off and had a whirlwind romance, but the family were against them marrying. The reason given is that they thought this gentleman travelled too widely and that once back in England Emma would be shelved or else made unhappy. The family loved Emma and it appears nothing ever came of the romance as she remained unmarried all her life.

ii. Eliza Margaret GUNN (2604) was born on 14 Apr 1857.
iii. Lucy GUNN (2605) was born in 1858. She died in 1878.
iv. Colin Roderick GUNN (2606) was born in 1863. He was christened on 03 May 1863 in Kildonan Church, Manitoba.
v. Alexander James GUNN (2607) was born on 30 Jun 1865. He died on 11 Jul 1865 in St Andrews, Manitoba.
vi. Donald GUNN (2608) was born on 31 Aug 1867. He married an unknown person. He married Leticia Margaret Muckle (2609), daughter of Alexander Montgomery Muckle (2564) and Janet Gunn (2563). He died on 08 Apr 1962 at age 94.

Leticia Margaret MUCKLE (2609) was born in 1877. She died in 1914.

vii. Alexander William Montgomery Muckle GUNN (2533) was born on 08 Jul 1873. He married Johanna Moriah Johnston (2534). He died in Jul 1952 in Selkirk, Manitoba.

Johanna Moriah JOHNSTON (2534) was born in 1878 in Little Britain, Manitoba. She died on 09 Sep 1974 in Winnipeg, Manitoba.

28. George GUNN (2555) was born on 11 Dec 1833 in Lot 163, St Andrews, Manitoba. He married Eliza Winechild (3445) circa 1870 in Red River Settlement, Manitoba.[963] He married Eliza Otterskin (2556) after 1873 in Fort Qu'appelle, Saskatchewan. He died on 13 Dec 1901 in Swift Current, Saskatchewan, at age 68.

Children of George Gunn (2555) and Eliza Winechild (3445) were as follows:

i. Donald Edward GUNN (2621) was born on 24 May 1877 in Mire Creek, North West Territory. He died in Nov 1954 in Shaunavon, Saskatchewan, at age 77.
ii. Eliza Margaret GUNN (2622) was born on 01 Apr 1879 in Dark Sand Hills, North West Territory. She died in Aug 1883 in Red Deer River, North West Territory, at age 4.
iii. Catherine Jane GUNN (2620) was born on 26 Aug 1882 in Parkberg, North West Territory. She died in Jan 1910 at age 27.
iv. Nancy GUNN (2624) was born in 1872 in Fort Garry, Manitoba. She died in 1959 in Maple Creek, Saskatchewan.

Eliza OTTERSKIN (2556) died in 1917.

Children of George Gunn (2555) and Eliza Otterskin (2556) were as follows:

i. Max GUNN (2623).
ii. William James GUNN (2625) was born on 24 May 1890 in Maple Creek, Saskatchewan. He died on 15 Feb 1989 in Swift Current, Saskatchewan, at age 98.

29. Margaret GUNN (2558) was born on 06 Apr 1838 in Lot 163, St Andrews, Manitoba. She married William Taylor (2559) on 19 Feb 1856 in Kildonan, Rupertsland, Manitoba. She died after 1881.

Children of Margaret Gunn (2558) and William Taylor (2559) were:

[963] This, and many subsequent citations, are by Caroline Armstrong in e-mails to Donald Gunn during 2006.

i. Elizabeth Mary TAYLOR (2603) was born on 22 Jan 1857. She married Benjamin McKenzie Gunn (2602), son of Alexander Gunn (2531) and Angelique MacKenzie (2532).

Benjamin McKenzie GUNN (2602) was born on 24 Dec 1855 in Lot 127, St Andrews, Manitoba. He died on 14 Apr 1930 in St Andrews, Manitoba, at age 74.

30. Donald GUNN (2560) was born on 17 May 1840 in Lot 163, St Andrews, Manitoba. He married Caroline Bellendine (2561) in 1867. He married Sarah Fidler (2581) on 22 Oct 1881 in St Pauls, Manitoba. He died on 26 Mar 1927 in Devils Lake, Saskatchewan, at age 86.

He left Manitoba and came west to to the Birdtail Creek in 1876. He was a sawmiller in 1876 in Saskatchewan. He moved to the Qu'Appelle Valley in 1881 in Saskatchewan. He was a homesteader in 1881 in Saskatchewan. He took up land under squatter's rights in 1887 in Devil's Lake, Saskatchewan. An obituary of him was published on 27 Mar 1927 in the Yorkton Enterprise.

Caroline BELLENDINE (2561) was born on 07 Aug 1846 in Grand Rapids, Manitoba. She died in 1878.

Children of Donald Gunn (2560) and Caroline Bellendine (2561) were as follows:

i. Donald James GUNN (2610) was born on 10 Jul 1868 in St Andrews, Manitoba. He married Mary Ellen Carragher (2611). He died on 14 Mar 1917 in Lintlaw, Saskatchewan, at age 48.

Mary Ellen CARRAGHER (2611) was born on 03 Sep 1886 in Bowden, Saskatchewan.

ii. George GUNN (2687) was born on 13 Jul 1870 in St Andrews, Manitoba. He died on 10 Oct 1943 in Preeceville, Saskatchewan, at age 73.

iii. Annabelle Ellen GUNN (2612) was born on 20 Jul 1871 in Little Britain, Manitoba. She married Arthur White (2613). She died on 29 Jul 1959 in Preeceville, Manitoba, at age 88.

Arthur WHITE (2613) died in 1928.

iv. William Henry GUNN (2614) was born on 28 Jul 1874 in Little Britain, Manitoba. He died on 04 Sep 1906 in Canora Area, Saskatchewan, at age 32.

v. Margaret Francis GUNN (2615) was born on 14 Jul 1876 in Little Britain, Manitoba. She died on 26 Aug 1964 in Preeceville, Manitoba, at age 88.

vi. Unnamed GUNN (2688) was born in 1878 in Little Britain, Manitoba. He/she died in 1878 in Little Britain, Manitoba.

Sarah FIDLER (2581) was born on 04 Mar 1851 in Rupertsland, Manitoba. She died on 12 Feb 1897 in Devils Lake, Saskatchewan, at age 45.

Children of Donald Gunn (2560) and Sarah Fidler (2581) all born in Fort Qu'appelle, Saskatchewan, were as follows:

i. Unnamed GUNN (2689) was born in Apr 1882. He/she died in Apr 1882 in Fort Qu'appelle, Saskatchewan.

ii. John Alexander GUNN (2582) was born on 21 Aug 1883. He married Margaret Ruth Walker (2583) circa 1920. He died on 12 Aug 1947 in Fort San, Saskatchewan, at age 63.

Margaret Ruth WALKER (2583) was born on 15 Mar 1898. She died on 24 Apr 1976 at age 78.

iii. Amelia Mary GUNN (2586) was born on 04 Dec 1885.

31. Janet GUNN (2563) was born on 09 Mar 1846 in Lot 163, St Andrews, Manitoba. She married Alexander Montgomery Muckle (2564). She died on 06 Nov 1930 in Muckle's Creek, Manitoba, at age 84.

She received a letter from her aunt Cecilia Cormack Gunn in 1893, see page 445.

Alexander Montgomery MUCKLE (2564) was born on 03 Dec 1844 in Quebec City, Quebec. He died on 14 Jan 1908 in Clandeboye, Manitoba, at age 63.

Children of Janet Gunn (2563) and Alexander Montgomery Muckle (2564) were as follows:

i. Anna Hollins MUCKLE (3367).

ii. Monty MUCKLE (3368).

iii. Alexander Montgomery MUCKLE (3365) married Katherine Boyd (3366).

iv. Robert James Tennant MUCKLE (3003) was born in 1875. He married Hannah Estelle Jensen (3363).

v. Leticia Margaret MUCKLE (2609) was born in 1877. She married Donald Gunn (2608), son of Alexander Gunn (2531) and Angelique MacKenzie (2532). She died in 1914.

Donald GUNN (2608) was born on 31 Aug 1867 in Lot 127, St Andrews, Manitoba. He married an unknown person. He died on 08 Apr 1962 at age 94.

32. William GUNN (2565) was born on 17 Aug 1848 in Lot 163, St Andrews, Manitoba. He married Catherine Ann Mowat (2566) in 1876 in Little Britain, Manitoba. He died on 26 Aug 1917 in Shaunavon, Saskatchewan, at age 69.

Catherine Ann MOWAT (2566) was born on 27 Nov 1857 in Kildonan, Manitoba. She died on 06 Jun 1950 in Shaunavon, Saskatchewan, at age 92.

Children of William Gunn (2565) and Catherine Ann Mowat (2566) were as follows:

i. Donald Edward GUNN (2616) was born on 02 Dec 1877 in St Andrews, Manitoba. He died in Nov 1954 in Spirit Lake, Shaunavon, Saskatchewan, at age 76.

ii. Mary Jane GUNN (2683) was born in Oct 1879 in St Andrews, Manitoba. She died on 26 Aug 1881 in St Andrews, Manitoba, at age 1.

iii. James GUNN (2684) was born in Mar 1881 in St Andrews, Manitoba. He died on 03 Apr 1882 in St Andrews, Manitoba, at age 1.

iv. Janet GUNN (2685) was born on 14 Nov 1884 in St Andrews, Manitoba. She died on 14 Mar 1886 in St Andrews, Manitoba, at age 1.

v. Isabella Catherine GUNN (2686) was born on 20 Nov 1886 in St Andrews, Manitoba. She died on 06 Mar 1887 in St Andrews, Manitoba.

vi. William GUNN (2619) was born on 02 Jul 1888 in St Andrews, Manitoba. He died on 09 Jun 1969 in Shaunavon, Saskatchewan, at age 80.

vii. Alexander Montgomery GUNN (2617) was born on 22 Mar 1891 in Selkirk, Saskatchewan. He died on 20 Apr 1959 in Shaunavon, Saskatchewan, at age 68.

viii. Victor John GUNN (2618) was born on 22 Jun 1897 in Gunview, Saskatchewan.

33. Murdoch MCDONALD (3566) was born in 1830 in Reay Parish, Caithness. He was christened on 17 Apr 1830 in Reay Parish, Caithness.[964] He married Annie McMullin (3567) on 08 May 1872 in Osclay, Peterboro, Ontario. He died on 17 Jan 1905 in Percy Township, Northumberland County, Ontario.

Annie MCMULLIN (3567) was born circa 1850 in Ontario.

Children of Murdoch McDonald (3566) and Annie McMullin (3567) were as follows:

i. Martha A. MCDONALD (3611) was born in 1844 in Percy Township, Northumberland County, Ontario.

ii. Peter MCDONALD (3607) was born in 1873 in Rawdon Township, Northumberland County, Ontario. He married Maude Greenley (3608) on 18 Jan 1899 in Percy Township, Northumberland County, Ontario. He died in 1946 in Percy Township, Northumberland County, Ontario. He was buried in Warkworth, Percy Township, Northumberland County, Ontario.

Maude GREENLEY (3608) was born in 1877. She died in 1953.

iii. Eleanor MCDONALD (3609) was born in 1877 in Percy Township, Northumberland County, Ontario.

iv. Abraham MCDONALD (3610) was born on 03 Mar 1878 in Percy Township, Northumberland County, Ontario. He died on 31 Aug 1908 in Percy Township, Northumberland County, Ontario, at age 30.

34. Jane MCDONALD (3513) was born circa 1845 in Upper Canada. She died on 14 Mar 1916 in Percy Township, Northumberland County, Ontario, at age 71.

She remained single. She is mentioned in a 1893 letter from C. C. Gunn in Australia to Mrs Muckle in Manitoba, Canada.

Children of Jane McDonald (3513) include:

i. Mary MCDONALD (3606) was born in 1862. She died on 11 Mar 1876.

35. William GUNN (377)[965] was born in 1853 in Wick Parish, Caithness.[966] He married Julia Janet Ingram (903), daughter of Robert Ingram (930) and Emma Gifford (931), in Aug 1889 in St Barnabas Church, South Melbourne, Vic.[967] and died on 16 Nov 1921 in Rushworth, Vic.[968]

He emigrated in 1857 to Melbourne with mother Cecilia. He and Alexander Gunn (906) were named as Lessees in Arrears under Sec 20 of the Land Act 1869, of lease no. 2970 Waranga

---

964Bill and Sharon Gurney, e-mail to Donald Gunn, 23 Apr 2009: Family of Marjory Gunn and Peter McDonald.

965See Part 7 for the biography of William Gunn, the son of William of Waranga, and his family, and letters from his grand daughter Janettie McMillan.

966Register of BDMs - Victoria, 1889 4812.

967*Melbourne Argus*, 02 Sep 1889: Marriages GUNN—INGRAM.—On the 10th ult., at St. Barnabas' Church, South Melbourne, by the Rev. H. Collier, W. Gunn, Esq., of Waranga-park, to Julia Janet, eldest daughter of Mr. R. Ingram, of Murchison, and granddaughter of the late Lieutenant-Governor Ingram of Her Majesty's Colonial service. No cards; Letter from Janettie McMillan to Donald Gunn, 24 Apr 1974; Register of BDMs - Victoria, 1889 4812.

968Register of BDMs - Victoria, 1921 15658; *Melbourne Argus*, 18 Nov 1921: Gunn - on the 16th November, at 'Waranga Park', Waranga, William Gunn, honoured chief of the Caledonian Society of Rushworth, and member of the council of Victorian Scottish Union (Inserted by the Rushworth Caledonian Society); *Melbourne Argus*, 18 Nov 1921: Gunn - on the 16th November, at 'Waranga Park', Waranga, William, loved husband of Julia J Gunn, aged 68 years.

and no. 2730 Murchison on 01 Apr 1888 in Rushworth, Vic. He was a beneficiary of the estate of William Gunn of Waranga (374) on 20 Dec 1888 in Supreme Court, Vic.[969] He was appointed as a Manager of the newly gazetted Waranga Common on 24 Feb 1891 in Waranga, Vic.[970] He was a Waranga Shire Councillor between 1897 and 1919 in Rushworth, Vic., and Shire President in 1899, again in 1908, and again in 1915. [971] He was the employer of two prospectors who discovered a corpse near his property on 21 Feb 1913 in Waranga Park, Vic.[972]

969*Melbourne Argus*, 20 Dec 1888 p3: NOTICE is hereby given that after the expiration of fourteen days from the publication hereof application will be made to the Supreme Court of the Colony of Victoria in its Probate jurisdiction, that PROBATE of the WILL of WILLIAM GUNN, late of Waranga, County of Rodney, in the colony of Victoria grazier, deceased, may be granted to William Gunn (the younger) and Alexander Gunn, both of Waranga aforesaid, landowners, sons of the said deceased, the executors named in and appointed by the said will. Dated this eighteenth day of December, 1888. BROMFIELD andFEDDEN, High Street, Rushworth, Proctors for the said executors.

970*New South Wales Government Gazette*), 1891: The Governor, with the advice of the Executive Council, has been pleased to appoint William Gunn [*with five others*] to be Managers of the Waranga Common. sgd A. McLean, Commissioner of Crown Lands and Survey.

971*Commemorative stone at Rushworth Mechanics Institute*, 'This stone was laid by William Gunn, Esq, President, July 18th 1915, D. Crothers, Builder A.J. Inches, Architect.'

972*Melbourne Argus*, 21 Feb 1913 p7: TRAGEDY OF THE BUSH. WOMAN'S REMAINS FOUND. HEAD AND ARM MISSING. SUPPOSED CASE OF MURDER. WANGARATTA, Thursday. --- By the discovery at Everton on Tuesday night of the decapitated body of a woman devoid of clothing, and with portion of the left arm missing, a sensation has been caused in the district. A ghastly murder, it is thought, has been brought to light, as the mutiilated condition of the remains point to a middle- aged woman having been brutally butchered, and after the body was stripped of all its clothing the corpse was thrown into a creek, to be carried away by the running water. So far the case is shrouded in mystery, as the body was in such an advanced state of decomposition that identification was an impossibility.
The prospectors James Mathieson and Charles Pratt, were responsible for the discovery of the remains. They spent Tue day searching for gold in the gullies along Stony Creek, not far from Everton. It was dark, save for the faint moon, when they started homeward. They were walking through the bush along the side of the creek which conveys water to the Ovens River from the sluicing claims around the Beechworth district, when they stumbled against a soft object. In the moon light it looked like a body, and , though it gave them an uncanny feeling, they did not examine the object to ascertain exactly what it was. When they arrived at the house of their employer, Mr. W. Gunn, later they related their experience, and one of them said he felt so positive that they had stumbled over a corpse that a party was organized to search the creek with a lantern. Then the mutilated remains of a woman of medium build was discovered lying face downwards on the bank of the creek. Decomposition was so far advanced that death had probably taken place six months previously. The head had been severed at the neck, and the left arm and two fingers of the right hand were missing. A search of the creek failed to discover the head or arm.
On the following morning Constable Strachan, who is temporarily in charge at Everton, was informed, and he, with the assistance of Constable Mallon, removed the body to the Morgue at the Wangaratta Hospital for medical examination. To-day an inquest was formally opened before Mr. Beaven, P.M., and on his suggestion the police telegraphed to Dr. Mollison, the Government pathologist in Melbourne, asking him to come and make a post-mortem examination of the remains. He left Melbourne for Everton later in the day, and will examine the body tomorrow.
Detective Sullivan has been despatched by Superintendent Davidson, at Benalla, to make investigations, and though much depends on the result of the post-mortem examination Detective Sullivan is of the opinion that the woman's death was not caused naturally. He does not think it possible for the water in the creek to have parted the head and arm from the body.
The locality where the body was found is a lonely one, situated at the foot of small range, two and a half miles from the Everton railway station. The nearest residence is that of Mr. W. Gunn, half a mile away, while the spot is a similar distance from the main road, which leads from Wangaratta to Beechworth. Evidence seems to point to the fact that, if a murder was committed, the deed was not perpetrated where the body was found, though the spot would have been suitable enough if concealment was desired. One theory is that the body was washed down the creek, which, allowing for windings through the ranges, has a course of 19 miles from Beechworth to Everton, seven miles from Beechworth.
Sluicing claims, with settling dams, are in the creek, and these obstructions reduce the distance along which the body might be carried to 12 miles.
Stony Creek, as the name implies, flows through rocky gullies on its course to Ever- ton, and there are several falls over little cliffs. These are localities frequently visited by picnic parties. One of these falls is 200 yards from where the body was found, but it is about four months since the last picnic was held there. The main road from Wangaratta to Beechworth crosses the creek a mile and a half above this fall, and the body could be easily carried that distance. So far only surmises can be made, but one that receives some acceptation by the police is that the body was placed in the creek some distance beyond Everton, and was washed down below the falls by the floods in December, and that, as the result of an inch and a half of rain on Saturday, the remains were dislodged from a tree, which at present holds much debris. This tree is seven yards away fiom the bank where the body was found by Mathieson and Pratt.
Inquiries shows that no residents of the district have been reported missing, but reports are given of at least two women who arrived in the district with swagmen during the past six months. In the absence of other suspicions, attention is being given to these cases at present. Tramps frequently visit the district in the company of women, who wander about from place to place. They are unknown, and their disappearance would not arouse suspicion unless the swagmen left behind them evidence of foul play.

Julia Janet INGRAM (903)[973] was born in 1860 in Rockford, Vic.[974] She died in 1957 in Murchison, Vic. She was a teacher in 1889 in Murchison, Vic.

Children of William Gunn (377) and Julia Janet Ingram (903) were as follows:

i. William Ingram GUNN (389) was born on 06 Dec 1890 in Rushworth, Vic.[975] He died on 04 Jan 1891 in Rushworth, Vic, aged 4 weeks.[976]

ii. Janettie GUNN (2494) was born in 1894 in Rushworth, Vic.[977] She married John Archibald Wyld McMillan (911), son of Robert Neil McMillan (2755) and Christina Wyld (2756), on 05 Sep 1925 in Holy Trinity Church, Oakleigh, Vic. She died in 1992 in Mooroopna, Vic, age 98.[978]

She was the informant at the death of Alexander Gunn (906) on 31 Aug 1915 in Rushworth, Vic; unmarried, no issue, following injury sustained after being thrown from a gig.[979]

John Archibald Wyld MCMILLAN (911) was born in 1900 in Murchison, Vic.[980] He died in 1953 in Tatura, Vic.

iii. William GUNN (909) was born on 25 Sep 1896. He died on 25 Sep 1896 of heart failure before birth.

36. Elizabeth GUNN (384) was born in 1859 in Rushworth, Vic.[981] She married Alexander Ingram (905) in 1888.[982]

Children of Elizabeth Gunn (384) and Alexander Ingram (905) both born in Rushworth, Vic, were as follows:

i. Cecelia Catherine INGRAM (386) was born in 1890.[983] She married William Tait (2995), son of William Tait (385) and Elizabeth Gunn Finlayson (2991), in 1936 in Vic.[984] She died in 1976 aged 86.[985]

William TAIT (2995) was born in 1872 in Mt Prospect, Vic.[986] He died in 1948 in Murchison, Vic, age 77.[987]

ii. Marie Elizabeth Gunn INGRAM (914) was born in 1898.[988] She married Frederick Esmond King (915) circa 1930. She died in 1957

---

973 Register of BDMs - Victoria, 1957 18279.

974 Letter, Edith Christoe to Donald Gunn, 06 Feb 2006 and for further information on this page.

975 Register of BDMs - Victoria, 1890 36133; *Melbourne Argus*, 10 Dec 1890 p1 Births GUNN. - On the 6th inst., at Waranga-park, the wife of William Gunn of a son.

976 Letter, Edith Christoe to Donald Gunn, 04 Mar 2008; *Melbourne Argus*, 14 Jan 1891 p1 Deaths GUNN.-On the 7th inst., at Waranga-park, the infant son of William and Julia Gunn, aged 1 month.

977 Register of BDMs - Victoria, 1894 6725.

978 Letters, Edith Christoe to Donald Gunn, 29 Nov 2005 and 06 Feb 2006.

979 Register of BDMs - Victoria, 1915 11067; *Melbourne Argus*, 03 Sep 1915: Gunn - on the 31st August, at Waranga Park, (result of accident) Alexander (Tal), youngest son of the late William Gunn, aged 54 years; *The Age*, 31 Aug 1915: A serious accident happened to Mr Alexander Gunn, of Waranga Park, Waranga, on Friday. While driving to Rushworth in company with his niece, the horse suddenly propped, and Mr Gunn was thrown out of the gig on the hard metal roadway, sustaining serious injury to the head, and he has not regained consciousness. The horse bolted, and Miss Gunn was also thrown out and injured.

980 Register of BDMs - Victoria, 1900 20996.

981 Register of BDMs - Victoria, 1859 3776.

982 Register of BDMs - Victoria, 1888 4595.

983 Register of BDMs - Victoria, 1890 7304.

984 Letter, Edith Christoe to Donald Gunn, 14 Jun 2009.

985 Letter, Edith Christoe to Donald Gunn, 04 Mar 2008.

986 Register of BDMs - Victoria, 1872 4425.

987 Register of BDMs - Victoria, 1948 23237.

Frederick Esmond KING (915) was a pastoralist in 1920 in Clermont, Qld.[989]

37. Margaret GUNN (1123) was born on 22 Nov 1841 in Carriside, Reay Parish, Caithness,[990] and was christened on 27 Nov 1841 in Carriside, Reay Parish, Caithness. She married Torquil Nicholson (1127), son of Euphemia (--?--) (3927), on 06 Sep 1870 in Edinburgh, Edinburgh Parish, Midlothian.[991] She died in 1892 in Durness Parish, Sutherland.

She appeared on the 1851 Census.[992]

Torquil NICHOLSON (1127) was born circa 1844 in Snizort, Inverness. He was a schoolmaster in 1871 in Durness, Sutherland. He was the informant at the death of his mother-in-law Catherine Gunn in Campster (1120) on 14 Oct 1871 in Durness, Sutherland, age 55.[993]

Children of Margaret Gunn (1123) and Torquil Nicholson (1127) both born in Durness, Sutherland, were as follows:

i. John NICHOLSON (Rev) (3928) was born on 25 Mar 1873. He married Catherine May Brown (3933), daughter of David Brown (3934) and Christina Carstairs (3936), on 23 Dec 1902.

ii. Donald NICHOLSON (Rev) (3929) was born on 25 Mar 1877. He married Catherine May Brown (3930) on 23 Dec 1902.

He was a draper's assistant in 1901 in Durness, Sutherland.

38. Alexander GUNN in Sangomore (887)[994] was born on 19 Nov 1859 in Sangomore, Durness Parish, Sutherland.[995] He married Georgina MacKay (2749) circa 1885 in Durness Parish, Sutherland[996] and died in 1945 in Sangomore, Durness Parish.[997]

He was a teacher.[998] He was the ground oficer in 1891 in Durness, Sutherland. He was the land steward in 1901.

Georgina MACKAY (2749) was born circa 1857 in Durness, Sutherland.

Children of Alexander Gunn in Sangomore (887) and Georgina MacKay (2749) were:

i. Catherine GUNN (3353) was born in 1888 in Durness, Sutherland. She died in 1930.

ii. Marianne GUNN (3355) was born circa 1890.[999] She died circa 1891 in infancy.

---

988 Register of BDMs - Victoria, 1898 28929.

989 Caroline Armstrong, e-mail to Donald Gunn, 20 March 2006.

990 Bill and Sharon Gurney, e-mail to Donald Gunn, 13 Sep 2008.

991 Michael J Gunn, "Descent of the Gunns"; Bill and Sharon Gurney, e-mail to Donald Gunn, 27 Jul 2010, Descendants of Alexander Gunn and Barbara Weir and for further information on this page.

992 Census 30 March 1851: John Gunn born Reay age 46, Catherine Gunn born Reay age 34, Margaret born Reay age 10, Donald born Reay age 6.

993 Bill and Sharon Gurney, e-mail to Donald Gunn, 21 Sep 2008; Balnakeil Cemetery: Text reads: In loving memory of John Gunn Land Steward Durness who died 10th Jany 1885 aged 77 years. Also Catherine Gunn his Spouse who died 14th Octr 1871 aged 55 years. Also their Sons John Gunn Inland Revenue Officer who died at Comber Ireland 9th January 1861 aged 23 years and interred there. Donald Gunn Teacher who died 21st Jany 1864 aged 20 years. Also their Daughters Johan [Gunn] who died 11th Octr 1868 aged 13 years. Barbara [Gunn] who died 3rd Novr 1905 aged 58 years. Catherine [Gunn] who died 3rd April 1907 aged 56 Erected by their Son Alexander [Gunn]. See page 372.

994 Chart from Colin Gunn;

995 Bill and Sharon Gurney, e-mail to Donald Gunn, 21 Sep 2008; Chart from Colin Gunn.

996 Michael J Gunn, "Descent of the Gunns."

997 Chart from Colin Gunn.

998 Bill and Sharon Gurney, e-mail to Donald Gunn, 21 Sep 2008.

iii. John Alexander GUNN (3354) was born in 1890 in Durness Parish, Sutherland.[1000] He died in 1890.

iv. Andrew Mackay GUNN (888) was born in 1894 in Durness Parish, Sutherland. He married Florence (--?--) (3357). He died in 1970 without issue.[1001]

v. Donaldina GUNN (3358) was born in 1896 in Durness, Sutherland. She died in 1974.

She was also known as Dolina GUNN (3358).

vi. Marion Ellen GUNN (3359) was born in 1899 in Durness, Sutherland. She died in 1975.

39. Williamina GUNN (889) was born on 19 Nov 1859 in Durness Parish, Sutherland.[1002] She married George Campbell (890) circa 1885. She died in 1951.[1003]

Children of Williamina Gunn (889) and George Campbell (890) were:

i. Catherine CAMPBELL (891) was born circa 1888.[1004] She married (--?--) Mackay (892) circa 1910.

(--?--) MACKAY (892) was born in Laid, Sutherland.

40. Catherine GUNN (119)[1005] was born on 13 May 1830 in Reay Parish, Caithness.[1006] She was christened on 18 May 1830 in Halkirk Parish, Caithness.[1007] She married James Miller (117), son of John Miller (934) and Elizabeth Dunnet (935), on 13 Mar 1857 in residence of John W Surman, Buninyong, Vic.[1008] She died in 1912 in Vic.[1009]

999Michael J Gunn, "Descent of the Gunns", Descent of the Gunns of Dalnaglaton and Braehour and for elsewhere on this page.

1000Bill and Sharon Gurney, e-mail to Donald Gunn, 27 Jul 2010, Descendants of Alexander Gunn and Barbara Weir and for further information on this page.

1001Chart from Colin Gunn; *Burke's Peerage*.

1002Chart from Colin Gunn.

1003Michael J Gunn, "Descent of the Gunns", Williamina b 1860 d 1951 m George Campbell. However a a gravestone at Balnakeil reads (in 2011)' In Loving Memory of George Campbell Who Died at Laid 8th April 1925 Aged 84 and his wife Williamina Gunn Who Died 20th April 1950 Aged 92 also their family John, Alexander, Margaret.' Given the names and 'Laid' it is possible this may be them.

1004Chart from Colin Gunn.

1005*LDS Church*, Christenings of children of Barbara Gunn, father Alexander Gunn. Catherine, 18 May 1830, Halkirk; Donald, 9 Jun 1832, Reay; Janet, 19 Aug 1834, Reay; John, 29 Feb 1836, Reay.

1006UK Census 06 June 1841: District of Brawlbin lying in the south part of the Parish of Reay. Each person who abode in each house on night of 6 June 1841: Alexander Gunn 50 farmer; Barbara Gunn 30; Kathrine Gunn 11; Donald Gunn 9; John Gunn 5; Janet Gunn 7; William Gunn 2; all born in Caithness. Note: Census instructions for recording age were that if under 15, actual age; if over 15, record to the nearest 5 years below actual ie Alexander Gunn was between 50 and 55 and Barbara between 30 and 35 on 6 June 1841. Birth years are thus Alexander 1786-1791 and Barbara 1806-1811.; Census 30 March 1851: County of Caithness, Parish of Reay. Residents at Brawlbinn. Donald Gunn head, unmarried 19, farmer, 16 acres, born Halkirk; Katherine Gunn sister, unmarried 20, general service, born Reay; Janet Gunn sister, unmarried 17, scholar, born Reay; John Gunn brother, unmarried 15, scholar born Reay; William Gunn brother, unmarried 12, scholar born Reay.; *Bible of Alexander Gunn*: my daughter Kitty born May 13 1830.

1007*LDS Church*, Christenings of children of Barbara Gunn, father Alexander Gunn
Catherine, 18 May 1830, Halkirk; Donald, 9 Jun 1832, Reay; Janet, 19 Aug 1834, Reay; John, 29 Feb 1836, Reay.

1008Certificate of Marriage, 1857 130 Marriages solemnized in the District of Buninyong: James Miller, Ship Chandler, age 28, born Wick Scotland, Bachelor resident Geelong, father John Miller, Builder, mother Elizabeth Dunnet, married Catherine Gunn, Servant, age 26, born Reay Scotland, Spinster resident Geelong, father Alexander Gunn, Farmer, Mother Barbara Gunn, according to the Rites of the Presbyterian Church.

1009Bruce A Smith, *The James Miller Story* (Prahran, Victoria: D.W.Paterson Co, 1962). The James Miller Story, published for the centenary of James Miller and Co, 1962: James Miller. Born in 1826 at Wick, Caithness, in the north of Scotland, he died in 1918 at the age of 92, after 54 years with the company. He arrived in Australia in 1850, tried his luck in the goldfields, and worked as a ship chandler before he established his rope business. In 1854, he sent home for his childhood sweetheart, Catherine Gunn, whom he married in Geelong. One of their sons, J D Miller, became secretary and a director of the company in 1918. James Miller's youngest daughter, Katherine, married W P Vine, and their son, F S Vine, was managing director until 1960. Today his

She appeared on the 1841 Census of Brawlbin, Reay Parish, Caithness, in the household of her parents Alexander Gunn of Bualchork and Brawlbin (1) and Barbara Gunn of Braehour (6). She appeared on the 1851 Census of Brawlbin, Reay Parish, Caithness, in the household of Donald Gunn in Brawlbin and Ballarat (3).[1010] James Miller sent home for his childhood sweetheart Catherine Gunn (119) in 1854.[1011] Catherine (119) and Donald (3) arrived in Melbourne, Vic, aboard the Herald of the Morning in Dec 1854. Catherine apparently travelled under her mother's name Barbara Gunn. She lived in 1857 in Geelong, Vic.[1012]

James MILLER (117)[1013] was born in 1826 in Wick Parish, Caithness; born in 1826 at Wick, Caithness, in the north of Scotland.[1014] He died in 1918 in Vic at the age of 92, after 54 years

---

son, James Miller Vine, a great grandson of James Miller, is with the company. James died at 92 in 1918, six years after Catherine's death.

[1010]Census 30 March 1851: County of Caithness, Parish of Reay. Residents at Brawlbinn. Donald Gunn head, unmarried 19, farmer, 16 acres, born Halkirk; Katherine Gunn sister, unmarried 20, general service, born Reay; Janet Gunn sister, unmarried 17, scholar, born Reay; John Gunn brother, unmarried 15, scholar born Reay; William Gunn brother, unmarried 12, scholar born Reay.

[1011]See Part 7 for the reminiscences of James Miller.

[1012]Register of BDMs - Victoria, 1857 879.

[1013]Certificate of Marriage, 1857 879 marriages solemnized in the District of Buninyong; Certificate of Marriage, 1857 879 marriages solemnized in the District of Buninyong.

[1014]Bruce A Smith, *James Miller Story*, James Miller, the son of a stonemason and builder, came to Australia in 1850 from Wick, a small seaport of Caithness in the north-east of Scotland. There he had learnt the age-old craft of sail making.

With only meagre savings behind him he worked for a while as a sailmaker in Van Diemen's Land, travelling on the ships trading between Van Diemen's Land and Norfolk Island. On one of these trips the cargo included a number of female convicts. The manner in which they were 'loaded' into the vessel, and the conditions under which they were carried, so disgusted the sailmaker that he left the ship in Sydney.

In the meantime the rush to the Victorian goldfields had set in. The discovery of the fabulously rich Ballarat and Bendigo fields, the first in Australia, resulted in fortunes for many diggers. James Miller decided to try his luck and, although he made no fortune, he was sufficiently successful to be able to establish his own small business as a ship chandler in Geelong.

In 1854 he sent home for his childhood sweetheart, Catherine Gunn, of Brawlbyn, Caithness, whom he married in 1857 in Geelong. They had six children, some of whom continued in the rope making business started by James.

James started his rope works at Emerald Hill, now South Melbourne, in 1862. A century later it was Australia's largest manufacturer of rope, cordage and associated products. Alexander Gray, another Scot, helped by providing capital for modern machinery. Then James brought to Australia his brothers-in-law: Peter Hogg, an experienced ropemaker, and George Murray, a carpenter.

In 1864, George Kinnear joined the staff to install and maintain machinery purchased from America. He was an engineer, but left the company in 1869 to establish his own successful enterprise.

With a nucleus of sound men, James was the first in Australia to introduce machinery for the preparing and spinning of vegetable fibres and the walk-laying of rope. The term 'ropewalk,' now a very old one, came from the spinner or ropemaker walking back and forth. The spinner wound a bunch of combed fibres around his waist, attached a few of the fibres to a hook and walked backwards while the driving wheel was turned by a fellow worker. As the hook revolved, the spinner fed out the fibre from the bundles around his waist. By the time he reached the end of the ropewalk a long piece of yarn had been spun. He repeated this operation until there were several yarns to twist together to form the 'strand.' Finally, three or more strands were twisted together thus 'laying' the rope. The James Miller enterprise was known originally not as a ropeworks but as a 'ropewalk.'

One day in 1888, James walked into the office and told the staff that he had sold the factory's South Melbourne site for £100,000. It was the height of the land boom. A deposit of £ 20,000 was paid and the purchaser promptly resold at £125,000. And then the boom burst. Miller had only his deposit. Moreover he had contracted to build new works on a river frontage at Yarraville.

In the tragic years that followed, bank after bank closed its doors - including Miller's own bank. Left with the now unsaleable South Melbourne property on his hands, James was committed to substantial expenditure in the middle of the worst depression the colony had known. It must have been heartbreaking. Somehow the firm survived, the banks reconstructured and opened again, and by the time the depression was over, James' operations had all been transferred to Yarraville.

Not only were all debts paid, but James and his partner, Alexander Gray, managed to help friends who also faced ruin.

As a result of the land boom and the large number of bankruptcies that followed the crash of the 1890's, James and Gray, both now in their 70's, dissolved the partnership and formed a limited company on 7 Sep 1898, with James as Chairman and Gray one of the other two directors.

James Miller was a compassionate man. At the end of the first world war, and shortly before his death, the company built a canteen at the Yarraville factory. This was one of the very first to be provided by a company in Melbourne - at a time when concessions and benefits extended by employers to employees were a rarity. Full meals were not supplied, but light refreshments could be purchased. At James' direction, soup was supplied free to juveniles and female workers. It was his opinion that many arrived for work having had little or no breakfast and he considered they needed more than just the cold lunch they brought with them. This consideration toward employees and their personal problems is one reason that many grandchildren of original employees are on the payroll of the company today.

James died at 92 in 1918, six years after Catherine's death, after 54 years with the company he founded.

with his company. He learned to be a ropemaker and sailmaker in Wick in 1845.[1015] He emigrated on 28 Jun 1850 from London in the sailing ship Australasia. He arrived in Hobart, Tas, in Oct 1850. He was employed as a sailmaker for three voyages in the Lady Franklin between Hobart and Norfolk Island in 1851. He settled in Melbourne one week before gold was discovered at Clunes in Jun 1851. He walked all the way from Melbourne to Ballarat in 1851, and left the diggings in 1852. He started a coal yard and ship chandler business in 1852 in Geelong, Vic. He sent for his childhood sweetheart, Catherine Gunn, of Brawlbiin in 1854. He lived on 13 Mar 1857 in Geelong, Vic.[1016] He was a ship chandler on 13 Mar 1857. He was the founder of Millers Ropes at Emerald Hill, now South Yarra, in partnership with Alexander Gray in 1862 in Vic. He sold the South Melbourne factory and bought river frontage at Yarraville in 1888. He dissolved the partnership and formed a limited company with son James as chairman and Gray as director on 07 Sep 1898. He retired as Chairman and Managing Director of Millers Ropes in 1916 in Melbourne, Vic. See 'The James Miller Story'and Part 7.

Children of Catherine Gunn (119) and James Miller (117) were as follows:

i. Elizabeth MILLER (278) was born in 1858 in Geelong, Vic.[1017] She died in 1918 in Vic unmarried.

ii. Alexander Gunn MILLER (279) was born in 1860 in Geelong, Vic.[1018] He died in 1938 in Apollo Bay, Vic.[1019]

iii. John William Gunn MILLER (280) was born in 1862 in Geelong, Vic.[1020] He died in 1925 in St Kilda, Vic.[1021]

iv. Jessie Barbara MILLER (284) was born in 1865 in Emerald Hill, Vic.[1022] She married Charles James Swears (282), son of William James Swears (4135) and Maria Sarah Simons (4136), in 1892 in London. She died on 03 Mar 1936 in Totnes, Devonshire, age 70.[1023] Her estate was probated on 03 Mar 1936. She and Charles James Swears (282) appeared on the 1901 Census of Linden Hall, Bournemouth,[1024] and on the 1911 Census of Totnes, Devonshire.[1025]. In 1936 she lived in Puddavine Court, Dartingdon, Totnes, Devonshire.

Charles James SWEARS (282) was born in 1857 in Bayswater, Greater London. He died on 01 Oct 1927 in Puddavine, Dartington, Devonshire. He left a will, valued at £28,876 6s to Jessie Barbara Swears and Herbert Swears.

v. James Dunnet MILLER (281) was born in 1868 in Emerald Hill, Vic.[1026] He died in 1933 in Heidelberg, Vic.[1027]

1015 *Unknown newspaper*, Mr James Miller's reminiscences. See Paart 7 for the complete article..

1016 Certificate of Marriage, 1857 879 marriages solemnized in the District of Buninyong.

1017 Register of BDMs - Victoria, 1858 2500.

1018 Register of BDMs - Victoria, 1860 3112.

1019 Register of BDMs - Victoria, 1938 17395.

1020 Register of BDMs - Victoria, 1862 14625.

1021 Register of BDMs - Victoria, 1925 15460.

1022 Register of BDMs - Victoria, 1865 8468.

1023 UK Probate Calendar 1861-1941, England and Wales National Probate Calendar 1861-1941 record reports Jessie Barbara Swears d. 5 March 1936 of Puddavine Dartington Devonshire ... (leaving) to Hubert Swears retired Bank Official £4219 19s 6d.'

1024 Census 1901.

1025 Census 1911.

1026 Register of BDMs - Victoria, 1869 2257.

1027 Register of BDMs - Victoria, 1933 460.

He was secretary and director of Millers Ropes in 1918.[1028]

vi. Katherine Margaret Mackay MILLER (285) was born in 1872 in Emerald Hill, Vic.[1029] She married William Porter Vine (283), son of James John Vine (1106) and Jane McDonald (1107), in 1895 in Vic.[1030]

She was also known as Catherine (285). She and William Porter Vine (283) were listed in the electoral roll in 1919 in 11 Redan Street, St Kilda, Vic. She and William Porter Vine (283) were listed in the electoral roll in 1924 in 10 Avondale Road, Armadale, Vic. She and Lesley Alison Vine (289) were listed in the electoral roll in 1936 in 10 Avondale Road, Armadale, Vic. She was listed in the electoral roll in 1937 in 10 Avondale Road, Armadale, Vic. She was listed in the electoral roll in 1943 living with her daughter and husband in 1 Fairfax Road, Bellevue Hill, NSW. She was listed in the electoral roll in 1949 in 59 Drumalby Road.

William Porter VINE (283) was born in 1857 in Port Melbourne, Vic; age 66 at death in 1923. He died in 1923 in Prahran, Vic.[1031]

41. Donald Gunn in Brawlbin and Ballarat (3) was born on 28 Mar 1832 in Brawlbin, Reay Parish, Caithness.[1032] He was christened on 09 Jun 1832 in Reay Parish, Caithness.[1033] He married Jane Surman (41), daughter of Daniel Surman (270) and Mary Ann Watkins (271), on 25 Mar 1859 in Presbyterian school residence, Buninyong, Vic.[1034] He died on 14 Feb 1901 in 185 Lydiard Street, Ballarat, Vic, at age 68 broncho pneumonia and heart disease.[1035] He was buried on 16 Feb 1901 in Old Cemetery Area DN Sec.14 Lot 5, Ballarat, Vic.[1036]

He appeared on the 1841 Census of Brawlbin, Reay Parish, Caithness, in the household of his parents Alexander Gunn of Bualchork and Brawlbin (1) and Barbara Gunn of Braehour (6).[1037] In Mar 1851 Donald Gunn in Brawlbin and Ballarat (3) was a farmer of 16 acres in

---

[1028] Bruce A Smith, *James Miller Story*.

[1029] Register of BDMs - Victoria, 1872 8854.

[1030] Register of BDMs - Victoria, 1895 880.

[1031] Register of BDMs - Victoria, 1923 16539.

[1032] Clan Gunn Parish Records: Births 1832 Donald Gunn, parents Alexander, Brawlbin - Barbara;
Bible of Alexander Gunn: Donald Gunn born 28 Mar 1832.

[1033] *LDS Church*, Christenings of children of Barbara Gunn, father Alexander Gunn
Catherine, 18 May 1830, Halkirk; Donald, 9 Jun 1832, Reay; Janet, 19 Aug 1834, Reay; John, 29 Feb 1836, Reay.

[1034] Register of BDMs - Victoria, 1859 827; "Notes by William Watkins Gunn"; Married by Rev J Hastie, (ca. 1902); Certificate of Marriage, no.157 of marriages solemnized in the District of Buninyong, Donald Gunn, 26, bachelor, of Buninyong, farmer, married Jane Surman, 23, spinster, of Buninyong, teacher, on 25 March 1859; Letter or email, Dougal Gilmour to Donald Gunn, 8 Apr 1999.

[1035] Register of BDMs - Victoria, 1901 253; *The Ballarat Courier*, Friday 15 Feb 1901, on the 14th February, at 185 Lydiard Street, Donald Gunn, aged 68 years. No flowers;
John William Gunn - notes, held in 1996 by Dorothy Margaret Jenkin (nee Milner):
Donald - whisky drinker and bought station near Ararat beyond Erildowne. Lost his money. Died about 1902 Ballarat; Dorothy Margaret Milner; Letter or email, Dougal Gilmour to Donald Gunn, 8 Apr 1999; Certificate of Death: Vic 1901 24552: 14 February 1901 at Lydiard Street, City of Ballarat, Donald Gunn, 68, insurance agent of broncho pneumonia, cardiac disease and asthma, duration about 3 months, father Alexander Gunn, farmer, mother Barbara Gunn, maiden name Gunn. Buried 16 February 1901 at Ballarat Old Cemetery. Born at Brawlbin, Reay, Caithness, Scotland, 47 years in Victoria, married at Buninyong at 27 years to Jane Surman, issue in order of birth, John Alexander, 41, William Watkins, 39, Mary Jane, 37, Donald, 35, Marcus Daniel, 32, Barbara, 30, Norman, 28, Hugh, died, Arthur Gilbert, 22, Catherine, 20. Signed by Donald Gunn, son, of Crossover, Gippsland.

[1036] Ballarat Old Cemetery records; *Ballarat Courier*, Friday 15 Feb 1901, the friends of the late Donald Gunn are respectfully informed that his remains will be interred in the old Ballarat Cemetery. The funeral cortage will leave his late residence, 185 Lydiard Street North, on Saturday 16th February at 2 o'clock. Funeral private;
Certificate of Death: Vic 1901 24552.

[1037] UK Census 06 June 1841: District of Brawlbin lying in the south part of the Parish of Reay. Each person who abode in each house on night of 6 June 1841: Alexander Gunn 50 farmer; Barbara Gunn 30; Kathrine Gunn 11; Donald Gunn 9; John Gunn 5;

Brawlbin, Reay Parish.[1038] He appeared on the Census of Brawlbin, Reay Parish, Caithness, dated 30 Mar 1851. Donald (3) received a preliminary form for List of Candidates for a Passage on 24 May 1853 in Reay Parish.[1039] He failed to gain passage to Australia on 30 Jun 1853 in Brawlbin, Reay Parish, Caithness. He was given a character reference by Minister on 29 Jun 1854 in Brawlbin, Reay Parish, Caithness. He was given a second character reference on 03 Jul 1854 in Brawlbin, Reay Parish, Caithness. He emigrated on 21 Aug 1854 from Liverpool, Merseyside, per the 'Herald of the Morning', 1291 t, which is the only ship with a Donald Gunn as an unassisted passenger arriving between the range of known dates of Oct 1854 and Jun 1856. He was 47 years in Victoria.[1040] Donald (3) and Catherine (119) arrived in Melbourne, Vic, aboard the Herald of the Morning in Dec 1854. Catherine apparently travelled under her mother's name Barbara Gunn.[1041] He bought a farm for £250 in partnership with John Surman, his future brother-in-law in 1857 in Cardigan, Vic. He was a farmer in 1857 in Buninyong, Vic.[1042] He was the foundation secretary of the Buninyong Highland Society on its formation on 01 Jan 1858.[1043] He was the judge for the first sports meeting on 01 Jan 1859,[1044] and was Secretary and the Gathering controller at the Second Gathering.[1045] He was awarded a silver

---

Janet Gunn 7; William Gunn 2; all born in Caithness. Note: Census instructions for recording age were that if under 15, actual age; if over 15, record to the nearest 5 years below actual ie Alexander Gunn was between 50 and 55 and Barbara between 30 and 35 on 6 June 1841. Birth years are thus Alexander 1786-1791 and Barbara 1806-1811. The summary notes that there were 40 occupied houses, 2 uninhabited houses, 78 males and 94 females comprising 40 families in the Brawlbin District.

[1038]Census 30 March 1851: County of Caithness, Parish of Reay. Residents at Brawlbinn.
Donald Gunn head, unmarried 19, farmer, 16 acres, born Halkirk; Katherine Gunn sister, unmarried 20, general service, born Reay; Janet Gunn sister, unmarried 17, scholar, born Reay; John Gunn brother, unmarried 15, scholar born Reay; William Gunn brother, unmarried 12, scholar born Reay. Brawlbin comprised 39 occupied houses with 70 males and 93 females. The census district of Brawlbin and Oldenbruch (?) was 12 miles in length and 2 miles in breadth. The majority of homes, 39, was in Brawlbin, with 3 in Oldenbruch accommodating 24 people.

[1039]See part 3 for much of the original documentation.

[1040]Letter or email, Dougal Gilmour to Donald Gunn, 8 Apr 1999; Certificate of Death: Vic 1901 2455214 February 1901 at Lydiard Street, City of Ballarat, Donald Gunn, 68, insurance agent of broncho pneumonia, cardiac disease and asthma, duration about 3 months, father Alexander Gunn, farmer, mother Barbara Gunn, maiden name Gunn. Buried 16 February 1901 at Ballarat Old Cemetery. Born at Brawlbin, Reay, Caithness, Scotland, 47 years in Victoria, married at Buninyong at 27 years to Jane Surman, issue in order of birth, John Alexander, 41, William Watkins, 39, Mary Jane, 37, Donald, 35, Marcus Daniel, 32, Barbara, 30, Norman, 28, Hugh, died, Arthur Gilbert, 22, Catherine, 20. Signed by Donald Gunn, son, of Crossover, Gippsland.

[1041]Unknown compiler, "Immigration to Victoria," *Ancestral File*, a Donald Gunn aged 27 arrived in Melbourne per the Herald of the Morning. This is the only recorded Donald Gunn of the approximate age to arrive between late '54 and early '56. The ship's passenger list records John Raps(?), 22; Walter Williamson, 20; John Sutherland,19; Hugh Murray, 22; Donald Gunn, 27; Barbara Gunn, 29 and Hugh Matheson, 36 all travelling together. There are no other names listed on the passenger list that could possibly be corruptions of Catherine or William. WW Gunn states Donald and Catherine travelled together - could Catherine for some reason travelled under her mother's name?

[1042]Certificate of Marriage, no.157 of marriages solemnized in the District of Buninyong, Donald Gunn, 26, bachelor, of Buninyong, farmer, married Jane Surman, 23, spinster, of Buninyong, teacher, on 25 March 1859.

[1043]The rules are reproduced in full on page 275.

[1044]William Bramwell Withers, *The History of Ballarat, from the First Pastoral Settlement to the Present Time* (40 Sturt Street: F W Niven and Co, 1887), The Caledonian Society was formed in November, 1858, and the first sports were held on New Year's Day, 1859, on what is now known as the Eastern Oval. Mr Hugh Gray was the first president, and with him as judges on that day were Charles Roy, Donald McDonald and Donald Gunn; "The Buninyong Highland Society."

[1045]*Melbourne Argus*, 05 Jan 1859 p6: SECOND GATHERING OF THE HIGHLAND SOCIETY OF BUNINYONG. (FROM THE BALLAARAT STAR.)
The second gathering of this society, which took place yesterday (Monday), in a paddock adjoining the Geelong road, about a mile beyond the township of Buninyong, was attended with much success. The day was calm and delightful, for the heat of the sun was pleasantly moderated by a cool sea breeze, which prevented those present from being oppressed by the weather. This fact was no doubt one of the great causes which produced an attendance of nearly all Buninyong has of pretty damsels, matronly dames, and stalwart men. Not a few Ballaarat men, too, were present, including most of those who joined in the Gathering on the Ballaarat cricket ground on New Year's Day, and tartan kilts, goat-skin sporrans and Highland caps, were nearly as numerous as on the latter occasion. There could not have been less than 800 or 1,000 people on the ground, who appeared to take the utmost interest in the proceedings. The arrangements, under the control of the energetic secretary, Mr. D. Gunn, were very good, as far as the clearing of the ground was concerned. A paddock was fenced in with palings, and no one was admitted but the competitors, the Committee, and a very few friends, mostly consisting of ladies. The Committee, in deciding upon this regulation, however, failed to provide proper accommodation for many ladies and gentlemen ineligible for admission within the sacred precincts without the payment of a guinea subscription, and who, therefore, were compelled to witness the sports from the hill afar off, at a manifest

medal by Buninyong Highland Society on 03 Jul 1859 in Ballarat, Vic.[1046] He was the recipient of a letter from Donald Gunn of Brawlbin and Dundee (976) written on 07 Nov 1859. The Buninyong Highland Society sports meeting realised £340 17s to give a balance of £60.[1047] The fourth Highland Games of the Buninyong Highland Society were held and well attended.[1048] He was the recipient of a letter from Donald Gunn of Brawlbin and Dundee (976)

---

disadvantage. Not a few grumbled loudly; and it is to be hoped the Committee will in future have more confidence in their own popularity, and provide far a larger attendance. The Secretary, however, very wisely insisted upon the carrying out of the regulations, such as they were, in their integrity, and thus a clear space was kept, without disorder. No untoward event interfered with the pleasantness of the occasion. The spectators mostly belonged to the respectable classes of society; and though Mr. Armltage's booth was filled with thirsty souls the whole day, a drunken man or an angry word were hardly to be seen or heard, nor were the decisions of Messrs. Stewart, M'Lachlan, and Gray, who were the judges, in any way questioned.
The medals of the society, which ware exhibited on the ground, were of the most handsome description, and were manufactured, we were informed, in Geelong. On the obverse was the figure of a Highlander in full costume, with the motto "Lainh na cear tais," the whole surrounded with the words "Highland Society, Instituted 1857." The reverse was left blank to admit of the names of the winners being engraved thereon. The day passed off in the most delightful manner, and though we were compelled to leave before the games were concluded, we doubt not the sports ended as pleasantly as they began. The following is a report of the day's proceedings:- '
PUTTING THE HEAVY STONE, 22 LB.
First prize, silver medal and £1 1s. Second prize, £1 1s.
Peter Haggart.28ft. 11in. Charles Nicholson. 28ft. 9in.
PUTTING THE LIGHT STONE, 16 LB.
First prize, silver medal and £1 1s. Second prize, £1 1s.
Peter Haggart. 86ft. 7in. Charles Nicholson . 85ft.1in.
THROWING THE HEAVY HAMMER, 18 LB.
First prize, silver medal and £1 1s Second prize, £1 1s.
Peter Haggart . 82ft. 6in. Charles Nioholson 76ft. 6in.
THROWING THE LIGHT HAMMER, 14 LB.
First prize, silver medal and £1 1s. Second prize, £1 1s.
Peter Haggart ... ... 95ft. 5in.
Charles Nicholson ... 94ft. 5in.
TOSSING THE CABER
First prize, silver medal and £1 1s. Second prize, £1 1s.
There was some difficulty in achieving this feat. It was at length accomplished by Mr. Fraser and Mr. Heggart; the former, however, was adjudged to take the best prize, and the latter the second.
PIPE MUSIC.
Piobaireachd-One prize, silver medal and £2 2s. It was won by Donald Rowan.
Strathspeys and Reels- First prize, silver medal and £2 2s. Second prize, £1 11s. 6i.
1. Andrew Wattie. 2. Donald Rowan.
COSTUME.
Best Dressed Highlander (ornaments not considered) - One prize, silver medal and
£2 12s 6d,
Hobart F. M'Lean. (This dress, we were informed, was 120 years old. It still looked fresh and handsome.)
Best Dressed Highland Boy (under 14 years) - £1 Is.
This was won by a lad whose name we could not hear. His dress was hardly complete, as it wanted the sporran and dirk.
DANCING.
Gillie Callum-First prize, sllver medal and £1 11s. 6d. Second prize, £1 1s.
1. William Coutts. 2. - Cameron.
Highland Fling-First prize, sllver medal and £1 11s. 6d. Second prize, £1 1s.
1. - Cameron.
2. William Coutts.
Strathspeys and Reels-First prize, silver medal and £1 11s. 6i Second prize, £1 1s.
We could not learn the names of those who gained the prizes for dancing. Two ladies attended the platform, and danced with Messrs. Coutts and Cameron, with great spirit and skill. There efforts were crowned with tremendous applause. They then danced the Reel of Tulloch, with equal success.
Foot Race of 600 yards-First prize, £2 2s Second prize, £1 1s.
1. - Emery. 2. L. Mount.
It was now fully 6 p.m., and, though several prizes remained to be competed for we were compelled to wend our way home, compelled of having spent a really pleasant day.

1046 See Part 3.

1047 *Melbourne Argus*, 17 Jan 1860 p5:
HIGHLAND SOCIETY OF BUNINYONG.-After paying all liabilities, the Highland Society of Buninyong have a balance of £60 in their favour. Tho total amount realised by the sports being £340 17s.-Ballarat Star.

1048 *Melbourne Argus*, 28 Dec 1860 p5:
GAMES.-The fourth grand gathering of the Buninyong Highland Society came off on Wednesday, on the grounds, which are situated at an easy distance from the "Ancient Township." About 2 000 persons were present, and the grand stand, which is capable of affording accommodation to about 310 persons, was quite crowded, while the awning overhead protected them from the

written on 24 Oct 1863. He was the recipient of letter from Donald Gunn of Brawlbin and Dundee (976) written on 25 Dec 1863. He was the recipient of a letter from Donald Gunn of Brawlbin and Dundee (976) written on 25 Apr 1864. He was first elected as a Shire Councillor on 30 Aug 1865 in Ballarat, Vic.[1049] He ended his first term as a Shire Councillor on 10 Jun 1867 in Ballarat, Vic. He was elected for second term as a Shire Councillor on 15 Aug 1870 in Ballarat, Vic. He was the President of the Ballarat Agricultural and Pastoral Society on 09 Nov 1872.[1050] Donald (3) was elected Shire President in Ballarat, Vic, on 11 Nov 1872. Donald (3) was appointed to a newly formed Ballarat Local Forest Board on 09 Sep 1873 in Ballarat, Vic.[1051] Donald (3) ended his service as Shire President on 12 Oct 1874 in Ballarat, Vic. Donald (3) ended service as a Shire Councillor in 1876 in Ballarat, Vic. Donald (3) was appointed as the sheep inspector of the Ballarat Agrictural Society on 11 Oct 1883 in Ballarat, Vic.[1052] He was involved in a dispute as the sheep inspector for the Ballarat Agricultural Society on 07 Apr 1884 in Ballarat, Vic.[1053] He was an insurance agent in 1900.[1054]

---

sun's rays. The band of the Western Fire Brigade lent the charms of music to the amusements of the day, and acquitted themselves right loyally, while the strain of the noisy bagpipes., more warlike than pleasing, was heard at intervals above both drum and brass instrumentation. Buninyong and its vicinity have the good fortune to be peopled with many of the sons of the mountain and heather, and, as may be imagined, there was a good gathering of the Gael. Men with brawny arms and stern resolve were there vieing with each other in those manly games which expand the limbs and give buoyancy and muscle to the body, many of them dressed in their national costume. The Grand Stand was decorated with a variety of bunting, while high overhead the standard of Scotland floated gaily in the breeze, in conjunction with Scotia's patron saint. The lessees of the booths did a good business all day, the extreme heat in no small degree contributing to swell their coffers. The only untoward event that occurred during the day was when throwing the heavy hammer, which slipped out of the hands of one of the persons flinging it, cleared the fence, and hit a person outside, but he miraculously escaped almost uninjured, and a little brandy and water appeared to make him all right again. At one time of the day there was a slight commotion among the ladies on the platform, at the creaking of a plank and tho ignition of some of the calico on the stand, caused by some gentleman's cigar; but in a very short time it was extinguished, and peace once more reigned paramount on the erection. Ballarat Star. Dec. 27.

1049See Part 7. Donald (1832-1901) had emigrated to Australia in approximately 1850 *[NB, must be after Jul 1854 and before Feb 1856. DG 06/01]* and had settled near Ballaarat which was then in the throes of a gold rush. Donald was a Councillor of the Shire of Ballaarat for two periods early in JA's life - 30 August 1865 until 10 June 1867 and 15 August 1870 until 12 October 1874. For the period 11 November 1872 until 12 October 1874 he was President of the Shire. Donald was also Foundation Secretary of the first Highland Society in Victoria - namely The Buninyong HIghland Society which was established in 1854 *[silver medal suggests correct date is 1857]* (the first Melbourne society was established in 1861 and the Victorian society was established in 1864). Donald's wife was Jane Surman of Oxford who was born on 18 January 1836. Donald's mother was Barbara (1810-1844) who was the second child of Donald the Sennachy (1770-1861) who was the oldest grandson of Alexander of Dalnaglaton and Strathmore (d 1765) who was the younger brother of George of Knockfinn from whom came the last chiefs of the Clan Gunn.

1050*The Age*, 09 Nov 1872.

1051*Melbourne Argus*, 09 Sep 1873, p6: BALLARAT FOREST BOARD. A Ballarat Local Forest Board, the Ballarat Courier states, has been appointed by the hon, the Minister of Lands. It will have the control and management of all state forests in the shires of Ballarat, Creswick, Bungaree, Buninyong, Ballan, and Meredith, and consist of the following members :- ... Donald Gunn, president, to represent the Council of the Shire of Ballarat; ... -provided that, if any person so appointed shall cease to hold office as specified, he shall thereupon also cease to be a member of the Ballarat Local Forest Board.

1052*Melbourne Argus*, 11 Oct 1883, p5: BALLARAT. WEDNESDAY. The Ballarat Agncultural Society has appointed Mr Donald Gunn of Burrumbeet an inspector of sheep which have been shorn and intended for exhibition at the Society's sheep show in September, 1884. Mr Gunn visits the stations and farms upon receipt of written notice and after satisfying himself that the sheep have been evenly, equally, and fairly shorn, will brand them and give the owner a certificate to that effect. The inspector's fee is £3 3s, to be paid at the time of inspection. The Ereildoune sheep have all been certified to, and next week the Carngham, Ellingrerrin, Barunah plains and Berry Bank stations will be visited.

1053*Melbourne Argus*, 07 Apr 1884, p7: THE BALLARAT SHOW SHEEP. BALLARAT, SATURDAY The dispute between the Ballarat Agricultural Society and Mr C Ayrey, of Woronooke station respecting his sheep entered for the next annual show was finally settled at the monthly meeting to-day. At the last meeting a resolution was carried that, as Mr Ayrey had withdrawn his refusal to allow his sheep to be inspected by the society's inspector, the original motion debarring him from competing, and returning his offer of a £50 donation, should be rescinded. There was a large attendance of members, in anticipation of an unfavourable report from the inspector when the minutes were read.
The President (Mr Philip Russell), sald the minutes were scarcely in accordance with the spirit of the resolution. It was understood that the motion for rescinding the action taken was carried conditionally upon the inspector's report being favourable to the state of Mr Ayrey's sheep. If the minutes were now confirmed, as just read, Mr Ayrey was entirely exonerated no matter what the tenor of Mr Gunn's report might be. If the meeting adopted them without hearing the report he should refuse to take any further responsibility, and vacate the chair.
Mr G G MORTON thought the chairman should not attempt to coerce the other members by threatening to vacate the chair.
Several members said the impression they were under was that the motion was carried
contingent upon the inspector's report.

Jane SURMAN (41) was born on 18 Jan 1836 in Hampton Poyle, Oxfordshire. She died on 14 Feb 1908 in 616 Lydiard St, Ballarat, Vic, at age 72.[1055] She was buried on 15 Feb 1908 in Old Cemetery Area DN, Sec.14, Lot 5, Ballarat, Vic.[1056] She appeared on the 1841 Census of Hampton Poyle, Oxfordshire, in the household of Daniel Surman (270).[1057] She appeared on the 1851 Census of Hampton Poyle, Oxfordshire, in the household of Daniel Surman (270).[1058] She emigrated with Daniel Surman (270) circa 1855; to Australia.[1059] She was 52 years in Victoria.[1060] She was a teacher in Feb 1859 in Buninyong, Vic.[1061] Wrote to her first grandson Alexander Donald, the son of John Alexander, referring to Arthur Gilbert.[1062] She lived in 1904 in 116 Doveton Street North, Ballarat, Vic.[1063] She lived in Oct 1906 in Doveton Street North, Ballarat, Vic. She was a beneficiary of the estate of The Honourable John Gunn (32) on 15 Oct 1910; Estate was valued at £31,690 which he left to his widow and children, with annuities of £150 to his mother for life and of £75 each to his sisters, Mary Jane Gunn and Katherine Alexandrina Gunn, and a bequest of £300 to his sister Mrs Barbara Padgett.[1064]

Children of Donald Gunn in Brawlbin and Ballarat (3) and Jane Surman (41) were as follows:

i. John Alexander GUNN (Hon.) (32) was born on 11 Feb 1860 in Buninyong, Vic.[1065] See Part 7. He married Jessie Marie Turner (104), daughter of

---

Mr ROWE said that if the minutes were adopted, Mr Ayrey would leave that meeting without the slightest stigma on his name.
Mr GUNN said the question was, were the minutes correct or incorrect? If they were correct then they must be confirmed.
After some further discussion a motion was carried confirming the minutes and the president then ruled that the inspector's report could not be read.
Mr MORTON remarked that whatever Mr Russell had done in this matter, they all gave him credit for acting in a disinterested manner, and wholly in the interests of the society. He had however, been carried away by over zeal and it was as well that the matter should be allowed to drop.
At a subsequent stage a letter was read from Mr Robert Simson owner of the Langi Kal Kal station with reference to the refusal to allow his sheep to be inspected. It transpired that the cause was a slight misunderstanding between the manager and the inspector and no action was taken.
In reply to a question, Mr Gunn, the inspector, said that as the system was on its trial he had refrained from selecting any station for special report; but he could inform the committee that with two exceptions there was not a holding on which he did not find the sheep improperly shorn - in some instances as much as 50 per cent.

1054 Letter or e-mail, Dougal Gilmour to Donald Gunn, 8 Apr 1999; Certificate of Death: Vic 1901 24552: 14 February 1901 at Lydiard Street, City of Ballarat, Donald Gunn, 68, insurance agent of broncho pneumonia, cardiac disease and asthma, duration about 3 months, father Alexander Gunn, farmer, mother Barbara Gunn, maiden name Gunn. Buried 16 February 1901 at Ballarat Old Cemetery. Born at Brawlbin, Reay, Caithness, Scotland, 47 years in Victoria, married at Buninyong at 27 years to Jane Surman, issue in order of birth, John Alexander, 41, William Watkins, 39, Mary Jane, 37, Donald, 35, Marcus Daniel, 32, Barbara, 30, Norman, 28, Hugh, died, Arthur Gilbert, 22, Catherine, 20. Signed by Donald Gunn, son, of Crossover, Gippsland.

1055 Register of BDMs - Victoria, 1908 219.

1056 Ballarat Old Cemetery records: Area DN, Sec.14, Lot 5.

1057 UK Census 06 June 1841: Daniel Surman 35 shoe maker, Mary Surman 30, John Surman 9, Jane Surman 5, Catherine Watkins 60.

1058 UK Census 30 March 1851: Hampton Poyle Daniel Surman head married 45 servant b Wokingham, Mary Surman wife married 40 schoolmistress b Oxford, Jane Surman daughter unmarried 15 scholar b Hampton Poyle, Catherine Watkins mother in law, widow 70 b Middlesex, London.

1059 *Unknown newspaper*, ...in 1855 he arrived in Victoria with his parents and only sister, the latter being Mrs Gunn, of Doveton Street North.

1060 Letter or email, Dougal Gilmour to Donald Gunn, 8 Apr 1999.

1061 Certificate of Marriage; Letter or email, Dougal Gilmour to Donald Gunn, 8 Apr 1999.

1062 See Part 3.

1063 *Victorian Post Office Directory 1904*.

1064 *Melbourne Argus*, 15 Nov 1910 p7: [:CR:The estate of the late Mr John Alexaander Gunn of Braehhour, near Wagga NSW, grazier and bacteriologist, has been valued for probate purposes at £31,690. He left his real and personal estate to his trustees upon trust for his widow and children subject to annuities of £150 to his mother for life and of £75 each to his sisters, Mary Jane Gunn and Katherine Alexandrina Gunn, and subject to a bequest of £300 to his sister Mrs Barbara Padgett, and of life insurance policies for £750 to Mr H H B Bradley, Solicitor, of Sydney.

1065 An extensive review of the life of John Alexander Gunn is given in Part 7.

William Turner (437) and Maria Reinhardt (440), on 08 Jun 1886 in North Brighton, Vic.[1066] He died on 21 Sep 1910 in Sydney, NSW, at age 50.[1067] He was buried on 26 May 1904 in Old Cemetery, Ballarat, Vic; J.A.Gunn of Borambola Station, Wagga Wagga, purchased Lot 5 Area DN, Sec. 14.[1068] He was buried in Rookwood cemetery, NSW. His estate was probated on 15 Oct 1910; Estate was valued at £31,690 which he left to his widow and children, with annuities of £150 to his mother for life and of £75 each to his sisters, Mary Jane Gunn and Katherine Alexandrina Gunn, and a bequest of £300 to his sister Mrs Barbara Padgett.[1069]

He lived between 1860 and 1878 in Burrumbeet, Ballarat, Vic; with his parents. He lived between 1878 and 1897 in South Yalgogrin Station, Ardlethan, NSW.[1070] He was a jackaroo for Goldsborough, Mort and Co in 1878 in South Yalgogrin Station, Ardlethan, NSW. He was the inventor of the first mechanical poison-bait layer, made from an old sausage machine, some cogs and a pair of wheels, which soon came into general use in various froms throughout the country between 1880 and 1885.[1071] John (32) was appointed a sheep inspector for the Ballarat Agricultural Society on 11 Oct 1883 in Ballarat, Vic.[1072] He became the manager South Yalgogrin Station, Ardlethan, NSW in 1886. Anthrax ravaged sheep at the Station in 1888. In 1892 Yalgogrin station comprised 129 000 acres running 26 600 sheep, 34 horses and 41 cattle.[1073] He created a double dose anthrax vaccine in Dec 1893 in Ardlethan, NSW. John Alexander (32) was given approval to introduce and

---

1066Register of BDMs - Victoria, 1886 3043.

1067*Unknown newspaper*, The death in Randwick (Sydney) private hospital of Mrs J.M.Gunn, formerly of Wagga, and widow of the late J.A.Gunn, M.L.C., recalls the debt owing by the sheep-owners of Australia to her late husband and McGarvie Smith, who collaborated in discovering a vaccine for combating anthrax in sheep. Gunn and McGarvie Smith experimented for years before succeeding, and the benefit to the pastoral industry in Australia cannot be assessed in figures. Gunn predeceased McGarvie Smith, who in his will devised the formula to the people, asking only that the State should provide the buildings necessary for the preparation of the vaccine. He had been offered £100,000 for the formula, but refused it; Rookwood cemetery records: Gunn John Alexander, died Sydney 22 Sep 1910.

1068Ballarat Old Cemetery records.

1069*Melbourne Argus*, 15 Nov 1910 p7:The estate of the late Mr John Alexaander Gunn of Braehhour, near Wagga NSW, grazier and bacteriologist, has been valued for probate purposes at £31,690. He left his real and personal estate to his trustees upon trust for his widow and children subject to annuities of £150 to his mother for life and of £75 each to his sisters, Mary Jane Gunn and Katherine Alexandrina Gunn, and subject to a bequest of £300 to his sister Mrs Barbara Padgett, and of life insurance policies for £750 to Mr H H B Bradley, Solicitor, of Sydney.

1070Letter from Nathalie Semmler (Euronga, Moombooldoal, NSW 2665) to Ian Marcus Gunn, 10 Jun 1991;...Yalgogrin South is now no more than a locality. It is officially named Gunn - but you know how difficult it is to get local folk to adopt a change of name - and so it remains S. Yalgogrin. Some sign boards have S. Yalgogrin, and some Gunn, so it must be very confusing for people trying to find the 'place'.
I take it that you have never visited S. Yalgogrin? There used to be a hall, school and tennis courts there, but now nothing remains, not even the old homestead nearby, as it was burned to the ground about 2 years ago. Peter Russell, the present owner told me the only original building on the station is the dog kennel! It is built from stone. The homestead itself was built on a stony rise, but the new home has been located in more hospitable surroundings. The memorial itself is only a cement post with a small plaque. I will enclose a photo of it and also one of the little child's head stone. The only grave that can be identified in the old cemetery.
... In 1988 I sent a photo of the memorial to the NSW Historical Society and it was published in their bicentennial book, 'Monuments of NSW' or some such title.

1071Rob Webster, *Bygoo and Beyond.*

1072*Melbourne Argus*, 11 Oct 1883, p5: BALLARAT. WEDNESDAY. The Ballarat Agncultural Society has appointed Mr Donald Gunn of Burrumbeet an inspector of sheep which have been shorn and intended for exhibition at the Society's sheep show in September, 1884. Mr Gunn visits the stations and farms upon receipt of written notice and after satisfying himsell that the sheep have been evenly, equally and fairly shorn, will brand them and give the owner a certificate to that effect. The inspector's fee is £3 3s, to be paid at the time of inspection. The Ereildoune sheep have all been certified to, and next week the Carngham, Ellingrerrin, Barunah plains and Berry Bank stations will be visited.

1073Rob Webster, *Bygoo and Beyond.*

keep microbes and to inoculate animals on 06 Dec 1893.[1074] He was superintendent for all Goldsborough Mort stations in southern NSW in 1895 in NSW. He was a Justice of the Peace in 1895 in NSW. In Apr 1895 John (32) entered into a partnership with John McGarvie Smith in NSW. He was Commissioned as a Justice of the Peace in 1896. He succeeded in developing a single dose anthrax serum in 1897 in South Yalgogrin Station, Ardlethan, NSW. He lived between 1897 and 1905 in Borambola Station, nr Wagga Wagga, NSW. He hosted a visit by Sidney and Beatrice Webb in 1898 in Borambola Station, NSW.[1075] He suffered burns during bushfires in 1902. He was listed in the electoral roll in 1903 in Borambola Station, NSW.[1076] He was resigned from Goldsborough Mort in 1905 in NSW. He lived in Jun 1905 in Braehour, nr Wagga Wagga, NSW. He was described as a grazier, bacteriologist and station inspector in Aug 1905 in NSW. John (32) was elected a vice president of the Murrumbidgee Fish and Game Protection and Anglers' Society on 22 Sep 1905 in Wagga, NSW. He was Chairman of the Council of Advice on Rabbit Extermination in 1908. On 21 Jul 1908 The Honourable John Gunn (32) was elected as a Member of the Legislative Council of NSW until his death on 21 Sep 1910.[1077] He gave a most patriotic speech in praise of Britain's navy at the time of the visit of the US Great White Fleet which was followed by the spontaneous singing of Rule Britannia.[1078] He is in *Bygoo and Beyond*.[1079] An article headed 'On the Land, Farm and Station, Destructive Weevil', drew attention to JA's long belief that poisoning of pests should be avoided.[1080] He was listed in the NSW Parliament's record of qualifications, occupations and interests.[1081]

1074 *Sydney Morning Herald*, 08 Dec 1893, p7: BOARD OF HEALTH. A meeting of the Board of Health was held on the 6th instant. Papers from the Lands Department, forwarding an application from Mr. J. A. Gunn, for licenses to introduce and keep microbes, and to inoculate animals, were read. After consideration, it was decided that 'the Lands Department should be recommended to issue to Mr. Gunn licenses under the 6th and 7th sections of the Animal Infections Diseases Act.

1075 See Part 7.

1076 Electoral Roll, 1903 Roll lists John Alexander Gunn, Station Manager, Marcus Daniel Gunn, Station Manager, Norman Gunn, Licensed Vaccinator, Mary Jane Gunn, Domestic Duties and Jessie Marie Gunn, Domestic Duties as residing at Borambula Station.

1077 NSW Parliament Members: Life Appointment under the Constitution Act. Date of Writ of Summons 10 July 1908.

1078 *Hobart Mercury*, 02 Sep 1908 p4: RULE, BRITANNIA The convivial serenity of the annual social at Wagga (New South Wales) last week, in connection with the show, was disturbed by an outburst of patriotic feeling as remarkable for its spontaneity as for its enthusiasm. Mr. P. McGarry, M.L.A., in the course of a response to the toast of the guests, said the crowd that watched the fleet's arrival at Sydney was not enthusiastic because it was dumbfounded with amazement at the magnificent spectacle. Australia was, like America, a young country, but America was self-contained, and able to put out the greatest fleet of any nation in tho world. (Loud cries of "No! No!"). They had the most up-to-date ships it was possible to have. (Uproarious dissent and interruption.) As Mr. McGarry resumed his seat, amid considerable uproar, Mr. J. A. Gunn, M.L.C., declared, with considerable emphasis: "I am proud to see the American fleet here. I am proud of our friendship with America; but I desire to enter the protest of this meeting against anyone, whether a guest or not, cracking up the American fleet as against the British. (Loud and continuous cheering.) The British fleet rules the world, and could beat any three fleets in the world. Whoever says the American fleet, or any other fleet, is the first in the world, let him go and live there." At this stage the assemblage, numbering about 300, rose as one man and lustily sang "Rule, Britannia. Britons never, never, shall be slaves,"
followed by deafening cheers. Mr. Mc Garry joined in.

1079 See Rob Webster, *Bygoo and Beyond*, Yalgogrin

1080 *Sydney Morning Herald*, 26 Nov 1913, p8: The increase of insect pests (every year some new ones appear) recalls a remark made some years ago by the late Mr J A Gunn, MLC, who had given years of study to stock diseases, and natural phenomena. Mr Gunn always strongly opposed the use of poisons for dealing with the rabbits. "If this practice is persisted in," he says, "the eventual effect will be the entire destruction of our useful birds, and after that we shall have plagues of insects which will be far more ruinous to rural interests than even the rabbit. "

1081 NSW Parliament Members: Qualifications, occupations and interests Pastoralist. Moved to New South Wales c.1878; employed by Goldsborough Mort and Company; managed Yalgogrin and other stations; late in life purchased Braehour near

Jessie Marie TURNER (104) was born on 01 Jul 1862 in Beechworth, Vic.[1082] She died on 05 May 1925 in Helene Pt Hospital, Randwick, NSW, at age 62.[1083] She was buried on 07 May 1925 in Rookwood cemetery, Sydney, NSW; alongside her husband. She was a dressmaker on 08 Oct 1885 in Arundel Street, Benalla, Vic.[1084] She was on the electoral roll with John Alexander Gunn (Hon.) (32) in 1903 in Borambola Station, NSW.[1085]

ii. William Watkins GUNN (33) was born on 26 Dec 1861 in Cardigan, Nr Ballarat, Vic.[1086] He married Margaret Jane Balharrie (42), daughter of John Balharrie (1314) and Jane Carmichael (1315), on 24 Jun 1891 in Bloomfield, Vic.[1087] He died on 24 Jun 1935 in Crossover, Vic, at age 73.[1088] He was buried on 26 Jun 1935 in Warragul Cemetery, Vic.

Wagga Wagga; known for collaboration with McGarvie Smith on anthrax vaccination; chairman of the Rabbit Destruction Fund committee which financed Dr Danysz; chairman of Narrandera Pastures Protection Board until 1897; afterwards of Wagga Wagga Board; for three years was chairman of the Pastures Protection Boards Advisory Council; Member of Stockowners and Farmers and Settlers Associations; president of the Murrumbidgee Pastoral and Agricultural Society.

1082Rookwood cemetery records: Gunn Jessie Marie born Beechworth, Victoria 1 Jul 1862.

1083*Unknown newspaper*, The death in Randwick (Sydney) private hospoital of Mrs J.M.Gunn, formerly of Wagga, and widow of the late J.A.Gunn, M.L.C., recalls the debt owing by the sheep-owners of Australia to her late husband and McGarvie Smith, who collaborated in discovering a vaccine for combating anthrax in sheep. Gunn and McGarvie Smith experimented for years before succeeding, and the benefit to the pastoral industry in Australia cannot be assessed in figures. Gunn predeceased McGarvie Smith, who in his will devised the formula to the people, asking only that the State should provide the buildings necessary for the preparation of the vaccine. He had been offered 100,000 pounds for the formula, but refused it; Rookwood cemetery records: Gunn Jessie Marie, died Sydney 5 May 1925; *Sydney Morning Herald*, 08 May 1925 p12: The funeral of the late Mrs. Jessie Maria Gunn, widow of the late Mr. J. A. Gunn, M.L.C., who died, in her 83rd year, at a private hospital at Randwick, took place yesterday, from Wood Coffil's mortuary chapel, where a short service was conducted by the Rev. W. J. Grant, of Randwick, who also officiated at the place of interment, in the Presbyterian Cemetery at Rookwood. Amongst those who attended the funeral yesterday were Messrs. Alexander D. Gunn, Angus W. Gunn, Mrs. F. Supton, Messrs. J. A. and W. Turner, and Mrs. W. Turner, senr., who were the chief mourners, and Messrs. A. Buchanan, P. H. Broadhurst, Norman Kyle, W. Bibs, Alec Davidson, Mr. and Mrs. F. A. Mackenzie, Mr. and Mrs. C. M. Davidson, and Mrs. Pennicuick.

1084*North East Ensign*, 08 Oct 1885 - Miss Jessie Turner, wishes to inform the Ladies of Benalla that she has started DRESSMAKING, In Arundel Street - all kinds of sewing done.

1085Electoral Roll: 1903 Roll lists John Alexander Gunn, Station Manager, Marcus Daniel Gunn, Station Manager, Norman Gunn, Licensed Vaccinator, Mary Jane Gunn, Domestic Duties and Jessie Marie Gunn, Domestic Duties as residing at Borambula Station.

1086Register of BDMs - Victoria, 1862 467.

1087Register of BDMs - Victoria, 1891 3581.

1088Register of BDMs - Victoria, 1935 15057; *Melbourne Argus*, 26 Jun 1935 p1: On the 24th June, at Crossover, William Watkins, beloved husband of Margaret Jane, and loving father of John, Jean (Mrs Milner), Violet (Mrs Wadeson), Edith (deceased), Marjorie and Allan, aged 73 years; *The Warragul Gazette*, The death occurred at Crossover on Monday of William Watkins Gunn, at the age of 73 years. He commenced a sawmilling business at Crossover more than 40 years ago. He leaves a widow, two sons and three daughters; *The Warragul Gazette*, W.W.Gunn Passing of a Pioneer One of the oldest pioneers in the timber industry of Gippsland in the person of Mr WW Gunn, of Crossover and Noojee, passed away last week, and the 'natural' body was placed to rest in the Warragul Cemetery. At the graveside on Wednesday last a number of relatives and friends of the family assembled to pay their last respects to one who had fought a good fight and a strenuous one, in the heavily timbered country of Gippsland. Tangible evidence of the affection and esteem felt for him was seen in the large number of beautiful wreaths which covered the casket. At the funeral which took place at the Warragul Cemetery on Wednesday, the coffin-bearers were:- Messrs A Aldersea, J Parker, J Byrnes, N McDougall, F Young and R Holmes, several of whom were old employees of the firm. The burial service was read by the Rev. Neil McDonald, of the Presbyterian Church, and all the arrangements were entrusted to Messrs JA McGilton Pty Ltd.

The late Mr Gunn came of a real old Highland family, who emigrated to Australia in the early days. He was born in the Burrumbeet district near Ballarat and came to Gippsland in the very early days about 1884, and engaged in sawmilling in what is now known as Lionel Young's farm. He moved over to Bloomfield, now called Nilma, and later still to Crossover and Noojee. In fact, he was a pioneer of this forest country, over 50 years ago. Notwithstanding his strenuous life and the hard work of handling timber, he enjoyed splendid health for over 70 years and was never happier than when among the giant Eucalypts.

One of the most memorable events of his life was his visit to the Old Highland homeland with the Scottish Delegation. There he met his cousin, Col. Gunn, a landed proprietor by whom he was introduced to, and enjoyed the hospitality of, many of the notabilities of the North.

By his marriage with Miss Balharrie, he became associated with another well-known pioneer family of Gippsland, Cr. Balharrie being her brother. The family consists of two sons and several daughters, John Gunn being the eldest son, is now in charge of the sawmilling business.

He lived in 1884 in Darnum, Vic.[1089] He was a timber miller with Amoss as partner circa 1888 in Bloomfield (now Nilma), Vic.[1090] He applied for a mining lease on 01 Jun 1892 in South Warragul, Vic.[1091] He was a member in 1894 in Cricket Club, Traralgon, Vic.[1092] He was a member in 1895 in Cricket Club, Traralgon, Vic.[1093] He lived between 1895 and 1935 in Brawlbin, Crossover, Vic. He took out a mining right circa 1895 in Crossover, Vic.[1094] He appeared at court on 28 Mar 1896 in Warragul, Vic, when a local shoemaker was accused of forging WW's cheque.[1095] He and Margaret Jane Balharrie (42) lived in 1903 in Crossover, Vic.[1096] He and Margaret Jane Balharrie (42) lived in 1904 in Albert Street, Sebastopol, Vic.[1097] He was a miner, Gippsland leases 5047 and 5048 in 1904.[1098] He brought the first car to Crossover district in 1912 in Crossover, Vic. He invented a method to destroy submarines in 1915.[1099] He was took part in a published discussion on oddities in Nature,

---

A man of sterling qualities, strong in his convictions and of the strictest integrity, the deceased pioneer has left behind him a name and character, which will be remembered with affection, by a very large circle of friends.

1089Dorothy Hunt, *A History of Neerim* : William Watkins Gunn first came to Darnum Gippsland in 1884. He married Margaret Jane Balharrie at Bloomfield in 1891. They settled in Crossover in 1895 and had six children - John, Jean, Violet, Edith, Marjorie and Marcus Allan. They all attended Crossover State School. William built and operated successful sawmills at Crossover, Shady Creek and districts, employing many men. He built a three foot six inch tramway for transporting the sawn timber from these mills to the rail-head at Crossover. William brought in the first car to the district in 1912. In 1921 he took up milling at Noojee, his son John was manager. During the First World War he invented a method for destroying submarines which was duly adopted by the British Admiralty with considerable success. He attempted to obtain recognition for this invention during a visit to England in 1928 but failed to do so. The Admiralty claimed it their right to commandeer such inventions in wartime. William also had a large interest in goldmining in Crossover and Buchan.
He died in 1945 aged 74 years.
(Typed notes written by Dorothy Margaret Jenkin (nee Milner) for A History of Neerim, and held by her - Mar 1996).

1090John William Gunn.

1091*Melbourne Argus*, 01 Jun 1892: GOLD IN WEST GIPPSLAND. FORMATION OF A COMPANY.WARRAGUL, Tuesday.
The recent discoveries of good prospecta of fine gold at South Warragul, as reported in The Argus a few days ago, continue to excite a considerable amount of local interest, and it is generally felt that although no very extensive developments may take place owing to the notoriously "patchy" character ot the country, the eventual results may be sufficiently important to materially benefit, the district. The local residents, at alll events, have great hopea in this direction, and some half-a-dozen oí them are demo strating their faith in the prospects by making application for a miners lease. Their names are W. A. Amos, A. Strang, and.J. Balharrie (Bloomtield), W. W. Gunn and D. Gunn (Darnum), and W. Edwards (Gainsborough). The land in which they seek the right to mine covers 30 acres, and is owned by J. V. Robertson. The minimum number of men to be employed for the first six months is six, and subsequently 150. It is proposed to invest £6,000 in the venture, and operations will be commenced immediately the lease is granted. The company will be designated "The South Warragul Gold-mining Company."

1092Photograph; Royal Historical Society of Victoria, Melbourne, Vic, Group of men belonging to Traralgon Cricket Club, Item No. MSPH-0498.

1093Photograph; Royal Historical Society of Victoria, Group of men belonging to Traralgon Cricket Club, Item No. MSPH-0499.

1094John William Gunn.

1095*Melbourne Argus*, 28 Mar 1896 p8: CHARGE OF FORGERY. WARRAGUL, FRIDAY. At the police court today, before Mr. W Love, JP, a local shoemaker named William Doddrell, was charged with forging the signature of W W Gunn, sawmiller, Darnum, to a cheque made out on the Commercial Bank for£8 5s in the name of one Dopa. The accused denies the charge, and alleges that a man named Dopar sent him the cheque in payment of repairs to his boots amounting to 7s, and that he (accused) cashed the cheque and subsequently gave the change to Dopar. The police however, cannot discover anyone in the district of this name. The cheque was cashed on the 4th inst., and last night Sergeant Hillard and Constable Steedman arrested the accused at his shop. The case was remanded till Thursday next, accused being admitted to bail himself in £50, and two sureties of £25 each.

1096Electoral Roll: 1903 Vic.

1097Archive CD Books, *Ballarat and District Directory 1904.*, CD-ROM, 2004; *P.O. Directory 1904.*

1098*Ballarat Directory 1904*; *Victoria Government Gazette*, 30 Dec 1936:
Mining Leases and Licence Declared Void
5047Gippsland, William Watkins Gunn
5048Gippsland, William Watkins Gunn.

1099Gunn, William Watkins - Power of Attorney from William Watkins Gunn to The Admiralty, 17 Oct 1928;, granted to Gunning Francis Plunkett Esq dated 17 October 1928 relating to claim against the Admiralty, prepared by Galbraith and Best, Australia House, Strand W.C.2. See Part 3 for the full document.

such as fish and frog showers on 19 Nov 1920.[1100] William (33) took up saw milling in 1921 in Noojee, Vic.[1101] He was a sawmiller. He and John William Gunn (133) appeared at court on 23 Jul 1925 in Warragul, Vic, accused of trespass by a neighbour.[1102] He was present when George Mackenzie (3435) gave details of family genealogy to William Watkins Gunn and Marcus Daniel Gunn of the Scottish Delegation on 19 Jun 1928 in Wick Parish, Caithness.[1103] He wrote to the Argus supporting hardwood cases for fruit exports to Britain on 30 Nov 1931.[1104] He was appointed as a member of a Committee of Management of a reserve for a Mechanics Institute on 27 Apr 1932 in Crossover, Parish of Neerim, Vic.[1105] He has personal history notes by John

---

1100 *Melbourne Argus*, 19 Nov 1920 p4: SHOWERS OF FISH. Referring to this subject. Mr. W. W. Gunn, of Crossover, says that in the late summer of 1870-71, while living at Burrnumbeet, there was a heavy storm during the night, and in the morning the tubs, buckets, plough furrows, and every depression that held water were full of a small fish similar to whitebait, and from 2½ in. to 3 in. in length on the average. "It is no exaggeration," remarks Mr. Gunn, "to say that they must have numbered hundreds of thousands, as the water in all depressions was thick with them. They were all alive, and apparently in perfect condition. The water was fresh, and the fish themselves lived without inconvenience in an ordinary fish globe. As the pools dried up the odour from the decaying mass of fish was most objectionable. In continuance of another note on this subject, Mr. Gunn says that he saw a shower of frogs near the Burrumbeet racecourse in 1870. There could be no mistake, as some of them fell in his spring-cart, and the remarkable thing was that they were not apparently injured. The shower included both brown and green frogs, the largest about 1½_in. in length. A second frog shower was seen near Burrumbeet Station, and Mr. Gunn says that some of the frogs struck him in falling.

1101 Letter or email from Sylvia Bairsto to Donald Gunn, Dec 1996. Norman (Sylvia's father, Norman Gunn Padgett) worked for William Watkins Gunn at Noojee and it was from there that Norman first went to Borneo; John William Gunn; Graeme Butler, *Buln Buln - a History of the Buln Buln Shire* (Drouin: Drouin Commercial Printers, 1979), p582: Two years later, the renowned sawmiller W W Gunn established a mill three miles away on the Red Hill Creek, north-east of the Crossover Railway station. Records show that William Watkins Gunn lived on the Crossover town reserve and by 1930 he had as well as his mill at Neerim, another at Noojee East on the Loch River. However it was just after the turn of the century that Gunn made his biggest splash when he laid down eight miles of steel track to a mill site at Shady Creek.

On this shiny three feet six inch highway, he launched a steam locomotive which he had bought from one Sanderson, at the timber town of Forest, in the west. He converted its four feet eight and an half inch gauge to suit his own; doing all of the conversion work necessary at his mill at Shady Creek.

The Depression beat Gunn, and his line closed in 1936. Two south Australian bogies, originally purchased with the lot of second-hand steel rails back about 1900, remained in the district, at McKenzie's property in Neerim South.

1102 *Melbourne Argus*, 23 Jul 1925 p18:

At the Warragul County Court on Tuesday, before Judge Williams, Mrs. M. E. Hendry, of Loch Valley, brought an action for damages for £100 against W. W. and J. W. Gunn, of Crossover, for trespass on her land at Noojee, and asked for an injunction to prevent defendants from further using her land. Mr. Fullagar (instructed by Messrs. Hall and Wilcox) appeared for plaintiff, and Mr. Clyne (instructed by Messrs. Courtney mid Dunn) for the defence. Defendants counter-claimed that the term of the contract of sale of January 1924, should be specifically performed, and the transfer of the land signed. After hearing evidence, Judge Williams said that plaintiff had not established her case, but there was the other issue whether the contract of sale definitely established a specific performance, and there had been no evidence to justify that. Plaintiff would be awarded 1/- damages for the trespass, but as the case had hinged on other issues, no costs would be allowed, and he would not grant an injunction. The counter-claim, based on the contract of sale in January 1924, had been established, and the pertormance must be carried out and the contract signed. On the counter-claim he felt justified Ingiving costs to defendants.

1103 WW and MD Gunn: William Watkins and Marcus Daniel Gunn, sons of Donald Gunn in Brawlbin and Ballarat, visited Caithness in 1928 as members of the Scottish Delegation See page 338 for the complete text.

1104 *Melbourne Argus*, 30 Nov 1931: HARDWOOD FRUIT CASES. TO THE EDITOR OF THF ARGUS.

Sir, With reference to the meeting of the Somerville Fruitgrowers' Association, reported on November 25th, I can corroborate Mr Wells's statement about hardwood cases. When in Great Britain recently, I made wide inquiries on this subject. More than 90 per cent of the firms handling Australian apples said that the hardwood cases were satisfactory, and that it would be a great mistake to dispense with them as they were distinctive, and the trade was used to them. The only improvements suggested were that the case could be made lighter, and that a distinctive label should be placed on the cases. With the assistance of Australia House a label was designed meting their requirmenets. This was submitted to the then Minister for Markets, and to the Victorian Department of Agriculture. It has remained in abeyance. In this connection I wish to acknowledge the msot valuable assistance I received from the staff at Australia House not only in this but in several other inquiries realting to Australian exports.

Yours etc

W.W.Gunn, Crossover.

1105 *Victoria Government Gazette*, 27 Apr 1932: Committees of Management of Reserves... William Watkins Gunn as a Committee of Management, for a period of three years, of the land permanently reserved by Order in Council of 11th October, 1904, as a site for a Mechanics Institute and Free Library in the Parish of Neerim, at Crossover.

William Gunn.[1106] His personal history notes derived from *Neerim - A History*.[1107]

Margaret Jane BALHARRIE (42)[1108] was born on 27 Dec 1860 in Blairgowrie, Perth, Tayside. She died on 16 May 1946 in Frankston, Vic, at age 85 cancer. She was buried in Springvale, Vic. She arrived in Melbourne, Vic, in 1862. As of 1904, she was also known as Nellie Gunn (42).[1109]

iii. Mary Jane GUNN (34) was born on 18 Jan 1864 in Cardigan Nr Ballarat, Vic.[1110] She died on 05 May 1934 in Braemore, Werribee, Vic, at age 70.[1111] She was buried on 07 May 1934 in Old Cemetery Area DN Sec.14 Lot 5, Ballarat, Vic.[1112]

She was on the electoral roll with John Alexander Gunn (Hon.) (32) in 1903 in Borambola Station, NSW.[1113] She was a beneficiary of the estate of The Honourable John Gunn (32) on 15 Oct 1910; Estate was valued at £31,690 which he left to his widow and children, with annuities of £150 to his mother for life and of £75 each to his sisters, Mary Jane Gunn and Katherine Alexandrina Gunn, and a bequest of £300 to his sister Mrs Barbara Padgett.[1114]

iv. Donald GUNN (35) was born on 20 Nov 1865 in Burrumbeet, Vic.[1115] He married Amy Agnes Wareham (43), daughter of James Wareham (1697) and

---

1106 John William Gunn, William Watkins Gunn - Jackaroo as J.A. on stations mainly around Ballarat eg Mt Eniur (?) and Creilaowne (?) then to Gippsland about 1888 to Bloomfield (now Nilma) timber milling with Amoss as partner. Dissolved partnership then to South of Darnum (Gainsborough). Married Margaret Jane Balharrie.
Land boom burst about 1893 - banks closed. Found Crossover whilst on expedition for gold. Took a milling right at Crossover about 1895 or 6 - built 'Brawlbin.' Bushfires 1898, 1908. Took up Noojee milling about 1921-2. John Willian married Jessie Eileen Evans 1925. Burnt out 1926, 32, 39.
William brought first car to district about 1912.
Goldmine. Brother Donald went to Buchan with Ralph Milner mining - returns were good, while Ralph was in charge. Milner retired and McRae part manager and then Mackieson came in. The family members retired but WW carried on with Mackieson as manager. Quartz reef formation caolinore rich gold. Abandoned about 1917 - got down to sulphides named Mt Tara, turn right before going down to Buchan about 3-4 miles.
(held by Dorothy Margaret Jenkin (nee Milner) - Mar 1996).

1107 Dorothy Hunt, *A History of Neerim*, William Watkins Gunn first came to Darnum Gippsland in 1884. He married Margaret Jane Balharrie at Bloomfield in 1891. They settled in Crossover in 1895 and had six children - John, Jean, Violet, Edith, Marjorie and Marcus Allan. They all attended Crossover State School. William built and operated successful sawmills at Crossover, Shady Creek and districts, employing many men. He built a three foot six inch tramway for transporting the sawn timber from these mills to the rail-head at Crossover. William brought in the first car to the district in 1912. In 1921 he took up milling at Noojee, his son John was manager. During the First World War he invented a method for destroying submarines which was duly adopted by the British Admiralty with considerable success. He attempted to obtain recognition for this invention during a visit to England in 1928 but failed to do so. The Admiralty claimed it their right to commandeer such inventions in wartime. William also had a large interest in goldmining in Crossover and Buchan. He died in 1945 aged 74 years.
(Typed notes written by Dorothy Margaret Jenkin (nee Milner) for A History of Neerim, and held by her - Mar 1996).

1108 *International Genealogical Index (IGI)*.

1109 *Ballarat Directory 1904*.

1110 Register of BDMs - Victoria, 1864 278.

1111 *Unknown newspaper*, on the 5th May, at Braemore, Werribee, Mary Jane, beloved eldest daughter of the late Donald and Jane Gunn, formerly of Burrumbeet. Deeply regretted; Register of BDMs - Victoria, 1934 15340.

1112 Ballarat Old Cemetery records: Area DN Sec.14 Lot 5.

1113 Electoral Roll: 1903 Roll lists John Alexander Gunn, Station Manager, Marcus Daniel Gunn, Station Manager, Norman Gunn, Licensed Vaccinator, Mary Jane Gunn, Domestic Duties and Jessie Marie Gunn, Domestic Duties as residing at Borambula Station.

1114 *Melbourne Argus*, 15 Nov 1910 p7: The estate of the late Mr John Alexaander Gunn of Braehour, near Wagga NSW, grazier and bacteriologist, has been valued for probate purposes at £31,690. He left his real and personal estate to his trustees upon trust for his widow and children subject to annuities of £150 to his mother for life and of £75 each to his sisters, Mary Jane Gunn and Katherine Alexandrina Gunn, and subject to a bequest of £300 to his sister Mrs Barbara Padgett, and of life insurance policies for £750 to Mr H H B Bradley, Solicitor, of Sydney.

1115 Register of BDMs - Victoria, 1865 20736; "William Watkins Gunn;" Certificate of Birth: 1865 Births in the District of Burrumbeet in the Colony of Victoria, 20 Nov 1865, Donald Gunn, father Donald Gunn, farmer 33, mother Jane, 29.

Mary Dalton (1114), on 16 Sep 1922 in St Anselms C of E, Middle Park, Vic.[1116] He died on 29 Dec 1933 in The Shack, Crossover, Vic, at age 68 cardiac failure.[1117] He was buried on 30 Dec 1933 in Warragul, Vic.[1118]

He was a partner when William Watkins Gunn (33) applied for a mining lease on 01 Jun 1892 in South Warragul, Vic. He was with Ralph Milner gold mining circa 1900 in Buchan, Vic.[1119] He lived between 1901 and 1922 in Crossover, Vic.[1120] He was Sawmill employee in 1922.[1121]

Amy Agnes WAREHAM (43)[1122] was born in Oct 1862 in Cheshire. She married Francis Gumley (1115) in 1887.[1123] She died in 1933 in Vic.

v. Marcus Daniel GUNN (36) was born on 11 May 1868 in Buninyong, Vic.[1124] He married Mary Jane Chenhall (105), daughter of Nicholas Chenhall (864) and Mary J Mills (865), on 19 May 1903 in residence of the bride's mother, Corowa, NSW.[1125] He died on 01 Dec 1952 in South Yarra, Vic, at age 84.[1126]

He was present with brother John (32) when anthrax ravaged sheep at the Station in 1888.[1127] Marcus (36) was granted a licence to inoculate animals with anthrax vaccine in Aug 1894.[1128] He was a temporary manager on

---

1116 Certificate of Marriage, No. 192 in Register of St Alsems C of E, Middle Park, 1922, BDM 7091
16 September 1922 between Donald Gunn, Bachelor, born Burrumbeet, sawmill employee age 56 of Crossover, and Amy Agnes Gumley, widow since 2 January 1901, 2 children, born Cheshire, England, house duties age 59 of Crossover, father James Walton (deceased), mother Mary (Dalton).

1117 *Unknown newspaper*, on the 29th December, at The Shack, Crossover, Donald, beloved husband of Amy, and son of late Donald and Jane Gunn, Burrumbeet; Certificate of Death: 1933 18730: On 29 December 1933 at The Shack, Crossover, Shire of Buln Buln, Donald Gunn, Timber Worker age 68, born Burrumbeet, married at Middle Park at age 56 to Amy Gumley, no issue, father Donald Gunn, Farmer, mother Jane Gunn formerly Surman.

1118 Certificate of Death: 1933 18730: On 29 December 1933 at The Shack, Crossover, Shire of Buln Buln, Donald Gunn, Timber Worker age 68, born Burrumbeet, married at Middle Park at age 56 to Amy Gumley, no issue, father Donald Gunn, Farmer, mother Jane Gunn formerly Surman.

1119 John William Gunn, Brother Donald went to Buchan with Ralph Milner mining - returns were good, while Ralph was in charge. Milner retired and McRae part manager and then Mackieson came in. The family members retired but WW carried on with Mackieson as manager. Quartz reef formation caolinore rich gold. Abandoned about 1917 - got down to sulphides named Mt Tara, turn right before going sown to Buchan about 3-4 miles.

1120 Certificate of Death: Vic 1901 24552 14 February 1901 at Lydiard Street, City of Ballarat, Donald Gunn, 68, insurance agent of broncho pneumonia, cardiac disease and asthma, duration about 3 months, father Alexander Gunn, farmer, mother Barbara Gunn, maiden name Gunn. Buried 16 February 1901 at Ballarat Old Cemetery. Born at Brawlbin, Reay, Caithness, Scotland, 47 years in Victoria, married at Buninyong at 27 years to Jane Surman, issue in order of birth, John Alexander, 41, William Watkins, 39, Mary Jane, 37, Donald, 35, Marcus Daniel, 32, Barbara, 30, Norman, 28, Hugh, died, Arthur Gilbert, 22, Catherine, 20. Signed by Donald Gunn, son, of Crossover, Gippsland; Electoral Roll: 1903 Vic.

1121 Certificate of Marriage, No. 192 in Register of St Alsems C of E, Middle Park, 1922, BDM 7091 16 September 1922 between Donald Gunn, Bachelor, born Burrumbeet, sawmill employee age 56 of Crossover, and Amy Agnes Gumley, widow since 2 January 1901, 2 children, born Cheshire, England, house duties age 59 of Crossover, father James Walton (deceased), mother Mary (Dalton).

1122 Certificate of Marriage, Amy Agnes Gumley, widow since 2 January 1901.

1123 Register of BDMs - Victoria, 1887 4462.

1124 Register of BDMs - Victoria, 1868 14645; "William Watkins Gunn."

1125 Letter or email from Ian M Gunn to Donald Gunn, Mar 1997; Register of BDMs - NSW, 1903 3446; *Melbourne Argus*, 06 Jun 1903 p9: GUNN - CHENHALL- On the 19th May, at the residence of the bride's mother, by the Ven. Archdeacon Hose, Marcus D., fourth son of the late Donald Gunn of Ballarat, to Marie, only daughter of the late Nicholas Chenhall, Corowa.

1126 *The Sun, Melbourne*, Wednesday 2 Dec 1953, Mr M. Gunn, pioneer grazier, dies. Marcus Daniel Gunn of Walsh St, South Yarra, a pioneer pastoralist, died yesterday, aged 85. Mr Gunn was born at Mt Banningong Station, near Ballarat, in 1868. He contributed much to the pastoral industry. He and his brother Mr J.A.Gunn, discovered and developed late last century the anti-anthrax vaccine still in use. He is survived by a daughter, Norma Caro and a son Keith Gunn. The funeral today will be private.

1127 Rob Webster, *Bygoo and Beyond*, one day in 1888 Gunn and his brother, Marcus Daniel Gunn, rode to a paddock on Yalgogrin where they saw hundreds of carcases of dead sheep.

1128 Letter from J H Todd to Ian Marcus Gunn, 27 May 1990; ... your grandfather, Mark. He assisted John Gunn with the vaccinating work. By the way, did you know that he (Marcus) was granted a licence to inoculate animals with anthrax vaccine in August 1894?

Borambola station on 01 Apr 1902.[1129] He was on the electoral roll with John Alexander Gunn (32) in 1903 in Borambola Station, NSW.[1130] He was a station master.[1131] He lived in Wagga Wagga, NSW. He witnessed the burial of Alfred Nicholas Chenhall (869) on 21 Sep 1921 in Waverley, NSW.[1132] He and Mary Jane Chenhall (105) lived in 17 Dec 1923 in Mittagong Station, Yerong Creek, Vic.[1133] He was present when George Mackenzie (3435) gave details of family genealogy to William Watkins Gunn and Marcus Daniel Gunn of the Scottish Delegation on 19 Jun 1928 in Wick Parish, Caithness.[1134]

Mary Jane CHENHALL (105)[1135] was born on 08 Oct 1873 in Doma Mungi, Chiltern, Vic.[1136] She died in 1941 in Melbourne, Vic.[1137] She was also known as Gay (105).

vi. Barbara GUNN (106) was born on 20 Jun 1870 in Burrumbeet, Vic.[1138] She married Isaac Padgett (103), son of George Padgett (2330) and Martha Turner (2331), on 29 Mar 1899 in 185 Lydiard Street, Ballarat, Vic.[1139] She died on 17 Jul 1941 in Braemore, Duncans Road, Werribee, Vic, at age 71.[1140] Her estate was probated.[1141]

She was a schoolteacher in 1898 in Mount Cole, Vic[1142] where she lived between 1898 and 1905. She was a schoolteacher and post mistress between

---

1129Rob Webster, *Bygoo and Beyond*

1130Electoral Roll: 1903 Roll lists John Alexander Gunn, Station Manager, Marcus Daniel Gunn, Station Manager, Norman Gunn, Licensed Vaccinator, Mary Jane Gunn, Domestic Duties and Jessie Marie Gunn, Domestic Duties as residing at Borambula Station.

1131Ian M Gunn to Donald Gunn, Mar 1997.

1132*Sydney Morning Herald*, 22 Sep 1921: The remains of the late Dr. Alfred Chenhall were buried in Waverley Cemetery yesterday afternoon, Canon Bellingham officiating at the grave. Members of the Newington Boat Club acted as pallbearers, and the chief mourners were: Mr. Fred. N. Chenball (son), Dr. William T. Cbenhall (brother), Dr. Hilton W. T. Chenhall (nephew), Dr. R. Schlink (brother-in-law), and Mr. M. D. Gunn (brother-in-law).

1133*Sydney Morning Herald*, 17 Dec 1923: Dr. William Thomas Chenhall, who died on Saturday after a very short illness, at his home, Wanaweena, Trelawney Street, Woollahra, was bom at Chiltern, Victoria. He was educated at Beechworth Grammar School, and entered the Melbourne University in residence at Ormond College, taking his M.B., B.S., degrees with first-class honours. Several years later he received the M.D. of Melbourne University. After practising at Stanmore for some years, he went to England and obtained the degree of F.R.C.S. of Edinbrough. Returning to Australia, he was appointed honorary surgeon to the Royal Hospital for Women, which position he held to hie death. He practised as surgeon in Macquarie Street. Dr. Chenhall leaves a widow, the daughter of the late Mr. J. T. Tlllock; one son, Dr. Hilton W. T. Chenhall; and one sister, Mrs. M. D. Gunn, of Mittagong Station, Yerong
Creek.

1134See page 338 for the complete text.

1135Ian M Gunn to Donald Gunn, Mar 1997.

1136Register of BDMs - Victoria, 1873 22731.

1137Letter or email from Jan Tracy to Donald Gunn, 20 Aug 2007.

1138Register of BDMs - Victoria, 1870 14268.

1139Register of BDMs - Victoria, 1899 983.

1140*Melbourne Argus*, 18 Jul 1941 p4: On 17 July, at her residence, Braemore, Duncans Road, Werribee South, Barbara, the dearly beloved wife of the late Isaac Padgett, and loving mother of Barbara (Mrs Bence), Norman, and Jean (Mrs Gilmour) aged 71 years - mother and father reunited. On 17 July, at her residence, Braemore, Werribee South, Barbara, relict of the late Isaac Padgett, loved mother of Barbara (Mrs Bence) Norman, and Jean (Mrs Gilmour), and loved sister of M.D., Norman and Catherine Gunn.

1141*Melbourne Argus*, 22 Jul 1941 p6: AFTER the expiration of 14 days from the publication hereof application will be made to the Supreme Court of the State or Victoria in its Probate Jurisdiction that PROBATE of the will dated 24th July 1939. and Codicil thereto dated the 22nd April 1940 of BARBARA PADGETT, late of "Braemore" Werribee in the said State widow deceased may be granted to Barbara Gunn Bence of Werribee foresaid poultry keeper, and Jean Gunn Gilmour formerly of Swansea in the said State of Tasmania but now of Narrandera in the State of New South Wales, married woman, the executrices named within.

1142Letter, Sylvia Bairsto to Donald Gunn, Dec 1996 Barbara and Isaac Padgett lived at Braemore, Werribee South, Victoria from some time after their marriage until their deaths. Son Norman (1903-1952) bought the house and farm from the estate. His family lived there through the war until selling the property in 1947. Barbara was a schoolteacher (and as such had secondary task - unpaid - of Post Mistress) at Mount Cole before marriage. Also at Point Arlington as school teacher. Isaac - dairy farmer with

1900 and 1930 in Vic. She was given a valedictory farewell on leaving Mount Cole, Vic circa 1905 .[1143] She lived between 1905 and 1910 in Cressy, Vic. She lived between 1910 and 1941 in Braemore, Werribee South, Vic. She was a beneficiary of the estate of The Honourable John Gunn (32) on 15 Oct 1910; Estate was valued at £31,690 which he left to his widow and children, with annuities of £150 to his mother for life and of £75 each to his sisters, Mary Jane Gunn and Katherine Alexandrina Gunn, and a bequest of £300 to his sister Mrs Barbara Padgett.[1144] She left a will on 24 Jul 1939.[1145] Barbara and Isaac Padgett lived at Braemore, Werribee South, Victoria from some time after their marriage until their deaths.

Isaac PADGETT (103)[1146] was born in 1867 in Mount Cole, Vic. He died on 30 Sep 1937 in Braemore, Werribee, Vic.[1147] His estate was probated on 09 Mar 1938.[1148] He left a will on 21 Apr 1938.[1149]

vii. Norman GUNN (37) was born on 11 May 1872 in Burrumbeet, Vic.[1150] He died on 15 Nov 1944 in Williamstown Hospital, Williamstown, Vic, at age 72.[1151]

---

pure bred Friesan cattle. Grand-daughter Sylvia was born in Wellington NZ when parents were taking delivery of a bull (Ferdinand Prince Domino) for her grandfather Isaac. Later grandson Arthur Bence (1926-1994), dairyfarmer, had progeny amongst his herd.

1143 *Unknown newspaper*, 1st July [Probably about 1905 - DG 7/97] On Thursday evening last, in the local Hall, a valedictory social was tendered to Mr and Mrs Isaac Padgett, who are leaving this district for their new home at Cressy. The hall was tastefully decorated with ferns, heath and wattle blossom, and a large number of local residents gathered to wish Mr and Mrs Padgett au revoir. Mr Padgett had for many years been our church organist, and his place will be very difficult to fill. Mr J Tait, as chairman, spoke in the highest terms of Mr Padgett, and his words faithfully expressed the sentiments of all present. Geo. Gordon also in a very humorous speech endorsed Mr Tait's remarks, but said that the one thing against Mr Padgett, inasmuch as he had done the younger part of the population of Mount Cole an irreparable injury, by taking from them their painstaking and popular school teacher, but he would forgive him. He had much pleasure, on behalf of their numerous friends, in presenting Mrs Padgett with a small token of their regard, in the shape of a very handsome hot water kettle. ... Mrs Padgett kindly acted as accompanist (to a programme of songs and recitations) in her usual efficient manner.

1144 *Melbourne Argus*, 15 Nov 1910 p7: The estate of the late Mr John Alexaander Gunn of Braehour, near Wagga NSW, grazier and bacteriologist, has been valued for probate purposes at £31,690. He left his real and personal estate to his trustees upon trust for his widow and children subject to annuities of £150 to his mother for life and of £75 each to his sisters, Mary Jane Gunn and Katherine Alexandrina Gunn, and subject to a bequest of £300 to his sister Mrs Barbara Padgett, and of life insurance policies for £750 to Mr H H B Bradley, Solicitor, of Sydney.

1145 *Melbourne Argus*, 22 Jul 1941 p6: After the expiration of 14 days from the publication hereof application will be made to the Supreme Court of the State or Victoria in its Probate Jurisdiction that PROBATE of the will dated 24th July 1939. and Codicil thereto dated the 22nd April 1940 of BARBARA PADGETT, late of "Braemore" Werribee in the said State widow deceased may be granted to Barbara Gunn Bence of Werribee foresaid poultry keeper, and Jean Gunn Gilmour formerly of Swansea in the said State of Tasmania but now of Narrandera in the State of New South Wales, married woman, the executrices named within.

1146 Letter from Margaret Bence to Donald Gunn, 17 Aug 2005.

1147 *Unknown newspaper*, On the 30th September, 1937 (suddenly) at Braemore, Werribee, Isaac, loved husband of Barbara, and loving father of Barbara, Norman and Jean.

1148 *Melbourne Argus*, 09 Mar 1938 p15: After the expiration of 14 days from the pubication hereof application will be made to the Supreme Court of the State of Victoria, in its Probate Jurisdiction, that PROBATE of the WILL (dated the 9th day of November, 1927) of ISAAC PADGETT, late of "Braemore," Werribee, in the said State, farmer, deceased, be granted to Norman Gunn Padgett, of Narbethong, in the said State, sawmller, and James Arthur Padgett, of Berrybank, in the said State, farmer, the executors appointed by the said will Dated the 9th day of March, 1938. LUCAS and MUMME.

1149 *Melbourne Argus*, 21 Apr 1938 p 17: NOTICE is hereby given, that all persons having claims in respect of the property or estate of ISAAC PADGETT, late of "Braemore," Werribee, in the State of Victoria, farmer, deceased, who died on the thirtieth day of September, 1937, and probate of whose will was granted by the Supreme Court of Victoria on the eighth day of April, 1938, to Norman Gunn Padgett, of Narbethong, in the said State, sawmller, and James Arthur Padgett, of Berrybank, in the said state, farmer, the executors appointed by the said will, are hereby required to SEND PARTICULARS of such CLAIMS to such executors, care of the undersigned, on or before the thirtieth day of June, 1938, after which date it is the intention of the said executors to convey or distribute such property or estate to or among the persons entitled thereto. Dated this 21st day of April, 1938 LUCAS and MUMME, Tavlock House.

1150 Register of BDMs - Victoria, 1872 7586.

1151 Register of BDMs - Victoria, 1944 11958; *Melbourne Argus*, Thu 01 Mar 1945 p13: NORMAN GUNN, Late of 82 Cromwell Road, South Yarra, Retired Manager, Who Died on 15th November, 1944. -Creditors, next of kin, and all other persons having CLAIMS in respect of the estate of the deceased are required by the executors, THE TRUSTEES EXECUTORS AND AGENCY

He was on the electoral roll with John Alexander Gunn (Hon.) (32) in 1903 in Borambola Station, NSW.[1152] He was a stock and station agent, unmarried in 1915.[1153] He began military service on 12 Apr 1915 in Melbourne, Vic, enlisted as Private, service number 1549, next of kin W.W.Gunn (brother).[1154] He was discharged from military service on 15 May 1918 in 22nd Battalion. He lived in 15 Gladstone Street, Sandringham, SA. He lived in 1944 in 82 Cromwell Road, South Yarra, Vic. Article in The Gunn Herald.

viii. Hugh GUNN (38) was born on 28 Oct 1875 in Burrumbeet, Vic.[1155] He died on 24 Jun 1879 in Burrumbeet, Vic, at age 3.[1156] He was buried on 25 Jun 1879 in Old Cemetery Area DN Sec.14 Lot 5, Ballarat, Vic.[1157]

ix. Arthur Gilbert GUNN (9) was born on 19 May 1878 in Burrumbeet, Vic.[1158] He married Louisa Maud Miriam Retallick (10), daughter of Edgar Retallick (100) and Louisa Miriam Hore (102), on 03 Dec 1901 in Scots Church, Lydiard St, Ballarat, Vic.[1159] He died on 18 Jun 1933 in Ivanhoe, Vic, at age 55.[1160] He was buried on 20 Jun 1933 in Brighton cemetery, Vic.[1161]

Arthur's mother Jane wrote to her first grandson Alexander Donald, the son of John Alexander, referring to Arthur Gilbert.[1162] He lived in 1901 in Clarendon Street, Ballarat, Vic. He was a commercial traveller.[1163] He lived between 1903 and 1912 in 923 Ward Street, Kalgoorlie, WA. He was listed in the electoral roll in 1903 in 65 Lygon Street Sth, Ballarat, Vic. He and Louisa Maud Miriam Retallick (10) lived in 1904 in 85 Lyons Street South, Ballarat

---

COMPANY LIMITED and Marcus Daniel Gunn to SEND PARTICULARS, addressed to them, at 401 Collins street, Melbourne, on or before 10th May, 1945, after which date they will dis- tribute the assets, having regard only to the claims of which they then have notice. DAVIES, CAMPBELL, and PIESSE, solicitors, 84 William street, Melbourne; *Melbourne Argus*, Sat 18 Nov 1944 p2: GUNN.- On November 15 at Williamstown Hospital, Norman Gunn, loved brother of M. D. and C. A. Gunn.

1152Electoral Roll: 1903 Roll lists John Alexander Gunn, Station Manager, Marcus Daniel Gunn, Station Manager, Norman Gunn, Licensed Vaccinator, Mary Jane Gunn, Domestic Duties and Jessie Marie Gunn, Domestic Duties as residing at Borambula Station.

1153The AIF Project, online http://www.aif.adfa.edu.au:8080/index.html.

1154National Archives of Australia Series B2455, control symbol Gunn N, barcode 4380098, born Ballarat; The AIF Project.

1155Register of BDMs - Victoria, 1875 21520.

1156Register of BDMs - Victoria, 1879 3921.

1157Ballarat Old Cemetery records: Area DN Sec.14 Lot 5.

1158Register of BDMs - Victoria, 1878 7226.

1159Register of BDMs - Victoria, 1901 7407; Certificate of Marriage, Scots Church Register No. 114 - Arthur Gilbert Gunn, 23, Warehouseman, of Clarendon Street, Ballarat, born Burrumbeet, and Louisa Maud Miriam Retallick, 26, Spinster, of Campbells Crescent, Ballarat, born Naseby, New Zealand, at Scots Church, Ballarat. Witnesses Alice Louisa Pascoe and Paul Hore.

1160*Unknown newspaper*, on the 18th June (suddenly), at Ivanhoe, Arthur Gilbert, dearly beloved husband of Louisa Maud Gunn, and beloved father of Malcolm, Kenneth, Angus, and Collier (deceased), late of Ballarat; Certificate of Death: 1933 4607: 18th June 1933 at Kenilworth Private Hospital, Kenilworth Parade, Ivanhoe, Shire of Heidelberg, Arthur Gilbert Gunn, Commercial Traveller, age 55 years, of coronary thrombosis, 1st attack 2 years ago, cardiac failure, father Donald Gunn, farmer, mother Jane Gunn formerly Surman, buried 20th June 1933 at Brighton Cemetery. Born Ballarat, 43 years in Victoria, 12 years in Western Australia. Married at age 24 years to Louisa Maud Retallack; children Malcolm Donald, 30 years, Kenneth Douglas, 28 years, Angus Norman, 21 years, Collier, deceased.

1161Certificate of Death: 1933 4607: 18th June 1933 at Kenilworth Private Hospital, Kenilworth Parade, Ivanhoe, Shire of Heidelberg, Arthur Gilbert Gunn, Commercial Traveller, age 55 years, of coronary thrombosis, 1st attack 2 years ago, cardiac failure, father Donald Gunn, farmer, mother Jane Gunn formerly Surman, buried 20th June 1933 at Brighton Cemetery. Born Ballarat, 43 years in Victoria, 12 years in Western Australia. Married at age 24 years to Louisa Maud Retallack; children Malcolm Donald, 30 years, Kenneth Douglas, 28 years, Angus Norman, 21 years, Collier, deceased.

1162See Part 3.

1163Electoral Roll: Arthur Gilbert Gunn, Traveller, 85 Lyon Street South; Louisa Maud Marion Gunn, Home Duties, 85 Lyon Street South.

West, Vic.[1164] He was a warehouseman on 03 Jan 1905 in Kalgoorlie, WA. He and Louisa Maud Miriam Retallick (10) lived on 30 Apr 1909 in Ward Street, Kalgoorlie, WA.[1165] He and Louisa Maud Miriam Retallick (10) were listed in the electoral roll in 1914 in Cnr Mair and Pleasant Streets, Ballarat, Vic. He was a business manager in Jan 1916 in Ballarat, Vic.[1166] He and Louisa Maud Miriam Retallick (10) were listed in the electoral roll in 1919 in Cnr Mair and Pleasant Streets, Ballarat, Vic. He and Louisa Maud Miriam Retallick (10) were listed in the electoral roll in 1931 in 189 Bambra Road, Caulfield, Vic. He was a traveller in 1931.[1167]

Louisa Maud Miriam RETALLICK (10) was born on 21 Nov 1875 in Naseby, Otago. She was christened on 07 Jan 1877 in St George's Church, Naseby, Otago.[1168] She died on 13 Nov 1959 in Elsternwick, Vic, at age 83. She was buried in Brighton cemetery, Vic. As of 1875, she was also known as Retallack (10) husband's death certificate of 1933 gives her surname as Retallack.[1169] She lived in 1901 in Campbells Crescent, Ballarat, Vic.[1170] She lived in 1935 in 23 Sandham Street, Elsternwick, Vic.[1171] She lived in 1958 in 21 Hope Street, Glen Iris, Vic.

x. Catherine Alexandrina GUNN (39) was born on 13 Sep 1880 in Burrumbeet, Vic.[1172] She died on 13 Aug 1960 in 13 Leila Road, Ormond, Vic, at age 79.

She was listed in the electoral roll in 1903 in Clarendon Street, Ballarat, Vic. She lived in 1904 in Clarendon Street, Ballarat West, Vic.[1173] She was listed in the electoral roll in 1909 in 505 Mair Street, Ballarat, Vic. She was a beneficiary of the estate of The Honourable John Gunn (32) on 15 Oct 1910; Estate was valued at £31,690 which he left to his widow and children, with annuities of £150 to his mother for life and of £75 each to his sisters, Mary Jane Gunn and Katherine Alexandrina Gunn, and a bequest of £300 to his sister Mrs Barbara Padgett.[1174] She was educated in 1911 in the University of

---

1164*Ballarat Directory 1904.*

1165Postcard from Caroline Pascoe , 30 April 1909; Ward St, Kalgoorlie, April 30th 1909,
Dear Miss Hocking,
Thank you very much for the p.card you sent me. I must apologise for not writing before. But Maud thought you would like the boys photos. Mother and Sylvia are in Melbourne with Alice. Maud sends her love to you. Trusting you are in the best of health. I remain, Yours sincerely, Caroline Pascoe
P.S. Kind regards to your Mother from both.

1166Certificate of Death: of son Colin.

1167Electoral Roll.

1168Certificate of Baptism: St George's, Naseby, New Zealand, No.89, Louisa Maud Miriam Retallick, born 21 Nov 1875, baptised 07 Jan 1877, daughter of Edgar and Louisa Retallick of Naseby, sponsored by James Hore, Silas Hore and mother.

1169Certificate of Death: 1933 4607 18th June 1933 at Kenilworth Private Hospital, Kenilworth Parade, Ivanhoe, Shire of Heidelberg, Arthur Gilbert Gunn, Commercial Traveller, age 55 years, of coronary thrombosis, 1st attack 2 years ago, cardiac failure, father Donald Gunn, farmer, mother Jane Gunn formerly Surman, buried 20th June 1933 at Brighton Cemetery. Born Ballarat, 43 years in Victoria, 12 years in Western Australia. Married at age 24 years to Louisa Maud Retallack; children Malcolm Donald, 30 years, Kenneth Douglas, 28 years, Angus Norman, 21 years, Collier, deceased.

1170Register of BDMs - Victoria, Louisa Maud Miriam Retallick Spinster Campbells Crescent.

1171*Melbourne Argus*, 18 Sep 1935: Jeanette, youngest daughter of Mr and Mrs Hugh Paton of Craigendowan, Thorn Street, Camberwell, to Angus Norman Gunn of Glenferrie, youngest son of the late Mr Arthur Gunn and of Mrs Gunn of 23 Sandham Street, Elsternwick.

1172Register of BDMs - Victoria, 1880 20818.

1173*Ballarat Directory 1904.*

1174*Melbourne Argus*, 15 Nov 1910 p7: The estate of the late Mr John Alexander Gunn of Braehour, near Wagga NSW, grazier and bacteriologist, has been valued for probate purposes at £31,690. He left his real and personal estate to his trustees upon trust

Sydney, Sydney, NSW; a massage student.[1175] She began military service on 06 Dec 1915 appointed as Member of Australian Army Masseuse Service with grade of Masseuse. She ended military service on 03 Apr 1925 in Prince of Wales Hospital, Randwick, NSW; resigned of own accord. She lived on 13 Apr 1942 in Burnt Pine, Norfolk Island, NSW. She was on the electoral roll with Alexander Donald Gunn (222) and Joan White Larkin (665) in 1949 in 20 Ridgeway Place, Melbourne, Vic. She was listed in the electoral roll in 1954 in 66 Evans Street, Port Melbourne, Vic. Recollections by Jan Tracy, nee Wilkinson, 2010: Served overseas, extreme deafness from gunfire, went to Norfolk Island, built hut, grew pineapples, refused to marry friend (Tolly) because of profound deafness, came back to Melbourne. See Part 3 for documents and photographs of her.

42. Janet 'Mcleod' GUNN (120)[1176] was born on 08 May 1834 in Brawlbin, Reay Parish, Caithness.[1177] She was christened on 19 Aug 1834 in Reay Parish, Caithness.[1178] She married John Watkins Surman (118), son of Daniel Surman (270) and Mary Ann Watkins (271), on 12 May 1864 in house of bride's brother, Donald Gunn, Esquire, Cardigan, Vic.[1179] She died on 30 May 1913 in Cardigan, Vic, at age 79.[1180] She was buried on 02 Jun 1913 in Old Cemetery Area DN Sec.14 Lot 5A, Ballarat, Vic.[1181]

She was also known as Jessie (120). She appeared on the 1841 Census of Brawlbin, Reay Parish, Caithness, in the household of her parents Alexander Gunn of Bualchork and Brawlbin (1) and Barbara Gunn of Braehour (6). She appeared on the 1851 Census of Brawlbin, Reay Parish, Caithness, in the household of Donald Gunn in Brawlbin and Ballarat (3). She was living with, and looking after, aged grandparents in Nov 1859.[1182] She planned to leave for Australia, but postponed in Mar 1863.[1183] She emigrated on 01 Oct 1863 from London per Chatsworth, 1129 tons register, 200 passengers. She arrived in Melbourne, Vic, aboard the Chatsworth in company with her cousin Donald Campbell 20 (3514) and Eliz K Huxton(?) 25 on 16 Jan 1864. She arrived safely and was treated kindly by family in Jan 1864 in Ballarat, Vic. She was a teacher in 1864.[1184]

---

for his widow and children subject to annuities of £150 to his mother for life and of £75 each to his sisters, Mary Jane Gunn and Katherine Alexandrina Gunn, and subject to a bequest of £300 to his sister Mrs Barbara Padgett, and of life insurance policies for £750 to Mr H H B Bradley, Solicitor, of Sydney.

1175Sydney University, online http://calendararchive.usyd.edu.au/Calendar/1911/PDF/1911%20-%200485.pdf, p 445.

1176*LDS Church*, Christenings of children of Barbara Gunn, father Alexander Gunn.
Catherine, 18 May 1830, Halkirk; Donald, 9 Jun 1832, Reay; Janet, 19 Aug 1834, Reay; John, 29 Feb 1836, Reay.

1177Clan Gunn Parish Records: Births 1834 Janet Gunn, parents Alexander, Brawlbin - Barbara; See Part 3 for UK census documents.

1178*LDS Church*, Christenings of children of Barbara Gunn, father Alexander Gunn
Catherine, 18 May 1830, Halkirk; Donald, 9 Jun 1832, Reay; Janet, 19 Aug 1834, Reay; John, 29 Feb 1836, Reay.

1179Certificate of Marriage, 1864 1914 marriages solemnized in the District of Ballarat, John Watkins Surman, Teacher age 33, Bachelor born Hampton-Poyle, Oxon, England, residence Cardigan, father Daniel Surman, Farmer, mother Mary Ann Watkins, married Janet Gunn, age 30, Spinster born Reay, Caithness, Scotland, residence Cardigan, father Alexander Gunn, Farmer, mother Barbara Gunn, at the house of the Bride's Brother, Donald Gunn, Esq, Cardigan, according to the rites of the Presbyterian Church of Victoria.

1180Register of BDMs - Victoria, 1913 4219; Letter or email, Dougal Gilmour to Donald Gunn, 8 Apr 1999.

1181Ballarat Old Cemetery records.

1182See Part 3.

1183See Part 3 for original documents and images.

1184Certificate of Marriage, 1864 1914 marriages solemnized in the District of Ballarat.

John Watkins SURMAN (118)[1185] was born on 09 Oct 1831 in Hampton Poyle, Oxfordshire.[1186] He died on 11 Oct 1906 in Cardigan, Ballarat, Vic, at age 75.[1187] He was buried on 13 Oct 1906 in Old Cemetery Area DN, Section 14, Lot 5A, Ballarat, Vic.[1188] He appeared on the 1841 Census of Hampton Poyle, Oxfordshire, in the household of Daniel Surman (270).[1189] He emigrated with Daniel Surman (270) circa 1855; to Australia.[1190] He arrived in Melbourne, Vic, say 1855. He lived in 1857 in Buninyong, Vic.[1191] He was a schoolmaster, the first teacher at Windermere State School No.668, which he helped build. He lived in 1860 in Cardigan, Vic.[1192] He was the postmaster on a salary of £35/a in Cardigan, Vic, in 1868. On 26 Jun 1878 John Watkins Surman (118) reported that two more cases of scarlet fever had occurred in the vicinity of Windermere School in Ballarat, Vic. He was presented with a citation from the Windermere community, signed by eight Windermere Church Elders, for his services on 27 Jun 1887.[1193]

Children of Janet Mcleod Gunn (120) and John Watkins Surman (118) were as follows:

i. Baby SURMAN (1550) was born in Feb 1865 in Ballarat, Vic.[1194] She died on 24 Feb 1865 in Ballarat, Vic.

ii. John Daniel SURMAN (272) was born in 1866 in Cardigan, Vic. He married Margaret Cowley (1553) in 1895. He died in 1935 in Dunolly, Vic.[1195]

He was registered as a dentist on 28 Aug 1891 in 18 Carlton Street, Carlton, Vic.[1196] He was listed in the electoral roll in 1903 in 18 Carlton Street, Carlton, Vic. He was listed in the electoral roll in 1909 in 18 Carlton Street, Carlton, Vic. He was listed in the electoral roll in 1914, 1919 and 1924 in Parkville, Vic.

Margaret COWLEY (1553)[1197] was born in 1866. She died on 17 Jul 1951 in Geelong, Vic. She was listed in the electoral roll in 1902 in Victoria Terrace, Geelong, Vic.[1198] She and Jessie Marguerite Surman (1554) were listed in the

---

1185 *Unknown newspaper*, Undated The death of another old resident, JW Surman, occurred on Thursday at his residence, Cardigan, aged 73 years. The deceased gentleman was born at Hampton Poyle, Oxfordshire, and was educated under Bishop Wilberforce at Oxford. In 1855 he arrived in Victoria with his parents and only sister, the latter being Mrs Gunn, of Doveton Street North. Two years later he settled in Buninyong, where he was engaged with the late Rev. J.Hastie in school work; and in August, 1860, he moved to Cardigan, opening a public school. Subsequently he entered the service of the Education Department, and retained his post until 1892, when he was retired. He was an earnest Sunday school and church worker, conducting the Sunday services for many years until the scattered congregations were able to build a church and obtain a settled minister. Deceased was married in 1864, and seven of his eight children survive. Of these five are sons and two daughters.

1186 Certificate of Marriage, 1864 1914 states age as 33; e-mail message from Judy Meyer to Donald Gunn, 02 Aug 2004.

1187 Register of BDMs - Victoria, 1906 11573 - gives mother's name as Mary Ann Watkins; Judy Meyer, 02 Aug 2004.

1188 Ballarat Old Cemetery records: Area DN, Section 14, Lot 5A.

1189 UK Census 06 June 1841: Daniel Surman 35 shoe maker, Mary Surman 30, John Surman 9, Jane Surman 5, Catherine Watkins 60.

1190 *Unknown newspaper*, ...in 1855 he arrived in Victoria with his parents and only sister, the latter being Mrs Gunn, of Doveton Street North.

1191 *Unknown newspaper*, ...Two years later he he settled in Buninyong, where he was engaged with the late Rev. J.Hastie in school work.

1192 *Unknown newspaper*, ...and in August, 1860, he moved to Cardigan, opening a public school.

1193 The J W Surman Citation, unknown repository, unknown repository address.

1194 Judy Meyer, 02 Aug 2004.

1195 Register of BDMs - Victoria, 1935 18026.

1196 *Victoria Government Gazette*, 31 Jan 1907, The Dentists' Register for 1907; John Daniel Surman of 18 Carlton Street, Carlton, was registered as a dentist on 28 August 1891, certificate No. 359.

1197 Judy Meyer, 02 Aug 2004.

1198 Electoral Roll: Margaret Surman home duties, Victoria Terrace, Geelong.

electoral roll in 1919 and in 1924 at 86 Western Beach, Geelong, Vic.[1199] She was listed in the electoral roll in 1936 in 49 The Esplanade, Geelong, Vic.[1200] She was listed in the electoral roll in 1942 in 38 Alexandra Avenue, Corio, Vic.[1201]

iii. Alexander Gunn SURMAN (273) was born in 1868 in Ballarat, Vic.[1202] He married Esther Kirk (676) on 16 Sep 1891 in Vic.[1203] He died in Dec 1909 in Ballarat, Vic.[1204] He was a farmer. He was buried on 31 Dec 1909 in New Cemetery, Ballarat, Vic.[1205]

Esther KIRK (676) was born in 1864. She died on 11 Mar 1938 in Cardigan, Vic.[1206] She and Stella Surman (681) were listed in the electoral roll in 1919 in Cardigan, Vic.[1207] She was on the electoral roll with Reginald Gunn Surman (678) in 1931 in Cardigan, Vic.

iv. Barbara Margaret McKay SURMAN (274) was born in 1870 in Ballarat, Vic.[1208] She married James Brewster (1559) in 1892 in Learmonth, Vic.[1209] She died in 1928 in Morwell, Vic.

She and James Brewster (1559) were listed in the electoral roll in 1909 in Middle Creek, Vic.[1210] She and James Brewster (1559) were listed in the electoral roll in 1914 in Middle Creek, Vic.

James BREWSTER (1559) was born on 09 Jun 1864 in Coghills Creek, Vic. He was listed in the electoral roll as a grazier in 1936 in Middle Creek, Vic.[1211]

v. Watkins SURMAN (405) was born in 1871 in Sago Hill/Cardigan, Vic.[1212] He died on 15 May 1875 in Cardigan, Vic.[1213]

vi. James William SURMAN (275) was born in 1873 in Sago Hill, Vic.[1214] He married Alice Maud Grace Curtis (677) on 21 Feb 1894 in Ballarat, Vic.[1215] He died on 05 Dec 1947 in Horsham, Vic.[1216]

1199 Electoral Roll: Margaret Surman home duties, Jessie Marguerite Surman dressmaker, 86 Western Beach, Geelong.

1200 Electoral Roll: Margaret Surman home duties, 49 The Esplanade, Geelong.

1201 Electoral Roll: Margaret Surman home duties, 38 Alexandra Avenue, Corio.

1202 Register of BDMs - Victoria, 1868 819.

1203 Register of BDMs - Victoria, 1891 5725; Judy Meyer, 02 Aug 2004.

1204 Register of BDMs - Victoria, 1909 11179.

1205 Ballarat Old Cemetery records: Area Presbyterian, Section 7 Lot 40.

1206 *Melbourne Argus*, 14 Mar 1938 p10: SURMAN.-On the 11th March, 1938, at private hospital, Ballarat, Esther, widow of the late Alexander G. Surman, of Cardigan, and loving mother of Jessie (Mrs. W. G. Stephens), Pearl (Mrs. W. G Johnson), Eric, Stella (Mrs. D. Draffin), Tettie (Mrs. R. Thompson), Rex and Margery (Mrs. C. Sharp), in her 76th year. -At rest.

1207 Electoral Roll: Esther and Stella Surman, Cardigan, home duties.

1208 Judy Meyer, 02 Aug 2004.

1209 Register of BDMs - Victoria, 1892 3269.

1210 Electoral Roll: James Brewster, grazier, Barbara Margaret mckay Brewster, home duties, Middle Creek.

1211 Electoral Roll: 1936 James Brewster, Middle Creek grazier.

1212 Register of BDMs - Victoria, 1871 19097.

1213 Register of BDMs - Victoria, 1875 5572.

1214 Register of BDMs - Victoria, 1873 5211.

1215 Register of BDMs - Victoria, 1894 1393.

1216 Register of BDMs - Victoria, 1947 22836.

He was educated in Windermere, now Cardigan, Vic. He was a teacher, spending 50 years in the Education Department in Vic. He began military service when war broke out in 1914 in Vic.[1217]

Alice Maud Grace CURTIS (677) was born in 1874 in Buninyong, Vic.[1218] She died on 02 May 1956 in Horsham, Vic.

vii. Irene Marian Catherine SURMAN (693) was born in 1874 in Sago Hill, Vic.[1219] She married William O'Connor (692) in 1918 in Vic.[1220] She died in 1940 in Melbourne, Vic.

viii. Theodore Oswald SURMAN (276) was born in 1876 in Cardigan, Vic.[1221] He died on 17 May 1918 in Melbourne South, Vic.[1222] He was buried in Morwell Cemetery, Plot D, Row R, Grave No. 282, Morwell, Vic.[1223]

Theodore Oswald SURMAN
Tree No. 207

Theodore Oswald Surman was born at Cardigan, via Ballarat. He enlisted on 4th December, 1914, at the age of 38 years and ten months.

Next of kin was Mrs. Barbara Brewster (sister) of Yinnar, Sth. Gippsland. Reg. No. 1614, Theodore was in 5th Battalion, 3rd Reinforcements on 16th January, 1915 at Broadmeadows, prior to embarking overseas on the HMTS "Barda" on the 18th October, 1915. Theodore returned to Australia on the HS "Ascanius" on 17th March, 1916, being discharged on 25th July, 1916 with rhuematism.

From Duty Nobly Done by the Learmonth & District Historical Society, used with permission.

He was a civilian subordinate attached to 38 Co. ASC, Boer War circa 1900.[1224] He lived in 1914 in Yinnar, Gippsland, Vic; unmarried.[1225] He began military service on 04 Dec 1914 in Vic enlisted as Corporal, Regimental number 1614, Next of Kin, Mrs Barbara Brewster, Yinnar, Gippsland. He ended military service on 25 Jul 1916 in 3rd M.D.[1226]

[1217] *Melbourne Argus*, 25 May 1918, Died in Service On the 17th May at Base Hospital, Theodore Oswald, ex sgt 5th Btn, AIF, fourth son of the late John and Jessie Surman of Cardigan, and brother of John (late AIF), the late Alex, Barbara, James (late AIF), Irene and Geoffery (late AIF) 'He answered his country's call.'

[1218] Judy Meyer, 02 Aug 2004.

[1219] Register of BDMs - Victoria, 1874 11626.

[1220] Register of BDMs - Victoria, 1918 5698.

[1221] Register of BDMs - Victoria, 1876 4937.

[1222] Register of BDMs - Victoria, 1918 5986; Judy Meyer, 02 Aug 2004

[1223] The AIF Project.

[1224] Army Attestation Paper.

[1225] The AIF Project.

[1226] Miscellaneous Army Form.

ix. Geoffrey Eustace SURMAN (277) was born on 29 Jun 1878 in Sago Hill, Vic.[1227] He married Winifred May Littlehales (458), daughter of John Littlehales (768) and Martha Young (767), on 25 Apr 1917 in St Peters Anglican, Ballarat, Vic.[1228] He married Ethel Stella Todd (1552) in 1926.[1229] He died in Jul 1951 in Heidelberg, Vic, at age 73.[1230] He was buried on 01 Aug 1951 in New Cemetery Area Private, Section 3 Lot 6R1, Ballarat, Vic.[1231]

He was listed in the electoral roll in 1909 in Curyo, Vic.[1232] He lived in 1914 in Cardigan, Ballarat, Vic.[1233] He was a farmer, unmarried in 1914 in Cardigan, Ballarat, Vic. He began military service on 25 Aug 1914 as a private, Regimental No. 129, next of kin, brother J O Surman, Cardigan.[1234] He was a billiards professional in 1920. He lived in 1921 in 210 Sturt Street, Ballarat, Vic. He was listed in the electoral roll in 1924 in 210 Sturt Street, Ballarat, Vic.[1235] He and Ethel Stella Todd (1552) were listed in the electoral roll in 1931 in 715 Sturt Street, Ballarat, Vic.[1236]

Winifred May LITTLEHALES (458) was born in 1892 in Vic.[1237] She died circa 20 Apr 1920 in Ballarat, Vic. She was buried on 24 Apr 1920 in New Cemetery, Ballarat, Vic.[1238]

Ethel Stella TODD (1552)[1239] was born in 1901.

43. Williamina GUNN (1130) was born on 03 Mar 1843 in Reay Parish, Caithness.[1240] She was christened on 07 Apr 1843 in Reay Parish, Caithness.[1241] She married James D Clarke (3411), son of William Clarke (3451) and Mary Chalmers (3452), on 23 Jul 1875 in Braehour, Halkirk Parish, Caithness. She died in 1909 in Lanarkshire.

She appeared on the census of 30 Mar 1851 in the household of Alexander Gunn (Capt.) of Braehour and Newton (572) and Mary Innes Campbell (1128) in Brawlbin, Reay Parish, Caithness.[1242] She appeared on the census of 30 Mar 1861 in the household of her parents Alexander (572) and Mary (1128) in Halkirk Parish, Caithness.[1243] She appeared on the census of 1871 in the household of her father Alexander (572) in Braehour, Halkirk Parish,

---

1227 Register of BDMs - Victoria, 1878 18658; Judy Meyer, 02 Aug 2004.

1228 Register of BDMs - Victoria, 1917 2043; *Ballarat BDMs CD.*, CD-ROM), register book 18/565.

1229 Register of BDMs - Victoria, 1926 572.

1230 Register of BDMs - Victoria, 1951 9171.

1231 Ballarat Old Cemetery records.

1232 Electoral Roll: Geoffrey Eustace Surman, farmer Curyo (near Birchip).

1233 The AIF Project.

1234 *Melbourne Argus*, 25 May 1918, Died in Service On the 17th May at Base Hospital, Theodore Oswald, ex sgt 5th Btn, AIF, fourth son of the late John and Jessie Surman of Cardigan, and brother of John (late AIF), the late Alex, Barbara, James (late AIF), Irene and Geoffery (late AIF) 'He answered his country's call.'

1235 Electoral Roll: Geoffrey Eustace Surman, billiad marker, 11 Sturt street, Ballarat.

1236 Electoral Roll: Geoffrey Eustace Surman and Ethel Stella Todd, 715 Sturt Street, Ballarat.

1237 Register of BDMs - Victoria, 1920 4167.

1238 Ballarat Old Cemetery records.

1239 Judy Meyer, 02 Aug 2004.

1240 *John O'Groat Journal*, 24 Jan 1861, Birth notice: Friday March 3, 1843, Gunn, Mrs Alex Brawlbin, a daughter.

1241 Bill and Sharon Gurney, e-mail to Donald Gunn, 07 Jan 2009.

1242 UK Census 30 March 1851: Brawlbin, Reay, Caithness: Alexander Gunn corn merchant born Braehour age 36, Mary aka Margaret Campbell born Reay age 36, Williamina age 8, Barbara age 6, Peter age 4, Catherine age 2.

1243 UK Census 30 March 1861: Alexr Gunn 46 farmer 600 acres; Mary Gunn 48; Williamina Gunn 17; Barbara Gunn 15; Peter Gunn 13; Catherine Gunn 11; Robertina Gunn 9.

Caithness.[1244] She appeared on the census of 1881 in 67 Quarry Street, Hamilton, Lanarkshire.[1245] She was a coal agent in 1881. She appeared on the census of 1891 in 151 Quarry Street, Hamilton, Lanarkshire.[1246] She appeared on the census of 1901 in the household of her son William (3453) in Old Monkland, Lanarkshire.[1247]

James D CLARKE (3411) died before 1881.[1248] He was a civil engineer on 23 Jul 1875 in Hamilton, Lanarkshire.[1249]

Children of Williamina Gunn (1130) and James D Clarke (3411) all born in Hamilton, Lanarkshire, were:

i. William CLARK (3453) was born in 1877. He appeared on the census of 1881 in the household of his mother Williamina (1130) in 67 Quarry Street, Hamilton, Lanarkshire. He appeared on the census of 1891 in the household of his mother Williamina (1130) in 151 Quarry Street, Hamilton, Lanarkshire. He appeared on the census of 1901 in Old Monkland, Lanarkshire.

ii. Alexander Gunn CLARK (3454) was born in 1878.[1250] He appeared on the census of 1881 in the household of his mother Williamina (1130) in 67 Quarry Street, Hamilton, Lanarkshire. He appeared on the census of 1891 in the household of his mother Williamina (1130) in 151 Quarry Street, Hamilton, Lanarkshire. He appeared on the census of 1901 in the household of his brother William (3453) in Old Monkland, Lanarkshire.

iii. Mary Campbell CLARK (3455) was born in 1880. She appeared on the census of 1881 in the household of her mother Williamina (1130) in 67 Quarry Street, Hamilton, Lanarkshire. She appeared on the census of 1891 in the household of her mother Williamina (1130) in 151 Quarry Street, Hamilton, Lanarkshire. She appeared on the census of 1901 in the household of her brother William (3453) in Old Monkland, Lanarkshire.

44. Catherine GUNN (1133) was born in 1849 in Reay Parish, Caithness. She married John Scott (3450), son of John Scott (3456) and Jessie Spalding (3457), on 18 Jun 1873 in Inverness.[1251] She died on 19 Sep 1929 in Edinburgh, Midlothian.

She appeared on the census of 30 Mar 1851 in the household of Alexander Gunn (Capt.) of Braehour and Newton (572) and Mary Innes Campbell (1128) in Brawlbin, Reay Parish, Caithness.[1252] She appeared on the census of 30 Mar 1861 in the household of her parents

---

[1244]UK Census 1871: Alexr Gunn 56 farmer 600 acres; Williamina Gunn 26; 3 servants.

[1245]Census 1881: Williamina Clark 36, coal agent, born Reay; William Clark 4 born Hamilton; Alexander Clark 3 born Hamilton; Mary Clark 1 born Hamilton.

[1246]Census 1891: Williama Gunn Clark 47 coal agent; William Clark 14 colliery shipper; Alexander Gunn Clark 13 colliery clerk; Mary Campbell Clark; 11 scholar.

[1247]Census 1901: Wm Clark head 24 clerk; Williamina G Clark mother 57; Alexander G Clark, brother 22 tester steel works; Mary C Clark sister 21.

[1248]Bill and Sharon Gurney, e-mail to Donald Gunn, 07 Jan 2009.

[1249]*The Owen Sound Advertiser*, Married: At Brayhour House, Scotland, on the 30th ult., by the Rev. Daniel Ferguson, Free Church, Westerdale, James D Clarke, Esq, C of E, Hamilton, to Williamina Gunn, daughter of Captain Gunn, Brayhour, and niece of R.I.Campbell, Owen Sound.

[1250]Bill and Sharon Gurney, e-mail to Donald Gunn, 07 Jan 2009.

[1251]Unknown translator, "unknown short register title", John Scott, contractor, age 25, Angus, married Catherine Gunn age 24, Braehour in the Parish of Halkirk on 18 June 1873 in Inverness. Witnesses were William Scott and Barbara Gunn.

[1252]Census 30 March 1851: Brawlbin, Reay, Caithness: Alexander Gunn corn merchant born Braehour age 36, Mary aka Margaret Campbell born Reay age 36, Williamina age 8, Barbara age 6, Peter age 4, Catherine age 2.

Alexander (572) and Mary (1128) in Halkirk Parish, Caithness.[1253] She was a housemaid in 1871 in 2 Park Place, Edinburgh, Midlothian.

John SCOTT (3450) was born circa 1848 in Forfarshire. He was a contractor in 1873. He was a contractor in 1881 in Falkirk, Stirling Parish. He was a railway contract manager in 1891 in Stirling, Stirling Parish. He was a railway contract manager in 1901 in Stirling, Stirling Parish.

Children of Catherine Gunn (1133) and John Scott (3450) were as follows:

i. Robertina G SCOTT (3458) was born in 1874 in Cupar, Angus. She married Alexander Munro (3459) circa 1901. She died in 1944 in Inverness

Alexander MUNRO (3459) was born in 1869. He died in 1962.

ii. John SCOTT (3460) was born in 1876 in Dalry, Ayrshire.

iii. Alexander S SCOTT (3461) was born in 1878 in Hamilton, Lanarkshire.

iv. Charles SCOTT (3462) was born in 1880 in Hamilton, Lanarkshire.

v. William SCOTT (3463) was born in 1882 in Falkirk, Stirlingshire.

vi. Patrick S SCOTT (3464) was born in 1885 in Perthshire.

vii. Walter SCOTT (3465) was born in 1887 in Ayrshire.

45. John St Clair GUNN (Dr) (3575) was born in 1854 in Dundee, Angus. He married Hester Easton (3713) circa 1890.[1254] He died on 10 Jul 1907 in Kaikoura, Marlborough.[1255]

He appeared on the 1871 Census.[1256] He was a medical practioner in 1876. He was educated on 20 Sep 1876 in University of Glasgow, Glasgow; qualified as a medical doctor. He was a member of the Arctic Expedition in 1879. He was the informant at the death of Donald Gunn of Brawlbin and Dundee (976) on 13 May 1879 in St Andrew, Dundee, Angus.[1257] He was a Fellow of the Meteorological Society, London. He appeared on the 1881 Census of 13 King Street, Dundee, St Andrew Parish, Angus, dated 1881.[1258] He emigrated after 1881 to New Zealand. He was appointed public vaccinator on 27 Jun 1896 in Kaikoura, Marlborough.

Hester EASTON (3713) was born circa 1867. She died in 1939 in Kaikoura. She was also known as Esther (3713).

Children of John St Clair Gunn (Dr) (3575) and Hester Easton (3713) were as follows:

[1253]Census 30 March 1861: Alexr Gunn 46 farmer 600 acres; Mary Gunn 48; Williamina Gunn 17; Barbara Gunn 15; Peter Gunn 13; Catherine Gunn 11; Robertina Gunn 9.

[1254]Bill and Sharon Gurney, e-mail to Donald Gunn, 23 Nov 2009: Family of Alexandrina and Donald Gunn.

[1255]*Unknown newspaper*, Kaikoura, July 10. The death is announced of Dr John St Clair Gunn, aged fifty-four, after a long illness. He was a Fellow of the Meteorological Society, London, and contributed largely to many English and Foreign scientific magazines and colonial journals. He served in the Arctic Expedition in 1879, and later practised in India and Burmah. He had a long and varied connection with military matters, and was surgeon-captain to the New Zealand Staff. He was also surgeon at the Kairkoura Mounted Rifles, which corps he parctically established, being the first captain. He was the patentee and inventor of Gunn's rain rejector, now in common use. He showed also a very warm interest in educational questions in scenery preservation. He leaves a widow and three children.

[1256]Census 1871: Donald Gunn head age 53 born Halkirk Governor; Alexandrina Gunn wife age 44 born Halkirk;John Gunn son age 17 Apprentice Druggist; Daniel A Gunn son age16 born Dundee Apprentice Merch. Clerk; Margaret Gunn dau. age 12 born Dundee Scholar; Catherine Gunn dau. age 10 born Dundee Scholar; Wilhelmina Gunn dau. age 5 born Dundee Scholar; Robertina Gunn niece age 18 born Dundee Matron's Asst.

[1257]Bill and Sharon Gurney, e-mail to Donald Gunn, 09 Feb 2009; The Descendants of Donald Gunn.

[1258]Census 30 March 1861: John Gunn head age 27 born Dundee General Medical Pract MB CM Glasgow; Kate Gunn sister age 20 born Dundee; Wilhelmina Gunn sister age 15 born Dundee.

i. Agnes Loeda GUNN (3715) was born in 1893. She married Walter Charles Cropp (3716) in 1916. Walter Charles CROPP (3716) died on 14 Apr 1918 and was buried in Apr 1918 in the Military Cemetery, Meteren.

ii. Alexandrina Margaret GUNN (3717) was born in 1896. She married William Alastair McQueen (3718) in 1920 and died in 1967. William Alastair MCQUEEN (3718) was born on 15 Nov 1886. He died in 1976.

iii. Donald St Clair GUNN (3719) was born on 29 Jul 1899. He died in 1973.

46. Catherine GUNN (3578) was born on 13 Sep 1860 in Dundee, Angus.[1259] She married Peter Munro (3714), son of Peter Munro (3720) and Jane MacKenzie (3721), on 13 Oct 1887 in Perthshire.[1260]

She appeared on the 1861 Census[1261] and on the 1871 Census.[1262] She appeared on the 1881 Census of 13 King Street, Dundee, St Andrew Parish, Angus, in the household of her brother John St Clair Gunn (3575).[1263] She was a nurse on 13 Oct 1887. She and Peter Munro (3714) emigrated circa 1888 to USA.

Peter MUNRO (3714) was born circa 1866. He was a commercial traveller on 13 Oct 1887.

Children of Catherine Gunn (3578) and Peter Munro (3714) were:

i. Peter Lascelles MUNRO (3722) was born in 1889 in Kansas.[1264] He died on 03 Apr 1918 in Communal Cemetery, Fouilloy, Somme, age 29.[1265]

He appeared on the 1891 Census and the 1901 Census of St Davids Private Orphanage, East Lothian. [1266]

47. Williamina GUNN (3579) was born on 14 Apr 1865 in Dundee, Angus.[1267] She married Thomas H Arthur (3581), son of Sturrock Arthur (3931) and Mary McHardy (3932), on 16 Apr 1885 in Aberdeen. She died in Omaha, Nebraska.

She was also known as Wilhemina (3579). She appeared on the 1871 Census.[1268] She appeared on the 1881 Census of 13 King Street, Dundee, St Andrew Parish, Angus, in the

---

1259 Bill and Sharon Gurney, e-mail to Donald Gunn, 23 Apr 2009: Family of Alexandrina Gunn and Donald Gunn.

1260 Bill and Sharon Gurney, e-mail to Donald Gunn, 23 Nov 2009: Family of Alexandrina and Donald Gunn; unknown translator, "unknown short register title", Peter Munro age 21, Commercial Traveller, res. 18 St Andrews Hall, Dundee, son of Peter Munro, marine engineer and Jane Munro m.s. MacKenzie, married Kate L Gunn, age 24 Nurse, res. 163 Shandon Place, Dundee, dauaghter of Donald Gunn, Govr. Dundee Poor House (decd) and Alexandrina Gunn m.s. Gunn (decd), on 13 October 1887 at no. 28 High Street, Perth by Declaration in presence of Alexander Forsyth.

1261 Bill and Sharon Gurney, e-mail to Donald Gunn, 23 Nov 2009: Family of Alexandrina and Donald Gunn; Census 30 March 1861: Donald Gunn head age 43 born Halkirk House Governor; Alexandrina Gunn Mat. age 35 born Halkirk Matron; Daniel A Gunn son age 7 born Dundee; Margaret Gunn dau. age 3 born Dundee; Catherine Gunn dau. age 7m born Dundee.

1262 Bill and Sharon Gurney, e-mail to Donald Gunn, 23 Nov 2009: Family of Alexandrina and Donald Gunn; Census 1871: Donald Gunn head age 53 born Halkirk Governor; Alexandrina Gunn wife age 44 born Halkirk;John Gunn son age 17 Apprentice Druggist; Daniel A Gunn son age16 born Dundee Apprentice Merch. Clerk; Margaret Gunn dau. age 12 born Dundee Scholar; Catherine Gunn dau. age 10 born Dundee Scholar; Wilhelmina Gunn dau. age 5 born Dundee Scholar; Robertina Gunn niece age 18 born Dundee Matron's Asst.

1263 Census 30 March 1861: John Gunn head age 27 born Dundee General Medical Pract MB CM Glasgow; Kate Gunn sister age 20 born Dundee; Wilhelmina Gunn sister age 15 born Dundee.

1264 Unknown title, Peter Munro age 21, Commercial Traveller, res. 18 St Andrews Hall, Dundee, married Kate L Gunn, age 24 Nurse, res. 163 Shandon Place, Dundee on 13 October 1887 at no. 28 High Street, Perth by Declaration in presence of Alexander Forsyth etc.

1265 Cemetery Marker: In memory of Sapper Peter Lascelles Munro, 162775, 217th Army Troops Coy, Royal Engineers who died age 29 on 03 April 1918. Grandson of Mrs Jane M Munro of Forfar Rd, Dundee. Remembered with honour, Fouilloy Communal Cemetery, Somme.

1266 Census 1901: St Davids Private Orphanage, East Lothian, age 12, born America, Scholar; Bill and Sharon Gurney, e-mail to Donald Gunn, 23 Nov 2009: Family of Alexandrina and Donald Gunn.

1267 Bill and Sharon Gurney, e-mail to Donald Gunn, 23 Apr 2009: Family of Alexandrina Gunn and Donald Gunn.

household of her brother John St Clair Gunn (Dr) (3575).[1269] She and Thomas H Arthur (3581) emigrated circa 1888 to USA. with Peter Munro (3714) and Catherine Gunn (3578).

Thomas H ARTHUR (3581) was born in 1866 in Angus.

Children of Williamina Gunn (3579) and Thomas H Arthur (3581) were as follows:

i. Thomas Hutton ARTHUR (3582) was born on 23 Nov 1885 in St Andrew, Angus. He emigrated with his parents circa 1888 to USA.

ii. Sturrock ARTHUR (3583) was born in Oct 1888 in Kansas.

iii. Douglas ARTHUR (3584) was born in Nov 1891 in Nebraska.

iv. Stanley ARTHUR (3585) was born in May 1894 in Nebraska.

v. Stewart ARTHUR (3586) was born in Mar 1899 in Nebraska.

[1268] Census 1871: Donald Gunn head age 53 born Halkirk Governor; Alexandrina Gunn wife age 44 born Halkirk;John Gunn son age 17 Apprentice Druggist; Daniel A Gunn son age16 born Dundee Apprentice Merch. Clerk; Margaret Gunn dau. age 12 born Dundee Scholar; Catherine Gunn dau. age 10 born Dundee Scholar; Wilhelmina Gunn dau. age 5 born Dundee Scholar; Robertina Gunn niece age 18 born Dundee Matron's Asst.

[1269]Census 30 March 1861: John Gunn head age 27 born Dundee General Medical Pract MB CM Glasgow; Kate Gunn sister age 20 born Dundee; Wilhelmina Gunn sister age 15 born Dundee.

Westerdale Old Presbyterian Church, 2011

Westerdale Mill, 2011

Part 6—Concerning the descendants of Donald Gunn, the Sennachie (708)

Descendants of Donald Gunn (708)

Bill and Sharon Gurney, February 2009

1. Donald Gunn, son of John Gunn and Marjory ('May') Dunbar, was born about 1769 in Caithness, Scotland and died on 3 Jan 1861 in Brawlbin, Reay, Caithness about age 92. Death Notes: Informant at death Alexander Gunn, Braehour (not present). (John O'Groat Journal, Jan. 24, 1861) General Notes: Donald was known as Donald the Sennachie of Braehour & Brawlbin. He was a farmer.

1841 a Farmer in Reay Parish, Brawlbin
Donald Gunn, age 72
Katherine Gunn, age 60
Alexr. Gunn, age 26
Mary Gunn, age 26
Margaret Gunn, age 22
Alexandrina Gunn, age 18
George Gunn, age 80
George Gunn, Servant, age 22
(5 servants)

1851 Reay Parish, Brawlbin
Donald Gunn, age 80, Farmer 60 Acres, born Halkirk
Catherine Gunn, age 68, born Latheron
Margaret Gunn, Dau. age 30, born Halkirk, House Maid
Alexandrina Gunn, Dau. age 28, born Halkirk, House Maid
George Gunn, Serv. age 28, born Halkirk, Servant
George Dunbar, age 30, born Halkirk, Servant
Mary Gunn, age 16, born Reay, Herd
Margaret Sutherland, age 24, born Halkirk, Outdoor Servant

Donald married Catherine Gunn, daughter of Alexander Gunn and Barbara Weir (Wheir), on 3 Mar 1807 in Halkirk Parish, Caithness. Catherine was born about 1781 in Latheron Parish, Caithness, Scotland and died on 24 Oct 1870 in Newton, Watten Parish, Caithness about age 89.

Marriage Notes: Marriage also recorded on 28 Feb. 1807 in Latheron.
Death Notes: Informant at death, Alexander Gunn, Braehour, son.
General Notes: In 1861 Catherine was living as a Lodger with Alexander Miller in Ulbster, Wick

Children from this marriage were:

+ 2 M **i. John Gunn** was born in 1808 in Halkirk Parish, Caithness and died in 1885 in Durness, Sutherlandshire at age 77. John married Catherine Gunn (b. Abt 1817, d. 1871) on 11 May 1836 in Wick, Caithness.

+ 3 F **ii. Barbara Gunn** was born in 1810 in Braehour, Halkirk Parish, Caithness, was christened on 30 Mar 1810 in Halkirk Parish, Caithness, and died on 28 Feb 1844 in Brawlbin, Reay, Caithness at age 34.
Barbara married Alexander Gunn (b. 1789, d. 29 Mar 1847) on 19 Mar 1829 in Halkirk Parish, Caithness.

+ 4 F **iii. May (Marjory) Gunn** was born in 1812 in Halkirk Parish, Caithness, was christened on 7 Feb 1812 in Halkirk Parish, Caithness, died on 13 Sep 1853 in Halkirk Parish, Caithness at age 41, and was buried in Dorrery Cemetery, Halkirk. May married John Campbell (b. Abt 1815) about 1837 in Caithness, Scotland.

+ 5 M **iv. Capt. Alexander Gunn** was born in 1814 in Halkirk Parish, Caithness, was christened on 23 Apr 1814 in Halkirk Parish, Caithness, and died on 3 Jan 1900 in Thurso, Caithness at age 86. Alexander married Mary Innes Campbell (b. 1808, d. 5 Sep 1864) in Apr 1841 in Caithness, Scotland.

+ 6 F **v. Jean (Jane) Gunn** was born in 1816 in Braehour, Halkirk Parish, Caithness, Scotland, was christened on 27 Jul 1816 in Halkirk Parish, Caithness, died on 10 Aug 1910 in Killimster, Parish of Wick at age 94, and was buried in Dirlot Cemetery. Jean married Hugh McKenzie (b. Abt 1802, d. 11 May 1870) on 18 Dec 1840 in Reay, Caithness, Scotland.

+ 7 F **vi. Margaret Gunn** was born in 1819 in Caithness, Scotland, died in 1888 in Newton, Watten Parish, Caithness at age 69, and was buried in Dirlot Cemetery. Margaret married John MacKay (b. Abt 1815, d. 20 Aug 1865) on 14 Feb 1860 in Brawlbin, Reay, Caithness, Scotland.

+ 8 F **vii. Lexy (Alexandrina) Gunn** was born in 1825 in Halkirk Parish, Caithness, was christened on 12 Jul 1825 in Halkirk Parish, Caithness, and died in 1876 in St. Andrew, Dundee, Angus at age 51. Lexy married Donald Gunn (b. Abt 1818, d. 13 May 1879) on 26 Apr 1852 in Reay, Caithness, Scotland.

The attachment on Barbara's siblings does not include a George Gunn.

Although a George Gunn was in the 1841 and 1851 census with Donald & Catherine's family, we think he was a great nephew of Donald's and grandson of the 80 year old George Gunn who was also in the 1841 census with Donald and Catherine.

Captain Alexander Gunn[1270] (572), Braehour; 'memories' and tradition

Bill and Sharon Gurney

1

(ID numbers inserted by the authors.)

Transcribed by B. Gurney from the handwritten notes of Captain Alexander Gunn, (340) Braehour from an undated manuscript. (For the most part spelling and punctuation are as on the original. Some wording is difficult to decipher.)

The rise of the value of land from 1700 to this date is considerable far beyond the idea of any hughman (sic) being. It seems that in the year 1710 that Dalgannchan was only paying £20 Scots equal to £ 1- 3/4 sterling at this date the rent is £ 1 07 sterling. I was an offered myself at £105. It will grase 800 sheep in summer and will keep about 400 sheep in winter. It was part of Ulbster Estate which Mr. Donald Horn Writer Edin. bought from Sir John Sinclair and now of late sold by Mr. Horn to Mr. John George Sinclair of Ulbster also Mr. Sinclair bought Glitt and Rumsdale from W. Horn at £ ?

Mr Sinclair bought also Dalglaton and Dalwillan from Sir George Dunbar of Hempriggs or rather exchanged(?) for the land of Tannoch and give £600 in the exchange to Dunbar. Immediately in Mr. Sinclair cause to posess these lands he Lett the farms of Dalgannchan and Dalwillan as one farm for £258. Stg. But the propositon part rent and Dalgannchan is £ 1 07 Stg. and considering the great prices for sheep it should be worth the present rent. Price of three year old wedden 35.

1712 my great great grandfather John Gun (569) called John McInis(?) McHemish entered this land of Dalgannchan on ?Loch on the agreement of getting 10 cows in calf and 10 ewes to be supplied from the Laird's cattle at Glitt. The person in charge of said cattle gave Gun 20 cows in calf in place of the ten of each kind and fortunately for Gun these cattle was never entered in books against Gun. Consequantly was never demanded, nor yet their value. His son Alexander (240) married Jannet (281) Daughter of McLeod (799) Tacksman of Dalglaton he said Alexr held the farm of Dalgannchan and was selling his butter at 5/ per stone, and there after possessed the farm of Dalglaton but before he got it, it was possessed by Willm Gunn Achlibster for some period of time after the death of McLeod Alexr Gun's Father in Law, however it seems that during the time that Achlibster had Dalglaton that Gun left Dalgannchan and became a subtenant there to Achlibster, which sub tenant was ruled by a rod of iron. Achlibster put the whole rent on the subtenants and keeped the most and best part of town, and grasing to himself, at last his period of Lease was about an end Alexr Gun went to Badenloch and told his chief the ill usage they receive at the hands of Achlibster. Alexander Gun the then Chief of the Guns sent him with a letter ot Sir Willm Dunbar of Hempriggs the proprieter, informing him of the bad usage they got from Achlibster and with request to give a Tack of Dalglaton to Alexr Gun which request was granted consequently

[1270] 'He was a 'notable antiquarian', p. 45 *The Sinclairs of Roslin, Caithness, and Goshen* however he could be 'very secretive' p.2 M. Rugg Gunn *History of the Clan Gunn.*

Achlibster was legally summoned at the proper time to quite the farm to which summons he gave a deaf ear and keeped possession beyond the legal time, and built the shielings and went and possess them as usual. Gun collected a good party and went and demolished them and fired the same and destroyed the whole content of the shelling of Cambeg(?). Gun and Achlibster had a sharp hand to hand fight, as Gun was one of the most powerfull men of the Highlands he soon got the upper hand, and collected all Achlibster's horses, cattle and every living animal and all down past Lochmore.

Alexr Gun (240) remained in Dalglaton during his life time, and died there in the year 1765 aged 75 years and was buried at Dirlot and a grave stone placed over his remains. He left three sons, viz. George (242), Angus (243) and John (707).

George the second son possessed the farm after his father's death, he married Donald Cruin's Daughter, by whom he had Alexander (2882) and Donald (4328), the former was the champion of the North of Scotland who died at the age of 28 years A.D. 1785 and was buried in Dirlot.

Donald succeeded his father who paid a rent of £16 yearly Stg. Donald formed the foolish notion of believing to better his condition by going to Canada N. America and gave over his lease to Capt. Robert Sinclair of Scots Calder for a trifling consideration. Sold off all about the year 1807 he had a large grown up respectable family by a daughter of William Crivach of McKay Forsnaid, the time of departing arrived and the ship and appeared the ships name "Lough Mohr America"

(Gurneys note—Donald "Cruin" Gunn was a notorious scoundrel. He is described in Alex Gunn's (Capt) notes.)

(Gurneys note—from Thomas Sinclair's[1271] *writing "a son Donald who was drowned with all his family in the loss of the emigrant ship on the Newfoundland coast which sailed from Scrabster in 1807, the "Lough Mohr America" agented by Donald Sinclair, tacksman of Isauld, and merchant in Thurso (her real name was the Linnet)." "It's worth noting that in the Mark Rugg Gunn 'History of the Clan Gunn'—page 204—Donald has left the ship just before sailing and was not drowned, although his wife and some children did. Some children had remained in Scotland.")*

(Margin: 1703)

[1271]See Part 8.

Donald Gunn, comanly called Donald Cruin was a descendant of the Braemore Gunns, he was for sometime a Servant to Angus Gunn Glutt he had a Brother called John Gun, Donald was a Farmer in Achorclate(?) year 1703. He held some land in Dalglation sometime after the above year. He was a man who possed strength and swiftness far above the commonality of people and was among those who could have their requirements whither right or wrong from those that could spare, as late as the above date even respectable people sheltered such caracters as Donald in order to procure Beef and mutton for them from their richer neighbours without money or price, Donald was such a man that would not scruple for taking a man's life on a slight provocation, which he did, providing tradition is true, among others he was charged with the murder of Paul Dauph at the foot of Dalglaton, Strathmore.

The murdered man was with named Daphan i.e.OH(?) and attempted to save his life by plunged to the river to a large stone still there to where Donald followed him and killed him and buried him on the East side of the River. His blood is to be seen on the stone for a long time, thereafter. This is a large stone, is still there and likely will remain.

On some other occasion his Servant maid left him and on his refusing to pay her, her wages, which was lawfully due to her. She remarked that she would in revenge inform and reveal some of his wicked doings, he pursured after her and overtook at a small stream running from the West in to Loch Eileanach where he killed her, the little stream is called ever since Sulhan na nighin Ril ie Small maid Burn.

On one occation he was down in the lowland and came to a Farmer's house after nightfall and found his way in to the Byre and selected the best and fatest cow being a black cow he applied whitning to the cow's head, and turn her to the out side and soon as he did so he entered to the house of the owner of the cow and requested them to give him a rope to lead away a fractious cow he had and also to assist him to which the inmate of the house consented, and give Donald all the assistance they could and assisted him to fasten the rope to the cow's horns and drove her away from the house, as the cow appeared as a white faced cow they never formed any idea that the cow was their own but behold in the morning the farmer found that he wanted one of the best cows he had and too late came to understand that he was fold (sic fooled) by Donald

[Gurneys note—Donald "Cruin" Gunn was a grandfather of Alexander Gunn who died 1785, age 28. Alexander was a son of George Gunn and ? Gunn.]

Part 7—Biographies

Hon. Donald Gunn, Canada

Hon. Donald Gunn (372)[1272], Canada

Donald Gunn[1273] (September 1797–30 November 1878) was a Manitoba politician and member of the Province's Legislative Council (which he helped to abolish).

Gunn was born in Orkney, Scotland, in 1797. He worked in the Canadian North West for the Hudson's Bay Company between 1813 and 1823, and was subsequently a Judge on the Court of Petty Sessions in Red River. He also wrote for the Smithsonian Institution[1274] and the Institute of Rupert's Land, and was a member of the Board of Management for Manitoba College (a Presbyterian institution).

Gunn was a supporter of Canadian Confederation and the Government of Adams George Archibald. In Manitoba's first general election (27 December 1870), he ran against Provincial Secretary and fellow Archibald-supporter Alfred Boyd. He was defeated by 58 votes to 28.

Gunn was appointed to the Province's new Legislative Council on 15 March 1871, one of seven members. In 1876, he supported the decision of the Robert A. Davis government to abolish the institution.

Donald Gunn died in 1878.

And for a fulsome, 'Victorian phrased', life—

SKETCH OF THE LIFE of the late HON. DONALD GUNN[1275]; *author presumably C.R. Tuttle*

Prominently one whose scholarly instinct was of a verity a part of his nature, the author of the History of which this brief notice is a prefix, Donald Gunn, was born in the Parish of Halkirk in the County of Caithness, Scotland, in the year 1797, and sprang from that strong and fertile class of peasant farmers whose health of body and mind-nurtured in the frugal simplicity of their native hill—has furnished so many worthy sons to the stout old land that gave them birth. A land whose scant nurture and limited scope, while it conserves so much, yet breeds a necessity enriching other shores than those of the rugged peninsula stretching its rocky arm into the wild northern seas, sending out, from time to time, to the great

---

[1272] Baptism: June 10, 1798, Halkirk, Caithness, Scotland (Source: Halkirk Christenings, Batch \#C11037-4 Ser\# 01255-1.) Burial: Little Britain Cemetery, St. Andrews, Manitoba, Canada. (Source: (1) Headstone in Cemetery., (2) *Joyce Anaka Family History Book.*, (3) Little Britain United Church Cemetery Transcripts.) Census: 1838, Manitoba Red River Settlement Elected: Bet. 1871 - 1876, Legislative Council (Source: *Joyce Anaka Family History Book.*) Immigration: June 28, 1813, Stromness, Scotland aboard the Eddystone (Source: *Joyce Anaka Family History Book*, page 6.) Occupation: Aft. 1822, Farmer (Source: *Joyce Anaka Family History Book.*) Retirement: 1822, Freeman from Hudson's Bay Company (Source: Hudson Bay Company Archives, Donald Gunn Bio Sheet.)

[1273] http://en.wikipedia.org/wiki/Donald_Gunn reproduced under license see http://creativecommons.org/licenses/by-sa/3.0/

[1274] Smithsonian Institution, *Annual report*, *1878* (Washington), 63–64. Donald Gunn, "Indian remains near Red River settlement, Hudson's bay territory," Smithsonian Institution, *Annual report*, *1867* (Washington), 399–100; "Notes of an egging expedition to Shoal lake, west of lake Winnipeg. Made under the direction of the Smithsonian Institution in 1867 . . ."

[1275] Being from Donald Gunn and C. R. Tuttle, *History of Manitoba from the earliest settlement to 1835 by the late Hon. Donald Gunn, and from the admission of the province into the Dominion by Charles R. Tuttle* (Ottawa, 1880).

unoccupied spaces her colonizing children, who achieve by virtue of inherent and trained qualities—that stand them ever instead—a success second to none, if equaled by any.

Of the children of the tenant of the old farm house in the strath of Braeholme, two furnish worth proof of this fact, an elder son seeking at an earl day his fortune in the wilds of Australia, becoming in due course of time one of the largest wool growers and sheep farmers in the colony: the other, the subject of our memoir, who turning his face to the west, wrought out amid the ice and snow of the northern land, not only fair fortune but an honored name.

It was in the Parish School of Halkirk that the blue-eyed, fair haired Scotch lad first mastered the mystic signs that were to prove to him in after years, such unvarying delight. Here the speech of the Hills took precedence, and the Gaelic (the tongue the Scotsmen fondly boast contains all others) found an apt and loving pupil; one who the latest years of his life knew no poet king save Ossian, no loftier flight than that of the strong wing of the early Scottish bard, whose bold imaginings conned by the boy on the mist clad heights of the tempestuous shore, resonant with the mighty music of the sea, found quick interpretation, and were framed kindred elevation, leaving a picture no time could fade.

Secondary, came the alien English—the strange classic spoken by the Southerns—that lent dignity to the little school-house, whose curriculum boasted these two alone, yet in themselves an education holding all of flexibility and power that written or spoken thought demands, an equipment, seeming slender, in reality full of pith.

Happily for the boy, the hills and valley, the storm and sunshine on the heather-clad braes, the glory and changeful lights of his mountain, sea grit home, these too were his teachers. Here following the herds, or watching the browsing, wandering sheep, he drank in a tranquil strength he little wot of, received the silent benison of nature, knitting together the robust tissues that make life a harmony, a forceful quietude, breeding strength for cheerful essay of all tasks, admirably fitted for the one that now came quickly to his youthful hand.

The Hudson's Bay Company, who had depots and shipping ports on the neighbouring islands, had long been in the habit of mainly recruiting their force of servants among the hardy, frugal people in the north of Scotland and the Orkney Isles. Their ships were the 'argosies' that freighted fortunes from the distant shores of Hudson's Bay; and their ships were to the simple youth of the coast—wearied with an unremunerative toil that held no future—the brave craft that would bear them to a better fate. The slender stipend promised seemingly, by home comparison, large indeed.

Young Donald, now some sixteen summers, urged by such thoughts, and a love of wandering that seems instinctive at a certain period of life, aware of the large number of families being sent out by the Earl of Selkirk, engaged with the local agent, and in the year of grace, 1813, found himself duly enrolled as servant of the great fur trading company, and bound for York Factory, on Hudson's Bay, in company with the Pilgrim Fathers of the North-West, now widely known as the Selkirk Settlers.[1276]

[1276]Note taken from Hudson's Bay Company Archives; Donald is described in 1814-1815 as with "dark brown hair, strong, well made", but "desires to return home".

The future historian will yet linger over the pages of this volume, in seeking to portray anew the story of these people. No record of colonial life is more affecting than the tearful embarkation of these cottagers, their hardships at the bay, and the culminating and dreadful distresses in which they and their helpless families were plunged on their arrival at the Red River, caused by their miserable and unexpected involvement in the deadly strife and murderous competition of the two great rival companies, their own protectors and the wild half-savage men of the "North-West"

The suffering is so real and persistent, their patience so admirable, their helpless acceptance of the most grievous situation so simple and unostentatious, that it hardly seems real; deepening our sympathy and admiration as we look upon the picture of to-day, the smiling farms of their children and descendants, where plenty and peace brood over the spot fraught to their progenitors with terror, flight and distress.

The life of a "Company man'—in the phrase of the country—is either fraught with incident or entirely uneventful, being simply a matter of locality. "The Severn District", abutting upon, "the Bay," in which Mr. Gunn passed his ten years of service, was the natural stronghold of the Hudson's Bay men, peopled by peaceful, inoffensive Indians, and productive of no marked event, while at the same time the plains to the west—as is seen in this narrative—were, with the Red River Country, the theatre of a warfare so fatal to the contestants as to impel the coalition of the great rivals, the North-West Company being merged into that of the Hudson's Bay in the year 1821.

But the time, to a man of Mr. Gunn's energetic character, and thirst for knowledge, was not—if barren of event—unprofitably spent. His vicinity to the great depot of the north, and his early promotion to the position of a lesser postmaster, threw him continually into the society of the leading men of the Company, from whose conversation he derived a great store of exact information touching the past and contemporaneous history of the great governing Corporation. He was also enabled to acquire, by loan or purchase, books, and the digest of his acquisitions at his period, as shown in conversation and reminiscences in after years, was of singular fullness and value. An immense amount of local character detail of the most unique and interesting description has by his decease, been forever lost to the lesser records of our colonial history, a loss as great to us in the future as would have been the early destruction of "Pepys' Diary" to the English people.

The year 1819 was to Mr. Gunn alike a memorable and happy one, he then marrying Margaret, the eldest daughter of James Swain, Esquire, the officer in charge of the York District, a union blessed and fortunate in every respect—one unbroken for a period of fifty years.

That the newly married couple were in no danger of being at the time of their marriage enervated by luxury, Mr. Gunn would, with a keen recollection of the time and their freedom from care and grief, amusingly relate. In addition to the usual allowance of small stores, their outfit of meats and breadstuffs was more suggestive than real, consisting of a "flint trade gun," ammunition, and twine for nets. The hardship was but in seeming, game and fish abounded, Indian and traders alike resorted to their well stocked "preserves" for subsistence, and, possibly, the jaded epicures of the city would have envied the young couple their keen enjoyment of their woodland fare.

A deprivation more felt was at times when in recent possession of a treasured book, to be without candles or oil, when thinly split pitch pine fagots would light up the house, drag from their shadowy coverts the finest print, and convert the snug log dwelling, nestled in evergreens, into a hall of learning, where each recurring page folded down and conserved satisfactions remembered through life.

It being found inexpedient by the Hudson's Bay Company after the absorption of the North-West, to maintain so large a force as the united employees of the late Company and its own, certain reductions were determined upon, and Mr. Gunn gladly availed himself of the opportunity to retire. With his wife and newly born son, he followed his old friends, the "Selkirk Settlers," to the Red River, settling in what is now the Parish of St. Andrews, but which he and a few friends of certainly ambitious loyalty for the time, named "Little Britain," scarce for seeing that their tiny speck of civilization would ripen so quickly, and assure here and to the west a "Greater Britain."

The locality chosen, however, proved to be a good one, and drew about it a more than usually intelligent class of "freemen," as the retired servants of the Company were called; among them Mr. William Smith, and English worthy full of strong, honest points, one of the most genial and humorous of men, who had also married a daughter of Mr. Swain, and was after appointed Secretary to the Council of Assiniboia and Clerk of the Local Courts, an office which he held until his death.

Happily for the new farmers, these were the halcyon days of the hunters. Buffalo were near and plenty, the net was ever in the water, sturgeon and "gold eyes" daily fare. Without ploughs, tools or cattle, their first attempts at agriculture were of the rudest description; putting down wheat with a hoe, the quantity of seed is not hard to surmise, yet from such a beginning ere many years—aided by his stout sons—spacious stone house with ample stabling for the large stock of horses and horned animals, and abundant grain, made the homestead of Donald Gunn one of the foremost in the entire settlement, one whose abundance made glad many a luckless soul.

After an interval of ten years spent in active farming, Mr. Gunn found himself, by the increasing size and usefulness of his large family so relieved from personal attention to the farm, that he was enabled to take charge of the Parish School established, and, with the exception of the very slight contributions of the parents, supported by the Mission Society of the English Church.

This task, one held in the highest honor and respect in those primitive days—to the shame of our own diminished and unwise estimate be it spoken—was one so congenial to his taste, that, fortunately for the youth of both sexes in his charge, it was continued without intermission by him for the long period of eighteen years.

A period of usefulness in one of the highest and most responsible functions possible to an individual, one which while training others had disciplined and fitted for distinction many of our best thinkers and actors in the world of statecraft and of letters.

This was, in the case of Mr. Gunn, very distinctly avouched, not only in the career of numbers of his pupils who attained to positions of public trust and honor, but even more certainly, if less marked, in the sustained life impress made upon all, intelligence bearing fruit by many a fireside, unseen rivulets trained to fertilize and make glad an otherwise barren field.

Had the classes in charge of Mr. Gunn been fired with the same student ardor—simple and pure love of knowledge for its own sake—as their teacher, his task, always an arduous one, would have been slight indeed. Its compensation lay in the fact that he was at least at the Centre of all literary lore in the North-West, in contact with such varied and sufficient printed erudition as made him more than content.

When, later, made custodian and librarian in his own house of the only public collection of books in the country, he was fairly environed with satisfaction, each tome a silent friend.

The spacious stone farm-house to which we have adverted, was always the hospitable home, alike of the purposeless tourist or the wandering Savant who sought its well known doors in search of special facts in the physical geography or natural history of the vast terra incognita of which the Red River settlement was the threshold.

At Donald Gunn's, the stranger found not only the warmth of a home, but an intelligence which threw light on all detail of purposed travel and entered into and discussed every them of scientific research.

The personal characteristics of Mr. Gunn were of the most engaging character. In an intercourse of nearly twenty years we fail to recall other than the most genial and unaffected cordiality to all; super added to this, his varied powers of conversation, replete with valuable matter gathered from all sources, his sense of humor lighting up old Gaelic lore, the traditions of the Viking race from whom he sprung, the rough adventures and eccentricities of the hero worthies of "the trade" the early and chequered life in the settlement, with a vein of grounded culture running through all, made him to be one of the most companionable and instructive of men.

An Elder in the Kirk for many years, Mr. Gunn's liberality of thought—in this direction—would have been marked were it not for the general charity and largest tolerance universal in the country. Latterly, when he had retired mainly from public affairs, nearly all of Mr. Gunn's time was occupied in the preparation of this history, arranging his collated facts and personal experience with such care and patience as will doubtless cause it to be—as he intended it should be—an authority upon all the matters coming under his hands. Towards the close of his life, his sight failing him, it was his greatest pleasure to have some one read aloud to him from his favorite authors, his mind retaining its force and clearness until a few hours before his death. This occurred on the last day of November, 1878, in his own house, surrounded by his family, the parting being so peaceful as to be literally falling asleep.

Two grandsons of the Hon. Donald Gunn

Rev. Henry George Gunn (2631) 1866-1945; John J. Gunn[1277] (2628) 1861-1907

Being sons of John Gunn (2551) and Emma Garrioch (2552).

[1277] Provisionally identified.

William Gunn (374) of Waranga Park

(Waranga[1278] is in the State of Victoria, Australia.
It is roughly in the triangle between Shepparton, Nagambie and Rushworth.)

Individual Narrative of William Gunn of Waranga Park (374)

William GUNN of Waranga (374)[1279] was born in 1804 at Halkirk Parish, Caithness, Scotland.[1280] He was christened on 28 Apr 1805.[1281] He was Messenger at Arms on 6 Jun 1841 at Wick Parish, Caithness, Scotland.[1282] [1283] He lived on 6 Jun 1841 at Bridge Street, Wick Parish, Caithness, Scotland. He married Cecilia CORMACK (375), daughter of Alexander CORMACK (928) and Elizabeth (--?--) (929), on 26 Jul 1850 at Aberdeen, Grampian, Scotland.[1284] He appeared on the census of 30 Mar 1851 at Wick Parish, Caithness, Scotland.[1285] He emigrated in 1853 from Scotland and settled at Waranga, near Rushworth by

---

1278 According to *The Argus* page 10, 1 Jul 1927, William Gunn was the second owner of Waranga Park and it was 'long known as Gunn's swamp' and the meaning of 'waranga' is the local aboriginal word for water, see http://newspapers.nla.gov.au/ndp/del/article/3864141?searchTerm=Gunn .

1279 Letter from Janettie McMillan to Donald Gunn, 24 Apr 1974 and for further information on this page.

1280 Granddaughter Janettie McMillan gives age as 84 at death in 1888.

1281 Caroline Armstrong, Descendants of Donald Gunn, e-mail message to Donald Gunn, 20 Mar 2006.

1282 Notes by William Watkin & Marcus Daniel Gunn during visit to Dirlot, 1928: William Gunn (Waranga Park) was cousin to my great (grandmother?). He was Messenger at Arms at Wick. Two young men committed a crime and a tinker named Cluny who was had up for stealing was with them. William Gunn was taking the three of them to Inverness and stopped the other side of Helmsdale for the night at an inn, putting the two prisoners and the tinker in an upstairs room while he and some more were drinking downstairs. The tinker told the other two if they wanted to go he would take the handcuffs off as he was too old to go himself, so he took their handcuffs off and they opened the window, jumped out and got away. William Gunn was held responsible and had to resign. He then went to Australia where he stayed with a man named Mackay who left him the place where he died.

1283 UK Census 06 June 1841.

1284 Letter from Edith Christoe to Donald Gunn; 06 Feb 2006.

1285 Census 30 March 1851: William Gunn born Halkirk age 42, messenger at arms; Cecilia Gunn born Wick age 31; Margaret Elizabeth Gunn born Wick age 5 mo.

the Goulburn River in Northern Victoria.[1286] Gold was found on the property in 1853.[1287] He was a farmer of 51,840 acres in 1856 at Waranga Park, Vic. [1288] [1289] He was appointed a magistrate in October 1863[1290]. He was issued with a Licence for 8,800 sheep under The Scab Act, with no fine imposed on 07 Jan 1874 at Waranga Park, Vic.[1291] He was granted a licence to transfer the mining lease of Sandhurst, lease no. 1976 to W. Gunn on 14 Feb 1874 at Vic.[1292] He was granted confirmation of a grazing licence for 18,970 acres at an annual rent of £64/5/- on 09 Jan 1888 at Waranga Park, Vic. [1293] He died in 1888 at Waranga, Vic.[1294] [1295] [1296] Waranga Park was sold by auction on 14 Sep 1953.

*****

Concerning William Gunn (374) of Waranga Park

(**1**) 'By the time the N.S.W. squatters were prepared to initiate large-scale capital outlays on fencing, Victorian attitudes had become reasonably explicit and clear-cut. A proposal to fence a section of Waranga Park in Victoria makes this essential point in 1870: 'The absence of this fence renders unavailable about 12,000 acres of useful but scrubby country in which sheep would thrive running at large .... This large area would feed 3,000 sheep .... Mr Gunn .... reckons .... He could make £400 a year of this additional country .... The erection of this fence would enable him to discharge the 4 shepherds he now employs and thus save £225...'[1297]

(2) 'Once known as Waranga Lagoon or Gunn's Swamp, the waters of Waranga Basin engulfed the former southern village of Waranga upon completion of works that converted a swamp into the major irrigation water storage as we see it today.

Former Waranga Run owner, William Gunn Snr. transported his original home from Waranga Village to Rushworth, built a new home and relocated his family onto what is now known as Finnigan's Island.'[1298]

[1286] Letter from Janettie McMillan to Donald Gunn, 24 Apr 1974; When my grandmother and father arrived out here in 1857 ... until grandfather was able to go for them - he came out here in 1853.

[1287] Caroline Armstrong, e-mail to Donald Gunn, 20 Mar 2006.

[1288] Letter, Edith Christoe to Donald Gunn, 29 Nov 2005.

[1289] Caroline Armstrong, e-mail to Donald Gunn, 20 Mar 2006.

[1290] *The Argus*, page 6, 17 October 1863.

[1291] *Victoria Government Gazette*), 1874.

[1292] *Victoria Government Gazette*, 1874.

[1293] *Victoria Government Gazette*, 1888.

[1294] Register of BDMs - Victoria, 1888 15610 father William Gunn, mother Janet Sinclair, age 84.

[1295] Letter from Janettie McMillan to Donald Gunn, 17 Oct 1974.

[1296] Letter from Janettie McMillan to Donald Gunn, 24 Apr 1974.

[1297] Being from p. 93 N. G. Butlin, *Investment in Australian Economic Development 1861-1900*, Cambridge University Press.

[1298] http://www.rushworthtourism.com.au/Stanhope.html

Modern transcript of a letter written by Cecilia Cormack Gunn (375) of Waranga Victoria to Janet Gunn Muckle (2563) in Canada

Letter written to Janet Muckle from her Aunt Cecelia who lived in Australia.
Waranga Park
October 6, 1893

My dear Mrs. Muckle

The last of your ever welcome letters dated March last reached me in due time. By it I was glad to hear that yourself and family and all belonging to you were then in good health and in the enjoyment of a share of the other blessings of life.
We are here moving along in the old way and each doing his and her duties as well as we can. Our boys are busy here preparing for the sheering which begins in a fortnight. We have had a very wet winter and the earth has got a fine soaking a state of things very desirable here and now as the warm weather advances everything looks lovely and green. Our garden looks charming at present the flowers these gems of the earth being all in bloom and in all their gayest hues of color. Our homestead is very pleasently situated on rising ground which slopes down to a small water course where Alexander made an embankment which conserves a fine sheet of water for our garden. But I am forgetting that Marnie has been with you for I am sure her valuble tongue will have described everything here about to you.
I suppose you hear from Marnie oftener than we do here for she seemed to enjoy hereself very much while with you. Don't you think it very queer of her staying there among strangers so far away from her own family more especially while her old mother is in the land of the living. I must tell you Janet that I was very angry with Marnie before she left here and I think you will say I had reason when I tell that she never entered her sister Bessie's home since she was married although her place is not two miles from here and I must tell you Bessie did not make a low marriage by any means. The Ingrams are all very respectable and Bessie chose Mr. Alex from among many other wooers. They are a very happy couple and she has a neat and pretty country home and a freehold of over 1000 acres of good land. Bessie has been in better health lately since the last operation was preformed, she has improved greatly. I forget whether I told you that Bessie had a second operation we had her over here for a time and two doctors attended her. Her side being probed four times while being under the influence of Chloraform. I don't know whether Marnie knows of all this or not as I never wrote her about it. As it seems to me Marnie estimation to be married is to have committed the unpardonable sin. I have no doubt but Marnie will be very much disappointed at her brother not taking the trip home that he intended taking when she left here. Since then our monetary institutions have been tumbling down one after another and causing a great deal of anxiety and loss to many who had their all invested in them. This state of things doubtless influenced Alex to give up his trip to the old country and to your big country and its big show. Some little time before I received your letter I noticed in a newspaper the death of your husband's relative Sir McClure and I was just wondering whether any of his wealth would come your way but in your letter you say it will not. Well never mind Janet as long as your own dear husband is spared and you and your young family around you and your own dear self reign Queen of hearts there- that is wealth of happiness than many cannot buy for the poet says "Mind hearts are more than Coronots and simple faith than to ??? blood" I am glad to hear you say that the dolman cape fitted you and pleased you so well. If I had thought it would ever reach you I would have had it lined. Our climate here is so hot for the most part of the year we are obliged to have our garments made as lightly as possible. I had a letter from Jane McDonald a short time complaining greatly of Marnie for not paying her a visit when she was so near. Do you think Marnie knew their whereabouts when she left you. As I have little to write about that would be of interest to you I must for the present conclude this scrawl. With kind love and regards to Mr. Muckle self and young folks. Believe me ever your affectly.
C. C. Gunn

"Waranga Park" Sale

One of the most important land sales of recent years was conducted at Murchison on Monday afternoon last, when Messrs John McNamara & Co. and Dalgety & Co. (agents in conjunction) submitted to auction the well-known property described as Waranga Park. The agents were acting under instructions from the executors of the late Mr William Gunn.

Waranga Park consisted of 2700 acres of splendid grazing land in the parishes of Murchison and Waranga, and the land was offered in eight separate lots. The sale created tremendous interest right throughout this district, and there was an exceptionally large attendance of the public at Messrs McNamara's & Co's. Murchison yards, where the auction was conducted.

The first lot offered is known as the Woolshed paddock, consisting of 171 acres, with a frontage to the Waranga Basin, and includes what is known as Gunn's Island. Bidding opened at £13 per acre, and quickly rose to £16, at which price it was knocked down to Mr Jim Finnigan, of Murchison, who owns the adjoining property.

Lot 2, known as the Big Paddock, containing 632 acres and situated on the north side of the Murchison-Rushworth road in the vicinity of Hammond's siding, was purchased by Mr Les. Hammond, of Murchison. Bidding started at £10 per acre and rose to £13, at which price it was knocked down to Mr Hammond's bid.

Lot 3 is known as Tals, and contains 299 acres. Bidding for this block also started at £10 per acre, and rose to £15/2/6, before it went to the bid of Mr Jim Hammond, of Murchison.

Lot 4, described as The Doctor's, and containing 320 acres on the south side of the Murchison-Rushworth road in the vicinity of Hammond's siding, was purchased by Mr Wallance Hamilton, of Murchison, at £13 per acre.

Lot 5 consisted of 624 acres of uncleared land on the boundary of the Moormbool State forest. Bidding started at 30/- per acre and rose to £4, at wiich price Mr D. Wilson, of Murchison, became the new owner.

Lot 6, known as Bowden's, in the parish of Waranga, contains 181 acres and was purchased by Mr W. Wilson, of Murchison, for £4 per acre.

Lot 7, described as Armstrong's, is situated on the south side of the Murchison-Rushworth road about three miles from Rushworth. It contains 175 acres. Bidding started at £4 per acre and quickly rose to £7/5/-, the purchaser being Mr W. Martin, of Tatura.

Lot 8, known as Kane's, contains 320 acres of good flat grazing land in the parish of Waranga, and is on the fringe of the Moormbool forest, a couple of miles south of the Waranga Basin. This block was purchased by Mr W. Wilson, of Murchison, at £8 per acre.

At the conclusion of the land sale, the agents conducted a sale of stock and plant on account of the executors of Waranga Park. About 1000 Merino and Merino - Corriedale Cross sheep were submitted in lots, and these brought splendid prices. 164 ewe weaners sold at £5/18/- each; 143 wether weaners, £5/0/6; 43 wethers, 2 and 3 years, £4/1/-; 116 wethers, 3 and 4 years, £5/7/-; 204 wethers, 4 years, £3/10/-; 33 mixed weaners, £3/15/-; 63 wethers, 5 yrs, £3/5/-; 8 Merino and Corriedale rams 8¾ guineas each.

Plant sold well. A 1951 model Vanguard Utility Truck brought £550; fencing posts sold at £20 per 100; Fordson Tractor, £200; Nicholson and Morrow Gardiner Wool Press £10; Wool Table £11; Platform scales £32; galvanised fencing wire £3 per coil, while numerous tools and sundries all sold at satisfactory prices

From an unknown newspaper

Letters from the Grand-daughter of William Gunn (374) of Waranga Park

… 21 Apr '74

Dear Mr Gunn,

A few months ago …[1299] gave me your address and suggested that I write to you … At the age of 80 I found the long sticky summer most trying and wrote as few letters as I could get away with. We are distantly related I understand.

I am the only Gunn grand-daughter of William Gunn Senr of Waranga Park, Waranga.

I am very keen of genealogy but did not begin early enough, while there were a few of the older generations on all sides still about. I am also dist. related to the family of the late Rev. Peter Gunn & Enid Gunn - Mrs Kirby - I have known for a lifetime who is one of his grand daughters.

When my grandmother and father arrived out here in 1857 they stayed with the Rev. Peter & Mrs Gunn at Campbellfield until grandfather was able to go for them - he came here in 1853.

I knew all the Millers in my early days very well. The years bring changes.

I have two books on the Clan, one by Thomas Sinclair MA 1890 and the recent one by Mark Rugg Gunn. I will enclose a tree of the family but that is about the best I can do about it - unfortunately.

I knew Rene Surman years ago & father & I met the brother in Ballarat after his return from the first war & also met Arthur Gunn then.

The best of our Waranga land is under the Waranga Basin & the rest I sold after my husband's death in 1953. My brother lived on until 1957 & in hospital for 3½ years.

I have tried so hard to get information from descs of grandfather's eldest brother Donald who was in Canada, though for years I wrote to several of the family & the only information I did get was so vague and of little help really.

The genealogical path is an uphill struggle. Donald had 5 sons. I hope you won't think I am intruding.

My son-in-law Jim Christoe had a Baglis mother & is a g.grandson of Henry Baglis, PM of Maffra (?) who was shot by Morgan & badly wounded. …[1300]

I do look forward to hearing from you,

Yours sincerely,

Janettie McMillan (*signed*)

Grandfather Gunn said to have been a cousin of Mrs James Miller but of what degree I don't know. … I met Gladys Gunn when she at MLC & again not long before her death.
Please excuse my blunders! *Hand drawn tree attached.*

[1299] A name is deleted here…

[1300] Some non-relevant personal discussion is deleted…

... 17 Oct '74

Dear Mr Gunn,

Thank you very much for your letter & family trees but I fear we are further apart than you think. I note that your ancestor Donald married a Jane Surman & her brother I expect it was who married Janet McLeod Gunn & Rene Surman & her brother Geoff in Ballarat must be their descs. Geoff died some years ago & probably Rene ??, a Mrs O'Connor or Connor I am not sure at this stage.
I will keep on trying to 'spread' our branch.
Mrs James Miller's brother was I expect I told you born Barbara Gunn - what family ? - again something to be found out if one can. I wonder can Jack Alex Gunn help. I have not yet been speaking to either since their return.
I may have told you that my aunt Margaret once told me that Mrs Miller was related to 3 Gunn families not related to each other.
I notice that Norman Gunn is on your tree - I met him at Miller's many years ago.
I have a strong idea that there is a McLeod & a Dunbar in my tree somewhere further back but if I ever prove it remains to be seen, anyway the sands of time are running out!
There was a ????? in early Scottish Genealogist (?) a few years ago about a George Gunn of Corrish & I will enclose a copy for you to think about, as to me it seems to suffist our line.
I go away next week to stay with my family for about a fortnight - my son-in-laws surname is Christoe & his ancestor from Swansea in Wales.
Kind regards from Janettie McMillan
According to the recent book by Mark Rugg Gunn the ancestors of my grandfather William Gunn of Waranga Park, Waranga & his brother Donald of Winnipeg & others is as follows but no wives or side lines are given.
Alexander McHamish -> George ->Alexander -> John -> William = Janet Sinclair.
Then Donald, died 1878 aged 81 = Margaret Swain whose father was a factor in the Hudson Bay Co and William, died Oct 88 aged 84=Cecelia Cormack, died 1906 aged 87 ->William 1853-1921 aged 68 = J.J.Ingram 1860 – 1957 aged 96½ ->Janettie

*****

William Gunn of Waranga Park's son; also called William Gunn.

His daughter was Janettie Gunn author of the preceding letters. William (Junior) was Waranga Shire Councillor 1897-1919 and President of the Waranga Shire1899, 1908 and 1915. He was also Chief of the Caledonian Society of Rushworth and a member of the council of the Victorian Scottish Union.

Sir John Gunn of Tormsdale (3250) 1837-1918[1301]

The biography of Sir John Gunn of Tormesdale is by P. R. Myers and is called "Sir John Gunn, the Cardiff Business Entrepeneur from Caithness," and it was published in 'The Caithness Field Club Journal' in October 1983. The complete article can be accessed at http://www.caithness.org/caithnessfieldclub/bulletins/1983/october1983/sirjohngunn.htm

It is an interesting, useful article and some of the key points are as follows—

'Sir John Gunn ... left his native county at the age of eighteen to begin his business apprenticeship in Newport, Monmouthshire in 1855. ...

John Gunn moved to Cardiff, coal exports had increased to two and a quarter million tons... The hundreds of ships ... required dry-docking facilities. The Mount Stuart Dry Dock was ... acquired in 1872 by a syndicate of which John Gunn was the principal promoter. Two years later, John was joined by his brother, Marcus who acted as manager ...

... the two brothers ... decided to enter shipowning themselves when they took delivery of the 1,481 gross tons iron steamer "Dunedin" ... By 1892, John and Marcus Gunn & Co. of 11 Mount Stuart Square, owned a further three vessels: the iron steamers "Cornelia" (894 gross tons, built 1872), "Dunbar" (1,774 gross tons, built 1876), and "Dunkeld" (2,791 gross tons, built 1880). ... The Gunns' tramp steamers were employed in the coal trade ... The Gunns were involved in a cut-throat business ... *(Steamers owned included the 'Lorna Doone' 1896-1898.)*

(John Gunn) was elected as president of the Cardiff Chamber of Commerce in 1886 and 1887 and again in 1897. In 1891 he was chairman of the Cardiff Shipowners' Association. As well as being chairman of the timber importers, John Bland & Co. Ltd., John Gunn held a number of directorships and he was to be found on the boards of the Cardiff Railway Company, the Bristol and West of England Bank, Cardiff Collieries (Llanbradach) Ltd. and several other public companies.

... In 1892 he unsuccessfully contested a Cardiff constituency on the Unionist ticket. For several years he was a member of Cardiff Town Council and in June 1898 ... the Cardiff Caledonian Society, of which he was founder, held a special banquet in celebration of the knighthood conferred upon him ... (he was) the principal founder of the Presbyterian Church in Windsor Place of which he was the senior elder for many years...

The Gunns' fleet of steamers always remained a modest one ... and by 1899 they had sold the elderly steamers "Cornelia", "Dunbar", and "Dunkeld", leaving them with their first ship, the "Dunedin". In 1903 the "Dunedin" was sold and was replaced by the "Renwick" (664 gross tons, built 1890) which in turn was sold two years later. For their subsequent tramp steamers, the Gunns adopted the limited liability system of ship ownership in which the ownership of each vessel was turned into a limited liability company. ... Honouring their birthplace in Caithness, the Gunn brothers had the steel screw steamer "Achlibster" (4,395 gross tons) built for them in 1906 by Richardson, Duck & Co. of Stockton-on-Tees. Her owners were the Achlibster S. S. Co. Ltd. and was managed by the Gunn brothers. A similar steamer, the "Bilbster", owned by the Bilbster. S. S. Co. Ltd., followed from the same builders in 1908.

In 1911 the managership ... was taken over by A. H. and E. Gunn. Arthur H. Gunn was one of Sir John's three sons (he also had six daughters) and I can only assume that E. Gunn was a son of Marcus Gunn[1302]. The younger Gunns

[1301] We would have included the complete article but we have not been able to find the copyright holder; the Caithness Field Club could not provide the required information.

added a third ship to the fleet, the steel screw steamers, "Chalister", which was built in 1913 by D. & W. Henderson & Co. Ltd., Partick, Glasgow. The "Chalister" was a typical shelter deck tramp steamer and was employed in the deep sea tramping trades throughout her career which lasted until 1942. She had a large cargo carrying capacity but like many such ships, she was underpowered and able to maintain only 8½ knots on 34 tons of coal per day.

The year in which the "Chalister" was built marked the peak of Cardiff's coal exporting prosperity when a staggering 10,576,506 tons of coal was exported. ... During the war itself, many ships were requisitioned by the Admiralty to serve as colliers which were needed to replenish the bunkers of the Royal Navy's warships. The s.s. "Bilbster" was requisitioned to perform this role .... While the "Achlibster" and "Chalister" survived the war, the "Bilbster" was not so fortunate because she was lost after a collision, east of the Azores on 21st November, 1917[1303].

Sir John Gunn died on 20th January, 1918 ...

A. H. & E. Gunn sold the "Achlibster" and "Chalister" in 1919 and never resumed shipowning although A. H. Gunn continued as a director of the Mount Stuart Dry Locks Ltd.'

In storage at 'The Historic Dockyard' in Chatham, Kent, is a builders' half-model of the s.s. "Chalister". It is available for viewing if one requests in advance.

It's a fascinating article about a major Gunn figure who has nearly disappeared from the history books. He deserves to be better remembered. The article is a little effusive but still very readable.

Further information can be found in—

- 'John O'Groat Journal' 8th February, 1918 (or the *South Wales Daily News* of a little earlier)
- *Who Was Who 1916-1928*
- *Who's Who* 1903

[1302] He was correct in this assumption; Ernest Gunn (3329) 1878-1916 was a son of Marcus Gunn and Mary Elizabeth Yeandle (3329).

[1303] http://newspapers.nla.gov.au/ndp/del/article/15614673?searchTerm=Gunn for a 1915 article concerning the 'Bilbster'; it carried 6710 tons of metal from the Australian Metal Company consigned to a company to London but really destined for Germany. The claim was whether the Gunns could claim the freight or whather it belonged to the Crown. It was reported in London on September 17. In October 'The Argus'of 8 October reports that J. and M. Gunn would get £2,546 of the proceeds and also see 'The Argus' of 20 September 1915, page 7.

S.S. Chalister. Reproduced with permission[1304].

S.S. Chalister 1924?

Marcus Gunn (brother of Sir John Gunn)

"The South Wales Daily News reported in 1899 the death, after a short illness, of Marcus Gunn, a native of Caithness and one of the most prominent business men in Cardiff. He was 54 years of age and best known in commercial circles outside Cardiff as a member of the firm of J. and M. Gunn, shipowners, his partner being his brother, Sir John Gunn. The firm was largely interested in the Mountstuart Dry Dock Company, who were entrusted with the work of raising the *City of Paris* from the Falmouth. The firm was also interested in Bland & Co. Timber merchants as well as other local enterprises. A remarkably able business man Marcus was often invited to devote time to public work, but the Free Library and Infirmary were the only institutions in whose management he took an active interest. His private library contained many rare volumes.

He was born at Westerdale, Caithness in 1845 and went to South Wales in 1864 as representative of a manufacturing firm in the North of England. After a short absence, when he filled the position of representative of an engineering firm at Glasgow he returned to Cardiff to join his brother in business at the Mountstewart Dry Dock and Engineering Works, subsequently becoming a partner in the undertaking. At the time of his death he was one of the directors of the company, as well as a director of Bland & Co. He left a widow and six children, the eldest son having attained his majority. *"Northern Ensign", undated, 1903*

[1304] Copyright http://www.clydebuiltships.co.uk and http://www.clydesite.co.uk (except where otherwise stated). Extracts from the database may be used so long as credit is given to this website with a full url published in printed material...

Ships / boats owned by J. and M. Gunn

'Caledon'; 384 gross tonnage and 303 net tonnage. 127.2 x 25.5 x 14.8 feet. She was a three mast planked on iron frame vessel. She was completed in August 1866 in Middlesborough by Harkass for Jones Bros. and named the '**R.H. Jones'**. In around 1875 she was sold to R. Cowell and Co of Cardiff who renamed her **'Richard Cowell'**. She was surveyed in Cardiff in 1878 and acquired by J. and M. Gunn who renamed it the '**Caledon**'. She was not in the Lloyds Register after 1884.

'Dunedin'; 2,284 gross tonnage and 1,412 net tonnage. 286 x 37.3 x 22.9 feet. She was an iron steamship, compound two cylinders by the builders. She was completed in September 1883 by W. Doxford and Sons, Sunderland for J. and M. Gunn as the **'Dunedin'**. In 1901 she was sold to the Bank of Athens and renamed the **'Beeby'**. She was wrecked in 1908.

'Dunbar'; 1,812 gross tonnage and 1,182 net tonnage. 280.2 x 34.0 x 24.0 feet. She was an iron steamship, compound two cylinders by R. Stephenson and Co. Newcastle. She was completed by W. Doxford and Sons, Sunderland for Farnham and Co. Newcastle and called **'Peer of the Realm'**. She was acquired J. and M. Gunn in 1885 and called the **'Dunbar'**, after various other companies had briefly owned her. She was posted missing in March 1898 on a voyage from Theodisia to Leith, with a cargo of barley.

'Dunkeld'; 2,796 gross tonnage and 2,117 net tonnage. 320.8 x 40.5 x 23.2 feet. She was an iron steamship, compound two cylinders by the builders. She was completed in 1880 by A. Stephens and Co. Glasgow and Called **'Katie'**. First trace of an owner is in 1887 where she was owned by Christopher Furness. In 1889 J. and M. Gunn acquired her and renamed her **'Dunkeld'**. She was lost east of Lobos Island, Uruguay, when on a voyage from Barry Dock, Wales, to Buenos Aires with a cargo of coal. (Check a map; they must all have walked to land!)

'Cornelia'; 903 gross tonnage, 553 net tonnage. 220.3 x 29.2 x 16.3 feet. She was an iron steamship, compound two cylinders by T. Richardson and Sons, Hartlepool. She was completed in January 1872 by Denton, Grays and Co. West Hartlepool for Fritz Herskind of West Hartlepool and was called the **'Cornelia'**. In 1886 the owners became Herskind and Woods. In 1889 she was acquired by J. and M. Gunn. On 13 August 1897 she was sold to Cornelia Steamship Co. Ltd. of Cardiff, being Guthrie, Heywood and Co. She was then sold to William Monroe of Cardiff on 8 May 1900. On 6 March 1917 she was captured by SM UC-43 (being a German Type 11 mine-laying submarine) and sunk by gunfire nine miles northwest of the Skelligs whilst on a voyage from Oporto to Cardiff with a cargo of pitwood. The SM UC-43 was sunk four days later at Muckle Flugga.

'Renwick'; 664 gross tonnage, 402 net tonnage. 180 x 28.1 x13.7 feet. She was a steel steamship; 3 cylinders by N.E. Marine Engineering Co of Newcastle. She was completed by Tyne 1 Shipbuilders of Newcastle for Renwick S.S. Co. (Fisher, Renwick and Co.) as **'Renwick'**. March 1903 she was stranded and wrecked. She was acquired by Sir John Gunn on 1 April 1904 and sold on 14 May 1906 to R. M. Horne-Payne of Walbrook, London which became the Renwick Co. Ltd (H.W. Harding) of Newcastle in c. 1907. She was sunk by collision in December 1911.

'Coronation'; 2,461 gross tonnage, 1,574 net tonnage. 286 x 40.7 x 18.2 feet. She was a steel steamship; 3 cylinders by Hutson and Son, Glasgow. She was completed by Grangemouth Dockyard Co in July 1894 for Macbeth and Gray, Glasgow and named **'Dunblane'**. In 1894 she was sold to M. Angel Cardiff and reamed the **'Phyllis Angel'**. On 26 May 1902 she was acquired by Sir John Gunn and renamed the **'Coronation'**. In 1903 she was onsold and renamed the **'Wilhelmine'**. There is no record of her in Lloyds Regsiter after 1904; perhaps she went to the Netherlands given the last name?

'**Achlibster'**; 4,395 gross tonnage and 2,820 net tonnage. 355.2 x 51.1 x 26.8 feet. She was a steel steamship; 3 cylinders by Blair and Co. Ltd. of Stockton-on-Tees. She was completed February 1906 by Richardson, Duck and Co. Stockton for Achlibster S.S. Co. Ltd (J. and M. Gunn and Co. Cardiff). She was later sold to Humphries of Cardiff and renamed **'Glofield'**. In c. 1927 she was then sold to Watts, Watts and Co and renamed **'Hampstead'**. Later she was sold to N. A. Cottakis of Greece and renamed **'Alecos'**. She was wrecked in 1935.

'Bilbster'; 4,478 gross tonnage and 2,790 net tonnage. 355.4 x 51.1 x 26.8 feet. She was a steel steamship; 3 cylinders by Blair and Co. Ltd. Stockton. She was completed January 1908 by Richardson, Duck and Co. of Stockton-on-Tees for Bilbster S.S. Co Ltd. (J. and M. Gunn Cardiff). In 1915 she was on Lloyds Register for A.H. Gunn and in 1917 for A.H. and E. Gunn. There are reports that she was naval collier during the First World War but another source says she carried oil fuel; she may have done both. On approximately 21 November 1919 she was lost in a collision east of the Azores.

'Chalister'; 5,344 gross tonnage and 3,369 net tonnage. She was a steel shelter deck steamship; 3 cylinders by the builders. She was completed by D. and W. Henderson and Co.Ltd of Glasgow for Chalister S.S. Co. Ltd (J. and M. Gunn and Co. Ltd.) in August 1913. In 1917 (possibly 1919) she was sold to Anglo-Newfoundland S.S. Co and in 1920 then sold to R.McLelland of Kingston, Ontario, Canada. She was then sold to Adam Bros., of Greenock in 1922. In 1924 she was sold to Turnbull, Scott Shipping and renamed the '**Haggersgate'**. In March 1936 she was sold to Seerederei Frigga of Germany and renamed the '**Hodur'**. On 20 April 1943 she was sunk by HM submarine 'Trident' northwest of Namsos, Norway.

John Gunn and Co. Registered vessels 1896-1899

These vessels were leased / hired.

'**Bonnie Doon'** a steam paddle steamer; 272 gross tonnage and 81 net tonnage. The builders were T. B. Scath and Co, in 1876; 1 cylinder by A. Campbell and Sons Glasgow. She was registered by John Gunn in October 1896 and certainly by 1899 was in other hands. She 'earlyon acquired the nickname 'Bonnie Beakdoon[1305]'' She was broken up in 1913 in Rotterdam.

S.S. Bonnie Doon

[1305] http://website.lineone.net/~tom_lee/bonniedoonimg.htm

'Lorna Doone' was a steam paddle steamer; 427 gross tonnage and 83 net tonnage. 220.05 x 26 x 9.2 feet; 2 cylinders by D. Rowan and Son Glasgow. In the name of J. Gunn October 1896, by 1899 sold to the Isle of Wight Steam Packet Co.

P.S. Lorna Doone

'Lord Tredegar' was an iron paddle steamer; 179 gross tonnage and 12 net tonnage. 192.1 x 18 x 7.4 feet. The vessel was completed by Fullerton and Co. Paisley for Lochgoil Stemaboat company, named '**Carrick Castle'**. It was also renamed **'Lady Margaret'** in 1888 and then **'Lord Tredegar'** in 1896. It was in the name of John Gunn in October 1896 as **'Lord Tredegar'** (being a minor aristocratic family with a notable eccentric to finish the line).

'Scotia' was an iron paddle steamer; 303 gross tonnage and 38 net tonnage. 211.2 x 21.8 x 8.3 feet. The vessel was in the name of John Gunn in October 1896 Llyods Rebister. In 1903 she became the **'Principessa Mafalda Epomea'**.

'Rover' was an iron paddle steamer; 188 gross tonnage and 87 net tonnage. 140.6 x 20.1 x 8.2 feet. She was originally called the **'Chepstow'** and built in 1874 for the Great Western Railway Co. She was in the name of John Gunn in 1896. It was wrecked in 1896.

Hon. John Alexander Gunn,[1306] (32)

John Alexander Gunn was born at Buninyong, near Ballarat in the state of Victoria, Australia on 11 February 1860. His father was Donald (1832-1901) who had emigrated to Australia (probably in December 1854) and who had then settled near Ballaarat which was then in the throes of a gold rush. Donald was a Councillor of the Shire of Ballaarat for two periods early in J.A.'s life - 30 August 1865 until 10 June 1867 and 15 August 1870 until 12 October 1874. For the period 11 November 1872 until 12 October 1874 he was President of the Shire. Donald was also Foundation Secretary of the first Highland Society in Victoria – namely The Buninyong Highland Society which was established in 1858. (The first Melbourne society was established in 1861 and the Victorian society was established in 1864.) Donald's wife was Jane Surman of Oxford who was born on 18 January 1836. Donald's mother was Barbara (1810-1844) who was the second child of Donald the Sennachie (1770-1861).

Little is known of the early years of J.A.'s life bar that his parents' home "Burrumbeet" was becoming more crowded—by the time he left it in 1878 to be a jackaroo at South Yalgogrin station near Ardlethan, New South Wales; he had six brothers and two sisters. One more sister, Catherine, was born in 1880 which was two years after J.A. had left home to drive cattle to Yalgogrin station.

In 1886 J.A. was promoted to the position of manager of the station, before this he had been the overseer. The station was then owned by the major Australian pastoral firm of Goldsborough, Mort and Company. Also, in this year, on 8 June[1307] he married Jessie Maria Turner at North Brighton in Melbourne. Jessie was born at Beechworth in Victoria which was then a small gold-mining, rural service town near the Victorian Alps. Her father, William, was born at Kirkconnell, Scotland and her mother Maria Reinhardt was born at Hessen Cassell in Germany. They were always much in love and Jessie had a major role in their marriage—she kept all of J.A.'s laboratory records and fought on his behalf for many years to try and gain recognition for J.A.'s scientific and public works after his comparatively early death.

Sometime between 1878 and 1888 it is believed that J.A. also wrote a novel called *The Conargo Blacks*. The Conargo region is near Wagga Wagga but nothing is known about the novel. His descendants do not have a copy, nor does any Australian library.

With the acceptance of the managerial position J.A.'s scientific instincts came to prominence. In 1888 J.A. rode in a Yalgogrin paddock with Marcus Daniel, one of his younger brothers. They saw sheep dead in what was a fine season. Initially they thought it was due to poison but it was due to anthrax. This was not unlikely as in 1885-1886 the area immediately around Yalgogrin, which is the Merool district of the Northern Riverina, was devastated by the disease. One could lose half of one's sheep a year and all sheep regions of Australia were being attacked. This was despite Pasteur discovering a vaccine in France in 1881.

[1306] By Alastair Gunn and first published in *The Ballarat Historian* vol.1, No.10 September 1983, with minor alterations 2009 / 2010.

[1307] *The Argus* 12 June 1886, page 1 and see the Nithsdale photograph on page 90. They were married by the Rev Hay, at Nithsdale.

Pasteur's vaccine, though, was inappropriate for Australian conditions—he demanded £38,000 for its use and it needed to be kept cool and injected twice, fourteen days apart. Australia had a small population so could not afford that amount of money. The summers were hot so the vaccine was not reliable and it was very difficult and quite expensive to round up stock twice for injections.

By the 1890s anthrax was rampant throughout the Australian colonies and only rarely would natural increases make up for losses caused by the disease. As a consequence the quality of most flocks was declining. Anthrax is a particularly nasty disease in that the better the season the worse is the anthrax. J.A. had many reasons to experiment. In 1892 Yalgogrin consisted of 129,000 acres and ran 26,600 sheep, 34 horse and 41 cattle - Goldsborough, Mort and Co. also owned many other properties.

Leslie W. Devlin, who lived at Junee, had tested Pasteur's vaccine in earlier years and he and J.A. were to become close friends. At Yalgogrin J.A. established a laboratory in which he attempted to conquer anthrax [1308]- it included a huge boiling down vat and a great brick chimney. Initially he used Devlin's notes which included some from Pasteur. (There is an apocryphal family story that J.A. locked himself in a room for four months and allowed no-one in and did not exit whilst he learnt adequate French to read Pasteur's notes; this I do not believe as his wife was fluent in French and helped her husband with the experiments.[1309]) J.A. boiled down old sheep until he gained a clear solution then, using a converted chicken brooder which is now held at the Glenfield Veterinary Research Station, he introduced the anthrax culture. By the 1893-1894 summer J.A. had created his own vaccine but it was still double dose like Pasteur's - it was used, though, to inoculate over half a million sheep in that season. In 1897 J.A. succeeded where Pasteur had not in that he did develop a single dose serum. This, basically, was to save the Australian livestock industry.

The serum did not keep as well as J.A. desired. Initially he tried to get Devlin to help him increase the longevity of the serum but he was not successful. John McGarvie Smith was then approached and within days the keeping quality of the serum was markedly improved. McGarvie Smith had previously worked on snake venene and there is a story that he used to get snake collectors to release all their snakes into one room and they would then have to accept McGarvie Smith's price or attempt to recapture all their stock.[1310]

McGarvie Smith expected and gained a partnership with J.A. for the production of the serum even though he had been involved with the research for a matter of days whereas J.A. had worked on it for years. J.A. was not happy about this - he talked it over with family and friends for some days but he had no alternative as McGarvie Smith knew the formula.[1311] The partnership was to greatly prosper financially but in human terms it was a disaster that got worse. Under the terms of the partnership each was to maintain a laboratory - McGarvie

---

[1308] J. A. Gunn applied for permission to keep microbes and inoculate animals in December 1893 and nothing equivalent can be found for McGarvie Smith. *The Sydney Morning Herald* 8 December 1893, page 7.

[1309] http://newspapers.nla.gov.au/ndp/del/article/15646852?searchTerm=Gunn

[1310] Quoted in R.Webster, *Bygoo and Beyond*, p.88.

[1311] Ibidem, p.87.

Smith was to vaccinate north of Sydney and J.A. was to vaccinate south of Sydney and in Victoria. The partnership was entered into in April 1895.

J.A. was to write of the immediate seasons that followed that

... last season we inoculated over a million sheep with one inoculation, and though this was the first season of its use ... less than 10 per cent had to receive the second inoculation to render them absolutely immune; and this season, as we are more and more perfecting the material, out of another million not 2 per cent required a second vaccination... (The) President of the New South Wales Board of Health stated that vaccine under the most favourable circumstances killed 5 per cent of the sheep treated; he undoubtedly referred to the published results of Pasteur's process as under no circumstances whatever will McGarvie Smith and Gunn's vaccine kill a sheep... (and we) have offered to give £1000 to the charities of Sydney if he can produce proof of any deaths having been caused by it out of the 3,750,000 sheep treated by us.[1312]

The challenge was never taken up: Pasteur's vaccine was now irrelevant as a cheap and foolproof method was now available.

J.A. continued to work for Goldsborough, Mort and Co. as well as working on the vaccine. In 1895 he was made a superintendent for all stations owned by the company in Southern New South Wales. This was as well as managing Yalgogrin. He was to continue being a manager and a superintendent until he resigned from the company in 1905. J.A. also had become a Justice of the Peace in 1896.

in 1897 J.A. moved from Yalgogrin to Borambola station which abuts the Murrumbidgee River, eighteen miles from Wagga Wagga. Sidney and Beatrice Webb visited him there. They wrote of their 1898 visit that J.A. and his

...family were already at lunch when we arrived about 12.30, the party consisting of the husband and wife, an unmarried sister, the book-keeper and a young jackaroo or "colonial experience" young man, together with various youngsters of all sizes and both sexes; later on a travelling school inspector and his friend drove up and joined the party in the usual free and easy Australian fashion. The meal was a scrimmagy mixture of mutton, tea, jam and buns, wire covers protecting some of the eatables from the depredations of the flies that swarmed through the room - (the Australians have not yet tumbled to wire netting over doorways and windows characteristic of the fly devastated districts of America). Our host proved to be an unusually interesting man. Australian born, of Scotch extraction, a successful manager of stations in different districts in New South Wales, he has devoted his leisure to a scientific investigation of Anthrax and had invented and patented a vaccine named after him - the Gunn vaccine. Last year he had vaccinated over one million sheep, receiving from 1½ d. to 2d. for each animal and supplying his own operators as well as his own vaccine. He was delighted to show us over his laboratory and glad enough to find someone interested in his hobby. He was a thorough-going individualist, objecting altogether to Government regulation and the necessity of taking out a license for his experimental work - a fine fellow for all that - hard working and upright, with that interesting combination of speculative intelligence and a keen commercial instinct which is so characteristic of the best type of Scotchman. For the rest he was a materialist in metaphysic, a reactionary in politics, and an autocrat in the home; keeping his woman kind in due subordination to his own requirements, his sister, a good-natured raw ugly Scotch girl, doing the housekeeping and looking after the children, and his wife, a delicate little bright minded Melbourne lady, devoting her whole time to keeping his

[1312] *The Australasian Pastoralists' Review* 15 January 1899.

laboratory in perfect order and watching, hour by hour, his "incubating" processes. As might have been expected, the elderly book-keeper was Scotch and the jackaroo was also Scotch and doubtless if we had enquired we would have discovered that the overseer was Scotch: this Station was in fact a little bit of Scotland transplanted; only religion had disappeared and free and easy colonial materialism had taken its place.[1313]

and on their return journey the Webbs again visited

...we again lunched with our friend Mr. Gunn. In the evening we dined with him and Mr. Mouritz at the little inn at Wagga. Our pleasant smoke with them in the evening on the balcony overlooking the main street of Wagga Wagga completed our impression that the "managers" formed one of the most hopeful sections of these Australian colonies.[1314]

It is an interesting picture of J.A. and his family but not, perhaps, entirely accurate. A.A. Phillips, a distinguished Australian critic, was later to write that Beatrice Webb's "portraits are a little unbalanced by her fondness for finding faults... Nevertheless she has a waspish acumen, and she almost always adds a vividness to our image of these personalities."[1315]

At Borambola J.A. was nearly burnt to death in a bushfire. The summer of 1901/1902 was particularly dry and the bushfires were immense. Of the party of three in which he was working to save Borambola pastures one was burnt to death, one survived unharmed and J.A. was burnt about the hands[1316]. In January 1903 Boer farmer delegates visited the property; 'which has several miles of frontage to the Murumbidgee and to Tarcutta Creek'.[1317]Bushfires also reappeared in the summer of 1903-1904 and in these only the Borambola homestead was left untouched. The local newspaper was stunned and believed that Borambola was the best protected property in the district.

Increasingly J.A. was leaving the Wagga Wagga area and generally in connection with his own business: he often visited Sydney where he stayed at the Hotel Metropole, and he regularly visited Melbourne (even being knocked unconscious by a tram when he was there in 1903.) J.A. was finding it increasingly difficult to fulfil all the demands on his time. He decided to employ his brother Marcus Daniel to act as a temporary manager on Borambola from April 1, 1902. Initially J.A. paid the salary from his own wage but the position was ratified with Goldsborough, Mort and Co. and Marcus was made a permanent employee. J.A.'s salary was cut from £350 to £150 to match the salary paid to the new employee.

[1313] ed. A.G.Austin, *The Webbs' Australian Diary 1898*, pp.58-60. The two extracts are used with the kind permission of the copyright holders The London School of Economics and Political Science and the publishers Pitman Publishing Pty. Ltd..

[1314] Ibid., p. 61.

[1315] A.A. Phillips, *Responses: Selected Writings*, "A Lady among the Yahoos," p.138 used with permission of the author.

[1316] *The Sydney Morning Herald* 30 December 1901, page 8) reports Mr J.A. Gunn, manager of Borambola, with his brother Norman Gunn, and three station hands, were watching the river for the anticipated crossing of the flames. About 4 p.m. the grass took fire by a point close to them. An attempt was immediately to suppress the outbreak, and for a time it appeared as if their efforts would be successful. The wind suddenly changed, and the men were trapped. Mr. Gunn shouted to the others to follow him and dashed through the flames. It was a frightful experience and those few awful moments are not likely to be forgotten by the unfortunate men... All with the exception of a young man named Frank Curley reached the break, but it appears Curley tried to avoid the flames by making a detour, and in doing so met a horrible death. His charred body was discovered some time later...Mr J.A. Gunn, the manager, also had his hands rather severely burnt...A futile effort was made to save their horses which had been tied up, but three were roasted to death and the other three had eventually to be destroyed...'.

[1317] http://newspapers.nla.gov.au/ndp/del/article/14521956?searchTerm=Gunn being for 'The Sydney Morning Herald' 15 January 1903, page 6. The confluence with the Murumbidgee is about six kilometres south of Oura in the Riverina area of NSW.

By mid-1905 J.A. had bought his own property which he called Braehour[1318] (it was previously called Gumly Gumly) and which adjoined the Borambola station. In August of this year he was to refer to himself as a "grazier residing at Braehour.., a Bacteriologist and Station Inspector."[1319] Increasingly he was leading the life of a wealthy pastoralist – his sons finished their schooling boarding at the leading rural Presbyterian school of Victoria namely Geelong College; he had become a member of various rural pressure groups;[1320] he had acquired property ranging from at least four houses in Sydney to land outside Geelong and, in particular, in 1908 he was appointed Chairman of the Council of Advice on Rabbit Extermination[1321]. This occurred to a large extent because of his work at Yalgogrin on a chicken cholera virus[1322] with which he inoculated rabbits. This disease became known as the "Yalgogrin disease" and was a forerunner of the myxamatosis control of rabbits—the disease also spread to France where it was known as "the Australian disease."

Relationships with McGarvie Smith had not improved. From late 1905 on letters to McGarvie Smith were going via J.A.'s solicitor - on November 12, 1906 J.A. wrote about McGarvie Smith that "the man is a devil neither more nor less and a mad one at that but with the cunning of the devil himself."[1323] In 1907 J.A. was writing to the Tax Commissioners apologising for sending in an incomplete return but his partner was not providing him with full financial information.(Interestingly, when the information did come, it seems that J.A.'s income for the 1907 financial year was £3100—an average income at this time could not have been much over £100.) The partnership was brought to arbitration in July 1907 and it still required an arbitrator's services when J.A. died. When the figures were produced for the arbitrator it was shown that J.A. had vaccinated nearly 2,000,000 more sheep than McGarvie Smith at a cost of more than £50 per 100,000 sheep less than McGarvie Smith. Over 13,000,000 sheep had been vaccinated at this time as had sundry other stock.

In many respects the public career of J.A. culminated in his appointment to the Upper House of the New South Wales parliament on 10 July, 1908. As a Member of the Legislative Council J.A. was in a position to exert even more influence[1324] over rural life than he had already, especially as then an M.L.C. although not paid was appointed for life. J.A. was, though, a Liberal Party[1325] nominee. He tried to help the rural community by taking a major part on a Closer Settlement Bill in 1909, he was on a select committee for a new Sydney abbatoir and he tried to improve rolling stock to rural areas. General ill-health was, though, restricting him.

1318 http://www.beleura.org.au/History.htm for information about a later owner of Braehour and http://adbonline.anu.edu.au/biogs/A120184b.htm

1319 Letter, August 1905, Deposit 55, A.N.U. archives.

1320 Before 1897 J.A. was Chairman of the Narrandera Pastures Protection Board. By his death he had been Chairman of the Wagga Wagga P.P.B., Chairman of the P.P.B. Council of Advice in Sydney, a member of the Kyeamba Shire Council, Vice President of the Murrumbidgee Pastoral and Agricultural Association and a member of the Council of the Stockowners' Association of N.S.W.. By 1902 he was a member of the Taxpayers' Union http://newspapers.nla.gov.au/ndp/del/article/14453128?searchTerm=Gunn . In 1905 he was a member of the Murrumbidgee Fish and Game Protection and Anglers' Society http://newspapers.nla.gov.au/ndp/del/article/14713190?searchTerm=Gunn

1321 http://newspapers.nla.gov.au/ndp/del/article/14784643?searchTerm=Gunn and http://newspapers.nla.gov.au/ndp/del/article/14845100?searchTerm=Gunn

1322 See *The Sydney Morning Herald*, page 6 8 April 1908.

1323 Letter to lawyer, 12 November 1906, Deposit 55, A.N.U. archives.

1324 http://newspapers.nla.gov.au/ndp/del/article/15070625?searchTerm=Gunn for a report on one of his activities.

1325 He was, though, like most of his class and time, an Anglophile. See 'The Mercury' 2 September 1908

He was a regular attender for the 1908 and 1909 sittings but J.A. attended only four times in 1910 before being given leave of absence in August 1910. J.A. died in Sydney on the 21st September 1910[1326] and was buried in the Presbyterian section of the Rookwood cemetery. His wife (Jessie) and three children (Gladys, Alexander and Angus) succeeded him. A fourth child (Jessie) was buried at Yalgogrin in 1891.

The disagreements with McGarvie Smith[1327], though, were to continue[1328]. Increasingly McGarvie Smith was to claim most responsibility for the vaccine—he even donated £10,000 to the government for the creation of a McGarvie Smith Institute which was to control the manufacture and use of the vaccine. This Institute was opened in 1918. Jessie[1329], on behalf of J.A.'s executors, had already attempted to donate the formula[1330] to the State Government however this offer was only accepted after McGarvie Smith's. When the Glenfield Veterinary Research Station was opened in 1923 one wing was to become the Gunn wing[1331] to commemorate Jessie's 1918 gift. (The only condition on the gift was that J.A.'s name be associated with it.) The McGarvie Smith Institute still exists and there was a wooden plaque over one door at Glenfield commemorating J.A.. The State Cabinet was involved in the McGarvie Smith - Gunn dispute in 1918—one newspaper was even headed "Anthrax vaccines - manacling the Government."[1332] The dispute with McGarvie Smith was never satisfactorily resolved—J.A. believed that "McGarvie Smith is simply green with jealousy and hatred."[1333] If so, he hated J.A. for a long time.

J.A. was a man of strong character and major achievements: he was dedicated to science, pastoral work and his family. He was exceptionally hard-working but very popular. He was also a man who achieved much for the Australian pastoral industry—he invented the first mechanical poison-bait layer for rabbit control which was manufactured in Sydney and widely copied; he attempted viral control of rabbits and he stopped anthrax from ruining the Australian livestock industry. He then went on to serve rural Australia from the Parliament of New South Wales. John Alexander Gunn was one of many Australians who made large contributions to a 'young' country with unfortunately little lasting recognition.[1334]

****

[1326] http://newspapers.nla.gov.au/ndp/del/article/15165918?searchTerm=Gunn for the burial notice and chief mourners.

[1327] *The Sydney Morning Herald* of 3 July 1896 gives the background to McGarvie Smith's assorted experiments (photography, electricity, assaying, originally a chronometer maker, snake poison…)

[1328] 'Jim Cunningham and other neighbours, who had no doubts at all as to who was mainly responsible for the final discovery, bitterly resented the way in which Gunn's share in it was overlooked.' P. 89, Rob Webster, *Bygoo and Beyond*. And http://newspapers.nla.gov.au/ndp/del/article/15652008?searchTerm=Gunn . And http://newspapers.nla.gov.au/ndp/del/article/15648133?searchTerm=Gunn. And http://newspapers.nla.gov.au/ndp/del/article/16136760?searchTerm=Gunn

[1329] Jessie continued to run Braehour for some years; for example it was reported in *The Argus* 27 December 1916 that one of the haystacks was hit by lightning and destroyed. It was worth £100. http://newspapers.nla.gov.au/ndp/del/article/1623825?searchTerm=Gunn

[1330] http://newspapers.nla.gov.au/ndp/del/article/15806715?searchTerm=Gunn and http://newspapers.nla.gov.au/ndp/del/article/1754029?searchTerm=Gunn

[1331] *The Sydney Morning Herald* 3 November 1923 page 15,

[1332] *Daily Telegraph* 25 October 1918.

[1333] Letter to lawyer, July 1908, Deposit 55, A.N.U. archives.

[1334] http://newspapers.nla.gov.au/ndp/del/article/15178029?searchTerm=Gunn or http://newspapers.nla.gov.au/ndp/del/article/10477323?searchTerm=Gunn for a summary of his will.

M'GARVIE-SMITH & GUNN'S

Anthrax Vaccine.

Approved of and used by the Governments of New South Wales, Victoria, and New Caledonia.

PROTECTION BY ONE INOCULATION.

Over Ten Million Sheep and Cattle Successfully Treated.

SEASON, 1906-1907.

MINIMUM RATES: Sheep, 1½d.; Cattle, 6d. per head.

Special Discounts on Lots of 20,000 and over

(Belonging to one Owner).

TERMS—CASH on COMPLETION OF INOCULATION.

The business carried on under the name of GUNN'S VACCINE being merged into the above, and the Vaccine being now manufactured with great improvements introduced by Mr. J. M'GARVIE-SMITH. The difficulty of carriage being overcome by the new process, uniformity of results is assured.

The Firm issue Certificates, approved of by the Stock Department of Victoria, to owners of stock vaccinated by them in New South Wales, which acts as a passport for such stock to cross the border into Victoria or into New Caledonia during the Anthrax Season. Such Certificates remain operative for twelve months from date of vaccination.

Owing to the great difficulty in preparing a sufficient supply of tested *Single* Vaccine during the rush of the Anthrax Season, the Firm wish it to be understood that, while giving owners the benefit of this process whenever practicable, they reserve the right to give two inoculations when necessary, the scale of rates being the same for either *single* or *double* inoculations. The Vaccine in all cases being administered by their thoroughly trained operators; owners finding and paying catchers.

References will be given on application to the owners of over eleven million five hundred thousand Sheep and Cattle successfully treated by the improved process.

We have much pleasure in stating that the giving protection by *one inoculation* introduced by our Mr. J. M'GARVIE-SMITH has, since its introduction, been successfully used over 10,500,000 (ten million five hundred thousand) Sheep and Cattle.

Full Particulars on Application to
J. McGARVIE-SMITH, Denison Street, Woollahra, Sydney,
or J. A. GUNN, Braehour, Wagga Wagga.

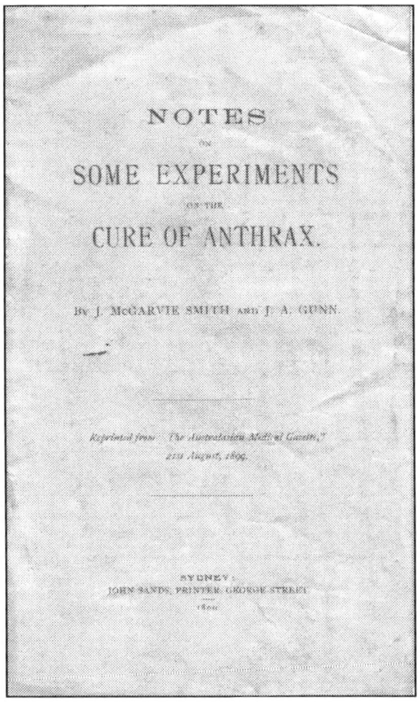

NOTES

ON

SOME EXPERIMENTS

ON THE

CURE OF ANTHRAX.

By J. McGARVIE SMITH and J. A. GUNN.

Reprinted from "The Australasian Medical Gazette,"

SYDNEY:

JOHN SANDS, PRINTER, GEORGE STREET.

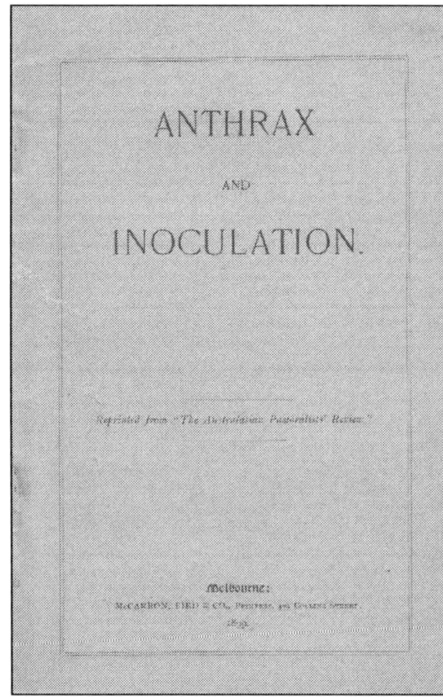

ANTHRAX

AND

INOCULATION.

Reprinted from "The Australasian Pastoralists' Review."

Melbourne:

Mr Gunn always strongly opposed the use of poisons for dealing with the rabbits. "If this practice is persisted in," he says, "the eventual effect will be the entire destruction of our useful birds, and after that we shall have plagues of insects which will be far more ruinous to rural interests than even the rabbit"

The Sydney Morning Herald, 26 November 1913

The original J.A. Gunn microscope, is in the family's ownership, 2007. A Carl Zeiss Jena 12213 model.

J. A. Gunn

Mr. James Miller's (117) Reminiscences

Being an extract from a newspaper (unknown). It is mainly about Mr James Miller[1335] *who was the husband of Catherine Gunn (1830-1912) who was Donald's (Scotland / Australia) elder sister.*

MELBOURNE BEFORE 1852

Of men who have seen Melbourme grow up to what it is, whose memories go back to Ballarat before the Eureka Stockade, there are only two or three - perhaps not that number - still engaged in business in the city. Mr James Miller, head of the well-known rope and mat manufacturing firm, in Little Collins Street is one of them. The period covered by his personal observation is of special interest to Australians, because it bridges the whole gulf between the Melbourne of blacks and bullock wagons and riverside humpies and the Melbourne of to-day. Before he came to Australia he can remember, as a child in Scotland, seeing school children go by with the word "Reform" printed on the sashes they were carrying. That was part of the First Reform Bill agitation of 81 years ago! He was himself a sympathiser in the Chartist riots, ten years later. As a young man in the twenties, Mr Miller has stood on the deck of the old Lady Franklin as she lay off Norfolk Island, and seen the convicts pulling out to the ship, with the heavily armed warders sitting at the stern. Strange weird-looking objects these convicts must have been, with their solitary garment a blanket, through which holes were pierced to give their arms egress. At Hobart in the early fifties, he has fraternised with John Mitchell, Smith O'Brien and O'Donahoo, three of the Irish patriots who narrowly escaped the gallows in 1849. In Tasmania, also, he has seen the "wild white man," Buckley, whose life among the blacks of Port Phillip has become the part of history. He was in Melbourne before the first electrifying news of the gold discoveries was made known, and he was a Ballarat miner some years prior to Peter Lalor and Lola Montez. Mr Miller, at the age of 87, speaks of these events, and of still earlier ones, with a keen appreciation of their significance, and with a memory that is still remarkably good - with something, too, of the typical Scotchman's eagerness to fight political and theological battles over again.

"One of my earliest recollections," he stated, recently,"is seeing the herring fleet go out from Wick, the town in the North-east of Scotland where I was born. It was at the time the largest fishing town in Scotland, and during the herring season more than a 1000 boats would go out together[1336]. Robert Louis Stevenson, who spent some time in Wick while his father built the pier there, says that the sailing of the herring fleet was one of the grandest sights he ever saw. I remember Elizabeth Fry coming to Wick, and also Dr Ritchie, but very few important visitors came so far north. There were no coaches, and the only means of communication

---

[1335] Further information on his life and times can be found in *The James Miller Story* (Prahran, Victoria: D.W.Paterson Co, 1962). *The James Miller Story*, published for the centenary of James Miller & Co, 1962: James Miller. Born in 1826 at Wick, Caithness, in the north of Scotland, he died in 1918 at the age of 92, after 54 years with the company. He arrived in Australia in 1850, tried his luck in the goldfields, and worked as a ship chandler before he established his rope business. In 1854, he sent home for his childhood sweetheart, Catherine Gunn, whom he married in Geelong. One of their sons, J D Miller, became secretary and a director of the company in 1918. James Miller's youngest daughter, Katherine, married W P Vine, and their son, F S Vine, was managing director until 1960. Today (*1960s*) his son, James Miller Vine, a great grandson of James Miller, is with the company. James died at 92 in 1918, six years after Catherine's death.

[1336] Neil M. Gunn's excellent novel *The Silver Darlings* evokes Caithness at this time.

with the South when I was a boy was a little schooner that came a few times a year. I learned to be a ropemaker in Wick, but made up my mind to get away to America or Australia. I was influenced in favour of Australia by hearing Dr. Lang lecturing about it. I don't know whether people now remember much about him—I met him in Melbourne years afterwards. I left Wick in the forties; spent some months in Glasgow, where I worked at my calling, and saw Fanny Kemble, Madame Vestris and Charles Matthews act; and going on to London left there on June 28th, 1850, in the sailing ship Australasia, partly working and partly paying my passage. Three and a half years later we reached Hobart, where the convict system was still in full swing."

Mr Miller saw Sydney for the first time in 1851-and was rather surprised to find it so large a place. He distinctly remembers seeing the bullock wagons in Pitt-street. For the best part of a year after reaching Tasmania he worked as a sail maker, on the Lady Franklin, and made three voyages on her between Hobart and Norfolk Island. He saw Martin Cash at Norfolk Island, and bought a cabbage tree hat that he had made. The Lady Franklin was engaged in taking men who had served their time back from Norfolk Island, and in taking stores, etc., out to that remote spot. Of the strange life stories represented by some of the passengers in that ship Mr. Miller could have said a good deal at one time. He recalls some of them now; but the passage of sixty years has swept the Norfolk Island prisoners, their misfortunes, their crimes and their life tragedies into oblivion. Only a shadow or two remains in the pages of Marcus Clarke and Price Warung, and in the memory of a diminishing remnant of people alive to-day.

Mr Miller gave up the sea, and came to settle in Melbourne about the end of June, 1851. He had been there just a week when news came of the discovery of gold, first at Clunes, and then at Ballarat. The stir and the tumult and the call to arms created by that astonishing discovery-one destined to remould and furnish Australia-are fresh in the mind of the Melbourne manufacturer to-day, though two generations of settlement have trodden in the wake of the pioneer settlers of 62 years ago.

Mr Miller tried his luck with others at the gold fields, and struck what might be considered an average of success. He did not become wealthy all at once, but his digging was not a total failure. "I remember," he said "when I went to Ballarat in 1851-I was with a party that walked all the way. When we arrived there were about 8000 or 9000 men on the field. Our party worked together for about four weeks, and in that time we got only about 8 oz. of gold. We decided to separate and each work for himself. I joined forces with a Cornishman, and as a result of the first day's digging, we got 2 oz. each. Next day a piece of clay fell as my mate was going down into the workings—they were not more than about six feet deep in those days, and he thought it a bad omen and left. I found another Cornishman for a partner, and worked on. After four months we had about 60 oz. each. We tried to sell it in Melbourne, having made the journey back there in a cart, but there was only one buyer, Mr. J. Hart and all he could offer was £2 10/ an oz.. My mate took this but I sent mine home through Mr. Fulton, and got the full £4 an oz. I had some months longer at the digging and left in 1852. Yes, that was before the Eureka Stockade; but I remember reading about that when I had gone into business in Geelong. The men who pioneered the diggings are gone now. I suppose there not many left of the 8000 or 9000 we found at Ballarat in 1851, but they were a fine lot of men, take them for all in all. They were good and bad, of course—any number of black sheep; but if you had sat around a mining camp fire in those days you would have met men of every kind, of good birth and bad birth, of great ability, some of them, and all sorts of attainments—men that you don't meet nowadays. Yes, I suppose, they have pretty well all gone."

Mr Miller's connections with Victorian manufacturers goes back 60 years. In the early fifties he left the diggings to go into business at Geelong. The town on Corio Bay was then threatening to rival Melbourne. Mr Miller started a coal yard and ship chandler business in Geelong, and, giving up a roving life, married a Miss Gunn, who, like himself, was a native of Scotland. Mrs Miller, who lived to be 82, died only a few months ago. In 1862 Mr Miller moved up to Melbourne. He turned his early experiences as sailer and sail maker to account by starting a rope and hemp business that was the parent of the one now carried on in his name. As a progressive Victorian he has done much for local industries, and it is largely due to him that the flax of Gippsland is now a valuable asset in local production. He still attends the fortnightly business meetings of his firm. His interest in all forms of activity-literary, political and social, as well as commercial-is that of a man who carries generous sympathies and abilities into a retirement well earned.

The detail here is largely repeated in 'The James Miller Story' (Prahran, Victoria: D.W.Paterson Co, 1962).

Part 8—*The Gunns* by Thomas Sinclair

There are various histories of the Clan Gunn; *The Gunns* by Thomas Sinclair being one of the earliest and best known. *The Gunns* by Robert Russell Gunn is of 171 pages with the first part being ageneral retelling of the Clan history, the second part being on various USA Gunn families. Much more readily available is Mark Rugg Gunn's *History of the Clan Gunn* which includes discussion of characters in this book; we recommend it.

THE GUNNS.

BY

THOMAS SINCLAIR, M.A.,

AUTHOR OF "HUMANITIES," ETC.

WICK:
WILLIAM RAE.
1890.

Extracts—

Another letter to the same, addressed, "George Gunn[1337], Esqre., Factor for the Marquis of Stafford, Assynt," is as follows:-

Thurso, 3rd September, 1821. Mr Gunn, Dear Sir,-Our intention of writing you and giving you this trouble is that our name was near to be buried in oblivion, and that in former times there was gaining the world by strength of arm, but now people must fall upon better method for providing for future accidents and distress. Therefore our intention (as proposed by some of our best men) was to form ourselves into a society, by which we should come to know the strength of our number. There are

[1337] George Gunn was the legally dubious Chief of the Clan Gunn at this time.

none to be admitted but those that can spell Gunn as their name. By several circumstances, and owing to the way that Sutherlandshire was flitted [cleared], we have most of the clan in this country, except a few in the army. We expect to muster about 200 men to form the society, who will, it is proposed, wear the clan tartan at the yearly meeting. The time of commencing thought to be most convenient is at or about Martinmas, when we shall look upon it as the greatest satisfaction that could be bestowed on us at the time, to have your presence as president at the meeting. It would also encourage the poor dispersed to gather from every corner, which they are very keen upon, so far as we have heard from them. We are to be looking for your opinion, and also if you are to attend, by course of post, when we shall know better what time we should meet together. We are at every exertion to gather names, but we do not intend to go further until we hear from you; so we must wait to have your letter to show to them to encourage them. No doubt we are strangers to you, but not altogether without relationship, which would be kept very affectionately by our forefathers. We remain, with Best wishes to you, Your most obedient servants, DONALD GUNN, Braehour; ALEXANDER GUNN, merchant, Thurso.

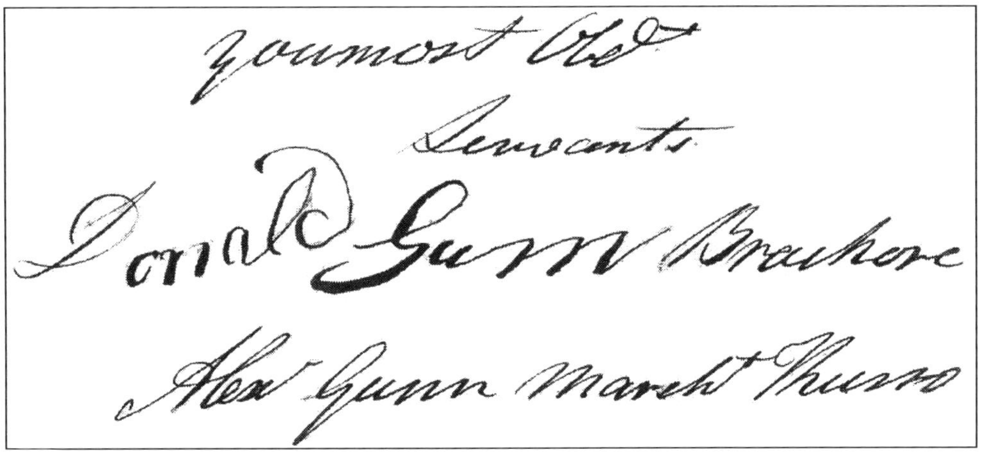
Your most Obedt
Servants
Donald Gunn Braehore
Alexr Gunn Marcht Thurso

The original of this document is held in the County Archives at Wick.

The former of these subscribers was father of Captain Gunn, the other being of the Achnakin family, Kildonan, son of the witness Robert of 1803. It was in 1820 that George, the McHamish, became factor in Assynt, and on getting the appointment he retired from the Royal Navy on half pay. In 1824 he was promoted to the factorship at Dunrobin Castle. Before giving some account of this Gunn Society, which anticipated the Mackay Society, the last of these Braehour invaluable MSS. must have its place. It is addressed, "George Gunn, Esqre., Lochinver," the factor of Assynt, and reads:-

Swiney, 1st April, 1823. My dear Sir,-It is now so long since we have communicated with each other that we are almost worn out of acquaintance. I intended to have written soon after your men left here, as I was very anxious to hear of their safety, which I did immediately on their arrival at home. I intend setting out to-morrow for Inverness, and will leave this and a copy of the regulations of our society at Ardgay. We will expect your attendance at the annual meeting on the last Thursday of June, for the day has been changed of purpose to secure your presence. We have only 61 members yet, but I expect that we shall make out 100 before the end of the year.

Have you no intention of getting spliced? The clan will absolutely mutiny unless you bestir yourself and leave a pistol to succeed you. To be serious, I fear you are becoming a determined bachelor. Perhaps you are only waiting to see the issue of Prince Hill's expedition lest you should be called off in the middle of the honeymoon.

May I request the favour from you to send Cathil McKenzie of the men who were here last season, as we shall not lay in any more stock than is exactly necessary for the number of boats we may expect. They will get the same price as is paid on this coast by any respectable curer. I regret that I could not send you any red herrings last year as we made none, but I hope this will not be the case again. Make offer of my best respects to Miss Gunn and to all my Assynt acquaintances. I shall expect to hear from you at your earliest convenience. I am, My dear Sir, Yours most truly, J. GUNN.

This Lieutenant John Gunn, merchant in Swiney, was the first president of the Loyal and United Benevolent Society of the Clan Gunn, instituted at Thurso, 18th December, 1821.

Pp. 171-172

*****

President, John Gunn, merchant in Swiney; treasurer, Alexander Gunn, merchant in Thurso; keymaster, Alexander Gunn in Osculay[1338]; stewards, Donald Gunn, farmer in Breahour; George Gunn, innkeeper in Thurso; William Gunn, farmer in Knockglass; John Gunn, messenger in Dunbeath; managers, Alexander Gunn, shoemaker in Buolkork; James Gunn, messenger in Thurso; Peter Gunn in Swiney; Robert Gunn, farmer in Olgrimbeg; clerk and secretary, John Gunn, Thurso.

On the blank back of the title-page is written, "No. I., George Gunn, Esq., Assynt, enrolled a member, 18th December, 1821, JOHN GUNN, *Preses*."

P. 174.

*****

His son George, Lieutenant of the Royal Navy, factor for the Duke of Sutherland, married Margaret, a daughter of Macdonald of Skeabost or Kingsborough, Skye, and was served heir in 1814. He died in 1859. His eldest son was Donald, a factor in Cornwall, who died without issue in 1863, chieftain four years. An only brother, Hector of the unfortunate Agra Bank, succeeded him, but he also died without issue in 1874. These two McHamishes do not seem to have taken the trouble and expense of serving themselves heirs. By one of the genealogical trees, which are always to be suspected till thoroughly established by legal inquisition, Captain Gunn traces his nephew back to a second son of John of Kinbrace, Alexander Gunn, Dalnaglaton, who died in 1765. His son John, Braehour, died in 1810. Donald, Braehour and Brawlbin, who died in 1861, was John's son and successor. Donald's eldest son was John in Durness, whose son Alexander is chieftan of the clan Gunn. Alexander's heirship goes back to the same McHamish as that of Hector Gunn, Thurso, did in 1803; the latter's *abavus* or great-great grandfather, their common ancestor. "Hector Gunn, Thurso, and my grandfather," Captain Gunn says, "were first cousins;" their fathers, George of Knockfinn, and Alexander, Dalnaglaton, being brothers, the son of John of Kilbrace, son of George of Borrobol, second son of Alexander of Killernan and Navidale in the middle of the 17th century, the above McHamish. If Alexander in Durness can back this genealogy with legal evidence from parish registers, public and private documents, or other sound sources, he is the McHamish of the time. Captain Gunn's accuracy, love of antiquities, and lineage enthusiasm give every hope that he could enable Alexander to establish his position before the most exacting and searching legal tribunals. Till this be done it is impossible to accept on his assertion, however detailed and probable, what may be only the tree mania which has attacked so many of the gallant Gunns. His interest in his ancestors has always been keenly intelligent, and a suggestive proof of the fact is that he possesses now a bed of George in Corrish's eldest brother Alexander, the McHamish

P. 176

We note that later analysis shows the above to be a good story, but not factually accurate.

[1338] It is possible that this might have been Catherine of Osclay's brother; she was the wife of Donald Gunn (Sennachie) (798).

Borrobol Estate, 2011

It is said that Alexander Gunn, Durness, clever, handsome, and well-to-do, has not asserted his rights as the real living McHamish, and chief of the clan, because he is only a subordinate official of the Duke of Sutherland. As ground-officer in his district, his modesty forbids him to assume the headship; but if fortune should further favour him, he would push to be returned heir to Factor Gunn's son, the last McHamish. Such diffidence is wholly unnecessary; for in the palmy days of the clan system it was the glory of a chief to have no property in land or goods, these belonging to the whole clan, who contributed to the sustentation of their leader, as Free Church and other congregations do now to that of their ministers. The chivalry of Celtic society lay precisely in this fact; and any modern Gunn who would object to his chief on the ground of not drawing thousands a year from land or from stocks or other investments, is out of court, as an ignorant and a Phliistine.

More promising credentials than Alexander's it would be difficult to desire. His uncle, Captain Gunn, Braehour, now seventy-six, is admitted to be, if not the greatest, at least a genuine, living authority on Gunn questions; and he is thoroughly assured of his nephew's being the rightful McHamish and chieftain. It were strange if the captain had not been well posted up in all historic points, seeing that his father, Donald Gunn, Braehour, was the acknowledged Sennachie or historian of his time, and that from him he has derived most of his traditional and other knowledge. So much had the Braehours been accepted, that Factor Gunn's son, that last McHamish, before his death, sent to Captain Gunn, as one of his nearest relatives, all the papers on the subject which he possessed, a few of which have appeared in this appendix. It is worth adding the as Donald Gunn's mother was May, a daughter of Dumbar of Hempriggs, he had thus interest and insight with respect to the ruling families as well as the Gunns, of which he took full advantage as an unusually learned Sennachie. Since it is to be hoped that the pedigree of Alexander in Durness will soon be submitted to public legal decision, it is unnecessary to state here the ample collateral details which exist, the persons of the main succession having been given. That there is no fear of failure of heirs to the chieftaincy in this branch may be gathered from the fact that the Hon. Donald Gunn, Manitoba, Canada, Captain Gunn's first cousin, and Alexander in Durness's, once removed, has himself seven or eight sons; and there are others, in Australia and elsewhere, of similar condition.

Pp. 185-186

Kinbrace, 2011

Appendices

1. Descendants of Hugh Gunn in Tormsdale (295)[1339]

Hugh Gunn in Tormsdale (295), b. 1787 Tormsdale, Halkirk Parish, Caithness, d. between 1841 and 1851 Halkirk Parish, Caithness
+**Henrietta MCGREGOR of Dalnawillan** (752), b. 1795 Latheron Parish, Caithness, m. 28 Oct 1814, d. 15 Apr 1890 Houstry, Dunbeath Parish, Caithness

├── **William GUNN** (807), chr. 24 Sep 1815 Inishmull, Halkirk Parish, Caithness
├── **Janet GUNN** (3230), chr. 04 Apr 1817 Inishmull, Halkirk Parish, Caithness, d. 15 Aug 1890 Houstry, Dunbeath Parish, Caithness
├── **Catherine GUNN** (3231), chr. 10 Jan 1819 Inishmull, Halkirk Parish, Caithness, d. 17 Mar 1913 Lybster, Latheron Parish, Caithness
│ +**Alexander MCDONALD** (3723), b. 1803 Latheron Parish, Caithness, m. 30 Oct 1857 Latheron Parish, Caithness, d. circa 1891 Latheron Parish, Caithness
│ ├── **Christina Sutherland MCDONALD** (3727), b. 13 Apr 1859 Latheron Parish, Caithness, d. 1876 Latheron Parish, Caithness
│ └── **Henrietta MCDONALD** (3728), b. 10 Jan 1861 Latheron Parish, Caithness
├── **Helen GUNN** (3232), b. 29 Sep 1822 Camster, Latheron Parish, Caithness
├── **Christina GUNN** (3233), b. 1825 Camster, Latheron Parish, Caithness, d. 24 Apr 1863 Houstry, Dunbeath Parish, Caithness
├── **Henrietta GUNN** (3234), b. 1827 Camster, Latheron Parish, Caithness
│ +**John CAMPBELL** (3730)
│ └── **Mary CAMPBELL** (3729), b. circa 1853 Latheron Parish, Caithness, d. 15 Mar 1934 Duthill, Inverness
│ +**Neil SINCLAIR** (3731), b. 03 Jan 1857, m. 09 Feb 1882 Houstry, Dunbeath Parish, Caithness, d. 11 Mar 1939
│ ├── **Alexander SINCLAIR** (3758), b. 1877 Latheron Parish, Caithness
│ ├── **Ann Gunn SINCLAIR** (3759), b. 1883 Latheron Parish, Caithness
│ ├── **Henrietta Janet SINCLAIR** (3760), b. 1885 Inverness
│ ├── **Elizabeth SINCLAIR** (3761), b. 1888 Inverness
│ ├── **Neil Francis SINCLAIR** (3762), b. 1890 Inverness, d. 22 Sep 1917 Frank, Alberta
│ ├── **Adam Robert SINCLAIR** (3764), b. 1894 Moy, Inverness
│ └── **Mary SINCLAIR** (3763), b. 1897 Moy, Inverness
├── **Donald GUNN** (3235), b. 1829 Camster, Latheron Parish, Caithness, d. 09 Jan 1912 Latheron Parish, Caithness
│ +**Williamina SINCLAIR** (3724), b. 07 Dec 1834 Halkirk Parish, Caithness, m. 13 Jan 1857 Halkirk Parish, Caithness, d. 20 Jun 1912 Latheron Parish, Caithness
│ ├── **Hugh GUNN** (3734), b. 13 Dec 1857 Halkirk Parish, Caithness
│ ├── **Alexander Henderson Robertson GUNN** (3735), b. 20 Sep 1859 Caithness
│ ├── **Elizabeth GUNN** (3738), b. 15 Oct 1861 Olrig Parish, Caithness
│ ├── **William GUNN** (3736), b. 08 Dec 1863 Halkirk Parish, Caithness
│ └── **John Waters GUNN** (3737), b. 29 Apr 1866 Halkirk Parish, Caithness
├── **Mary GUNN** (3236), b. 1835 Camster, Latheron Parish, Caithness
│ +**James SUTHERLAND** (3725), b. 1819 Latheron Parish, Caithness, m. 20 Feb 1857 Latheron Parish, Caithness
│ └── **Andrew George SUTHERLAND** (3741), b. 28 Jan 1861 Latheron Parish, Caithness
├── **John GUNN** (3237), chr. 10 Feb 1837 Wick Parish, Caithness
│ +**Ann MCINTOSH** (3726), b. circa 1835, m. 26 Nov 1858 Latheron Parish, Caithness
│ ├── **Hugh GUNN** (3744), b. 11 Sep 1859 Latheron Parish, Caithness
│ │ +**Margaret DUNNET** (3747), b. circa 1861 Wick Parish, Caithness, m. 28 Sep 1883 Wick Parish, Caithness
│ │ └── **Elizabeth Smith GUNN** (3767), b. 1888 Wick Parish, Caithness
│ ├── **John GUNN** (3749), b. 15 Jun 1861 Latheron Parish, Caithness
│ ├── **Adam GUNN** (3750), b. 07 Jul 1864 Latheron Parish, Caithness
│ ├── **Donald GUNN** (3742), b. 15 Apr 1866 Latheron Parish, Caithness
│ ├── **Alexander GUNN** (3743), b. 18 Jan 1868 Latheron Parish, Caithness

[1339] From a December 2009 email by Sharon and Bill Gurney.

├── **Ann GUNN** (3751), b. 11 Sep 1871 Latheron Parish, Caithness

└── **George GUNN** (3748), b. 24 Jan 1873 Latheron Parish, Caithness

└── **Alexander GUNN** (3238), chr. 27 Jul 1839 Wick Parish, Caithness, d. 06 Mar 1916 Houstry, Dunbeath Parish, Caithness

+**Christina GUNN** (3239), b. circa 1854 Halkirk Parish, Caithness, m. 1893 d. 15 May 1920 Latheron Parish, Caithness

├── **Henrietta GUNN** (808), b. 1894 Latheron Parish, Caithness, d. 28 Mar 1975 Dunbeath, Latheron Parish, Caithness

└── **Alexander M K GUNN** (3240), b. 1896 Latheron Parish, Caithness, d. 23 Oct 1915 Latheron Parish, Caithness

2. Descendants of Alexander Gunn of Osclay[1340] (3424)

Alexander GUNN of Osclay (3424), b. 1752 Caithness, d. 1820 Latheron Parish, Caithness
+**Barbara WEIR (WHEIR)** (797), b. circa 1760, m. say 1775, d. 1833 Latheron Parish, Caithness

- **Robert GUNN** (3558), b. say 1776
- **John GUNN** (3559), b. say 1778
- **Alexander GUNN** (3560), b. say 1779
- **Adam GUNN** (3561), b. say 1780
- **Catherine GUNN of Osclay** (3423), b. circa 1781 Latheron Parish, Caithness, d. 1870 Newton, Watten Parish, Caithness
  +**Donald GUNN (the Sennachie) of Braehour & Brawlbin** (708), b. circa 1769 Caithness, m. 1807 Halkirk Parish, Caithness, d. 1861 Brawlbin, Reay Parish, Caithness
  - **John GUNN in Durness** (878), b. 1808 Halkirk Parish, Caithness, d. 1885 Durness Parish, Sutherland
    +**Catherine GUNN in Camster** (1120), b. circa 1817 Reay Parish, Caithness, m. 1836 Caithness, d. 1871 Sutherland
    - **John GUNN** (1122), chr. 1837 Lamesdale, Reay Parish, Caithness, d. 1861 Combes, County Down
    - **Margaret GUNN** (1123), b. 1841 Carriside, Reay Parish, Caithness, d. 1892 Durness Parish, Sutherland
      +**Torquil NICHOLSON** (1127), b. circa 1844 Snizort, Inverness, m. 1870 Edinburgh, Edinburgh Parish, Midlothian
      - **John NICHOLSON (Rev)** (3928), b. 1873 Durness, Sutherland
        +**Catherine May BROWN** (3933), m. 1902
        - **Christina Gunn NICHOLSON** (3937), b. 1904
        - **Margaret Gunn NICHOLSON** (3938), b. 1905
        - **Ian Torquil NICHOLSON** (3939), b. 1912, d. 1916
        - **Alastair David NICHOLSON** (3940), b. 1913
      - **Donald NICHOLSON (Rev)** (3929), b. 1877 Durness, Sutherland
        +**Catherine May BROWN** (3930), m. 1902
    - **Donald GUNN** (1116), b. 1844 Brawlbin, Reay Parish, Caithness, d. 1864 Durness, Sutherland
    - **Barbara GUNN** (1124), chr. 1847 Carriside, Reay Parish, Caithness, d. 1905
    - **Catherine GUNN** (1125), b. 1849 Carriside, Reay Parish, Caithness, d. 1907
    - **Joan GUNN** (1126), b. 1855 Reay Parish, Caithness, d. 1868
    - **Alexander GUNN in Sangomore** (887), b. 1859 Sangomore, Durness Parish, Sutherland, d. 1945 Sangomore, Durness Parish, Sutherland
      +**Georgina MACKAY** (2749), b. circa 1857 Durness, Sutherland, m. circa 1885 Durness Parish, Sutherland
      - **Catherine GUNN** (3353), b. 1888 Durness, Sutherland, d. 1930
      - **Marianne GUNN** (3355), b. circa 1890, d. circa 1891
      - **John Alexander GUNN** (3354), b. 1890 Durness Parish, Sutherland, d. 1890
      - **Andrew Mackay GUNN** (888), b. 1894 Durness Parish, Sutherland, d. 1970
        +**Florence (--?--)** (3357)
      - **Donaldina GUNN** (3358), b. 1896 Durness, Sutherland, d. 1974
      - **Marion Ellen GUNN** (3359), b. 1899 Durness, Sutherland, d. 1975
    - **Williamina GUNN** (889), b. 1859 Durness Parish, Sutherland, d. 1951
      +**George CAMPBELL** (890), b. circa 1860, m. circa 1885
      - **Catherine CAMPBELL** (891), b. circa 1888
        +**? MACKAY** (892), b. Laid, Sutherland, m. circa 1910
        - **Williamina MACKAY** (893), b. after 1910
  - **Barbara GUNN of Braehour** (6), b. 1810 Halkirk Parish, Caithness, d. 1844 Brawlbin, Reay Parish, Caithness
    +**Alexander GUNN of Bualchork and Brawlbin** (1), b. 1789 Halkirk Parish, Caithness, m. 1829 Halkirk Parish, Caithness, d. 1847 Brawlbin, Reay Parish, Caithness
    - **Catherine GUNN** (119), b. 1830 Reay Parish, Caithness, d. 1912 Vic
      +**James MILLER** (117), b. 1826 Wick Parish, Caithness, m. 1857 Buninyong, Vic, d. 1918 Vic
      - **Elizabeth MILLER** (278), b. 1858 Geelong, Vic, d. 1918 Vic
      - **Alexander Gunn MILLER** (279), b. 1860 Geelong, Vic, d. 1938 Apollo Bay, Vic

---

[1340] We are unsure whether he is correctly 'in' or 'of' Osclay. Much of the detail is from the Gurneys.

John William Gunn MILLER (280), b. 1862 Geelong, Vic, d. 1925 St Kilda, Vic
Jessie Barbara MILLER[1341] (284), b. 1865 Emerald Hill, Vic d. 1936 Devon, UK
+ **Charles James SWEARS** (282), m. circa 1885 Vic or London 1892, d.1927 Devon, UK
Hugh Miller SWEARS (286), b. 1894, d. 1917 France
Marjorie Gertrude SWEARS (287), b. 1896 London d. Jan 1948 Worcs., England.
James Dunnet MILLER (281), b. 1868 Emerald Hill, Vic, d. 1933 Heidelberg, Vic
Katherine Margaret Mckay MILLER (285), b. 1872 Emerald Hill, Vic
+**William Porter VINE** (283), b. 1857 Port Melbourne, Vic, m. 1895 Vic, d. 1923 Prahran, Vic
James Miller VINE (288), b. 1896 St Kilda, Vic
William Alan VINE (290), b. 1898 St Kilda, Vic, d. 1917
Catherine Noel VINE (291), b. 1900 St Kilda, Vic, d. 1903 Melbourne South, Vic
Francis Seymour VINE (292), b. 1904 St Kilda, Vic, d. 1961 Somersby, Vic
Reginald Vernon VINE (694), b. 1908 St Kilda, Vic, d. 1987 NSW
Lesley Alison VINE (289), b. 1914 St Kilda, Vic
Donald GUNN of Brawlbin & Ballarat (3), b. 1832 Brawlbin, Reay Parish, Caithness, d. 1901 Ballarat, Vic
+**Jane SURMAN** (41), b. 1836 Hampton Poyle, Oxfordshire, m. 1859 Buninyong, Vic, d. 1908 Ballarat, Vic
John Alexander GUNN (Hon.) (32), b. 1860 Buninyong, Vic, d. 1910 Sydney, NSW
+**Jessie Marie TURNER** (104), b. 1862 Beechworth, Vic, m. 1886 North Brighton, Vic, d. 1925 Randwick, NSW
Gladys Emily GUNN (225), b. 1887 North Brighton, Vic, d. 1968 Melbourne, Vic
Jessie Jean GUNN (221), b. 1890 Ballarat, Vic, d. 1891 NSW
Alexander Donald GUNN (222), b. 1892 Ballarat, Vic, d. 1956 Melbourne, Vic
Angus William GUNN (223), b. 1895 Ballarat, Vic, d. 1926 Perth, WA
William Watkins GUNN (33), b. 1861 Nr Ballarat, Vic, d. 1935 Crossover, Vic
+**Margaret Jane BALHARRIE** (42), b. 1860 Perth, Tayside, m. 1891 Bloomfield, Vic, d. 1946 Frankston, Vic
John William GUNN (133), b. 1895 Ballarat, Vic, d. 1981 Frankston, Vic
Jean Margaret GUNN (139), b. 1896 Ballarat, Vic, d. 1975 Glenhuntly, Vic
Violet Helen GUNN (141), b. 1898 Warragul, Vic, d. 1968 Frankston, Vic
Edith Mary GUNN (134), b. 1899 Warragul, Vic, d. 1901 Sandringham, Vic
Marjorie May GUNN (135), b. 1904 Warragul, Vic, d. 1970 Launching Place, Vic
Marcus Allan GUNN (136), b. 1906 Crossover, Vic, d. 1981 Melbourne, Vic
Mary Jane GUNN (34), b. 1864 Cardigan Nr Ballarat, Vic, d. 1934 Werribee, Vic
Donald GUNN (35), b. 1865 Burrumbeet, Vic, d. 1933 Crossover, Vic
+**Amy Agnes WAREHAM** (43), b. 1863 Cheshire, m. 1922 Middle Park, Vic, d. 1933 Vic
Marcus Daniel GUNN (36), b. 1868 Buninyong, Vic, d. 1952 South Yarra, Vic
+**Mary Jane CHENHALL** (105), b. 1873 Chiltern, Vic, m. 1903 Corowa, NSW, d. 1941 Melbourne, Vic
Keith Lindsay GUNN (121), b. 1904 Corowa, NSW, d. 1967 Melbourne, Vic
Norma Mary GUNN (125), b. 1907 Corowa, NSW, d. 1971 Melbourne, Vic
Barbara GUNN (106), b. 1870 Burrumbeet, Vic, d. 1941 Werribee, Vic
+**Isaac PADGETT** (103), b. 1867 Mount Cole, Vic, m. 1899 Ballarat, Vic, d. 1937 Werribee, Vic
Barbara Gunn PADGETT (184), b. 1901 Ballarat, Vic, d. 1960
Norman Gunn PADGETT (180), b. 1903 Ballarat, Vic, d. 1952 Princhester, Qld
Jean Gunn PADGETT (186), b. 1913 Vic, d. 2002
Norman GUNN (37), b. 1872 Burrumbeet, Vic, d. 1944 Williamstown, Vic
Hugh GUNN (38), b. 1875 Burrumbeet, Vic, d. 1879 Burrumbeet, Vic
Arthur Gilbert GUNN (9), b. 1878 Burrumbeet, Vic, d. 1933 Ivanhoe, Vic
+**Louisa Maud Miriam RETALLICK** (10), b. 1875 Naseby, Otago, m. 1901 Ballarat, Vic, d. 1959 Elsternwick, Vic
Malcolm Donald GUNN (11), b. 1903 Ballarat, Vic, d. 1961 Heidelberg, Vic
Kenneth Douglas GUNN (23), b. 1905 Kalgoorlie, WA, d. 1951 Longreach, Qld

[1341] A third child, Dorothy Catherine Swears, was borm in Devon in 1903.

| | | | |—— **Angus Norman GUNN** (24), b. 1912 Kalgoorlie, WA, d. 1994 Caringbah, NSW
| | | | └—— **Colin GUNN** (29), b. 1915 Ballarat, Vic, d. 1916 Ballarat, Vic
| | | └—— **Catherine Alexandrina GUNN** (39), b. 1880 Burrumbeet, Vic, d. 1960 Ormond, Vic
| | |—— **Janet MacLeod GUNN** (120), b. 1834 Brawlbin, Reay Parish, Caithness, d. 1913 Cardigan, Vic
| | | +**John Watkins SURMAN** (118), b. 1831 Hampton Poyle, Oxfordshire, m. 1864 Cardigan, Vic, d. 1906
Ballarat, Vic
| | | |—— **Baby SURMAN** (1550), b. 1865 Ballarat, Vic, d. 1865 Ballarat, Vic
| | | |—— **John Daniel SURMAN** (272), b. 1866 Cardigan, Vic, d. 1935 Dunolly, Vic
| | | | +**Margaret COWLEY** (1553), b. 1866, m. 1895, d. 1951 Geelong, Vic
| | | | |—— **Jessie Marguerite SURMAN** (1554), b. 1896 Armadale, Vic, d. 1955 Geelong, Vic
| | | | └—— **Thomas William SURMAN** (1555), b. 1899 Carlton, Vic, d. 1965 Melbourne, Vic
| | | |—— **Alexander Gunn SURMAN** (273), b. 1868 Ballarat, Vic, d. 1909 Ballarat, Vic
| | | | +**Esther KIRK** (676), b. 1864, m. 1891 Vic, d. 1938 Cardigan, Vic
| | | | |—— **Jessie Beatrice SURMAN** (680), b. 1892 Ballarat, Vic, d. 1954 Caulfield, Vic
| | | | |—— **Linda Pearl SURMAN** (682), b. 1893 Ballarat, Vic
| | | | |—— **Eric SURMAN** (683), b. 1895 Haddon, nr Ballarat, Vic, d. 1959 Ballarat, Vic
| | | | |—— **Stella SURMAN** (681), b. 1897 Haddon, Vic, d. 1968 Ballarat, Vic
| | | | |—— **Tettie SURMAN** (679), b. 1898 Ballarat, Vic
| | | | |—— **Reginald Gunn SURMAN** (678), b. 1899 Haddon, Vic, d. 1943 Ballarat, Vic
| | | | └—— **Margery SURMAN** (687), b. 1904 Ballarat, Vic
| | | |—— **Barbara Margaret McKay SURMAN** (274), b. 1870 Ballarat, Vic, d. 1928 Morwell, Vic
| | | | +**James BREWSTER** (1559), b. say 1865, m. 1892
| | | | |—— **Renee Grace Daphne BREWSTER** (1577), b. 1893 Learmonth, Vic, d.1978 Doncaster, Vic
| | | | |—— **James William Ashley BREWSTER** (1578), b. 1895 Ballarat, Vic, d. 1957 Sale, Vic
| | | | |—— **John Watkins Surman BREWSTER** (1579), b. 1897 Ballarat, Vic, d. 1975 Leongatha, Vic
| | | | |—— **David Baxter BREWSTER** (1580), b. 1899 Yinnar, Vic
| | | | |—— **Janet Barbara BREWSTER** (1581), b. 1902 Yinnar, Vic
| | | | |—— **George Alan BREWSTER** (1582), b. 1904 Yinnar, Vic, d. 1985 Leongatha, Vic
| | | | |—— **Hugh Gordon BREWSTER** (1583), b. 1906 Leongatha, Vic, d. 1976 Leongatha, Vic
| | | | |—— **Oswald Geoffrey BREWSTER** (1584), b. 1912 Morwell, Vic
| | | | └—— **Robert Norman BREWSTER** (1585), b. 1913 Morwell, Vic
| | | |—— **Watkins SURMAN** (405), b. 1871 Sago Hill/Cardigan, Vic, d. 1875 Cardigan, Vic
| | | |—— **James William SURMAN** (275), b. 1873 Sago Hill, Vic, d. 1947 Horsham, Vic
| | | | +**Alice Maud Grace CURTIS** (677), b. 1874 Buninyong, Vic, m. 1894 Ballarat, Vic, d. 1956 Horsham,
Vic
| | | | |—— **Grace Jessie Frances SURMAN** (684), b. 1895 Wonwondah South, Vic, d. 1895 Mount
Jeffcott, Vic
| | | | |—— **Leslie Watkins SURMAN** (685), b. 1896 Horsham, Vic, d. 1939 Sydney, NSW
| | | | |—— **Hazel Marion SURMAN** (686), b. 1901 Dunolly, Vic, d. 1984 Horsham, Vic
| | | | └—— **Jack SURMAN** (1561), d. after 1947 Bairnsdale, Vic
| | | |—— **Irene Marian Catherine SURMAN** (693), b. 1874 Sago Hill, Vic, d. 1940 Melbourne, Vic
| | | | +**William O'CONNOR** (692), m. 1918 Vic
| | | |—— **Theodore Oswald SURMAN** (276), b. 1876 Cardigan, Vic, d. 1918 Melbourne South, Vic
| | | └—— **Geoffrey Eustace SURMAN** (277), b. 1878 Sago Hill, Vic, d. 1951 Heidelberg, Vic
| | | +**Winifred May LITTLEHALES** (458), b. 1892 Vic, m. 1917 Ballarat, Vic, d. circa 1920 Ballarat, Vic
| | | |—— **Geoffrey Oswald SURMAN** (4), b. 1918 Ballarat, Vic, d. 1921 Sale, Vic
| | | └—— **John Watkins SURMAN** (689), b. 1920 Ballarat, Vic, d. 1996 Brisbane, Qld
| | | +**Ethel Stella TODD** (1552), b. 1901, m. 1926
| | |—— **John GUNN** (12), b. 1836 Reay Parish, Caithness, d. circa 1854 Port Melbourne, Vic
| | └—— **William GUNN** (220), b. 1839 Reay Parish, Caithness, d. after 1864 Vic
| |—— **Mary (May) GUNN** (487), chr. 1812 Halkirk Parish, Caithness, d. 1853 Halkirk Parish, Caithness
| | +**John CAMPBELL** (3505), b. circa 1815 Reay, Caithness, m. circa 1837 Caithness
| | |—— **Johan CAMPBELL** (3570), b. 1838 Thurso, Thurso Parish, Caithness

Donald CAMPBELL (3514), b. 1840 Thurso, Thurso Parish, Caithness
William CAMPBELL (3515), b. 1843 Halkirk Parish, Caithness, d. 1873 Halkirk Parish, Caithness
John CAMPBELL (3571), b. circa 1850 Halkirk Parish, Caithness, d. 1851 Halkirk Parish, Caithness
Alexander GUNN (Capt.) of Braehour & Newton (572), chr. 1814 Halkirk Parish, Caithness, d. 1900 Thurso, Thurso Parish, Caithness
+**Mary Innes CAMPBELL** (1128), b. 1808 Reay Parish, Caithness, m. 1841 Caithness, d. 1864 Braehour, Halkirk Parish, Caithness
Catherine GUNN (1129), b. 1842 Reay Parish, Caithness, d. before 1849
Williamina GUNN (1130), b. 1843 Reay Parish, Caithness, d. 1909 Lanarkshire
+**James D CLARKE** (3411), m. 1875 Braehour, Halkirk Parish, Caithness, d. before 1881
William CLARK (3453), b. 1877 Hamilton, Lanarkshire
Alexander Gunn CLARK (3454), b. 1878 Hamilton, Lanarkshire
Mary Campbell CLARK (3455), b. 1880 Hamilton, Lanarkshire
Barbara GUNN (1131), b. 1844 Reay Parish, Caithness, d. 1879 Glasgow, Lanarkshire
Peter GUNN (1132), b. 1846 Reay Parish, Caithness
Catherine GUNN (1133), b. 1849 Reay Parish, Caithness, d. 1929 Edinburgh, Midlothian
+**John SCOTT** (3450), b. circa 1848 Forfarshire, m. 1873 Inverness
Robertina G SCOTT (3458), b. 1874 Cupar, Angus, d. 1944 Inverness
+**Alexander MUNRO** (3459), b. 1869, m. circa 1901, d. 1962
Mabel Scott MUNRO (3466), b. 1910, d. 2002
John SCOTT (3460), b. 1876 Dalry, Ayrshire
Alexander S SCOTT (3461), b. 1878 Hamilton, Lanarkshire
Charles SCOTT (3462), b. 1880 Hamilton, Lanarkshire
William SCOTT (3463), b. 1882 Falkirk, Stirlingshire
Patrick S SCOTT (3464), b. 1885 Perthshire
Walter SCOTT (3465), b. 1887 Ayrshire
Robertina GUNN (1134), b. 1852 Reay Parish, Caithness, d. 1872
Margaret GUNN (880), b. 1819 Caithness, d. 1888 Newton, Watten Parish, Caithness
+**John MACKAY** (3467), b. circa 1815 Halkirk Parish, Caithness, m. 1860 Brawlbin, Reay Parish, Caithness, d. 1865 Newton, Watten Parish, Caithness
Hector MACKAY (3468), b. 1863 Watten Parish, Caithness, d. 1892 Halkirk Parish, Caithness
+**Mary Ann MACKINNON** (3469), b. circa 1861 Watten Parish, Caithness, m. circa 1888, d. 1946 Watten Parish, Caithness
Alexandrina (Lexy) GUNN of Braehour (554), b. 1825 Halkirk Parish, Caithness, d. 1876 Dundee, Angus
+**Donald GUNN of Brawlbin & Dundee** (976), b. circa 1818 Brawlbin, Halkirk Parish, Caithness, m. 1852 Brawlbin, Reay Parish, Caithness, d. 1879 Dundee, Angus
John St Clair GUNN (Dr) (3575), b. 1854 Dundee, Angus, d. 1907 Kaikoura, Marlborough
+**Hester EASTON** (3713), b. circa 1867, m. circa 1890, d. 1939 Kaikoura
Agnes Loeda GUNN (3715), b. 1893
+**Walter Charles CROPP** (3716), m. 1916, d. 1918 Meteren
Alexandrina Margaret GUNN (3717), b. 1896, d. 1967
+**William Alastair MCQUEEN** (3718), b. 1886, m. 1920, d. 1976
Donald St Clair GUNN (3719), b. 1899, d. 1973
Daniel Alexander GUNN (3576), b. 1855 Dundee, Angus, d. circa 1890
Margaret GUNN (3577), b. 1859 Dundee, Angus, d. 1881 Dundee, St Andrew Parish, Angus
Catherine GUNN (3578), b. 1860 Dundee, Angus
+**Peter MUNRO** (3714), b. circa 1866, m. 1887 Perthshire
Peter MUNRO (3722), b. 1889 Kansas
Francis Molison GUNN (1137), b. 1863 Dundee, Angus, d. 1864 Dundee, Angus
Williamina GUNN (3579), b. 1865 Dundee, Angus, d. Omaha, Nebraska
+**Thomas H ARTHUR** (3581), b. 1866 Angus, m. 1866 Aberdeen
Thomas Hutton ARTHUR (3582), b. 1885 St Andrew, Angus
Sturrock ARTHUR (3583), b. 1888 Kansas
Douglas ARTHUR (3584), b. 1891 Nebraska

- **Stanley ARTHUR** (3585), b. 1894 Nebraska
- **Stewart ARTHUR** (3586), b. 1899 Nebraska
- **Francis Molison GUNN** (1138), b. 1867 Dundee, Angus, d. before 1871 Dundee, Angus
- **Alexander GUNN** (1139), b. 1868 Dundee, Angus, d. 1868 Dundee, Angus
- **Jean (Jane) GUNN** (941), b. 1816 Braehour, Halkirk Parish, Caithness, d. 1910 Killimister, Wick Parish, Caithness
- +**Hugh MACKENZIE** (3433), b. circa 1802 Farr, Sutherland, m. 1840 Reay Parish, Caithness, d. 1870 Winless, Caithness
- **Donald MACKENZIE** (3434), b. 1841 Reay Parish, Caithness, d. 1915 Bonar Bridge, Sutherland
- **Catherine MACKENZIE** (3437), b. 1843 Reay Parish, Caithness, d. before 1848 Reay Parish, Caithness
- **Barbara MACKENZIE** (3438), b. 1845 Reay Parish, Caithness, d. 1926 Killimister, Wick Parish, Caithness
- **George MACKENZIE** (3435), b. 1846 Reay Parish, Caithness
- +**Margaret (--?--)** (3441), b. circa 1846 Wick Parish, Caithness, m. 1892 Wick Parish, Caithness
- **Catherine MACKENZIE** (3439), b. circa 1848 Reay Parish, Caithness, d. 1924 Wick Parish, Caithness
- **Jessie/Janet MACKENZIE** (3440), b. 1850 Reay Parish, Caithness, d. 1926 Wick Parish, Caithness
- **William MACKENZIE** (3400), b. 1853 Reay Parish, Caithness, d. 1902 Cradock
- **Hugh MACKENZIE** (3401), b. 1855 Reay Parish, Caithness, d. 1868 Stemster, Latheron Parish, Caithness
- **Alexander MACKENZIE** (3436), b. 1856 Reay Parish, Caithness, d. 1860 Brawlbin, Reay Parish, Caithness
- **William GUNN** (3696), b. 1818, d. 1838
- **George GUNN** (3553), b. 1784 Dunbeath, Latheron Parish, Caithness, d. 1855 Pultneytown, Wick Parish, Caithness
- +**Anne RHIND** (3554), m. 1814 Wick Parish, Caithness, d. before 1871
- **Anne GUNN** (3834), b. 1815 Wick Parish, Caithness, d. 1855 Wick Parish, Caithness
- +**John LEITH** (3835), b. circa 1815, m. 1846 Wick Parish, Caithness
- **Ann LEITH** (3867), b. circa 1847 Wick Parish, Caithness
- **Christina LEITH** (3868), b. circa 1849 Wick Parish, Caithness
- **William LEITH** (3870), b. 1851 Wick Parish, Caithness
- **George LEITH** (3869), b. 1853 Wick Parish, Caithness
- **Barbara GUNN** (3836), b. 1817 Wick Parish, Caithness, d. 1817 Wick Parish, Caithness
- **Joanna GUNN** (3518), b. 1818 Wick Parish, Caithness, d. 1905 Wick Parish, Caithness
- +**Peter MACALLAN** (3837), b. 1819 Thurso, Caithness, m. 1844 Wick Parish, Caithness
- **James MACALLAN** (3871), b. 1846 Wick, Caithness
- **Ann MACALLAN** (3872), b. 1850 Wick, Caithness
- **Margaret GUNN** (3685), b. 1820 Wick Parish, Caithness, d. 1914 Wick Parish, Caithness
- +**John Millne FLETCHER** (3838), b. circa 1820, m. 1844 Wick Parish, Caithness
- **George FLETCHER** (3875), b. circa 1846 Wick Parish, Caithness
- **Ann FLETCHER** (3879), b. circa 1851 Wick Parish, Caithness
- **John FLETCHER** (3876), b. circa 1853 Wick Parish, Caithness
- **Alexander Gunn FLETCHER** (3877), b. 1855 Wick Parish, Caithness
- **Charles FLETCHER** (3878), b. 1857 Wick Parish, Caithness
- **Margaret FLETCHER** (3881), b. 1860 Wick Parish, Caithness
- **Harriet Gunn FLETCHER** (3880), b. 1863 Wick Parish, Caithness
- **Alexander GUNN** (3839), b. 1821 Wick Parish, Caithness
- **George GUNN** (3686), b. 1824 Wick Parish, Caithness, d. 1840 Wick Parish, Caithness
- **John GUNN** (3786), b. 1826 Wick Parish, Caithness, d. 1826 Wick Parish, Caithness
- **Harriet GUNN** (3840), b. 1832 Wick Parish, Caithness, d. 1924 Wick Parish, Caithness
- **Jessie GUNN** (3841), b. 1835 Wick Parish, Caithness, d. 1835 Wick Parish, Caithness
- **William GUNN of Osclay** (3557), b. circa 1796 Caithness, d. 1848 Latheron Parish, Caithness
- +**Margaret CORMACK** (3831), b. 1811 Latheron Parish, Caithness, d. 1898 Edinburgh, Edinburgh Parish, Midlothian
- **James GUNN** (3844), b. 1843 Latheron Parish, Caithness, d. 1888 Colombo
- **William GUNN** (3845), b. 1848 Latheron Parish, Caithness
- +**Helen H** (3846), b. circa 1858, d. before 1891 Edinburgh Parish, Midlothian
- **William GUNN** (3882), b. 1880 Glasgow, Lanarkshire
- **James GUNN** (3883), b. 1882 Edinburgh, Edinburgh Parish, Midlothian
- **Alice GUNN** (3884), b. 1886 Edinburgh, Edinburgh Parish, Midlothian

├── **Margaret GUNN** (3562), b. 1797 Breakachie, Latheron Parish, Caithness, d. before 1851
│ +**Alexander SUTHERLAND** (3563), m. 1827 Latheron Parish, Caithness
│ ├── **John SUTHERLAND** (3850), b. 1827 Pultneytown, Wick Parish, Caithness, d. 1869 Lybster, Latheron Parish, Caithness
│ ├── **Alexandrina SUTHERLAND** (3851), b. 1829 Pultneytown, Wick Parish, Caithness, d. 1905 Helmsdale, Sutherland
│ │ +**Gilbert MITCHELL** (3852), b. 1827 Kildonan Parish, Sutherland, m. 1849 Loth, Sutherland, d. 1861 Kildonan Parish, Sutherland
│ │ ├── **Margaret MITCHELL** (3887), b. 1851 Helmsdale, Kildonan Parish, Sutherland
│ │ ├── **Marjory MITCHELL** (3888), b. 1854 Kildonan Parish, Sutherland
│ │ ├── **William MITCHELL** (3889), b. 1857 Helmsdale, Kildonan Parish, Sutherland
│ │ └── **Alexander MITCHELL** (3890), b. 1860 Kildonan Parish, Sutherland
│ ├── **Barbara SUTHERLAND** (3853), b. 1832 Pultneytown, Wick Parish, Caithness, d. 1900 Berridale, Latheron Parish, Caithness
│ │ +**Adam MCPHERSON** (3854), b. circa 1832, m. say 1854, d. 1911 Latheron Parish, Caithness
│ │ ├── **Barbara MCPHERSON** (3891), b. Berriedale, Latheron Parish, Caithness, d. Berriedale, Latheron Parish, Caithness
│ │ ├── **Margaret MCPHERSON** (3892), b. 1857 Latheron Parish, Caithness, d. 1876 Berriedale, Latheron Parish, Caithness
│ │ ├── **Adam MCPHERSON** (3894), b. 1858 Latheron Parish, Caithness, d. 1880 Berriedale, Latheron Parish, Caithness
│ │ ├── **Annie MCPHERSON** (3893), b. 1861 Latheron Parish, Caithness, d. 1949 Berriedale, Latheron Parish, Caithness
│ │ ├── **William MCPHERSON** (3899), b. 1863 Latheron Parish, Caithness
│ │ ├── **Alexander MCPHERSON** (3895), b. 1864 Berriedale, Latheron Parish, Caithness, d. 1882 Berriedale, Latheron Parish, Caithness
│ │ ├── **John MCPHERSON** (3896), b. 1866 Latheron Parish, Caithness, d. 1953 Latheron Parish, Caithness
│ │ ├── **James MCPHERSON** (3897), b. 1868 Berriedale, Latheron Parish, Caithness, d. 1934 Edinburgh Parish, Midlothian
│ │ ├── **Sophia MCPHERSON** (3900), b. 1871 Latheron Parish, Caithness
│ │ └── **George MCPHERSON** (3898), b. 1873 Latheron Parish, Caithness, d. 1936 Berriedale, Latheron Parish, Caithness
│ ├── **Alexander SUTHERLAND** (3855), b. 1835 Pultneytown, Wick Parish, Caithness, d. before 1841
│ └── **William SUTHERLAND** (3856), b. 1838 Pultneytown, Wick Parish, Caithness, d. 1895 Auckland
│ +**Mary BEAVAN** (3857), m. 1868 Auckland
│ ├── **Alexandrina SUTHERLAND** (3901), b. 1869, d. 1944
│ ├── **Kenneth SUTHERLAND** (3906), b. 1871, d. 1941
│ ├── **Leopold SUTHERLAND** (3907), b. 1873, d. 1948
│ ├── **Ernest SUTHERLAND** (3908), b. 1874, d. 1945 London
│ ├── **Ira Joseph SUTHERLAND** (3909), b. 1876, d. 1957
│ ├── **Bessie SUTHERLAND** (3902), b. 1877, d. 1939
│ ├── **Edwin SUTHERLAND** (3910), b. 1880, d. 1946
│ ├── **Mary SUTHERLAND** (3903), b. 1882, d. 1932
│ ├── **Richard SUTHERLAND** (3911), b. 1883, d. 1944
│ ├── **Laura SUTHERLAND** (3904), b. 1885, d. 1886
│ ├── **Ella SUTHERLAND** (3905), b. 1887, d. 1963
│ └── **Frank SUTHERLAND** (3912), b. 1892, d. 1962
└── **James GUNN** (3555), b. circa 1801 Dunbeath, Latheron Parish, Caithness, d. 1870 Latheron Parish, Caithness
+**Christina MACLEOD** (3556), b. circa 1830 Braemore, Latheron Parish, Caithness, m. 1856 Osclay, Latheron Parish, Caithness, d. 1884 Latheron Parish, Caithness
├── **Janet GUNN** (3860), b. 1857 Latheron Parish, Caithness
├── **Barbara GUNN** (3861), b. 1858 Latheron Parish, Caithness
├── **Alexander GUNN** (3862), b. 1860 Latheron Parish, Caithness, d. 1864 Latheron Parish, Caithness
├── **Donald GUNN** (3863), b. 1863 Latheron Parish, Caithness
│ +**Catherine GANSON** (3864), b. 1864 Latheron Parish, Caithness, m. 1890 Newlands of Clyth, Latheron Parish, Caithness, d. 1898 Upper Lybster, Latheron Parish, Caithness
│ ├── **Elizabeth GUNN** (3915), b. 1893 Latheron Parish, Caithness

- **David GUNN** (3916), b. 1894 Latheron Parish, Caithness, d. 1907 West Clyth, Latheron Parish, Caithness
- **Donald GUNN** (3917), b. 1896 Latheron Parish, Caithness, d. 1930 Dundee, Angus
- **Alexander GUNN** (3918), b. 1898 Latheron Parish, Caithness

Alexandrina GUNN (3865), b. 1865 Latheron Parish, Caithness, d. 1913 Latheron Parish, Caithness
+**John STEVEN** (3866), b. 1863 Latheron Parish, Caithness, m. 1890 Lybster, Latheron Parish, Caithness

- **Christina STEVEN** (3921), b. 1891 Latheron Parish, Caithness
- **Donald STEVEN** (3923), b. 1893 Latheron Parish, Caithness
- **John STEVEN** (3924), b. 1895 Latheron Parish, Caithness
- **Jamessina STEVEN** (3922), b. 1897 Latheron Parish, Caithness
- **George STEVEN** (3925), b. 1899 Latheron Parish, Caithness
- **William STEVEN** (3926), b. 1900 Latheron Parish, Caithness

3. Adventures of an Eagle in Search of Prey[1342]

A few days ago, while several dogs and a lot of ravens were enjoying a feast on the carcase of a horse at Braehour, they were suddenly disturbed by the presence of a fine large eagle, at whose appearance the dogs ran off and the ravens flew away, one of the latter carrying off a portion of the entrails, part being swallowed. The raven being unable either to separate or disgorge her booty, she had to fly away with about half a yard dangling from her mouth. The eagle observing this, immediately gave chase, and soon after succeeded in seizing hold of the end of the piece, and in dragging both it and the raven to the ground, on reaching which he struck and killed the raven, and soon after made a meal of it and the carrion, returning towards the carcase. In the meantime, however, two of the dogs had returned, and possession being nine points of law, they growled defiance at the invader, and prepared to defend their rights. The eagle, bent on obtaining possession, for a short time hovered near to the spot, and suddenly descending gave the dogs two blows with its wings and expelled them. It fed for a short time, and then flew off with a large piece of carrion, which it deposited on a distant eminence, thereafter descending into the neighbouring loch, and enjoying a bath with evident relish. This, however, did not finish the eagle's adventures of the day. After slowly rising out of the loch, it descended upon a flock of sheep and lambs, and carried off in its talons a young lamb from the stock of Mr. Gunn, Braehour, disappearing on the top of Dorrery. Mr. Gunn, having observed the theft, gave chase, accompanied, strange to say, by the ewe whose lamb had been taken away. Whether the mother had observed the direction the eagle took, or merely followed Mr. Gunn after being deprived of its lamb, it is impossible to say: but it is certainly singular that she should have, at once, without invitation, accompanied him in the chase after her young one. On arriving at the top of Dorrery, the eagle was observed resting, while the lamb was skipping about uninjured. The eagle maintained its position until Mr. Gunn was within fifty yards of it, when it took its flight; and Mr. Gunn, with ewe and lamb, returned to Braehour, the lamb being none the worse for its aerial voyage in the talons of the eagle.

*****

We cannot, with assurance, know exactly which Gunn of Braehour is described here…

[1342] Being from page 306, *The Boy's Miscellany; An Illustrated Journal of Useful and Entertaining Literature for Youth Vol. 1.*

4. Pedigree of Barbara Gunn of Braehour (6)

┌── **William mac Sheumais mhic Crunar GUNN of Kilearnan, 1st Mackeamish** (3008)
┌── **Alexander GUNN of Kilearnan, 2nd Mackeamish** (2546)
┌── **William mor mac Allister GUNN of Kilearnan, 3rd Mackeamish** (793)
┌── **Iye Dubh MACKAY of Farr** (1716)
└── **Barbara MACKAY** (1853)
└── **Christina SINCLAIR of Dun** (1717)
┌── **Alexander GUNN of Kilearnan & Navidale, 4th Mackeamish** (574)
┌── **John GUNN of Kilearnan & Navidale, 5th Mackeamish** (573)
┌── **John GORDON of Backies & Kilcalmcill** (1873)
└── **Catherine GORDON** (792)
┌── **George GUNN of Borrabol and Achintoul** (568)
┌── **Francis SINCLAIR fiar of Dun** (795)
└── **Catherine SINCLAIR** (567)
┌── **John SINCLAIR of Ulbster** (2842)
└── **Jean SINCLAIR** (1324)
┌── **John GUNN of Knockfinn** (569)
┌── **Alexander GUNN of Dalnaglaton** (240)
┌── **John GUNN in Dalnaha, Strathmore & Braehour** (707)
┌── **Alexander MACLEOD of Dalnate** (799)
└── **Janet/Jean MACLEOD of Dalnate** (241)
┌── **Donald GUNN (the Sennachie) of Braehour & Brawlbin** (708)
┌── **Alexander DUNBAR of Rowens** (798)
└── **Marjory DUNBAR of Rowens** (706)
Barbara GUNN of Braehour (6)
┌── **Alexander GUNN of Osclay** (3424)
└── **Catherine GUNN of Osclay** (3423)
└── **Barbara WEIR (WHEIR)** (797)

Navidale, 2011

5. Pedigree of William mac Sheumais mhic Crunar Gunn of Kilearnan, 1st Mackeamish (3008)

```
                                                            ┌── Gunni ANDRESON 1st Chief and
                                                                     name-father of the Clan (3014)
                                              ┌── Snaekoll GUNNISON of Ulbster, 2nd Chief (3013)
                                              │   └── Ragnhild (--?--) (4058)
                                          ┌── Ottar (--?--) 3rd Chief (3012)
                                      ┌── James/Jakop (--?--) 4th Chief (2975)
                                  ┌── (--?--) GUN 5th Chief (2949)
                              ┌── John GUNN (Sir) 6th Chief (2805)
                          ┌── Donald GUNN (Sir) of Clyth, 7th Chief (2804)
                      ┌── James GUNN (Sir) of Clyth & Ulbster, 8th Chief (2593)
                  ┌── Magnus GUNN of Easter Clyth, Crowner, 9th Chief (3011)
              ┌── Thomas Crunair Ghall GUNN of Easter Clyth, 10th Chief (1427)
          ┌── James GUNN of Easter Clyth, Crowner of Caithness (3010)
      ┌── James Sheumais mac Crunar GUNN 12th Chief (3009)
William mac Sheumais mhic Crunar GUNN of Kilearnan, 1st Mackeamish (3008)
```

6. Descendants of William mac Sheumais mhic Crunar Gunn of Kilearnan, 1st Mackeamish (3008)

```
William mac Sheumais mhic Crunar GUNN of Kilearnan, 1st Mackeamish (3008)
└── Alexander GUNN of Kilearnan, 2nd Mackeamish (2546)
    +Barbara MACKAY (1853)
    └── William mor mac Allister GUNN of Kilearnan, 3rd Mackeamish (793)
        └── Alexander GUNN of Kilearnan & Navidale, 4th Mackeamish (574)
            +Catherine GORDON (792)
            └── John GUNN of Kilearnan & Navidale, 5th Mackeamish (573)
                +Anne MACLEOD (566)
                └── Alexander GUNN 6th Mackeamish (571)
                    +Christina MACKAY (790)
                    ├── Donald Crotaich GUNN of Killearnan (789)
                    │   +Margaret SUTHERLAND (791)
                    │   ├── Alexander GUNN of Badinloch & Wester Helmsdale, 7th Mackeamish (2464)
                    │   ├── George GUNN of Corrish (2465)
                    │   ├── William GUNN (Lt Col) (2466)
                    │   └── Esther GUNN (2467)
                    └── George GUNN in Borrobol (800)
                        +Barbara MACKAY (801)
                        ├── George GUNN in Achnahua (4056)
                        └── John GUNN in Kinbrace (2884)
                +Catherine SINCLAIR (567)
                └── George GUNN of Achintoul (568)
                    └── John GUNN of Knockfinn (569)
                        ├── Alexander GUNN of Dalnaglaton (240)
                        └── John GUNN (938)
            +Mary MACKAY Lady Fowlis (1871)
            ├── George GUNN of Borrobol (1874)
            │   +Joan MACKAY (1875)
            ├── John GUNN (380)
            └── Catherine GUNN (1846)
                +Angus MACKAY (Lt Col.) of Melness (1845)
    +Margaret ROSS (4057)
    └── William Beg GUNN (3413)
        ├── Donald GUNN (the Scholar) (3417)
        └── William GUNN of Kinbrace (3418)
            ├── William GUNN (3419)
            └── John GUNN of Kinbrace (3420)
                └── William GUNN of Kinbrace (3421)
                    └── Aeneas GUNN (3422)
                        └── William GUNN in Ascaig, Kildonan (3412)
```

Bibliography

We have, overall, restricted this bibliography to print materials which have been significantly used; websites are given throughout the text. The National Library of Australia's digitized archives have, however, been invaluable; http://trove.nla.gov.au/. Mention must also be made of the County Archives at Wick, Caithness, Scotland.

Manuscript sources:

Deposit 55, J.A.Gunn personal papers, Archives of Business and Labour, Australian National University, Canberra, A.C.T.
Assorted Deposits, Goldsborough, Mort and Co., Archives of Business and Labour, Australian National University, Canberra, A.C.T.

Newspapers and periodicals:

The Australasian 2.5.1898
The Australasian Pastoralists Review 15.6.1895, 15.3.1898, 16.5.1925
The Bulletin 9.5.1956
Daily Telegraph 25.10.1918
Highland Notes and Queries; The Gunn Papers, The Northern Chronicle, 11.1.1911, 1.2.1911, 8.2.1911, 15.2.1911, 22.2.1911, 1.3.1911, 8.3.1911, 15.3.1911,
Narrandera Argus 20.2.1894
New South Wales Hansard 1908-1910
The Sydney Stock and Station Journal 26.4.1895
Manitoba Free Press 2.12.1878
The Gunn Herald, No.70, October 2006 and assorted others.
J.A.Gunn et. al., 'Anthrax and Inoculation', being reprinted from *The Australasian Pastoralists' Review*, McCarran Bird and Co., (1899, Melbourne)
P R Myers, "Sir John Gunn, the Cardiff Business Entrepeneur from Caithness," *The Caithness Field Club Journal*, (October 1983, Caithness)

Other print material:

Burke's Peerage, Baronetage & Knightage, 107th edition (Wilmington, Delaware, U.S.A.: Burke's Peerage (Genealogical Books) Ltd, 2003) esp. pp.1705-1707

Duty Nobly Done, (Learmonth & District Historical Society 1995)

The Boy's Miscellany; An Illustrated Journal of Useful and Entertaining Literature for Youth Volume 1, (London, E. Harrison, 1863)

The James Miller Story (Prahran, Victoria: D.W.Paterson Co, 1962)

The New Statistical Account of Scotland Vol. XV, (William Blackwood and Sons Ltd., Edinburgh and London, 1845)

Ye Booke of Halkirk (A Ross Institute Souvenir, issued by the Bazaar Publications Committee, 1911)

Auckland, Bruce, ed. Stables, R., *Postal Markings of Scotland to 1840* (Second Edition, Scottish Postal History Society, 1995)

Austin, A.G. ed., *The Webbs' Australian Diary 1898* (Sir Isaac Pitman and Sons Ltd., Melbourne, 1965)

Beattie, M. and Shalders B. compiled by, *Mt. Cole – Warrak. A history and its people (*1990)

Bryce, George LL.D., *Worthies of Red River* (The Historical and Scientific Society of Manitoba, Winnipeg Free Press Print, 1896)

Bumsted, J. M., *Dictionary of Manitoba Biography* (University of Manitoba Press, 1999)

Butlin, N. G., *Investment in Australian Economic Development 1861-1900* (Cambridge University Pres , Cambridge, 1964)

Davies, A. and Stanbury, P. with assistance from Tanre, C., *The Mechanical Eye in Australia Photography 1841-1900* (Oxford University Press, Melbourne, 1985)

Devine, T.M., *Scotland's Empire 1600-1815* (Penguin Books, London, 2003)

Foden, Frank, Wick of the North; The Story of a Scottish Royal Burgh (North of Scotland Newspapers, Wick, 2006)

Gunn, Donald and Tuttle, C. R., History *of Manitoba from the ealiest settlements to 1835* by the late Hon. Donald Gunn, *and from the admission of the province into the Dominion* by Charles R. Tuttle (Ottawa, 1880).

Gunn, Robert P., *Tales from Braemore; Caithness legends and mysteries* (Whittles Publishing, Caithness, 2008)

Robert Russell Gunn, *The Gunns*[1343] (Moore's Print Shop Georgia, 1925)

Harper, Marjory, *Adventurers and Exiles: The Great Scottish Exodus* (Profile Books Ltd., London, 2003)

Keith, B.R. ed., *The Geelong College 1861-1961* (Geelong, 1961)

Maclean Sinclair Rev. A., *The Sinclairs of Roslin, Caithness, and Goshen* (The Examiner Publishing Company, 1901)

[1343]This book being detailed on some early U.S.A. Gunn families.

Phillips A. A., *Responses: Selected Writings* (Australia International Press and Publications Pty. Ltd., Melbourne, 1978,)

Phillips, Alastair, *My Uncle George; the Respectful Recollections of a Backslider in a Highland Manse* (Pan, London 1986)

Rugg Gunn, Mark, *Clan Gunn* (privately published, 1982)

Sinclair, Thomas*, The Gunns* (William Rae, Wick, 1890) *(and the further articles)*

Sutherland, Ian, *Caithness 1770 to 1832* (Signal Enterprises, Wick, 1995)

Swan, K., *A History of Wagga Wagga*, Hogbin (Poole and Co., Wagga Wagga, 1970)

Todd, J., *Colonial Technology; Science and the transfer of innovation to Australia* (Cambridge University Press, Melbourne, 1995)

Todd, J., and Inkster, I, 'Support for the scientific enterprise, 1850-1900' in Home, R.W., *Australian Science in the Making* (Cambridge University Press, Melbourne, 1988)

Webster R., *Bygoo and Beyond* (private publication, Bygoo, 1957)

Withers, W.B., *History of Ballarat* (Queensbury Hill Press, Hawthorn, facsimile edition 1980)

Printed in Great Britain
by Amazon

65074962R00276